Digitalization and Artificial Intelligence in Courts

Digitalization and Artificial Intelligence in Courts

Opportunities and Challenges

Edited by

FERNANDO ESTEBAN DE LA ROSA
Professor of Private International Law, University of Granada, Spain

PABLO CORTÉS
Professor of Civil Justice, University of Leicester, UK

NURIA MARCHAL ESCALONA
Chair in Private International Law, University of Granada, Spain

OXFORD
UNIVERSITY PRESS

OXFORD
UNIVERSITY PRESS

Great Clarendon Street, Oxford, OX2 6DP,
United Kingdom

Oxford University Press is a department of the University of Oxford.
It furthers the University's objective of excellence in research, scholarship,
and education by publishing worldwide. Oxford is a registered trade mark of
Oxford University Press in the UK and in certain other countries.

Published in the United States of America by Oxford University Press
198 Madison Avenue, New York, NY 10016, United States of America.

British Library Cataloguing in Publication Data
Data available

Library of Congress Control Number: 2025938006

ISBN 9780198918721

DOI: 10.1093/9780198918752.001.0001

The manufacturer's authorised representative in the EU for product safety is
Oxford University Press España S.A., Parque Empresarial San Fernando de Henares,
Avenida de Castilla, 2 – 28830 Madrid (www.oup.es/en or product.safety@oup.com).
OUP España S.A. also acts as importer into Spain of products made by the manufacturer.

For Mia and Eric

For Tristan, Alice and Ruben

For Ainhoa

Foreword

This is a quite outstandingly welcome and timely book.

It is welcome because it contains, in the writings of a large and distinguished team of commentators from all around the world, a scholarly and well-researched compendium of insights into a fast growing and, to most of us, bafflingly opaque pair of related legal subjects, digitilization and artificial intelligence. A dedication to the Rule of Law and Access to Justice is what unites lawyers all over the world into a single family. We are most of us dimly aware that the inexorable advance of digitalization and AI in the court and dispute resolution environment carries with it large potential benefits, alongside equally large and (because we know so little about the subject) frightening risks. We can see the same happening in many other aspects of our individual and shared lives.

The book is timely because it arrives at a crossroads in the advance of these two technologies. Most of us have already experienced at first hand the benefits and occasional frustrations of digitalization. It is well on the way to ending the tyranny of paper, but its arrival has (in the UK at least) been patchy and, until very recently, lacking in any overall planning or direction. Its performance is seldom as flawless as its designers and cheerleaders wish for. But few now doubt its potential and increasingly visible benefits, or question that it is here to stay, mainly for the good, provided it is truly accessible to litigants without lawyers, and to the public.

But much larger questions still surround the introduction of AI. As Sir Geoffrey Vos MR recently said, AI is the wild card. We can all see that AI may have much to do with making justice more accessible and in particular more speedy and affordable. We may be entirely happy for an AI robot judge to resolve small disputes, such as may attend the purchase of a second-hand electric kettle on Ebay. But do we want robot judges to decide whether we lose our homes, our children, or our liberty?

These democratic, ethical, philosophical, and practical questions were just coming up over the horizon when I conducted my Civil Courts Structure Review in 2015–16. But now, ten years later, they stare us in the face, and IT (including AI) is developing so fast that the time to address them is right now, and as a matter of urgency. All these problems, hopes, and fears are squarely addressed in the chapters of this book, based upon the truly encyclopaedic knowledge of its contributors, and backed up by a comprehensive bibliography that could take any one of us years to read.

So I would describe this book as compulsory reading for all those, young and old, anywhere in the world, who share a respect for the Rule of Law as something which does not just regulate but can enhance all our lives, for Access to Justice and for the crying need for better public legal education. In all those fields digitalization and AI have so much to contribute, if only those who may play a critical democratic role in accepting or rejecting them do so from a properly informed viewpoint. That is what this book provides.

Lord Briggs of Westbourne
Justice of the Supreme Court of the United Kingdom
March 2025

Acknowledgements

This collection originated from an international workshop organized by Fernando Esteban de la Rosa and Nuria Marchal at the Law Faculty of the Universidad de Granada in October 2022, just weeks before the ground-breaking launch of ChatGPT, which highlighted the transformative potential of Artificial Intelligence in revolutionizing legal practice and dispute resolution. The workshop explored the intersection of digital technologies and the legal field, offering a timely and critical examination of the challenges and opportunities posed by technology and AI, while laying the groundwork for broader discussions on its ethical, procedural, and human rights implications in the justice system. This event served as the foundation for the ideas and collaborations that underpin this book. We extend our heartfelt thanks to the participants of that workshop and to those who attended the follow-up event in November 2024, where the findings of this book were presented amidst the rapidly evolving prominence of AI and its exciting potential to broaden access to justice.

The editors are profoundly grateful to the authors of the chapters in this book for their intellectual contributions and personal dedication. Their willingness to engage with and thoughtfully respond to feedback during the editing process has significantly enriched the quality of this volume.

We would also like to acknowledge the reviewers at Oxford University Press, whose insightful suggestions broadened the scope of the collection and enhanced its coherence and depth. For the revision of chapters authored by non-native speakers, we benefited from the combined assistance of professional proof-readers.

Our gratitude further extends to the *Unidad de Excelencia de Investigación Sociedad Digital: Seguridad y Protección de Derechos* (Centre of Excellence for Digital Society Research: Security and Protection of Rights) and the TED2021 research project, which provided the essential framework and support for this initiative.

We also wish to thank the fellows of the National Center for Technology and Dispute Resolution, particularly Colin Rule, and the co-directors Ethan Katsh and Leah Wing, for their leadership in the field of Online Dispute Resolution.

We are also grateful to Begoña Fernández Rodríguez and Ozana Olariu for their invaluable contributions as coordinators in preparing the accompanying documents that complement this book, including the table of contents, list of abbreviations, and tables of cases and legislation.

It is our hope that this book will make a meaningful contribution to the evolving discourse on the digitalization of justice, offering valuable insights for researchers, practitioners, and policymakers alike.

Finally, we dedicate this book to our children, the digital natives who will undoubtedly expect digital justice, and whose unconditional love sustained us throughout the journey of bringing this work to fruition.

Contents

Table of Cases

AUSTRALIA

CHINA

EUROPEAN COURT OF HUMAN RIGHTS

COURT OF JUSTICE OF THE EUROPEAN UNION

SPAIN

UNITED KINGDOM

UNITED STATES OF AMERICA

Table of Documents

EUROPEAN DATA PROTECTION BOARD (EDPB) AND EUROPEAN DATA PROTECTION SUPERVISOR (EDPS)

EUROPEAN PARLIAMENT

EUROPEAN PARLIAMENT, THE COUNCIL AND THE COMMISSION

COUNCIL OF EUROPE

COUNCIL OF EUROPE

COUNCIL OF EUROPE COMMISSIONER FOR HUMAN RIGHTS

EUROPEAN COMMISSION FOR THE EFFICIENCY OF JUSTICE (COUNCIL OF EUROPE)

EUROPEAN COMMITTEE ON LEGAL CO-OPERATION (COUNCIL OF EUROPE)

EUROPEAN BARS FEDERATION

MEXICO

ORGANISATION FOR ECONOMIC CO-OPERATION AND DEVELOPMENT (OECD)

PAKISTAN

GOVERNMENT OF PAKISTAN

SUPREME COURT OF PAKISTAN

SPAIN

COTEC FOUNDATION-UGR

GENERAL COUNCIL OF THE JUDICIARY

GOVERNMENT

HIGH COURT OF JUSTICE OF ASTURIAS

MINISTRY OF ECONOMIC AFFAIRS AND DIGITAL TRANSFORMATION

SPANISH DATA PROTECTION AGENCY

WORKING GROUP: BASES FOR INTEROPERABILITY AND SECURITY (BIS)

UNIDROIT AND ELI

UNITED KINGDOM

CIVIL JUSTICE COUNCIL

DEPARTMENT FOR BUSINESS, ENERGY & INDUSTRIAL STRATEGY

GOVERNMENT

HM COURTS & TRIBUNALS SERVICE (HMCTS)

JUDICIARY OF ENGLAND AND WALES

MINISTRY OF JUSTICE UK

OTHER

THE ADVISORY, CONCILIATION AND ARBITRATION SERVICE (ACAS)

UNITED NATIONS

UNITED NATIONS HUMAN RIGHTS COUNCIL (UNHRC)

UNITED NATIONS COMMISSION ON INTERNATIONAL TRADE LAW (UNCITRAL)

NATIONAL CENTER FOR TECHNOLOGY AND DISPUTE RESOLUTION (NCTDR)

STATE OF FLORIDA'S DISTRICT COURTS

STATE OF MICHIGAN'S DISTRICT COURTS

SUPREME COURT OF OHIO

THE CALIFORNIA COMMISSION ON ACCESS TO JUSTICE

THE PEW CHARITABLE TRUSTS

UTAH COURTS

MISCELANEOUS

Abbreviations

A2J	Access to Justice
ABA	American Bar Association
ACAS	Advisory, Conciliation and Arbitration Service
ACHPR	African Commission on Human and Peoples' Rights
ACHR	American Convention on Human Rights
ADB	Asian Development Bank
ADM	Automated Decision-making
ADR	Alternative Dispute Resolution
AI	Artificial Intelligence
AI Act	Artificial Intelligence Act Regulation (EU) 2024/1689
AIAs	Algorithmic Impact Assessments
AIDA	Artificial Intelligence and Data Act
APEC	Asia Pacific Economic Cooperation
AV	Audio-visual
B2B	Business to Business
B2C	Business to Consumer
BATNA	Best Alternative to a Negotiated Agreement
BeA	Special Electronic Attorney Mailbox (Besonderes Elektronisches Anwaltspostfach) (Germany)
BOE	Official State Gazette (Boletín Oficial del Estado) (Spain)
BRAO	Bundesrechtsanwaltsordnung (Federal Code for Lawyers) (Germany)
CDR	Consumer Dispute Resolution
CE	Constitution (Constitución Española)
CEPEJ	European Commission for the Efficiency of Justice (Council of Europe)
CETS	Council of Europe Treaty Series
CFMS	Case Flow Management System
CJEU	Court of Justice of the European Union
CMMC	China Mobile Mini Court
CoE	Convention Council of Europe Framework Convention on Artificial Intelligence and Human Rights, Democracy and the Rule of Law of 17 May 2024
CoE	Council of Europe
COMPAS	Correctional Offender Management Profiling for Alternative Sanctions
COVID-19	Coronavirus Disease 2019
CPA	Civil Procedure Act, Ley 1/2000, 7 January, de Enjuiciamiento Civil (Spain)

CPR	Civil Procedure Rules
CRT	British Columbia Civil Resolution Tribunal
Cth	Commonwealth
Digital Services Act	Regulation (EU) 2022/2065 of the European Parliament and of the Council of 19 October 2022 on a Single Market for Digital Services and amending Directive 2000/31/EC
Digitalization Regulation	Regulation (EU) 2023/2844 on the Digitalization of Judicial Cooperation and Access to Justice in Cross-Border Civil, Commercial, and Criminal Matters, Amending Certain Legal Acts in the Field of Judicial Cooperation
DRL	Democracy and the Rule of Law
ECFR	European Charter of Fundamental Rights
ECHR	European Convention for the Protection of Human Rights and Fundamental Freedoms of 4 November 1950
ECJ	European Court of Justice
ECLC	European Committee on Legal Co-operation
e-CODEX Regulation	Regulation (EU) of the European Parliament and of the Council of 30 May 2022, regarding a Computerized System for the Cross-Border Electronic Exchange of Data in the Field of Judicial Cooperation in Civil and Criminal Matters, Which Amends Regulation (EU) 2018/1726
e-CODEX	Electronic Cross-Border Exchange
eDelivery	Certified Electronic Delivery Services
EDIW	European Digital Identity Wallet
EDPB	European Data Protection Board
EDPS	European Data Protection Supervisor
EIDAS Regulation	Regulation (EU) 910/2014 of the European Parliament and of the Council of 23 July 2014 on Electronic Identification and Trust Services for Electronic Transactions in the Internal Market and Repealing Directive 1999/93/EC
eIDAS2	Regulation Proposal for a Regulation of the European Parliament and of the Council amending Regulation (EU) 910/2014 as regards establishing a framework for a European Digital Identity
ENE	Early Neutral Evaluation
EP	European Parliament
ES	Expert System
eSeal	Electronic Seals
eSignature	Electronic Signatures
eTimestamp	Electronic Timestamps
EU	European Union
EVID	Escritorio Virtual de Inmediación Digital (Virtual Digital Immediacy Desk)
FDR	Financial Dispute Resolution
FJA	Federal Judicial Academy
FRIA	Fundamental Rights Impact Assessment
GBP	British Pound/Sterling

GDPR	General Data Protection Regulation
GDU	User Administration
GPAI	General-Purpose Artificial Intelligence
GPT-3.5	Generative Pre-trained Transformer Series 3.5
GPT-4	Generative Pre-trained Transformer Series 4
HART	Harm Assessment Risk Tool
HMCTS	His Majesty's Courts & Tribunals Service
HR	Human Rights
HRIA	Human Rights Impact Assessment
IACHR	Inter-American Commission on Human Rights
ICODR	International Council for Online Dispute Resolution
ICT	Information and Communications Technology
ID card	Identity Card
IJODR	International Journal on Online Dispute Resolution
IPR	Intellectual Property Rights
IPRax	Practice of private international and procedural law (Praxis des Internationalen Privat- und Verfahrensrechts) (Germany)
IT	Information Technology
LED	Directive Directive (EU) 2016/680 of the European Parliament and of the Council of 27 April 2016 on the protection of natural persons regarding the processing of personal data by competent authorities for the purposes of the prevention, investigation, detection, or prosecution of criminal offences or the execution of criminal penalties, and on the free movement of such data, and repealing Council Framework Decision 2008/977/JHA
LGBTY	Lesbian, Gay, Bisexual, Transgender, and Youth
LLM	Large Language Model
LOPJ	Organic Law on the Judiciary Power (Ley Orgánica 6/1985, 1 July, del Poder Judicial) (Spain)
MIAMs	Mediation, Information, and Assessment Meetings
MSME	Micro, Small, and Medium-Sized Enterprise
NADRA	The National Database Registration Authority
NCSC	National Center for State Courts
NFT	Non-Fungible Token
NIS Directive	Directive (EU) 2016/1148 of the European Parliament and of the Council of 6 July 2016 concerning measures for a high common level of security of network and information systems across the Union
NIS 2 Directive	Directive (EU) 2022/2555 of the European Parliament and of the Council of 14 December 2022 on measures for a high common level of cybersecurity across the Union, amending Regulation (EU) No 910/2014 and Directive (EU) 2018/1972, and repealing Directive (EU) 2016/1148
NJAC	National Judicial Automation Committee
NJPMC	National Judicial Policy Making Committee of Pakistan
NODS	National Open Court Data Standards
NPL	Natural Language Processing

NSW	New South Wales
OCMC	Online Civil Money Claims
ODR 2.0	Online Dispute Resolution Version 2
ODR	Online Dispute Resolution
OECD	Organisation for Economic Co-operation and Development
OJ	Official Journal of the European Union
OTP	One-Time Passwords
P2BR	Regulation (EU) 2019/1150 of the European Parliament and of the Council of 20 June 2019 on promoting fairness and transparency for business users of online intermediation services
PCP	Pakistan Citizen Portal
PIN	PIN Code
PNC	Police National Computer
Product Liability Directive	Directive (EU) 2024/2853 of the European Parliament and of the Council of 23 October 2024 on liability for defective products and repealing Council Directive 85/374/EEC
Q/A	Question-Answer
QR code	Quick Response Code
RAG	Retrieval Augmented Generation
RCTs	Randomized Control Trials
REDI	Spanish Journal of International Law (Revista Española de Derecho Internacional) (Spain)
REEI	Electronic Journal of International Studies (Revista Electrónica de Estudios Internacionales) (Spain)
RETE 2001	Council Regulation (EC) 1206/2001 of 28 May 2001 on Cooperation Between the Courts of the Member States in the Taking of Evidence in Civil or Commercial Matters [2001] OJ L 174/1
RETE 2020 1	Parliament and of the Council Regulation (EU) 2020/1783, of 25 November 2020 on Cooperation Between the Courts of the Member States in the Taking of Evidence in Civil or Commercial Matters (Taking of Evidence) [2020] OJ L 405
RGDA	General Journal of Administrative Law (Revista General de Derecho Administrativo) (Spain)
Riv.dir.int.priv.proc	Journal of Private International Law and Procedure (Rivista di Diritto Internazionale Privato e Processuale) (Italy)
RMB	Chinese Renminbi
Royal Decree Law 6/2023	Spanish Royal Decree-Law 6/2023 of 19 December approving urgent measures for the implementation of the Recovery, Transformation and Resilience Plan in the areas of the Judiciary, the Civil Service, Local Government and Patronage (Real Decreto-ley 6/2023, de 19 de diciembre, por el que se aprueban medidas urgentes para la ejecución del Plan de Recuperación, Transformación y Resiliencia en materia de servicio público de justicia, función pública, régimen local y mecenazgo) (Spain).
RSI	Resolution System Institute

SANDI	Self-Help Assistant Navigator for Digital Interactions
SARA network	System of Applications and Networks for Administrations
SCAAR	Apud Acta Appearances in Remote System (Sistema de Comparecencias Apud Acta en Remoto) (Spain)
TC	Spanish Constitutional Court
SCP	Supreme Court of Pakistan
SDGs	Sustainable Development Goals
SDP Act	Spanish Data Protection Act
SDPA	Spanish Data Protection Agency
Service of Documents Regulation	Regulation (EU) No. 2020/1784 of the European Parliament and of the Council of 25 November 2020, Concerning the Service and Transfer of Judicial and Extrajudicial Documents in the Member States in Civil or Commercial Matters
SLRs	Self-Represented Litigants
SMS	Short Message Service
SOPs	Standard Operating Procedures
SPC	Supreme People's Court of China
TFEU	Treaty on the Functioning of the European Union [2010] OJ C 83/47
US	United States of America
UK	United Kingdom
UN	United Nations
UNCITRAL	United Nations Commission on International Trade Law
UNCTAD	United Nations Conference on Trade and Development
UNDP	United Nations Development Program
UNGPs	United Nations Guiding Principles on Business and Human Rights
UPL	Unauthorized Practice of Law
USD	United States Dollar
WAS	Website Authentication Service
WP29	Working Party Article 29 (replaced by EDPB)

Contributors

Ella Sourdin Brown, Juris Doctor, BA Arts is Law Graduate, Monash University, University of Melbourne, Melbourne, Australia

Jose Antonio Castillo Parrilla, PhD is Ramón y Cajal Fellow, University of Granada, Granada, Spain. https://orcid.org/0000-0002-8527-999X

Alex Chung, PhD is Partner at Scopium, London, United Kingdom and former Consumer Policy and Law Expert, UN Trade and Development, Geneva, Switzerland

Pablo Cortés is Professor of Civil Justice, University of Leicester, United Kingdom. https://orcid.org/0000-0002-5981-5189

Fernando Esteban de la Rosa is Professor of Private International Law, University of Granada, Spain. https://orcid.org/0000-0002-2647-9086

Begoña Fernández Rodríguez is PhD student in Legal Sciences: International, European Union and Comparative Law, University of Granada, Spain. https://orcid.org/0000-0002-4702-3758

María José Fernández-Fígares Morales, PhD is Profesora Titular de Derecho Procesal. Departamento de Derecho Procesal, Universidad de Granada, GRANADA, Spain. https://orcid.org/0000-0001-6024-7740

David Freeman Engstrom, JD, PhD is Professor of Law, Stanford Law School, Stanford University, Stanford, CA, USA

Natalie Knowlton, JD/MA is Associate Director of Legal Innovation, Deborah L. Rhode Center on the Legal Profession, Stanford Law School, Stanford, CA, USA

Nuria Marchal Escalona, Phd is Chair in Private International Law, University of Granada, Spain. https://orcid.org/0000-0002-0353-664X

Roberta Montinaro is Professor of private law, Department of Humanities and Social Sciences, University of Naples L'Orientale, Naples, Italy

Ozana Olariu is Lecturer in Public International Law and International Relations, University of Granada, Granada, Spain

Orna Rabinovich-Einy, JSD is Law Professor, PI DRA Lab, University of Haifa, Israel. https://orcid.org/0000-0002-9855-0072

Nauman Reayat is Lecturer in Law, Leicester Law School, University of Leicester, United Kingdom. https://orcid.org/0000-0002-9426-4300

Amy J. Schmitz, BA, JD is Professor & John Deaver Drinko-Baker & Hostetler Chair in Law, Director, JusticeTech, Co-Director, Translational Data Analytics Institute Responsible Data Science CoP, Moritz College of Law, The Ohio State University, Columbus, United States

Ayelet Sela is Lecturer (Assistant Professor), Faculty of Law, Bar-Ilan University, Ramat Gan, Israel, Stanford University, Tel Aviv, United States, Israel. https://orcid.org/0000-0003-4287-9191

Tania Sourdin, BA, LLB, LLM, PhD is Professor Emerita, University of Newcastle, Australia, Newcastle, Australia. https://orcid.org/0000-0001-8620-1513

Javier Valls-Prieto, PhD is Professor, Criminal Law, University of Granada, Granada, Spain

Ying Yu, PhD is Distinguished Professor at Beijing Normal University's (BNU) Internet Institute, Beijing, China and former Legal Officer at the United Nations, Geneva, Switzerland

John Zeleznikow, B Sc (Hons), PhD, Grad Dip Comp is Professor, Law School, La Trobe University, Bundoora, Australia

Introduction

Fernando Esteban de la Rosa, Pablo Cortés, and Nuria Marchal Escalona

The Demand for Digital Transformation in Justice Systems to Improve Access to Justice

The catalyst for the digital transformation in legal services is fuelled by the growth in other economic sectors, such as education, finance, and commerce. In an era where technology permeates every aspect of society, this shift has created a pressing demand for modernization in the justice sector, aiming to enhance efficiency, accessibility, and responsiveness while addressing growing caseloads and persistent barriers to justice.

Successive waves of technological advancements have influenced justice systems in many countries around the world. In the 1990s, the use of office tools, such as computers and word processors, became widespread. In the second decade of the 21st century, the deployment of electronic case management systems began. In that moment, the onset of digitalization in courts evolved from mere digitalization of records to the adoption of comprehensive case management systems. These systems revolutionized how courts operate, starting to enable electronic filing, scheduling, and tracking of cases. By the mid-2010's, experimentation with the creation of the first pilot projects for online courts was underway in many jurisdictions.[1] Mobility restrictions imposed in the aftermath of the Covid 19 pandemic was another important factor that encouraged the digitalization of the court process. Even though digital tools were used before in courts, it was after the pandemic that the implementation of remote work and the use of videoconferencing emerged as effective widespread tools for conducting hearings, gathering evidence, and serving the public. Other technological tools that are transforming judicial systems include electronic communications, which have evolved from emails to electronic portals, the adoption of Cloud Computing and ODR (Online Dispute Resolution) Platforms, and the Modalities for Identity Management, evolving from a Username and Password model to the use of biometric technologies. Furthermore, the nowadays implementation of 5G networks is enhancing connectivity, enabling faster data transmission, and real-time interactions, which are essential for remote hearings, video conferencing, and digital case management systems. Steps have also been taken to advance system interoperability, facilitating interconnection between judicial bodies and other institutions such as registries, the prosecution

[1] See Remote Courts Worldwide. Available at <https://remotecourts.org>, hereinafter, last accessed 6 January 2025.

Fernando Esteban de la Rosa, Pablo Cortés, and Nuria Marchal Escalona, *Introduction* In: *Digitalization and Artificial Intelligence in Courts*. Edited by: Fernando Esteban de la Rosa, Pablo Cortés, and Nuria Marchal Escalona, Oxford University Press.
DOI: 10.1093/9780198918752.001.0001

service, and the police. This interoperability also enables cross-border communications, enabling an easier international cooperation.

Running in parallel Artificial Intelligence (AI) systems and blockchain technology have also emerged. The last momentous driver in the digitalization process has been the recent developments with AI, notably with the advances of Large Language Models (LLMs), such as ChatGPT, have begun to carve out its role within the legal system. AI's application ranges from automating routine tasks to providing sophisticated tools for legal research, predictive analytics in litigation outcomes, providing legal information to users and facilitating dispute resolution. AI technologies, such as expert systems, natural language processing and machine learning, are not just auxiliary tools but may also be increasingly central to the functioning of courts and legal practices. They offer the promise of making legal processes more efficient and are poised to redefine the nature of legal research, evidence analysis, and even some aspects of judicial decision-making.

The use of technology offers new opportunities to transform judicial systems and widen access to justice. Digitalization can improve the efficiency of work within the administration of the justice system and contribute to a justice system that is closer to the citizens, promoting also greater transparency and accessibility. The traditional structure of a justice system, based on face-to-face, paper-based, and labour-intensive processes is no longer the only option, as new opportunities for streamlined, efficient, and accessible forms of justice administration are increasingly being embraced. Digitalization can enable remote access to court rulings, judicial files by professionals and users of the justice system, online payment of judicial fees, and the submission of requests for legal aid. It may also facilitate the provision of virtual hearings, allow users to track their proceedings, and promote settlements. Furthermore, the integration of chatbots can provide legal information, guidance on filing lawsuits, assistance in selecting relevant documents, and support in drafting legal documents, improving the accessibility, efficiency, and user experience within the judicial process.

The use of technology can facilitate the simplification of procedures, overcome physical and temporal barriers, accelerate judicial processes, reduce costs, and enhance litigation prevention and containment by promoting settlements. As a result, digitalization offers the opportunity to reimagine the judicial system by integrating technology into its processes. Documents-only processes, such as money claims, have already started transitioning online. In a similar vein, the digitalization also reached other court processes, often starting with small claims where the low value of the claims requires proportionate processes that minimize litigants' costs. Notably, in China blockchain technology is routinely being used before the Internet courts to certify the authenticity of electronic transactions, providing reliable evidence for the judiciary.

Technology is also transforming the work of lawyers. Freeman Engstrom and Vogt identified three waves of legal-tech tools. The first wave is the use of generic technologies that are already being used in different business sectors, such as word processors and spreadsheets; the second wave consists of legal tech tools that have been designed for lawyers, such as e-discovery software; and the third wave, which is expected to revolutionize the legal market, consists of AI tools and other natural language processing (NPL) tools which can complement, and sometimes replace, the role of lawyers.[2] They argue that all these legal-tech tools deploy two main tasks: research and analytics. NLP tools can offer a Q&A tool for disputants and lawyers, while the most advance systems can draft legal documents and predict case outcomes.[3] Yet, it has been observed that currently the most cutting-edge tools tend to concentrate within specific, compact domains, which are frequently self-contained and often characterized by technocratic expertise, like tax or employment law.[4]

The Emergence of Standards for the Digitalization and Use of Artificial Intelligence in Justice Systems

The digitalization and integration of AI systems in justice systems are not without challenges. As this collective book highlights, these include difficulties arising from insufficient digital connectivity and literacy (the digital divide). In this regard, doubts may emerge about users' ability to effectively navigate web-based procedures, whose treatment raises concerns closely linked to due process requirements. These issues exist alongside general concerns related to how organizational elements must fulfil the requirements arising from keeping data privacy and cybersecurity. The use of AI systems also raises concerns, including a lack of transparency, the potential for bias, and the controversial compatibility of automated decisions with democratic principles. Moreover, this transformation raises deeper questions about the fundamental nature of justice administration, including the balance between human judgment and automated processes, and the need to preserve the human elements that are critical to the adjudication process. Moreover, these concerns extend to encompass matters of professional deontology in the use of AI systems by legal professionals.

As access to justice is a crucial component of the rule of law, the most important international organizations have expressed—and continue to express—concern about ensuring that the digitalization of justice systems delivers tangible results in the form of improved access to justice without leaving anyone behind. Among them, the United Nations, the Council of Europe, the European Union, the OECD, or the World Bank have addressed and continue to focus on this matter.[5] Accordingly, the technological

[2] David Freeman Engstrom and Robert Vogt, 'The New Judicial Governance: Courts Data, and the Future of Civil Justice' (2023) 72 De Paul Law Review 198–200.

[3] ibid, 200–01. See, also, Rob Carty, 'Computer-Written Legal Briefs Are Closer Than You Think' Artificial Lawyer (11 April 2019). Available at <https://www.artificiallawyer.com/2019/04/11/computer-written-legal-briefs-are-closer-than-you-think>; and Leonor Moral Soriano, 'Legal Intelligence at the Intersection between AI and Law', in Fernando Esteban de la Rosa and others (ed.), *Justice, Trade, Security and Individual Freedoms in the Digital Society* (2021 Thomson Reuters) 29.

[4] Freeman et al (n 2) 202. See also Benjamin Alarie, Anthony Niblett, and Albert Yoon, 'Using Machine Learning to Predict Outcomes in Tax Law' (2016) 58 Canadian Business Law Journal 253.

[5] See United Nations (General Assembly), 'Transforming our world: the 2030 Agenda for Sustainable Development', (Resolution) A/RES/70/1; UNCITRAL, Technical Notes on Online Dispute Resolution [2017]; UNDP 'e-Justice. Digital Transformation to Close the Justice Gap' [2022]; ECLC, 'Guidelines on online dispute resolution mechanisms in civil and administrative court proceedings', 1407th meeting, 16 June 2021; CEPEJ, 2022–2025 CEPEJ Action plan: 'Digitalisation for a better justice' CEPEJ(2021) 12 Final; European Commission, *Digitalisation of justice in the European Union: A toolbox of opportunities*, COM(2020) 710 final, 2/12/2020; EP, Council and Commission, European Declaration on Digital Rights and Principles for the Digital Decade, OJEU 23/01/2023 C23/1; OECD, 'OECD Online Dispute Resolution Framework', OECD Public Governance Policy Papers, No 59, OECD Publishing, Paris, [2024].

developments and their application in the justice space is resulting in the emergence of guidelines and rules that seek to ensure that these digital processes do not discriminate amongst users and comply with due process.

This emerging regulation is particularly notable in the AI space, a field in which binding regulations and soft law are overlapping at the conventional, supranational, and national levels, with the aim of promoting its use and controlling the harms that may result from the use of AI systems in the justice field. It is a movement that finds exponents all around the world. In America, the US is developing guidelines from a soft law approach. Notably, the US AI Bill of Rights is highly relevant for digital courts, offering a framework to guide the ethical use of artificial intelligence within judicial systems.[6] Key principles for AI use in digital courts include ensuring safe and unbiased systems, protecting against algorithmic discrimination, safeguarding data privacy, providing transparency about AI roles, and offering human review options to maintain fairness and trust. In China, on 8 December 2022, the Supreme People's Court issued the Opinions on Regulating and Strengthening the Applications of Artificial Intelligence in the Judicial Fields with the aim of promoting the deep integration of artificial intelligence with judicial work, enhancing the development of smart courts, and striving to achieve a higher level of digital justice.[7]

The European regional framework provides significant examples of texts establishing standards for the use of AI systems in the judicial domain. The 2021 Council of Europe's Guide on the use of ODR in legal proceedings has focused on the need to disclose the automated nature of a decision as well as the right to have it reviewed by a human,[8] an approach that goes beyond the requirements provided by Article 22 of the GDPR. In a similar vein, human review of automated decisions is required in out-of-court processes. In the EU, the Digital Services Act[9] and the Consumer ADR Directive[10] ensure users can request human oversight when decisions

Available at <https://doi.org/10.1787/325e6edc-en>; OECD, 'Recommendation on Access to Justice and People-Centred Justice Systems', [2023], <https://legalinstruments.oecd.org/en/instruments/OECD-LEGAL-0498>; European Union, European e-Justice Strategy 2024–2028, C/2025/437, OJEU 16.1.2025. In December 2024, the World Bank's Digital Justice Working Group was created with the aim of improving the performance of justice systems and delivering better services to citizens by digitalizing the justice systems. See <https://www.worldbank.org/en/programs/global-program-on-justice-and-rule-of-law/digital-justice-working-group>.

[6] The White House, *Blueprint for an AI Bill of Rights—Making Automated Systems Work for the American People* (October 2022). Available at <https://www.whitehouse.gov/wp-content/uploads/2022/10/Blueprint-for-an-AI-Bill-of-Rights.pdf>.

[7] The Supreme People's Court, The Opinions on Regulating and Strengthening the Applications of Artificial Intelligence in the Judicial Fields (2022). Available at <https://www.chinajusticeobserver.com/law/x/the-supreme-people-s-court-the-opinions-on-regulating-and-strengthening-the-applications-of-artificial-intelligence-in-the-judicial-field-20221208>.

[8] European Committee on Legal Cooperation, Guidelines of the Committee of Ministers of the Council of Europe on online dispute resolution mechanisms in civil and administrative court proceedings—Explanatory Memorandum (16 June 2021) para. 53.

[9] Regulation (EU) 2022/2065 of the European Parliament and of the Council of 19 October 2022 on a Single Market for Digital Services and amending Directive 2000/31/EC [2022] OJ L 277/1.

[10] Directive 2013/11/EU of the European Parliament and of the Council of 21 May 2013 on alternative dispute resolution for consumer disputes and amending Regulation (EC) No 2006/2004 and Directive 2009/22/EC (Directive on consumer ADR) [2013] OJ L 165/63.

are made by automated systems.[11] However, practical challenges arise, as the volume of automated decisions often exceeds the capacity for comprehensive human review. In many cases, humans may simply approve AI-generated outcomes without meaningful scrutiny.[12] This problem may be particularly acute in scenarios where the law prohibits fully automated decisions, such as the GDPR's stipulation that processing personal data affecting legal rights cannot rely solely on automation.

Following the path set by the CEPEJ European Ethical Charter on the Use of Artificial Intelligence in Judicial Systems and Their Environment, the Council of Europe has adopted the first-ever international legally binding treaty to ensure that the use of AI systems upholds human rights, democracy, and the rule of law. This ground-breaking treaty mandates that European countries implement measures to prevent AI from undermining democratic institutions and processes. The treaty establishes a legal framework covering the entire lifecycle of AI systems in both the public and private sectors, offering compliance mechanisms that align with international human rights obligations. Key provisions include requirements for transparency and oversight, measures to identify and mitigate risks, and accountability for adverse impacts. Additionally, the treaty ensures that AI systems respect principles of equality and privacy rights, and it provides legal remedies for victims of human rights violations.

The new European Regulation on AI,[13] often referred to as the AI Act, stands out as it establishes a mandatory framework for AI systems designed for justice systems. The underlying idea of the Regulation is to promote the ethical use of AI systems. The AI Act focuses on data quality, transparency, human oversight, and robustness. It aims to ensure that AI systems adhere to principles of transparency, accountability, and non-discrimination. To that end, it requires prior authorization for the use of AI systems in those fields, such as justice, which are categorized as high-risk uses due to their significant impact on individual safety or fundamental rights. Thus, the EU AI Act holds significant relevance for the digitalization of the courts as it is hoped to support the transformation of courts into more efficient, accessible, and equitable institutions by using AI systems. In theory, the AI Act provides guidelines for integrating AI systems that could speed up processes and make it easier for people to get justice. At the same time, it seeks to prevent AI from violating fundamental rights, undermining democracy, or weakening the rule of law. However, as this book explores whether the AI Act can actually deliver on these promises remains to be seen.

[11] Regulation (EU) 2022/2065 of the European Parliament and of the Council of 19 October 2022 on a Single Market for Digital Services and amending Directive 2000/31/EC (Digital Services Act) Recital 58 and art 20. See also European Commission, A Proposal for a Directive amending Directive 2013/11/EU, COM(2023) 649 final.

[12] Geoffrey Vos, MR, 'Are Rights Sufficiently Human in the Age of the Machine' Blackstone Lecture, Pembroke College, Oxford (27 November 2024) para 24.

[13] Regulation (EU) 2024/1689 of the European Parliament and of the Council of 13 June 2024 laying down harmonized rules on artificial intelligence and amending Regulations (EC) No 300/2008, (EU) No 167/2013, (EU) No 168/2013, (EU) 2018/858, (EU) 2018/1139 and (EU) 2019/2144 and Directives 2014/90/EU, (EU) 2016/797 and (EU) 2020/1828 (Artificial Intelligence Act) [2024] OJ L 1689/1.

Purpose and Structure of the Book

The book's main objective is to describe how digitalization and AI are transforming, and may transform, the courts' functioning, the legal profession, and access to justice. The book observes how the role of managing disputes is increasingly shared with technological tools, which are gradually displacing the functions of legal professionals, judges, and other third-party neutrals. This is particularly evident when AI is embedded in the resolution process, either as a tool to inform judicial decisions or even to replace judges altogether. Accordingly, the book seeks to contribute to understanding how the digitalization of court proceedings affects litigants' ability to access the courts and engage in the dispute resolution process. It also aims to explore how the digital transformation of justice systems can be implemented to maximize efficiency, improve transparency, and expand access to justice. By leveraging the possibilities offered by existing technology, this transformation seeks to bring justice closer to citizens. At the same time, it must carefully avoid risks such as the loss of rights or the undermining of the fundamental role that courts play in our societies.

With this purpose, the book seeks to examine the main opportunities arising from the transition from face-to-face and conventional technology-assisted justice systems to advanced digital justice systems and to explore how digitalization and AI may reshape courts, prompting a re-evaluation of traditional practices and opening new avenues for delivering justice in the twenty-first century. In the same vein, the book addresses the current challenges in the digital transformation of justice systems, considering the possibilities offered by technology within the existing legal and ethical frameworks. Thus, the book considers both technological innovations and the ethical, legal, and social implications of their application in courts. In doing so, it seeks to analyse both the potential benefits and the challenges or drawbacks that accompany these technologies, providing recommendations to address possible shortcomings. This approach aims to ensure that the steps taken are consistent with regulatory frameworks, fundamental rights, and ethical principles, while correctly guiding progressive steps to ensure that digitalization becomes an ally in improving access to justice; the main goal it should serve. Given the global nature of the topic, this book brings together the specialized perspectives of academic experts from various countries around the world, reflecting opportunities and concerns about the digitalization of justice systems in diverse contexts and at different stages of development.

This book aims to inform readers about the impact of technology on the functioning of courts. Given its global scope and the broad range of potential topics, the subjects have been carefully selected to provide a comprehensive and inclusive overview of the key debates and tensions shaping the configuration, design, and direction of advanced digitalization in justice systems. It seeks to help readers understand the social, legal, and ethical issues surrounding the digital transformation of justice.

The book highlights emerging topics in digital justice, with a particular focus on the digital transformation of courts and the integration of AI systems. To achieve this goal, the book is organized into the following three sections:

Part I: Building Foundations for the Digitalization of the Justice Systems

First part aims to shed light on the need for digitalization initiatives to explain their methodological foundations and the guiding principles underpinning them. In addition, it seeks to identify the new needs arising from the digitalization process, the ways in which progress can be achieved, as well as how it is possible to legally and technically ensure a better access to justice and the protection of rights that may be impacted by their implementation. Chapters 1 and 2 propose conceptual frameworks to support a thoughtful integration of technological tools into dispute resolution processes. Chapter 1, by Fernando Esteban de la Rosa, explores the growing potential of the people-centred approach to guiding digitalization initiatives. Through various examples of national regulatory measures and proposals, it highlights this approach as a guiding principle for identifying legal solutions that support advanced digitalization. In Chapter 2, Orna Rabinovich demonstrates how technology can provide tailored solutions for different contexts, enhancing the effectiveness of dispute resolution while promoting accessibility and ensuring fairness. Chapter 3, by José Antonio Castillo Parrilla, examines the critical task of designing a digital justice system that meets the requirements of personal data protection and cybersecurity. Finally, Chapter 4, by Begoña Fernández Rodríguez, delves into the challenge of building a digital justice system that fosters trust and legal certainty in a virtual environment. It also explores the potential role of biometric technology in achieving these objectives.

Part II: The impact of Technology in Transforming National Courts and Cross-border Litigation

The digitalization of justice systems is a practical process, led primarily by States that are experimenting with the best ways to implement technology in their dispute resolution processes. Its future orientation should be largely based on learning from both successful and unsuccessful experiences, reflecting on the reasons for these outcomes, and continuously considering new paths forward, including the most disruptive technologies, such as AI and blockchain. Accordingly, the second part of the book turns its attention to offer knowledge regarding selected national innovative experiences on digitalization of dispute resolution processes. It examines national developments in transformative digitalization initiatives within court processes, showcasing examples of the integration of digital tools and ODR. Accordingly, the following chapters offer an analysis of how different legal systems are adapting to the integration of technology, examining the resulting shifts towards a plurality of processes that seek to increase access to justice. In addition, they critically assess the challenges that accompany these advancements, including concerns about digital divides, algorithmic bias, and the need for robust regulatory frameworks.

This Part II of the book thus explores how technology is changing the way we resolve disputes. It looks at how technology is creating a wider range of options for people to find solutions, beyond traditional courtrooms. The authors examine the impact of these changes on access to justice in different legal systems around the world, including England, the United States, and China. They also look at the specific challenges faced by developing countries like Pakistan in adopting these new technologies. Finally, it analyses the European Union's leading role in creating laws and digital systems for handling legal cases across borders.

In Chapter 5 Pablo Cortés considers the contribution that technology is making in England and Wales to the amicable resolution of disputes, providing an alternative to more costly and adversarial court adjudication, particularly in relation to personal injury claims and small claims. Amy Schmitz, in Chapter 6, examines ODR initiatives in US courts, reviewing notable programs such as Florida's pilot program, Utah's small claims ODR system, and Michigan's traffic dispute ODR platform. Chapter 7 by Alex Chung and Ying Yu discuss the approach China has taking to adapt its judicial system to address disputes arising from the digital economy, a pathway supported by the establishment of Internet Courts specifically designed to resolve such disputes, along with the integration of AI systems and blockchain technology. Chapter 8, by Nauman Reayat, addresses the challenges commonly hindering the digitalization of justice systems in low- and middle-income countries, using Pakistan as a case study. The chapter aims to offer proposals tailored to countries with large populations and significant case backlogs, aiming to enhance access to justice and improve efficiency in managing the substantial number of pending cases. Chapter 9, by Nuria Marchal Escalona, and Chapter 10, by María José Fernández-Fígares Morales, analyse the EU's efforts to improve judicial cooperation in civil matters through technology and to make justice more accessible, efficient and user-friendly for citizens involved in cross-border judicial proceedings. The chapters describe the legal, technological, and coordination innovations being implemented by the European Union to electronically facilitate access to justice in cross-border cases. While Nuria Marchal provides a general overview of the new system and focuses on judicial services, the submission of documents, and the use of videoconferencing for hearings, María José Fernández-Fígares Morales specifically addresses the legal possibility for judges in one European country to conduct evidence-gathering via videoconferencing with individuals located in other Member State.

Part III: The Rise of AI in Digital Courts

Given its great potential to impact the administration of justice, the book dedicates an entire section to the emergence of the use of AI in courts of justice. Part III explores the versatile potential of AI within digital courts, examining both theoretical and practical considerations. The section examines the implications of the use of AI systems for international human rights processes, the evolving theoretical underpinnings of justice in a digital society, and the crucial need for the effective governance of intelligent systems.

Chapter 11, by Ozana Olariu and John Zeleznikow, highlights the risks that the use of AI can pose to individuals, including perpetuating bias, discriminating against vulnerable groups, and undermining fundamental freedoms, such as privacy, freedom of expression, and the right to a fair trial. It also provides a global overview of the emerging multi-level regulatory framework, encompassing global, regional, and domestic initiatives for protection. This chapter examines the key principles underpinning a human rights-centric approach to AI governance, and the mechanisms necessary for effective implementation. This introductory chapter sets the stage for a deeper exploration of these critical issues in the subsequent chapters of this book. Chapter 12 by Javier Valls-Prieto examines the growing use of AI in the judicial system, focusing on its potential benefits and risks, particularly regarding fundamental human rights. It discusses AI's impact on rights such as freedom, equality, and privacy, with specific attention to pre-trial detention and sentencing.

Chapter 13 by Roberta Montinaro examines the use of AI systems, particularly LLMs, in processing judicial decisions and legal data within the EU legal framework. In particular, Montinaro reviews the EU AI Act and the Council of Europe Framework Convention on Artificial Intelligence and Human Rights, Democracy, and the Rule of Law. The discussion extends to the use of LLMs' capabilities in legal research, document generation, and natural language understanding.

In Chapter 14 John Zeleznikow discusses the transformative integration of AI into the ongoing digitalization of justice administration, with a particular focus on its potential to enhance access to justice for self-represented litigants (SRLs). The chapter reviews various ODR systems, including the pioneering British Columbia Civil Resolution Tribunal and the Dutch Rechtwijzer and explores the integration of AI into ODR systems, discussing both research prototypes and systems in use, such as Split-Up and Amica, which leverage AI to provide negotiation support and advice on asset division.

Chapter 15 by David Freeman Engstrom, Ayelet Sela, and Natalie Knowlton explores the evolving landscape of AI within American courts, focusing on its potential to enhance access to justice. The chapter identifies the numerous challenges to realizing AI's full potential in courts, among them a 'checkerboard' of varying data infrastructures across jurisdictions and courts, courts limited technical capacity, legal-cultural barriers, and norms of court neutrality.

Finally, chapter 16 by Tania Sourdin and Ella Sourdin Brown explores the ethical and societal challenges associated with integrating AI into judicial decision-making, particularly focusing on the controversial concept of 'Judge AI.' The chapter evaluates the EU's AI Act and examines areas where Judge AI would be suitable. The authors set the stage for a discussion on how AI can be responsibly incorporated into judicial systems while safeguarding fundamental legal principles.

We hope that the diverse perspectives presented in the chapters of this book will inspire readers to explore the fascinating world of the digitalization of justice systems, a subject that is far more than a mere technical matter and one that has the potential to profoundly impact the future of humanity.

PART I
BUILDING FOUNDATIONS FOR THE DIGITALIZATION OF THE JUSTICE SYSTEMS

1

Towards a People-Centric Digitalization of Justice Systems

Fostering Empowerment, New Rights, and Fair Treatment amid the Digital Divide

*Fernando Esteban de la Rosa**

A. Introduction

The unstoppable digitalization of societies in the Fourth Industrial Revolution[1] has impacted justice systems. Information and Communications Technology (ICT) represents a crucial element in the functioning of many justice systems in Europe, the Americas, and Asia.[2] Prior to the COVID-19 pandemic, electronic communications

* Professor of Private International Law. Director of the Research Unit of Excellence 'Digital Society: Security and Protection of Rights' of the University of Granada. Member of the Digital Justice Working Group (The World Bank). This research has been supported by Spanish Ministry of Research, Innovation and Universities, within the project TED2021-131127B-I00 'Building the foundations for an efficient, legal and safeguards digitalisation of alternative dispute resolution systems for consumer disputes through technological platforms' (COBADIRALCO).

[1] Klaus Schwab, *La cuarta revolución industrial* (Debate 2016).

[2] For an overview of the current status of the digital transformation of justice systems in 14 countries, see Antonio Garrido Reus, *Online Courts: Comparative Study* (PRK Partners & Masaryk University, 2022) <https://www.prkpartners.com/files/0-final-version-online-courts-comparative-study-antonio-garrido-reus-prk-partners-masaryk-university.pdf> last accessed 25 October 2024.

Fernando Esteban de la Rosa, *Towards a People-Centric Digitalization of Justice Systems* In: *Digitalization and Artificial Intelligence in Courts*. Edited by: Fernando Esteban de la Rosa, Pablo Cortés, and Nuria Marchal Escalona, Oxford University Press. © Fernando Esteban de la Rosa 2025. DOI: 10.1093/9780198918752.003.0001

and procedural management systems had already made key progress. Many justice systems rely on remote electronic interactions, justice officials working from home, and videoconferencing.[3] 5G networks, cloud computing, user geolocation, system access traceability, infrastructure interoperability, online dispute resolution (ODR) platforms, new possibilities for identity management, expert systems, AI systems, new foundational models, cybercomputing, blockchain technology, and gigabit connectivity offer new potential for transforming the civil justice system, improving efficiency in dispute resolution, and enhancing access to justice.[4] According to the 2023 EU Justice Scoreboard,[5]

> The use of ICT may strengthen the Member States' justice systems and make them more accessible, efficient, resilient, and ready to face current and future challenges.

Digitalization enables access to judgments, online payment of court fees, online filing of legal aid applications, citizens' access to their court files, remote public services and hearings, notices, information on the average length of proceedings,[6] chatbots for legal information, case diagnosis, steps to file a complaint, and assistance with selecting relevant files. These innovations may increase transparency and contribute to overcoming time and geographical barriers, including borders. The most recent developments in European Judicial Cooperation in Civil and Commercial matters include several key enhancements: using videoconferencing for direct evidence collection and hearings involving individuals from countries outside the court's jurisdiction, the cross-border service of judicial documents, and the electronic submission of pleadings to courts in other European Union member states.[7]

Justice initiative digitalization contributes to the achievement of Goal 16 of the UN 2030 Agenda to promote peaceful and inclusive societies and facilitate access to justice.[8] The development of digitalization must take place in compliance with the legal framework, without jeopardizing the enjoyment of fundamental rights and without leaving anyone behind. In addition, the concern of ensuring that ODR and the use of technology comply with ethical principles has been reaffirmed since the middle of the last decade, and it has led to guidelines and standards development.[9] However,

[3] Tania Sourdin and John Zeleznikow, 'Courts, Mediation and COVID-19' (2020) 48(2) Australian Business L Rev 138.

[4] Aura Esther Vilalta Nicuesa, 'Acceso a la justicia y su transición digital: hacia una justicia abierta al ciudadano (A2J4all)' (2021) 58 Revista General de Derecho Administrativo 2.

[5] Commission, 'The 2023 EU Justice Scoreboard' (Communication) COM (2023) 309.

[6] Information provided by the Hungarian Electronic Administration Portal <https://e-ugyintezes.birosag.hu/eljaras-idotartam-kalkulator> last accessed 25 October 2024.

[7] Commission, 'Digitalisation of justice in the European Union: A toolbox of opportunities' (Communication) (2020) 710 final; EP and Council Regulation 2020/1783 on taking of evidence [2020] OJ L405/1; EP and Council Regulation 2020/1784 on service of judicial and extrajudicial documents [2020] OJ L405/40; EP and Council Regulation (EU) 2023/2844 on digitalisation of judicial cooperation and access to justice [2023] OJ L 27.12.2023.

[8] General Assembly of the United Nations, 'Transforming our world: the 2030 Agenda for Sustainable Development' (Resolution) A/RES/70/1. See also UNDP, 'e-Justice: Digital Transformation to Close the Justice Gap' 2022.

[9] UNCITRAL, 'Technical Notes on Online Dispute Resolution' (2017); APEC, 'Collaborative Framework For ODR of Cross-Border B2B Disputes' (2019); OECD, 'OECD Online Dispute Resolution Framework'; OECD Public Governance Policy Papers, No. 59, OECD Publishing, Paris, (2024) <https://

a single roadmap does not exist. ICT innovation in justice systems does not always follow the same path because of the diverse factors that influence system digitalization.[10] Although the objectives of digital transformation are generally shared, the implementation processes must consider the political and technological starting points, as well as the cultural, territorial, and legal circumstances of the affected societies. For instance, online courts face different development prospects in continental countries than in common law countries, where litigation without legal representation is more widely accepted.[11] This disparity may lead to significant differences in the design of platforms to accommodate users who lack legal knowledge. Country-specific analyses and assessments, accompanied by policy recommendations, are becoming increasingly valuable for the successful implementation of digitalization projects.[12]

Today's intensification of digitalization has given rise to a movement aimed at proclaiming the need to put people at the centre. In June 2021 the Council of Europe[13] proclaimed that: 'ODR should be easily understood, affordable and user-friendly so that it can be used comfortably by as many people as possible'. On 9 December 2021 the European Commission for the Efficiency of Justice (CEPEJ) adopted its 2022–25 Action Plan, titled 'Digitalisation for a Better Justice'. The plan prioritizes supporting States and courts in transitioning to digital justice systems in line with European standards, particularly Article 6 of the European Convention on Human Rights. A key focus is people-centred justice, which emphasizes training for justice professionals and users to effectively utilize digital tools. There it is submitted that while users should be supported through training, digital proficiency should not become a prerequisite for access to justice.[14]

doi.org/10.1787/325e6edc-en> last accessed 25 October 2024. Given its focus on studying and analysing ODR systems worldwide, the initiatives developed by the National Center for Technology and Dispute Resolution (https://odr.info/ethics-and-odr/) and the International Council for Online Dispute Resolution (https://icodr.org/standards/) are particularly valuable.

10 Among them are tensions between local versus centralized solutions, the development of specialized tools versus more global and generic systems, data security versus external access by users and competences between the executive power in this area and judicial power. CEPEJ, 'European judicial systems. Evaluation Report' (2020) Evaluation cycle (2018 data) 95.

11 Rabeea Assy, *Injustice in Person: The Right to Self-representation* (OUP 2015).

12 NCSC, 'A guide to help design your ODR' <https://nationalcenterforstatecourts.app.box.com/s/ypjzrnfohwao3j1httwoa6mjlgxxeimw> and 'Request for Information (RFI) Toolkit for Courts Procuring Online Dispute Resolution (ODR) Technology' <https://nationalcenterforstatecourts.app.box.com/s/gtyiz0m5vjv76pykn1z5q51jhukp11yt> last accessed 11 July 2025. ; Mexico Evalua, 'Guía de Buenas Prácticas en el uso de nuevas tecnologías para la impartición de justicia' (7/10/2020) <www.mexicoevalua.org/guia-de-buenas-practicas-en-el-uso-de-nuevas-tecnologias-para-la-imparticion-de-justicia> last accessed 25 October 2024; Fernando Esteban de la Rosa (ed), 'Guía Justicia Digital' (Fundación COTEC-UGR 2022) <https://cotec.es/proyectos-cpt/guia-para-la-justicia-digital> last accessed 25 October 2024; OECD, 'Developing Effective Online Dispute Resolution in Latvia, Paris, 2024, <https://doi.org/10.1787/75ef5c4c-en> last accessed 25 October 2024; OECD, 'Measuring and improving access to justice in court services: Learning from the United Kingdom's experience', OECD Public Governance Policy Papers, No 60, OECD Publishing, Paris, 2024, <https://doi.org/10.1787/a8226ccc-en> last accessed 25 October 2024. For the European judicial cooperation in civil and commercial matters see COM(2020) 710 final.

13 ECLC, 'Guidelines on online dispute resolution mechanisms in civil and administrative court proceedings', 1407th meeting, 16 June 2021.

14 CEPEJ, 2022–25 CEPEJ Action plan: 'Digitalisation for a better justice' CEPEJ (2021) 12 Final.

As a prominent expression of this trend, the European Declaration on Digital Rights and Principles for the Digital Decade declares that '[p]eople are at the centre of the digital transformation in the European Union. Technology should serve and benefit all people living in the EU and empower them to pursue their aspirations, in full security and respect for their fundamental rights'.[15] In a more daring way, the *Recommendation on Access to Justice and People-Centred Justice Systems* adopted by the OECD in 2023 includes the meaning of people-centricity.

> People-centricity refers to a human-centred approach that adopts the perspective of people as a starting point and places people at the core when designing, delivering, implementing and evaluating public policies, services and legal procedures within and beyond the justice system. It takes into account the perspectives and needs of specific communities, including marginalised, underserved and groups in vulnerable situations (e.g. women, children, indigenous groups, elderly and people with disabilities).

According to this, it is recommended that adherents

> Design and deliver people-centred legal and justice services by: a) ensuring the availability, accessibility, and quality of a continuum of legal and justice-related services; b) ensuring that legal, justice and related services are: i. designed with people at the centre, taking into account their rights and possible vulnerabilities, and based on empirical understanding of their legal and justice needs, preferences and capabilities.

The European e-Justice Strategy 2024–2028,[16] aiming to identify strategic and operational objectives and the principles that should be respected when carrying out this digital transformation process, establishes as three of the substantial principles the following:

> c. People centricity: In line with the Declaration on Digital Rights and Principles for the Digital Decade, any efforts in the area of the digitalisation of justice should be focused on the needs of the people. People are at the centre of the digital transformation in the European Union. People-centred services are accessible to all, are tailored to people's needs and comply with high quality standards. The needs of all people, including those lacking digital skills or tools, should be met equally by enabling effective participation and engagement in judicial proceedings. Shifting the focus to the people's perspective and making justice systems more accessible, effective and transparent will therefore be essential for strengthening trust between the people and public institutions.
>
> d. Bridging the digital divide. To promote a fair and balanced justice landscape across Europe, it is essential to reduce the digital divide that creates inequality in access to justice. This is not only a potential source of exclusion for citizens, but also an obstacle to the exercise of their rights. This principle also covers the need to work

[15] OJEU 23/01/2023 C23/1.
[16] Document C/2025/437, OJEU 16.1.2025.

towards an aligned level of justice digitalisation in all EU Member States. By sharing best practices and efforts, we can collectively advance the digital transformation of justice, while maintaining a people-centred perspective, ensuring that everyone's rights are protected and upheld.

e. Digital empowerment of users. 46 % of European citizens (9) currently lack basic digital skills and resources. To enable them to make full use of their rights and opportunities, they should be provided with the digital skills needed to access digital services. The digital transformation of justice must therefore include the digital empowerment of and capacity-building among users. Special attention should be paid to training for justice professionals. Promoting the use of digital tools and resources among justice professionals will enhance their ability to navigate both national and European legal frameworks effectively, thereby ensuring consistency.

It is important to understand well that the human-centred approach includes, but goes beyond, respect for the right to a fair trial and the right to an effective remedy, as proclaimed in Articles 6 (1) and 13 of the European Convention on Human Rights (ECHR). Although this perspective is not defined by specific measures, it has valuable consequences and mandates for justice system digitalization.

First, a people-centred perspective requires gathering information and data on the limitations of the current justice system regarding access to justice, whether by subject matter or by specific vulnerable groups. Data collection is thus a prerequisite for digitalization initiatives. Therefore, it is essential that judicial systems implement a robust policy for collecting justice system data—an approach increasingly adopted by international organizations and state judiciaries.[17]

Second, once these limitations are identified, the current challenges of the justice system must be considered when setting priorities for improvement.[18] Third, the people-centred perspective requires digitalization measures be designed with users in mind. Test phases or pilot projects should be implemented to assess the proper functioning of the system and ensure that it meets the needs of the people it serves. There is also a need for an empirical evaluation of the results obtained through digitalization, comparing the baseline situation with new outcomes. Finally, the human-centric approach implicitly integrates access to justice and procedural justice, recognizing that legislative changes in the field must prioritize people's needs rather than focus solely on system efficiency.[19] To this end, justice system digitalization must adopt measures

[17] UNDP 15 (n 8); for the United Kingdom see OECD, 'Measuring and improving access to justice in court services' (n 12); for Spain see Royal Decree-Law 6/2023 of 19 December approving urgent measures for the implementation of the Recovery, Transformation and Resilience Plan in the areas of the Judiciary, the Civil Service, Local Government and Patronage (2023) (Real Decreto-ley 6/2023, de 19 de diciembre, por el que se aprueban medidas urgentes para la ejecución del Plan de Recuperación, Transformación y Resiliencia en materia de servicio público de justicia, función pública, régimen local y mecenazgo) (SPA). The preamble emphasizes the critical importance of data in a modern digital society, highlighting the commitment to its rational use for generating evidence and certainty in shaping effective public justice policies.

[18] Leah Wing, 'Ethical Principles for Online Dispute Resolution: A GPS Device for the Field' (2016) 3 IJODR 1, 20.

[19] For the Chinese justice system see Liyuan Wang, 'Application of Information Technology in Judicial Field: The Development Model of Online Litigation in China' (2024) 52 Computer Law & Security Review 105936.

that both support digitalization while considering new or special people's needs and address new challenges introduced by justice system digitalization.

This chapter focuses on identifying good practices, safeguards, and measures to achieve a truly people-centred digitalization of justice systems, aiming to enhance efficiency and achieve user empowerment that leaves no one behind. Advanced digitalization increases user exposure to digital technologies, a debate that was once overshadowed by the allure of digitalization but is now gaining renewed relevance based on recent experiences. Addressing the digital divide caused by a lack of equipment or connectivity and by insufficient digital literacy, along with protecting rights in human–machine interactions, is paramount. This issue is critical in judicial situations involving self-represented litigants (SRLs). This chapter aims to identify good practices, regulations, and measures that contribute to a people-centred adjustment of the functions offered by the digital public justice system. To achieve this, we review the models used for the digitalization of electronic communications, videoconferencing, and online courts, assessing the extent to which they address the digital divide fairly and comply with data protection regulations.

B. People-centred Practices in Digital Communications

1. The judicial service

With the widespread use of remote communication methods and their high social acceptance, many judicial systems have adopted electronic communication to deliver justice. The influence of the social and technological context on the interpretation of fundamental rights has been recognized by the ECHR. In the case *Stichting Landgoed Steenbergen and Others v the Netherlands*, it was determined that the introduction of electronic services did not contradict the principle of due process recognized by most Western legal systems. This finding is contingent on high internet penetration, lack of significant evidence of computer illiteracy, and a solid normative basis for electronic services.[20]

Efficiency improves when electronic services become the standard or default system, a model adopted by several judicial systems for specific procedures or particular groups.[21] The focus shifts when technology is emphasized as a means of empowering individuals and justice system users. Accordingly, recent guidelines recommend a strategic approach that moves away from a digital-by-default policy.[22]

[20] App no 19732/17 (ECHR, 16 February 2021) paras 48–52.

[21] Estonia is among the pioneers. In the Netherlands, the Basic Plan for Digitalisation (November 2019) introduces a new digital solution for civil and administrative law jurisdictions, facilitating the implementation of compulsory digital litigation as outlined in the Quality and Innovation of the Judiciary (KEI) programme <https://cms.law/en/int/expert-guides/cms-expert-guide-to-digital-litigation/netherlands> last accessed 25 October 2024. In Spain since 2017 the system of mandatory electronic judicial service has been gradually extended to different groups (professionals, legal persons, entities without legal personality, now civil servants litigating in their own name on their statutory rights). See art 273 CPA 2000 (Ley de Enjuiciamiento Civil). In China see Fang Xuhui, 'Recent Development of Internet Courts in China' (2018) (5) IJODR 1-2 55.

[22] See first point of the European Declaration on Digital Rights and Principles for the Digital Decade. OECD, 'Developing Effective Online Dispute Resolution in Latvia' (n 12); at the national level see art

Despite proclamations, the widespread adoption of digital channels across all sectors of society, including judicial systems, is expected within a few years, contingent on the level of commitment and investment. In a highly digitalized environment, the rules that most effectively respect individual needs are those requiring the recipient's informed consent as a condition for service validity.[23] An intermediate dual-service system may provide a satisfactory solution to facilitate a smooth transition without causing any difficulties. This system, in which service occurs in both traditional and digital formats without mandating the latter, aligns more closely with the idea of digitalization tailored to people's needs.[24] The optional dual system optimizes efficiency and appears to have minimal impact on protection against vulnerability. However, digital formats require skills that are not universally available to all users.

Professionals, on the other hand, are increasingly excluded from this flexibility, as judicial systems mandate electronic notifications for them by categorizing them de facto as part of the judicial system. In this way, the Spanish Constitutional Court noted the following:

> It is difficult to identify any legal obstacles that the shift from an in-person to an electronic system, accessible from various devices and locations for individual convenience, might pose to the welfare of lawyers. Given their commitment and professional duties, these professionals are expected to check their electronic mailboxes daily or almost every day.[25]

As a balancing mechanism and widely recognized as good practice, judicial systems are beginning to counter the categorical nature of this obligation by acknowledging the right to digital disconnection for professionals. Beyond considering digital literacy, this measure aims to facilitate a healthy balance between work and personal life among those associated with administration of justice.[26]

Email was one of the first electronic tools adopted by judicial systems to advance judicial service digitalization. However, experience has shown that email does not fully meet all the requirements related to judicial services. Specifically, email does not adequately support the cybersecurity and data protection requirements essential to uphold the right to effective judicial protection.[27] Messages often arrive in inboxes that can be last accessed without re-entering passwords, and most email addresses are provided by large companies in the private sector. Further, notifications may be

XVIII para 4 of the Spanish Government's Charter of Digital Rights adopted in 2021; in China, see the Online Litigation Rules of the People's Courts, Fa Shi [2021] no 12 (Adopted at the 1,838th meeting of the Adjudication Committee of the Supreme People's Court on 18 May 2021, and effective as of 1 August 2021).

[23] Para 33 of the Preamble of Regulation 1784/2020. In Spain, see new wording of art 155.2 b) CPA.

[24] In Spain see art 50.3 First Book of the Royal Decree-Law 6/2023 (n 17). For the effectiveness of the service (the first date on which the notification was verified) see art 152.6 CPA.

[25] Spanish Constitutional Court Judgment 6/2019 17 January BOE 39 14 February 2019. Lorenzo Cotino Hueso, 'La preocupante falta de garantías constitucionales y administrativas en las notificaciones electrónicas' (2021) RGDA Iustel 1.

[26] Art 6.2 f) First Book Royal Decree-Law 6/2023 (n 17).

[27] 'Guidelines on online dispute resolution mechanisms in civil and administrative court proceedings' paras 31–34 ECLC (n 14); Esteban de la Rosa (n 12) 42–44.

filtered into the recipient's spam folder without their knowledge and never reach the inbox. It is worth discussing the compatibility of certain practices with digitalization efforts that prioritize people's needs, such as regulations for automatic receipt generation upon email delivery[28] or mechanisms that lock mobile devices until notifications have been read.[29]

The increasing availability of dedicated portals, folders, and electronic offices provided by judicial administrations, accessible through various devices, offers better compliance with security and data protection regulations. This finding should prompt a gradual shift away from using email in judicial services, as seen in digitally advanced justice systems, such as those in Estonia[30] or Spain.[31] Accordingly, the Service of Documents Regulation permits member states to establish conditions and limitations on using email for judicial notifications, where their national laws impose stricter requirements for email services or prohibit it altogether.[32] Singapore has also had a positive experience with Notify-Singpass, an in-app messaging service requiring greater identity assurance than SMS or other third-party services. The service provides access through authentication and verifies the recipient's consent via their signature. The system then automatically records the date and time the notified content was received by both the recipient and the court.[33] In any case, since in electronic judicial services the receipt of a notification is not always simultaneous with its delivery, and technical or material failures can hinder the effectiveness of the process, national procedural laws that allow recipients to claim non-receipt or lack of awareness of the communication more effectively uphold due process requirements.[34]

Additionally, electronic judicial services raise cybersecurity and trust concerns[35] that should be addressed through special measures. Because these functionalities may lead to the use of cloud computing, this progress must be accompanied by

[28] Vicente Pérez Daudí, 'La justicia civil ante el reto de las TIC' in Jesús Conde Fuentes y Gregorio Serrano Hoyo (eds), *La justicia digital en España y la Unión Europea* (Atelier 2019) 98–99; Rafael San Bruno Casuso, 'El Tribunal Constitucional limita el uso del correo electrónico en los procedimientos judiciales' Rödl & Partner 2021) <www.roedl.es/es/articulos/el-tribunal-constitucional-limita-el-uso-del-correo-electronico-en-los-procedimientos-judiciales> last accessed 28 October 2024.

[29] This system is currently used for judicial service practices by the internet courts established in Hangzhou, Beijing, and Guangzhou, China. See Fang Xuhui (n 21).

[30] See the information related to the Estonian Public E-File <https://www.kohus.ee/sites/default/files/tekstidokumendid/the_public_e-file_questions_and_answers.pdf> last accessed 29 October 2024.

[31] Art 50.1 First Book Royal Decree-Law 6/2023 (n 17). The Beta version of Carpeta Justicia, a personal online platform that enables users to receive notifications, is currently being tested in Spain <https://www.administraciondejusticia.gob.es/carpeta-justicia> last accessed 29 October 2024.

[32] Such conditions could address issues like verifying the identities of the sender and recipient, ensuring document integrity, and protecting transmissions from outside interference. However, completely excluding email notifications is not an option for the European cooperation. This means that European countries must continue to accept email service for judicial cooperation in civil matters, even if it is excluded domestically.

[33] The Singapore government's information related to Singpass <https://www.tech.gov.sg/products-and-services/for-citizens/digital-services/singpass/> last accessed 10 August 2024.

[34] Rosa Cernada Badía, 'La notificación judicial electrónica: garantía del derecho fundamental a la tutela judicial efectiva y retos que plantea a la administración de justicia en España' (thesis, University of Valencia 2016) 202–03; Cotino Hueso (n 25).

[35] The risk of identity theft, whether by one of the parties involved or a third party, is a significant drawback of online courts. Doron Menashe, 'A Critical Analysis of the Online Court' (2018) University of Pennsylvania Journal of International Law 921.

technological advancements and safeguards to ensure the highest cybersecurity by design and default, as well as data protection measures to prevent identity theft and unauthorized access. People must trust the legitimacy of court documents and websites.[36] As a complementary measure to a human-centric approach, the establishment of a Secure Verification Code is considered good practice. When included in an electronic document, this code enables the verification of the authenticity of the document by providing access through designated websites. To meet the special needs of this area, measures such as watermarks, anti-copying systems, and personalized document versions that trace the origin of unauthorized distribution have been adopted in the digitalization of courts.[37]

The crucial importance of the first service in guaranteeing the right to defence is a good reason to exclude electronic communications. In fact, in procedures designed to occur entirely online, such as the Online Civil Money Claims in England and Wales, the defendant is notified of a claim filed online via certified mail.[38] The exception to the first service was also recognized until December 2023 by the Spanish judicial system for legal persons and entities without legal personality who, according to the law, are required to interact electronically with the administration of justice.[39] Consequently, the requirement for the email addressee to check their email address to become aware of its content was dismissed.[40] Banning traditional channels for initial notifications may lead to situations of defencelessness, despite the availability of procedural resources to address notification unawareness. These concerns are particularly pressing, given the low reliability of technological processes for initial electronic notifications, as seen in the Spanish judicial system. Starting from 20 March 2024, if the addressee did not access the electronic service within three days, the notice was published on an online bulletin board.[41] To mitigate unawareness, the new system should allow users to subscribe to alerts and receive court notices. However, these alerts may become ineffective if the ID number is missing or incorrectly entered or if the addressee updates their mobile phone number or email address without updating this information in the alert system. Such issues underscore the need to reconsider the ban on traditional first-time notifications and explain how quickly Spain has changed the aforementioned system, including a reform in the new Organic Law 1/2025, of January 2, on measures for the efficiency of the Public Justice Service.[42] According to the new wording of article 155 CPA, if the communication is intended

[36] Resolution System Institut (RSI), 'Making ODR More Accessible to Self-Represented Parties: Focus Group Perspectives' (2024). The research found that a lack of trust, identified as a secondary barrier, significantly impacted participants' perceptions of the legitimacy of court documents and websites.

[37] In Spain, see art 26 First Book Royal Decree-Law 6/2023 (n 17).

[38] Pablo Cortés, 'El acceso a la justicia del consumidor inglés a través de las comunicaciones electrónicas' in Fernando Esteban de la Rosa (ed), *Justicia Digital, Mercado y Resolución de Litigios de Consumo. Innovación en el Diseño del Acceso a la Justicia* (Aranzadi 2021) 97.

[39] Arts 155.1 and 155.2 of the former version of the CPA. See Julio Pérez Gaipo, 'El proceso laboral ante la era digital' in Jesús Conde Fuentes and Gregorio Serrano Hoyo (eds), *La justicia digital en España y en la Unión Europea* (Atelier 2019) 79.

[40] Judgments of the Spanish Constitutional Court 47/2019 8 April BOE n 116 15 May 2019; 40/2020 27 February BOE n 83 26 March 2020; and 9/2021 25 January 2021 BOE n 46 23 February 2021.

[41] The Single Edictal Board can be last accessed through the following link: <www.boe.es/notificaciones/notificaciones_historico.php> last accessed 29 October 2024.

[42] BOE 3, 3 January 2025.

as the first summons and three days pass without the recipient accessing its content, domiciliary communication will be carried out. Only if this domiciliary communication proves unsuccessful will publication in the Electronic Judicial Edict Board be pursued. A more human-centred approach can also be seen in Estonian practice, where if the defendant does not use Public E-File, notifications are served by conventional means.[43]

The use of email as the first service has also brought about other kinds of disadvantages in online court cases, where the service is made directly by the claimant to the defendant. In a survey by the Resolution Systems Institute[44] many defendants expressed scepticism about receiving an initial claim statement from an unknown claimant. This is significant, because lenders often sell debt to third parties that file claims. When this happens, the defendants may not recognize the claimant, raising concerns about potential fraud. In such cases, users often lack a way to verify whether the letter of claim is legitimate, addressed to them, or scammed. Therefore, as a human-centred practice, it is crucial that courts always include contact information in the documentation provided.

Using electronic services with only the user's consent is a human-centred practice. This practice is followed in national judicial systems[45] as well as in European Judicial Cooperation in Civil Matters.[46] Along with the proclamation of the principle of voluntariness, a people-centred approach should include additional protective measures. First, one such measure involves requiring consent for each specific procedure rather than obtaining general consent for the service of documents across various legal proceedings.[47] The latter option covertly obliges the user to monitor the information systems used for notifications continually within a short time frame, potentially indefinitely. Second, a people-centred system that acknowledges the digital divide should ensure that users opting for electronic services have adequate digital literacy. One useful way to assess this is by requiring consent to be provided online. Therefore, it is not considered good practice to enforce an offline contractual agreement that obliges parties to use electronic means.[48] Third, it should be considered good practice to allow the interested party, especially SRLs, to choose their preferred method of communication with the administration of justice at any time, including the option to decide whether subsequent communications should be conducted electronically.[49] For this right to be fully effective, the person concerned should be informed in each subsequent communication of their options to make this choice and the steps to do so.

[43] <www.kohus.ee/sites/default/files/tekstidokumendid/the_public_e-file_questions_and_answers.pdf> last accessed 29 October 2024.

[44] RSI (n 36).

[45] Including Netherlands, Singapore, and Spain. In Spain, see arts 152.2 b) and c) CPA and art 49.3 First Book Royal Decree-Law 6/2023 (n 17). In China, see Litigation Rules of the People's Courts 1,838th meeting of the Adjudication Committee of the Supreme People's Court on 18 May 2021 <https://cicc.court.gov.cn/html/1/219/199/201/2208.html> last accessed 29 October 2024.

[46] Para 29 Regulation 2023/2844; art 4.6 Regulation 2023/2844; art 13.2 Regulation 861/2007.

[47] Art 19 Regulation 2020/1784. See Nuria Marchal Escalona, 'El nuevo marco europeo sobre notificación y obtención de pruebas en el extranjero: hacia un espacio judicial europeo digitalizado' (2022) REDI 155.

[48] However, this measure is envisaged in Spain by new version of art 152.2 b) CPA as amended by Royal Decree-Law 6/2023 (n 17).

[49] In Spain, see art 49.3 of the First Book Royal Decree-Law 6/2023 (n 17).

2. Court notices

Electronic communication allows for differentiated treatment between judicial services and court notices. This distinction has become increasingly important in advanced digital justice systems tailored to people's needs. Owing to the immediacy of notice communication, notices bring justice closer to citizens. They serve multiple purposes: reminding parties, witnesses, and others to appear in court, particularly for videoconferences; providing updates on the online availability of new information such as witnesses and expert reports or appeals; and notifying involved parties about hearing schedules, cancellations, or suspensions.[50] Even without the requirement to indicate their receipt, and despite lacking procedural consequences, court notices are crucial for supporting e-Justice. They aid judicial services, promote transparency, and make justice more accessible to citizens. Implementing a system of court notices that supports automatic transmission and accommodates user preferences for receiving notifications—whether via SMS, email, web browser notifications, downloadable apps, WhatsApp, social network (Facebook), or other means—should be considered a human-centred practice. This approach ensures that the system adapts to the social customs of each country and aligns with the preferences of individual users.[51] Unlike document services, access to court notices does not require the completion of an authentication procedure; therefore, it is crucial to limit the information provided to details about the issuing court and the relevant case identification data. Additionally, including a website or link where the addressee can access a full file is a useful measure.

3. Submitting electronic pleadings

Greater efficiency in the judiciary is achieved exclusively using electronic channels to submit pleadings. In this framework, both users and professionals within the justice system play crucial roles as collaborators in its operations. Although no court system has fully established electronic filings as standard practice, many have made significant strides towards this goal. Some systems mandate electronic filing for specific groups, including professionals and, in some cases, SRLs.[52] Electronic filing is

[50] In Spain, see art 56 of the First Book Royal Decree Law 6/2023 (n 17). In Hungary, the electronic system for judicial information and alerts allows registered users and their representatives to access up-to-date information on the status of their proceedings, as well as on key procedural actions, such as the submission of expert reports or the filing of an appeal <https://e-ugyintezes.birosag.hu/informacio> last accessed 6 November 2024.

[51] According to article 5 of First Book Royal Decree-Law 6/2023 (n 17) it is recognized 'the right k) to choose the applications or systems to interact with the Administration of Justice as long as they use open standards or, where appropriate, those others that are widely used by citizens and, in any case, provided that they are compatible with those available to the judicial bodies and the guarantees and requirements provided for in the procedure in question'.

[52] In Germany, lawyers are obliged to file pleadings electronically with the BeA. See art 31a, 6 BRAO <https://tinyurl.com/ybeynvx5> last accessed 6 November 2024. The Spanish system has imposed on lawyers, legal persons and other entities without legal personality the obligation to file pleadings electronically, with the consequence that failure to comply with this obligation means that the pleadings will be deemed not to have been filed if they are not remedied (art 275.5 CPA).

mandated for certain specific procedures. For example, the English[53] and Estonian[54] systems introduced mandatory electronic filing for specific types of procedures. When considering efficiency optimization, it is important to recognize that for the electronic filing of pleadings to be truly progressive and not merely a measure to reduce paper use, it must be integrated with advanced filing systems, ensuring that documents are accurately organized to facilitate the work of judges, court officials, and other justice system users. Implementing entry systems that are compatible with procedural management systems should be recognized as good practice to ensure a more effective and organized judicial workflow.

Public health emergencies during the COVID-19 pandemic have prompted many countries to introduce an obligation to submit documents electronically.[55] However, because such a system does not address the digital divide, this regulation should be considered temporary and reviewed as circumstances normalize. Introduction of the obligation to file documents electronically presents challenges that the legal system must address. The first stems from the need to fairly address the digital divide, as it is unrealistic to assume that everyone has access to the necessary equipment, digital skills, and internet connectivity. This risk can be effectively mitigated by maintaining a traditional channel to submit briefs as an alternative. Examples of this regulatory model can be found in Europe (Spain and the Netherlands),[56] the United States, and in European judicial cooperation.[57]

The second challenge arises from technological anomalies that may hinder the successful submission of briefs. These issues can vary widely and include system crashes, slow loading times, incompatibilities across different browsers or devices, overly complicated procedures, file size restrictions, and limitations on the character usage of file names. Such technical difficulties often stem from the complexity of the system or a non-intuitive interface. To address these challenges, constant monitoring of communication systems and implementation of special measures are essential. A human-centred approach should offer remote assistance, both online and via telephone, to help users navigate the system during document submission, or handle emergency situations that may prevent timely submission. This approach has been successfully implemented in the Netherlands.[58] Alternatively, a website can be provided on which users can report incidents. It is also considered good practice to issue an electronic receipt to users confirming their submission or, if unsuccessful, to detail the reasons for the failure to facilitate potential challenges. Moreover, when anomalies detected during transmission or when delivery cannot be completed, it is advisable to implement an error message system to notify users of any issues during the

[53] The filing of documents using the electronic court filing system (CE-File) is mandatory for professional users in the High Court, the Court of Appeal and the Costs Office of the High Court <https://tinyurl.com/2tpbe33z> last accessed 17 November 2024.

[54] Among them, in claims for payment, order for payment proceedings and maintenance proceedings.

[55] Sourdin and Zeleznikow (n 3).

[56] Xandra E Kramer, Emma van Gelder, and Erlis Themeli, 'e-Justice in the Netherlands: the Rocky Road to Digitised Justice' in M Weller and M Wendland (eds), *Digital Single Market: Bausteine eines Rechts in der Digitalen Welt* (Mohr Siebeck 2018) 209.

[57] Art 4.1 Regulation 861/2007 as amended by Regulation 2023/2844.

[58] Support is available from the Judicial Service Center (rechtsspraakservicecentrum) online and by telephone from 8:00 to 20:00.

submission process. This allows the user to make corrections or opt for alternative submission methods. Further, it is prudent for the judicial system to establish a clear and explicit protocol for handling service interruptions and technical failures. This protocol should include provisions for the in-person submission of pleadings, when necessary.[59] In the event of a planned interruption, an announcement of this protocol should be made on the website through which the document is to be filed.

4. The use of videoconferencing

SRLs may participate in hearings through video conferences. According to European Law, videoconferencing refers to audio–visual transmission technology that allows two-way and simultaneous communication of images and sounds, thereby enabling visual, audio, and oral interactions.[60] Judicial systems do not consider metaverse interactions because of the challenges involved in their implementation.[61] A prerequisite for widespread adoption of videoconferencing in the justice system is the availability of adequate equipment and bandwidth. This will be facilitated by 5G networks and, importantly, by specific agreements between the judiciary and telecommunications companies.

During the COVID-19 pandemic, many civil courts conducted online hearings when both parties consented or when the judge deemed it appropriate. With the health emergency now over, it is essential to evaluate these experiences to justify the continued use of videoconferencing. Videoconferencing empowers justice system users by overcoming temporal and geographical barriers. However, because individuals may have legitimate reasons for preferring face-to-face interactions, protecting the rights of justice users from being heard in-person is considered good practice.

Videoconferencing is useful for conducting nonjudicial activities involving judges, serving justice system users, and performing procedural activities. In all cases, videoconferencing must adhere to the highest technological standards for cybersecurity, data protection, confidentiality, and reliable user identification. Without these measures, there is a risk of cyberattacks, such as those that have paralysed the deliberations of the Spanish Constitutional Court.[62] Most cloud-based systems manage data collection and retention at the local application level. If the judiciary cannot use its own infrastructure, it must thoroughly understand and influence the specific terms of its contract with the service provider.[63]

The use of videoconferencing in court proceedings poses challenges to the protection of due process and proper performance of judges' duties, which extend beyond

[59] These measures are outlined in Spain under art 135.2 CPA.

[60] Art 2.6 Regulation 2023/2844.

[61] On the challenges of using the metaverse in Online Dispute Resolution (ODR), see Mayu Watanabe and Colin Rule, 'ODR in the Metaverse' (2022) IJODR 21.

[62] Jose Maria Brunet, 'El Constitucional alega temor a un "hackeo" y decide paralizar los plenos' (15 May 2020) <https://elpais.com/espana/2020-05-15/el-constitucional-alega-temor-a-un-hackeo-y-decide-paralizar-los-plenos.html> last accessed 29 October 2024.

[63] Oscar Daniel Franco Conforti, 'Diseño de una plataforma de resolución de conflictos por medios electrónicos en el ámbito de consumo' in Fernando Esteban de la Rosa (ed), *Justicia digital, mercado y resolución de litigios de consumo. Innovación en el diseño del acceso a la justicia* (Aranzadi 2021) 133.

the scope of the people-centred digitalization of the justice system.[64] One of the issues to be resolved concerns the right to a public hearing, as recognized in Article 6.1 of the ECHR. Although various models have been tested, recording and publication on the internet are appropriate ways to achieve open justice while respecting data protection and evidence intangibility.[65] It is important to remember that the ECHR has held that using videoconferencing in court proceedings is compatible with fundamental rights provided that it pursues a legitimate aim and the rights of the defence are respected.[66] This perspective is a focal point in the Guidelines on the Use of Videoconferencing in Judicial Proceedings adopted by the European Commission for the Efficiency of Justice (CEPEJ) in 2021.

By using videoconferencing, a people-centred design should help overcome challenges related to a lack of equipment, insufficient broadband, and, most importantly, a lack of digital training. As an example of good practice in Hungary, 215 remote hearing points (remote hearing endpoints) have been installed in the country's courts, national and district offices, national user services, and prisons.[67] In particular, the measures are aimed at enabling people with disabilities living in institutions or residential care facilities to communicate remotely with the justice system. These measures allow them to give statements and, where appropriate, sign documents to formalize their appearances.[68] The latest technological innovations also enable the appropriate management of user identities, allowing videoconferencing from outside the office, whether from work or home.

Models for regulating the use of videoconferencing in judicial hearings can vary in how people-centred they are. Some models view videoconferencing as a way to rationalize and modernize the judicial system by enhancing principles such as procedural economy, focus, and efficiency. Accordingly, the court may authorize using videoconferencing ex officio, depending on the circumstances, even if the parties have not requested it.[69] More people-centred systems make using videoconferencing dependent on the wishes of the parties[70] involved and recognize the right to appear via videoconference without assuming the impossibility of physical presence, thereby offering additional benefits. The recommended rules should protect the rights of those appearing before the court to interact personally with the administration of justice,[71] allow parties to request a face-to-face hearing and state their reasons,[72] offer them the

[64] María José Fernández-Fígares Morales, *Audiencias telemáticas en la Justicia. Presente y futuro* (Tirant Lo Blanch 2021) 124–42.

[65] Esteban de la Rosa (n 12) 59.

[66] *Marcello Viola v Italy* App no 45106/04 (ECHR, 5 October 2006) 6, §72.

[67] This took place under the project Electronic Solution for the Improvement of Work Organization and Communication for Procedures with the Public Administration (VIKI), led by the National Infocommunications Service.

[68] This System has been implemented in Spain through the EVID (Virtual Desktop for Digital Immediacy) <https://www.youtube.com/watch?v = 6Dg7b66-exA last accessed 29 October 2024.

[69] Art 129 bis, second para letter a) CPA Spain.

[70] Art 5.1 Regulation 2023/2844.

[71] Para 3 (1) of the Austrian Federal COVID-19 Accompanying Justice Act gives an example. Until 30 June 2022 the court may, with the consent of the parties, conduct negotiations and oral hearings without the personal presence of the parties or their representatives, using appropriate technical means of communication. Consent is deemed to have been granted unless the parties object within a reasonable period set by the court.

[72] Para 11 CEPEJ 'Guidelines on videoconferencing in judicial proceedings'.

opportunity to consult with the court about the possibility of holding the hearing via videoconferencing, and provide information on the procedure to address security concerns. These rules should ensure that the decision to hold a meeting by videoconference is reasonable and may be subject to appeal.

C. The Emergence of Online Courts

1. Approach to the meaning of online court

The spearhead of digitalizing the administration of justice comprises 'online courts'. Richard Susskind explains[73] that the online court is distinct from the courts' use of technology to replicate certain online activities, such as videoconferencing or remote communications. This term is reserved for judicial proceedings that do not involve paper or physical court hearings. Instead, evidence and arguments are submitted through an online platform and court hearings are conducted virtually. As an exception, online courts may use papers to conduct in-person hearings. Judges issue their decisions through an online platform, and the procedure takes place via video, audio, or real-time chats rather than face-to-face hearings. Online courts provide comprehensive services that are accessible through all types of electronic devices, including mobile phones. As Leah Wing expressed, dispute resolution is no longer tied to the courthouse or physical space.[74]

In a narrower sense, an online court designates an extended court that provides justice system users with functionality beyond the competencies of traditional courts.[75] The court can offer legal information, diagnose cases, present available options for action, assist in completing court forms and gathering evidence, facilitate negotiations, help complete litigation though party agreements, and assist in drafting agreements. Case management may include referrals to an electronic alternative resolution channel, case assessment tools for direct negotiations without a facilitator, and the facilitation of agreements with third-party support. Among the online courts are a great number of pilot projects developed in the United States;[76] the Civil Resolution Tribunal (CRT) of British Columbia, Canada; the UK's Online Civil Money Claim; the Traffic Penalty Tribunal; and the internet courts created in Hangzhou, Beijing, and Guangzhou. Online courts limit their material jurisdiction to small or specific types of claims.

The creation of online courts is closely related to the acceptance of SRLs, a rule characteristic of court systems in common law countries, and connected to the do-it-yourself principle.[77] In line with this idea, there are examples in which the general rule

[73] Richard Susskind, *Tribunales online y la justicia del futuro* (Spanish translation, Wolter Kluwers 2020) 26–27.

[74] Leah Wing, 'Mapping the Parameters of Online Dispute Resolution' (2022) (9) 1 IJODR 11.

[75] Susskind (n 73).

[76] Amy J Schmitz, 'Expanding Access to Remedies, Voice, and Possibly Justice in United States Court Online Dispute Resolution' (2024) Ohio State Legal Studies Research Paper.

[77] Although common law courts do not require legal representation, they are not necessarily more accessible, unless we are referring to small claims. In the UK and US, in around 50 per cent and 70 per cent of the cases, respectively, there is one party without a lawyer. House of Commons Library, 'Litigants

is for parties to appear without a representative before the court.[78] In common law countries, parties do not recover the cost of legal representation in tribunals (unlike in courts), which discourages legal counsel and makes the process more informal.[79] Behind this change in philosophy is the conviction that operating online courts in this way can simplify and reduce the cost of dispute resolution and preserve equality of arms between parties. This approach is clearly aligned with the argument for economic efficiency and can overshadow the difficulties of conducting a completely online process.

The integration of technology into judicial systems, particularly online courts, is increasingly considered vital for promoting conflict resolution through negotiations and mutual agreements. This shift emphasizes efficiency over the traditional pursuit of factual truth, favouring 'truth as consensus' over 'truth as correspondence'.[80] The focus on resolving legal issues efficiently—often through ADR—sidelines the process of establishing factual accuracy. This approach aligns well with the human-centric perspective, which focuses on empowering individuals involved in disputes. By leveraging technology, these systems enable parties to resolve disputes more efficiently and with greater autonomy, especially since the COVID-19 pandemic demonstrated that negotiations and agreements could also be achieved remotely.[81] For example, the Online Civil Money Claim provided confidential settlement proposals and telephone mediation services, ensuring that parties received support throughout the negotiation process.[82] The CRT even informs parties and guides them through the negotiation phases, reducing the need for judicial intervention. These systems may help to reduce the stress, cost, and time associated with traditional court proceedings, making dispute resolution more accessible and focused on achieving fair and mutually agreeable outcomes. Interactions with machines, primarily through chatbots or conversational agents, may be fundamental to human-centred approaches. Naturally, such systems cannot be developed simultaneously; they require an incremental process, starting with prototypes and followed by ongoing improvements and evaluations.

Supported by technology, the online court may increase system efficiency and enhance user experience, reinforcing the principle that justice should be responsive to the needs of the people it serves. According to this characterization, a helpful ODR

in person: the rise of the self-represented' (Briefing Paper Number 07113, 14 March 2019). Civil Justice Council, 'Access to Justice for Litigants in Person (or self-represented litigants)' (2011). USA: National Center for State Courts, 'Self-Representation in U.S. Family Law Cases' (2017); American Bar Association, 'The State of Self-Representation in Civil Cases' (2016).

[78] It is the case in the CRT. As exceptions to the general rule a lawyer is allowed when the party is a minor or when the court considers it necessary due to specific circumstances. Art 20 CRT Act <www.bclaws.ca/civix/document/id/complete/statreg/12025_01#section20> last accessed 6 November 2024.

[79] In the US, the general rule is that each party pays their own costs regardless of the outcome, which incentivizes self-representation. In the UK and elsewhere, small claims have very restricted allocation of costs, hence the growth of self-representation.

[80] Tomás J Aliste Santos, 'ADR y digitalización como premisas para la transformación eficiente de nuestro sistema de justicia civil' (2023) 11 Actualidad Civil.

[81] Noam Ebner, 'The human touch in ODR: Trust, empathy and social intuition in online negotiation and mediation' in Daniel Rainey, Ethan Katsh, and Mohamed S Abdel Wahab (eds), *Online Dispute Resolution: Theory and Practice* (2nd edn, Eleven International Publishing 2021) 73–136.

[82] Cortés, (n 38) 92–98.

system for SRLs should include six key features: (1) case management, enabling users to enter information, track the case, and know required documents; (2) triaging, providing guidance on timely action, especially in high-risk cases like domestic abuse; (3) advisory tools, offering resources like legal information and calculators to help users understand potential outcomes;[83] (4) communication tools, facilitating negotiation, mediation, and conciliation; (5) decision support tools, using AI or game theory to guide trade-offs when legal advice is not available; (6) and drafting software, to create agreements once a resolution is reached.[84]

Online courts are a significant innovation that enhances access to justice, particularly for low-value claims, online evidence, and geographically distant parties. However, implementing online courts poses key challenges. If everything moves online, and it is impossible to guarantee access to devices, internet connections, and digital literacy for all users, videoconferencing cannot be systematically relied upon. Instead, communication should rely on asynchronous methods or telephonic contact, which poses challenges to real-time participation in hearings. Consequently, online processes should focus on cases that do not require a judge's control over live hearings and that involve limited, primarily documentary evidence. Concerns exist regarding preserving due process, public trials, and adversarial principles in civil procedures.[85] The model assumes that laypersons can articulate legal issues, identify relevant documents, and present evidence independently; however, these tasks often require legal expertise. There is no empirical support that intuitive interfaces can fully substitute legal assistance. Facilitators involved in the prejudicial phase raise concerns about neutrality, cost-effectiveness, and impartiality, especially when redefining the dispute's factual basis. Moreover, the role of the plaintiff in defining the subject matter is essential for judicial protection.[86] Online litigation also faces challenges, particularly regarding judges' authority to conduct evidence investigations. There is a need to reassess the relationship between the evidence investigation and adversarial systems to establish clearer guidelines for online trials. Therefore, a sound policy for implementing online courts should start with simpler processes, ensuring a smoother transition and more effective evaluation before incorporating more complex matters.

2. Dispute system design options for a people-centred online court

2.1. The case for implementing online courts

In online courts, a people-centred perspective should begin with the decision of whether to create a specialized process or court to operate online. Crucial to this

[83] Advice tools are a key part of supporting litigants who do not have legal aid. John Zeleznikow, 'An Australian Perspective on Research and Development Required for the Construction of Applied Legal Decision Support Systems', (2002) 10 Artificial Intelligence and Law 237–60.

[84] Fernando Esteban de la Rosa and John Zeleznikow, 'Making Intelligent Online Dispute Resolution Tools available to Self-Represented Litigants in the Public Justice System: Towards and Ethical use of the AI technology in the administration of Justice' (Eighteenth International Conference for Artificial Intelligence and Law, 2021).

[85] Huang-Chih Sung, 'Can Online Courts Promote Access to Justice? A Case Study of the Internet Courts in China' (2020) 39 Computer Law & Security Review 105, 461.

[86] Esteban de la Rosa (n 12) 66.

decision is the identification of areas where barriers to accessing justice exist, where data point to procedural bottlenecks, or when circumstances can be identified that make it especially appropriate to establish such a court. In all cases, online courts empower justice system users by allowing them to follow procedures without the need to travel or appear in court. The intention to overcome barriers to access justice is evident in the establishment of online courts designed to resolve small claims or debt claims, such as the Online Civil Money Claim of England and Wales, the CRT of British Columbia, Canada;[87] and most of the online courts created in the United States.[88] For instance, the Online Civil Money Claim system in England and Wales was established following several reports, notably Lord Briggs' 2015 and 2016 reviews, which highlighted inefficiencies in handling claims under £25,000 due to the disproportionate costs of legal representation. The report recommended creating an online solution court that is accessible to SRLs to improve access and reduce costs. After public consultations and government approval (Ministry of Justice, 2016), the online court pilot was launched in 2018 under the official name 'Online Civil Money Claim', aimed at streamlining civil claims under £25,000.[89]

The suitability of implementing online courts is also influenced by their potential to overcome geographical barriers in large territories, integrate an online phase into procedures for quicker resolution, better address the delocalization of internet-related cases, and resolve international business disputes. Geographic and territorial factors, such as the need to serve vast areas and reach users of the remote justice system, are compelling reasons for the establishment of online courts. As an example of the first, CRT is particularly beneficial because most of the population lives in Vancouver, sparing many people the need to travel to Victoria, which requires a nearly three-hour boat trip. The Online Civil Money Claim process allows debt claims to be handled entirely online. The defendant must submit their responses online, and the procedure continues digitally unless there is opposition. The Chinese government centralized disputes arising from delocalized relationships stemming from the internet in newly established online courts. For example, the Beijing Internet Court handles cases involving internet-related disputes such as e-commerce contracts, online services, financial loans, copyright and domain name issues, infringements on personal and property rights, product liability, and administrative disputes concerning internet regulations.[90] On 1 January 2019 the Netherlands launched the Netherlands Commercial Court (NCC), which conducts cases and renders judgments in English. The NCC employs judges, counsellors, and legal assistants from across the Netherlands who possess specific expertise in commercial law and a strong command of English. The electronic NCC (eNCC) portal allows users to submit procedural motions, documents, exhibits, and messages online. Use of the eNCC is mandatory for all written communications, including correspondence and document submissions, in all NCC cases, unless directed otherwise by the court. Hearings may occur in a

[87] The CRT has jurisdiction over most small claims disputes up to $5,000 <https://civilresolutionbc.ca/solution-explorer/small-claims/> last accessed 30 October 2024.

[88] <https://datawrapper.dwcdn.net/TAM4u/1/> last accessed 17 November 2024.

[89] See Cortés (n 38) 94.

[90] The jurisdiction of the Beijing internet court <https://english.bjinternetcourt.gov.cn/2019-03/25/c_23.htm> last accessed 30 October 2024.

digital courtroom with options for videoconferencing for pretrial hearings or remote attendance.[91]

2.2. Measures to ensure that no one is left behind

The need for measures to ensure that no one is left behind is critical in the creation of online courts. Insufficient connectivity, lack of equipment, and limited digital literacy among users may exacerbate barriers to access to justice. As noted earlier, this issue goes beyond respecting the right to effective judicial protection, a fair trial, and an effective remedy—as proclaimed in Articles 6.1 and 13 of the ECHR. Inequalities stemming from the digital divide could further intensify restrictions on the right to effective judicial protection and lead to potential deficiencies in legal defences.

ODR systems must prioritize a user-centric approach for wide adoption. Margaret Hagan, from Stanford University Law School, has been a strong advocate of integrating user-centric design principles to enhance access to justice in ODR.[92] Human-centric design focuses on user experience to develop solutions that are both experimental and iterative.[93] Margaret Hagan's research on improving judicial systems for SRLs has led to seven key recommendations for courts and self-help centres to make their systems more accessible and efficient. First, courts should coordinate 'navigable pathways' to give SRLs a clear understanding of the entire legal process and provide effective support along the way. Additionally, people require more robust and user-friendly tools for navigating the court system and a welcoming and supportive experience to encourage them to complete the necessary procedures. Paperwork should be redesigned to be visually clear, prioritized, and manageable. Hagan suggested developing online tools to help SRLs prepare for court visits and ensure that tasks are completed correctly. Within courts, better workstations and materials are needed to help SRLs prepare for appearances. Finally, fostering a culture of usability, testing, and feedback within the court system is essential to enhance accessibility and efficiency for SRLs.[94]

Maintaining the same procedure or court in a non-digital format is likely, if possible, the best measure to achieve people-centred digitalization. In Spain, through the electronic judicial office,[95] individuals and legal entities can claim the payment of debts in a money claims procedure, without a limit on the amount, without needing a lawyer or solicitor, and without the conventional procedure ceasing to exist.[96] When circumstances make an alternative to the online court infeasible or when the suppression of the in-person channel is adopted to enhance efficiency and save resources, it

[91] The website of the NCC <https://www.rechtspraak.nl/english/ncc/Pages/default.aspx> last accessed 17 November 2024.

[92] Margaret D Hagan, 'A Human-Centered Design Approach to Access to Justice: Generating New Prototypes and Hypotheses for Interventions to Make Courts User-Friendly' (2018) 6 Indiana Journal of Law and Social Equality 199, 200.

[93] Tim Brown, 'Design Thinking' (2008) 86(6) Harvard Business Review 84.

[94] Hagan (n 92) 201.

[95] < https://sedejudicial.justicia.es> last accessed 30 October 2024.

[96] The process requires a written statement from the interested party and a document proving the debt between the creditor and debtor, such as an invoice. After entering the relevant data, users can view and confirm a draft of the document to be submitted. For amounts exceeding 2,000 euros, the involvement of a lawyer and solicitor is required, and the procedure cannot be completed through the electronic platform <https://sedejudicial.justicia.es/-/procedimiento-monitorio-1> last accessed 30 October 2024.

is crucial to intensify the adoption of measures that ensure the people-centric digitalization of online courts. Among the fundamental best practices is informing users whether the process before the online court is an alternative to the traditional court, and if so, whether it follows an opt-in or opt-out approach.

When implementing online courts, the standards highlight the need to guarantee the easy use of digital systems, which should be sufficiently tested before being fully implemented. This is why pilot projects are helpful for these purposes, as seen in the many projects launched in the United States in recent years, as well as in the case of the Online Civil Money Claims in England.[97] These projects enable the testing of an electronic procedure or parts of it (such as a prenegotiation phase or online mediation) with a limited group of users. This approach helps gather feedback and evaluate the digital process, ensuring that the final design meets its objectives optimally. During the pilot phase, only a limited number of individuals were granted access to online court platforms. By evaluating their experiences, improvements can be made to the system before its official launch.

Given that the entire process takes place online, the easy-to-use resources of the online court must meet the needs of individuals with limited digital literacy, including older adults and various other groups that may have technological limitations. Courts and ODR providers should ensure that their sites are accessible through all types of electronic devices and optimized for smartphones and tablets, including the formatting for these devices. Public policies that guarantee the availability of mobile devices (such as tablets) and public places where the internet can be accessed are appropriate for implementing online courts.

Usability, especially for SRLs, should also involve avoiding languages based on legal jargon. The 2023 OECD recommends providing information in clear, plain, and inclusive language, while avoiding unnecessary complexity. The development of foundational language models combined with voice recognition makes it possible to use a conversational agent prepared to answer questions regarding the basic operation of the system.

An important accompanying measure is the establishment of technological assistance services to overcome digital literacy deficits among system users. With the implementation of online courts, the need for telephone assistance has increased, given the variety of tools that users can use and the greater complexity of the procedures. Consequently, online courts should implement measures that assist users in accessing and navigating technological tools. In these instances, assistance should focus on digital justice platforms rather than on providing legal advice. The UK Traffic Penalty Tribunal serves as a good example, as individuals can call for help by completing the application form or even having someone complete the application on their behalf.[98] In a slightly different role, the CRT envisions appointing a case manager to assist with dispute resolution. The case manager's responsibilities include helping the parties

[97] For the English experience see Pablo Cortés, 'The English Online Court: A Research Proposal for Its Evaluation' (2022) 9 (2) IJODR 138–44; Pablo Cortés and Toru Takagi, 'The Civil Money Claim Online: The Flagship Project of Court Digitalization in England and Wales' (2019) 25(8) Computer and Telecommunications L Rev 207–12.

[98] Cortés (n 38) 101.

reach a resolution through facilitated settlement, as outlined in the rules; reviewing the claims and aiding the parties in identifying facts and issues critical to the dispute; determining the evidence or information that will aid in resolving the dispute; and recommending an appropriate hearing process to the tribunal if the tribunal has jurisdiction to make such determinations.[99] The above response from the judicial system is insufficient for individuals with cognitive, visual, or hearing impairments (persons with disabilities) or for those who find it difficult or impossible to use the available online programmes and interfaces.[100] In these cases, it is a human-centric practice to allow conventional or face-to-face channels of communication or to provide a judicial agent or the cooperation of someone to assist in proceeding online.[101] The online court experience of Utah is an example of this approach. The West Valley Justice Court's ODR Pilot Project Regulations mandate participation in ODR platforms for small claims cases. However, the court may grant an exemption to one or both parties if they face exceptional difficulties accessing the online process, allowing the case to proceed through traditional in-person court hearings.[102]

2.3. The empirical evaluation of the users

The human-centred approach emphasizes the need for an empirical evaluation of the results obtained through digitalization. Therefore, reports on the operation of online courts are becoming increasingly valuable, with significant interest in the results of projects seeking feedback from online courts users.[103] Among these, RSI Report 2024 offers an essential benchmark for future research and evaluation.[104] The report is likely to provide critical insights into how effectively new online courts meet users' needs, offering a standardized framework for assessing the performance of various online judicial systems globally. In addition, it sheds light on how well these platforms align with a human-centric approach to justice by assessing their responsiveness to users' real-world needs and expectations.

The findings were as follows: Most of the surveyed participants in ODR processes had reservations about text-based ODR, although this was also seen as an advantage by some of them. They were worried about misunderstandings or the other party

[99] Civil Resolution Tribunal Act [SBC 2012] chapter 25, part 4, division 1, para 23 <https://www.bclaws.gov.bc.ca/civix/document/id/complete/statreg/12025_01> last accessed 30 October 2024.

[100] On the advantages and challenges of ODR for persons with disabilities, see Nivedita Krishna, Krithika Sambasivan, Upasana Nath, Pragya Sahay, and Shanti Raghavan, 'Delivering Justice Solutions to Persons with Disabilities through Online Dispute Resolution Platforms' 2023 (10) International Journal on Online Dispute Resolution 1, doi: 10.5553/IJODR/235250022023010001004, 1–22.

[101] For Spain, see the example in n 68.

[102] Para 5 of Utah Supreme Court Order 13 on the Small Claims ODR Pilot Project: inability of a party to access the online system and participate in the process without incurring substantial hardship or expense.

[103] NCSC, 'Impact of the Utah Online Dispute Resolution (ODR) Pilot Program: Final Report', 19 December 2020. See also Stacy Butler, Sarah Mauet, Christopher L Griffin and Mackenzie Pish, 'The Utah Online Dispute Resolution Platform: A Usability Evaluation and Report' [2020] Arizona Legal Studies Discussion Paper No. 21-06. The report contains findings and recommendations from usability testing of the State of Utah's online dispute resolution (ODR) platform. The State of Utah is piloting the use of ODR in small claims cases at 37 select courts throughout the state <www.sji.gov/utah-pilots-odr-in-select-courts-for-small-claims-caseload/> last accessed 17 November 2024.

[104] See the report in n 36.

becoming uncivil during negotiations. To keep people in check and accountable, many wanted someone to moderate or facilitate communication with other parties.

When presented with the prospect of being sued, participants were almost unanimous in saying that they felt overwhelmed or intimidated. These feelings were often associated with the amount of information provided, formatting of court documents, and a general lack of confidence in their ability to navigate ODR without the help of court staff. Many participants expressed a strong desire to contact someone who could answer their questions and help them feel more confident in navigating the ODR. To enhance access to justice and increase participation in ODR programmes, it may be necessary for courts to provide parties with a contact person who is knowledgeable about ODR to answer their questions.

One area where users feel that improvements are needed in online courts is the provision of information on how the procedure works. The report highlighted that users of online courts often feel overwhelmed when informed of a lawsuit and find it difficult to follow the steps in the online procedure, which represents a barrier to ODR use. To overcome this, the report recommends using simple pictures to depict the next steps, enhancing information with videos, and providing the same information in a written form. The conclusions also highlight the importance of providing information in more than one way (text and video) and offering alternatives for parties without reliable internet access or digital literacy.[105]

Another concern expressed by users in the RSI research relates to websites used in online courts.[106] Many participants were concerned about being scammed and wanted reassurance that the mailed court documents such as the Notice, and the ODR platforms were legitimate. In this respect, the conclusions submit that it is necessary to ensure that court websites and documents appear trustworthy by including an official seal and the name of the court and by providing court contact information on all communications. Online courts should highlight the correct place to start ODR on each platform and platforms should use large buttons or other design elements to clearly indicate what parties should do next. Having help links prominently placed on the homepage and blue or underlined hyperlinks, or formatted as bottoms, were among the preferences of the surveyed users.

Survey respondents expressed concerns regarding security and the possibility of scams, making it necessary for online courts to ensure platform security.[107] Information should be provided in compliance with data protection regulations regarding the data to be stored and saved. In countries such as the United States, the negative impact of using third-party logins, such as Facebook or Google, when registering with an online court has been noted. However, creating a new account and having to remember a new password are also considered inconvenient. Consequently, electronic certificates or biometric systems that allow access without the need to use a new account or a third-party account may be of high interest.

Complying with the safeguards defined by international standards, consistently monitoring and learning from users' experiences, incorporating the necessary

[105] ibid 6–9.
[106] ibid 6–9.
[107] ibid 6–9.

reforms to overcome the identified shortcomings, and maintaining a constant focus on improvement should be the way forward for the worldwide implementation and design of a people-centred online court. This approach demonstrates how technology facilitates citizens' access to justice in a human-centric manner.

D. Conclusions

This chapter aimed to identify the best practices, safeguards, and measures for the people-centred digitalization of justice systems, with a focus on improving efficiency while empowering users and ensuring inclusivity. The idea that people should be at the centre of justice digitalization projects is gaining ground, as reflected in the OECD's 2023 Recommendation on Access to Justice and People-Centred Justice Systems. People centredness is defined as a human-centred approach that considers people's perspectives and needs in the design, delivery, implementation, and evaluation of public policies and legal processes.

The human-centred approach to the digitalization of justice systems goes beyond respecting the right to a fair trial and an effective remedy, as enshrined in Articles 6(1) and 13 of the ECHR. While this approach is not defined by specific measures, it has considerable implications for how justice systems should be transformed through digitalization. To achieve a truly people-centred digitalization of justice systems, good practices, safeguards, and measures need to be identified. This is critical for SRLs, who are increasingly exposed to digital technologies. Addressing the digital divide, protecting rights in human–machine interactions, and adapting the digital features of public justice systems to people's needs are paramount.

Although the goals of digital transformation are generally the same, implementation must consider the unique political, technological, cultural, territorial, and legal contexts of each society. Changing the complex machinery of the justice administration in any country is difficult. The successful implementation of digital transformation requires careful planning, the involvement of professionals in technological design, developing pilot projects to validate these designs, and special attention to the training and motivation of professionals.

The key mandates of this approach include comprehensive data collection; setting priorities for improvement; conducting empirical evaluations; and identifying good practices, safeguards, and measures to address the difficulties encountered. A human-centred perspective requires an understanding of the current barriers to accessing justice, particularly for specific issues or vulnerable groups. Collecting these data is essential to accurately assess where barriers exist and tailor digitalization efforts accordingly. Therefore, justice systems should implement robust data collection strategies. These data will both inform the design and implementation of digital tools and ensure that these systems are responsive to the needs of all individuals, including marginalized communities, and improve access to justice in a meaningful and equitable way. Without such data, efforts to digitalize justice systems may miss critical areas for improvement or overlook vulnerable populations, undermining the goal of truly human-centred transformation. This approach requires addressing the current limitations and challenges, setting priorities for improvement, and designing digital interventions with users in mind. Test phases or pilot projects should assess the functionality of these systems and empirical evaluations are required to compare the results with baseline conditions. This approach emphasizes access to justice and procedural fairness and ensures that legislative changes prioritize people's needs, not just the efficiency of the system.

This chapter evaluated different models for court notifications and videoconferencing, highlighting the need to prioritize people's preferences in legal frameworks to better align with a human-centred perspective. Court notifications can serve several purposes, including reminding parties to appear in court, providing updates, and notifying them of hearings. The importance of notices in the digitalization of justice systems has been highlighted as they serve as a key element that aligns with and supports the human-centred approach. Automatic delivery of court notices, considering user preferences for receiving notices, is considered the best practice. Security and data protection are crucial for e-Justice and require dedicated portals and electronic offices provided by judicial administrations. Maintaining the traditional submission of pleadings is important to address the digital divide and ensuring fairness for those without digital access or skills. It provides an alternative in case of technical problems, supports a smoother process, and ensures that users can still file in-person in case of service disruptions or emergencies.

Online courts represent a major advancement in justice system digitalization, providing a platform where legal proceedings can be conducted without paper or in-person hearings. Online courts such as British Columbia's CRT and the English Online Civil Money Claim emphasize user empowerment by enabling self-representation and simplifying the legal process, reducing costs, and increasing access to justice. A people-centred approach is essential for these courts, ensuring inclusivity by providing user-friendly interfaces and support for those with limited digital literacy. Their design, focused on small claims and geographically remote users, addresses barriers such as travel and complexity. Online Courts are reshaping justice systems by promoting accessibility, efficiency, and user empowerment through technology. However, they must ensure that they do not exacerbate the digital divide by offering non-digital alternatives where possible. The standards highlight the need for easy-to-use ODR systems, continuous monitoring, and timely upgrades. Pilot projects and empirical studies on user experience should provide valuable insights for improvements.

The ongoing digitalization of justice systems offers considerable potential to improve civil justice and dispute resolution efficiency. A collaborative approach involving all stakeholders—the government, professionals, users, and companies—is essential for transformation success. Although the process is long term and still in its early stages, starting with appropriate strategies is critical. A human-centred approach must guide this effort, ensuring inclusivity and preventing anyone from being left behind. Technology can enhance access to justice globally by adopting best practices, addressing the digital divide, safeguarding rights, and continuously improving user feedback.

Bibliography

Aliste Santos TJ, 'ADR y digitalización como premisas para la transformación eficiente de nuestro sistema de justicia civil' (2023) 11 Actualidad Civil.

Assy R, '*Injustice in Person: The Right to Self-representation* (OUP 2015).

Brown T, 'Design Thinking' (2008) 86:6 Harvard Business Review 84.

Butler S, Mauet S, Griffin CL and Pish M, 'The Utah Online Dispute Resolution Platform: A Usability Evaluation and Report" [2020] Discussion Paper No. 21-06 Arizona Legal Studies.

CEPEJ, 'European judicial systems. Evaluation Report', [2020] Evaluation cycle (2018 data).

CEPEJ, 'Guidelines on the use of videoconferencing in judicial proceedings' (June 2021). Available at <https://rm.coe.int/cepej-2021-4-guidelines-videoconference-en/1680a2c2f4>.

CEPEJ, '2022–2025 CEPEJ Action plan: Digitalisation for a better justice' CEPEJ (2021) 12 Final.

China, Online Litigation Rules of the People's Courts, Fa Shi [2021] No 12 (Adopted at the 1,838th meeting of the Adjudication Committee of the Supreme People's Court on 18 May 18 2021, and effective as of 1 August 2021). <https://cicc.court.gov.cn/html/1/219/199/201/2208.html>.

Cernada Badía R, 'La notificación judicial electrónica: garantía del derecho fundamental a la tutela judicial efectiva y retos que plantea a la administración de justicia en España', (thesis, University of Valencia 2016) URI: <http://hdl.handle.net/10550/57638>.

Cortés P, 'The English Online Court: A Research Proposal for Its Evaluation' (2022) 9(2) IJODR 138.

Cortés P and Takagi T, 'The Civil Money Claim Online: The Flagship Project of Court Digitalization in England and Wales' (2019) 25(8) Computer and Telecommunications L Rev 207.

Cortés P, 'El acceso a la justicia del consumidor inglés a través de las comunicaciones electrónicas' in Esteban de la Rosa F (ed), *Justicia digital, mercado y resolución de litigios de consumo. Innovación en el Diseño del Acceso a la Justicia* (Aranzadi 2021) 89.

Cotino Hueso L, 'La preocupante falta de garantías constitucionales y administrativas en las notificaciones electrónicas' (2021) RGDA Iustel 1.

Conforti ODF, 'Diseño de una plataforma de resolución de conflictos por medios electrónicos en el ámbito de consumo' in Esteban de la Rosa F (ed), *Justicia digital, mercado y resolución de litigios de consumo. Innovación en el diseño del acceso a la justicia* (Aranzadi 2021) 133.

Ebner N, 'The human touch in ODR: Trust, empathy and social intuition in online negotiation and mediation' in Rainey D, Katsh E, & Wahab MA (eds), *Online Dispute Resolution: Theory and Practice* (2nd edn) (2021 Eleven International Publishing) 73.

ECLC, 'Guidelines on online dispute resolution mechanisms in civil and administrative court proceedings', 1407th meeting, 16 June 2021, <https://search.coe.int/cm?i=0900001680a2cf96>.

Esteban de la Rosa F and Zeleznikow J, 'Making Intelligent Online Dispute Resolution Tools available to Self-Represented Litigants in the Public Justice System: Towards and Ethical use of the AI technology in the administration of Justice' Eighteenth International Conference for Artificial Intelligence and Law (2021) <https://doi.org/10.1145/3462757.3466077 >.

European Union, *European e-Justice Strategy* 2024–2028, C/2025/437, OJEU 16.1.2025.

European Commission, *Digitalisation of justice in the European Union: A toolbox of opportunities*, COM(2020) 710 final, 2/12/2020; EP and Council Regulation (EU) 2020/1783 on taking of evidence [2020] OJUE L405/1.

EP and Council Regulation 2020/1784 on service of judicial and extrajudicial documents [2020] L405/40; EP and Council Regulation (EU) 2023/2844 on digitalisation of judicial cooperation and access to justice [2023] OJUE L 27.12.2023.

European Commission, 'The 2023 EU Justice Scoreboard', (Communication) COM (2023) 309.

EP, Council and Commission, European Declaration on Digital Rights and Principles for the Digital Decade, OJEU 23/01/2023 C23/1.

EP and Council Regulation 2020/1783 on taking of evidence [2020] OJ L405/1.

EP and Council Regulation 2020/1784 on service of judicial and extrajudicial documents [2020] OJ L405/40.

EP and Council Regulation (EU) 2023/2844 on digitalisation of judicial cooperation and access to justice [2023] OJ L 27.12.2023.

Fundación COTEC-UGR Esteban de la Rosa F (ed), 'Guía Justicia Digital', 2022 <https://cotec.es/proyectos-cpt/guia-para-la-justicia-digital>.

Fernández-Fígares Morales MJ, *Audiencias telemáticas en la Justicia. Presente y futuro* (2021 Tirant Lo Blanch).

Garrido Reus A, *Online Courts: Comparative Study*, PRK Partners & Masaryk University, 2022. Available at <https://www.prkpartners.com/files/0-final-version-online-courts-comparative-study-antonio-garrido-reus-prk-partners-masaryk-university.pdf>.

Hagan MD, 'A Human-Centered Design Approach to Access to Justice: Generating New Prototypes and Hypotheses for Interventions to Make Courts User-Friendly' (2018) 6 Indiana Journal of Law and Social Equality 199.

Hungary, Courts section of the Hungarian Electronic Administration Portal, available at <https://e-ugyintezes.birosag.hu/kalkulator and https://e-ugyintezes.birosag.hu/eljaras-idotartam-kalkulator>.

Kramer XE, Van Gelder E, and Themeli E, 'e-Justice in the Netherlands: the Rocky Road to Digitised Justice' in Weller M and Wendland M (eds), *Digital Single Market: Bausteine eines Rechts in der Digitalen Welt* (Mohr Siebeck 2018) 209. Available at <https://papers.ssrn.com/sol3/papers.cfm?abstract_id=3167543>.

Krishna N., Sambasivan K, Nath U, Sahay P, and Raghavan S, 'Delivering Justice Solutions to Persons with Disabilities through Online Dispute Resolution Platforms', (2023) 10(1) International Journal of Online Dispute Resolution doi: 10.5553/IJODR/235250022023010001004 20.

Marchal Escalona N, 'El nuevo marco europeo sobre notificación y obtención de pruebas en el extranjero: hacia un espacio judicial europeo digitalizado' (2022) REDI 155.

Menashe D, 'A Critical Analysis of the Online Court' (2018) University of Pennsylvania Journal of International Law 921.

Mexico Evalua, 'Guía de Buenas Prácticas en el uso de nuevas tecnologías para la impartición de justicia' (7/10/2020) <www.mexicoevalua.org/guia-de-buenas-practicas-en-el-uso-de-nuevas-tecnologias-para-la-imparticion-de-justicia>.

NCSC, 'Impact of the Utah Online Dispute Resolution (ODR) Pilot Program: Final Report', December 19, 2020, available at <https://ncsc.contentdm.oclc.org/digital/collection/adr/id/66/rec/1>.

NCSC, (the States), 'A guide to help design your ODR" <https://nationalcenterforstatecourts.app.box.com/s/ypjzrnfohwao3j1httwoa6mjlgxxeimw>.

NCSC, (the States) '*Request for Information (RFI) Toolkit for Courts Procuring Online Dispute Resolution (ODR) Technology* <https://nationalcenterforstatecourts.app.box.com/s/gtyiz0m5vjv76pykn1z5q51jhukp11yt >.

OECD, 'Developing Effective Online Dispute Resolution in Latvia' (OECD Publishing 2024) <https://doi.org/10.1787/75ef5c4c-en>.

OECD, 'Measuring and improving access to justice in court services: Learning from the United Kingdom's experience', OECD Public Governance Policy Papers, No 60 (OECD Publishing 2024) <https://doi.org/10.1787/a8226ccc-en>.

OECD, 'OECD Online Dispute Resolution Framework', OECD Public Governance Policy Papers, No 59 (OECD Publishing 2024) <https://doi.org/10.1787/325e6edc-en>.

OECD, 'Recommendation on Access to Justice and People-Centred Justice Systems', [2023], <https://legalinstruments.oecd.org/en/instruments/OECD-LEGAL-0498>.

Pérez Daudí V, 'La justicia civil ante el reto de las TIC' in Jesús Conde Fuentes and Gregorio Serrano Hoyo (eds), *La justicia digital en España y la Unión Europea* (Atelier 2019) 87.

Pérez Gaipo J, 'El proceso laboral ante la era digital' in Jesús Conde Fuentes and Gregorio Serrano Hoyo (eds), *La justicia digital en España y en la Unión Europea* (Atelier 2019) 79.

Resolution System Institut Rachel Feinstein and Jennifer Shack (2024) 'Making ODR More Accessible to Self-Represented Parties: Focus Group Perspectives' <https://s3.amazonaws.com/aboutrsi/591e30fc6e181e166ffd2eb0/Final-Report-OPEN-Making-ODR-More-Accessible-20May2024-R.pdf>.

San Bruno Casuso R., 'El Tribunal Constitucional limita el uso del correo electrónico en los procedimientos judiciales' (Rödl & Partner 2020) <www.roedl.es/es/articulos/el-tribunal-constitucional-limita-el-uso-del-correo-electronico-en-los-procedimientos-judiciales>.

Schmitz AJ, 'Expanding Access to Remedies, Voice, and Possibly Justice in United States Court Online Dispute Resolution' (2024) Ohio State Legal Studies Research Paper.

Schwab K, *La cuarta revolución industrial,* (Debate 2016).

Sourdin T and Zeleznikow J, 'Courts, mediation and COVID-19' (2020) 48-2 Australian Business L Rev 138.

Spanish Government, Charter of Digital Rights (2021)

Sung H-C, 'Can Online Courts Promote Access to Justice? A Case Study of the Internet Courts in China', Computer Law & Security Review (2020) 39 105461.

Susskind R, *Tribunales online y la justicia del futuro* (spanish translation, Wolter Kluwers 2020).

UK House of Commons Library, 'Litigants in person: the rise of the self-represented' (Briefing Paper Number 07113, 14 March 2019).

UK Civil Justice Council, 'Access to Justice for Litigants in Person (or self-represented litigants) ' (2011). Available at <https://www.judiciary.uk/wp-content/uploads/2014/05/report-on-access-to-justice-for-litigants-in-person-nov2011.pdf>.

United Nations (General Assembly), 'Transforming our world: the 2030 Agenda for Sustainable Development', (Resolution) A/RES/70/1.

UNCITRAL, *Technical Notes on Online Dispute Resolution* (2017).

UNDP "e-Justice. Digital Transformation to Close the Justice Gap' (2022).

USA: National Center for State Courts, 'Self-Representation in U.S. Family Law Cases' (2017).

USA American Bar Association, 'The State of Self-Representation in Civil Cases' (2016).

Vilalta Nicuesa AE., 'Acceso a la justicia y su transición digital: hacia una justicia abierta al ciudadano (A2J4all)' (2021) 58 Revista General de Derecho Administrativo 2.

Watanabe M and Rule C, 'ODR in the Metaverse' (2022) IJODR 21.

Wang L, 'Application of Information Technology in Judicial Field: The Development Model of Online Litigation in China' (2024) 52 Computer Law & Security Review, 105–936.

Wing L, 'Ethical Principles for Online Dispute Resolution. A GPS Device for the Field' (2016) 3 IJODR 1, 20.

Wing, L, 'Mapping the Parameters of Online Dispute Resolution' (2022) (9) 1 IJODR 11.

Xuhui F, 'Recent Development of Internet Courts in China", (2018) (5) 1-2, IJODR 49.

Zeleznikow J, 'An Australian perspective on research and development required for the construction of applied legal decision support systems', Artificial Intelligence and Law, (2002) 10 237–60 <https://doi.org/10.1023/A:1025450828280>.

2

Process Pluralism in the Post-Covid Dispute Resolution Landscape

Orna Rabinovich-Einy[*]

A. Introduction

Among her numerous contributions as a founder of the field, Professor Menkel-Meadow coined and developed the term 'process pluralism', one of the most influential concepts in the dispute resolution arena. Process pluralism serves both as a descriptive lens in observing the dispute resolution landscape and as a normative prism through which various procedural schemes can be evaluated and procedural reform can be devised.[1]

In the last few years process pluralism has gained new meaning as diversity in procedural avenues increasingly encompassed a broader range of mediums, procedural options, and roles with the spread of new technologies. Initially, such additional procedural choices existed mainly in written asynchronous form and with the facilitation of human third parties. Over time, two main developments expanded procedural choice. With the onset of COVID-19, a plethora of remote proceedings emerged,

* Associate Professor, Law Faculty, University of Haifa. This chapter draws significantly on an article published at 10 Tex A&M L Rev 55 (2022) and also entitled 'Process Pluralism in the Post-COVID Dispute Resolution Landscape.' This research was made available by the Israel Science Foundation (Grants No. 492/17; 2381/22) 'Online Courts: An Empirical Analysis', and 'Online Courts in the Post-Covid Era: An Empirical Analysis'.

[1] See Carrie Menkel-Meadow, 'When Litigation Is Not the Only Way: Consensus Building and Mediation as Public Interest Lawyering' (2002) 10 Wash UJL & Pol'y 37, 37–39; Carrie Menkel-Meadow, 'From Legal Disputes to Conflict Resolution and Human Problem Solving: Legal Dispute Resolution in a Multidisciplinary Context' (2004) 54 J Legal Ed 7, 7–9.

Orna Rabinovich-Einy, *Process Pluralism in the Post-Covid Dispute Resolution Landscape* In: *Digitalization and Artificial Intelligence in Courts*. Edited by: Fernando Esteban de la Rosa, Pablo Cortés, and Nuria Marchal Escalona, Oxford University Press. © Orna Rabinovich-Einy 2025. DOI: 10.1093/9780198918752.003.0002

varying from synchronous and asynchronous written proceedings to audio and video-based processes.[2] In addition, with the growth of artificial intelligence, extra technological roles are being introduced into on- and offline dispute resolution, operating alongside, or displacing, human actors. These developments have raised a host of questions as to the desirability of such plurality.[3] For the readers of Menkel-Meadow's work these questions are not new. Years ago, she asked whether more procedural options are necessarily a good thing, ultimately underscoring the need for sensitivity to context in modern and complex societies, thereby making the case that the time has come to move from the Fuller-shaped approach of process integrity to one in which procedural hybridization reflects 'an integrity of its own'.[4]

This chapter proceeds as follows. Section B describes the concept of process pluralism, the backdrop against which it emerged, and the new reality in which this term is grounded. Section C elaborates on the connection between process pluralism and technology over the years. In sections D and E, studies conducted on online and remote proceedings, as well as research on the impact of introducing artificial intelligence into the legal and dispute resolution contexts, illuminate the ways in which different designs of online schemes can significantly shape the degree of access to justice, procedural fairness, and the fairness of outcomes that such processes provide. Finally, section F concludes the chapter.

B. The Concept of Process Pluralism

The concept of process pluralism emerged in response to two alternative views of dispute resolution mechanisms in our society. The first was what might be termed a traditional view under which courts presented the preferred route for addressing a wide range of individual and social disputes that would fall under the rubric of 'legal disputes'. For many years this view was assumed but not pronounced, as courts were the dominant means for resolving disputes in modern societies in which social and religious ties have disintegrated.[5]

The alternative approach emerged in response to what were seen as the failings and limitations of the courts in addressing conflict. It hailed the role of alternative processes, mostly mediation that emerged as of the last quarter of the twentieth century, and viewed these new forms of justice as superior to the court.[6] In response to the

[2] See The Pew Charitable Trusts, 'How Courts Embraced Technology, Met the Pandemic Challenge, and Revolutionized Their Operations' (*The Pew Charitable Trusts | The Pew Charitable Trusts*, 1 December 2021) <www.pewtrusts.org/en/research-and-analysis/reports/2021/12/how-courts-embraced-technology-met-the-pandemic-challenge-and-revolutionized-their-operations> last accessed 20 May 2024.

[3] See Alicia Bannon and Janna Adelstein, 'The Impact of Video Proceedings on Fairness and Access to Justice in Court' (*Brennan Center for Justice*, 10 September 2020) <www.brennancenter.org/our-work/research-reports/impact-video-proceedings-fairness-and-access-justice-court> last accessed 20 May 2024.

[4] Carrie Menkel-Meadow, 'Hybrid and Mixed Dispute Resolution Processes: Integrities of Process Pluralism' in Maria Moscati, Micael Palmer and Marian Roberts (eds), *Comparative Dispute Resolution* (Edward Elgar Publishing 2020) 13, 13–15 <http://dx.doi.org/10.4337/9781786433039.00038> last accessed 20 May 2024.

[5] Jerold S Auerbach, *Justice Without Law?* (OUP 1983) 10–11.

[6] See generally Carrie Menkel-Meadow, 'The Trouble with the Adversary System in a Postmodern, Multicultural World' (1996) 38 Wm & Mary L Rev 5.

adoption of alternatives, some critics expressed the traditional view in objecting to the adoption of mediation and the encouragement of settlement in the courts.[7] Over time, as alternatives were institutionalized in the court setting, the dichotomous approach to 'courts' on the one hand and 'alternatives' on the other hand was transposed with an understanding that we were now in an era in which formal and informal avenues often comingled (or as Professor Menkel-Meadow described it, we saw the rise of 'semi-formal' procedures).[8]

Process pluralism connotes the idea that it is desirable to have a wide selection of processes in our justice system, capturing a unique mix of goals and values, and allowing for a contextualized tailoring of processes to the particulars of the dispute and characteristics of the parties, thereby creating 'an integrity of its own—seeking flexibility and variability.'[9] In other words, we need to figure out, as Menkel-Meadow emphasizes, '[w]hat human problems are best resolved, handled, or solved by what processes.'[10]

All of this, as Menkel-Meadow has been telling us for many years, will enhance justice. '[O]ne size does not fit all,' she writes, and 'new forms of hybridity, variation and mixed processes may enhance human problem solving, increase creativity and flexibility in outcomes and dispute prevention, as well as resolution—and, hopefully, strengthen both peace and justice in their different forms.'[11] Modern societies with all their diversity, she emphasizes, require pluralism and diversity in process.[12] Indeed, in recent decades this insight has permeated not only into the alternative (or appropriate) dispute resolution realm, but also the formal court arena, a distinction which has in itself been blurred by the growing array of procedures offered along the dispute resolution continuum.[13]

[7] Owen M Fiss, 'Against Settlement' (1984) 93 Yale LJ 1073, 1075 <http://dx.doi.org/10.2307/796205> last accessed 21 May 2024; Richard Delgado et al, 'Fairness and Formality: Minimizing the Risk of Prejudice in Alternative Dispute Resolution' (1985) 1369 Wis L Rev 1359, 1360–61, n 8; Trina Grillo, 'The Mediation Alternative: Process Dangers for Women' (1991) 100 Yale LJ 1545, 1601 <http://dx.doi.org/10.2307/796781> last accessed 21 May 2024.

[8] Carrie Menkel-Meadow, 'Regulation of Dispute Resolution in the United States of America: From the Formal to the Informal to the "Semi-formal"' in Felix Steffek and Hannes Unberath (eds), *Regulating Dispute Resolution: ADR and Access to Justice at the Crossroads* (Hart Publishing 2013) 419.

[9] Menkel-Meadow, 'Hybrid and mixed dispute resolution processes' (n 4) 15.

[10] Carrie Menkel-Meadow, 'Peace and Justice: Notes on the Evolution and Purposes of Legal Processes' (2006) 94 Geo LJ 553, 565.

[11] Menkel-Meadow, 'Hybrid and mixed dispute resolution processes' (n 4) 3.

[12] ibid 13.

[13] Carrie Menkel-Meadow, 'Pursuing Settlement in an Adversary Culture: A Tale of Innovation Co-Opted or "The Law of ADR"' (1991) 19 Fla St UL Rev 1, 1–5. See also Menkel-Meadow, 'Regulation of Dispute Resolution' (n 8) 419–28. See also Deborah R Hensler, 'Our Courts, Ourselves: How the Alternative Dispute Resolution Movement Is Re-Shaping Our Legal System' (2003) 108 Dick L Rev 165, 174–89. See also Nancy A Welsh, 'The Thinning Vision of Self-Determination in Court-Connected Mediation: The Inevitable Price of Institutionalization?' (2001) 6 Harv Negot L Rev 1, 3–7. See also Leonard L Riskin and Nancy A Welsh, 'Is That All There Is? "The Problem" in Court-Oriented Mediation' (2008) 15 Geo Mason L Rev 863, 863–67. See also Bobbi McAdoo and Nancy A Welsh, 'Look Before You Leap and Keep on Looking: Lessons from the Institutionalization of Court-Connected Mediation' (2005) 5 Nev LJ 399, 399–401. See also Orna Rabinovich-Einy, 'The Legitimacy Crisis and the Future of Courts' (2015) 17 Cardozo J Confl Resol 23, 23.

Why would process pluralism enhance justice? This is because procedures shape access to justice, procedural justice, and, ultimately, shape the outcomes reached. In terms of access to justice, procedural arrangements determine whether we can effectively access and use avenues of redress, and different design choices will leave a different group of people outside the reach of specific dispute resolution processes because of such features as their cost, complexity, location, jurisdiction, and language employed. Since different people have different capabilities and preferences, a wide choice of processes that differ along these axes should enhance access to justice, particularly for those members of disempowered groups who have traditionally faced higher barriers in accessing the courts.

In terms of procedural justice, different procedural schemes could impact whether parties experience processes as fair and as ones that provide them with an opportunity to express voice. Over the years, research has demonstrated the significance of procedural justice perceptions not only to parties' assessments of whether the particular procedure was fair, but also its centrality in shaping parties' perceptions of the legitimacy of the entity delivering such dispute resolution processes. While the pillars of procedural justice have been found to remain significant across social groups, locales, and settings, the levels of access to justice experienced by different parties under varying procedural structures can be expected to differ. Therefore, here too, more options can enhance parties' sense of fairness.

Finally, different procedures are bound to lead parties to different outcomes. In some cases, third parties render these decisions, while in other instances parties devise their own resolutions. In court and arbitration, rights-based outcomes are sought, while in mediation the goal is oftentimes to reach interest and needs-based outcomes. Indeed, a principal driver for the adoption and use of mediation is its ability to produce outcomes that are different from those reached in court and that expand our 'remedial imagination'.[14] So here also, if we believe that different problems could be resolved in various ways, depending on parties' needs, rights, situation, and choices, then we would view process pluralism as a positive development.

When Menkel-Meadow wrote about process pluralism, she referred to a wide array of contexts which crossed familiar distinctions and categorizations, with disputes ranging from domestic to international[15] and from civil to criminal,[16] and functions ranging from dispute resolution to rule-making and consensus building.[17] In the second decade of the twenty-first century, process pluralism took on a new meaning as technology became another layer of process diversification, as we shall see in the following part.

[14] Menkel-Meadow, 'Pursuing Settlement in an Adversary Culture' (n 13) 7.

[15] See generally Carrie Menkel-Meadow, 'Correspondences and Contradictions in International and Domestic Conflict Resolution: Lessons from General Theory and Varied Contexts' (2003) 2003 J Disp Resol 319.

[16] See generally Carrie Menkel-Meadow, 'Restorative Justice: What Is It and Does It Work?' (2007) 3 Ann Rev L & Soc Sci 161 <http://dx.doi.org/10.1146/annurev.lawsocsci.2.081805.110005> last accessed 21 May 2024. See generally Carrie Menkel-Meadow, 'Process Pluralism in Transitional/Restorative Justice' (2015) 3 Int'l J Confl Engagement & Resol 3.

[17] See generally Carrie Menkel-Meadow, 'The Lawyer's Role(s) in Deliberative Democracy' (2004) 5 Nev LJ 347.

C. Legal Pluralism and Online Proceedings

1. First wave: the 1990s

While online dispute resolution (ODR) had already emerged in the 1990s, it was seen as a discrete arena, fit for disputes that emerged in the online setting, which at the time was a milieu that was separate from face-to-face interactions.[18] Indeed, even for the online disputes, mostly in the context of e-commerce, online proceedings were perceived as inferior to the richer and fuller opportunities for engagement offered through physical encounters. Nevertheless, it was also clear that there needed to be dispute resolution processes available for those engaging in online activities that could provide effective, low-cost redress.

Some online entities quickly realized that they needed to take responsibility for problems that arose on their platforms if they wished to draw in users and engender trust in their services. eBay, whose elaborate dispute resolution scheme is often viewed as the 'poster child' of ODR, was a pioneer in the field. After conducting a pilot experiment on its site, eBay offered a full-fledged ODR system to its users. First, through an external start-up, and, later, through its internal trust and safety program, it created an ODR system that has come to address over 60 million disputes a year.[19]

But the significance of the eBay ODR system extends beyond its primacy and scope; it has to do mainly with its use of technology to expand process pluralism. While most other ODR entities at the time tried to create online equivalents to familiar face-to-face processes, eBay was probably the first entity to embrace the unique qualities of online digital communication to rethink the nature of processes employed,[20] their qualities,[21] and the values and goals they advance.[22] Indeed, this mind shift was an important development, which paved the way for the second wave of ODR.

2. Second wave: early 2000s

It was only with the spread of smartphones and social media that online and offline activities began to comingle. As habits and expectations evolved and technology improved (not only in terms of connectivity, but also in terms of interface and user experience), it became possible, and in some cases even expected, to have online resolution

[18] Orna Rabinovich-Einy, 'The Past, Present, and Future of Online Dispute Resolution' (2021) 74 Current Legal Probs 125, 129–30 <http://dx.doi.org/10.1093/clp/cuab004> last accessed 21 May 2024.

[19] Ethan Katsh and Orna Rabinovich-Einy, *Digital Justice: Technology and the Internet of Disputes* (OUP 2017) 34–35.

[20] eBay was a pioneer in designing an 'automated negotiation' process, which did not have an offline equivalent. See Rabinovich-Einy, 'The Past, Present, and Future of ODR' (n 18) 133.

[21] Online processes differ from offline ones in their degree of structure and the level of confidentiality they afford. See Orna Rabinovich-Einy, 'Technology's Impact: The Quest for a New Paradigm for Accountability in Mediation' (2006) 11 Harv Negot L Rev 253, 268–83.

[22] The digital trail that comes with online proceedings, can promote the goal of dispute prevention by detecting pattern of recurring disputes and reforming the environment in which transactions are formed or interactions occur so as to reduce or eliminate such disputes altogether. See ibid 273.

avenues available for a growing array of contexts and disputes.[23] Even concerns over the digital divide diminished somewhat with growing evidence of the widespread use of online communication by members of disempowered groups for various ends.[24]

During this time, courts and tribunals were adopting ODR; Modria and Matterhorn began operating across growing numbers of local and state courts,[25] and the Civil Resolution Tribunal in British Columbia provided a proof of concept for a diagnosis phase in formal proceedings.[26] Outside courts, novel types of online proceedings were emerging in diverse settings ranging from smart contracts[27] to school bullying.[28] Menkel-Meadow was, of course, ahead of the game and saw the opportunities for process pluralism enhanced through the novel dimension of choice of medium, but she was also duly cautious in recognizing the challenges and dangers associated with the widespread adoption of online processes.[29]

At the same time, we started seeing assessments of ODR proceedings that gave reason to think that in some contexts, for some parties, such processes could increase various dimensions of justice, including: access to justice (due to the convenience of handling proceedings online, from anywhere and anytime people engage more with the process when it is conducted online, as parties raise more problems and are more responsive to complaints against them, rather than just 'lumping it' or defaulting);[30] procedural justice (in those cases where parties felt they were better able to express themselves in writing, asynchronously);[31] and even substantive justice, with the

[23] See Orna Rabinovich-Einy and Ethan Katsh, 'The New New Courts' (2017) 67 Am UL Rev 165, 203–12.

[24] See 'Mobile Fact Sheet' (*Pew Research Center*, 31 January 2024) <www.pewresearch.org/internet/fact-sheet/mobile/> last accessed 21 May 2024.

[25] Rabinovich-Einy, 'The Past, Present, and Future of ODR' (n 18) 135–36.

[26] ibid 133–34.

[27] See 'The Justice Protocol' (*Kleros*) <https://perma.cc/GP4B-SXVW> last accessed 21 May 2024. See also Amy J Schmitz and Colin Rule, 'Online Dispute Resolution for Smart Contracts' (2019) 2019 J Disp Resol 103, 114–21. See also Orna Rabinovich-Einy and Ethan Katsh, 'Blockchain and the Inevitability of Disputes: The Role for Online Dispute Resolution' (2019) 2019 J Disp Resol 47, 57–71.

[28] 'Resolving Digital Conflicts, Together' (*Agree Online*) <https://www.facebook.com/p/Agree-Online-100064071970062/> last accessed 29 May 2024.

[29] Carrie Menkel-Meadow, 'Is ODR ADR?' (2016) 3 Int'l J Online Disp Resol 4, 5 <http://dx.doi.org/10.5553/ijodr/235250022016003001002> last accessed 21 May 2024.

[30] JJ Prescott, 'Improving access to justice in state courts with platform technology' (2017) 70 Vand L Rev 1993, 2030–34, 2037–39. It should be noted, however, that where the participation in such proceedings is voluntary, as is often the case with asynchronous ODR processes usage rates can be disappointing. Where participation rates are low, not only is it difficult to provide meaningful evaluation of such programs' accessibility, but it may also reflect the existence of access barriers that prevent more widespread use of these processes; See Donna Shestowsky and Jennifer Shack, 'Online Dispute Resolution for Debt and Small Claims Cases: A Report on a Pilot Program in a Justice of the Peace Court in Collin County, Texas' (2022) SSRN Electronic Journal <http://dx.doi.org/10.2139/ssrn.4173414> last accessed 21 May 2024; Renee Danser et al, 'Online Dispute Resolution of Low-Level Court Proceedings: Two Broken Field Experiments, One Unexpected Result' (2023) SSRN Electronic Journal <https://ssrn.com/abstract = 4375081>.

[31] Ayelet Sela, 'Streamlining Justice: How Online Courts Can Resolve the Challenges of Pro Se Litigation' (2016) 26 Cornell J L & Pub Pol'y 331, 375–80; Avital Mentovich, JJ Prescott and Orna Rabinovich-Einy, 'Legitimacy and online proceedings: Procedural Justice, Access to Justice, and the Role of Income' (2023) 57 L & Soc'y Rev 189 <http://dx.doi.org/10.1111/lasr.12653> last accessed 21 May 2024; Katie Sykes et al, 'Civil Revolution: User Experiences with British Columbia's Online Court' (2022) 37 Windsor Y B Access Just 161, 186–88 <http://dx.doi.org/10.22329/wyaj.v37i1.7192> last accessed 21 May 2024; Donna Shestowsky and Jennifer Shack, 'Online Dispute Resolution for Post-Judgment Family Law Cases. A Report to the Ottawa County, Michigan, Friend of the Court' (2022) SSRN Electronic Journal <http://dx.doi.org/10.2139/ssrn.4173424> last accessed 21 May 2024.

elimination of race-based outcome disparities, as we have seen in one study of ODR in the traffic arena,[32] and a finding that parties were far more likely to reach an agreement through ODR than those not using the ODR platform in certain family disputes.[33]

3. Third wave: COVID–19

The dawn of the third decade of the 21st century brought about yet another development: the rise of remote proceedings in the wake of COVID–19. Clearly, the health, economic, and social-related consequences we experienced were devastating. The pandemic had, however, accelerated some developments, and one could say that it has been a positive force in spreading and mainstreaming the use of technology in courts (as well as outside the formal legal system), further buoying the previous move to adopt ODR in courts. Such use was not limited to what was traditionally seen as ODR, but came to encompass what was termed by Richard Susskind 'remote courts'.[34]

Suddenly, everyone began conducting remote proceedings. Many courts were forced to shut down completely while others restricted their hearings to urgent cases in light of social distancing requirements. Even where in-person court sessions continued to take place, the use of online proceedings became essential to prevent extreme backlogs and delays, as court personnel contracted COVID or were exposed to people who were later diagnosed with COVID.

The adoption of remote proceedings in courts and for alternative proceedings outside the courts quickly became a global phenomenon, although local variations existed in terms of scope and types of proceedings adopted. Some courts employed videoconferencing platforms such as Zoom and Skype; others relied on audio and paper-based decision-making, while others still chose to adopt and expand ODR systems and processes that do not rely on real-time communications and are mostly text-based.[35]

Whatever the strategy adopted, it seems fair to say that internationally, courts had substantially expanded their use of technology, employing some form of online or remote proceedings during the pandemic.[36] As courts reopened, with many resuming full-scale operations in person, it became clear that online and remote proceedings were not going away; they are here to stay as part of the plurality of options offered by our modern-day 'multidoor courthouse'.[37] The following part expands on the desirability of such developments.

[32] Avital Mentovich, J Prescott, and Orna Rabinovich-Einy, 'Are Litigation Outcome Disparities Inevitable? Courts, Technology, and the Future of Impartiality' (2020) 73 Ala L Rev 893, 961–67.

[33] Shestowsky and Shack, 'ODR for Post-Judgment Family Law Cases' (n 31).

[34] Richard Susskind, 'The Future of Courts—Harvard Law School Center on the Legal Profession' (*Harvard Law School Center on the Legal Profession*, July/August 2020) <https://clp.law.harvard.edu/knowledge-hub/magazine/issues/remote-courts/the-future-of-courts/> last accessed 21 May 2024.

[35] ibid; David Freeman Engstrom, 'Post-COVID Courts' (2020) 68 UCLA L Rev 246, 250–51; Tania Sourdin, Bin Li, and Donna Marie McNamara, 'Court Innovations and Access to Justice in Times of Crisis' (2020) 9 Health Pol'y & Tech 447, 448 <http://dx.doi.org/10.1016/j.hlpt.2020.08.020> last accessed 21 May 2024.

[36] See Engstrom, 'Post-COVID Courts' (n 35) 250–51. See also Pew, 'How Courts Embraced Technology' (n 2) 1.

[37] Frank EA Sander, 'Varieties of Dispute Processing' in Art Hinshaw, Andrea K Schneider, and Sarah Rudolph (eds), *Discussions in Dispute Resolution* (OUP 2021) 321.

D. Evaluating [Online] Process Pluralism

How should we view these developments from a process pluralism perspective? As Menkel-Meadow tells us, 'process pluralism also has its dangers'.[38] For many ODR enthusiasts, the widespread adoption of remote proceedings was a mixed blessing. They feared that ODR was being equated with Zoom or with videoconferencing, erasing many years of serious work in terms of process design and plurality of options, which relied heavily on asynchronous communication.[39]

At the same time, the ODR community came to realize the significance some users attach to the availability of easy to use, readily available synchronous video communication and came to adjust their thinking on the need for such options as part of the procedural choices that are made available to users and providers.[40]

Another lesson for ODR was the need to adjust and spread quickly—this required an infrastructure that involved not only designers and platforms that could scale their operations and adjust to new arenas, but also dedicated individuals and groups that could offer guidance on training, ethical standards, and dispute system design principles. The implications of the shift from face-to-face proceedings to real time video communication on existing principles, values, and goals needed to be explored and addressed. This shift was very different from the impact of the previous move to asynchronous written communication in ODR, and existing guidelines and trainings from the ODR context were often inadequate to address these novel developments that were occurring quickly and at mass scale.[41]

Thus, for example, questions of accessibility arise with respect to the ability of people from low socio-economic backgrounds to join a videoconferencing session due to insufficient bandwidth.[42] At a time of quarantine, their ability to find a private

[38] Menkel-Meadow, 'Hybrid and Mixed Dispute Resolution Processes' (n 4) 3.

[39] Ana Goncalves and Daniel Rainey, 'Mediating Online Is Much More Than "Doing It On Zoom"' (*Kluwer Mediation Blog*, 28 February 2021) <https://mediationblog.kluwerarbitration.com/2021/02/28/mediating-online-is-much-more-than-doing-it-on-zoom/> accessed 21 May 2024. See also Simon Boehme, 'You Mediate on Zoom. Now What?' (*Mediate.com*, 14 September 2020) <https://mediate.com/you-mediate-on-zoom-now-what/> last accessed 21 May 2024. See also Amy J Schmitz and John Zeleznikow, 'Intelligent Legal Tech to Empower Self-Represented Litigants' (2022) 23 Colum Sci & Tech L Rev 142, 146.

[40] Indeed, for some operating in the dispute resolution field, ODR and remote proceedings fall under the same heading. See Meredith McBride, 'ODR in the Era of COVID-19' (*American Bar Association*, 27 October 2020) <www.americanbar.org/groups/family_law/committees/alternative-dispute-resolution/odr/> last accessed 21 May 2024.

[41] See generally Jean R Sternlight and Jennifer K Robbennolt, 'In-Person or Via Technology? Drawing on Psychology to Choose and Design Dispute Resolution Processes' (2022) 71 DePaul L Rev 701. The following guidelines were developed by the International Council for Online Dispute Resolution (ICODR) as the use of Zoom began to spread. See The International Council for Online Dispute Resolution, *ICODR Video Mediation Guidelines* (2020) <https://icodr.org/guides/videomed.pdf> last accessed 21 May 2024. See also The International Council for Online Dispute Resolution, ICODR Video Arbitration Guidelines (2020) <https://icodr.org/guides/videoarb.pdf> last accessed 21 May 2024.

[42] See The California Commission on Access to Justice, *Remote Hearings and Access to Justice During COVID-19 and Beyond* (The California Commission on Access to Justice 2020) 13, 13–14 <www.ncjfcj.org/wp-content/uploads/2020/06/2020-Remote-Hearings-Guide.pdf> last accessed 21 May 2024. See also 'Internet, Broadband Fact Sheet' (*Pew Research Center*, 31 January 2024) <www.pewresearch.org/internet/fact-sheet/internet-broadband/> last accessed 21 May 2024 (presenting data on bandwidth use in the US across demographics); Alicia L Bannon and Douglas Keith, 'Remote Court: Principles for Virtual

area within what is often a small living space that may be occupied with young children was limited and made the prospect of meaningful participation in a live session via video challenging, to say the least.[43] COVID also made it more difficult, in some cases impossible, to find a public space from which parties could connect to a hearing, let alone a quiet and discrete one.[44] Even post-COVID, concerns over access to video technology remain for a 'substantial minority'.[45]

Interestingly, a National Center for State Courts (NCSC) study of remote proceedings in Texas found that access to the courts actually increased in remote proceedings—not only of parties, but also of witnesses, victims, and others, all of whom found it easier to participate and defaulted less frequently.[46] At the same time, we know that mere participation is an insufficient measure of access, and the question arises as to what extent such participation was effective. There is reason for concern given some of the other studies of video proceedings—describing frequent connectivity problems for tenants in landlord–tenant cases, lack of preparation,[47] as well as concerns over more elusive challenges to access such as the ability to decipher more subtle cultural expectations from disputants in these settings (dress code, language use, and the like).[48] While courts made an effort to generate codes of conduct for the remote setting, these rules left much room for confusion and misunderstanding for pro se litigants.[49]

Alongside troubling findings in terms of access, more recent developments give room for optimism as process design and structured support for users evolve. Thus,

Proceedings During the COVID-19 Pandemic and Beyond' (2021) 115 NW UL Rev 1875, 1891. See also Pew, 'How Courts Embraced Technology' (n 2) 2, 13–14.

[43] One difficulty that is particularly acute for disempowered parties has to do with the use of interpreters in a remote hearing. See Nuffield Family Justice Observatory, *Remote hearings in the family justice system: a rapid consultation* (Nuffield Family Justice Observatory 2020) 15 <www.nuffieldfjo.org.uk/resource/remote-hearings-rapid-consultation> last accessed 21 May 2024. See also Alicia Summers and Sophia Gatowski, *Remote Hearing Study* (Nevada Court Improvement Program 2020) 9 <https://nevadacurrent.com/wp-content/uploads/2022/01/21-17924.pdf> last accessed 21 May 2024.

[44] Bannon and Keith, 'Remote Court' (n 42) 1890.

[45] Victor D Quintanilla et al, *Accessing Justice with Zoom: Experiences and Outcomes in Online Civil Courts* (Maurer School of Law 2023) 31.

[46] National Center for State Courts, *The Use of Remote Hearings in Texas State Courts: The Impact on Judicial Workload* (National Center for State Courts 2021) <www.ncsc.org/consulting-and-research/areas-of-expertise/access-to-justice/remote-and-virtual-hearings/resources-docs/TX-Remote-Hearing-Assessment-Report.pdf> last accessed 22 May 2024. See also Pew, 'How Courts Embraced Technology' (n 2) 1 (finding that default rates of defendants in legal proceedings dropped, meaning that participation by them increased). This was also noted in the context of online mediation, where a principal advantage mentioned by those involved was the ability to have key stakeholders participate. See Deborah Thompson Eisenberg, Donna Shestowsky, and Robert R Niccolini, 'What Matters to Employment Attorneys When Considering Online or In-Person Mediation?' (2023) 41 Alt High Cost Litig 151 <http://dx.doi.org/10.1002/alt.22020> last accessed 22 May 2024.

[47] Pew, 'How Courts Embraced Technology' (n 2) 12–13.

[48] In addition, discomfort with technology could inhibit willingness to engage with the process. Sternlight and Robbennolt, 'In-Person or Via Technology' (n 41) 732. The ability to present an organized version of one's story could prove crucial in videoconferencing, given such phenomena as zoom fatigue. ibid 740. Both capabilities may be lacking with disempowered parties.

[49] See Judiciary of England and Wales, *Good Practice for Remote Hearings* 2–4 (Judicial College 2020) <www.judiciary.uk/wp-content/uploads/2020/03/Good-Practice-for-Remote-Hearings-May-2020-1.pdf[https://perma.cc/UU5P-63NT]> last accessed 22 May 2024.

the NCSC has devised principles and guidelines for courts and judges to overcome some of the technical and cultural barriers that are typical of remote proceedings, alongside tools and principles that allow courts to integrate solutions for bridging language- and disability-related access barriers.[50] The NCSC has worked with courts to improve their technological infrastructure, layout and capabilities, to enhance their users' experience and access.[51] Also, some courts are using remote technology to create more tailored and accessible solutions for parties. For example, there are courts that have set up 'satellite access points' and 'customer service centers,' as well as 'mobile access points' to accommodate petitioners in cases such as domestic violence that require confidentiality and privacy.[52] Nevertheless, concerns over access to technology for disempowered parties remain.[53]

An important concern in terms of access to justice has to do with the difficulty of accessing counsel. In the case of represented parties who were not in the same room as their counsel, the new medium has presented many challenges to their ability to consult their lawyer in confidence (access to telephone communication with counsel could prove inferior in light of the thin nature of such communication).[54] For those who could not afford hiring a lawyer, the shift to remote proceedings presented new barriers to obtaining legal aid and for such counsel to operate remotely.[55]

At the same time, it should be noted that some studies have found that remote processes are preferred for their increased convenience and comfort.[56] This is true even for disempowered parties, as shown by a recent large-scale study comparing the experiences of pro-se litigants (particularly defendants) in face-to-face versus remote high-volume civil cases, which found positive perceptions of online proceedings. Specifically, remote processes were seen as more convenient, less stressful, more

[50] National Center for State Courts, *Hybrid Hearings Improvement Initiative* (National Center for State Courts 2024) 16, 44–45 <www.ncsc.org/__data/assets/pdf_file/0040/98896/HybridHearings_Report_2024.pdf> last accessed 22 May 2024.

[51] ibid 43.

[52] ibid 16, 29.

[53] See Meghan M O'Neil et al, 'Treatment Court Staffs' Perceptions in Support of the Use of Virtual Services in Court Post-Pandemic' (2024) 51 Crim Just & Behav 286 <https://doi.org/10.1177/00938548231219807> last accessed 23 May 2024. See also Ayelet Sela and Hadar Dancig-Rosenberg, 'The Right to Presence, via Screens: Court Observations in Remote Criminal Detention Hearings' (2022), 54 Hebrew UL Rev (forthcoming). See also Roni Factor et al, 'Videoconferencing in Legal Hearings and Procedural Justice' (2023) 18 Victims & Offenders 1557 <www.tandfonline.com/doi/full/10.1080/15564886.2023.2248465> last accessed 23 May 2024.

[54] While this complaint was voiced most strongly in the criminal context, it also presented a significant challenge in civil proceedings. Taylor Benninger et al, *Virtual Justice? A National Study Analyzing the Transition to Remote Criminal Court* (Standford Law School 2021) 7–9 < https://law.stanford.edu/wp-content/uploads/2021/08/Virtual-Justice-Final-Aug-2021.pdf> last accessed 15 June 2025. See also Cynthia Alkon, 'Criminal Court System Failures During COVID-19: An Empirical Study' (2022) 37 OSJDR 453, 489 <https://scholarship.law.tamu.edu/cgi/viewcontent.cgi?article = 2610&context = facscholar> last accessed 24 May 2024; Quintanilla et al (n 45) 31.

[55] See Bannon and Adelstein, 'The Impact of Video Proceedings' (n 3) 9–10. See also Natalie Byrom, Sarah Beardon, and Abby Kendrick, *The Impact of COVID-19 Measures on the Civil Justice System* (Judiciary College 2020) 22 <www.judiciary.uk/wp-content/uploads/2022/07/CJC-Rapid-Review-Final-Report-f-1.pdf> last accessed 24 May 2024. See also Jenia Iontcheva Turner, 'Remote Criminal Justice' (2021) 53 Tex Tech L Rev 197, 217 <https://papers.ssrn.com/sol3/papers.cfm?abstract_id = 3699045> last accessed 24 May 2024.

[56] Eisenberg et al (n 46).

satisfactory, and more desirable for future use.[57] Also, the technical problems were rare.[58] Interestingly, while in face-to-face processes plaintiffs' perceptions were more positive than those of defendants, this gap decreased substantially in the online setting due to defendants' positive experiences.[59]

Alongside the issue of access, another important layer of justice has to do with parties' procedural experiences and their perceptions of procedural justice.[60] In this context, the impact of having to turn off their video due to limited bandwidth can be detrimental for parties who feel unheard and unseen when giving testimony and hearing others.[61] The impact on voice and a sense of fairness of real-time communication where only some of the parties are shown is very different from both physical proceedings and from ODR settings in which everyone communicates asynchronously in writing.[62] Similar concerns arise where parties' words are cut off due to connectivity problems,[63] and perhaps more acute concerns arise over audio proceedings, particularly in those proceedings in which some of the parties use video.[64] At the same time, it should be noted that recent reports on remote proceedings in the employment and eviction contexts, find that parties' procedural justice experiences and satisfaction levels are positive, often not very different from those of equivalent offline proceedings, at times surpassing them.[65]

[57] Quintanilla et al (n 45) 31. The report notes that 'for many unrepresented parties, accessing court remotely decreased structural barriers encountered by those who attended court in person and provided conveniences. These conveniences included reducing time off work, traveling, and childcare burdens. At the same time, a smaller percentage of litigants, including perhaps the most technologically disadvantaged persons, reported new barriers to participation not encountered by those who attended court in person. As a result, these persons may experience the decision to participate in-person/remotely as a tradeoff: attending remote proceedings affords the conveniences described. Still, it may entail other barriers, such as the need to borrow a phone/computer or travel for Wi-Fi' (ibid 27).

[58] ibid 32–33.

[59] ibid 17–18.

[60] Turner, 'Remote Criminal Justice' (n 55) 264–65; Byrom, Beardon and Kendrick, *The impact of COVID-19 measures on the civil justice system* (n 55).

[61] Celia Kitzinger, 'Remote justice: a family perspective' (*The Transparency Project*, 29 March 2020) <https://transparencyproject.org.uk/remote-justice-a-family-perspective/[https://perma.cc/> last accessed 24 May 2024. See also Nuffield Family Justice Observatory, *Remote hearings in the family justice system* (n 43) 10. See also Judiciary of England and Wales, *Good Practice for Remote Hearings* (n 49) 3. See also Elizabeth G Thornburg, 'Observing Online Courts: Lessons from the Pandemic' (2020) SSRN Electronic Journal 193 <http://dx.doi.org/10.2139/ssrn.3696594> accessed 24 May 2024; Sela and Dancig-Rosenberg, 'The Right to Presence, via Screens' (n 53); Factor et al, 'Videoconferencing in Legal Hearings and Procedural Justice' (n 53).

[62] Mentovich, Prescott and Rabinovich-Einy, 'Legitimacy and online proceedings' (n 31) 31; Sela, 'Streamlining Justice' (n 31) 375–79.

[63] Indeed, research has shown that connectivity problems have not decreased over time. See Luis C Torres, Elizabeth M Lyne and Ashley M Appleby, 'On the (zoom) record: the role of videoconferencing in detention hearing proceedings' (2024) 47 J Crime & Just 613 <http://dx.doi.org/10.1080/0735648x.2024.2321588> last accessed 25 May 2024.

[64] See Sternlight and Robbennolt, 'In-Person or Via Technology?' (n 41) 745. See also Bannon and Keith, 'Remote Court' (n 42) 1891. See also Ruth Higgins 'Courts in the Pandemic–A View from the Bench' (2020) Winter Bar News 34 <https://www5.austlii.edu.au/au/journals/NSWBarAssocNews/2020/55.pdf> last accessed 15 June 2025.

[65] See E Patrick McDermott and Ruth Obar, 'The Equal Employment Opportunity Commission Mediation Participants' Experience in Online Mediation and Comparison to In-Person Mediation' (2022) SSRN Electronic Journal 13 <http://dx.doi.org/10.2139/ssrn.4130612> accessed 25 May 2024; Quintanilla et al (n 45) 17–18.

In addition to the impact on one's sense of voice, concerns have been raised that the characteristics of videoconferencing may diminish parties' sense of dignity and their ability to establish whether the judge was impartial.[66] At the same time, others have highlighted the positive psychological impact of participating from a familiar and relaxed setting, as well as the mitigation of adversarial tactics when proceedings are conducted remotely.[67] One study based on mock video proceedings finds that they can not only meet procedural justice standards, but even surpass the traditional physical gathering on certain dimensions.[68]

Another question has to do with substantive outcomes. Various past studies have shown empirically that disempowered parties fare substantially worse in videoconferencing proceedings.[69] This could be attributed to several causes. One source impacting the favourability of outcomes reached through videoconferencing for parties belonging to disempowered groups has to do with the effectiveness of such parties' performance through this medium, whether those parties are perceived as reliable and whether communication problems affect their ability to tell a coherent and comprehensible story.[70] Interestingly, one lab experiment demonstrated that the volume level can impact the credibility assigned to the speaker,[71] and another study

[66] Sternlight and Robbennolt, 'In-Person or Via Technology' (n 41) 750–52.

[67] Berkeley Research Group, *The Psychological Impact of Remote Hearings* (Berkeley Research Group 2021) 5–6 <https://media.thinkbrg.com/wp-content/uploads/2021/08/05105717/BRG-Remote-Hearing-Impact-2021-Final.pdf> last accessed 25 May 2024.

[68] Linda Mulcahy, Emma Rowden, and Wend Teeder, *Exploring the case for Virtual Jury Trials during the COVID-19 crisis: An evaluation of a pilot study conducted by JUSTICE* (Oxford Faculty of Law 2020) <https://files.justice.org.uk/wp-content/uploads/2020/04/06165956/Mulcahy-Rowden-Virtual-trials-final.pdf> last accessed 25 May 2024. But see also Byrom, Beardon, and Kendrick, *The impact of COVID-19 measures on the civil justice system* (n 55), which portrays a more mixed picture of the impact of video proceedings on procedural justice and user satisfaction.

[69] Anne Bowen Poulin, 'Criminal Justice and Videoconferencing Technology: The Remote Defendant' (2004) 78 Tul L Rev 1089, 1089; Frank M. Walsh and Edward M. Walsh, 'Effective Processing or Assembly-Line Justice? The Use of Teleconferencing in Asylum Removal Hearings' (2008) 22 Geo Immigr LJ 259, 259; Shari Seidman Diamond et al, 'Efficiency and Cost: The Impact of Videoconferenced Hearings on Bail Decisions' (2010) 100 J Crim L & Criminology 869, 898 <https://scholarlycommons.law.northwestern.edu/cgi/viewcontent.cgi?article = 7365&context = jclc> last accessed 25 May 2024; Dane Thorley and Joshua Mitts, 'Trial by skype: A Causality-oriented Replication Exploring the Use of Remote Video Adjudication in Immigration Removal Proceedings' (2019) 59 Int'l Rev L & Econ 82, 82 <https://doi.org/10.1016/j.irle.2019.05.002> last accessed 25 May 2024; Jean-Pierre Douglas-Henry and Ben Sanderson, *Virtual Hearings Report* (DLA Piper 2020) 13 <http://viewer.zmags.com/publication/051503a3#/051503a3/1> accessed 25 May 2024. But see Meredith Rossner and David Tait, 'Presence and Participation in a Virtual Court' (2021) 23 Criminology & Crim Just 136 <http://dx.doi.org/10.1177/17488958211017372> last accessed 25 May 2024, where an experiment demonstrated that mock jurors' perceptions of defendant culpability were not influenced by defendant's appearing on video, whether on their own or with counsel (in what they termed a 'distributed court').

[70] Bannon and Keith, 'Remote Court' (n 42) 1895–96; Sternlight and Robbennolt, 'In-Person or Via Technology?' (n 41) 737–38. Attorneys discussing online mediation also referred to the fact that they were less able to read cues and body language online. See Eisenberg et al (n 46). While research has cast significant doubt on the ability to discern truthful from dishonest testimony through verbal and nonverbal cues, existing beliefs in the professional-legal milieu continue to support such perceptions, potentially hindering the widespread adoption of remote proceedings. See João Ilhão Moreira and Liwen Zhang, 'Assessing Credibility in Online Arbitration Hearings: Determining Facts and Justice by Zoom' (2023) 37 IJSL 887 <http://dx.doi.org/10.1007/s11196-023-10046-7> last accessed 25 May 2024.

[71] Elena Bild et al, 'Sound and credibility in the virtual court: Low audio quality leads to less favorable evaluations of witnesses and lower weighting of evidence' (2021) 45 L & Hum Behav 481, 481 <http://dx.doi.org/10.1037/lhb0000466> accessed 25 May 2024.

highlighted the impact of the camera angle on credibility assessment,[72] features which the speaker may not even have control over, let alone be aware of. Even regarding those aspects of the camera over which parties do exert control, usage may reflect knowledge gaps. A study observing eviction cases, found that lawyers appeared much more often with 'staged backgrounds' than non-represented parties (plaintiffs and defendants).[73] A study comparing face-to-face arbitrations with remote ones—both video and written proceedings—found that individual plaintiffs whose cases are arbitrated remotely win less often and recover lower sums than those whose cases are conducted face-to-face, a phenomenon the author terms the 'remote penalty'.[74] On the other hand, a more recent study conducted on thousands of Zoom hearings involving pro se litigants found that pro-plaintiff judgements and eviction rates dropped in remote proceedings compared to physical court proceedings, as in Zoom proceedings agreements were more frequent.[75] Another study evaluating outcomes in the criminal context found that while technical problems were prevalent in remote proceedings, they did not shape outcomes in pretrial detention hearings.[76]

Another source of influence on outcomes are structural issues, which can shape the manner in which remote proceedings are conducted. Thus, for example, the fact that remote proceedings lack opportunities offered by in–person proceedings—such as forms to fill out, additional information garnered through physical observation, or in-person information and support—means that disadvantaged disputants may obtain worse outcomes.[77]

An additional factor that could negatively impact outcomes reached through remote proceedings is implicit bias by judges. Judges, like all other human beings, are subject to biases and heuristics that impact the way in which they process, understand, and weigh information.[78] Such biases operate against members of disempowered groups and are what explain the persistent phenomenon of disparities in legal outcomes where minorities are involved.[79] While written asynchronous proceedings have been found to eliminate outcome disparities in one context, video proceedings are likely to operate differently.[80] This is because videoconferencing not only exposes judges to parties' identity features, but also to legally irrelevant information about the parties, such as their living conditions (messy house, noisy kids, etc). This state of affairs may

[72] See Bannon and Adelstein, 'The Impact of Video Proceedings' (n 3) 7; See also Sternlight and Robbennolt, 'In-Person or Via Technology?' (n 41) 725–26.

[73] Quintanilla et al (n 45) 36.

[74] David Horton, 'Forced Remote Arbitration' (2022) 108 Cornell L Rev < http://dx.doi.org/10.2139/ssrn.4035835> last accessed 15 June 2025. This was found to be the case even after controlling for case type and representation; ibid.

[75] Quintanilla et al (n 45) 23–24, 36.

[76] See Torres, Lyne and Appleby, 'On the (zoom) record' (n 63).

[77] Bannon and Adelstein, 'The Impact of Video Proceedings' (n 3) 5; Turner, 'Remote Criminal Justice' (n 55) 218; Benninger et al, *Virtual Justice?* (n 54) 9. Interestingly, some lawyers also reported missing the opportunity to meet opposing counsel in person or 'head for the door' in an online mediation. See Eisenberg et al (n 46).

[78] Jeffrey J Rachlinski and Sheri Lynn Johnson, 'Does Unconscious Racial Bias Affect Trial Judges?' (2009) 84 Notre Dame L Rev 1195, 1195 <https://scholarship.law.nd.edu/ndlr/vol84/iss3/4/> last accessed 26 May 2024.

[79] Thornburg, 'Observing Online Courts' (n 61) 201–02.

[80] See eg, Sternlight and Robbennolt, 'In-Person or Via Technology' (n 41) 741–42.

prove most detrimental for parties belonging to disadvantaged groups both because they may not have a quiet and secluded space at home from which to conduct the proceeding and because they may be less aware of the need to obscure such information (and potentially less experienced in employing technological tools to that end).[81] It should be noted, though, that some studies have underscored the levelling effect that a display of all participants from afar could have on the proceedings, assuming all those taking part in the process participate remotely.[82]

Finally, another important dimension relating to case outcomes is the manner in which the parties perceive and evaluate them, as opposed to an 'objective' outcome evaluation. This measure would not compare actual outcomes reached through processes conducted on different mediums but would compare parties' evaluations of the fairness and favourability of such outcomes, or parties' sense of satisfaction with the outcome of their case. Some recent studies have found that remote proceedings fare extremely well in this respect. One study found that attorneys perceive on- and offline dispute resolution processes similarly, including the nature of their outcomes—settlement rates and values,[83] another found that unrepresented defendants in Zoom court proceedings have reported greater satisfaction with their outcomes in remote proceedings than in physical ones,[84] and a third found that remote mediation proceedings were associated with higher levels of outcome satisfaction by both sides of the mediation compared to in person mediations.[85]

Given the mixed findings described above, how can we ensure that process pluralism does indeed promote justice? Menkel-Meadow tells us that we need 'to analyze, understand, and implement both process values . . . and substantive justice values'.[86] Initially, in remote proceedings, this was not carefully thought through. Many of those adapting face-to-face processes to the reality of COVID had not realized there is an entire field of practice and study that deals with the shift in medium of dispute resolution proceedings, formal and informal.

Such oversight had several implications. For one, the opportunity to expand the use of ODR was overlooked, and the immediate desire was to allow proceedings to continue operating in a mode that was as similar as possible to that conducted face-to-face. This has meant that the entire premise of ODR—reimagining processes for enhancing justice—was overlooked and altered. The emphasis instead was placed mainly on conducting the proceeding as planned under emergency conditions,[87] sometimes at a cost to justice. Even where levels of access were sustained, though, opportunities for enhancing effective access and fairness might not have been realized.[88]

[81] See ibid 761. But see Andrew Guthrie Ferguson, 'Courts Without Court' (2022) SSRN Electronic Journal 33 <http://dx.doi.org/10.2139/ssrn.4051790> last accessed 27 May 2024.
[82] Mulcahy, Rowden, and Teeder, *Exploring the case for Virtual Jury Trials during the COVID-19 crisis* (n 68).
[83] Eisenberg et al (n 46).
[84] Quintanilla et al (n 45) 20.
[85] McDermott and Obar, 'The Equal Employment Opportunity Commission Mediation Participants' Experience in Online Mediation and Comparison to In-Person Mediation' (n 65) 13–14.
[86] Menkel-Meadow, 'From Legal Disputes to Conflict Resolution and Human Problem Solving' (n 1) 19.
[87] Sykes et al, 'Civil Revolution' (n 31) 162.
[88] Pew, 'How Courts Embraced Technology' (n 2) 12.

A second implication was that, initially, some of those behind the adoption of remote proceedings understood the change in medium as a technical change. Those engaged in ODR have had a head start in realizing the connection among medium, values, and justice.[89] This is the entire premise of process pluralism—the mix of traits matters, precisely because the right mix can or may (but not necessarily) enhance justice.

Indeed, as we have seen, change of medium can dramatically impact access, perceptions of justice, and outcomes of dispute resolution proceedings, but such impact may operate in different directions. As opposed to some of the rather promising findings on the impact of certain court ODR processes on justice, in the case of remote proceedings, the limited research conducted has raised some questions. Early research has shown significant challenges in terms of access for the less privileged who have difficulty with real-time synchronous video communication,[90] as well as some anecdotal reason for concern in terms of procedural justice.[91] There is also some evidence, mostly from past research, that parties belonging to disempowered groups fare worse when their case is being heard remotely through video.[92] More recent research on video-based proceedings, which may reflect already some of the design and structural changes that have taken place over time in their adoption as well as growing familiarity and comfort with their operation,[93] have generated positive findings related to access to justice for pro se parties, as well as improved procedural experiences and substantive outcomes for such parties.[94] Interestingly, while efficiency is a dominant driver for the adoption of remote proceedings,[95] empirical findings have been mixed.[96] Most notably, concerns regarding the impact of the shift online on the weakest parties, and, in the criminal context, on the defendants' side,

[89] Ethan Katsh and Janet Rifkin, *Online Dispute Resolution: Resolving Conflicts in Cyberspace* (Jossey-Bass 2001); Orna Rabinovich-Einy, 'Beyond Efficiency: The Transformation of Courts Through Technology' (2008) 12 UCLA JL & Tech 1, 4-5 <https://ssrn.com/abstract = 3457265> last accessed 27 May 2024 (2008).

[90] Bannon and Adelstein, 'The Impact of Video Proceedings' (n 3) 5, 10.

[91] See (n 61)–(n 64) and accompanying text.

[92] See Sternlight and Robbennolt, 'In-Person or Via Technology?' (n 41) 744; Turner, 'Remote Criminal Justice' (n 55) 264–65; Byrom, Beardon and Kendrick, *The impact of COVID-19 measures on the civil justice system* (n 55) 266 (finding in a survey of criminal defense attorneys that in terms of perceptions of fairness of outcomes in remote proceedings '[m]ore than two-thirds of defense attorneys believe that online proceedings lead to less favorable results for defendants'). It should be noted that in other arenas as well, perceptions of professionals of the effectiveness of video-based dispute resolution processes are less favorable than those of face-to-face ones, as seen in a recent survey of professionals engaged in online and traditional arbitration. See Ferreira Daniel Brantes et al, 'Arbitration chambers and technology: witness tampering and perceived effectiveness in videoconferenced dispute resolution proceedings' (2023) 31 IJLIT 75 <http://dx.doi.org/10.1093/ijlit/eaad012> last accessed 27 May 2024.

[93] Quintanilla et al (n 45) 34 (stating that the decline in frequency of people dialing in rather than appearing on video could be attributed to the changes in 'increased familiarity and saturation of these technologies' over time). But see Torres, Lyne, and Appleby, 'On the (zoom) record' (n 63) (finding that connectivity problems on the defendants' end in remote proceedings increased over time).

[94] Quintanilla et al (n 45).

[95] Turner, 'Remote Criminal Justice' (n 55) 212.

[96] Horton, 'Forced Remote Arbitration' (n 74) 4; McDermott and Obar, 'The Equal Employment Opportunity Commission Mediation Participants' Experience in Online Mediation and Comparison to In-Person Mediation' (n 65) 13.

Table 2.1 ODR vs Remote Proceedings (author's own)

	ODR	Remote Proceedings
Early motivation for Adoption	Choice, reimagine	Forced, sustain
Principal Goal	Access, efficiency	Maintain activity, efficiency
Communication	Asynchronous, written	Real-time video/audio, written document exchange

remain,[97] requiring more inclusive design efforts in launching and improving remote proceedings.[98]

In Table 2.1 above, the author presents a comparison of the early motivation for the adoption of ODR and remote proceedings. The table demonstrates the different rationales and goals for their initial adoption, which could explain some of the differences in terms of justice levels achieved for each type of process during the pandemic and in its immediate aftermath. This is, of course crude, as not all ODR processes operate under the 'reimagining processes for delivering justice' paradigm, and, as we can see in the more recent studies, remote proceedings may be successful in fulfilling (more than merely maintaining) the ongoing activities of courts. Also, recent studies have uncovered the conditions under which access and fairness can be enhanced in video proceedings through better court architecture, appropriate procedural design, and tailored training.[99] Indeed, this is precisely why we need to be sensitive to context and apply the conceptual framework of process pluralism—to tailor procedural characteristics to the context, while ensuring that goals and values are defined and met through system design.

E. The Next Frontier: AI and Dispute Resolution

The recent launch of ChatGPT has demonstrated that the connection between new technologies and dispute resolution runs deeper than the realm of procedural medium. The introduction of artificial intelligence (AI) into dispute resolution processes,

[97] Quintanilla et al (n 45); Elizabeth Webster et al, '"Court Can Happen Anywhere": Courtroom Workgroup Members' Perceptions of the Challenges and Opportunities of a Transformed Workplace' (2023) 50 Crim Just & Behav 1737 <http://dx.doi.org/10.1177/00938548231196574> accessed 14 June 2025. Indeed, research has found that there is a lack of consistency in the adoption of remote proceedings and that such models need to be adapted to the needs of unrepresented parties. See Katherine LW Norton, 'Accessing Justice in Hybrid Courts: Addressing the Needs of Low-Income Litigants in Blended in-Person and Virtual Proceedings' (2023) 30 Geo J Poverty L & Pol'y 499.

[98] Cynthia Alkon, 'Designing for Justice: Pandemic Lessons for Criminal Courts' (2022) 52 Stetson L Rev 185.

[99] Sela and Dancig-Rosenberg, 'The Right to Presence, via Screens' (n 53). See also Factor et al, 'Videoconferencing in Legal Hearings and Procedural Justice' (n 53); National Center for State Courts, *Hybrid Hearings Improvement Initiative* (n 50).

promises to curtail some of the functions traditionally performed by human third parties (eg, judges, arbitrators, and mediators) as well as lawyers, now being relegated to the 'fourth party'.[100] The functions performed by AI can range anywhere from technical ones (such as assistance in filing a case) to more impactful ones (such as sentiment analysis or presenting similar outcomes reached in previous cases), to ultimately deciding the outcome of a case through automated decision-making (ADM). While the role of AI in general and of ADM in particular has thus far been limited in the courts, its use has begun to expand in informal settings, as well as in the formal administrative realm.[101]

The employment of AI in formal and informal dispute resolution has evolved through two main routes. The first is the legal tech industry, which has been focused on the needs of legal actors in developing and deploying various products, such as risk assessment tools for judges and tools that are employed by lawyers and their clients in predicting legal outcomes and/or the likely success of a particular lawyer or argument before a judge, arbitrator, or mediator. The second route is ODR, where AI is seems like a natural expansion of the already existing software-based infrastructure. Here, 'lighter' tools could include negotiation support tools and sentiment analysis, while at the other end of the spectrum; blind-bidding processes offer full-fledged ADM.[102] After the launch of ChatGPT, possibilities for deploying LLMs in dispute resolution are also being explored.[103]

Despite heated debates over the performance of AI and the risk of biased outcomes,[104] hallucinations,[105] and data privacy and security breaches,[106] we can expect AI to play a growing role in dispute resolution in- and outside courts, both in early stages and technical capacities, and in later stages in more substantive realms. These developments may offer substantial benefits in terms of accessible and accurate outcomes, but also raise questions regarding the accessibility of such tools for those who are not AI-literate, the degree of procedural fairness associated with such processes, and the fairness of the outcomes they produce. Perhaps the most interesting questions

[100] Katsh and Rifkin, *Resolving Conflicts in Cyberspace* (n 89); Leah Wing et al, 'Designing Ethical Online Dispute Resolution Systems: The Rise of the Fourth Party' (2021) 37 Negot J 49 <http://dx.doi.org/10.1111/nejo.12350> last accessed 27 May 2024.

[101] Orna Rabinovich-Einy and Ethan Katsh, 'Artificial Intelligence and the Future of Dispute Resolution: The Age of AI-DR' (2021) SSRN Electronic Journal <http://dx.doi.org/10.2139/ssrn.3830033> last accessed 27 May 2024.

[102] ibid.

[103] Hannes Westermann, Jaromir Savelka, and Karim Benyekhlef, 'LLMediator: GPT-4 Assisted Online Dispute Resolution', *Proceedings of the ICAIL 2023 Workshop on Artificial Intelligence for Access to Justice co-located with 19th International Conference on AI and Law* (ICAIL 2023) <https://doi.org/10.48550/arXiv.2307.16732> last accessed 27 May 2024.

[104] Julia Angwin et al, 'Machine Bias' (*ProPublica*, 23 May 2016) <www.propublica.org/article/machine-bias-risk-assessments-in-criminal-sentencing> accessed 27 May 2024; Luca Oneto and Silvia Chiappa, 'Fairness in Machine Learning' in Luca Oneto, Nicolo Navarin, Alessandro Sperduti, and Davide Anguita (eds), *Recent Trends in Learning From Data* (Springer International Publishing 2020) <http://dx.doi.org/10.1007/978-3-030-43883-8_7> last accessed 27 May 2024.

[105] Matthew Dahl et al, 'Large Legal Fictions: Profiling Legal Hallucinations in Large Language Models' (forthcoming, *arXiv:2401.01301*, 2 January 2024) <https://doi.org/10.48550/arXiv.2401.01301> last accessed 27 May 2024.

[106] Daniel J Solove, 'Artificial Intelligence and Privacy' (2025) 77 Fla L Rev 1 <https://dx.doi.org/10.2139/ssrn.4713111> last accessed 14 June 2025.

arise with respect to those measures that have to do with subjective perceptions of these processes' accessibility and fairness. While we know very little on the perception of such processes by real users in real cases, the now robust literature that exists on ADM in legal and dispute resolution processes tells us that the answer to what makes an AI-based dispute resolution process fair depends on context. Expectations differ depending on such elements as the type of dispute,[107] party characteristics,[108] model attributes,[109] the complexity of the dispute,[110] and the stage of the process in which AI is employed.[111] As we can see, AI is fast becoming another domain in which process pluralism comes into play.

Does 'more' process pluralism also mean more justice in this context? Or more generally, how do we view process pluralism in the age of new technologies? Does it present a positive development? I would say that it depends. The devil is in the design. Technology offers another important layer for the plurality of designs of dispute resolution processes. Like other design features, it can work to enhance or reduce justice. Change in medium, process, or role, is far from technical; it can have far-reaching effects on the accessibility and fairness of dispute resolution processes. If we want our justice system to maintain its commitment to basic values and goals of fairness, equality, and justice, we need to systematically study the impact of design choices on justice across settings, dispute types, and disputant characteristics.[112]

Despite generating many negative outcomes, the COVID crisis has nevertheless opened up new and exciting opportunities. Up until the spread of the Coronavirus, the ODR community tended to overlook the potential of video communication to address some disputants' process needs in various contexts. The introduction of video hearings, certainly in lieu of some in-person court hearings, can significantly reduce barriers to accessing court and, where designed accordingly, could sustain or enhance perceptions of procedural fairness and the attainment of just outcomes. The recent leap in AI capabilities presents another set of promises and challenges for realizing the

[107] Gizem Yalcin et al, 'Perceptions of Justice by Algorithms' (2023) 31 AI & L 269 <http://dx.doi.org/10.1007/s10506-022-09312-z> last accessed 27 May 2024; Ayelet Sela, 'Can Computers Be Fair? How Automated and Human-Powered Online Dispute Resolution Affect Procedural Justice in Mediation and Arbitration' (2018) 33 Ohio St J Disp Resol 91 <https://ssrn.com/abstract = 3074311> last accessed 27 May 2024.

[108] Dovilė Barysė and Roee Sarel, 'Algorithms in the Court: Does it Matter Which Part of the Judicial Decision-Making is Automated?' (2022) SSRN Electronic Journal <http://dx.doi.org/10.2139/ssrn.4208203> last accessed 27 May 2024; Theo Araujo et al, 'In AI we trust? Perceptions about automated decision-making by artificial intelligence' (2020) 35 AI & Soc'y 611 <http://dx.doi.org/10.1007/s00146-019-00931-w> accessed 27 May 2024; Michael C Horowitz and Lauren Kahn, 'What influences attitudes about artificial intelligence adoption: Evidence from US local officials' (2021) 16 PLoS ONE e0257732 <http://dx.doi.org/10.1371/journal.pone.0257732> last accessed 27 May 2024.

[109] Ari Waldman and Kirsten Martin, 'Governing Algorithmic Decisions: The Role of Decision Importance and Governance on Perceived Legitimacy of Algorithmic Decisions' (2022) 9 Big Data & Soc'y <http://dx.doi.org/10.1177/20539517221100449> accessed 27 May 2024; Ryan P Kennedy, Philip D Waggoner, and Matthew Ward, 'Trust in Public Policy Algorithms' (2021) 84 J Pol 1132 <http://dx.doi.org/10.1086/716283> last accessed 27 May 2024.

[110] Yalcin et al (n 107).

[111] Barysė and Sarel, 'Algorithms in the Court' (n 107).

[112] See Janet Martinez, Lisa Blomgren Amsler, and Stephanie E Smith, *Dispute System Design: Preventing, Managing and Resolving Conflict* (Stanford University Press 2020) 37. See also David Freeman Engstrom and Robert Vogt, 'The New Judicial Governance: Courts, Data, and the Future of Civil Justice' (2022) SSRN Electronic Journal 8 <http://dx.doi.org/10.2139/ssrn.4024511> last accessed 27 May 2024.

goal of delivering justice. Technology presents us with an opportunity to reimagine our dispute resolution landscape in a way that is focused on disputants and addresses the deepest, most persistent problems that have plagued our system, which previous transformations have failed to eradicate.

To fulfil their potential, technology-based proceedings, whether online or offline, asynchronous or synchronous, formal or informal, human- or AI-based, need to adhere to the principles of process pluralism by:

(1) Recognizing plurality *within* technological dispute resolution options, including hybrid forms of online-offline proceedings, an option that has not received sufficient attention in the design of online proceedings, treating such choice as a dichotomous one;[113]
(2) Pushing our imagination in generating new types of processes that are not limited to familiar structures, by adopting such processes as diagnosis (which was pioneered in the Civil Resolution Tribunal in British Columbia)[114] or crowdsourced dispute resolution (first developed by eBay in its negative feedback removal process, but also adopted in the smart contract context);[115]
(3) Embracing context and refraining from procedural imperialism—we should not employ the same online / technology-based process across courts, case types, and party distinctions. Indeed, we should remember that we did not seek to displace courts with mediation, but to expand parties' options and offer a multitude of procedural options, allowing us to 'fit[] the forum to the fuss;'[116] and
(4) adopting processes that realize both procedural and substantive aspects of justice—a goal that must be evaluated continuously and may require procedural reforms over time.[117]

F. Conclusion

The rise of alternative dispute resolution presented a watershed moment in the evolution of our justice system. The institutionalization of 'alternatives' in courts, tribunals, and organizations have served to undermine the long-held view that equated courts with justice, and that saw court proceedings as appropriate for addressing a

[113] Carrie Menkel-Meadow, 'Hybrid and mixed dispute resolution processes' (n 4) 7 (highlighting the significance of hybrid procedural schemes). Recently, this option is being employed in courts post COVID, see National Center for State Courts, *Hybrid Hearings Improvement Initiative* (n 50).

[114] Shannon Salter and Darin Thompson, 'Public-Centred Civil Justice Redesign: A Case Study of the British Columbia Civil Resolution Tribunal' (2017) 3 McGill J Disp Resol 113, 114 <https://ssrn.com/abstract = 2955796> last accessed 27 May 2024.

[115] See generally Carrie Menkel-Meadow, 'Aha? Is Creativity Possible in Legal Problem Solving and Teachable in Legal Education?' (2001) 6 Harv Negot Law Rev 97.

[116] See generally Frank EA Sander and Stephen B Goldberg, 'Fitting the Forum to the Fuss: A User-Friendly Guide to Selecting an ADR Procedure' (1994) 10 Negot J 49 <http://dx.doi.org/10.1111/j.1571-9979.1994.tb00005.x> last accessed 27 May 2024.

[117] Menkel-Meadow, 'From Legal Disputes to Conflict Resolution and Human Problem Solving' (n 1).

wide range of disputes. By advancing the notion that justice could be found 'in many rooms'[118] and that 'one size does not fit all,' such developments have served as a foundation for process pluralism.

In the last few decades, and more strongly since the onset of COVID and the evolution of artificial intelligence, the permeation of technology into dispute resolution in and outside the courts has added another important dimension to the notion of process pluralism: choice of medium, and the availability of new types of processes and roles that are free from the constraints that have come with the need to rely on synchronous communication, human capacity, physical space, and geographical location.

But novel technological processes are far from a panacea to the problems that have plagued the justice system for years—inaccessibility, complexity, high costs, and a fairness deficit. While new technologies promise to enhance efficiency, lower costs, and enhance convenience for many, they also inevitably impact the ability of various individuals and, more significantly, the ability of members of different social groups, to initiate and effectively utilize dispute resolution processes. Context and design matter; therefore, if we are to realize technology's empowering and equalizing potential, its use and design must be tailored to the particulars of the case and the characteristics and needs of the parties. This could mean refraining from employing technology in one context, while tailoring the medium and nature of online communication employed to parties' capabilities in another context. The implication of various design schemes needs to be studied systematically, over time, and across contexts and demographics to generate meaningful insights regarding the impact of design choices on the values embodied in our procedures and the goals advanced by our systems.

At the end of the day, the procedural backbone of our justice system is what ultimately shapes its fairness—whether the processes can be used by all echelons of society, how procedures are experienced by different users, and what type of outcomes can be reached and enforced by various members of society.

Bibliography

Alkon C, 'Designing for Justice: Pandemic Lessons for Criminal Courts' (2022) 52 Stetson Law Review 185.

Alkon C, 'Criminal Court System Failures During COVID-19: An Empirical Study' (2022) 37 Ohio State Journal on Dispute Resolution 453 <https://scholarship.law.tamu.edu/cgi/viewcontent.cgi?article = 2610&context = facscholar>.

Angwin J et al, 'Machine Bias' (*ProPublica*, 23 May 2016) <www.propublica.org/article/machine-bias-risk-assessments-in-criminal-sentencing>.

Araujo T et al, 'In AI we trust? Perceptions about automated decision-making by artificial intelligence' (2020) 35 AI & Society 611 <http://dx.doi.org/10.1007/s00146-019-00931-w>.

Auerbach JS, *Justice without Law?* (OUP 1983).

Bannon AL and Keith D, 'Remote Court: Principles for Virtual Proceedings During the COVID-19 Pandemic and Beyond' (2021) 115 Northwestern University Law Review 1875.

118 Marc Galanter, 'Justice in many Rooms: Courts, Private Ordering, and Indigenous Law' (1981) 13 J Legal Pluralism & Unofficial L 1 <http://dx.doi.org/10.1080/07329113.1981.10756257> last accessed 27 May 2024.

Bannon A and Adelstein J, 'The Impact of Video Proceedings on Fairness and Access to Justice in Court' (*Brennan Center for Justice*, 10 September 2020) <www.brennancenter.org/our-work/research-reports/impact-video-proceedings-fairness-and-access-justice-court>.

Barysė D and Sarel R, 'Algorithms in the Court: Does it Matter Which Part of the Judicial Decision-making is Automated?' (2022) SSRN Electronic Journal <http://dx.doi.org/10.2139/ssrn.4208203>.

Benninger T et al, *Virtual Justice? A National Study Analyzing the Transition to Remote Criminal Court* (Standford Law School 2021) <https://law.stanford.edu/wpcontent/uploads/2021/08/Virtual-Justice-Final-Aug-2021.pdf>.

Berkeley Research Group, *The Psychological Impact of Remote Hearings* (2021) <https://media.thinkbrg.com/wp-content/uploads/2021/08/05105717/BRG-Remote-Hearing-Impact-2021-Final.pdf>.

Bild E et al, 'Sound and credibility in the virtual court: Low audio quality leads to less favorable evaluations of witnesses and lower weighting of evidence' (2021) 45 Law and Human Behavior 481 <http://dx.doi.org/10.1037/lhb0000466>.

Boehme S, 'You Mediate on Zoom. Now What?' (*Mediate.com*, 14 September 2020) <https://mediate.com/you-mediate-on-zoom-now-what/>.

Bol SH, 'Ethan Katsh and Janet Rifkin, Online Dispute Resolution, Resolving Conflicts in Cyberspace' (2003) 11 Artificial Intelligence and Law 69 <http://dx.doi.org/10.1023/b:arti.0000013403.91418.92>.

Bowen Poulin A, 'Criminal Justice and Videoconferencing Technology: The Remote Defendant' (2004) 78 Tulane Law Review 1089.

Brantes FD et al, 'Arbitration Chambers and Technology: witness tampering and perceived effectiveness in videoconferenced dispute resolution proceedings' (2023) 31 International Journal of Law and Information Technology 75 <http://dx.doi.org/10.1093/ijlit/eaad012>.

Byrom N, Beardonm S, and Kendrick A, *The Impact of COVID-19 Measures on the Civil Justice System* (Judiciary College 2020) <www.judiciary.uk/wp-content/uploads/2022/07/CJC-Rapid-Review-Final-Report-f-1.pdf> .

Danser R et al, 'Online Dispute Resolution of Low-Level Court Proceedings: Two Broken Field Experiments, One Unexpected Result' (2023) SSRN Electronic Journal <https://ssrn.com/abstract = 4375081>.

Delgado R et al, 'Fairness and Formality: Minimizing the Risk of Prejudice in Alternative Dispute Resolution' (1985) 1369 Wisconsin Law Review 1359.

Douglas-Henry JP and Sanderson, B, Virtual Hearings Report (DLA Piper 2020) <http://viewer.zmags.com/publication/051503a3#/051503a3/1>.

Eisenberg DT, Shestowsky D, and Niccolini RR, 'What Matters to Employment Attorneys When Considering Online or In-Person Mediation?' (2023) 41 Alternatives to the High Cost of Litigation 151 <http://dx.doi.org/10.1002/alt.22020>.

Engstrom DF and Vogt, R, 'The New Judicial Governance: Courts, Data, and the Future of Civil Justice' (2022) SSRN Electronic Journal <http://dx.doi.org/10.2139/ssrn.4024511>.

Factor R et al, 'Videoconferencing in Legal Hearings and Procedural Justice' (2023) 18 Victims & Offenders 1557 <www.tandfonline.com/doi/full/10.1080/15564886.2023.2248465>.

Ferguson AG, 'Courts Without Court' (2022) SSRN Electronic Journal <http://dx.doi.org/10.2139/ssrn.4051790>.

Fiss OM, 'Against Settlement' (1984) 93 Yale Law Journal 1073 <http://dx.doi.org/10.2307/796205>.

Freeman Engstrom D, 'Post-COVID Courts' (2020) 68 UCLA Law Review 246.

Galanter M, 'Justice in many Rooms: Courts, Private Ordering, and Indigenous Law' (1981) 13 The Journal of Legal Pluralism and Unofficial Law 1 <http://dx.doi.org/10.1080/07329113.1981.10756257>.

Goncalves A and Rainey D, 'Mediating Online Is Much More Than "Doing It On Zoom"' (Kluwer Mediation Blog, 28 February 2021) <https://mediationblog.kluwerarbitration.com/2021/02/28/mediating-online-is-much-more-than-doing-it-on-zoom/>.

Grillo T, The Mediation Alternative: Process Dangers for Women' (1991) 100 Yale Law Journal 1545 <http://dx.doi.org/10.2307/796781>.

Hensler DR, 'Our Courts, Ourselves: How the Alternative Dispute Resolution Movement Is Re-Shaping Our Legal System' (2003) 108 Dickinson Law Review 165.

Higgins R, 'Courts in the Pandemic–A View from the Bench' (2020) Winter Bar News 34 <https://www5.austlii.edu.au/au/journals/NSWBarAssocNews/2020/55.pdf>.

Horowitz MC and Kahn L, 'What Influences Attitudes about Artificial Intelligence Adoption: Evidence from US Local Officials' (2021) 16 PLoS ONE e0257732 <http://dx.doi.org/10.1371/journal.pone.0257732>.

Horton D, 'Forced Remote Arbitration' (2022) 108 Cornell Law Review 1 <http://dx.doi.org/10.2139/ssrn.4035835>.

'Internet, Broadband Fact Sheet' (*Pew Research Center*, 31 January 2024) <www.pewresearch.org/internet/fact-sheet/internet-broadband/>.

Judiciary of England and Wales, *Good Practice for Remote Hearings* (Judiciary College 2020) <www.judiciary.uk/wp-content/uploads/2020/03/Good-Practice-for-Remote-Hearings-May-2020-1.pdf[https://perma.cc/UU5P-63NT]>.

Katsh E and Rabinovich-Einy O, *Digital Justice: Technology and the Internet of Disputes* (OUP 2017).

Katsh E and Rifkin R, *Online Dispute Resolution: Resolving Conflicts in Cyberspace* (Jossey-Bass 2001).

Kennedy RP, Waggoner PD and Ward M, 'Trust in Public Policy Algorithms' (2021) 84 The Journal of Politics 1132 <http://dx.doi.org/10.1086/716283>.

Kitzinger C, 'Remote Justice: a Family Perspective' (*The Transparency Project*, 29 March 2020) <https://transparencyproject.org.uk/remote-justice-a-family-perspective/>.

M Walsh F and M Walsh E, 'Effective Processing or Assembly-Line Justice? The Use of Teleconferencing in Asylum Removal Hearings' (2008) 22 Georgetown Immigration Law Journal 259.

Martinez J, Amsler LB and Smith SE, *Dispute System Design: Preventing, Managing and Resolving Conflict* (Stanford University Press 2020).

McAdoo B and Welsh NA, 'Look Before You Leap and Keep on Looking: Lessons from the Institutionalization of Court-Connected Mediation' (2005) 5 Nevada Law Journal 399.

McBride M, 'ODR in the Era of COVID-19' (*American Bar Association*, 27 October 2020) <www.americanbar.org/groups/family_law/committees/alternative-dispute-resolution/odr/>.

McDermott EP and Obar R, 'The Equal Employment Opportunity Commission Mediation Participants' Experience in Online Mediation and Comparison to In-Person Mediation' (2022) SSRN Electronic Journal <http://dx.doi.org/10.2139/ssrn.4130612>.

Menkel-Meadow C, 'Correspondences and Contradictions in International and Domestic Conflict Resolution: Lessons from General Theory and Varied Contexts' (2003) 2003 Journal of Dispute Resolution 319.

Menkel-Meadow C, 'From Legal Disputes to Conflict Resolution and Human Problem Solving: Legal Dispute Resolution in a Multidisciplinary Context' (2004) 54 Journal of Legal Education 7.

Menkel-Meadow C, 'Hybrid and mixed dispute resolution processes: integrities of process pluralism' in Maria Moscati M, Palmer M and Roberts M (eds), *Comparative Dispute Resolution* (Edward Elgar Publishing 2020) 13 <http://dx.doi.org/10.4337/9781786433039.00038>.

Menkel-Meadow C, 'Is ODR ADR?' (2016) 3 International Journal on Online Dispute Resolution 4 <http://dx.doi.org/10.5553/ijodr/235250022016003001100>.

Menkel-Meadow C, 'Peace and Justice: Notes on the Evolution and Purposes of Legal Processes' (2006) 94 The Georgetown Law Journal 553.

Menkel-Meadow C, 'Process Pluralism in Transitional/Restorative Justice' (2015) 3 The International Journal of Conflict Engagement and Resolution 3.

Menkel-Meadow C, 'Pursuing Settlement in an Adversary Culture: A Tale of Innovation Co-Opted or "The Law of ADR"' (1991) 19 Florida State University Law Review 1.

Menkel-Meadow C, 'Regulation of Dispute Resolution in the United States of America: From the Formal to the Informal to the "Semi-formal"' in Steffek F and Unberath H (eds), *Regulating Dispute Resolution: ADR and Access to Justice at the Crossroads* (Hart Publishing 2013) 419.

Menkel-Meadow C, 'Restorative Justice: What Is It and Does It Work?' (2007) 3 Annual Review of Law and Social Science 161 <http://dx.doi.org/10.1146/annurev.lawsocsci.2.081805.110005>.

Menkel-Meadow C, 'The Lawyer's Role(s) in Deliberative Democracy' (2004) 5 Nevada Law Journal 347.
Menkel-Meadow C, 'The Trouble with the Adversary System in a Postmodern, Multicultural World' (1996) 38 William and Mary Law Review 5.
Menkel-Meadow C, 'When Litigation Is Not the Only Way: Consensus Building and Mediation as Public Interest Lawyering' (2002) 10 Washington University Journal of Law & Policy 37.
Menkel-Meadow C, 'Aha? Is Creativity Possible in Legal Problem Solving and Teachable in Legal Education?' (2001) 6 Harv Negotiation Law Review 97.
Mentovich A, Prescott J and Rabinovich-Einy O, 'Are Litigation Outcome Disparities Inevitable? Courts, Technology, and the Future of Impartiality' (2020) 73 Alabama Law Review 893.
Mentovich A, Prescott J and Rabinovich-Einy O, 'Legitimacy and Online Proceedings: Procedural Justice, Access to Justice, and the Role of Income' (2023) 57 Law & Society Review 189 <http://dx.doi.org/10.1111/lasr.12653>.
'Mobile Fact Sheet' (*Pew Research Center*, 31 January 2024) <www.pewresearch.org/internet/fact-sheet/mobile/>.
Moreira JI and Zhang L, 'Assessing Credibility in Online Arbitration Hearings: Determining Facts and Justice by Zoom' (2023) 37 International Journal for the Semiotics of Law 887 <http://dx.doi.org/10.1007/s11196-023-10046-7>.
Mulcahy L, Rowden E and Teeder W, *Exploring the case for Virtual Jury Trials during the COVID-19 crisis: An evaluation of a pilot study conducted by JUSTICE* (Oxford Faculty of Law 2020) <https://files.justice.org.uk/wp-ontent/uploads/2020/04/06165956/Mulcahy-Rowden-Virtual-trials-final.pdf>.
National Center for State Courts, *Hybrid Hearings Improvement Initiative* (2024) <www.ncsc.org/__data/assets/pdf_file/0040/98896/HybridHearings_Report_2024.pdf>.
National Center for State Courts, *The Use of Remote Hearings in Texas State Courts: The Impact on Judicial Workload* (2021) <www.ncsc.org/consulting-and-research/areas-of-expertise/access-to-justice/remote-and-virtual-hearings/resources-docs/TX-Remote-Hearing-Assessment-Report.pdf>.
Norton KLW, 'Accessing Justice in Hybrid Courts: Addressing the Needs of Low-Income Litigants in Blended in-Person and Virtual Proceedings' (2023) 57 Georgetown Journal on Poverty Law & Policy 499.
Nuffield Family Justice Observatory, *Remote hearings in the family justice system: a rapid consultation* (2020) <www.nuffieldfjo.org.uk/resource/remote-hearings-rapid-consultation>.
O'Neil MM et al, 'Treatment Court Staffs' Perceptions in Support of the Use of Virtual Services in Court Post-Pandemic' (2024) 51 Criminal Justice & Behavior 286 <https://doi.org/10.1177/00938548231219807>.
Oneto L and Chiappa S, 'Fairness in Machine Learning' in Oneto L, Navarin N, Sperduti A and Anguita D (eds), *Recent Trends in Learning From Data* (Springer International Publishing 2020) 155 <http://dx.doi.org/10.1007/978-3-030-43883-8_7>.
Prescott JJ, 'Improving Access to Justice in State Courts with Platform Technology' (2017) 70 Vanderbilt Law Review 1993.
Quintanilla VD et al, *Accessing Justice with Zoom: Experiences and Outcomes in Online Civil Courts* (Maurer School of Law 2023).
Rabinovich-Einy O and Katsh E, 'Artificial Intelligence and the Future of Dispute Resolution: The Age of AI-DR' (2021) SSRN Electronic Journal <http://dx.doi.org/10.2139/ssrn.3830033>.
Rabinovich-Einy O and Katsh E, 'Blockchain and the Inevitability of Disputes: The Role for Online Dispute Resolution' (2019) 2019 Journal of Dispute Resolution 47.
Rabinovich-Einy O and Katsh E, 'The New New Courts' (2017) 67 American University Law Review 165.
Rabinovich-Einy O, 'Technology's Impact: The Quest for a New Paradigm for Accountability in Mediation' (2006) 11 Harvard Negotiation Law Review 253.
Rabinovich-Einy O, 'The Legitimacy Crisis and the Future of Courts' (2015) 17 Cardozo Journal of Conflict Resolution 23.
Rabinovich-Einy O, 'The Past, Present, and Future of Online Dispute Resolution' (2021) 74 Current Legal Problems 125 <http://dx.doi.org/10.1093/clp/cuab004>.

Rabinovich-Einy O, 'Beyond Efficiency: The Transformation of Courts Through Technology' (2008) 12 UCLA Journal of Law and Technology 1 <https://ssrn.com/abstract = 3457265>.

Rachlinski JJ and Johnson SL, 'Does Unconscious Racial Bias Affect Trial Judges?' (2009) 84 Notre Dame Law Review 1195 <https://scholarship.law.nd.edu/ndlr/vol84/iss3/4/>.

'Resolving Digital Conflicts, Together' (*Agree Online*) <https://www.facebook.com/p/Agree-Online-100064071970062/>.

Riskin LL and Welsh NA, 'Is That All There Is? "The Problem" in Court-Oriented Mediation' (2008) 15 George Mason Law Review 863.

Rossner M and Tait D, 'Presence and Participation in a Virtual Court' (2021) 23 Criminology & Criminal Justice 136 <http://dx.doi.org/10.1177/17488958211017372>.

Salter S and Thompson D, 'Public-Centred Civil Justice Redesign: A Case Study of the British Columbia Civil Resolution Tribunal' (2017) 3 McGill Journal of Dispute Resolution 113 <https://ssrn.com/abstract = 2955796>.

Sander FEA and Goldberg SB, 'Fitting the Forum to the Fuss: A User-Friendly Guide to Selecting an ADR Procedure' (1994) 10 Negotiation Journal 49 <http://dx.doi.org/10.1111/j.1571-9979.1994.tb00005.x> accessed 27 May 2024.

Sander FEA, 'Varieties of Dispute Processing', in Hinshaw A, Schneider AK and Rudolph S (eds), *Discussions in Dispute Resolution* (OUP 2021) 321.

Schmitz AJ and Rule C, 'Online Dispute Resolution for Smart Contracts' (2019) 2019 Journal of Dispute Resolution 103.

Schmitz AJ and Zeleznikow J, 'Intelligent Legal Tech to Empower Self-Represented Litigants' (2022) 23 Columbia Science and Technology Law Review 142.

Seidman Diamond S et al, 'Efficiency and Cost: The Impact of Videoconferenced Hearings on Bail Decisions' (2010) 100 The Journal of Criminal Law and Criminology 898 <https://scholarlycommons.law.northwestern.edu/cgi/viewcontent.cgi?article = 7365&context = jclc>.

Sela A and Dancig-Rosenberg H, 'The Right to Presence, via Screens: Court Observations in Remote Criminal Detention Hearings' (2022) 54 Hebrew University Law Review (forthcoming).

Sela A, 'Can Computers Be Fair? How Automated and Human-Powered Online Dispute Resolution Affect Procedural Justice in Mediation and Arbitration' (2018) 33 Ohio State Journal on Dispute Resolution 91 <https://ssrn.com/abstract = 3074311>.

Sela A, 'Streamlining Justice: How Online Courts Can Resolve the Challenges of Pro Se Litigation' (2016) 26 Cornell Journal of Law and Public Policy 331.

Shestowsky D and Shack J, 'Online Dispute Resolution for Debt and Small Claims Cases. A Report on a Pilot Program in a Justice of the Peace Court in Collin County, Texas' (2022) SSRN Electronic Journal <http://dx.doi.org/10.2139/ssrn.4173414>.

Shestowsky D and Shack J, 'Online Dispute Resolution for Post-Judgment Family Law Cases A Report to the Ottawa County, Michigan, Friend of the Court' (2022) SSRN Electronic Journal <http://dx.doi.org/10.2139/ssrn.4173424>.

Solove DJ, 'Artificial Intelligence and Privacy' (2025) 77 Florida Law Review 1 <http://dx.doi.org/10.2139/ssrn.4713111>.

Sourdin T, Li B and McNamara DM, 'Court innovations and access to justice in times of crisis' (2020) 9 Health Policy and Technology 447 <http://dx.doi.org/10.1016/j.hlpt.2020.08.020>.

Sternlight JR and Robbennolt JK, 'In-Person or Via Technology?: Drawing on Psychology to Choose and Design Dispute Resolution Processes' (2022) 71 DePaul Law Review 701.

Summers A and Gatowski S, *Remote Hearing Study* (Nevada Court Improvement Program 2020) <https://nevadacurrent.com/wp-content/uploads/2022/01/21-17924.pdf>.

Susskind R, 'The Future of Courts - Harvard Law School Center on the Legal Profession' (*Harvard Law School Center on the Legal Profession*, July/August 2020) <https://clp.law.harvard.edu/knowledge-hub/magazine/issues/remote-courts/the-future-of-courts/>.

Syke K et al, 'Civil Revolution: User Experiences with British Columbia's Online Court' (2022) 37 The Windsor Yearbook of Access to Juststice 161 <http://dx.doi.org/10.22329/wyaj.v37i1.7192>.

The California Commission on Access to Justice, *Remote Hearings and Access to Justice During COVID-19 and Beyond* (2020) <www.ncjfcj.org/wp-content/uploads/2020/06/2020-Remote-Hearings-Guide.pdf>.

The International Council for Online Dispute Resolution, *ICODR Video Mediation Guidelines* (2020) <https://icodr.org/guides/videomed.pdf>.

'The Justice Protocol' (*Kleros*) <https://perma.cc/GP4B-SXVW>.

The Pew Charitable Trusts, 'How Courts Embraced Technology, Met the Pandemic Challenge, and Revolutionized Their Operations' (*The Pew Charitable Trust*, 1 December 2021) <www.pewtrusts.org/en/research-and-analysis/reports/2021/12/how-courts-embraced-technology-met-the-pandemic-challenge-and-revolutionized-their-operations>.

Thorley D and Mitts J, 'Trial by skype: A causality-oriented replication exploring the use of remote video adjudication in immigration removal proceedings' (2019) 59 International Review of Law and Economics 82 <https://doi.org/10.1016/j.irle.2019.05.002>.

Thornburg EG, 'Observing Online Courts: Lessons from the Pandemic' (2020) SSRN Electronic Journal <http://dx.doi.org/10.2139/ssrn.3696594>.

Torres LC, Lyne EM, and Appleby AM, 'On the (zoom) record: the role of videoconferencing in detention hearing proceedings' (2024) 47 Journal of Crime and Justice 613 <http://dx.doi.org/10.1080/0735648x.2024.2321588>.

Turner JI, 'Remote Criminal Justice' (2021) 53 The Texas Tech Law Review 217 <https://papers.ssrn.com/sol3/papers.cfm?abstract_id = 3699045>.

Waldman A and Martin K, 'Governing algorithmic decisions: The role of decision importance and governance on perceived legitimacy of algorithmic decisions' (2022) 9 Big Data and Society <http://dx.doi.org/10.1177/20539517221100449>.

Webster E et al, '"Court Can Happen Anywhere": Courtroom Workgroup Members' Perceptions of the Challenges and Opportunities of a Transformed Workplace' (2023) 50 Criminal Justice and Behavior 1737 <http://dx.doi.org/10.1177/00938548231196574>.

Welsh NA, 'The Thinning Vision of Self-Determination in Court-Connected Mediation: The Inevitable Price of Institutionalization?' (2001) 6 Harvard Negotiation Law Review 1.

Westermann H, Savelka J and Benyekhlef K, 'LLMediator: GPT-4 Assisted Online Dispute Resolution', *Proceedings of the ICAIL 2023 Workshop on Artificial Intelligence for Access to Justice co-located with 19th International Conference on AI and Law* (ICAIL 2023) <https://doi.org/10.48550/arXiv.2307.16732>.

Wing L et al, 'Designing Ethical Online Dispute Resolution Systems: The Rise of the Fourth Party' (2021) 37 Negotiation Journal 49 <http://dx.doi.org/10.1111/nejo.12350>.

Yalcin G et al, 'Perceptions of Justice by Algorithms' (2023) 30 Artificial Intelligence and Law 269 <http://dx.doi.org/10.1007/s10506-022-09312-z>.

3

Challenges of Using AI Tools in the Digitalization of Advanced Justice Systems

Beyond Data Protection and Cybersecurity

*Jose Antonio Castillo Parrilla**

A. The Boost to the Digitalization of Justice and the Need to Direct it towards Better Protection of Rights

The digital transformation of justice systems brings several advantages, particularly highlighted during the COVID-19 pandemic.[1] Key benefits include improved jurisdictional efficiency—streamlining procedures, reducing delays, and enhancing the quality of judicial decisions. It may also foster transparency and greater accessibility

* Ramón y Cajal Fellow at University of Granada. This publication is part of the contract RYC2021-031430-I, funded by MCIN/AEI/10.13039/501100011033 and by the European Union, 'NextGenerationEU'. It is developed in the framework of the GOIA Project, funded by MCIN/AEI/TED2021- 12902B-C22 and by the European Union, 'NextGenerationEU'.

[1] Commission, 'The 2024 EU Justice Scoreboard: Communication from the Commission to the European Parliament, the Council, the European Central Bank, the European Economic and Social Committee and the Committee of the Regions' (2024) 4 <https://commission.europa.eu/document/download/84aa3726-82d7-4401-98c1-fee04a7d2dd6_en?filename = 2024%20EU%20Justice%20Scoreboard.pdf> last accessed 26 December 2024; Directorate-General for Justice and Consumers, 'Digitalisation of Justice in the European Union A Toolbox of Opportunities' (European Commission 2020) <https://eur-lex.europa.eu/legal-content/EN/ALL/?uri = COM:2020:710:FIN> last accessed 26 December 2024.

Jose Antonio Castillo Parrilla, *Challenges of Using AI Tools in the Digitalization of Advanced Justice Systems* In: *Digitalization and Artificial Intelligence in Courts*. Edited by: Fernando Esteban de la Rosa, Pablo Cortés, and Nuria Marchal Escalona, Oxford University Press. © Jose Antonio Castillo Parrilla 2025. DOI: 10.1093/9780198918752.003.0003

for citizens, while optimizing the work of judicial staff through better workflow management and training opportunities.[2]

However, the process of digitalization in justice must go beyond simply introducing new technologies. It requires a fundamental shift in practices, prioritizing accessibility, transparency, and interoperability of systems. All of this can help for better and more efficient communication between legal professionals. The European Commission for the Efficiency of Justice (CEPEJ) outlines several principles for a successful digital transformation, a technique that has recently been replicated in the European e-Justice Strategy 2024–28.[3] The CEPEJ outlines as principles for a successful digital transformation the following: (1) efficiency of justice, (2) transparency of justice, (3) collaborative justice, (4) human justice, (5) people-centred justice, (6) informed justice, and (7) responsible and reactive justice. On the other hand, the European e-Justice Strategy 2024–28 lists as principles: (1) respect for fundamental rights, (2) access to justice, (3) people centricity, (4) bridging the digital divide, (5) digital empowerment of users, and (6) sustainability. These principles are more or less explicitly included in the different regulations promoting the digitalization of justice, as can be seen in this and other works in this work.

An example of this is the importance of respecting fundamental rights outlined in the European Charter of Fundamental Rights (ECFR),[4] as underlined by the European e-Justice Strategy, which stresses that initiatives for the digital transformation of justice must respect judicial independence and the rule of law, which includes the need to carry out a thorough assessment of their impact on fundamental rights. The European e-Justice Strategy underlines that the emergence of innovative technologies may give rise to new challenges and risks, such as cybersecurity breaches, deepening of the digital divide or unconscious discrimination due to biased algorithms or datasets. Key concerns include ensuring effective judicial protection and the right to effective judicial protection,[5] which could be undermined by the opacity of algorithms used in decision-making or due to lack of data security. Tools like risk assessment systems (eg, RisCanvi in Spain[6]) must be transparent and not lead to

[2] Joaquín Delgado Martín, 'Una Concepción Integral Del Expediente Judicial Electrónico' [2012] Revista Aranzadi de derecho y nuevas tecnologías 119, 11; '2022–2025 CEPEJ Action Plan: 'Digitalisation for a Better Justice' (European Commission for the Efficiency of Justice (CEPEJ) 2021) <https://rm.coe.int/cepej-2021-12-en-cepej-action-plan-2022-2025-digitalisation-justice/1680a4cf2c> last accessed 26 December 2024; John Zeleznikow, 'Can Artificial Intelligence and Online Dispute Resolution Enhance Efficiency and Effectiveness in Courts' (2017) 8 International Journal for Court Administration 8 <https://iacajournal.org/articles/10.18352/ijca.223> last accessed 26 December 2024; Cristina San Miguel Caso, 'Inteligencia Artificial y Algoritmos: La Controvertida Evolución de La Tutela Judicial Efectiva En El Proceso Penal' [2023] Estudios penales y criminológicos <https://revistas.usc.gal/index.php/epc/article/view/8859/13292> last accessed 26 December 2024.

[3] European Commission (n 2) 4; 'European e-Justice Strategy 2024–28' (ST/15509/2023/INIT, OJ C, C/2025/437, 16.01.2025) <https://eur-lex.europa.eu/eli/C/2025/437/oj> last accessed 20 January 2025.

[4] Charter of Fundamental Rights of the European Union [2000/C] 364/01.

[5] San Miguel Caso (n 2); 'Presidency Conclusions—The Charter of Fundamental Rights in the Context of Artificial Intelligence and Digital Change' (Council of the European Union 2020) 11481/20 13 <https://data.consilium.europa.eu/doc/document/ST-11481-2020-INIT/es/pdf> last accessed 26 December 2024; Guillermo Schumann Barragán, 'La Inteligencia Artificial Aplicada al Proceso Penal Desde La Perspectiva de La UE', en S Pereira Puigvert, F Ordóñez Ponz (dirs), *Investigación y proceso penal en el siglo XXI: nuevas tecnologías y protección de datos* (Aranzadi 2021).

[6] Pere Simón Castellano, *La Prisión Algorítmica: Prevención, Reinserción Social y Tutela de Derechos Fundamentales En El Paradigma de Los Centros Penitenciarios Inteligentes* (Tirant lo Blanch

discriminatory or unjust outcomes. Additionally, digital literacy for both practitioners and citizens is critical in reducing the digital divide and ensuring access to justice.[7] Last but not least, that data are accessible electronically without filters or basic security measures, or that access to justice is compulsory in all cases are factors that contribute to lower data security.

In this chapter we will focus on certain specific vulnerabilities in terms of data protection that some of the well-known tools for the digitalization of justice may present, such as remote access to documents and courts, electronic communications, or the use of artificial intelligence tools (understood in a broad sense).

We will focus our attention on four main areas: (1) the guarantee of the right to data protection in the process of digitalization of justice; (2) cybersecurity in the use of digital tools by practitioners, courts and users; (3) right to data protection in the use of AI tools; and (4) transparency and explainability of AI tools. After the appropriate considerations in the respective sections, we will conclude with a proposal for a brief impact assessment of AI tools in the administration of justice.[8] When referring to the digitalization of justice, we do so in a broad sense, including alternative dispute resolution (ADR) procedures, to which we will make specific references when necessary. The aim is that this model can be used by practitioners and public authorities in the study and implementation of digitalization of justice tools.

B. Personal Data Protection in the Process of Digitalization of Justice

According to the ECFR, individuals have the right to the protection of their personal data[9] and the right to respect for their private and family life, home, and communications.[10] While the right to data protection is closely related to privacy, they are distinct. The Spanish Constitutional Court (TC)[11] distinguishes between the two: privacy protects against invasions into personal and family matters that individuals wish to keep private, while data protection ensures control over personal data and its processing. The right to data protection covers all personal data, not just sensitive information, and aims to give individuals control over how their data is used.

2022) 100; Lorena Alemán Aróstegui, 'El uso de RISCANVI en la toma de decisiones penitenciarias' (2023) 44 Estudios Penales y Criminológicos 1; Ángel Gordo López and María José Rubio Martín, 'Incertidumbres algorítmicas en torno a las violencias de género. El caso del sistema VioGén y otros sistemas de predicción del riesgo' (2024) 33 Revista Española de Sociología 1.

[7] [1983] Spanish Constitutional Court Case 292/1982, para 2.

[8] Fernando Esteban de la Rosa et al, 'Justicia Digital, Guía Para El Diálogo Sobre El Diseño y El Uso Eficiente, de Calidad y Ético de Herramientas Tecnológicas En La Justicia Civil' (*Fundación COTEC para la Innovación*, 2022) 75 <https://cotec.es/proyectos-cpt/guia-para-la-justicia-digital/> last accessed 26 December 2024.

[9] Art 8 ECFR.

[10] Art 7ECFR.

[11] *Infringement of the fundamental right to the protection of personal data Partial nullity of several precepts of the Organic Law* [2000] Spanish Constitutional Court Case 292/2000, paras 6 and 7.

The process of digitalization of justice systems implies a considerable increase in data processing operations of all kinds, and particularly of personal data. This entails the need to be particularly mindful of both the principles relating to the processing of personal data and the General Data Protection Regulation (GDPR) as a whole. The GDPR[12] outlines a broad understanding of personal data and its processing, emphasizing the expansive nature of the right to data protection. Data processing must comply with principles like lawfulness, fairness, transparency, purpose limitation, data minimization, accuracy, retention limitation, integrity, confidentiality, and accountability[13]. The accountability principle requires data controllers to demonstrate compliance with these principles.[14] Additionally, data subjects have rights to information, access, objection, limitation of processing, data rectification, erasure, and protection from automated decisions.

The principle of lawfulness, fairness, and transparency means that data must be processed lawfully, fairly, and transparently toward the data subject.[15] Lawfulness is further defined in Arts 6 and 9 of the GDPR, which specify that data processing must be justified by a legal basis, such as fulfilling a legal obligation or performing a task in the public interest, especially in the justice sector. For special categories of data, exceptions are required. For example, processing personal data in the justice sector is permissible for formulating, exercising, or defending claims, or when courts act in their judicial capacity.[16] Fairness and transparency are achieved when individuals are informed about what data is being processed and for what purpose. This is particularly relevant for the digitalization of justice, where clear rules and 'digital-ready' regulations ensure transparency in processing.

The purpose limitation principle dictates that personal data should only be collected for specified, legitimate purposes and should not be used in ways incompatible with those purposes. Further processing may be allowed for archiving in the public interest, scientific research, or statistical purposes, provided safeguards like pseudonymization are in place.[17] Adequate anonymization is crucial to prevent data from being traced back to individuals once made public. Anonymization techniques and measures like firewalls are essential for protecting the purpose limitation principle. A firewall is a computer system or program that automatically prevents an unauthorized person from gaining access to a computer when it is connected to a network such as the internet.[18] There are different anonymisation techniques with variable degrees of robustness. Broadly speaking there are two different approaches: randomization and generalization. Randomization alters the veracity of the data in order to remove the

[12] Regulation (EU) 2016/679 of the European Parliament and the Council of 27 April 2016 on the protection of natural persons with regard to the processing of personal data and on the free movement of such data, and repealing Directive 95/46/EC (General Data Protection Regulation) [2016] OJ L119/1.

[13] Art 5.2 GDPR.

[14] In accordance with Art 236 sexies.2 OLJ, the competent administration will be the one that has the status of data controller, which means that it will be the justice departments of the respective autonomous communities that will have the status of data controller.

[15] Art 5.1.a and Rec 39 GDPR.

[16] Art 9.2.f GDPR.

[17] Arts 5.1.b and 81.1 GDPR.

[18] Collins Dictionary, 'Firewall' <https://www.collinsdictionary.com/dictionary/english/firewall> last accessed 26 December 2024.

strong link between the data and the individual. The main randomization techniques are noise addition, permutation, and differential privacy. Generalization consists of generalizing, or diluting, the attributes of data subjects by modifying the respective scale or order of magnitude (ie a region rather than a city, a month rather than a week). The main generalization techniques are aggregation, K-anonymity, L-diversity and T-closeness.[19] While there is always an inherent residual risk of re-identification,[20] data where it is no longer possible to identify the data subject are technically considered anonymous, otherwise the GDPR would end up applying to unwanted or unforeseen situations.[21] Respecting this principle is key if we take into account that it is increasingly encouraged that decisions are not only in open, but also in a machine-readable format in order to achieve an algorithm-friendly justice system.[22] In Spain, court judgments are anonymized before publication unless they involve specific exceptions like decisions from the Constitutional Court, the European Court of Human Rights (ECHR), or the European Court of Justice (ECJ). The reversion of personal data is prohibited in Spain.[23] Beyond anonymization techniques, other measures should be adopted to protect the purpose limitation principle, such as firewalls to prevent data leakage or unintended uses of data. A general example of this is article 5.a.4 of EU Regulation eIDAS 2,[24] according to which European Digital Identity Wallets shall enable citizens to perform certain tasks in a user-friendly, transparent, and traceable manner.[25] Additionally, the principle of further processing requires a compatibility check to ensure any new use of personal data aligns with the original purpose for which the data was collected. This is particularly relevant in the use of artificial intelligence (AI) tools, where data usage needs to be carefully examined.

The principle of data retention limitation mandates that personal data should be kept only for as long as necessary to fulfil the purpose for which it was collected.[26]

[19] WP29, 'Opinion 05/2014 on Anonymisation Techniques' (2014) 11–19 <https://ec.europa.eu/justice/article-29/documentation/opinion-recommendation/files/2014/wp216_en.pdf> last accessed 26 December 2024.

[20] WP29, 'Opinion 05/2014 on Anonymisation Techniques' (2014) 7 <https://ec.europa.eu/justice/article-29/documentation/opinion-recommendation/files/2014/wp216_en.pdf> last accessed 26 December 2024.This risk of re-identification can be seen in particularly well-known cases such as that of Mario Costeja, which paradoxically gave rise to the jurisprudence on which the right to be forgotten is built.

[21] WP29, 'Opinion 04/2007 on the Concept of Personal Data' (2007) 5 <https://www.pdp.ie/docs/1030.pdf> last accessed 26 December 2024.

[22] Esteban de la Rosa et al (n 8) 75.

[23] By Act 37/2007, on the re-use of public sector information, following its amendment by Law 18/2015 (art. 8.f). See [2017] SDPA E/02554/2017.

[24] Regulation (EU) 2024/1183 of the European Parliament and the Council of 11 April 2024 amending Regulation (EU) No 910/2014 as regards establishing the European Digital Identity Framework [2024] OJ L 1183.

[25] Tasks such as the following: '(a) securely request, obtain, select, combine, store, delete, share and present, under the sole control of the user, person identification data and, where applicable, in combination with electronic attestations of attributes, to authenticate to relying parties online and, where appropriate, in offline mode, in order to access public and private services, while ensuring that selective disclosure of data is possible; (c) securely authenticate another person's European Digital Identity Wallet, and receive and share person identification data and electronic attestations of attributes in a secured way between the two European Digital Identity Wallets; (e) sign by means of qualified electronic signatures or seal by means of qualified electronic seals'. We highlight those that seem to us to be most relevant for the purpose of promoting progress in the digitalization of justice.

[26] Art 5.1.e GDPR.

This is especially relevant in communication history logs or platforms used in justice digitalization. Data should be deleted once it is no longer necessary, but it is important that deletion is not automatic. Alerts should be generated to notify users when data is no longer needed, allowing them to assess whether deletion is appropriate. This ensures better data protection through design alongside with human intervention.

The data minimization principle[27] requires data collected to be adequate, relevant, and limited to what is necessary for the processing purpose. This principle is closely linked to purpose limitation, and data controllers must assess whether fewer personal data can achieve the intended purpose. In the context of justice digitalization, this principle suggests avoiding the collection of biometric data when less invasive alternatives are available.[28] In the area of digitalization of justice this criterion should be borne in mind in several respects, such as for example: (1) the avoidance of the use of biometric data when less invasive identification alternatives exist;[29] (2) in the design of ODR platforms, telematics connection tools, or electronic communications only the data necessary to launch the court should be collected, and only for these purposes;[30] (3) the image of the parties (eg in a video conference or on an ODR platform) should be required only when necessary, and the use of facial recognition tools and processing of other biometric data should be prevented.[31]

The accuracy principle mandates that personal data must be accurate and kept up to date. If data is inaccurate, it should be corrected or deleted promptly.[32] This requires active involvement from data subjects, who are best positioned to know the accuracy of their data. However, data controllers should implement mechanisms like contact details or online access to facilitate the correction of inaccurate data.

Finally, all these criteria should serve to guide compliance with a preventive principle that is essential for proper compliance: data protection by design and by default.[33] The principle of data protection by design and by default should take into account the state of the art, the cost of implementing the different measures and the purposes of processing,[34] and should therefore be subject to periodic review to incorporate possible advances or cost reductions. In any event, it should assess criteria such as the following:

- what data are necessary for the tool in view of the purpose for which it is to be applied in the administration of justice;

[27] Art 5.1.c GDPR.

[28] EDPB, 'Guidelines 4/2019 on Article 25 Data Protection by Design and by Default Version 2.0' (2020) 22 <https://www.edpb.europa.eu/sites/default/files/files/file1/edpb_guidelines_201904_dataprotection_by_design_and_by_default_v2.0_en.pdf> last accessed 26 December 2024.

[29] EDPS, 'Guidelines 3/2019 on Processing of Personal Data through Video Devices Version 2.0' (2020) 18 <https://www.edpb.europa.eu/sites/default/files/files/file1/edpb_guidelines_201903_video_devices_en_0.pdf> last accessed 26 December 2024; Esteban de la Rosa et al (n 8) 34.

[30] Esteban de la Rosa et al (n 8) 69; *Online Dispute Resolution Mechanisms in Civil and Administrative Court Proceedings* (Council of Europe 2021) 11 <https://rm.coe.int/publication-guidelines-and-explanatory-memoreandum-odr-mechanisms-in-c/1680a4214e> last accessed 26 December 2024.

[31] Esteban de la Rosa et al (n 8) 73; EDPS (n 29); EDPS and EDPB, 'Joint Opinion 5/2021 on the Proposal for a Regulation of the European Parliament and of the Council Laying down Harmonised Rules on Artificial Intelligence (Artificial Intelligence Act)' (2021) 11.

[32] Art 5.1.d GDPR.

[33] Art 25 GDPR.

[34] Art 25.1 GDPR.

- what impact the use of the tool will have, taking into account the nature of the process (administrative, civil, criminal, mediation, arbitration, etc.) and the characteristics of the parties involved (minors, people with disabilities, vulnerable groups, etc.);
- what risks may be involved in the use of the tool, based on the principle of zero reliance;
- what recommendations for improvement can be made and how regularly they will be checked to see if they are being implemented.

C. Cybersecurity and Data Protection in the Use of Digital Tools by Practitioners, Courts and Users

Cybersecurity is a multidisciplinary field, and its application involves all sectors, industries and stakeholders, both vertically and horizontally. To increase the development of national capabilities, political, economic and social forces must make efforts. This can be achieved through the efforts of good actors within the ecosystem, such as law enforcement, justice departments, educational institutions, ministries, private sector operators, ICT developers, public–private partnerships and intra-state cooperation.[35] An adequate level of cybersecurity is indispensable in the process of digitalization of services in general, as these processes can be viewed with suspicion prior to their implementation. These considerations are not unrelated to the progressive digitalization of the public sector (including the administration of justice), which must also take into account its size (and, therefore, the enormous volume of data processed) and the sensitivity of the information it handles.[36]

According to art 5.1.f GDPR, data shall be 'processed in a manner that ensures appropriate security of the personal data, including protection against unauthorised or unlawful processing and against accidental loss, destruction or damage, using appropriate technical or organizational measures ('integrity and confidentiality')'. This principle is further developed in arts 32, 33, and 34 GDPR, relating to risk-based security of processing and the data breach notification obligation. The controller must implement measures to protect against unauthorized access to personal data as well as against loss, destruction or damage to personal data,[37] including, for example, pseudonymisation and encryption of data, or the quality of processing systems and services, as well as the regular review of all implemented measures. The implementation of technical and organizational measures to protect data integrity and

[35] International Telecommunication Union, 'Global Cybersecurity Index 2024 5th Edition' (2024) 128 <https://www.itu.int/en/ITU-D/Cybersecurity/Documents/GCIv5/2401416_1b_Global-Cybersecurity-Index-E.pdf> last accessed 26 December 2024.

[36] Arturo Ribagorda Garnacho, 'La seguridad del tratamiento en el ámbito de las Administraciones Públicas: la ciberseguridad (Comentario al artículo 32 RGPD y a la Disposición adicional primera LOPDGDD)' in *Comentario al Reglamento General de Protección de Datos y a la Ley Orgánica de Protección de Datos personales y Garantía de los Derechos Digitales* (Thomson Reuters Aranzadi 2021) 2010 <https://dialnet.unirioja.es/servlet/articulo?codigo = 7915633> last accessed 26 December 2024.

[37] Art 32.2 GDPR.

confidentiality must take into account the state of the art and the cost of implementation. This also results in the need to periodically review the implemented measures. Considering the speed of advances in computer development, it seems advisable to implement annual review protocols.

The NIS 2 Directive[38] establishes the obligation for essential and important entities to adopt 'cyber hygiene' measures, aimed at ensuring cybersecurity through staff training and awareness.[39] Regardless of whether or not the NIS 2 Directive is applicable to the means of the administration of justice,[40] cyber hygiene measures are very important criteria to be taken into account in order to achieve adequate levels of cybersecurity in the use of digital tools in the administration of justice. The cyber hygiene measures proposed by the NIS 2 Directive are the following:

- Zero trust principle
- Regular software updates
- Proper configuration of devices
- Network segmentation
- User awareness about identity and access management
- Staff training and awareness of cyber threats.

The zero trust principle is a cyber security and systems management strategy based on the premise that threats exist both inside and outside the network boundaries, implying that organizations should not trust anything inside or outside their perimeters, and verify anything before granting access. It represents a shift in philosophy from traditional security, which focuses on protection against external threats (eg through firewalls) and automatically relies on internal users. Implementing zero trust strategies entails a number of advantages, such as: (1) enabling the workplace for secure and flexible access; (2) reducing security costs in a sustainable way; (3) preventing the spread of malware and lateral movement by creating more granular

[38] EU Directive 2022/2555 of the European Parliament and of the Council of 14 December 2022 on measures for a high common level of cybersecurity across the Union, amending Regulation (EU) No 910/2014 and Directive (EU) 2018/1972, and repealing Directive (EU) 2016/1148 (NIS 2 Directive) [2022] OJ L333.

[39] European Commission for the Efficiency of Justice (CEPEJ), 'Digitalisation for a Better Justice' (2021) 2 <https://rm.coe.int/cepej-2021-12-en-cepej-action-plan-2022-2025-digitalisation-justice/1680a4cf2c> last accessed 26 December 2024.The training of legal professionals contributes not only to the efficiency of the justice system but also to its independence, insofar as it enables them to act in full knowledge of the law and procedures.

[40] This issue may not be entirely clear in the rule. According to art 3.1.d EU Directive NIS 2, entities of the central public administration are considered to be essential, and other entities mentioned in Annexes I and II that do not have the status of essential are considered to be important entities. In Annex I, public administration entities (state and regional) are considered as high criticality sectors, excluding the judiciary, parliaments and banks. However, the exclusion of the 'judiciary' can be interpreted in a broad or narrow sense: the Spanish Constitutional Court in its Rulings 56/1990 and 62/1990 distinguishes between the administration of justice in the narrow and the broad sense. The Administration of Justice in the strict sense is identified with the judicial power, that is to say, with the function of judging and enforcing what has been judged, which is the responsibility of independent judges and magistrates, who are irremovable and subject only to the rule of law (art 117 SC). The administration of justice in the broad sense refers to the material and personal resources necessary for the correct exercise of the judicial function. With regard to the latter, the Ministry of Justice and the Autonomous Communities with jurisdiction over justice must provide courts and tribunals with the personnel, facilities and means necessary for the proper performance of the judicial function.

micro-perimeters and network rules; and (4) mitigating the damage of data breaches.[41] Looking at the suggestions in the NIS 2 Directive Recital 89, one could argue that they are consequences of implementing a zero trust strategy. Perhaps of these, the last two may require some further comment: awareness of the staff using the tools is essential to prevent bad practices acquired over time from jeopardising the entire designed cybersecurity architecture. It is of little use, for example, to implement technical and organizational measures aimed at protecting the integrity and confidentiality of personal data if the people who have access to them share them or communicate them to third parties who should not know them. In Spain, art 5.1 SDP Act[42] reinforces the duty of confidentiality that exists in certain professional sectors and extends it to all persons who in the exercise of their functions have access to personal data.[43] It is, therefore, also an obligation regarding data protection from the design and by default, to train and make staff aware of this duty of confidentiality. For example, it is advisable to use watermarks, anti-copying systems or personalized versions of documents that make it possible to detect the specific person who has disseminated a document in an unauthorized manner. These recommendations have already been formulated in the COTEC Guide[44] and have been incorporated into Spanish legislation.[45]

In terms of identification and authentication, EU Regulation eIDAS[46] has incorporated utilities for the digitalization of justice, such as the mutual acceptance of national electronic identification systems for natural and legal persons that have been notified to the European Commission by the Member States.[47] This mechanism has made it possible to overcome the incompatibility between national identification systems developed within the framework of Unfair Terms Directive[48,49] It has also established

[41] William Yeoh et al, 'Zero Trust Cybersecurity: Critical Success Factors and A Maturity Assessment Framework' (2023) 133 Computers & Security 103412.

[42] Organic Law 3/2018 of 5 December, on the protection of personal data and guarantee of digital rights [2018] BOE num. 294 6.12.2018 (Ley Orgánica 3/2018, de 5 de diciembre, de Protección de Datos Personales y garantía de los derechos digitales) (SPDPA).

[43] Antonio Troncoso Reigada, 'Los Principios Relativos al Tratamiento (Comentario al Artículo 5 RGPD y al Artículo 4 LOPDGDD)' in Antonio Troncoso Reigada (ed), *Comentario al Reglamento General de Protección de Datos y a la Ley Orgánica de Protección de Datos personales y Garantía de los Derechos Digitales*, Vol 1 (Thomson Reuters Aranzadi 2021).

[44] Esteban de la Rosa et al (n 8) 36.

[45] Art 26.5 Royal Decree-Law 6/2023 of 19 December approving urgent measures for the implementation of the Recovery, Transformation and Resilience Plan in the areas of the Judiciary, the Civil Service, Local Government and Patronage (2023) (Real Decreto-ley 6/2023, de 19 de diciembre, por el que se aprueban medidas urgentes para la ejecución del Plan de Recuperación, Transformación y Resiliencia en materia de servicio público de justicia, función pública, régimen local y mecenazgo) (SPA).

[46] Regulation (EU) 910/2014 of the European Parliament and the Council of 23 July 2014 on electronic identification and trust services for electronic transactions in the internal market and repealing Directive 1999/93/EC [2014] OJ L 257/73.

[47] The electronic identification schemes notified by EU Member States can be found at the following website: <https://administracionelectronica.gob.es/pae_Home/pae_Estrategias/pae_Identidad_y_firma electronica/Nodo-eIDAS/Sistemas-de-identificacion-electronica-notificados.html> last accessed 26 December 2024.

[48] Council Directive 93/13/EEC of 5 April 1993 on unfair terms in consumer contracts [1993] OJ L 95/29.

[49] EU Regulation eIDAS 2 consolidates this trend when it states in the new art 24a that qualified electronic signatures and qualified electronic seals based on a qualified certificate, as well as their respective qualified creation devices, issued by one Member State shall be recognised as such in all other Member States.

qualified trust certificates, which enjoy a presumption of authenticity, such as website authentication certificates, signature certificates and seal certificates.[50] Qualified trust services are regulated in arts 20 et seq of eIDAS, which have been modified by EU Regulation eIDAS 2 in order to offer greater guarantees of cybersecurity and integrity,[51] as well as greater guarantees of authentication of the identity of the subjects.[52] Spanish law establishes[53] the right of citizens to interact with the Administration of Justice by electronic means, and within the framework of this right, to use electronic identification and signature systems before the Administration of Justice to facilitate their authentication.[54] On the other hand, the protection of the integrity and confidentiality of personal data cannot, by its very nature, be complete. Not only, as we have already said, because a weighing of measures must be carried out based on both the risk and the cost of implementation and the state of the art, but also because it is impossible to achieve absolute certainty that a system will not be attacked. This leads to looking at cyber security not from the question of whether a breach will occur, but to delay as much as possible the moment when it does occur and to develop alert and rapid response mechanisms when it does occur.[55] These mechanisms are provided for in arts 33 and 34 GDPR, concerning the obligation to notify data breaches to both the supervisory authority[56] and the data subject.[57] This notification shall take place without undue delay in either case, although in the case of notification to the supervisory authority a time limit of 72 hours is set,[58] starting from the time the data controller has a reasonable degree of certainty that a security incident has occurred that has led to personal data being compromised.[59]

EU Regulation eIDAS 2 amends certain articles of eIDAS, and incorporates some new features, such as the European Digital Identity Wallet (EDIW)[60] or a new trust service called 'electronic attestations of attributes'.[61] The 'electronic attestation of attributes' is a new electronic document that guarantees the authenticity

[50] Art 1.c eIDAS.

[51] See art 24.2.f.b eIDAS 2. This rule establishes the obligation to notify, without undue delay and no later than 24 hours after the occurrence of the incident, the supervisory body, identifiable affected persons, as well as other competent bodies and the general public as appropriate, of any breach of security or disruption of service that has a significant impact on the trusted service or the data held therein.

[52] See new wording of art 24, according to eIDAS 2.

[53] Royal Decree-Law 6/2023 of 19 December approving urgent measures for the implementation of the Recovery, Transformation and Resilience Plan in the areas of the Judiciary, the Civil Service, Local Government and Patronage (2023) (Real Decreto-ley 6/2023, de 19 de diciembre, por el que se aprueban medidas urgentes para la ejecución del Plan de Recuperación, Transformación y Resiliencia en materia de servicio público de justicia, función pública, régimen local y mecenazgo) (SPA).

[54] Art 5.i SPA.

[55] In the words of Dr. Carlos Galán Pascual, the question is not whether or not they are going to attack a system, but when they are going to attack it.

[56] Art 33 GDPR.

[57] Art 34 GDPR.

[58] Art 33.1 GDPR.

[59] WP29, 'Guidelines on Personal Data Breach Notification under Regulation 2016/679' (2018) 10–11 <https://ec.europa.eu/newsroom/article29/items/612052> last accessed 26 December 2024. See also Rec. 85 GDPR.

[60] Arts 5.a to 5.f eIDAS 2.

[61] Arts 1.c and art 3.16.g and 3.16.h eIDAS 2.

of information, for information with full legal value from authentic sources. Given the guarantee provided by this document, it can only be issued by (1) public sector bodies responsible for authentic sources, or on their behalf, and (2) qualified trust service providers. Furthermore, these documents will have the same legal value throughout the EU.[62] The guarantee of authenticity of the information (both sender and content) contained in this document is supported by the requirements it must fulfil, which are set out in Annexes V–VII eIDAS 2. The introduction of the EDIW, on the other hand, is intended to be an instrument that facilitates the achievement of many of the objectives relating not only to the correct identification and authentication of citizens, but also to the principle of data integrity and confidentiality, and other objectives highlighted here. This can be seen in art 5.a.4 eIDAS 2, which sets out the objectives of the EDIW. Interesting to note in the EIDW for personal data protection purposes is the mandate to establish a logical separation between personal data related to the provision of EIDW and other data held by the portfolio provider.[63] This allows for a better respect of the purpose limitation principle[64] by ensuring that each set of data is specifically fulfilling the function for which it was collected. Respecting this principle from the outset in turn respects the principle of data protection by design and by default[65] from the standard, which in turn meets one of the objectives set by the European Commission in 2024 (digital-ready rules).[66]

Based on the criteria and considerations developed in the COTEC Guide and those just mentioned, we can take into account safeguard measures (which should be reviewed on a regular basis) such as the following:

- designing a strategy based on the principle of zero trust;
- training and awareness-raising of staff on cyber-security, especially on proper identity and access management and on external and internal cyber-threats;
- establish protocols for pseudonymization and encryption of personal data;
- ensure the continued confidentiality, integrity, availability and resilience of processing systems and services;
- ensure availability and rapid access to personal data in case of incidents;
- ensuring identification of users and preventing unauthorized access to confidential data;
- preventing unwanted alteration or deletion of data;
- ensuring the interoperability of documents;
- ensure the performance of programmes by staff;
- enable notification of data breaches to the supervisory authority and the data subject without undue delay.

[62] Rec 10 eIDAS 2.
[63] Art 5.a.14 eIDAS 2.
[64] Art 5.1.b GDPR.
[65] Art 25 GDPR.
[66] European Commission (n 2) 35.

D. Artificial Intelligence and the Rights to Data Protection and Effective Judicial Protection in Digital Justice

In a broad sense, an AI tool can be understood as any software capable of generating output information such as content, predictions, recommendations, or decisions with the ability to influence the environment in a similar way to a human being. AI tools are divided into two main groups: (1) expert systems, based on logical rules; and (2) data-driven systems, based on the analytics of large amounts of data. Within the latter, a distinction can be made between machine learning and deep learning, depending on whether the system is to be guided through the phases of the data analysis process (machine learning) or whether it is able to learn by itself with each new input of information (deep learning).[67] The AI Act[68] adopts a restrictive notion of what it calls 'AI Systems', focusing only on data-driven systems.[69] This may affect its possible application in the Administration of Justice, at least at the present time, when most AI tools are expert systems. For the purposes of this paper, we will always refer to AI tools as both expert systems and data-driven systems, so that the term cannot be confused with that of art 3.1 AI Act.

AI tools have limitations. In the case of expert systems, they often encounter limitations in areas of high discretion:[70] while it is true that these limitations can be partially overcome by incorporating expert knowledge to model decision trees, the results are still unsatisfactory. The limitations of data-driven systems have to do with the quality of the data that feed them and with the transparency and explainability of the algorithms.[71] In either case, it is important to differentiate between fully automated suggestions and decisions and to avoid any kind of discrimination, for which it will be particularly important to take into account the provisions of arts 22 GDPR and 11 LED[72] on automated decision-making and suggestions.

The AI Act defines artificial intelligence models and systems as 'machine-based system that is designed to operate with varying levels of autonomy and that may exhibit adaptiveness after deployment, and that, for explicit or implicit objectives,

[67] Javier Valls Prieto, *Inteligencia artificial, Derechos humanos y bienes jurídicos* (Thomson Reuters Aranzadi 2021) 18–20 <https://dialnet.unirioja.es/servlet/libro?codigo = 847600> last accessed 26 December 2024.

[68] Regulation (EU) 2024/1689 of the European Parliament and the Council of 13 June 2024 laying down harmonised rules on artificial intelligence and amending Regulations (EC) No 300/2008, (EU) No 167/2013, (EU) No 168/2013, (EU) 2018/858, (EU) 2018/1139 and (EU) 2019/2144 and Directives 2014/90/EU, (EU) 2016/797 and (EU) 2020/1828 (Artificial Intelligence Act) [2024] OJ L2024/1689.

[69] Art 3.1 AI Act.

[70] Richard E Susskind, 'Expert Systems in Law: A Jurisprudential Approach to Artificial Intelligence and Legal Reasoning' (1987) 49 The Modern L Rev 168; Fernando Esteban de la Rosa, 'Construyendo El Marco Legal Europeo Para El Diseño y Uso de Herramientas de Inteligencia Artificial En El Entorno de La Justicia Civil-Administrativa', in *El derecho y la inteligencia artificial* (Editorial Universidad de Granada 2022) 431 <https://digibug.ugr.es/bitstream/handle/10481/82089/VERSION%20PUBLICADA%20EN%20DIGIBUG.pdf?sequence = 1&isAllowed = y> last accessed 26 December 2024.

[71] Esteban de la Rosa et al (n 8) 79–81.

[72] Directive (EU) 2016/680 of the European Parliament and the Council of 27 April 2016 on the protection of natural persons with regard to the processing of personal data by competent authorities for the purposes of the prevention, investigation, detection or prosecution of criminal offences or the execution of criminal penalties, and on the free movement of such data, and repealing Council Framework Decision 2008/977/JHA (LED) [2016] OJ L119/89.

infers, from the input it receives, how to generate outputs such as predictions, content, recommendations, or decisions that can influence physical or virtual environments'.[73] This definition does not cover all AI tools, and leaves out expert systems or weak AI.[74] As far as the use of AI in justice is concerned, the restricted objective scope of application in the AI Act makes it necessary to examine the different tools to determine whether or not the standard is applicable to them. However, regardless of the applicability of the AI Act depending on the type of AI used by the tool, we should not lose sight of the fact that any AI tool used for automated decision-making or suggestions in the field of justice involves the processing of personal data.[75] This data processing will take place at least at the end of the data value chain, ie when the suggestion or decision, in abstract, is applied to the case of a specific data subject. But typically, personal data processing will also take place during the feeding and validation of the tool. In this regard, the GDPR is applicable, and in particular art 22 and Rec. 71 on the right not to be subject to a fully automated decision. As regards the AI Act, its articles and recitals can serve as interpretative criteria for the content of some of the GDPR's rules, regardless of whether or not they are applicable depending on the type of tool in question, and we will use them in this section.

Starting with the rules on data protection, it is important to bear in mind and treat art 22 GDPR and art 11 LED together. They are almost identical rules, so the considerations on art 22 GDPR apply to art 11 LED as far as they do not differ. Let us briefly look at the differences in order to be able to subsequently analyse their common content and the considerations this entails in the area of justice.

Firstly, the GDPR is a Regulation, while the LED is an EU Directive, which conditions its wording: the LED mandates States, leaving them to choose the form and means of achieving the result, while the GDPR is directly applicable and mandatory in all its elements.[76] On the other hand, the scope of application of the two standards is different: the LED refers only to the processing of personal data for the purposes of the prevention, investigation, detection or prosecution of criminal offences or the execution of criminal penalties;[77] whereas the GDPR refers generally to the processing of personal data and their free movement.[78] As far as justice is concerned, this implies that the LED will be applicable in criminal proceedings, but that for processing operations other than those referred to in Art1 LED, whether in criminal proceedings or in other proceedings, the GDPR will be applicable as a supplementary rule.[79]

As to the content of the prohibition, art 22 GPDR prohibits fully automated decisions that entail legal effects or significant effects,[80] while art 11 LED prohibits fully automated decisions that entail negative legal effects,[81] and the compilation of files resulting in discrimination of natural persons when these profiles have been compiled

[73] Art 3.1 AI Act.
[74] See art 2.1 AI Act.
[75] On the topic, Esteban de la Rosa (n 70) 445.
[76] Art 288 TFEU. Consolidated Version of the Treaty on the Functioning of the European Union [2008] OJ C326.
[77] Art 1 LED.
[78] Art 1 GDPR.
[79] Rec 11 LED.
[80] Art 22.1 GDPR.
[81] Art 11.1 LED.

using special categories of data.[82] Personal data revealing racial or ethnic origin, political opinions, religious or philosophical beliefs or trade union membership, genetic data, biometric data intended to uniquely identify a natural person, data concerning health, and data concerning a natural person's sex life or sexual orientation are considered to be special categories of data.[83]

The exceptions to the general prohibition of fully automated decision-making are more restricted in the case of the LED, which only provides that such decisions may take place if they are authorized by EU or Member State law.[84] Generally speaking, art 22 GDPR adds two more: (1) explicit consent of the data subject and (2) that the automated decision is necessary for the conclusion or performance of a contract to which the data subject is a party. When the procedure (judicial or administrative) is part of formal justice and therefore of public administration, the only exception to the prohibition of fully automated decision-making is that it is authorized by EU or Member State law by virtue of the principle of legality.[85] It should be borne in mind, on the basis of the Schufa case, that the legal protection referred to in art 22.2.b GDPR must respect the limits of the GDPR as well as the case law interpretation of the GDPR, among which the data processing principles of art 5 GDPR should be highlighted.[86]

More and more jurisdictions are proposing combined systems of AI tools aimed at providing a diagnosis or prediction of the outcome of the process for future direct online negotiation, such as the Dutch platform Rechtwijzer in the Netherlands, the CRT in British Columbia in Canada, or the three Internet courts set up in China. These systems are intended to assist in decision-making, to facilitate negotiation (or even to automate it as much as possible), or to calculate possible compensation in the same way as a professional from whom advice is sought.[87] As regards alternative dispute resolution systems (ADR), the explicit consent of the data subject should not be considered as the only legal basis for the processing of personal data, or even the main one if we take into account the weak position of the data subject as a party to a dispute. Perhaps a better alternative is legitimate interest.[88] In any case, according to the principle of lawfulness, fairness, and transparency in the processing of personal data,[89] the use of AI tools for fully automated decision-making in the context of an ADR procedure (whether for decisions or procedural steps) must be sufficiently highlighted so that the data subject is aware of their existence and scope and can, if necessary, object to them.

As regards the common aspects of both provisions that are of interest to us here, it should first be noted that a general prohibition of fully automated decision-making

[82] Art 11.3 LED.

[83] Arts 9.1 GDPR and 10.1 LED.

[84] Art 11.1 LED.

[85] By virtue of the principle of legality, the public administration, including the administration of justice, can only relate to citizens when a regulation with the status of law delimits the respective rights and obligations, the scope of the power exercised and the correlative duty (Francisco Rubio Llorente, 'El principio de legalidad' (1993) 13 Revista española de derecho constitucional 9, 21). On the topic, for Spanish legislation see arts 103.1, 103.2, and 106.1 SC, and 8 OLJP.

[86] Case C-634/21 OQ v Land Hessen [2005] ECJ (Shufa Case), paras 67–69.

[87] Esteban de la Rosa (n 70) 441.

[88] Art 6.1.f GDPR.

[89] Art 5.1.a GDPR.

is established, and not only a subjective right in the hands of the data subject.[90] Considering it as a subjective right in the hands of the data subject could undermine the objectives of art 22 GDPR, leading in practice to situations contrary to the rights and interests of the data subject in this respect,[91] since if art 22 is interpreted as a prohibition, data controllers will not be allowed to make automated decisions about a data subject until one of the three specified in art 22 is met;[92] while if art 22 is interpreted as a right to object, automated decision-making is restricted only to cases in which the data subject actively objects.[93]

It should be clarified that while profiling facilitates or assists automated decision-making and suggestions, there is no full identity between profiling and automated decision-making, hence arts 11 LED and 22 GDPR prohibit both automated individual decision-making and profiling, when they entail legal or significant effects on the data subject. Automated decisions can take place with or without profiling, and profiling as such will not necessarily result in an automated decision or suggestion (although this is its main utility).[94] In short, they are independent but strongly interrelated activities.[95] In relation to profiling, it should be stressed that it involves data processing activities such as (1) data collection and deposit, (2) automated data analysis to identify correlations, and (3) application of the correlations to specific natural persons. This latter data processing activity is very close to automated decision-making or suggestions, although it does not go as far as that: only a similarity between a profile and a specific individual is made explicit, and inferences are made; but it is not yet formulated in the form of an automated suggestion or decision. It should be recalled that inferred data, as long as they relate to an identified or identifiable person, are also personal data,[96] and therefore the entire GPDR is fully applicable to them. For example, profiles relating to the likelihood of recidivism such as those produced by RisCanvi, or relating to the voting behaviour of a judge or magistrate such as those produced by the Supreme Court Forecasting Project[97] are, according to GDPR, personal data.

An important aspect in relation to the use of AI tools in the field of justice, and particularly in relation to the aforementioned arts 11 LED and 22 GDPR, is the difference between fully automated decisions and suggestions. The intensity and freedom

[90] WP29, 'Guidelines on Automated Individual Decision-Making and Profiling for the Purposes of Regulation 2016/679' (2018) 21 <https://ec.europa.eu/newsroom/article29/items/612053/en> last accessed 26 December 2024.

[91] Mónica Vilasau Solana, 'La Realización de Perfiles y La Salvaguardia de Los Derechos y Libertades Del Afectado' in Agustí Cerrillo i Martínez and Miguel Peguera Poch (eds), *Retos jurídicos de la inteligencia artificial* (Thomson Reuters Aranzadi 2020) 182.

[92] As we have seen in this section, the three circumstances are (1) the provision by State or EU law, (2) that the automated decision is necessary for the performance of a contract to which the data subject is a party, or (3) the explicit consent of the data subject.

[93] Sandra Wachter, Brent Mittelstadt, and Luciano Floridi, 'Why a Right to Explanation of Automated Decision-Making Does Not Exist in the General Data Protection Regulation' (Social Science Research Network, 28 December 2016) <https://papers.ssrn.com/abstract = 2903469> last accessed 26 December 2024.

[94] WP29, 'Guidelines on Automated Individual Decision-Making and Profiling for the Purposes of Regulation 2016/679' (n 89) 7–9.

[95] ibid 8.

[96] Art 4.1 GDPR.

[97] See later in this section.

of human intervention differentiates an automated suggestion from an automated decision: meaningful human intervention prevents us from talking about a fully automated decision, and we move into the realm of suggestions. Meaningful human intervention may also take place before the production of legal or significant effects (human in the loop), or at the review stage.[98] The controller must ensure, by virtue of the principle of accountability, that human intervention, if foreseen, is meaningful and takes place before the production of any effects.[99] In the case of the administration of justice, the court or office where the proceedings are being heard shall have the status of data controller. In the case of ADR systems, the status of data controller can be attributed to the entity managing the system.

But when is a human intervention meaningful? First of all, we must be clear that a mere formal or symbolic human intervention should not be considered meaningful.[100] The Schufa case establishes a broad interpretation of what is to be understood by an automated decision. It arguably allows for a 'veil piercing' of this term that forces a more restrictive interpretation of when there is significant human intervention. This criterion favours a better achievement of the objectives of art 22 GDPR, which is particularly significant in the field of public law and particularly in the digitalization of justice.[101]

If the AI tool is being used in an alternative dispute resolution process, we must differentiate between arbitration and mediation. Mediation is a self-compositional procedure, where a third party helps the disputing parties to reach an agreement, but it is the parties themselves who reach, voluntarily and expressly, the agreement.[102]

[98] See art 14.1 Organic Law 7/2021 of 26 May on the protection of personal data processed for the purposes of the prevention, detection, investigation and prosecution of criminal offences and the execution of criminal penalties (2023) (Ley Orgánica 7/2021, de 26 de mayo, de protección de datos personales tratados para fines de prevención, detección, investigación y enjuiciamiento de infracciones penales y de ejecución de sanciones penales).

[99] Guillermo Lazcoz Moratinos, 'Gobernanza y supervisión humana de la toma de decisiones automatizada basada en la elaboración de perfiles/governance and human oversight of automated decision-making based on profiling' (http://purl.org/dc/dcmitype/Text, Universidad del País Vasco - Euskal Herriko Unibertsitatea 2023) 194 <https://dialnet.unirioja.es/servlet/tesis?codigo = 318838> last accessed 26 December2024.

[100] WP29, 'Guidelines on Automated Individual Decision-Making and Profiling for the Purposes of Regulation 2016/679' (n 89) 23; SDPA, 'Adecuación al RGPD de Tratamientos Que Incorporan Inteligencia Artificial. Una Introducción' (2020) 10 <https://www.aepd.es/guias/adecuacion-rgpd-ia.pdf> last accessed 26 December 2024; Maja Brkan, 'Do Algorithms Rule the World? Algorithmic Decision-Making and Data Protection in the Framework of the GDPR and Beyond' (2019) 27 International Journal of Law and Information Technology 91, 101; Lazcoz Moratinos (n 99) 192; Esteban de la Rosa (n 70) 443–48.

[101] Lorenzo Cotino Hueso, 'La Primera Sentencia Del Tribunal de Justicia de La Unión Europea Sobre Decisiones Automatizadas y Sus Implicaciones Para La Protección de Datos y El Reglamento de Inteligencia Artificial' [2024] Diario La Ley <https://diariolaley.laleynext.es/Content/Documento.aspx?params = H4sIAAAAAAAEAFWNMQ7CMBAEf-P6YpCAwlXMD9yjJLdGJ6w7dAFEfk9SpGDLkWZWmFMutO5wITqdwwc-i2mKFI_UdTGoMUru01sZVRQc2jCi9RvG95XuULhMV3fzzZa6ZJvK8kSqQ5sRMJo9_k5ue_wHc7CJiX4AAAA = WKE>. last accessed 26 December 2024.

[102] Pablo Cortés and Fernando Esteban de la Rosa, 'La Normativa Europea de Resolución de Conflictos de Consumo y Su Transposicióin En España: Una Oportunidad Para Mejorar Los Derechos de Los Consumidores Aprovechando Las Experiencias Positivas En El Derecho Comparado' (ADICAE 2016) <https://www.congreso.es/docu/docum/ddocum/dosieres/sleg/legislatura_12/spl_5/pdfs/46.pdf> last accessed 26 December 2024; Silvia Barona Vilar, 'Las ADR En La Justicia Del Siglo XXI, En Especial La Mediación' (2011) 18 Revista de derecho (Coquimbo) 185.

In arbitration proceedings, on the other hand, the parties to a present or future dispute agree to submit to the decision of a third party, which they accept by mutual agreement, and also fix the terms under which the arbitration proceedings are to be resolved.[103] Both procedures have in common the need for human intervention. However, the agreement in the case of arbitration refers to the submission of the dispute to a third party, whereas in the case of mediation it extends to the content of the agreement itself. This is relevant for the assessment of whether or not there is significant human intervention, not by the third party (whether arbitrator or mediator), but by the parties. In mediation, meaningful human intervention is guaranteed to the extent that it is the parties who intervene in a meaningful way by accepting or rejecting the agreement. This is not the case in arbitration, where the assessment of whether or not there is significant human intervention follows the same considerations as in the case of institutional justice. The guarantee of the mediator's or arbitrator´s independence (be it human or an AI tool) is a different matter,[104] but this goes beyond the doubts about how to assess meaningful human intervention, and the certainty that this is guaranteed in mediation procedures by their very nature.

In addition to excluding formal or symbolic intervention, we can look at the following criteria to determine whether meaningful human intervention is warranted in the automated decision:

- The decision must be made by a competent person who is authorized to modify the suggestion proposed by the AI tool.[105] This implies not only formal capacity, but also the person's material capacity and willingness to question the tool's suggestion.
- It must be avoided that the person using the AI tool routinely applies the suggestions of the AI tool (complacency and automation bias).[106] Complacency bias is understood as the belief of human operators in the reliability of the system, which causes them to pay insufficient attention to monitoring the process and verifying the results of the system.[107] This complacency usually occurs under conditions of task accumulation, when manual tasks compete with the automated task for the human operator's attention, over more factors and causes that lead to this complacency.[108] The aim of avoiding such biases can be achieved

[103] Bernardo María Cremades Sanz-Pastor, 'Arbitraje' in Benigno Pendás (ed), *Enciclopedia de las Ciencias Morales y Políticas para el siglo XXI: Ciencias Políticas y Jurídicas (con especial referencia a la sociedad poscovid 19)* (Real Academia de Ciencias Morales y Políticas 2020) <https://racmyp.es/wp-content/uploads/2023/06/2020-0592_enciclopedia_ciencias_morales_acc_ee_final.pdf> last accessed 26 December 2024.

[104] The inclusion of private entities in ADR should not preclude the establishment of elements to guarantee independence through control over the financing of the private entity (Cortés and Esteban de la Rosa (n 102) 16).

[105] SPDA (n 100) 10.

[106] Michael Veale and Lilian Edwards, 'Clarity, Surprises, and Further Questions in the Article 29 Working Party Draft Guidance on Automated Decision-Making and Profiling' (2018) 34 Computer Law & Security Review 398, 400; Lazcoz Moratinos (n 99) 197.

[107] Judith Simon, Pak-Hang Wong and Gernot Rieder, 'Algorithmic Bias and the Value Sensitive Design Approach' (2020) 9 Internet Policy Review 13 <https://policyreview.info/concepts/algorithmic-bias> last accessed 26 December2024.

[108] Raja Parasuraman and Dietrich H Manzey, 'Complacency and Bias in Human Use of Automation: An Attentional Integration' (2010) 52 Human Factors 381, 382–90.

through training programmes for the promotion of AI literacy, and also through automatic alert systems that generate warnings to the user when they detect a higher than acceptable level of follow-up of suggestions.

Taking into account the above criteria, we propose the following checklist to ensure meaningful human intervention in the use of AI tools in justice:

(1) the person has the formal authority to challenge the proposal received,
(2) that the person has sufficient training in the subject matter of the suggestion to be able to rebut it,
(3) the person has sufficient AI literacy to be able to challenge and rebut the suggestion,
(4) the suggestion is accompanied by arguments as to why it was made (transparency and explainability), and
(5) that training and warning measures are taken to avoid accommodating bias on the part of the controller.

The digitalization of justice also involves automating processes, so automated decision-making must be integrated, in accordance with the following rule: the more significant the human intervention, the more significant the effects on the citizen. This criteria has been incorporated in the Spanish legislation,[109] which we will take as a case study in relation to the reasonable level of meaningful human intervention depending on the importance of the specific procedure. Thus, the following scale (see Table 3.1) can be proposed as a traffic light according to three degrees of significance of the act:[110]

Table 3.1 Level of human intervention depending on proceedings

Relevance of the proceedings	Level of human intervention
Resolutive acts that require a deliberative and argumentative process	Meaningful human intervention
Qualifying or resolutive acts, but which do not require a special deliberative and argumentative process	Individualized human supervision
Acts of mere formality, communications and non-final acts	General passive human supervision

These three levels correspond to the traffic light we have just summarized:

- Proactive automated actions are considered to be a subcategory of automated actions, self-initiated by information systems without human intervention that take advantage of information incorporated in a file to generate limited effects, such as notifications or notices.[111]

[109] See arts 56 to 58 SPA, on automated actions in the Administration of Justice, distinguishing between proactive automated actions, automated actions and assisted automated actions.
[110] Esteban de la Rosa et al (n 8) 88.
[111] Art 56.3 SPA.

- Automated actions are considered to be those procedural actions produced by programmed systems without the need for human intervention in each individual case, and will be encouraged in respect of procedural actions or simple decisions that do not require legal interpretation (eg pagination of files, referral of cases to the archive[112] or declaration of finality of a decision, in accordance with the corresponding procedural law).
- Finally, assisted actions are considered to be those in which an information system generates a total or partial draft of a complex data-based document that can serve as a basis or support for a judicial or procedural decision that requires a deliberative process.[113] With regard to the latter, meaningful human intervention is guaranteed when art 57.2 requires that the systems of the administration of justice ensure that the draft is only generated at the will of the user and can be freely and entirely modified by the user.

The right to human intervention with regard to automated actions is guaranteed, even at the review stage, when art 56.4 requires that automated actions can be identified as such, that it is possible to act on them in a non-automated way, and that it is possible to disable, reverse, or render them ineffective. It should be borne in mind that the production of automated sentences could be contrary to the Spanish Constitution, in such important aspects as the right to effective judicial protection (and particularly the duty to motivate sentences as part of this right) or the exclusive attribution of jurisdictional power to courts and tribunals.[114] Therefore, even in the case of substantially complete drafts of judgments, meaningful human review by Judges and Courts must be ensured.[115]

The use of AI tools and systems in justice has generated phenomena such as the so-called 'predictive justice', a term that is certainly used for a multitude of purposes, all associated with improving procedural efficiency and the quality of decision-making.[116] Within these purposes, the use of AI tools and systems in the inference of

[112] This would allow better compliance with the principle of storage limitation of personal data.

[113] Art 57.1. Spanish Royal Decree-Law 6/2023 of 19 December approving urgent measures for the implementation of the Recovery, Transformation and Resilience Plan in the areas of the Judiciary, the Civil Service, Local Government and Patronage (Spanish Royal Decree-Law 6/2023 of 19 December approving urgent measures for the implementation of the Recovery, Transformation and Resilience Plan in the areas of the Judiciary, the Civil Service, Local Government and Patronage (Real Decreto-ley 6/2023, de 19 de diciembre, por el que se aprueban medidas urgentes para la ejecución del Plan de Recuperación, Transformación y Resiliencia en materia de servicio público de justicia, función pública, régimen local y mecenazgo) (Spain).

[114] See arts 24 and 120.3 Spanish Constitution for the right to effective legal protection, and art 117.3 Spanish Constitution for the exclusive attribution of jurisdictional power to courts and tribunals. Also, as a general remark, art 18.4 Spanish Constitution states that the law shall limit the use of information technology in order to guarantee the honour and personal and family privacy of citizens and the full exercise of their rights. Esteban de la Rosa (n 70) 447.

[115] In France, although not in the judicial field but in the field of alternative dispute resolution, it has been established by law that companies providing online mediation or arbitration services are prohibited from leaving the final decision entirely to machine decision to be left entirely in the hands of machine algorithms. Therefore, there must always be a final phase to ensure human presence (art. 4.3 Act num 2019-222 of 23 March 2019 of programming 2018–22 and reform for justice—LOI n° 2019-222 du 23 mars 2019 de programmation 2018–22 et de réforme pour la justice).

[116] Jordi Gimeno, 'Instrumentos actuales de policía y justicia predictiva en el proceso penal español: análisis crítico y reflexiones de lege ferenda ante aplicaciones futuras' (2023) 44 Estudios Penales y Criminológicos 1, 7–8.

future judicial decisions stands out for its (hopeful and risky) potential. The hopeful potential lies in the improvement of procedural quality and efficiency. The main risk factors are possible discriminatory uses and a new form of infringement of the right of access to justice: if a citizen consults a predictive AI tool on their chances of success in court and receives low probability results, it is very likely that this will discourage them to the point that in many cases they will desist from initiating proceedings.

Some examples of predictive justice tools have been available since the beginning of this century. The first example was the Supreme Court Forecasting Project (2004), which aimed to predict the outcome of judicial decisions based on two parameters: (1) whether the court would affirm or reverse the appeal, and (2) how each individual judge would vote. It combined the use of a panel of expert analysts and a statistical model based on data from precedent cases. The model first analysed whether the cases met the characteristics of precedent with unanimous or conflicting rulings. Then, nine decision trees were used to predict each judge's vote, taking into account six different variables, the most decisive of which was the ideology of each judge. The model predicted the direction of the Court's ruling by 75 per cent (compared to 59.1 per cent for the expert panel), and the direction of each judge's vote by 66.7 per cent (compared to 67.9 per cent for the expert panel).[117] In 2017 the system was improved by applying machine learning techniques applied to almost 30,000 judgments and more than 240,000 individual votes of the Supreme Court from 1816 to 2015. The reliability of the direction of the judgment decreased (70.2 per cent), but the reliability of the direction of the individual votes of the judges increased (71.9 per cent).[118] In Europe, a predictive model has been developed on the jurisprudence of the European Court of Human Rights, using as a data set the jurisprudence of this Court in relation to three cases: prohibition of torture (Art. 3 ECHR), right to a fair trial (Art. 6 ECHR), and right to personal and family privacy (Art. 8 ECHR). The model achieved 79 per cent reliability about the direction of the judgment and showed that judges are strongly influenced by extra-legal factors related to the facts and circumstances of each case.[119] Other examples are the Lex Machina tool designed by Stanford University and owned by Lexis Nexis since 2015, Ravel Law, designed by Standford Law School students with support from the Harvard Law Library, or Jurimetrics, owned by Wolters Kluwer.[120]

The elaboration of quantifications on data relating to the decisions of individual judges and magistrates affects their rights to privacy and private life and to the protection of personal data. It should not be forgotten that according to the broad notion of personal data established in art 4.1 GPDR, profiles, whether of judges, arbitrators, mediators, or citizens, are also personal data. This consideration has been taken to the

[117] Theodore Ruger et al, 'Supreme Court Forecasting Project: Legal and Political Science Approaches to Supreme Court Decision-Making' [2004] Columbia L Rev <https://scholarship.law.upenn.edu/faculty_scholarship/672> last accessed 26 December 2024.

[118] Daniel Martin Katz, Michael J Bommarito Ii, and Josh Blackman, 'A General Approach for Predicting the Behavior of the Supreme Court of the United States' (2017) 12 PLOS ONE <https://journals.plos.org/plosone/article?id = 10.1371/journal.pone.0174698> last accessed 26 December 2024.

[119] Masha Medvedeva, Michel Vols, and Martijn Wieling, 'Using Machine Learning to Predict Decisions of the European Court of Human Rights' (2020) 28 Artificial Intelligence and Law 237.

[120] Íñigo Gutiérrez Gómez, 'La Justicia Predictiva: Límites y Usos Procesales' (Universidad de Cantabria 2023) 27–31.

extreme in France, where the use of AI machines to create profiles and predict the behaviour of judges has been criminalized.[121]

Both the use of profiling with special categories of data that may cause discriminatory effects in criminal proceedings and, in general, the use of profiling that may cause discriminatory effects in all types of proceedings should be avoided. We support this assertion on the following grounds:

- Art 22 GDPR prohibits fully automated decision-making that entails legal or significant effects, and discriminatory treatment is significant. art 21 ECFR prohibits all forms of discrimination, and thus also discrimination that takes place in the context of fully automated decision-making or suggestions. It should be added that many of the discriminatory factors listed in art 21.1 ECFR coincide with the so-called special categories of personal data.
- The right to an effective judicial protection[122] and the presumption of innocence must be guaranteed in all proceedings,[123] and a profile, an automated suggestion or an automated decision leading to discriminatory effects may jeopardize both the right to an effective remedy (in particular the right not to be defenceless) and the right to the presumption of innocence.

It should be borne in mind that discrimination exists not only when a person is treated less favourably because of one or more of his or her characteristics (direct discrimination), but also when an apparently neutral rule, criterion, or usual practice places persons from certain groups at a disadvantage or in front of treatment that is unfavourable in relation to others in a similar situation without a justified reason or, if such a reason exists, when the means are not proportionate and appropriate (indirect discrimination). It is very difficult to find situations of direct discrimination in the case of the use of AI tools, which is understandable in view of the right to equality before the law,[124] although it cannot be ruled out. The protection against indirect discrimination in the use of AI tools in the field of justice allows greater focus on the overall effects of these tools and not so much on specific details about their parameters and functioning. However, some of the challenges related to situations of indirect discrimination in the use of AI tools are group privacy or the use of proxy data.

The notion of group privacy has been coined by Luciano Floridi. The 'group' is a functional or ad hoc concept that depends on the choices previously established in each data analytics operation in terms of (1) observable elements, (2) purposes for which they are observed, and (3) limitations of the analyzed sets). These ad hoc groups may refer to very specific groups that are difficult to protect by anti-discrimination rules, even if we focus on protection against indirect discrimination.

The use of 'proxy' data or indicators to circumvent prohibitions on weighting special category data. Proxies are alternative indicators that allow inferences to be made about an individual's characteristics. Consider, for example, the prohibition in many countries on using cancer data in insurance contracts or in assessing creditworthiness

[121] Esteban de la Rosa et al (n 8) 82.
[122] ibid.
[123] Art 47 and 48 ECFR.
[124] Art 20 ECFR.

for loan applications.[125] However, there may be less problematic data that allow inferring that the person has suffered from cancer, and it is precisely this other data (proxies) that the AI tool uses and evaluates. Below are some examples (see Figure 3.1) for illustrative purposes only, but above all it should be emphasized that although this type of discrimination is more difficult to detect, it is nonetheless a form of discrimination, as Weerts et al show:[126]

Automated decisions and suggestions may be based on data provided by the data subject, observed data, or inferred data (including conclusions derived from profiling). It is particularly important to monitor the quality of the data both in profiling and in automated decision-making and suggestions. Quality data are data that are relevant, sufficiently representative, free of errors as far as possible and complete for the intended purpose of use,[127] and that take into account the particular characteristics of the specific geographic, contextual, behavioural, or functional environment in which the AI tool is intended to be used.[128] High-quality data and access to high-quality data play an essential role in providing structure and ensuring the performance of many AI tools, especially when techniques involving model training are employed.[129] If the AI tool is not trained with good quality data, does not meet adequate requirements in terms of performance, accuracy, or robustness, or is not properly designed and tested before it is introduced to the market or put into service, it is possible that it will discriminatorily, incorrectly, or unfairly single out individuals.[130] The data quality principle as expressed by the AI Act is clearly related to the GDPR's principle of accuracy in data processing,[131] according to which data shall be accurate and up to date taking into account the purpose of the processing. If the data used in an automated decision or elaboration process are inaccurate, any resulting decision or profile will be flawed and may lead to incorrect inferences that would result in an equally wrong decision (automated or not). Art 3 AI Act specifies what is to be understood by 'accurate and up-to-date' data in the case of its use in AI tools, and thus serves as an interpretative criterion for art 5.1.d GDPR regardless of whether or not the AI Act is applicable to the specific tool.

Notwithstanding the above, the preservation of data quality should not be an argument for hiding from the users of the tool or those affected by the suggestions or decisions that the tool makes (1) the data from which it draws, or (2) the operating parameters of the model. This was the argument made by the Dutch government in the SyRI case.[132] In this case, the District Court of The Hague found that: (1) it is lawful

[125] A brief list of these initiatives is available at Jose Antonio Castillo Parrilla, 'Crédito Ao Consumo, Avaliação Da Solvabilidade e Esquecimento Oncológico à Luz Da Diretiva 2225/2023' (28 November 2023) <https://novaconsumerlab.novalaw.unl.pt/credito-ao-consumo-avaliacao-da-solvabilidade-e-esquecimento-oncologico-a-luz-da-diretiva-2225-2023/> last accessed 26 December 2024.

[126] Hilde Weerts et al, 'Unlawful Proxy Discrimination: A Framework for Challenging Inherently Discriminatory Algorithms', *Proceedings of the 2024 ACM Conference on Fairness, Accountability, and Transparency* (Association for Computing Machinery 2024) 1853 <https://dl.acm.org/doi/10.1145/3630106.3659010> accessed 30 October 2024.

[127] Art 3.1 AI Act.

[128] Art 3.4 AI Act.

[129] Rec 67 AI Act.

[130] Rec 59 AI Act.

[131] Art 5.1.d AI Act.

[132] *SyRI Case* [2020] The Hague District Court C-09-550982-HA ZA 18-388.

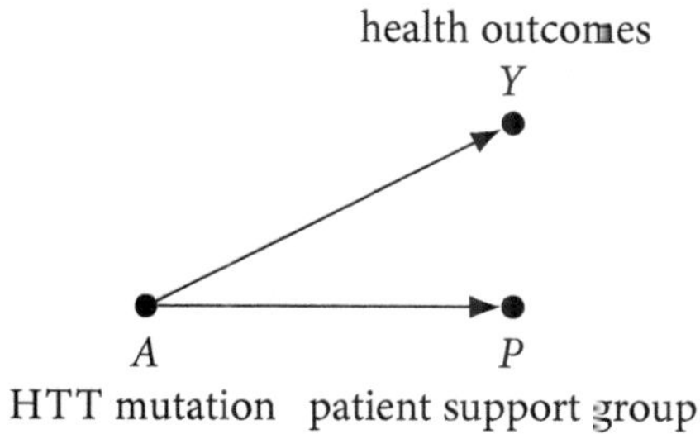

(a) Example of proxy discrimination as defined by [47]. P **is associated with** Y**, due to a direct causal link between** A **and** Y **(via path** $Y \leftarrow A \rightarrow P$**).**

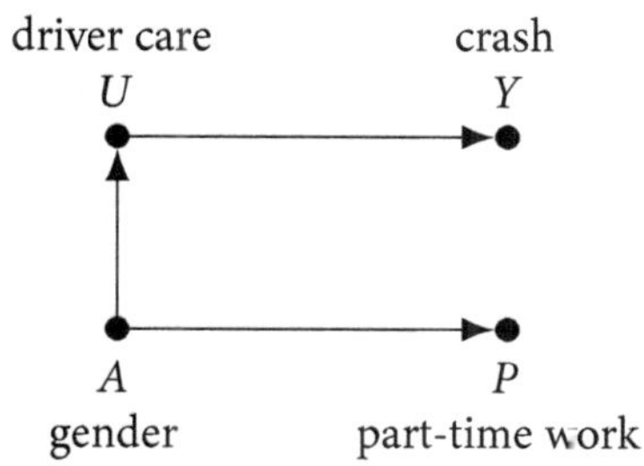

(b) Example of proxy discrimination as defined by [47]. P **is associated with** Y**, due to an indirect causal link between** A **and** Y **(via path** $Y \leftarrow U \leftarrow A \rightarrow P$**).**

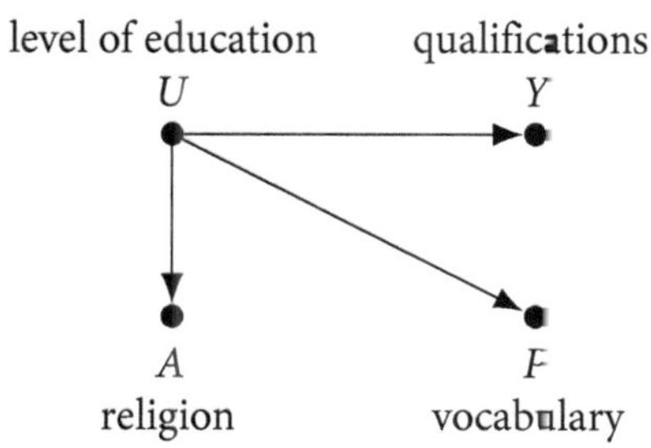

(c) Example of indirect non-proxy discrimination, according to [47]. P **is associated with** Y**, but the predictive power is not derived from its relationship with** A **but its relationship with** U **(via path** $P \leftarrow U \rightarrow Y$**).**

Figure 3.1 Proxy discrimination scheme (Weerts et al, 2024)

to use such instruments as long as there is a justifiable public interest and appropriate measures are taken to ensure the minimum necessary interference with the right to privacy; and (2) that the implementation of SyRI does not provide sufficient guarantees to consider that this particular system respects the necessary proportionality test that any interference with privacy must pass under Article 8 of the European Convention on Human Rights (ECHR).[133] According to the Dutch government's argumentation, the functioning of the algorithm had to be obscure, otherwise mass data on citizens' behaviour of sufficient quality would not be obtained.[134] The case as a whole, and also the surprising argumentation of the Dutch government, underline the need to emphasize the importance of transparency as an essential tool for the protection of the rights and interests of individuals affected by its use, in general, and certainly also when the tool is used in judicial or ADR proceedings.

Transparency is a polysemous and instrumental concept, and above all it can be considered from different points of view. As far as this paper is concerned, the important aspects are (1) transparency of data processing,[135] and (2) transparency of the AI tool.[136] Transparency and explainability are treated together in much of the various AI policy documents, although they are neither absolute synonyms nor fully interrelated. Among other documents, the Ethical Guidelines for Trustworthy AI[137] deserve special attention, which includes a checklist to verify the degree of transparency and explainability of AI tools that we will take as a reference in the final section of this paper. Transparency means that AI tools are developed and used in a way that allows for adequate traceability and explainability, while at the same time making individuals aware that they are communicating or interacting with an AI tool and duly informing those responsible for deployment about the capabilities and limitations of the AI tool and affected individuals about their rights.[138] Explainability implies intelligibility of the input, output, and operation of each algorithmic component and its importance in the results; that is, it makes it possible to describe how the model generates predictions in such a way that the system is understandable to its users and that they have the possibility of tracing (and questioning) the decisions or suggestions produced. Although, in principle, less transparency also means less explainability, transparency by itself does not guarantee explainability. In this paper we will speak of transparency to refer to both transparency and explainability.

It should also be borne in mind that transparency, both in data processing and with respect to the functioning of AI, is instrumental: it allows a better guarantee of data protection rights as well as others, such as the right to equality and non-discrimination or the right to effective judicial protection; and it also allows verification of the proper functioning of the AI tool by all subjects in the value chain. For example, if we do not know that an AI tool is using outdated data, we will not be able to request its rectification or detect biases derived from poor data quality, and if we do not know the

[133] Guillermo Lazcoz Moratinos and José Antonio Castillo Parrilla, 'Valoración Algorítmica Ante Los Derechos Humanos y El Reglamento General de Protección de Datos: El Caso SyRI' (2020) 9 Revista chilena de derecho y tecnología 207.

[134] Paragraph 6.49 of the Judgment.

[135] Art 5.1.a and Rec 71 GDPR.

[136] Art 13.1 AI Act.

[137] HLEG on Artificial Intelligence, 'Ethics Guidelines for Trustworthy AI | Shaping Europe's Digital Future' (European Commission 2019) <https://digital-strategy.ec.europa.eu/en/library/ethics-guidelines-trustworthy-ai> last accessed 7 January 2025.

[138] Rec. 27 AI Act.

operating parameters, we will not be able to detect forms of discrimination; all of which can lead to situations of defencelessness in a process.

The transparency of AI tools is especially important in the public sector, of which the administration of Justice is part, allowing a better respect of the guarantees of administrative action and due process; including the possibility to challenge the decision to the extent that such challenge will be on the reasons for the decision. It is also a fundamental instrument for the generation of trust in the AI systems, as well as for accountability, which is required of any AI tool insofar as it processes personal data under art 5.2 GDPR. Moreover, it should be added that if AI tools translate the law into code, the principle of publicity of the rules must be understood to apply not only to the 'translated law' but also to the translating tool. If ignorance of the rules does not exempt from compliance with them,[139] the minimum is that these rules (and the AI tools that enable their more or less automated application) are understandable to the citizens who will have to comply with them.

It is worth asking about the specific content of transparency: how much transparency is required. It should be remembered that transparency is an instrumental concept, and therefore the level of transparency required will depend on the purpose that transparency is intended to achieve. In addition to this, criteria such as the following can be taken into account to determine the greater or lesser degree of transparency required: (1) the impact of the AI tool on the decision, the outcome and the citizen; (2) the degree of human intervention in the decision making; and (3) the type and complexity of the algorithm. Finally, despite what it may seem, an excess of transparency can be counterproductive for the better knowledge and understanding of the AI tool. Therefore, the above criteria must be taken into account to set the advisable level of transparency, both minimum and maximum. In other words, the transparency and explainability binomial does not require total transparency of the model, but rather that its recipients be informed in a broad sense of its main operating parameters and the reasons why some are more important than others. This balance can be seen, beyond the AI Act, in art 5.1 P2BR.[140]

AI tools must be sufficiently transparent so that their output results can be correctly interpreted and used (cf art 13.1 AI Act), ie that the practitioners in charge of interpreting and using the automated suggestions or decisions have elements of judgment to question the result (internal transparency), and that in the same way the citizens affected by them can control (and, if necessary, appeal) such decisions (external transparency). On generative AI tools, from the perspective of both internal and external transparency, it is important that their respective users (either judges, justices, arbitrators, mediators, or even lawyers) communicate that they are using generative AI tools in their writings. Not only transparency is important when using generative AI tools, but also subsequent human review should be monitored in order to avoid hallucinations or inventions of the AI, such as reference to non-existent rulings or bibliography.

[139] Art 6.1 TC.

[140] Regulation (EU) 2019/1150 of the European Parliament and of the Council of 20 June 2019 on promoting fairness and transparency for business users of online intermediation services [2019] OJ L186.

The transparency of AI tools used in justice brings significant benefits beyond the strictly digital. In the first place, the right to effective judicial protection[141] contemplates the right to a decision that is reasoned on the merits and founded in law, as well as the right to appeal, to the presumption of innocence and not to suffer defencelessness. The resolution must be motivated by a human being, and an opaque tool does not allow the person receiving it to know (and, above all, have the opportunity to share or not) the reasons for the suggestion. Therefore, it is essential for an AI tool not to make fully automated decisions not only to allow human review, but for it to be meaningful; and it will be meaningful, (1) if the tool clearly states the reasons why it suggests one thing or another, and (2) if the human in charge of receiving the suggestion has the capacity (because the rule allows it, and because it does not impose particularly burdensome additional obligations if he does not follow the AI suggestion), and sufficient training (in law, and in AI) to decide freely whether or not to share the criterion.

The adequate training of the user of the tool is part of the so-called AI Literacy. AI Literacy is understood as

> skills, knowledge and understanding that allow providers, deployers and affected persons, taking into account their respective rights and obligations in the context of this Regulation, to make an informed deployment of AI systems, as well as to gain awareness about the opportunities and risks of AI and possible harm it can cause.[142]

Like transparency, AI literacy is instrumental: it allows obtainment of the greatest benefits from the use of AI tools while protecting fundamental rights, health and safety, and democratic control.[143] Also in the same way as transparency, AI literacy can be projected on the users of the AI tool or on the citizenship in general, requiring different degrees of intensity: (1) basic AI literacy so that citizens have the necessary knowledge to interpret it, and (2) more advanced AI literacy that allows the users of the tool to correctly interpret and apply its results, for which voluntary codes of conduct can be useful.

Those responsible for the deployment of AI systems shall take measures to ensure that, to the greatest extent possible, their personnel and other persons in charge of using the AI tool have a sufficient level of AI literacy taking into account the knowledge, experience, and training level required in each specific position.[144] As we have already stated above, the AI Act can act as an interpretative criterion for rules already in force, such as the GDPR. To the extent that AI literacy allows a better protection of fundamental rights (particularly, of art 22 GDPR), the data controller must provide its staff with a sufficient level of AI literacy of the users of the AI tool to ensure the adequate respect of art 22 GDPR and the rest of the data protection rights as well

[141] Art 24 Spanish Constitution. (CE) Spanish Constitution (Constitución Española) (Spain)
[142] Art 3.56 AI Act.
[143] Rec 20 AI Act.
[144] Art 4 AI Act.

as, indirectly, the right to effective judicial protection. In the case of the administration of justice, art 236 bis Organic Law of the Judiciary Power (OLJ)[145] considers each competent body (court or tribunal) responsible for the processing of personal data, although further on, art 236 *sexies* OLJ specifies that the Endowment Administration will be responsible for providing the technological means and the appropriate organizational measures for the correct processing of personal data, so that the said Endowment Administration will be responsible for ensuring the adequate AI Literacy of Judges and Magistrates. In the case of ADR systems, the ADR platform itself, in its capacity as data controller, will be responsible for providing the appropriate and necessary AI Literacy to arbitrators and mediators.

E. Conclusions: development of a traffic light to inform on the impact of the incorporation of certain AI tools in advanced justice systems

In this last section we do not intend to carry out an impact assessment per se, but rather to use the impact assessment technique to systematize as conclusions what has been seen in this chapter through a model that allows the most complete assessment possible through common parameters of the different tools that can be implemented to advance the digitalization of justice.

The tables we propose synthesize the key aspects described in this chapter regarding the protection of personal data and cybersecurity in the use of AI tools, focusing on four major aspects: (1) protection of personal data in general (see Table 3.2); (2) cybersecurity (see Table 3.3); (3) automated decision-making and suggestions (see Table 3.4), and (4) transparency and explainability of AI tools (see Table 3.5). We have taken into account not only the criteria strictly related to personal data protection and cybersecurity, but also the various documents and reports of international organizations and Spanish initiatives on the digitalization of the Administration of Justice. The answers that can be inserted in the proposed checklist are binary (yes/no). We have tried to ensure that each item has an equivalent weight in the set, so that later it can be assessed in a global way how the specific tool responds to the protection of each specific aspect in a percentage. This answer would then allow a classification of the tools according to a traffic light system similar to the one proposed in the COTEC Guide for AI tools in justice[146]: red (below 50 per cent), yellow (from 50 to 80 per cent) and green (above 80 per cent).

[145] Organic Law 6/1985 of 1 July, on the Judiciary Power (Ley Orgánica 6/1985, de 1 de Julio, del Poder Judicial (OLJP).

[146] Esteban de la Rosa et al (n 8) 84–86.

Table 3.2 Questionnaire on how AI tools affect justice. Principles on data processing (author's own)

Principles on data processing		
Principle	**Item**	**Answer (yes/no)**
Lawfulness, fairness and transparency	Are there rules that provide a legal ground for the processing of the data subject's data through the tool?	
	Are there mechanisms to clearly and comprehensibly inform the data subject about the processing of his/her personal data through the tool?	
Purpose limitation & storage limitation	Is adequate anonymization of personal data ensured prior to the publication of resolutions for general knowledge?	
	Are firewalls in place to prevent data leakage or unintended use of data? For example, logical separation between data packages according to their intended purpose.	
	Does the tool have alerts to warn of the desirability of deleting data that no longer needs to be retained?	
Data minimisation	Does the tool collect only the data necessary for the court to function?	
	Does the tool avoid collecting biometric or image data, unless strictly necessary?	
Accuracy	Are there mechanisms in place to facilitate the data subject's reporting of any inaccuracies in personal data?	
Accountability	Has the provisioning Administration of the tool trained and made its staff aware of the need to accredit and document the correct use of digital tools from the perspective of the principles related to data processing?	
	Does the tool have self-registration mechanisms that facilitate compliance with the principle of accountability?	
Data protection by design and by default	Has a general impact assessment of the tool been carried out?	
	If yes, will the recommendations for improvement be reviewed on an annual basis?	

Table 3.3 Questionnaire on how AI tools affect justice. Integrity and confidentiality (author's own)

Integrity and confidentiality Have protocols been established		
Items		**Answer (yes/no)**
Based on a zero trust strategy?		
For staff training and awareness	About identity and access management	
	About cyberthreats, internal and external	
To pseudonymize and encrypt personal data		
To ensure the permanent confidentiality, integrity, availability and resilience of processing systems and services?		
To ensure the availability and rapid access to personal data in the event of incidents?		
To ensure identification of users and prevent unauthorized access to confidential data?		
To prevent unwanted alteration or deletion of data?		
To ensure the interoperability of documents?		
To ensure software updates by justice administration staff and practitioners?		
To enable notification of data breaches to the supervisory authority without undue delay?		
To enable notification of data breaches to the data subject without undue delay?		
To periodically review the measures taken to ensure the security and integrity of the data and its processing?		

Table 3.4 Questionnaire on how AI tools affect justice. Automated decisions and data protection (author's own)

Automated decisions and data protection when using AI tools in Justice systems		
Item		**Answer (yes/no)**
Are the results of the AI tool likely to produce significant or negative legal effects on the data subject?		*If the answer is no, the test ends here. In compliance with data protection by design and by default (art. 25 GDPR), it must be sufficiently reasoned why there are no significant or negative legal effects possible.
Are measures established to prevent the AI tool from causing discrimination (direct, indirect or functional)? *Criteria are detailed in a separate table	Internal transparency* External transparency* Exclusion of unwanted bias Data quality monitoring	
Does the context in which the tool is used allow for fully automated decisions (e.g., procedural decisions)?	If yes, is it clearly indicated?	*If yes, the test ends here.
Are measures in place to ensure meaningful human intervention in the use of the tool? For example . . .	AI Literacy of the persons who will be using the tool Rules guaranteeing the independence of judgment of the decision maker (e.g., no direct or indirect retaliation for departing from the automated suggestion)	

Table 3.5 Questionnaire on how AI tools affect justice. Transparency and explainability (author's own)

Transparency and explainability of AI tools		
Items		**Answer (yes/no)**
Design traceability - Have the methods for design and development of the AI tool been documented?	*In expert systems, the programming method and the way the model was created should be documented ** In machine learning systems, the method of training the algorithm, and the collection and selection of input data must be documented.	
Test and validation traceability - Have the methods for testing and validating the AI tool been documented?	*In rule systems, use cases used for testing and validation should be documented ** In machine learning systems, information on data used for testing and validation should be documented	
Traceability of results	Have the results of the decisions or suggestions produced been documented? Have the results been compared on a case-by-case basis?	
Interpretability - Has the principle of interpretability been taken into account in...	...the design of the AI tool? ...the testing and validation of the AI tool?	
Internal transparency - Has it been assessed whether the results (and their motivations) are understandable to the users of the AI tool?		
External transparency	Has it been assessed whether the results (and their motivations) are understandable to the citizens affected by the AI tool? Has it been assessed whether the motivation is sufficient to make it easier for the person concerned to appeal?	
Transparency and impact of the decision - Has the expected impact of the decision or suggestion been taken into account when assessing all the above parameters? *The deeper the impact, the more transparency is required.		
External transparency - Writing assistants	Are citizens or those affected by the decision informed that their rationale has been written in whole or in part by a generative AI tool? Are practitioners using the tool obliged to a subsequent human review of the result? Are they informed of the professional liability they may incur if they fail to carry out this subsequent human review?	

Bibliography

Alemán Aróstegui L, 'El uso de RISCANVI en la toma de decisiones penitenciarias' (2023) 44 Estudios Penales y Criminológicos 1.

Article 29 Data Protection Working Party, 'Opinion 04/2007 on the Concept of Personal Data' (2007) <https://www.pdp.ie/docs/1030.pdf> .

'Opinion 05/2014 on Anonymisation Techniques' (2014) <https://ec.europa.eu/justice/art.-29/documentation/opinion-recommendation/files/2014/wp216_en.pdf>.

'Guidelines on Automated Individual Decision-Making and Profiling for the Purposes of Regulation 2016/679' (2018) <https://ec.europa.eu/newsroom/art.29/items/612053/en>.

'Guidelines on Personal Data Breach Notification under Regulation 2016/679' (2018) <https://ec.europa.eu/newsroom/art.29/items/612052>.

Barona Vilar S, 'Las ADR En La Justicia Del Siglo XXI, En Especial La Mediación' (2011) 18 Revista de derecho (Coquimbo) 185.

Brkan M, 'Do Algorithms Rule the World? Algorithmic Decision-Making and Data Protection in the Framework of the GDPR and Beyond' (2019) 27 International Journal of Law and Information Technology 91.

Castillo Parrilla JA, 'Crédito Ao Consumo, Avaliação Da Solvabilidade e Esquecimento Oncológico à Luz Da Diretiva 2225/2023' (28 November 2023) <https://novaconsumerlab.novalaw.unl.pt/credito-ao-consumo-avaliacao-da-solvabilidade-e-esquecimento-oncologico-a-luz-da-diretiva-2225-2023/>.

Cortés P and Esteban de la Rosa F, 'La Normativa Europea de Resolución de Conflictos de Consumo y Su Transposicióin En España: Una Oportunidad Para Mejorar Los Derechos de Los Consumidores Aprovechando Las Experiencias Positivas En El Derecho Comparado' (ADICAE 2016) https://www.congreso.es/docu/docum/ddocum/dosieres/sleg/legislatura_12/spl_5/pdfs/46.pdf.

Cotino Hueso L, 'La Primera Sentencia Del Tribunal de Justicia de La Unión Europea Sobre Decisiones Automatizadas y Sus Implicaciones Para La Protección de Datos y El Reglamento de Inteligencia Artificial' [2024] Diario La Ley <https://diariolaley.laleynext.es/Content/Documento.aspx?params=H4sIAAAAAAAEAFWNMQ7CMBAEf-P6YpCAwlXMD9yjJLdGJ6w7dAFEfk9SpGDLkWZWmFMutO5wITqdwwc-i2mKFI_UdTGoMUru01sZVRQc2jCi9RvG95XuULhMV3fzzZa6ZJvK8kSqQ5sRMJo9_k5ue_wHc7CJiX4AAAA=WKE>.

Council of Europe, 'Online Dispute Resolution Mechanisms in Civil and Administrative Court Proceedings' (2021)< https://rm.coe.int/publication-guidelines-and-explanatory-memoreandum-odr-mechanisms-in-c/1680a4214e>.

Council of the European Union, 'Presidency Conclusions—The Charter of Fundamental Rights in the Context of Artificial Intelligence and Digital Change' (2020) 11481/20 <https://data.consilium.europa.eu/doc/document/ST-11481-2020-INIT/es/pdf>.

Cremades Sanz-Pastor BM, 'Arbitraje' in Pendás M (ed), Enciclopedia de las Ciencias Morales y Políticas para el siglo XXI: Ciencias Políticas y Jurídicas (con especial referencia a la sociedad poscovid 19) (Real Academia de Ciencias Morales y Políticas 2020) <https://racmyp.es/wp-content/uploads/2023/06/2020-0592_enciclopedia_ciencias_morales_acc_ee_final.pdf>.

Delgado Martín J, 'Una Concepción Integral Del Expediente Judicial Electrónico' [2012] Revista Aranzadi de derecho y nuevas tecnologías 119.

Directorate-General for Justice and Consumers, 'Digitalisation of Justice in the European Union A Toolbox of Opportunities' (European Commission 2020) <https://eur-lex.europa.eu/legal-content/EN/ALL/?uri=COM:2020:710:FIN>.

European Commission, 'The 2024 EU Justice Scoreboard: Communication from the Commission to the European Parliament, the Council, the European Central Bank, the European Economic and Social Committee and the Committee of the Regions' (2024) https://commission.europa.eu/document/download/84aa3726-82d7-4401-98c1-fee04a7d2dd6_en?filename=2024%20EU%20Justice%20Scoreboard.pdf.

European Commission for the Efficiency of Justice, '2022–2025 CEPEJ Action Plan: "Digitalisation fr a Better Justice"' <https://rm.coe.int/cepej-2021-12-en-cepej-action-plan-2022-2025-digitalisation-justice/1680a4cf2c>.

'European Judicial Systems CEPEJ Evaluation Report' (2020) <https://rm.coe.int/evaluation-report-part-1-english/16809fc058>.

'European Judicial Systems CEPEJ Evaluation Report—Part 1, General Analyses' (2024) <https://rm.coe.int/cepej-evaluation-report-2024-general-analyses/1680b1e91d>.

European Commission for the Efficiency of Justice, 'Digitalisation for a Better Justice' (2021) <https://rm.coe.int/cepej-2021-12-en-cepej-action-plan-2022-2025-digitalisation-justice/1680a4cf2c>.

European Court of Justice, 'Case C-634/21 OQ v Land Hessen' [2005] ECJ (Shufa Case).

European Data Protection Board, 'Guidelines 4/2019 on Article 25 Data Protection by Design and by Default Version 2.0' (2020) <https://www.edpb.europa.eu/sites/default/files/files/file1/edpb_guidelines_201904_dataprotection_by_design_and_by_default_v2.0_en.pdf>.

European Data Protection Supervisor, 'Guidelines 3/2019 on Processing of Personal Data through Video Devices Version 2.0' (2020) <https://www.edpb.europa.eu/sites/default/files/files/file1/edpb_guidelines_201903_video_devices_en_0.pdf>.

European Data Protection Supervisor and European Data Protection Board, 'Joint Opinion 5/2021 on the Proposal for a Regulation of the European Parliament and of the Council Laying down Harmonised Rules on Artificial Intelligence (Artificial Intelligence Act)' (2021).

Esteban de la Rosa F., 'Construyendo El Marco Legal Europeo Para El Diseño y Uso de Herramientas de Inteligencia Artificial En El Entorno de La Justicia Civil-Administrativa', *El derecho y la inteligencia artificial* (Editorial Universidad de Granada. 2022) <https://digibug.ugr.es/bitstream/handle/10481/82089/VERSION%20PUBLICADA%20EN%20DIGIBUG.pdf?sequence=1&isAllowed=y>.

Esteban de la Rosa F et al, 'Justicia Digital, Guía Para El Diálogo Sobre El Diseño y El Uso Eficiente, de Calidad y Ético de Herramientas Tecnológicas En La Justicia Civil' (*Fundación COTEC para la Innovación*, 2022) <https://cotec.es/proyectos-cpt/guia-para-la-justicia-digital/>.

'Guidelines on Automated Individual Decision-Making and Profiling for the Purposes of Regulation 2016/679' (2018) <https://ec.europa.eu/newsroom/art.29/items/612053/en>.

'Guidelines on Personal Data Breach Notification under Regulation 2016/679' (2018) <https://ec.europa.eu/newsroom/art.29/items/612052>.

Gimeno J, 'Instrumentos actuales de policía y justicia predictiva en el proceso penal español: análisis crítico y reflexiones de lege ferenda ante aplicaciones futuras' (2023) 44 Estudios Penales y Criminológicos 1.

Gutiérrez Gómez I, 'La Justicia Predictiva: Límites y Usos Procesales' (Universidad de Cantabria 2023) <https://revistas.usc.gal/index.php/epc/article/view/9027>.

International Telecommunication Union, 'Global Cybersecurity Index 2024 5th Edition' (2024) <https://www.itu.int/en/ITU-D/Cybersecurity/Documents/GCIv5/2401416_1b_Global-Cybersecurity-Index-E.pdf>.

Katz DM, Bommarito Ii MJ, and Blackman J, 'A General Approach for Predicting the Behavior of the Supreme Court of the United States' (2017) 12 PLOS ONE <https://journals.plos.org/plosone/article?id=10.1371/journal.pone.0174698>.

Lazcoz Moratinos G, 'Gobernanza y supervisión humana de la toma de decisiones automatizada basada en la elaboración de perfiles/governance and human oversight of automated decision-making based on profiling' (Universidad del País Vasco - Euskal Herriko Unibertsitatea 2023) <https://dialnet.unirioja.es/servlet/tesis?codigo=318838>.

López ÁG and Martín MJR, 'Incertidumbres algorítmicas en torno a las violencias de género. El caso del sistema VioGén y otros sistemas de predicción del riesgo' (2024) 33 Revista Española de Sociología 1.

Medvedeva M, Vols M, and Wieling M, 'Using Machine Learning to Predict Decisions of the European Court of Human Rights' (2020) 28 Artificial Intelligence and Law 237.

'Opinion 05/2014 on Anonymisation Techniques' (2014) <https://ec.europa.eu/justice/art.-29/documentation/opinion-recommendation/files/2014/wp216_en.pdf>.

Parasuraman R and Manzey DH, 'Complacency and Bias in Human Use of Automation: An Attentional Integration' (2010) 52 Human Factors 381.

Ribagorda Garnacho A, 'La seguridad del tratamiento en el ámbito de las Administraciones Públicas: la ciberseguridad (Comentario al artículo 32 RGPD y a la Disposición adicional primera LOPDGDD)', *Comentario al Reglamento General de Protección de Datos y a la Ley Orgánica de*

Protección de Datos personales y Garantía de los Derechos Digitales, Vol. 1, 2021, ISBN 978-84-9197-925-8, págs. 2009-2032 (Thomson Reuters Aranzadi 2021) <https://dialnet.unirioja.es/servlet/articulo?codigo=7915633>.

Rubio Llorente F, 'El principio de legalidad' (1993) 13 Revista española de derecho constitucional 9.

Ruger T, Pauline K, Andrew M, and Kevin Q, 'Supreme Court Forecasting Project: Legal and Political Science Approaches to Supreme Court Decision-Making' [2004] Columbia L Rev <https://scholarship.law.upenn.edu/faculty_scholarship/672>.

San Miguel Caso C, 'Inteligencia Artificial y Algoritmos: La Controvertida Evolución de La Tutela Judicial Efectiva En El Proceso Penal' [2023] Estudios penales y criminológicos <https://revistas.usc.gal/index.php/epc/article/view/8859/13292>.

Schumann Barragán G, 'La Inteligencia Artificial Aplicada al Proceso Penal Desde La Perspectiva de La UE' en Pereira Puigvert S, Ordóñez Ponz, F (dirs),

Investigación y proceso penal en el siglo XXI: nuevas tecnologías y protección de datos (Aranzadi 2021).

Simón Castellano P, *La Prisión Algorítmica: Prevención, Reinserción Social y Tutela de Derechos Fundamentales En El Paradigma de Los Centros Penitenciarios Inteligentes* (Tirant lo Blanch 2022).

Simon J, Wong P-H, and Rieder G, 'Algorithmic Bias and the Value Sensitive Design Approach' (2020) 9 Internet Policy Rev <https://policyreview.info/concepts/algorithmic-bias>.

Spanish Constitutional Court, Case 292/2000.

Spanish Constitutional Court, Case 292/1982.

Spanish Constitutional Court, Case E/02554/2017.

Spanish Data Protection Agency, 'Adecuación al RGPD de Tratamientos Que Incorporan Inteligencia Artificial. Una Introducción' (2020) <https://www.aepd.es/guias/adecuacion-rgpd-ia.pdf>.

Susskind RE, 'Expert Systems in Law: A Jurisprudential Approach to Artificial Intelligence and Legal Reasoning' (1987) 49 The Modern L Rev 168.

The Hague District Court, 'SyRI Case' [2020] C-09-550982-HA ZA 18-388 International Telecommunication Union, 'Global Cybersecurity Index 2024 5th Edition' (2024) <https://www.itu.int/en/ITU-D/Cybersecurity/Documents/GCIv5/2401416_1b_Global-Cybersecurity-Index-E.pdf>.

Troncoso Reigada A, 'Los Principios Relativos al Tratamiento (Comentario al Artículo 5 RGPD y al Artículo 4 LOPDGDD)' in Troncoso Reigada A (ed), *Comentario al Reglamento General de Protección de Datos y a la Ley Orgánica de Protección de Datos personales y Garantía de los Derechos Digitales, Vol. 1* (Thomson Reuters Aranzadi 2021).

Valls Prieto J, *Inteligencia artificial, Derechos humanos y bienes jurídicos* (Thomson Reuters Aranzadi 2021) <https://dialnet.unirioja.es/servlet/libro?codigo=847600>.

Veale M and Edwards L, 'Clarity, Surprises, and Further Questions in the Article 29 Working Party Draft Guidance on Automated Decision-Making and Profiling' (2018) 34 Computer Law & Security Rev 398.

Vilasau Solana M, 'La Realización de Perfiles y La Salvaguardia de Los Derechos y Libertades Del Afectado' in Cerrillo i Martínez A and Peguera Poch M (eds), *Retos jurídicos de la inteligencia artificial* (Thomson Reuters Aranzadi 2020).

Wachter S, Mittelstadt B, and Floridi L, 'Why a Right to Explanation of Automated Decision-Making Does Not Exist in the General Data Protection Regulation' (Social Science Research Network, 28 December 2016) <https://papers.ssrn.com/abstract=2903469>.

Weerts, H, Binns R, Kelly-Lyth A, Adams-Prassl J, 'Unlawful Proxy Discrimination: A Framework for Challenging Inherently Discriminatory Algorithms', *Proceedings of the 2024 ACM Conference on Fairness, Accountability, and Transparency* (Association for Computing Machinery 2024) 1853 <https://dl.acm.org/doi/10.1145/3630106.3659010> accessed 30 October 2024.

Yeoh W et al, 'Zero Trust Cybersecurity: Critical Success Factors and A Maturity Assessment Framework' (2023) 133 Computers & Security 103412.

Zeleznikow J, 'Can Artificial Intelligence and Online Dispute Resolution Enhance Efficiency and Effectiveness in Courts' (2017) 8 International Journal for Court Administration <https://iacajournal.org/articles/10.18352/ijca.223>.

4

Biometric Breakthroughs

Transforming Electronic ID and Trust in Courts

*Begoña Fernández Rodríguez**

A. Introduction

Traditional identification systems accredit a person by presenting a physical document to a human operator. The physical relationship with the administration of justice does not usually pose a problem for its operators (ie users, administrators, and professionals) beyond the bureaucracy they face. The possibility of going to a physical place, such as a court and interacting directly with people creates trust for all parties involved in the relationship. However, when these relationships become virtual, they can lead to mistrust as users cannot confirm with their senses the reality of the formalities and procedures they are undergoing.

* PhD student. Doctoral Programme in Legal Sciences: International, European Union and Comparative Law. University of Granada. This research has been supported by the Spanish Ministry of Research, Innovation and Universities, within the project TED2021-131127B-I00 'Building the foundations for an efficient, legal and safeguards digitalisation of alternative dispute resolution systems for consumer disputes through technological platforms' (COBADIRALCO).

Begoña Fernández Rodríguez, *Biometric Breakthroughs* In: *Digitalization and Artificial Intelligence in Courts*.
Edited by: Fernando Esteban de la Rosa, Pablo Cortés, and Nuria Marchal Escalona, Oxford University Press.
 DOI: 10.1093/9780198918752.003.0004

Although online procedures have been a reality since the late 1990s,[1] the impact of the health emergency caused by COVID-19 has increased the need to conduct procedures in a nonphysical, face-to-face manner. In practice, many judicial situations require digital identity management, such as remote access to court files, personal identification during videoconferences outside court premises, remote access to the judicial system by court officials during teleworking sessions, and the filing of pleadings.

The right to effective legal protection and access to justice must be consistent with the social reality to which they apply. The functioning of a digital justice system raises important security challenges that must be addressed. One of the most important aspects of remote identification is ensuring its reliability and security. Digital relationships must be trustworthy for all parties involved, both the concerned parties and the justice system officials. Reliability has two aspects: personal and material.

The personal aspect refers to the ability to confirm the identity of the person interacting and their affiliation to avoid fraudulent situations such as identity theft or impersonation. For example, the official with whom we interact should belong to the administration of justice, or the professional should be a member of a certain professional association.

Material reliability corresponds to the confidence the user has in the space where the relationship is developed and in the elements that are exchanged, such as confidence that the website or platform through which we communicate with the administration of justice and its operators is reliable, secure, and belongs to the administration itself, not a third party—that it is not a fraudulent copy where data are stolen or document exchanges are intercepted; that the origin and integrity of the documents we receive, such as judicial notices, are guaranteed—ensuring they come from the administration of justice and have not been altered by a third party. Additionally, it ensures that documents sent or received through the platform are not at risk of being lost, damaged, or altered and can be traced or tracked at any time by the interested party. Moreover, it allows for the certification at any moment of the existence of certain information or data, such as when exchanging draft agreements or confirming a person's consent to the content of a document.

Digital tools such as electronic identification systems and trust services reduce both types of uncertainty. These tools enable safe and conscious interaction with the administration of justice, eliminating the need for operators to visit judicial offices. As stated by the European Commission,[2] since its entry into force, eIDAS regulation has become an essential building block for European judicial cooperation.[3] At the same

[1] With digital communication and document submission.

[2] European Commission, 'Digitalisation of justice in the European Union. A toolbox of opportunities' (Communication) COM (2020) 710 final.

[3] European Parliament and Council Regulation (EU) 910/2014 on electronic identification and trust services for electronic transactions in the internal market and repealing Directive 1999/93/EC [2014] OJ L257/73 (eIDAS Regulation). As a reference for the use of identification systems and trust services: European Parliament and Council Regulation (EU) 2023/2844 on the digitalisation of judicial cooperation and access to justice in cross-border civil, commercial and criminal matters, and amending certain acts in the field of judicial cooperation [2023] OJ L 2844/1, European Parliament and Council Regulation (EU) 2020/1784 on the service in the Member States of judicial and extrajudicial documents in civil or commercial matters (service of documents Regulation) (recast) [2020] OJ L405/40, and European Parliament and Council Regulation (EU) 2020/1783 on cooperation between the courts of the Member

time, the identification systems included in the eIDAS Regulation are becoming the foundation for the advanced digitization of the judicial systems of Member States.

For example, in Spain, Royal Decree-Law 6/2023[4] has adapted electronic identification to the content of the eIDAS Regulation, by updating the identification and authentication systems, including a secure identification service during videoconferencing and establishing that electronic judicial offices must use qualified website authentication certificates or equivalent means for encrypted communications.

Digital legal systems respond differently to these challenges. User identification methods include usernames and passwords, one-time passwords (OTP) for two-factor authentication, cryptographic digital certificates on computers or ID cards, and biometric data such as fingerprints, voice, iris, or facial images. Countries that have taken this last step include Canada, Spain, Estonia, and the UK (as discussed further in this chapter). Web authentication certificates, electronic seals, and electronic signatures are commonly used to ensure physical trust.

As justice systems advance technologically and adopt diverse digital tools, it is crucial to evaluate how well each system ensures certainty in identification, fosters trust in the digital justice process, and complies with existing legal frameworks.

This chapter identifies good policies and practices for an advanced digital justice system. First, it presents the main elements of this policy framework for identification systems and trust services and discusses European Union (EU) legal developments supporting biometric identity management. Second, it outlines the innovations introduced by the proposed eIDAS2 Regulation regarding the European Digital Identity. Third, the developments used by Member States for identity management in the field of justice are presented. Finally, it examines the digital identity management needs in administration of justice.

B. European Regulatory Framework for European Digital Identity Management

1. Coordination by means of the eIDAS Regulation

A legal framework is essential for communication technologies to manage digital identities. This framework must ensure security, instil confidence among stakeholders and define valid digital tools for justice. In the EU, the eIDAS Regulation provides this legal framework.

The eIDAS Regulation repeals Directive 1999/93/EC on electronic signatures, providing a comprehensive cross-border and cross-sectoral framework to ensure secure,

States in the taking of evidence in civil or commercial matters (taking of evidence Regulation) (recast) [2020] OJ L405/1.

[4] Royal Decree-Law 6/2023 of 19 December, approving urgent measures for the implementation of the Recovery, Transformation and Resilience Plan for the public service of justice, civil service, local government and patronage, 2023. *Real Decreto-ley 6/2023, de 19 de diciembre, por el que se aprueban medidas urgentes para la ejecución del Plan de Recuperación, Transformación y Resiliencia en materia de servicio público de justicia, función pública, régimen local y mecenazgo (SPA).*

reliable, and user-friendly electronic transactions.[5] Among the novelties introduced by the Regulation is the creation of a European legal framework for identification systems and trust services, promoting the elimination of operational barriers between Member States by establishing a common legal framework of mandatory compliance and a new interoperability framework, developed through the Commission Implementing Regulation on the interoperability framework in accordance with Article 12(8) of eIDAS Regulation.[6]

It addresses the issue of undefined national supervision obligations for service providers under the Electronic Signature Directive, which has hindered the use of electronic signatures across Member States due to varying validity and recognition mechanisms. The new text eliminates legal and technical barriers to the use of certificates issued by one Member State in another Member State.

The eIDAS Regulation defines and clarifies the legal framework for trust services, including electronic signatures, seals, timestamps, documents, certified deliveries, and website authentication certificates.[7] These services instil user confidence in digital interactions and facilitate document exchanges. It also sets rules for recognizing electronic identification systems, requiring Member States to acknowledge the identification means notified to the European Commission by other Member States. Trust service recognition extends to entities in third countries.

2. Electronic identification systems and means of electronic identification supported by the eIDAS Regulation

An electronic identification system identifies individuals by issuing and using identification methods for online authentication.[8] These means can be tangible (such as an ID card) or intangible (such as an electronic certificate). The most common systems used to interact with public administrations are based on electronic certificates or agreed-upon keys.

The eIDAS Regulation does not list specific electronic identification systems but outlines technical requirements to categorize them by security level. These technologically neutral requirements support various digital identity solutions, such as biometric IDs, non-cryptographic IDs, and two-factor systems. Biometric identification systems recognize individuals using physical, physiological, or behavioural data, comparing them with database records using AI and machine learning algorithms. To operate these systems, the software relies on a physical device such as a sensor to capture biometric data. Once captured, the system creates and compares a biometric template.

This comparison may be 1:1 or 1:n. In a 1:1 comparison, a person's biometric data are matched against their own stored data, confirming their identity with a yes/no

[5] European Parliament and Council Directive 1999/93/CE on a community framework for electronic signatures [1999] OJ L13/12.

[6] European Commission implementing Regulation (EU) 2015/1501 on the interoperability framework pursuant to art 12(8) of Regulation (EU) 910/2014 of the European Parliament and of the Council on electronic identification and trust services for electronic transactions in the internal market [2015] OJ L235/1.

[7] Art 1 eIDAS Regulation.

[8] Art 3.4 eIDAS Regulation.

decision. In a 1:n comparison, the data are compared with multiple entries in a database to identify a person without certainty they are present. In both cases, the technique used is based on the estimated match between the similarity of the biometric templates and the system.

Each Member State determines the means of electronic identification it will accept, choosing what is deemed most appropriate for each situation. In Spain, to reduce the risk of fraudulent use, only electronic certificates issued by the Fábrica Nacional de Moneda y Timbre, electronic ID cards, and *Cl@ve* passwords are accepted in digital relations with public administration.

The eIDAS Regulation offers three security levels for electronic identification systems: low, substantial, and high,[9] which correlate with the confidence level provided in a person's claimed identity. The classification of these levels depends on the system's technical standards, specifications, and procedures. The categorization of these trust levels is set out in the Annex to the Regulation on the establishment of minimum technical specifications and procedures for security levels of electronic identification means, in accordance with article 8(3) of the eIDAS Regulation.[10] This classification addresses the reliability and quality of enrolment, management of electronic identification means, authentication, and management and organization of the identification system. For example, the conditions for using electronic identification means are provided to the applicant at the time of registration or enrolment in the system; the person must physically visit an agency for the issuance, delivery, or activation of the electronic identification means; or the implemented authentication mechanism includes security controls to verify the electronic identification means.

In the eIDAS Regulation model, an identification system only receives a security level if all its components merit it. For instance, an electronic certificate cannot attain a high security level if it is delivered via a downloadable web link accessible to all users, thereby warranting a low security level.

In authentication mechanisms, the Annex provides a high level of security to the proof and verification of a natural person's identity when they possess or present evidence of biometric identification, such as enrolment in a biometric identification system.

The system of mutual recognition of electronic means of identification between Member States established by the eIDAS Regulation is linked to the security level of the means. In any case, it is a *sine qua non* condition in which the identification system issuing the means of identification to be recognized is included in the list published by the Commission,[11] derived from the notification of Member States. Thus, Member States are obliged to recognize, for the purpose of cross-border authentication for access to an online service provided by a public sector body, electronic identification means of a substantial or high level issued in another Member State, provided that the public body of the state where recognition is requested uses a substantial or high level

[9] Art 8 eIDAS Regulation.

[10] Commission Implementing Regulation (EU) 2015/1502 on setting out minimum technical specifications and procedures for assurance levels for electronic identification means pursuant to Article 8(3) of Regulation (EU) 910/2014 of the European Parliament and of the Council on electronic identification and trust services for electronic transactions in the internal market [2015] OJ L235/7.

[11] Pursuant to art 9 eIDAS Regulation.

of security for access to that online service. However, the means by which recognition is requested must have a level of security equal to or higher than that required for online access by the public body of the state where recognition is requested.

In cases where Spanish public bodies require a means of identification with a high level of security to access online services, they are obliged to recognize, for example, the Portuguese electronic means of identifying Portuguese eID cards from the Portuguese notified system *Cartão de Cidadão* (citizen card), which has a high level of security.

For equivalent means of identification with a low level of security, such recognition is at the discretion of each Member State and is not linked to the level of security used by the public body of the state where recognition is requested.

3. Trust services: the significance of electronic signatures

In physical interactions, users can easily confirm their identities through official badges, thereby fostering trust. In the digital world, it is difficult to establish trust without tangible cues. Trust services under the eIDAS Regulation aim to build confidence by verifying data origin, integrity, and website authenticity in digital interactions. This regulation establishes a general legal framework for the use of trust services without creating a general obligation to use them. Only trust services provided to the public that impact third parties must comply with the obligations laid down; those used to manage internal procedures do not.

The eIDAS Regulation facilitates various tools to enhance trust and confidence, including electronic signatures (eSignature), electronic seals (eSeal), electronic timestamps (eTimestamp), certified electronic delivery services (eDelivery), website authentication (WAC) and certificates for all these services.[12]

Although trust services usually aim to ensure material trustworthiness, they can also contribute to personal trustworthiness through certificates and electronic statements linking the validation data of a trust service to the identity data of a natural or legal person, usually their name.

As with handwritten signatures, digital signatures require a third element (eg a national identity card in Spain for handwritten signatures) to associate the e-signature with the identity of a person. The third component comprises digital certificates. The e-signature certificate links the validation data of an e-signature to a natural person and confirms their identity or, at least, the name or pseudonym of that person.

The eIDAS Regulation covers digital certificates for electronic signatures, electronic seals, and web authentication. Typically, individuals acquire digital certificates by personally visiting official entities and presenting a valid national ID. However, owing to the COVID-19 pandemic, some countries, such as Spain, have adapted to allow remote identification via video calls.[13]

[12] Art 3.16 eIDAS Regulation.

[13] Order ETD/465/2021, 6th May, on remote video identification methods for the issuance of qualified electronic certificates, 2021. *Orden ETD/465/2021, de 6 de mayo, por la que se regulan los métodos de identificación remota por vídeo para la expedición de certificados electrónicos cualificados* (SPA).

For individuals, an electronic signature involves electronic data for signing (eg checking a box or using unique passwords from apps or emails). It serves as a digital equivalent to a physical signature, signifying agreement or consent to the document's content.

An electronic seal, which is common among legal entities, ensures document origin and integrity using electronic data. It functions like a traditional stamped seal, but in digital form, identifying the submitting company or entity without requiring the inclusion of personal data.

Electronic timestamps offer digital evidence of a document's existence at a specific date and time, confirming that it remains unaltered thereafter. Typically integrated into digital signatures, they are widely used for document registration, particularly for digital submissions.

Certified electronic delivery services, akin to certified mail, operate in the digital realm, and facilitate secure data transmission between parties. They provide evidence of data handling, including sending and receipt, and safeguard against risks such as loss or alteration, akin to delivery proof or slips in electronic records. Finally, web authentication confirms the authenticity and legitimacy of a website for visitors.

Trust services can be categorized as basic, advanced, or qualified, based on the security level offered.[14] Trust service providers offer these services alongside digital certificates. Qualified service providers complete the ecosystem. The 'qualified' status is conferred by the national supervisory authority, such as Spain's Ministry of Economy and Digital Transformation. The EU Trust Mark, which is voluntarily used, identifies qualified trust services and fosters user trust in electronic services.

The eIDAS Regulation mandates standardized supervision requirements for all Member States to maintain an equivalent security level for qualified trust services. However, Member States retain the freedom to define additional trust service types for national recognition as qualified trust services.

Regarding electronic identification means, the eIDAS Regulation outlines the recognition rules for trust services from providers, including those in third countries. It stipulates that qualified trust services provided by EU-established providers under agreements with third countries or international organizations are legally equivalent and recognized.[15]

Regarding electronic signatures, the eIDAS Regulation outlines three levels of validity: simple, advanced, and qualified.[16] They all aim to verify the signer's ownership, reflecting consent to document content or actions.

The lowest level of security is observed for simple electronic signatures. In this case, the signature consists of data in electronic form attached to or logically associated with other electronic data used by the signatory. Examples include the use of a scanned document with a handwritten signature or a digitizer board on which a handwritten signature is created.

[14] See requirements for advanced electronic signatures (art 26 eIDAS Regulation); qualified trust services (s 3, chapter III eIDAS Regulation).

[15] Art 14 eIDAS Regulation.

[16] As stated in n 15.

Advanced signatures must satisfy additional requirements to guarantee higher security than simple signatures.[17] They identify signatories and detect subsequent data changes. Uniquely linked to the signatory, they are created using means under their sole control. This type of signature includes biometric signatures or OTP codes received via SMS, email, or an application that, once used, are no longer valid.

A qualified electronic signature is an advanced electronic signature generated by a qualified device using a corresponding certificate (see Annexes I and II of the eIDAS Regulation). These certificates can reside on various signatory devices, such as computers and smartphones. With top-notch security, they are supported by qualified service providers, including professional associations issuing digital certificates (eg the Bar Association's card-based certificate used with a card reader).

The eIDAS Regulation does not restrict valid signatures, thus allowing for biometric integration. Biometric data can sign documents, such as by confirming the content with fingerprints, irises, or voice recognition, or by using biometric signatures.

Biometric signatures are behavioural biometric techniques. They can establish relationships with identity based on the process of the user's handwritten signature by analysing dynamic data such as signature pressure, handwriting, direction, and inclination of the stroke. The signature must be made on a biometric capture device (eg digitizer board) ensuring signatures match written patterns. The significance of each analysed dynamic characteristic is determined at the system designer's discretion.

4. Innovations in eIDAS2 Regulation

The European Commission proposed amending the eIDAS Regulation to streamline the creation of trusted digital identities for all EU citizens.[18] The eIDAS2 Regulation aims to boost security in digital identity management and foster infrastructure development for collecting, storing, and sharing digital identity data.[19] It seeks to improve the usability, security, and reliability of electronic identification and trust services in the EU. This paper highlights the significance of using biometric technologies for electronic signatures and identification. In this regard, biometrics have been recognized as a highly reliable and secure authentication method.

The eIDAS2 introduces the concept of European digital identity wallets and Regulation (EU) 2019/1157 identity documents as potential means of electronic identification.[20] These innovations allow data storage, including personal information and credentials, for online and offline authentication, facilitating cross-border services and qualified electronic signatures and seals through an application (European

[17] Art 26 eIDAS Regulation.

[18] Commission, 'Shaping Europe's digital future' (Communication) COM (2020) 67 final.

[19] Commission, 'Proposal for a Regulation of the European Parliament and of the Council amending Regulation (EU) 910/2014 as regards establishing a framework for a European Digital Identity' COM (2021) 281 final. The proposal has been finally adopted as Regulation (EU) 2024/1183 of the European Parliament and of the Council of 11 April 2024 amending Regulation (EU) 910/2014 as regards the establishment of the European Digital Identity Framework (OJ L, 2024/1183, 30.4.2024).

[20] European Parliament and Council Regulation (EU) 2019/1157 on strengthening the security of identity cards of Union citizens and of residence documents issued to Union citizens and their family members exercising their right of free movement [2019] OJ L188/67.

Digital Identity Wallets). Thus, it enables QR code identification via mobile phones for face-to-face interactions with officials, such as confirming identity by physically accessing judicial files in court.

Biometric data storage involves preserving the biometric template created during the initial capture, typically during user enrolment in the relevant database. Among the categories of data that can be stored in the European Digital Identity Wallet, biometric data can be included in the category of identity data because they are considered personal data under the General Data Protection Regulation (GDPR)[21]. They can also be considered attributes (traits, characteristics, or qualities of a natural or legal person in electronic form), as the GDPR defines them as data related to the physical, physiological, or behavioural characteristics of a natural person that enables or confirms the unique identification of that person.[22] They are deemed more suitable for inclusion in the European Digital Identity Wallet as identity data because they are intricately linked to the fundamental data essential for person identification.

C. Experiences of Digital Identity Management in Courts: A Comparative View

1. Solutions without biometric technology

The administration of justice addresses digital identity management using both traditional and innovative approaches. Traditional methods use personal passwords or digital certificates, whereas newer methods incorporate biometric technology. Currently, most of the administrations of justice favour traditional solutions.

Various justice systems have implemented solutions to ease access to the digital administration of justice. These can be categorized into three groups: username/password combinations, specific access systems, and digital certificates. However, these categories often overlap based on the sophistication of the system.

Access to the administration of justice occurs primarily through private networks. This affords greater control over digital interactions, allowing the administration to dictate access methods based on security and functionality levels and facilitating the establishment of trust services, such as the use of timestamps in the exchange of documents. In Spain, access to the administration of justice occurs primarily through its internal network, or the System of Applications and Networks for Administrations (SARA) network.

When a service offers multiple applications, users have the freedom to choose an identification method that aligns with their preferences and requirements. To gain access to digital services, users must first register on specific platforms or databases with personal usernames and passwords. In the Spanish judicial system, to access the

[21] European Parliament and Council Regulation (EU) 2016/679 on the protection of natural persons with regard to the processing of personal data and on the free movement of such data, and repealing Directive 95/46/EC (General Data Protection Regulation) [2016] OJ L119/1.

[22] Art 4, s 14 GDPR.

Integrated Desktop,[23] users must register their usernames and passwords on a specific platform or database. Prior registration on the user management platform (GDU) at a judicial office or authorized body is also required to access the Electronic Archive of Court Powers of Attorney.[24] The Canadian justice system employs a registration-based approach to access the Civil Resolution Tribunal (CRT) of British Columbia.[25] Upon registration on a platform with a username and password, individuals receive a PIN along with claim notifications, facilitating access to litigation files and account setup. To access the Online Civil Money Claims service for financial claims submissions or responses in England and Wales, users must obtain an account on the UK government portal by registering with a username and password.[26] During account creation, users verify their email addresses by clicking on the link sent to their registered email accounts.

In other instances, the administration has considered using specific systems. The Spanish administration has resorted to the *Cl@ve* system with the objective of unifying the identification, authentication, and electronic signatures of users in digital procedures to use online services such as file status queries or the Digital Services Portal.[27] This eliminates the necessity for users to register separately in each public administration system or to create and retain distinct passwords. The system registration process can be completed digitally. Users must acquire their electronic identification credentials either in person at participating registration offices or online via recognized methods, such as certificates, video calls, or invitation letters. Upon registration, users receive two access codes: *Cl@ve PIN*, which offers occasional access with a time-limited password, and *Cl@ve Permanente*, which allows regular access and signatures reinforced with SMS single-use codes for certain services. The *Cl@ve* application facilitates *Cl@ve Móvil*, enabling password-free identification via QR codes or application confirmation on mobile phones.

The Ministry of Justice recently implemented *Cl@ve Justicia*, a method of authentication for users to access the Virtual Digital Immediacy Desk (EVID)[28] using a mobile phone and national ID or national foreign number data. Furthermore, the system

[23] Centralizes access to justice personnel applications and includes functionalities such as an alert service, a messaging service between users and access to relevant links. See <https://www.administraciondejusticia.gob.es/-/soluciones-escritorio-integrado?inheritRedirect = true&redirect=> last accessed 21 May 2024.

[24] Information system for the registration, consultation, and modification of court powers of attorney. See <https://www.administraciondejusticia.gob.es/-/soluciones-archivo-electronico-de-apoderamientos-judiciales?inheritRedirect = true&redirect=> last accessed 21 May 2024.

[25] <https://civilresolutionbc.ca/> last accessed 21 May 2024.

[26] <https://www.gov.uk/make-court-claim-for-money/make-claim> last accessed 21 May 2024.

[27] See Guide for Dialogue on the Efficient, Quality and Ethical Design and Use of Technological Tools in Civil Justice, by COTEC Foundation and Unidad de Excelencia de Investigación Sociedad Digital: Seguridad y Protección de Derechos, University of Granada. *Guía para el diálogo sobre el diseño y uso eficiente, de calidad y ético de herramientas tecnológicas en la justicia civil, de la Fundación COTEC y la Unidad de Excelencia de Investigación Sociedad Digital: Seguridad y Protección de Derechos, Universidad de Granada.* <https://sd2.ugr.es/guia-para-una-justicia-digital/> last accessed 21 May 2024.

[28] More information at: <https://www.administraciondejusticia.gob.es/-/soluciones-escritorio-virtual-de-inmediacion-digital?inheritRedirect = true&redirect=> last accessed 21 May 2024.

is designed to accommodate the use of pseudonym certificates that are particularly suited to the needs of state security forces and professionals.[29]

EVID is an online service that facilitates professional-citizen communication via videoconferences. It helps civil servants conduct procedures and manage appointments remotely. Targeting vulnerable groups such as older adults and those with disabilities, the system aims to alleviate the digital divide. Currently operational in various Spanish courts, it facilitates asset auctions, family matter ratifications (primarily divorces and custody arrangements), expert witness role acceptance, and mixed meetings by combining a physical court presence with remote videoconference participation. In these proceedings, identification and signatures are conducted using signature-capturing devices, allowing the entire proceeding to be carried out digitally.[30]

The *Cl@ve* access system serves as the default identification method for public services accessible via external networks, such as the internet. It is particularly utilized in areas where the administration of justice lacks the authority to implement control mechanisms.

Finally, access can be achieved using digital certificates issued by a recognized certification authority. In Spain, the Ministry of Industry, Trade, and Tourism issues digital certificates that permit access to tools used for the submission of pleadings and documents, transfer of copies, and execution of communications and notifications by electronic means (eg *LexNET*[31] or *Acceda-Justicia*).[32]

Mexican judiciaries have crafted bespoke digital signature systems to access judicial platforms, allowing autonomy at the security level.[33] For instance, the Federal Judiciary of Mexico employs the Certified Electronic Signature of the Federal Judiciary (Firel) to access its platform, file amparo proceedings, receive notifications, and consult electronic files.

In Nuevo León, pre-existing digital signatures from the Tax Administration Service and Firel are utilized via agreements with internal users.[34] Additionally, Nuevo León's Judicial Branch has its own electronic signature, comprising a username, password, and code card updated every three months for external platform users.

[29] 'El Ministerio de Justicia implanta nuevas actualizaciones en el Escritorio Virtual de Inmediación Digital', 26th September 2023 avalaible at: <https://www.mjusticia.gob.es/es/institucional/gabinete-comunicacion/noticias-ministerio/actualizaciones-evid> last accessed 21 May 2024.

[30] 'Justicia implanta nuevas actualizaciones en el Escritorio Virtual de Inmediación Digital', 26th September 2023. Avalaible at: <https://elderecho.com/justicia-implanta-nuevas-actualizaciones-en-el-escritorio-virtual-de-inmediacion-digital> last accessed 21 May 2024.

[31] See LexNET. <https://www.administraciondejusticia.gob.es/-/soluciones-lexnet?inheritRedirect = true&redirect=> last accessed 21 May 2024.

[32] See Acceda Justicia. <https://www.administraciondejusticia.gob.es/-/soluciones-acceda-justicia?inheritRedirect = true&redirect=> last accessed 21 May 2024.

[33] See Guide to Good Practices in the Use of New Technologies for the Delivery of Justice in Mexico (Mexicoevalúa). *Guía de buenas prácticas en el uso de nuevas tecnologías para la impartición de justicia mexicana* (Mexicoevalúa), available at <https://www.mexicoevalua.org/wp-content/uploads/2021/02/guia-buenas-practicas-okisbn.pdf> last accessed 21 May 2024.

[34] Ibid.

2. Identification with biometric technology

For decades, the EU has focused on biometrics, integrating this technology into immigration and asylum policies. Recently, biometrics have been used for identity management in courts, both physically and online. Although implementation in criminal proceedings, it is important to note that the biometric system's functionality remains consistent regardless of the type of proceeding.

Spain and Estonia are two European countries that have initiated the implementation of biometric identification in their justice systems. Spain has introduced this technology in several ways. First, it has incorporated biometric signatures within the Atlante Web judicial and procedural management system. Second, it has implemented the *Comparecencias Apud Acta en Remoto* (SCAAR) system. Finally, it has introduced machines such as 'biometric kiosks' physically located within the courts.[35]

Atlante Web is a procedural and judicial management system developed by the Government of the Canary Islands with the objective of implementing the Electronic Judicial File and facilitating the provision of new digital judicial services. This system allows remote access to the judicial system, including the use of digital signatures, for both individual and collegiate purposes. It also facilitates teleworking among officials in the administration of justice and enables interested parties to view electronic judicial files.

To optimize the management of the Electronic Judicial File, the Regional Ministry of Public Administrations, Justice, and Security,[36] in collaboration with the Directorate General of Telecommunications and New Technologies of the Canary Islands Government, is developing the implementation of biometric signatures in judicial proceedings.[37]

In 2021, the Canarian government implemented the SCAAR system for remote appearances apud acta in the Courts of Instruction of Las Palmas de Gran Canaria.[38] This system replaces the physical appearance of a person with biometric identification through their mobile phone when a judicial measure has been filed against them, which implies their regular appearance. The system is optional, allowing interested parties to reject its use and appear in person before the corresponding judicial authority.

To proceed, an interested party must first verify their identity by presenting a valid document. Subsequently, they generate their biometric credentials through a facial recognition system integrated into their mobile devices. This credential is employed to authenticate the identity of the individual in question and ascertain their geographical location, thereby corroborating their presence at the designated location. SCAAR

[35] See document: <https://www.mjusticia.gob.es/es/JusticiaEspana/ProyectosTransformacionJusticia/Documents/20221019%20TD%20> last accessed 21 May 2024.

[36] Consejería de Administraciones Públicas, Justicia y Seguridad.

[37] 'Desarrollo del Sistema de Gestión Judicial Atlante web y su evolución', <https://www.gobiernodecanarias.org/justicia/Formacion/FormacionAtlante/FormacionDesarrollo/> last accessed 21 May 2024.

[38] 'El Gobierno canario implanta un sistema de comparecencias judiciales a distancia y con identificación biométrica', 16 March 2023 <https://www3.gobiernodecanarias.org/noticias/el-gobierno-canario-implanta-un-sistema-de-comparecencias-judiciales-a-distancia-y-con-identificacion-biometrica/> last accessed 21 May 2024.

is integrated into the court's procedural management system, allowing notifications and alerts to be generated immediately for both the person and the court itself.

The use of biometric kiosks in Spanish courts commenced in 2022 with their implementation in Salamanca.[39] The objective was to avoid congestion in the courtroom by enabling individuals to complete their legal obligations remotely. The terminals are equipped with a facial, fingerprint, and iris identification system (1:1), as well as a national identity card reader. Individuals insert their valid national identity cards into the machine, after which biometric credentials are generated through the integrated identification system. The biometric credential is employed to verify the identity of the individual in question. Unlike the SCAAR system, the terminal is not dependent on geolocation because it is installed within the courthouse. Once identified, the user can receive notifications or summons from judicial bodies, collect documents electronically, or complete precautionary measures, such as physical appearances in court.

In Estonia, the implementation of the Salme tool in court proceedings has facilitated the use of biometric identification systems in the Estonian judicial system.[40] Salme is a voice recognition system specifically designed to transcribe court hearings in Estonian courts, whether conducted in person or remotely. The system's operation necessitates initial human intervention through an operator who manually introduces the previously validated participants to the judicial session and assigns them a microphone. This assignment enables the system to identify speakers and microphones to be recorded at any given moment. Finally, the system transcribes the session in real time or offline.

Although Salme cannot be considered a standalone biometric identification system because it requires prior identification, it relies on one in its operation. Prior identification for microphone assignment is done through the Estonian digital identity system, which is based, among other things, on citizens' biometric data, such as voice.

One of the objectives for 2024 for the Estonian judiciary is to achieve full digital competence in court hearings using only screens, Salme, and transcripts of hearings, regardless of whether they are conducted in a physical courtroom or remotely.[41]

Finally, it is notable that China stands out as a non-EU country in the use of biometric identification systems within the administration of justice. In 2019, the Chinese government implemented the 'China Mobile MiniCourt'[42] which allows disputing parties to conduct various online procedures, such as filing pleadings, notifications, or consulting case files through their devices. Access to the platform is through the Chinese WeChat application, which uses biometrics (facial and fingerprint recognition) for authentication.

[39] 'El innovador dispositivo de Justicia que permite al ciudadano tramitar procedimientos sin ser atendido personalmente por los funcionarios', 15 September 2022 <https://www.lagacetadesalamanca.es/salamanca/el-innovador-dispositivo-de-justicia-que-permite-al-ciudadano-tramitar-procedimientos-sin-ser-atendido-personalmente-por-los-funcionarios-GE12072466> last accessed 21 May 2024.

[40] 'Introducing Salme, Estonian courts' speech recognition assistant', 26 January 2022. <https://e-estonia.com/introducing-salme-estonian-courts-speech-recognition-assistant/> last accessed 21 May 2024.

[41] Raivo Tammus, IT Manager of the Estonian Courts when asked about Estonia's digital competence in courts. For more information: <https://investinestonia.com/introducing-salme-estonian-courts-speech-recognition-assistant/> last accessed 21 May 2024.

[42] See <https://es.chinajusticeobserver.com/a/chinese-courts-on-smart-phones> last accessed 21 May 2024.

3. Potential benefits and drawbacks of alternative methods of identification

Traditional digital identity management systems that avoid biometrics are user-friendly and adaptable to different security needs. However, they can be unreliable, as they may be used by someone other than the rightful owner without requiring fraudulent actions to obtain the necessary data.

User- and password-based systems are straightforward and intuitive. However, these systems have several drawbacks. Primarily, the user is required to set and remember their credentials, which can be inconvenient when new username and password must be created for each platform. It is common for passwords to be stolen, either through cyberattacks (phishing) or physical theft, especially if the user writes them down. Furthermore, users may lose access to their accounts due to forgetfulness. In such cases, initiating password recovery or changes can be costly, often requiring answers to security questions or the input of data that the user may not have readily available.

Username-password systems can be made more secure with a second step, such as ticking confirmation boxes (e.g. 'I am not a robot'), requesting personal data (eg date of birth), using dynamic or one-time passwords, or sending a random key via SMS to proceed with access after entering the ID on a platform. However, they share the same disadvantages as non-enforced systems in terms of user identity certainty. Users can voluntarily share data with a third party to conduct procedures on their behalf, which is a widespread practice among non-digital natives who provide information to family members.

Systems based on digital certificates offer more reliable identification because of the procedures for obtaining them. Users must verify their identity with an official body for reinforced confirmation. Once verified, the certificate can be downloaded to the device. However, the extensive formalities and documentation required can hinder digital access to justice.

After the certificate is issued, ensuring that the user matches the certificate holder faces challenges similar to those in other systems. Individuals often share credentials with legal advisors for court filings or with colleagues for network actions, leading to significant reliability issues in identity management systems. Consequently, in non-biometric systems, security depends on the user's possession and control of credentials. The holder must take necessary precautions to prevent misuse, as all credentials can be used by third parties.

Biometric identification systems have revolutionized security and personal identification by offering physical and virtual solutions. By associating an individual's identity with unique physical, physiological, or behavioural traits, these systems enhance the reliability of identity confirmation using intrinsic biometric data.

Biometric systems offer superior security and reliability in user identification compared to traditional methods. The inherent difficulty in forging or replicating biometric data reduces the risks of identity theft. Users benefit from rapid and straightforward identification without the need to memorize passwords or carry cards, as the process relies on their innate traits rather than external factors.

However, biometric identification technology is not devoid of risks, as emphasized by various national and European entities. The European Data Protection Board (EDPB) has extensively addressed these concerns, highlighting issues such as algorithmic biases and privacy rights as particularly detrimental to its societal implementation.[43]

In recent amendments to the Artificial Intelligence Act, the European Parliament banned the use of AI for real-time remote biometric identification in public areas, citing potential biases and discriminatory outcomes.[44] Nevertheless, this chapter focuses on systems performing 1:n comparison rather than 1:1 authentication.

In its White Paper on AI: A European Approach to excellence and trust,[45] the European Commission advocates for the use of AI only when justified, proportionate, and safeguarded. Spain's Guide for Digital Justice echoes these concerns, emphasizing the need for caution and appropriate safeguards in AI deployment.[46]

The risks of identification systems can be categorized into two types: those intrinsic to technology and those related to data protection. The processing and nature of personal data utilized by such systems pose data-protection risks. The EDPB outlines several concerns, including unauthorized use, excessive data collection, citizen surveillance perception, lack of transparency, legal justifications, and significant repercussions of biometric data breaches or misuse.[47] Unlike other forms of identification, individuals cannot issue new biometric data if it has been exposed, stolen, or misappropriated.

Regarding the risks associated with technology, it is important to note that discrimination owing to biases developed during algorithmic learning is a significant concern. The disparity in identification accuracy between different demographic groups may stem from the lack of diversity in the datasets used to train the biometric algorithms. If the training data are biased towards certain ethnic or gender groups, the systems may be less accurate in identifying individuals from underrepresented groups. Nevertheless, controlling and ensuring the quality of training data can mitigate this risk.

The operation of biometric technologies is based on the percentage of similarity between the data analysed by the system and those previously recorded in a database. Despite the high reliability of these systems, overall reliability is not guaranteed. Incorrect identifications (false positives) or missed identifications (false negatives) may occur. In both instances, there is potential for decisions that could impact individuals' rights. This risk can be mitigated by incorporating human reinforcement to the identification process, such as immediate visual verification of identification by a technician.

[43] Art 29 of Directive 95/46/EC Data Protection Working Party, 'Opinion 3/2012 on developments in biometric technologies' [2012] 00720/12/EN WP193.

[44] European Parliament, 'Report on the proposal for a regulation of the European Parliament and of the Council on laying down harmonised rules on Artificial Intelligence (Artificial Intelligence Act) and amending certain Union Legislative Acts' COM (2021)0206 – C9-0146/2021 – 2021/0106(COD).

[45] European Commission, 'White Paper on Artificial Intelligence—A European approach to excellence and trust' COM (2020) 65 final.

[46] See Guide to e-Justice.

[47] Art 29 of Directive 95/46/EC Data Protection Working Party. 'Working Document on Biometrics' [2003] 12168/02/EN WP 80.

However, the potential risks associated with biometric systems should not serve as barriers to their acceptance. Instead, these considerations should be incorporated into the development and implementation of these systems to conduct a rigorous analysis of the potential risks.

D. The Necessity of Digital Management in the Field of Administration of Justice: Identification of Good Practices

The administration of justice bears the responsibility of establishing a secure and reliable digital environment for all users. This requires the development of a digital framework that promotes trustworthiness. Users should be able to perceive and comprehend the environment's security through robust identification systems and trust services.

Trustworthiness and security should be foundational in designing a virtual space; however, user convenience must also be considered. No single identification method fits all e-justice actions. Analysing the relevance and consequences of digital actions helps identify the most suitable identification means based on reliability and security. In civil judicial cooperation, remote communication technology enables authorities to authenticate individuals for videoconferencing hearings, facilitating visual, audio, and oral communication. However, no established minimum security standards exist for such identification systems.[48]

Considering the security standards in the eIDAS Regulation, it is prudent for legislation to mandate electronic identification means with varying security levels. For basic platform access, substantial security is sufficient, whereas high security is required to confirm critical procedures, such as accepting electronic notifications or verifying identity for video calls.

Requiring a means of identification with a high level of security, which is cumbersome to obtain and use, would be counterproductive—both for authenticating users accessing a video call for judicial statements and for allowing users to view only the status of their file.

In Spain, it is sufficient to prove identity through any means of identification provided for in Law 39/2015 on the Common Administrative Procedure of Public Administrations,[49] the eIDAS Regulation, and Law 6/2020 regulating certain aspects of electronic trust services,[50] in actions where a signature is not required according to procedural regulations.[51]

[48] Regulation (EU) 2023/2844.

[49] Law 39/2015, 1st October, on the Common Administrative Procedure of Public Administrations, 2015. *Ley 39/2015, de 1 de octubre, del Procedimiento Administrativo Común de las Administraciones Públicas* (SPA).

[50] Law 6/2020, 11 November 2020, regulating certain aspects of electronic trust services, 2020. *Ley 6/2020, de 11 de noviembre, reguladora de determinados aspectos de los servicios electrónicos de confianza* (SPA).

[51] Royal Decree-Law 6/2023, 19th December, approving urgent measures for the implementation of the Recovery, Transformation and Resilience Plan for the public service of justice, civil service, local government and patronage, 2023. *Real Decreto-ley 6/2023, de 19 de diciembre, por el que se aprueban medidas urgentes para la ejecución del Plan de Recuperación, Transformación y Resiliencia en materia de servicio público de justicia, función pública, régimen local y mecenazgo* (SPA).

Biometric identification systems are ideal for both levels of security. For example, access to a platform through facial analysis or the acceptance of an electronic court notice by speaking to a voice-recognition device exemplifies this. The digital justice system must address errors in biometric identification systems, such as false positives granting unauthorized access (eg in the case of twins) or false negatives denying access (e.g. due to age-related changes). Training and refining recognition algorithms can mitigate false positives and enhance system reliability, while maintaining updated data or human support can address false negatives.

To enhance the security of identification systems and prevent fraud, strong or two-factor user authentication is recommended. This involves using multiple known, possessed, or inherent elements for authentication and dispersing the risk across several factors. For instance, combining fingerprint and password authentication ensures system reliability even if one element is compromised.

To ensure trust in the digital sphere, it is crucial that the trust services used for interactions with the administration of justice are qualified. Qualified trust services, issued by entities approved by national supervisory authorities, offer heightened security and reliability in digital relations. In judicial cooperation in civil matters, Regulation (EU) 2023/2844 emphasizes that competent authorities prefer the use of qualified electronic seals or signatures on documents transmitted as part of an electronic communication requiring a seal or signature.

The eIDAS Regulation does not detail the procedural aspects of evidentiary value or validity levels of unqualified electronic signatures. It acknowledges that they cannot be dismissed solely for not being handwritten or meeting qualified signature criteria, but for treating qualified electronic signatures similarly to handwritten ones.

In interactions with the administration of justice, using an advanced or qualified electronic signature is recommended based on the document type, procedural stage, and legal consequences. To receive judicial communications with procedural deadlines, a qualified signature may be required as evidence of receipt. However, for procedural submissions, such as hearing suspension requests or debt payment notifications, an advanced signature suffices.

In Spain, the Guide to Interoperability and Security for Authentication, Certificates, and Electronic Signatures proposes recommendations and good practices for actions related to the administration of justice, depending on the security level of the signature.[52] For example, it rightly points out, given the scope of the relationship, the preference for qualified certificates when using certificate-based signature systems.

Biometric signatures can be considered eIDAS advanced electronic signatures, as they fulfil the requirements of Article 26 of the eIDAS Regulation. Compared to other types of advanced signatures, such as OTP signatures or those based on public key infrastructure, where the user receives a password on a device via an application or message on a device to sign documents (such as the *Cl@ve* system), biometric

[52] Interoperability and Security Guide for Authentication, Certificates and Electronic Signatures of the State Technical Committee for Electronic Judicial Administration. *Guía de interoperabilidad y seguridad de autenticación, certificados y firma electrónica del comité técnico estatal de la administración judicial electrónica* (SPA), <https://www.administraciondejusticia.gob.es/documents/7557301/7558179/CTEAJE-GIS-707-Autenticaci%C3%B3n%2C + Certificados+y + Firma+electr%C3%B3nica.pdf/f153895d-a126-2529-ba07-0eabeb527a68?t = 1695723050866> last accessed 21 May 2024.

signatures are more reliable in terms of ensuring that the person signing is indeed the data subject.

In practice, the use of biometric signatures has drawbacks that can complicate or hinder the identification process, such as that individuals do not always sign in the same manner, or their physiological characteristics change over time. This means the newly issued signature may not match the person's previously recorded biometric data, thus preventing identification. A device is also required to capture biometric signatures and process the data.

To overcome these drawbacks, using biometric signature data such as irises and fingerprints has been proposed as a good practice. The proposal to use this type of biometric data instead of a dynamic signature is based on two reasons. First, facial, fingerprint, and iris characteristics of individuals are more constant than those of signatures. These biometric characteristics can change with the passage of time or remote external factors, such as accidents or illnesses, resulting in physical changes. The greater the immutability of the characteristics being analysed, the higher the matching rate, as the biometric data, barring exceptional changes, will continue to match a person's previously recorded data. Only when physical changes cause the registered biometrics to no longer match the person, as with the photograph on an ID card, must biometric databases be updated. If the biometric characteristic being analysed is no longer present due to an accident, illness, or chance event, another biometric characteristic can be registered; for example, switching from fingerprint to facial analysis.

Second, biometric enrolment devices are more integrated and accessible to society, as they are embedded in everyday devices, such as mobile phones and laptops. This eliminates the need to purchase a new biometric reader device, as with the digitizer board in a biometric signature, and increases user convenience, as they typically carry the reader device with them and can use it at any time.

Given the potential risk of discrimination from the digital divide in society, terminals could be set up in official bodies, such as Spanish biometric kiosks, equipped with biometric capture devices, and connected to digital justice platforms, allowing interested parties to conduct their procedures.

As a good practice, it is recommended that identification and/or signature systems using biometrics not be used in isolation within the administration of justice, but as an enhancement or in a subsidiary role. For example, biometric data are inherent to a person and form a key part of a strong authentication system.

The main drawback of biometric technology systems is that biometric data are inherent to users. Once compromised through theft or unauthorized access, it is difficult to restore normal and secure operations. These systems must have robust security features and protocols for handling breaches.

The ultimate security of biometric technology systems, unlike traditional systems, shifts from the user to the developers and administrators, as it relies on system security protocols—from the accuracy of biometric data capture to data storage, as well as the quality and training of the algorithms that recognize biometric characteristics.

Given the high risks involved in breaches of biometric data, it is essential that society be made aware of the dangers of theft or unintentional transfer of such data. Education should be promoted to prevent situations such as those recently reported, where individuals allowed their irises to be scanned in exchange for cryptocurrencies, unaware of how their data might be used.[53]

E. Conclusions

The integration of biometric systems into the administration of justice offers substantial benefits in identification, user authentication, and electronic signatures. As part of the ongoing digitalization of judicial systems, it is crucial to establish a secure and reliable digital framework that serves both judicial administrations and their users. This requires the implementation of advanced digital tools, such as electronic identification systems and trust services, which are essential for ensuring security and trustworthiness in digital interactions.

The security of these digital tools must be calibrated carefully, considering the nature of the judicial process or action, its potential impact on users, and the ease with which users can access or retrieve their data. Given the importance and potential legal ramifications of actions within the justice system, medium-to high-level security is generally advisable. For personal identification processes, systems with substantial or high security levels provide greater assurance, thereby minimizing the risk of impersonation or unauthorized access.

In terms of trust services, preference should be given to those with qualified status, as they are issued by entities certified by national supervisory authorities, ensuring a higher degree of security and reliability. For electronic signatures, the security level should correspond to the significance of the action being undertaken. Although lower levels may be sufficient for routine procedural matters, more significant actions require more advanced or qualified signatures. Biometric technology offers marked improvement in the reliability of both identification systems and electronic signatures, although it must be safeguarded by strict security measures due to the sensitive nature of biometric data and the high risks associated with potential data breaches.

The adoption of biometric recognition systems for electronic identification and trust services in judicial processes represents a major advancement in the digital transformation of justice. Biometric technology enhances the reliability, security, and efficiency of various judicial functions, such as remote access to court records and virtual hearings. The European regulatory framework, particularly the eIDAS Regulation and its proposed amendments, provides a solid foundation for deploying biometric technologies across Member States to ensure interoperability, security, and trust.

However, the use of biometric systems presents challenges, particularly in terms of data protection, potential biases, and operational risks. Comparative analyses of digital identity management practices across countries have underscored the need for a balanced approach. Although biometric technologies offer superior security and user convenience, they require stringent data protection measures and careful management of associated risks. The successful implementation of biometric systems in

[53] 'Escanear el iris a cambio de criptomonedas: los jóvenes atiborran las colas mientras los expertos piden andarse con ojo' <https://www.huffingtonpost.es/life/escanear-iris-cambio-criptomonedas-jovenes-atiborran-colas-expertos-piden-andarse-ojo.html> last accessed 2 March 2024.

judicial contexts depends on a combination of technological innovation, robust governance, and user education. This integrated approach facilitates the development of a more accessible, efficient, and trustworthy digital justice system.

Bibliography

Committee of Ministers of the Council of Europe, 'Guidelines on Online Dispute Resolution Mechanisms in Civil and Administrative Court Proceedings' (2021).

Conforti O DF, 'Diseño de una plataforma de resolución de conflictos por medios electrónicos en el ámbito de consumo' in Esteban de la Rosa F (ed), *Justicia digital, mercado y resolución de litigios de consumo. Innovación en el diseño del acceso a la justicia* (Aranzadi 2021) 133, 158.

Cortés P, 'Using Technology and ADR Methods to Enhance Access to Justice' (2018) 1(2) International Journal of Online Dispute Resolution 103, 121.

Cotino Hueso L, 'La preocupante falta de garantías constitucionales y administrativas en las notificaciones electrónicas' (2021) 57 Revista General de Derecho Administrativo RGDA Iustel.

Data Protection Working Party Opinion 3/2012 on developments in biometric technologies [2012] 00720/12/EN WP193.

De Asís Pulido M, 'La incidencia de las nuevas tecnologías en el derecho al debido proceso' (2020) 6(2), Ius et Scientia 186, 199.

Esteban de la Rosa F and Zeleznikow J, 'Making Intelligent Online Dispute Resolution Tools Available to Self-Represented Litigants in the Public Justice System: Towards an Ethical Use of the AI Technology in the Administration of Justice' in Proceedings of the Eighteenth International Conference for Artificial Intelligence and Law (São Paulo 2021).

Esteban de la Rosa F, '¿Quo vadis plataforma europea de resolución en línea de litigios de consumo? Nuevos pasos en la instauración de un acceso universal digital a la justicia alternativa de consumo en Europa' in Esteban de la Rosa F (ed), *Justicia digital, mercado y resolución de litigios de consumo: Innovación en el diseño de acceso a la justicia* (Aranzadi 2021) 35, 60.

European Commission, 'Digitalisation of justice in the European Union. A toolbox of opportunities' (Communication) COM (2020) 710 final.

European Commission, 'Proposal for a Regulation of the European Parliament and of the Council amending Regulation (EU) 910/2014 as regards establishing a framework for a European Digital Identity' COM (2021) 281 final.

European Commission, 'Shaping Europe's digital future' (Communication) COM (2020) 67 final.

European Commission, 'White Paper on Artificial Intelligence—A European approach to excellence and trust' COM (2020) 65 final.

European Parliament, 'Report on the proposal for a regulation of the European Parliament and of the Council on laying down harmonised rules on Artificial Intelligence (Artificial Intelligence Act) and amending certain Union Legislative Acts' COM (2021)0206 – C9-0146/2021 – 2021/0106(COD).

Fernández-Fígares Morales Mª.J, *Audiencias telemáticas en la justicia: Presente y futuro* (Tirant Lo Blanch 2021).

Galindo Ayuda F, 'Inteligencia artificial y acceso a documentación jurídica: sobre el uso de las TICs en la práctica jurídica' (2019) 1(18) Democracia Digital e Governo Electrônico 144, 166.

García Sanz J González Guimaraes-da Silva J, 'Las "vistas telemáticas" en el proceso civil español: visión comparada, regulación y cuestiones prácticas que suscita su celebración', Diario La Ley (2020).

Guide for Dialogue on the Efficient, Quality and Ethical Design and Use of Technological Tools in Civil Justice, by COTEC Foundation and Unidad de Excelencia de Investigación Sociedad Digital: Seguridad y Protección de Derechos, University of Granada (Guide to e-Justice). Guía para el diálogo sobre el diseño y uso eficiente, de calidad y ético de herramientas tecnológicas en la justicia civil, de la Fundación COTEC y la Unidad de Excelencia de Investigación Sociedad Digital: Seguridad y Protección de Derechos, Universidad de Granada.

Guide to Good Practices in the Use of New Technologies for the Delivery of Justice in Mexico (Mexicoevalúa). Guía de buenas prácticas en el uso de nuevas tecnologías para la impartición de justicia mexicana (Mexicoevalúa).

Interoperability and Security Guide for Authentication, Certificates and Electronic Signatures of the State Technical Committee for Electronic Judicial Administration. *Guía de interoperabilidad y seguridad de autenticación, certificados y firma electrónica del comité técnico estatal de la administración judicial.*

Larson DA, 'Designing and Implementing a State Court ODR System: From Disappointment to Celebration' (2019) 2, Journal of Dispute Resolution 77, 102.

Marchal Escalona N, 'El nuevo marco europeo sobre notificación y obtención de pruebas en el extranjero: hacia un espacio judicial europeo digitalizado' (2022) 74(1) Revista Española de Derecho Internacional 155, 179.

Marchal Escalona N, 'La nueva normativa europea relativa a la notificación y traslado de documentos y obtención de pruebas en el extranjero: los Reglamentos (UE) 2020/1783 y 2020/1784 de 25 de noviembre de 2020' (2021) 41 Revista Electrónica de Estudios Internacionales 10, 19.

Moreno García L, 'Las notificaciones procesales por medios electrónicos a la luz de la reciente doctrina constitucional' in Conde J and Serrano G (eds), *La justicia digital en España y la Unión Europea* (Atelier 2019) 61, 70.

Order ETD/465/2021, 6th May, on remote video identification methods for the issuance of qualified electronic certificates, 2021. *Orden ETD/465/2021, de 6 de mayo, por la que se regulan los métodos de identificación remota por vídeo para la expedición de certificados electrónicos cualificados* (SPA).

Parra García JL, 'Modernización tecnológica del proceso judicial. Lecciones aprendidas en el contexto europeo' in Gómez MF and Fernández M (eds), *Modernización digital e innovación en la Administración de Justicia* (Aranzadi 2019) 315, 342.

Romeo Casabona CM, 'Datos personales (Comentario al artículo 4.1 RGPD)' in Reigada AT (ed), *Comentario al Reglamento General de Protección de Datos y a la Ley Orgánica de Protección de Datos Personales y Garantía de los Derechos Digitales, tomo I* (Thomson-Reuters, Aranzadi 2018) 573, 589.

Susskind R, *Online Courts and the Future of Justice* (OUP 2019).

Smith R, 'Digitalisation and the Courts of England and Wales' (2018) Law, Technology and Access to Justice.

Pirttilä T et al, *Caseflow Management Handbook. Guide for Enhanced Court Administration in Civil Proceedings* (Lappeenranta University of Technology, The Research Institute on Judicial System of the National Research Council of Italy (IRSIG-CNR) 2016).

Pérez Daudí V, 'La justicia civil ante el reto de las TIC' in Conde J and Serrano G (eds), *La justicia digital en España y la Unión Europea* (Atelier 2019) 87, 101.

Picó i Junoy J, *Las garantías constitucionales del proceso* (Bosch 2012).

Valero Canales AL, 'Consideraciones procesales del expediente judicial electrónico' in Gómez MF and Fernández M (eds), *Modernización digital e innovación en la Administración de Justicia* (Aranzadi 2019) 343, 367.

PART II

THE IMPACT OF TECHNOLOGY IN TRANSFORMING NATIONAL COURTS AND CROSS-BORDER LITIGATION

5
Technology as an Instrument to Promote Settlement in Advance of Court Adjudication—Developments in England and Wales

*Pablo Cortés**

A. Introduction

The English civil justice system has increasingly emphasized early settlements as a key objective, driven by the constraints of limited court resources and the high costs associated with adversarial litigation.[1] This policy reflects a strategic move to alleviate the burden on the judicial system and reduce financial and time expenditures for the parties involved.[2] In England and Wales, the Civil Procedure Rules (CPR) actively promote the pursuit of settlements from the moment a claim emerges up to the trial

* Professor of Civil Justice, University of Leicester. An earlier version of parts of this chapter has already appeared in Pablo Cortés, 'Embedding alternative dispute resolution in the civil justice system: a taxonomy for ADR referrals and a digital pathway to increase the uptake of ADR' (2023) 43(2) Legal Studies 312–30.

[1] Neil Andrews, *The Modern Civil Process: Judicial and Alternative Forms of Dispute Resolution in England* (Mohr Siebeck 2008).

[2] Lord Woolf, *Access to Justice, Final Report* (Lord Chancellor's Department 1995).

Pablo Cortés, *Technology as an Instrument to Promote Settlement in Advance of Court Adjudication—Developments in England and Wales* In: *Digitalization and Artificial Intelligence in Courts*. Edited by: Fernando Esteban de la Rosa, Pablo Cortés, and Nuria Marchal Escalona, Oxford University Press. © Pablo Cortés 2025. DOI: 10.1093/9780198918752.003.0005

stage.[3] This encouragement extends to alternative dispute resolution (ADR) methods, and in particular to mediation. Given that legal expenses can be disproportionately high for claims of low and medium value, English litigants are increasingly required to engage in more cost-effective ADR options in advance of having their dispute adjudicated by a judge. However, while ADR may be chosen by well-informed commercial parties or take place out of concern for potential cost penalties, its adoption is more common among parties who are referred to an ADR process at some point during the dispute life cycle, typically as part of a court annexed or sponsored ADR process.

The referral task is progressively being supported by technology, which directs parties to ADR processes that are gradually operating online. These digital ADR processes are collectively known as online dispute resolution (ODR). This chapter examines how English law encourages, and at times requires, parties to explore a settlement in advance of court adjudication throughout their dispute life cycle. This approach acknowledges that most civil disputes are suited for party agreement, and accordingly, it deserves promotion as it brings important cost and times savings for both the parties and the courts, and a higher party satisfaction with the resolution of their disputes.[4] The push towards referring civil disputes to out-of-court methods has gained momentum with the rollout of court digitalization in England, known as the Reform Program.[5] A number of initiatives are strategically designed to enhance the adoption of ADR and ODR processes. Key among them is the imposition of mandatory participation in ADR, accompanied by the introduction of sanctions for instances of non-compliance. Furthermore, the integration of an online negotiation module in the pre-action stages of most personal injury claims and in the digital court process for small claims exemplify these efforts, promoting a shift towards more digitalized and consensual-based dispute resolution approach.[6] A further pivotal component of the English Reform program is the use of a unified digital platform for Civil, Family, and Tribunal proceedings, which runs on a shared database infrastructure. Despite the appearance of bespoken court processes tailored to accommodate distinct case types—thereby presenting varied 'front ends'—they fundamentally operate as different interfaces to a singular, underlying system.[7]

This chapter observes that the ongoing digitalization of English courts is integrating ADR and ODR further in the civil justice system, and it suggests that referrals will be particularly beneficial for court users when they are timely. This chapter examines the evolving reliance of the English civil justice system on technological advancements

[3] Civil Procedure Rules (CPR), r 1.4(1), (2), 26.4 and 44.2(5)(a).

[4] Roselle Wissler, 'The Effects of Mandatory Mediation: Empirical Research on the Experience of Small Claims and Common Pleas Courts' (1997) 33(3) Willamette L Rev 565, and M Galanter, 'The Hundred-Year Decline of Trials and the Thirty Years War' (2005) 57(5) Stan L Rev 1255–75, 1266.

[5] GOV.UK, Guidance—The HMCTS Reform Programme (2024). Available at <https://www.gov.uk/guidance/the-hmcts-reform-programme> last accessed 9 October 2024.

[6] CPR PD 51R introduced an Online Court pilot scheme for money claims in the County Court. Michael Briggs LJ, *Civil Courts Structure Review: Interim Report* (December 2015) and *Final Report* (July 2016) (hereinafter Briggs IR and Briggs FR). See also Ministry of Justice, *Transforming Our Justice System: Summary of Reforms and Consultation* (September 2016) and Government Response (February 2017). Ministry of Justice, 'Increasing the Use of Mediation in the Civil Justice System' (July 2022) 12–18.

[7] Colin Briss, 'The 24th Competition Law Association Burrell Lecture: Is a focus on data the way to improve access to justice in a multifaceted world?' (30 November 2023) para 41.

to mandate parties' engagement in settlement discussions prior to the initiation of expensive trial proceedings. It delineates the junctures within the dispute resolution continuum at which parties might be directed towards ADR processes—ranging from pre-litigation stages, as a prerequisite for filing a court claim, to post-defence stages in tandem with ongoing court proceedings and up to the trial stage. The analysis illustrates how strategic ADR referrals are being embedded throughout various phases of a dispute's lifecycle, highlighting a systemic shift towards integrating conciliatory mechanisms facilitated by technological platforms, aimed at mitigating the financial and time burdens traditionally associated with court litigation. Accordingly, the first section of this chapter examines when the ADR referrals take place before parties contemplate litigation. This is the case when sectorial laws require businesses to offer an ODR to consumers in many regulated sectors. The second section of the chapter discusses the scenario when the claimant has decided to issue a claim in court, but the court rules require them first to comply with pre-action ADR/ODR. Namely, the requirement for divorcing couples to attend mediation, information, and assessment meetings (MIAMs); the employees' obligation to notify the Advisory, Conciliation and Arbitration Service (ACAS) which in turn informs them about their early conciliation scheme; and the pre-action claims portals that require parties to negotiate digitally the financial settlement of personal injury claims resulting from road traffic accidents. Lastly, the third and final section of the chapter discusses the small claims telephone mediation that has become mandatory for most civil claims under £10,000 before parties can progress to trial. The chapter concludes noting that the court digitalization program is further eroding the 'alternative' element of ADR by embedding it deeper into the civil justice system, and notably by making participation in ADR mandatory and by developing an online referral system that seeks to prioritize settlements as the preferred outcome for resolving civil disputes, resulting in a more process-pluralistic approach within the English civil justice system.

B. Mandatory ADR: Consumer Dispute Resolution

Informal and accessible consumer ADR and ODR processes are widely considered to be more suitable than courts for resolving most consumer disputes in a cost-efficient and proportionate manner. This is why there is a growing number of sectorial legislations that require businesses to be adhered to a certified ADR entity;[8] this is especially so for those businesses working in regulated sectors where they are subject to specific rules, standards, and oversight by governmental bodies, and they are often required to obtain a licence to operate. In sectors, such as banking, telecommunications, and

[8] See Department for Business, Energy & Industrial Strategy (BEIS) 'Modernising Consumer Markets' Consumer Green Paper (April 2018) para 145. Available at <https://tinyurl.com/yd7me6bq> last accessed 9 October 2024. On 26 February 2024 the European Parliament introduced in its first reading an amendment on the ADR Directive 11/2013 to make mandatory the participation of airlines in an ADR scheme. See proposal for a directive of the European Parliament and of the Council amending Directive 2013/11/EU on alternative dispute resolution for consumer disputes, as well as Directives (EU) 2015/2302, (EU) 2019/2161 and (EU) 2020/1828. Available at <https://www.europarl.europa.eu/doceo/document/A-9-2024-0060_EN.pdf> last accessed 9 October 2024.

energy, consumers can often decide whether to bring a claim to their local court or via the certified ADR entity, which in most cases is free for the consumer, operates online, promotes early consensual settlements, and leaves the door open to the consumer to pursue the claim in court should they become dissatisfied with the ADR/ODR outcome.[9]

Consumer ADR entities are sometimes referred to as consumer dispute resolution (CDR) providers as they are remarkably different from commercial ADR schemes, and they often operate as the only realistic dispute resolution option available to consumers given the unsuitability of formal courts adjudication for many low-value consumer claims.[10] Hence, CDR is replacing the courts in the sectors where they operate because they are informal, specialized, and normally free. Most CDR bodies operate on a documents-only basis, and they are gradually employing technology as a filter to ensure that claims fall within the scope of the claims covered by the ADR scheme. These CDR entities are normally accessible online and by telephone, where consumers can reach out to trained staff that answer queries, provide information, and even some legal advice.[11]

Whilst there is a long history of consumer CDR in the UK, its development sped up in the last decade as a consequence of changes in regulated sectors requiring traders to be adhered to certified ADR entities. Within the substantial reform of the CDR landscape, a major development took place with the ADR Directive, which was transposed into UK law.[12] In a similar vein to the revocation of the Mediation Directive,[13] the UK Government decided to amend the consumer ADR legislation as a result of a wider policy of repealing the aspects from EU laws that provided preferential treatment to parties residing in the EU.[14] However, the changes have not been very significant thus far, as the regulation of CDR in the UK follows the EU model whereby regulators certify CDR providers in accordance to the legal standards that largely follow those set in the Directive.

The ADR regulations for CDR in England,[15] which essentially derives from the EU ADR Directive, seek the policy objective of stimulating trade, especially in the online arena, by ensuring that consumer complaints can be resolved by certified ADR bodies.[16] Although at the time of writing the certification process is voluntary, the Government announced its intention to require all CDR providers to be publicly certified so that they can be better monitored by the regulators.[17]

[9] Pablo Cortés, *The Law of Consumer Redress* (CUP 2017).

[10] Christopher Hodges, *Delivering Dispute Resolution—A Holistic Review of Models in England and Wales* (Hart 2019).

[11] ibid.

[12] The Alternative Dispute Resolution for Consumer Disputes (Competent Authorities and Information) Regulations 2015, which implemented the Directive 2013/11 on alternative dispute resolution for consumer disputes and Regulation 524/2013 on online dispute resolution.

[13] Cross-Border Mediation (EU Directive) (EU Exit) Regulations 2019.

[14] The Consumer Protection (Amendment etc.) (EU Exit) Regulations 2018.

[15] The Alternative Dispute Resolution for Consumer Disputes (Competent Authorities and Information) Regulations 2015, s 19(2).

[16] Communication on ADR for Consumer Disputes in the Single Market COM(2011) 791. See generally, Pablo Cortés (ed), *The New Regulatory Framework for Consumer Dispute Resolution* (OUP 2016).

[17] Department for Business, Energy and Industrial Strategy, 'Consultation outcome—Reforming competition and consumer policy: government response' (April 2022) CP 656.

While the ADR regulations do not make the participation in CDR compulsory, English traders are required to participate in a certified ADR entity in many regulated sectors, including energy, estate agents, financial services, higher education, gambling, legal services, pensions, postal services, property letting agents, and telecommunications. These CDR processes require consumers first to elevate their complainants to the traders' internal complaint system before they can escalate them to a certified CDR process, which frequently offers parties the option to settle the case before is adjudicated. In addition, traders adhered to CDR schemes are required to inform consumers about a certified CDR entity once they have rejected a complaint and they are required to participate in the CDR process. But if the business is not adhered to an ADR scheme, then the only option left for consumers is to seek redress in court. Indeed, consumer disputes are one of the main categories of small claims reaching the courts.

CDR processes for consumers vary significantly, but the most predominant model in the UK is the ombudsman, who operates mostly on digital communications, adopts an inquisitorial approach, and employs a tiered process that provides a conciliatory stage in advance of adjudication. The other main consumer ADR process is adjudication, which, akin to the final ombudsman stage, issues decisions that are normally only binding when accepted by the consumer complainant, who can instead refuse the outcome and pursue the claim in court. Both processes encourage parties to consider an amicable settlement in advance of the adjudication by a third party. Moreover, these CDR processes have often built-in economic incentives, which principally consist of reducing or eliminating the business case fee when parties settle the complaint.

The ombudsman procedure is characterized by providing a diagnosis stage, where a case handler advises consumers on whether they may have a claim that falls within its scope.[18] Although this stage is currently performed manually, there is clear potential for automation, which could be effectively supported by artificial intelligence systems. After this initial triage, most disputes are resolved informally by a case handler acting as a facilitator. The procedure is akin to an informal mediation carried out through caucus discussions over the phone or in writing—increasingly through asynchronous email and web-chat communications. Claims that are not settled move to the next stage, where the case handler issues a reasoned recommendation (often called a 'provisional assessment') based on what is considered to be a fair and reasonable outcome. This phase of the process is similar to early neutral evaluation (ENE),[19] but some ombudsman processes invite parties to comment on the provisional assessment before the case handler issues the decision. If one of the parties is not satisfied with the decision, then the dispute escalates to a more senior case handler (ie, an ombudsman) who will issue a final decision, which will normally be binding on the trader when the consumer has accepted the decision.

[18] Christopher Hodges, 'Consumer Ombudsmen: Better Regulation and Dispute Resolution' (2014) 15(1) ERA Forum 593–608.

[19] ENE is an ADR process whereby an independent evaluator, who is often a judge, provides the parties with a preliminary assessment of the facts and legal merits. While the outcome is not binding, the impartial assessment often helps parties to reach a settlement.

The UK Government considered the need to enhance the quality standards of certified CDR schemes and discussed the necessity of expanding mandatory CDR schemes to include traders in sectors where consumers face significant issues.[20] In doing so, it recognized the need to provide consumers with greater access to more CDR processes that allow them to circumvent expensive court proceedings.[21] The main hurdle for consumers seeking redress is to persuade businesses from non-regulated markets to opt in, and pay for, CDR.[22] It is thus not surprising that the main reason why consumers do not use ADR before going to court is because businesses normally refuse to participate in CDR unless they are legally or contractually required to do so.[23]

The Government is considering the extension of mandatory CDR model to other sectors where there is a high volume of consumer grievances. For example, a mandatory railway ombudsman[24] was approved in this sector, and in a similar vein it became mandatory for private landlords to be part of an ADR scheme to deal with complaints relating to repairs and maintenance.[25] In addition, the Government signalled plans to extend mandatory participation for businesses in the motor vehicles sector (to include the sale of new and used vehicles as well as their repair) and in the home improvements market.[26] Yet, the Government believes that it would be disproportionate to make CDR mandatory in every sector due to the costs imposed upon business.[27]

Therefore, a crucial limitation of the current signposting system is the voluntary nature of CDR in non-regulated sectors, especially as the cost of CDR is typically covered by a trader who has already rejected the claim and knows that the consumer is unlikely to contemplate the escalation of a low value claim through the courts. Effective and accessible courts can thus help to fill these gaps ensuring consumer redress, and when appropriate, referring parties to CDR. Some of these gaps may be covered by the increasingly digitalized small claims court (ie, the Online Civil Money Claim), but as it has been noted elsewhere, there is a need to coordinate the existing CDR infrastructure with the courts, especially in light of its current digitalization.[28] Furthermore, as it is examined below, there are other areas where considering ADR or ODR is a precondition to issue a claim in court—namely in family, employment, and in personal injury claims from road traffic accidents.

[20] See Department for Business, Energy & Industrial Strategy (BEIS) 'Resolving Consumer Disputes—Alternative Dispute Resolution and the Court System' Final Report (April 2018) 4. Available at <https://tinyurl.com/ybgxnjdh> last accessed 9 October 2024.

[21] ibid para 10.

[22] The consultation noted that the voluntary Consumer Ombudsman received only 5,600 complaints from non-regulated sectors in 2017, and businesses agreed to participate in only 6 per cent of these cases. ibid para 145.

[23] The most common reasons given by consumers for not using ADR (70 per cent) were that the trader refused to participate. See BEIS (n 20).

[24] See <https://www.railombudsman.org/about-us/> last accessed 9 October 2024.

[25] See The Property Ombudsman <https://www.tpos.co.uk> and the Property Redress Scheme <https://www.theprs.co.uk/Consumer> last accessed 9 October 2024.

[26] The Property Ombudsman <https://www.tpos.co.uk> and the Property Redress Scheme <https://www.theprs.co.uk/Consumer> last accessed 9 October 2024.

[27] BEIS (n 20) para 155.

[28] Pablo Cortés, 'The Online Court: Filling the Gaps of the Civil Justice System?' (2017) 36(1) Civil Justice Quarterly 54–71. See also the discussion in section D of this chapter.

C. ADR Referrals as a Pre-Condition to Start Litigation: Pre-action Requirements in Family, Employment and Personal Injury Cases

1. Family mediation

Similar to developments in the consumer sector, family law has become a focal point for public policy efforts aimed at transforming the culture of dispute resolution. This includes mandating couples that are going through a divorce to explore mediation before initiating court proceedings.[29] The enactment of the Family Law Act signified the beginning of official support for amicable resolutions. Echoing the Civil Procedure Rules, the Family Procedure Rules explicitly state that judges possess case management authority to encourage the parties to use a non-court dispute resolution procedure as a primary objective.[30] This shift in language from 'ADR' to 'non-court dispute resolution,' mirroring changes in the Commercial Court's terminology,[31] underscores the intention to position mediation and similar mechanisms not as alternatives to, but as integral components of, the legal process.

In matters of divorce and child custody, the legal structure supports the use of ADR. Both the First Hearing and Dispute Resolution Appointment and the Financial Dispute Resolution (FDR) session involve a specially trained district judge to facilitate a resolution in an expedient, cost-effective, and amicable manner.[32] Settlement proposals are required to be exchanged seven days before these sessions. The FDR proceedings are conducted 'without prejudice' (ie, the information exchanged is confidential and cannot be shared with the trial judge), with the District Judge acting as a mediator—or more accurately, a conciliator, offering settlement suggestions—without further participation in the case. The FDR approach has been praised by the Master of the Rolls, who is the judicial head of civil justice in England and Wales, as an effective form of ADR integrated within the court system.[33] Although these ADR processes have been primarily utilized for property division and child arrangements for over 25 years, the adoption of pre-action mediation represents a newer initiative.[34]

Since 2014 the Family Procedure Rules require individuals seeking to issue proceedings to attend a Mediation Information and Assessment Meeting (MIAM) to discuss with a private certified mediator whether their dispute is capable of being resolved through mediation or another ADR process.[35] Attendance is mandatory, barring exceptions such as domestic violence or child protection issues.[36] The court application form's first page requires applicants to confirm their participation in a

[29] Part III, Family Law Act 1996.

[30] Family Procedure Rules (FPR) 2010 r 1(4)(2)(f) and Part 3.

[31] HMCTS, The Business and Property Courts of England and Wales, The Commercial Court Guide, 11th edn, (2022).

[32] FPR r 9.17(1).

[33] Geoffrey Vos, 'The Relationship between Formal and Informal Justice', Hull University (26 March 2021) para 21. Available at <https://www.judiciary.uk/announcement-type/speeches/> last accessed 9 October 2024.

[34] Practice Direction Supplementing FPR Pt 3 (Pre-Application Protocol for Mediation Information and Assessment), Annex B.

[35] FPR r 3.7.

[36] FPR r 3.8.

MIAM, increasingly available online, especially following the surge in demand for remote communication methods during the period of COVID-19 restrictions.

The online MIAMs rely on video conferencing tools like Zoom and Microsoft Teams, alongside digital document sharing and electronic signing. These digital tools have enhanced accessibility and convenience for participants, especially those facing mobility issues or residing in remote areas. The Family Mediation Council and other regulatory bodies have facilitated this shift by providing comprehensive guidelines and best practices, ensuring the quality and security of online sessions.[37] While the digital approach has demonstrated significant benefits in terms of efficiency, cost-effectiveness, and inclusivity, challenges such as technology access and ensuring confidentiality remain critical considerations. This development illustrates a broader trend towards integrating digital solutions in ADR processes, aiming to make dispute resolution more accessible and responsive to the needs of a modern and increasingly digital society.

MIAMs foster a collaborative atmosphere, urging parties to pursue interest-based resolution strategies before their positions become rigid within the legal system. Despite a high settlement rate from family mediations, the conversion rate from MIAMs to actual mediations remains below its potential.[38] With the goal of increasing conversions, the Ministry of Justice launched in 2021 a voucher scheme whereby parties attending a MIAM will be informed of the possibility of applying for a £500 voucher towards the cost of their mediation.[39] This scheme is not means tested and it is administered by the Family Mediation Council. This incentive quickly proved effective with 27,000 families supported through this voucher scheme which resulted in two-thirds of families participating in the mediation to spare court proceedings.[40] Its success indicates that reducing mediation costs can significantly motivate individuals, in contrast to commercial entities, to engage in mediation.

However, the participation levels in MIAMs are low,[41] partly because attendance is not compulsory for respondents, and a significant number of claimants also

[37] Family Mediation Council, Guidance for Online Video Mediation (September 2016). Available at <https://www.familymediationcouncil.org.uk/wp-content/uploads/2016/09/FMC-Guidance-for-Online-Video-Mediation-September-2016.pdf> last accessed 9 October 2024. See also Family Mediation Standards Board, Guidance on Information and Assessment Meetings During Coronavirus Social Distancing Period (19 March 2020). Available at <https://www.familymediationcouncil.org.uk/wp-content/uploads/2020/03/FMSB-Guidance-on-Information-and-Assessment-Meetings-During-Coronavirus-Social-Distancing-Period-19.03.20.pdf> last accessed 9 October 2024.

[38] An empirical study found that a full or partial agreement was reached in 68 per cent of cases. See Becky Hamlyn, Emma Coleman, and Mark Sefton, 'Mediation Information and Assessment Meetings (MIAMs) and mediation in private family law disputes—Quantitative research findings' (Ministry of Justice Analytical Series, 2015) 3.

[39] Ministry of Justice, '£1 million voucher scheme to help families resolve disputes outside of court' Press release (26 March 2021). Available at <https://www.gov.uk/government/news/1-million-voucher-scheme-to-help-families-resolve-disputes-outside-of-court?utm_medium = email&utm_source=> last accessed 9 October 2024. See also The Law Society, 'Family Mediation Week 2022: further investment for mediation voucher scheme' (17 January 2022). Available at <https://www.lawsociety.org.uk/topics/family-and-children/family-mediation-week-2022-further-investment-for-mediation-voucher-scheme> last accessed 9 October 2024.

[40] Ministry of Justice, 'Thousands of families spared from damaging courtroom conflict' Press Release (3 April 2024). Available at <https://www.gov.uk/government/news/thousands-of-families-spared-from-damaging-courtroom-conflict> last accessed 9 October 2024.

[41] Hamlyn et al (n 38) 3.

bypass this step. Additionally, the discontinuation of legal aid for family matters has resulted in a significant reduction of the number of parties being referred by solicitor to MIAMs, contrary to the assumption that lawyers may have economic incentives to discourage parties from using ADR. Briggs LJ noted this paradoxical decline in the family mediation uptake following the reduction of legal aid, attributing this to a lack of awareness among self-represented litigants about the benefits of ADR.[42]

The limited engagement with MIAMs can also be attributed to several factors: judges do not impose cost penalties as these family disputes are not non-adversarial processes; the timing of MIAMs, occurring in the pre-action phase, limits their perceived value; and, as Hodges pointed out, the external provision of MIAMs by certified mediators from the private sector are minimally integrated into the dispute resolution landscape.[43] Addressing these challenges requires a more cohesive approach, including further integration of private MIAMs into legal procedures (aided by ongoing digitalization efforts) and proactive judicial encouragement of ADR, particularly when MIAM attendance is lacking.[44]

2. Employment conciliation

Conciliation represents a significant form of pre-action ADR in employment disputes, functioning under the broader category of non-adjudicatory resolution methods where a conciliator, acting as a neutral third party, may adopt a proactive role. This includes suggesting potential settlements, a practice reminiscent of evaluative mediation. In the UK, this service is provided by the Advisory, Conciliation and Arbitration Service (ACAS), an independent statutory entity financed by the Government, delivering conciliation for cases within the Employment Tribunal's scope.[45] Since 2014, claimants are required to inform ACAS, either online or via telephone, before submitting a claim to the Employment Tribunal. Thus, technology is used once again as a means to inform parties about ADR. ACAS assigns a conciliator within two working days. Participation in this early conciliation phase is voluntary, with parties free to join or withdraw at any point, and it remains an option even after a tribunal claim has been initiated.[46]

The primary aim of conciliation is to preserve the employment relationship, ideally resolving disputes before the tribunal proceedings begin. Its key benefits include cost-free service and, upon successful resolution, reduced expenses and time in settling the

[42] Michael Briggs IR (n 6) para 6.11. See also National Statistics, Legal Aid in England and Wales (Ministry of Justice, January to March 2017) 28.

[43] Hodges (n 10) 337.

[44] Under FPR r 3.3(1) the court must consider, at every stage of the proceedings, whether ADR is appropriate.

[45] The Employment Tribunals Act 1996 s 18 (as amended by the Enterprise and Regulatory Reform Act 2013). For the online notification see <www.acas.org.uk/earlyconciliation> last accessed 9 October 2024.

[46] This service is known as 'post-ET1 conciliation' since it occurs following the submission of an Employment Tribunal claim form, ie, 'ET1'. See 'Evaluation of ACAS Conciliation in Employment Tribunal Applications 2016', ACAS Research Paper, Ref: 04/16, 12. Most of these claims relate to unfair dismissal claims, workplace discrimination, redundancy payments or disputes around selection procedures, deductions from wages or unpaid notice/holiday pay, rights to time off or flexible working, and equal pay.

claim.[47] Additionally, conciliation offers the possibility of reaching agreements that extend beyond tribunal remedies, such as securing a positive job reference, apologies, or modifications in workplace behaviour or conditions.

The initial conciliation period is limited to one month, with a possible two-week extension. If needed, conciliation can be extended up to the tribunal hearing date (ie, the trial). ACAS reports that three-quarters of cases are resolved before requiring a tribunal hearing, with a 96 per cent user satisfaction rate highlighting the effectiveness of this service.[48]

Most early conciliation notifications to ACAS are made via an online form available in their website.[49] At the time of writing this ODR platform is operating in BETA, which means that it is still a testing platform released to a limited audience to identify issues, gather user feedback, and make improvements before its full-scale launch. If ACAS conciliation fails, parties can opt for a judicial mediation in a private preliminary hearing before a trained employment judge, where over 65 per cent of cases settle at this session or soon thereafter.[50] In addition, after the first case management hearing, parties can opt in for a 'judicial assessment', which similar to ENE, consists of an independent and confidential assessment of the strengths and weaknesses of the parties' claims.[51] While all these ADR processes may be conducted by the same judge, a different judge will be allocated if the case proceeds to trial.

Accessibility to the Employment Tribunal plays a pivotal role in mediation uptake. The Supreme Court's ruling in the UNISON case, which eliminated tribunal fees due to access to justice concerns, underscores this point.[52] The court noted that negotiation or mediation's effectiveness hinges on the assurance of a fair adjudication system if these measures fail, ensuring equitable bargaining between parties.[53] The removal of tribunal fees post-UNISON not only increased tribunal claims but also boosted early conciliation engagements by a quarter, compared to the previous year.[54]

[47] Linda Dickens, 'Employment Tribunals and Alternative Dispute Resolution' in Linda Dickens (ed), *Making Employment Rights Effective. Issues of Enforcement and Compliance* (Hart Publishing 2012).

[48] ACAS, Annual Report and Accounts 2021–22, 23. Available at <https://assets.publishing.service.gov.uk/government/uploads/system/uploads/attachment_data/file/1089912/acas-annual-report-accounts-2021-2022-web-optimised.pdf> 5, last accessed 9 October 2024.

[49] Available at <https://www.acas.org.uk/notify/wizard/individual/form> last accessed 9 October 2024.

[50] Ministry of Justice, *Judicial Mediation Employment Tribunals* (July 2014). Accessed via <https://formfinder.hmctsformfinder.justice.gov.uk/t612-eng.pdf> last accessed 9 October 2024. See also Andrew Boon, Peter Urwin, and Valeriya Karuk, 'What Difference Does It Make? Facilitative Judicial Mediation of Discrimination Cases in Employment Tribunals' (2011) 40 Industrial LJ 45.

[51] Presidential Guidance, Protocol on Judicial Assessments (3 October 2016). See also Employment Tribunals Regulations 2013 r 7.

[52] *UNISON, R v Lord Chancellor* [2017] UKSC 51 (26 July 2017). It must be noted that since this decision, the Government issued a consultation to re-introduce tribunal fees but at a much lower level with the objective of complying with the ruling of the Supreme Court. See Ministry of Justice, 'Introducing fees in the Employment Tribunals and the Employment Appeal Tribunal' (29 January 2024). Available at <https://tinyurl.com/yf53b3dd> last accessed 9 October 2024.

[53] Ministry of Justice, 'Introducing fees' (n 52) para 91.

[54] See ACAS, Quarterly Reports (April 2016–December 2016) and (April 2017–December 2017). Available at <http://www.acas.org.uk/index.aspx?articleid = 5203> last accessed 9 October 2024

Albeit it is not common to make a cost order in the employment tribunals,[55] the uptake of ADR would increase in employment disputes if tribunals issue cost sanctions to parties who refuse participation in ADR. The Employment Lawyers Association has suggested that non-participation in ADR could be considered unreasonable behaviour, potentially leading to a costs award, signifying a significant step towards promoting ADR in employment law.[56]

3. Online claim portals: the damages portal and the whiplash portal

Under the English Civil Procedure Rules parties are required to consider ADR from the pre-litigation stage in accordance with the prescribed conduct requirements contained in the pre-action protocols. These protocols provide claimants with clear guidelines on what they need to do prior to the issue of a claim. If parties do not comply with the protocols, they may not be awarded their costs in the event of succeeding.[57] As the Civil Justice Council observed:[58]

> There was broad support for the idea that a digital justice system will lead to significant savings in costs. Digitisation should facilitate early effective communication between parties and resolution of the dispute, or at least narrowing of the issues, before court proceedings are commenced. Costs has a role to play to encourage two things: the use of digital pre-action dispute resolution portals and compliance with pre-action protocols.

Several pre-action protocols now require prospective litigants to explore a settlement before they are allowed to escalate their claims to court. These pre-action processes are increasingly supported by ODR platforms that facilitate the negotiation between the parties and their legal representatives. Two important initiatives in this area in England are the Claims Portal for personal injury claims from road traffic accidents, and the Whiplash Portal for low-value personal injury claims also resulting from road traffic accidents.

The Claims Portal, aimed at road traffic accident-related personal injury claims under £25,000, facilitates settlements where the defendant admits liability, but the quantum of compensation is in dispute. Should the defendant insurer deny liability, the case may proceed to the County Court.[59]

The whiplash portal, introduced in 2021 and managed by the Motor Insurers' Bureau, a private professional association, which operates the portal at the Ministry of

[55] Tribunals will only make a cost order if one party has acted vexatiously, abusively, disruptively, or otherwise unreasonably in the bringing or conducting of the proceedings. See Employment Tribunals Rules of Procedure 2013, r 76.

[56] See Employment Lawyers Association, 'ADR and Employment Disputes' (November 2017) 41. Available at <tinyurl.com/tk386pyk> last accessed 9 October 2024.

[57] Practice Direction Pre-Action Conduct and Protocols para 13 and CPR rr 44.3 and 44.4.

[58] See Civil Justice Council, Cost Review, Final Report (July 2023) para ix. Available at <http://tinyurl.com/mv42tszx> last accessed 9 October 2024.

[59] The portal is governed by two pre-action protocols, the Pre-Action Protocol for Low Value Personal Injury Claims in Road Traffic Accidents.

Justice's behest, processing online low-value personal injury claims from road traffic accidents for free.[60] It targets minor personal injuries like whiplash, aiming to curb fraudulent claims and consequently reduce insurance premiums. The portal is accessible for claims involving minor personal injuries seeking compensation under £5,000, and for other losses up to £10,000.[61] The portal provides guidance on claim submission, offers parties a database of expert witnesses that can issue independent medical reports, assists with the claim processing, and to identify suitable compensation, which is largely dictated by fixed tariffs established in the Whiplash Injury Regulation 2021.

The introduction of this portal coincided with a revision to the CPR, raising the small claims track limit for personal injury cases from £1,000 to £5,000, a move that significantly limits the recoverability of legal representation costs.[62] The whiplash portal's objective is to expedite the resolution of small claims, avoiding the costs and delays associated with County Court litigation. Unlike the claims portal, the whiplash portal accommodates disputed liability claims and facilitates a novel and more flexible application of ADR, extending it beyond the pre-action phase. This portal allows for specific claim elements, such as contested liability, to be sent out of the portal to be adjudicated by a judge who will then send back the case to the portal once the discrete element of the dispute has been resolved, thereby enabling parties to settle remaining issues, notably the financial compensation, post-adjudication. Additionally, the portal permits up to three settlement offers, although, distinct from the claims portal, the final offer does not entail cost sanctions due to the nature of these small claims, which are typically exempted from cost orders.[63]

D. ADR Referrals during Court Proceedings: Integrating ADR in the Civil Justice System

Referrals to ADR and ODR processes are not confined solely to the period before the initiation of court proceedings. They can also occur via judicial referrals during the proceedings or be incorporated as part of the court process. The latter is exemplified in England through the integration of ADR in the Online Civil Money Claims process for small claims. As ADR becomes increasingly embedded in the court process, a phenomenon accelerated by the digitalization of court procedures, this chapter posits that ADR has transcended its status as merely an alternative to court processes. As is discussed later in this chapter, in England ADR has become an increasingly essential component of the civil justice system.

[60] See <https://www.officialinjuryclaim.org.uk> last accessed 9 October 2024.

[61] See MIB, Official Injury Claim. Available at <https://www.mib.org.uk/managing-insurance-data/mib-managed-services/whiplash-reforms-programme> last accessed 9 October 2024.

[62] Civil Procedure (Amendment No 2) Rules 2021. See also Pre-Action Protocol for Road Traffic Accidents and Civil Liability Act 2018.

[63] Under the English Civil Procedure Rules of 1998, Part 36 includes a provision about offers to settle. These offers come with automatic implications for legal costs if they are refused. Specifically, if a party turns down this formal offer, which is made without the judge's knowledge, and then fails to achieve a better result at trial, the offeree will have to pay all the legal costs from the moment the offer was refused.

English courts promote settlements by mandating that parties exchange their arguments and supporting evidence. Additionally, the imposition of a 'pay as you go' system for court fees—which are required to be paid by the claimant at various procedural stages, such as claim submission, track allocation, and trial[64]—along with legal fees, which are generally paid to counsel on an hourly basis, encourage settlements. Should a case proceed to trial, the majority of these costs can be recovered from the losing party, with two primary exceptions. The first exception arises when a party declines a reasonable settlement offer, which is not subsequently bettered in the judgment.[65] This penalty is predicated on the principle that the refusing party should have accepted a suitable settlement offer rather than allowing the claim to progress unnecessarily through the expensive court process. The second exception occurs when a party behaves unreasonably, either by failing to comply with a court order or by refusing an invitation to engage in mediation or an ADR process.[66] However court sanctions are less relevant when the ADR/ODR process is embedded into the legal proceedings, as discussed in the next section.

1. Compulsory ADR for small claims within the Online Civil Money Claims

His Majesty's Courts & Tribunals Service (HMCTS), which is an executive branch of the Ministry of Justice, administers a well-established Small Claims Mediation Service. Initiated in 2014, this service offers cost-free telephone mediation, facilitated by court staff trained in mediation techniques. Through a series of bilateral telephone conversations, the goal is to explore the potential for a settlement that would eliminate the need for trial attendance.[67] The popularity of this mediation scheme among litigants stems from several advantages: it provides a one-hour mediation at no charge, it is conducted via telephone (eliminating the need to attend court), allows parties to mediate without direct contact, and maintains confidentiality.

If the parties reach an agreement during the mediation, it is not legally binding by itself. However, the mediator will help draft a settlement agreement, which both parties will sign. This agreement then becomes a binding contract between the parties. In addition, if the settlement agreement is presented to the court at the hearing, the judge can make an order in the terms of the settlement. This converts the agreement into a binding court order, which can be enforced like any other court judgment.

The Small Claims process has been digitalized as part of the Online Civil Money Claims (OCMC) service, a crucial element of the judicial reform program. The

[64] Simon Roberts, 'Listing Concentrates the Mind': the English Civil Court as an Arena for Structured Negotiation 29(3) (2009) OJLS 457–79.

[65] CPR Pt 36.

[66] *Halsey v Milton Keynes General NHS Trust* [2004] EWCA Civ 576 and *PGF II SA V OMFS* [2013] EWCA Civ 1288.

[67] See HMCTS, Civil Mediation Service Manual (February 2009). Available at <https://www.judiciary.gov.uk/wp-content/uploads/JCO/Documents/Guidance/civil_court_mediation_service_manual_v3_mar09.pdf> last accessed 9 October 2024, and Sue Prince, 'Mediating Small Claims: Are We on the Right Track?' (2007) 26(2) CJQ 328–40.

OCMC, available for claims under £25,000[68] embeds ADR within its procedural framework, comprising three distinct steps: (1) claim submission and response via an online platform, enabling defendants to propose 'without prejudice' settlement offers; (2) referral of claims under £10,000 to telephone mediation, followed by case management assistance from a legal adviser or judge if a settlement is elusive; and (3) adjudication of unresolved claims by a judge through remote or in-person hearings, or based on document review.

The first step is designed to facilitate the electronic filing of claim statements and defence responses, ensuring claims fall within the specified scope and that the necessary information to process the case is submitted. It also aims to prevent dispute escalation by allowing defendants to make 'without prejudice' settlement offers, recorded within the online proceedings but not disclosed to the judge. Future developments could include an automated triage process, akin to British Columbia's Civil Resolution Tribunal's Solution Explorer,[69] aiming for periodic enhancements and relying on advanced software, potentially augmented by machine learning and AI, to recommend settlements.

In the second step, telephone mediation, which is at the time of writing due to become mandatory for most small claims, with parties automatically allocated a one-hour mediation slot.[70] This requirement aims to ensure active mediation participation, with non-compliance attracting sanctions.[71] This step applies to all small claims (under Part 7 of the CPR) in the County Court, typically valued under £10,000, and includes housing conditions and personal injury claims but excludes certain claims like possession claims issued under different procedures.[72] Currently, under the opt-out model, whereby parties may expressly opt out of the mediation without a sanction, parties reach a settlement in nearly half of the mediations.[73]

The online medium may impact on the existing incentives built into the small claims track. For example, presently the telephone mediation model has a powerful incentive for parties to use it because it is free and, if successful in reaching a settlement, parties obviate the need to take a day off work to attend a court hearing, which may be quite intimidating, especially for self-represented litigants (also known as litigants in person or LIPs). This incentive may dissolve once the third step is fully operational with digital hearings and documents-only adjudication becoming more prevalent. Furthermore, evidence-based research found that LIPs are less likely to settle and create additional work for court staff and judges, taking on average 50 per cent more

68 See <https://www.moneyclaims.service.gov.uk/eligibility> last accessed 9 October 2024.

69 Shannon Salter and Darin Thomson, 'Public-Centred Civil Justice Redesign: A Case Study of the British Columbia Civil Resolution Tribunal' (2017) 3 McGill Journal of Dispute Resolution 113. The Law Society, '21st Century Justice Project' Interim Report (April 2024) 7–9.

70 Practice Direction 51R – Online Civil Money Claims Pilot, s 6.

71 Ministry of Justice, (n 6) 14.

72 Ministry of Justice, 'Increasing the use of mediation in the civil justice system: Government response to consultation' (Updated 20 December 2023) para 5. Available at <http://tinyurl.com/bdhu5eyp> last accessed 9 October 2024. For possession claims, see CPR Pt 55.

73 HMCTS reported that out of the 10,250 mediation appointments attended in 2023, 48 per cent resulted in settlement. See HMCTS, Guidance, HMCTS services: Online Civil Money Claims (27 February 2024), available at <https://www.gov.uk/guidance/hmcts-services-online-civil-money-claims> last accessed 9 October 2024.

court time than legally represented litigants.[74] Hence, LIPs need not only referrals, but also incentives and sanctions, to increase further their participation in ADR. This view is being endorsed in the Government which plans to introduce mandatory mediation for small claims, with a view to extend it to all claims falling within the jurisdiction of the County Courts,[75] which include many civil claims under £100.00. The Government noted that the requirement to participate in mediation beyond small claims would entail referrals to external mediators outside the court service, and thus the Government is considering how to develop a system that would ensure the quality and accountability of private mediation services. Participation in the small claims mediation is incentivized by providing a convenient process (ie, over the phone and free of cost), and which refusal under the current proposal would trigger sanctions in terms of costs or the harsher sanction of striking down a party's claim or defence.[76] However, the Master of the Rolls has recently noted that compulsion is less likely to be required as the digitalization of the justice system develops automated referrals, which may include a further invitation to a face-to-face mediation when the telephone mediation has failed.[77]

For disputes that remain unresolved through mediation or other preliminary stages, they advance to the final third step of the legal process, where adjudication by a district judge occurs. These small claims represent the largest share of cases determined at trial in civil courts.[78] Judges can determine claims after a hearing which may take place via the telephone, video link, or after a face-to-face hearing. Under a new sub-pilot, a judge may also decide a case under £1,000 without a hearing, based on the documents submitted by the parties.[79] The removal of the oral hearing without the parties' consent represents a major shift from the traditional adversarial model of the common law system where orality has been a main pillar of the court proceedings. Moreover, it could potentially even amount to a breach of article 6 of the European Convention of Human Rights (unless the hearing is offered on an unrestricted appellate level) as stated in the guidelines developed by the Council of Europe for the use of ODR in the courts.[80]

In 2023 the Ministry of Justice conducted an evaluation of the OCMC.[81] At the time of the evaluation there was not a full online process for most claims as only steps one

[74] National Audit Office, 'Implementing Reforms to Civil Legal Aid' HC 784 (20 November 2014) 14–15.

[75] See Ministry of Justice (n 6).

[76] ibid 12–18.

[77] Geoffrey Vos, 'Mandating mediation: the digital solution' Chartered Institute of Arbitrators: Roebuck Lecture 2022 (8 June 2022) para 41.

[78] In the year to February 2021 small claims make up 77.8 per cent of the total number of final hearings in the civil courts. See Ministry of Justice, Civil Justice Statistics Quarterly. Available at <https://www.gov.uk/government/collections/civil-justice-statistics-quarterly> last accessed 9 October 2024.

[79] Practice Direction 51ZC—The Small Claims Paper Determination Pilot (1 June 2022).

[80] Guideline 23: 'The use of ODR in courts should not in itself deprive parties of a right to request an oral hearing before at least one level of jurisdiction.' See Council of Europe, Online Dispute Resolution Mechanisms in Civil and Administrative Proceedings, Guidelines (16 June 2021), available at <https://rm.coe.int/publication-guidelines-and-explanatory-memoreandum-odr-mechanisms-in-c/1680a4214e> last accessed 9 October 2024.

[81] Ministry of Justice, HMCTS, Corporate report: Assessing Access to Justice in HMCTS Services—Summary Report (12 December 2023) Part 5. Available at https://www.gov.uk/government/publications/assessing-access-to-justice-in-hmcts-services/assessing-access-to-justice-in-hmcts-services-summary-report#_ftn1 last accessed 9 October 2024.

and two were fully digitalized for all cases. The main problem identified in the evaluation of the data captured by the common platform was that only half of the cases completed the digital process, and thus, there was lack of information on the other half, some of which would have settled outside the system, but for the remaining it is unclear why the claimant did not apply for a default judgment or why the case was withdrawn.[82] The reasons behind the lack of completion remain unclear, but HMCTS observed that some users may have encountered usability challenges with OCMC. Such challenges could stem from technical difficulties, problems comprehending the content, issues providing the necessary information, or choosing to discontinue the claim for various other reasons.[83]

Despite the existing shortcomings, it must be acknowledged that this innovative judicial process reflects a broader shift in the English civil procedure, which seeks to reduce costly judicial involvement in the preliminary stages, which instead they now focused more on enabling dispute settlements, and reserving the involvement of a judge for a minority of cases that escalate to this third and final step of the court proceedings. Thus, OCMC aims to lessen the judicial time devoted to dispute resolution by reducing the frequency of judicial hearings (including trials) and enhancing the facilitation of settlements.[84]

The OCMC departs from the adjudicative paradigm and follows the basic premise of a 'multi-door courthouse' envisaged by Sander in the 1970s,[85] whereby the courts role extends to the provision of dispute resolution options that go beyond preparing the parties for trial.[86] Instead of directly assigning disputes to specific processes, the OCMC requires parties to engage in a series of procedural steps designed to encourage early settlements, thereby averting the need for more costly adjudication.[87] Therefore, the OCMC, akin to family proceedings, incorporates dispute resolution steps as part of its proceedings. This approach is due to be extended as part of the Reform Program to all non-criminal cases from the pre-court stage of the dispute life cycle.

A key aspect of the court digitalization program is the intensified referral to ADR at all three stages of the process. The Master of the Rolls initially announced the development of an 'online funnel' aimed at channelling civil, family, and tribunal claims through this digital platform.[88] Endorsed by the Judicial Review and Courts Act 2022[89] this initiative is poised to significantly enhance access to justice.[90] In a similar vein, Lord Briggs and the Law Society of England and Wales have called for a single digital entry point that provides legal information and advice on dispute resolution options.[91] However, the high public cost for developing and maintaining

[82] ibid 5.3.
[83] ibid 5.3.
[84] See UCL Laws and the Legal Education Foundation, 'Workshop Briefing Paper: Measuring Success in Online Courts: An Empirical Challenge' (October 2018).
[85] Frank Sander 'Varieties of Dispute Processing' (1976) 70 FRD 111.
[86] See John Sorabji, 'The Online Solutions Court—A Multi-door Courthouse for the 21st Century (2017) 36(1) CJQ 86–108.
[87] ibid 100. See, also, Dorcas Quek Anderson, 'The Convergence of ADR and ODR within the Courts: The Impact on Access to Justice' (2019) 38(1) CJQ 136.
[88] Geoffrey Vos MR, 'London International Disputes Week 2021: Keynote Speech' (10 May 2021) para 10.
[89] Chapter 2 Online procedure.
[90] Vos (n 88) para 36.
[91] The Law Society, '21st Century Justice Project' Interim Report (April 2024) 7–9.

such 'Solution Explorer' (ie, inspired by the online tool used by the Civil Resolution Tribunal in British Columbia) has been ruled out in favour of interconnecting a number of interoperable websites and apps from public and private providers that will provide authoritative and targeted advice on how to bring a claim against another party. Whether it is one or various websites, their goal is to inform disputants about the relevant pre-action protocols and ADR services. Should these initial attempts at resolution fail, cases will progress to pre-action court portals. In instances where disputes remain unresolved, a digital bundle, facilitated through an interoperable Application Programming Interface (API), will be prepared for transfer to the court, where additional ADR referrals may be made as the case moves towards trial.[92]

2. The fate of the 'alternative' element in 'alternative' dispute resolution

As ADR is being integrated into the court process, either by making it mandatory or making the refusal subject to cost sanctions, ADR can no longer be seen as an alternative to the court process, but rather as an integral part of the civil justice system. Indeed, the removal of the 'alternative' attribute of ADR has already happened in the Commercial Court and in the family courts which changed their nomenclature to 'negotiated dispute resolution' and 'non-court dispute resolution' because these consensual processes are no longer seen as an alternative or secondary to the court proceedings, but as a central part of it. This view has been endorsed by the Master of the Rolls, who stated that ADR 'should really be renamed as "Dispute Resolution" since it is not alternative at all.'[93]

This chapter highlights that dispute resolution integration is occurring at the pre-action stage, either through a statutory ADR/ODR option for consumers or as a prerequisite before filing a claim in court as it is the case for many family, employment, and personal injury claims. Additionally, ADR integration happens alongside court proceedings. The synergy between ADR and court processes is most effective when technology bridges both redress pathways. This is evident with the rise of pre-court portals, like the whiplash portal, which maintain a flexible connection with the court system, as parts of a claim may be referred for court adjudication before the case is directed back to the portal for the parties to negotiate a final settlement.

Therefore, the court digitalization program is increasing the ADR offering within the judicial process, which in turn is blurring the lines between ADR and the court process. In so doing, it is changing ADR's nature from being an alternative option to a judicial process, to being an essential part of the court proceedings, especially when the participation in ADR is a compulsory element of the proceedings. The mandatory nature, which thus far mostly applied to information sessions in family and employment cases, has recently been extended beyond the family domain to the participation in ADR for small claims, which captures most civil claims. These ADR referrals will be more effective when they are timely and when coupled with suitable incentives and

[92] Geoffrey Vos MR, 'Reliable Data and Technology: The Direction of Travel for Civil Justice', Law Society Webinar on Civil Justice and LawTech (28 January 2021) para 38.

[93] Geoffrey Vos MR, 'Recovery or Radical Transformation: The Effect of Covid-19 on Justice Systems' London School of Economics (17 June 2021) para 19.

sanctions, but sanctions ought to be accompanied by adequate safeguards that avoid LIPs from being unduly penalized.

The Master of the Rolls said that in the near future pre-action portals (including some consumer ADR schemes) will be linked to the court system via an online channel, which will provide court and tribunal users with an online end to end solution.[94] He envisages that once cases reach a court or a tribunal, technology-powered processes will continue making timely ADR referrals when it is believed that the cases are ripe for settlement, such as after expert evidence is submitted or once liability has been accepted.[95]

The push towards blending various processes, notably formal judicial proceedings with informal ADR processes, which has been referred to as process pluralism,[96] recognizes the necessity of offering multiple pathways to justice beyond traditional litigation.[97] However, this approach has encountered criticism. Critics argue that while ADR processes may broaden access to redress, they could result in a diminished quality of justice for the weaker party.[98] Essentially, this criticism highlights a potential compromise between the objectives of efficiency (ie, access) and fairness (ie, justice),[99] a concern that becomes more pronounced with the integration of technology in the dispute resolution process.[100] To mitigate these risks whilst still encouraging settlements, there is an increasing trend towards the regulation and supervision of court-annexed and certified ADR processes. This monitoring process seeks to ensure procedural fairness, especially in sectors like family, employment, and consumer disputes, where power imbalances between disputants are common. The point at which disputants are guided towards ADR is also crucial. Therefore, an online system could play a key role in ensuring that disputants evaluate the appropriateness of ADR processes at various stages of the dispute lifecycle.

E. Conclusion

The increasing state endorsement of ADR and ODR reflects a widespread acknowledgment that traditional judicial and private adjudication mechanisms often fall short in

[94] ibid para 28.

[95] ibid para 38.

[96] Carrie Menkel-Medow, Larry Love, Alon Kupfer, and Jean Sternlight, *Dispute Resolution: Beyond the Adversarial Model* (2nd edn, Aspen 2011).

[97] Marc Galanter, 'Justice in Many Rooms: Courts, Private Ordering, and Indigenous Law' (1981) 13 Legal Pluralism and Unofficial Law 1; and Mauro Cappelletti, 'Alternative Dispute Resolution Processes within the Framework of the World-Wide Access-to Justice Movement' (1993) 56 MLR 282–84.

[98] Owen Fiss, 'Against Settlement' (1984) 93 Yale LJ 1073; Trina Grillo 'Mediation alternative: process dangers for women' (1991) 100 Yale LJ 1545; and Michael Palmer, 'Formalisation of Alternative Dispute Resolution Processes: Some Socio-Legal Thoughts' in J Zekoll, M Balz, and I Ambling (eds), *Formalisation and Flexibilisation in Dispute Resolution* (Brill 2014) 21. See also The European Law Institute and the European Network of Councils for the Judiciary, 'The Relationship between Formal and Informal Justice: the Courts and Alternative Dispute Resolution' (2018), available at <https://www.europeanlawinstitute.eu/fileadmin/user_upload/p_eli/Publications/ADR_Statement.pdf> last accessed 9 October 2024.

[99] Debbie De Girolamo 'Sen, Justice and the Private Realm of Dispute Resolution' (2017) International Journal of Law in Context 1–21 (First-View 20 December 2017).

[100] Ethan Katsh and Orna Rabinovich, *Digital Justice* (OUP 2017) 39–54.

efficiently resolving private disputes. The effectiveness of ADR largely depends on the timing of referrals, which can significantly influence the parties' readiness to engage with the process. This chapter has examined the critical junctures within a dispute's lifecycle at which parties are directed towards ADR, highlighting the concurrent rise in such referrals with the digitalization of dispute resolution mechanisms as part of the reform programme in England and Wales.

Initially, in many regulated sectors, consumers are guided towards ADR as the primary dispute resolution method, usually before contemplating court litigation. Here, ADR serves as an autonomous redressal framework, recognizing that the judicial litigation of such consumer disputes is frequently unsuitable due to their low value and the claimants' preference for a non-formal and expedited process. Within the consumer domain, litigation typically emerges as an option of last resort when a business declines to participate in ADR. Conversely, referrals to ADR might act as an adjunct to, or in place of, court adjudication. These referrals can be mandated as a precondition for filing a court claim or may proceed concurrently with court actions once a defence is lodged.

Moreover, this chapter posits that the digitalization process, particularly through the interoperability of pre-action ODR platforms with digital court processes, is poised to seamlessly incorporate ADR further into the Civil Justice System by prompting parties to consider ADR and ODR at each stage of their dispute life cycle. This evolving referral mechanism, now obligatory for the majority of small claims, blurs the traditional demarcation between court proceedings and ADR, challenging the perception of ADR as merely an 'alternative' to the formal dispute resolution process.

Bibliography

ACAS, Annual Report and Accounts 2021–22.

ACAS, Quarterly Reports (April 2016–December 2016) and (April 2017–December 2017).

Boon A, Urwin A, and Karuk V, 'What Difference Does It Make? Facilitative Judicial Mediation of Discrimination Cases in Employment Tribunals' (2011) 40 Industrial LJ 45.

Briggs LJ M, *Civil Courts Structure Review: Final Report* (July 2016).

Briggs LJ M, *Civil Courts Structure Review: Interim Report* (December 2015).

Briss LJ, 'The 24th Competition Law Association Burrell Lecture: Is a focus on data the way to improve access to justice in a multifaceted world?' (30 November 2023).

Cappelletti M, 'Alternative Dispute Resolution Processes within the Framework of the World-Wide Access to Justice Movement' (1993) 56 MLR 282–84.

Civil Justice Council, Cost Review, Final Report (July 2023).

Communication on ADR for Consumer Disputes in the Single Market COM (2011) 791.

Cortés P (ed), *The New Regulatory Framework for Consumer Dispute Resolution* (OUP 2016).

Cortés P, 'The Online Court: Filling the Gaps of the Civil Justice System?' (2017) 36(1) Civil Justice Quarterly 54–71.

Cortés P, *The Law of Consumer Redress* (CUP, 2017).

Cortés P, 'Embedding Alternative Dispute Resolution in the Civil Justice System: a Taxonomy for ADR Referrals and a Digital Pathway to Increase the Uptake of ADR' (2023) 43(2) Legal Studies 312–30.

Council of Europe, Online Dispute Resolution Mechanisms in Civil and Administrative Proceedings, Guidelines (16 June 2021).

De Girolamo D., 'Sen, Justice and the Private Realm of Dispute Resolution' (2017) International Journal of Law in Context 1–21 (First-View 20 December 2017).
Department for Business, Energy and Industrial Strategy, 'Consultation Outcome—Reforming Competition and Consumer Policy: Government Response' (April 2022) CP 656.
Department for Business, Energy & Industrial Strategy, 'Modernising Consumer Markets' Consumer Green Paper (April 2018).
Department for Business, Energy & Industrial Strategy, 'Resolving Consumer Disputes—Alternative Dispute Resolution and the Court System' Final Report (April 2018).
Dickens L, 'Employment Tribunals and Alternative Dispute Resolution' in Dickens L (ed), *Making Employment Rights Effective. Issues of Enforcement and Compliance* (Hart Publishing 2012).
Employment Lawyers Association, 'ADR and Employment Disputes' (November 2017).
European Law Institute and European Network of Councils for the Judiciary, 'The Relationship between Formal and Informal Justice: The Courts and Alternative Dispute Resolution' (2018).
Fiss O, 'Against Settlement' (1984) 93 Yale LJ 1073.
Galanter M, 'Justice in Many Rooms: Courts, Private Ordering, and Indigenous Law (1981) 13 Legal Pluralism and Unofficial Law 1.
Galanter, M, 'The Hundred-Year Decline of Trials and the Thirty Years War' (2005) 57(5) Stan L Rev 1255–75, 1266.
Gov.uk, Guidance—The HMCTS Reform Programme (2024). Available at <https://www.gov.uk/guidance/the-hmcts-reform-programme>.
Grillo T, 'Mediation Alternative: Process Dangers for Women' (1991) 100 Yale LJ 1545.
Hamlyn B, Coleman E, and Sefton M, 'Mediation Information and Assessment Meetings (MIAMs) and mediation in private family law disputes—Quantitative research findings' (Ministry of Justice Analytical Series 2015).
HMCTS, Civil Mediation Service Manual (February 2009).
HMCTS, Corporate report: Assessing Access to Justice in HMCTS Services - Summary Report (12 December 2023).
HMCTS, Guidance, HMCTS services: Online Civil Money Claims (27 February 2024).
HMCTS, The Business and Property Courts of England and Wales, The Commercial Court Guide, 11th edn, (2022).
Hodges C, 'Consumer Ombudsmen: Better Regulation and Dispute Resolution' (2014) 15(1) ERA Forum 593–608.
Hodges C, *Delivering Dispute Resolution—A Holistic Review of Models in England and Wales* (Hart 2019).
Katsh E and Rabinovich O, *Digital Justice* (OUP 2017).
The Law Society, 'Family Mediation Week 2022: further investment for mediation voucher scheme' (17 January 2022).
Menkel-Medow C, Love L, Kupfer A, and Sternlight J, *Dispute Resolution: Beyond the Adversarial Model* (2nd edn, Aspen 2011).
Ministry of Justice, '£1 million voucher scheme to help families resolve disputes outside of court' Press release (26 March 2021).
Ministry of Justice, 'Increasing the Use of Mediation in the Civil Justice System' (July 2022).
Ministry of Justice, 'Increasing the Use of Mediation in the Civil Justice System: Government. Response to Consultation' (Updated 20 December 2023).
Ministry of Justice, 'Introducing fees in the Employment Tribunals and the Employment Appeal Tribunal' (29 January 2024).
Ministry of Justice, 'Thousands of families spared from damaging courtroom conflict' Press Release (3 April 2024).
Ministry of Justice, 'Judicial Mediation Employment Tribunals' (July 2014).
Ministry of Justice, 'Transforming Our Justice System: Summary of Reforms and Consultation' (September 2016).
Ministry of Justice, 'Transforming Our Justice System: Summary of Reforms and Consultation' - Government Response (February 2017).
National Audit Office, 'Implementing Reforms to Civil Legal Aid' HC 784 (20 November 2014).
National Statistics, Legal Aid in England and Wales (Ministry of Justice, January to March 2017).

Palmer M, 'Formalisation of Alternative Dispute Resolution Processes: Some Socio-Legal Thoughts' in Zekoll J, Balz M, and Ambling I (eds), *Formalisation and Flexibilisation in Dispute Resolution* (Brill 2014).
Prince S, 'Mediating Small Claims: Are We on the Right Track?' (2007) 26(2) CJQ 328–40.
Quek Anderson D, 'The Convergence of ADR and ODR within the Courts: The Impact on Access to Justice' (2019) 38(1) CJQ 136.
Roberts S, 'Listing Concentrates the Mind': the English Civil Court as an Arena for Structured Negotiation 29(3) (2009) OJLS 457–79.
Salter S and Thomson D, 'Public-Centred Civil Justice Redesign: A Case Study of the British Columbia Civil Resolution Tribunal' (2017) 3 McGill Journal of Dispute Resolution 113.
Sander F, 'Varieties of Dispute Processing' (1976) 70 FRD 111.
Sorabji J, 'The Online Solutions Court—A Multi-door Courthouse for the 21st Century (2017) 36(1) CJQ 86–108.
UCL Laws and the Legal Education Foundation, 'Workshop Briefing Paper: Measuring Success in Online Courts: An Empirical Challenge' (October 2018).
Vos MR G, 'Reliable Data and Technology: The Direction of Travel for Civil Justice', Law Society Webinar on Civil Justice and LawTech (28 January 2021).
Vos MR G, 'Recovery or Radical Transformation: The Effect of Covid-19 on Justice Systems' London School of Economics (17 June 2021).
Vos MR G, 'The Relationship between Formal and Informal Justice', Hull University (26 March 2021).
Vos MR G, 'London International Disputes Week 2021: Keynote Speech' (10 May 2021).
Vos MR G, 'Mandating Mediation: The Digital Solution' Chartered Institute of Arbitrators: Roebuck Lecture 2022 (8 June 2022).
Wissler RL, 'The Effects of Mandatory Mediation: Empirical Research on the Experience of Small Claims and Common Pleas Courts' (1997) 33(3) Willamette L Rev 565.
Woolf LJ, HK, *Access to Justice, Final Report* (Lord Chancellor's Department, 1995).

6

Designing to Expand Access to Remedies, Voice, and Possibly Justice in United States Court Online Dispute Resolution (ODR)

Amy J. Schmitz[*]

A. Introduction

New technologies have disrupted many established industries and institutions in recent years, testing our imaginations and expectations.[1] The advent of ChatGPT and generative AI, for example, is threatening to replace jobs in marketing, and legal AI tools are already replacing the need for an army of lawyers to review documents. Furthermore, generative AI and video platforms are disrupting traditional judicial processes. Moreover, the COVID-19 pandemic generated new disputes and a need for expanded access to online means for resolving disputes—especially when most courts were closed to in-person processes for health and safety reasons. As a result, lawyers, judges, software developers, and policymakers have been exploring ways to use technology to expand access to the courts and dispute resolution.[2]

* John Deaver Drinko-Baker & Hostetler Endowed Chair in Law, The Ohio State University Moritz College of Law, Co-Director of the Translational Data Analytics Institute, The Ohio State University. Thank you to Kelly Adams, Lara Esteves, and Favour Oluwafisayo Osa Oni for their research assistance.

1 See (2020) 123(2) MIT Technology Review, March–April, at 15 and previous annual reviews back to 2001.

2 Richard Susskind, *Tomorrow's Lawyers: An Introduction to Your Future* (OUP 2013).

Amy J. Schmitz, *Designing to Expand Access to Remedies, Voice, and Possibly Justice in United States Court Online Dispute Resolution (ODR)* In: *Digitalization and Artificial Intelligence in Courts*. Edited by: Fernando Esteban de la Rosa, Pablo Cortés, and Nuria Marchal Escalona, Oxford University Press. © Amy J. Schmitz 2025. DOI: 10.1093/9780198918752.003.0006

Consistent with this evolution, alternative or appropriate dispute resolution (ADR) processes are now yielding to online dispute resolution (ODR). ODR includes automated decision-making, as well as online negotiation, mediation, arbitration, community courts, and variations thereof. ODR processes' efficiency, accessibility, and ease open new avenues to remedies and access to justice (A2J).[3] Some of us have been researching and writing about ODR for many years because we hoped that technology could be a 'fourth party' in dispute resolution that could lower the barriers to obtaining remedies. The technology could add a 'virtual' door to the multidoor courthouse in the vein of the Pound Conference.[4] We proposed a 'human-centric' design aimed at helping real people with real problems. This is ODR that is designed based on research that addresses what people want in an ODR system in terms of access and interface and is continually adjusted based on user feedback and experience.

This conception of ODR allows individuals to resolve disputes more quickly, cheaply, and, hopefully, fairly. For example, the ability to resolve disputes using simple and accessible technologies, such as a cellphone, saves significantly on the costs, stress, and hassles of in-person processes usually associated with court cases.[5] Furthermore, many individuals feel more comfortable and calm seeking remedies from behind their computers or mobile devices at times that fit their schedules. This is especially true for smaller dollar claims or minor infractions, such as parking tickets and driving misdemeanors. This ODR should be user-friendly and empower individuals through online 'wizards' for case diagnostics and means for quickly filling out forms and uploading related documents to obtain timely resolutions.

In reality, however, not all ODR programs are helpful or well-designed. Some online processes may become 'click-through' sifters that perhaps fall outside what is rightfully 'ODR' because there is no facilitation involved. Click-through forms that provide limited options with no ability to explain one's case may not provide a real opportunity to be heard, and may cause frustration for users instead of offering 'justice' in a system that is largely legal.[6] However, some may argue that quick 'click' remedies provide a type of rough justice that some prefer due to efficiency. Still, choice is essential. ODR is not for all people or all problems. Self-empowerment and facilitated solutions enhance fairness and process satisfaction for some. Still, there should be accreditation rules for systems designers and the neutrals who may facilitate online mediations and arbitrations.[7]

[3] ibid. See also Amy J Schmitz and Colin Rule, *The New Handshake: Online Dispute Resolution and the Future of Consumer Protection* (American Bar Association Section on Dispute Resolution 2017). See also Amy J Schmitz, 'Building on OArb Attributes in Pursuit of Justice' in Maud Piers and Christian Aschauer (eds), *Arbitration in the Digital Age: the Brave New World of Arbitration* (CUP 2018) 182–208.

[4] Amy J Schmitz, '"Drive-Thru" Arbitration in the Digital Age: Empowering Consumers through Regulated ODR' (2010) 62 Baylor L Rev 178.

[5] Ethan Katsh and Colin Rule, 'What We Know and Need to Know About Online Dispute Resolution' (2016) 67 SCL Rev 329, 330. See also Ethan Katsh and Orna Rabinovitch-Einy, *Digital Justice: Technology and the Internet of Disputes* (OUP 2017) 1–25.

[6] Rebecca L Sandefur, 'The Fulcrum Point of Equal Access to Justice: Legal and Nonlegal Institutions of Remedy' (2009) 42 Loyola of Los Angeles L Rev 949, 950–54.

[7] Amy J Schmitz, 'Building Bridges to Remedies for Consumers in International eConflicts' (2012) 34 University of Arkansas Little Rock L Rev 779.

Nonetheless, ODR has gained significant traction in the United States (US) and elsewhere.[8] Many jurisdictions in the US have developed court ODR projects, and some have even moved to '2.0' with ODR redesign projects.[9] An increasing number of courts offer online processes for case types ranging from traffic tickets to small claims, to divorce. In many cases, this use of technology includes asynchronous text-based systems as well as video options in some cases.[10] Some ODR programs may also go beyond facilitating communication to provide problem diagnosis and assist parties in online negotiation empowered by digital advice. Online court systems also encourage participation by incorporating automatic notices and payments into the case management system.[11]

Again, some e-courts and public ODR pilots have demonstrated promise for helping people access remedies. However, others have not, which should encourage further research to help revise ODR processes to reimagine A2J. Accordingly, this chapter provides examples of US court ODR initiatives and the limited research results that have emerged—and calls for a focus on human-centric design based on solid research. Court ODR development should not simply consist of purchasing an off-the-shelf program based on price. Instead, courts must actively engage in the design and continually gather research to help tailor the program and improve it over time. This is essential if ODR aims to expand A2J.

Section B will provide examples of ODR in the US courts and explain some of the areas where ODR has flourished. Section C then notes movements toward research and development of ethical guardrails for ODR in the US. Section D highlights the need for functional analysis, careful planning, and attention to human-centric system design for ODR. Section E concludes.

B. Examples of ODR in US Courts

Local and state courts in the US have recognized that the justice system has not been working for many, leading some people to miss out on remedies or to otherwise forego their rights. In response, some US courts have adopted, and in some cases created, ODR programs. These programs aim to increase judicial access for individuals who

[8] Amy J Schmitz, 'Expanding Access to Remedies through E-Court Initiatives' (2019) 67 Buffalo L Rev 101; Rebecca Love Kourlis and Riyaz Samnani, 'A Court Compass for Litigants' (*IAALS*, May 2017) <https://iaals.du.edu/sites/default/files/documents/publications/court_compass_mapping_the_future.pdf> last accessed 28 September 2024.

[9] P Embley, 'NCSC, Presentation at the First Int'l Forum on Online Courts', 3 December 2018, US Courts and Online Dispute Resolution 13 <https://assets.publishing.service.gov.uk/government/uploads/system/uploads/attachment_data/file/761379/US.pdf>; see also Utah Courts Recent Press Notifications. 13 August 2020. 'Utah Courts.' <http://www.utcourts.gov/utc/news/2020/08/13/to-tackle-the-unmet-legal-needs-crisis-utah-supreme-court-unanimously-endorses-a-pilot-program-to-assess-changes-to-the-governance-of-the-practice-of-law/> last accessed 28 September 2024.

[10] Schmitz (n 4) 120–70.

[11] ibid. See also Amy J Schmitz, 'A Blueprint for Online Dispute Resolution System Design' (2018) 21 J Internet L 3; Amy J Schmitz, 'There's an "App" for That: Developing Online Dispute Resolution to Empower Economic Development' (2018) 32 Notre Dame Journal of Law, Ethics & Public Policy 1.

cannot afford attorneys and the costs of traditional litigation.[12] Furthermore, the National Center for State Courts (NCSC) partnered with PEW Charitable Trust to assist and assess judicial ODR projects.[13] Some ODR programs have had successes, while others have not. An analysis of these programs can help assess how best to design these programs. The next section discusses the available evidence for programs in Florida, Utah, and Michigan.

1. Florida

Florida provides a great example of ODR in action. In 2018, The Florida Supreme Court began a study of ODR for the courts and directed the Florida Commission on Trial Court Performance and Accountability and the Committee on Alternative Dispute Resolution Rules and Policy to conduct a review of ODR solutions.[14] By 2019, ODR pilot projects began in several Florida jurisdictions in a variety of areas: civil traffic infractions, small claims, and divorce with no children. ODR is defined for the program as an 'online platform hosted and supported by the judicial branch where used can easily access informational legal resources, engage with the other party of the dispute or officer of the court to address a legal issue, submit documents and evidence as needed, and generate an agreement that can be filed with the court, if applicable'.[15] The initial pilot program had six participating district courts, three of which withdrew from the program because of the vendor's inability to provide a functioning platform. Initially the third, fifth, ninth, tenth, eleventh, and seventeenth districts participated. Florida published its report in 2021.[16]

The report includes lessons learned and recommendations for implementing ODR in the state. First, the report recommends that courts prioritize ODR for 'high volume and low complexity cases'.[17] The report proposes a two-tiered approach to the application of ODR. The first-tier is recommended for simpler cases such as:

- Small claims
- Customer debt issues
- Real property actions, including commercial evictions
- Traffic-related disputes

[12] Individual state, county, and city courts act as laboratories for new initiatives aimed at improving access to justice as well as judicial efficiency. This is one of the tenets of federalism. *New State Ice Co v Liebmann*, 285 US 262, 311 (1932).

[13] See 'NSCS/PEW Charitable Trusts ODR Project Announcement' (*NCTDR*, 10 July 2018) <https://odr.info/ncscpew-charitable-trusts-odr-project-announcement/> last accessed 29 September 2024.

[14] 'Online Dispute Resolution Resources' (Florida Courts, 6 April 2023) <https://www.flcourts.gov/Administration-Funding/Performance-Accountability/Online-Dispute-Resolution-Resources> last accessed 29 September 2024.

[15] Amy Schmitz, 'Expanding Access to Remedies, Voice, and Possible Justice in United States Court Online Dispute Resolution (ODR)' in F Esteban de la Rosa, P Cortés, and N Marchal (eds), *Digital Courts: Integrating Human and Artificial Intelligence* (OUP forthcoming).

[16] 'Online Dispute Resolution Workgroup, 'Online Dispute Resolution Pilot Report' (Florida Courts, January 2021) <https://www.flcourts.gov/content/download/725954/file/Online%20Dispute%20Resolution%20Pilot%20Program%20Report%20-%20Final%20with%20Appendices.pdf> last accessed 29 September 2024.

[17] ibid.

- Dissolution of marriage cases without children involved
- County criminal cases, specifically those related to compliance with local ordinances

The report suggests that ODR may not be the optimal solution for certain types of cases due to their complexity or the number of parties involved. These include:

- Highly complex cases
- Cases involving more than two parties
- Cases where an insurance company is a party, except in debt collection scenarios
- County criminal misdemeanors
- Any circuit criminal cases
- Cases involving physician violence
- Probate or guardianship cases

Given Florida's vast geographical spread, which includes many rural areas, the report emphasizes the potential of ODR to increase A2J. It could be particularly beneficial for citizens who may find it challenging to travel to physical court locations due to financial constraints or other barriers. The report underscores the importance of considering these factors when planning the implementation of ODR in Florida.

The second recommendation was that the Supreme Court pursue amendments to the Florida Rules of Court Procedure. Florida's statutes do not define ODR. Thus, the Court would have to clearly define what ODR is to differentiate it from other dispute resolution methods. Accordingly, the report recommends the inclusion of an online notarization system. It also recommends the need for a user fee model to sustain the service in order to mitigate the fiscal impact on the courts, while protecting individuals from high fees that may hinder A2J. The report elaborates in the footnotes that a per-case processing fee for the pilot could vary from $10.00 for traffic infractions up to $25.00 for small claims cases. Low cost was key, but the courts still need to cover costs.[18]

At the same time, Florida notes that the courts should establish a project management team led by a court administrator with technology experience to oversee the implementation. The report suggests that a project team can function as a mechanism by which stakeholders have input and receive updates on the ODR project progress. The ODR management team should create a design framework at the project's outset, paying attention to the minimum criteria for desired functionality and a clearly stated goal.[19] Florida had the foresight to note that courts should include a data collection component that provides clear metrics by which the court can capture the information needed to evaluate usage and assess performance. Such data should include number of cases processed in ODR, average case processing time, staff workload associated with processing cases in ODR versus traditional methods, nature, and duration of engagement in the platform by user type and user satisfaction.[20]

[18] ibid 34.
[19] ibid 35.
[20] ibid 35.

Some pilots used the platform Modria[21] from Tyler Technologies, while others used Matterhorn, especially for traffic violation cases.[22] Nonetheless, users did not engage with the process to the extent that Florida hoped. In one district, for example, there were 622 cases uploaded onto Modria, but this engagement was only 43 per cent of all possible cases. One of their main issues was launching the program without back-end integration between the platform and the clerk's system. They also did not have a launch page or proper marketing.[23] Of all the pilot programs, the Eleventh Circuit civil traffic infraction online case resolution process had the best outcome and seems to still be operating.[24]

Other districts within Florida, not included in the report, have implemented their own ODR programs, and virtual mediation is being used more frequently for certain case types. Nonetheless, this report seems to indicate dissatisfaction with the implementation of the 'off-the-shelf' text-based ODR programs offered by the major ODR vendors.

2. Utah

Utah has implemented an ODR program for small claims cases statewide.[25] The Utah Judicial Council formed an ODR Steering Committee in June 2016 to create means for improving access to remedies in small claims cases. Still, the project gained traction once Justice Constandinos 'Deno' Himonas of the Utah Supreme Court supported the effort.[26] The ODR program follows a stepped process, beginning with 'Education and Evaluation,' moving to direct negotiation, and then allowing for mediation if the parties are unable to resolve their dispute on their own.[27] Early evaluations indicated that the number of in-person hearings dropped by 27 per cent.[28] Additionally, a 2018 report indicated that 22 per cent more cases were resolved than before the program began, and 36 per cent fewer warrants were issued for failure to appear.[29] In the small claims/tax department, 93 per cent of cases reached an agreement with ODR, versus only 46 per cent for those cases without the help of ODR.[30] These statistics indicate that ODR can be helpful in particular contexts, especially when championed by leaders, such as Justice Himonas, who guide system design aimed at expanding access to remedies.

[21] Upon further research I found that the 18th Florida Judicial Circuit also uses Modria: see 18th Judicial Circuit-Brevard County-Florida, *Small Claims Resolution Center* <https://flcourts18sc.modria.com/> last accessed 14 October 2023.

[22] 'Online Case Resolution' (Eleventh Judicial Circuit of Florida) <https://www.jud11.flcourts.org/About-the-Court/Court-Divisions/Traffic/Online-Case-Resolution> last accessed 29 September 2024.

[23] Susskind (n 2) 20.

[24] 'Alternative Dispute Resolution Services' (Florida's 10th Judicial Circuit Court) <https://www.jud10.flcourts.org/mediation> last accessed 29 September 2024.

[25] Melisse Stiglich, 'Utah Online Dispute Resolution Pilot Project' NCSC (December 2017), 1–3.

[26] ibid 6–7. Justice Himonas has since left the bench and is now in private practice of law.

[27] ibid 9.

[28] Embley (n 9) 13.

[29] ibid 13.

[30] ibid 15.

Utah was unique in that it built its own process, instead of purchasing an off-the-shelf program, and Utah engaged researchers to examine usability. System designers hoped to empower individuals to engage in the process without the time and cost of attending court in person. As one court administrator explained, 'half the battle is getting people to appear in court'.[31] ODR saves the parties from the time and hassles of in-court proceedings and allows for communication at convenient times and places.[32] However, Utah recognized that this savings would be meaningless if the system was not usable or intuitive. Specifically, Utah worked with researchers who studied the usability of the system. The usability testing of the Utah ODR system focused on functionality, usability, accessibility, and comprehension issues.[33] Based on this research, a 2020 report made five overall recommendations for improvement: (1) ease the transition from paper to platform; (2) streamline the registration process; (3) simplify document sharing and review; (4) improve ODR information and help; and (5) clarify legal information and user options.[34]

The observation-based usability testing was conducted in two rounds.[35] First, researchers established a baseline test in which participants used the original ODR platform. Next, after receiving data from the baseline test and implementing changes, a 'prototype' test was conducted.[36] In both tests, participants were asked to complete a set of tasks and give feedback vocally as they completed the tasks.[37] Researchers were careful to categorize metrics: (1) critical errors; (2) non-critical errors; (3) time-on-task; (4) task completion; and (5) subjective evaluations.[38] The researchers analyzed severity of problems in order to flag and prioritize correcting errors.

After receiving data from the previously mentioned baseline test, researchers conducted workshops to test and brainstorm for solutions to problems encountered during the user testing.[39] The workshops focused on different aspects of the platform that were deemed most problematic.[40] Workshop participants discussed ideas and voted on solutions for a redesign of the ODR system.[41] For example, a major flaw in the original system was its invitation system. The URL provided to parties invited to use the ODR system was long and unwieldy, causing some to see it as a possible scam. It was unclear that it was legitimately connected to the court, and it failed to highlight

[31] Email from Clayson Quigley, District Court Program Administrator in the Greater Salt Lake City area, in the Administrative Office of Utah Courts, to Andrew Johnson, Research Assistant to Professor Schmitz (9 August 2018).

[32] Amy J Schmitz, 'Measuring "Access to Justice" in the Rush to Digitize' (2020) 88 Fordham L Rev 2381–406.

[33] Stacy Butler et al, 'The Utah Online Dispute Resolution Platform: A Usability Evaluation and Report' (Innovation for Justice Program, 8 September 2020) ii <https://law.arizona.edu/sites/default/files/i4J_Utah_ODR_Report.pdf> last accessed 29 September 2024.

[34] ibid.

[35] ibid 7.

[36] ibid 8.

[37] ibid 7–8.

[38] ibid 16. Participants measured their satisfaction with each task (regardless of completion status) on a Likert scale.

[39] ibid 17.

[40] ibid 17. Including (1) affidavit, summons, and ODR homepage; (2) the ODR website registration process; and (3) the chat feature and document sharing.

[41] ibid 17–18.

key information to make it easier for registration on the website.[42] This was contrary to user-centric design, which would require a readily understandable invitation and website with attention to text location and size, color pallet, and consistent visual information.[43] The study also suggested reducing the number of steps required for registration and including a progress indicator to help individuals track their progress. User testing also uncovered bugs related to smartphone accessibility and researchers had ideas for providing better ODR information and help resources.

Armed with this research, Utah has been revising its program to address these shortcomings. The system is now much more user-friendly. The website has a clean application, and attendant information provided for parties using the ODR system. Utah also did user-testing and redesign based on that research is essential to user-centric design of ODR systems. Even before the testing in Utah, 15 of 16 participants said they would prefer using a website over going to physical court.[44] Therefore, the challenge is not to gain support for online platforms, but rather to create effective online platforms that are user-friendly.[45] The report stresses that it is crucial to customize to the needs of the most vulnerable populations to ensure that the legal needs of all users are met.[46] This is essential for design that aims to expand access to remedies, and justice.

3. Michigan

In 2014, Michigan was one of the first US states to launch an ODR pilot program in collaboration with Matterhorn, a private ODR vendor based in Michigan. The first ODR pilot was used to resolve traffic disputes.[47] The core of the program was an online portal for defendants to address traffic tickets online, including the ability to present arguments contesting their tickets or explanations for why they could not pay their fines. The system was text-based and asynchronous so that parties could participate at any time of day, on their own schedules. Police and prosecutors could review cases through the portal before the traffic issues were resolved.[48]

Research in 2017 conducted by one of Matterhorn's founders regarding the program was positive.[49] Surveys and interviews at that time indicated that 90 per cent of Matterhorn users found it 'easy to use' and 92 per cent said they understood the status of their claims while using the online process. Furthermore, more than a third of users who responded to surveys said they would have been unable to participate in a traditional in-person adjudication. Additionally, 30 per cent of participation on

[42] ibid 17–18.
[43] ibid 17–18.
[44] ibid 91.
[45] ibid 91.
[46] ibid 92.
[47] John Nevin, 'Online Ticket Review Helps Make Courts More Accessible and Efficient' (Michigan Courts News Release, 8 June 2015) <https://www.courts.michigan.gov/49c6b5/siteassets/news-releases/online-ticket-review-news-release.pdf> last accessed 3 October 2024.
[48] ibid.
[49] James J Prescott, 'Improving Access to Justice in State Courts with Platform Technology' (2017) 70 Vanderbildt L Rev 1993, 1994–96.

the platform was outside of business hours. This 2017 research also stated that 80 per cent of survey respondents who used the software indicated that they would recommend it to a friend and 40 per cent said they would not have addressed their legal issue without it.[50]

Since then, ODR has expanded in Michigan, and the process has changed in some respects. Some jurisdictions offer ODR that covers warrants and parking citations, in addition to general traffic tickets.[51] Additionally, parties can request and establish online payment plans using ODR, subject to court approval.[52] Nonetheless, individuals with out-of-state licenses face ineligibility for the online case review in some districts.[53] Still, no uniform ODR system is implemented across all courts or counties in Michigan.[54] However, the majority of courts have adopted some form of the Matterhorn service, with MI-Resolve being the primary platform for text-based ODR in Michigan.[55]

MI-Resolve is offered in two variants: the MI-Resolve Family System and the MI-Resolve Civil System.[56] These services are facilitated by the Michigan Supreme Court's Administrative Office and are typically provided free of charge to eligible participants.[57] The MI-Resolve Family System is used to help families work together to create parenting time agreements, revise current court-ordered plans, or create a plan for making up missed time with the help of a trained mediator.[58] The program is free and confidential, with cases usually mandated by the court or suggested by Friends of the court.[59] The MI-Resolve Civil System applies for certain small claims disputes, such as claims involving monetary debts, contract disputes, neighborhood conflicts, and landlord/tenant matters.[60] The service involves mediation with a third party and negotiation with just the parties. It is available any time of day, which is seen as a plus for many individuals who would be unable to attend formal processes during the workday.

Additionally, certain districts within Michigan have also embraced online case reviews for eligible warrants, traffic citations, and parking citation reviews.[61] Courts

[50] ibid 2021–30.

[51] 'Online Case Review' (61st District Court) <https://cii2.courtinnovations.com/MID61> last accessed 30 September 2024; 'Online Case Review' (8th District Court) <https://cii2.courtinnovations.com/MID08> last accessed 30 September 2024.

[52] 'Online Review' (41B District Court) <https://cii2.courtinnovations.com/MID41B> last accessed 30 September 2024.

[53] 'Online Ticket Review/Online Warrant Resolution' (16th District Court) <https://cii2.courtinnovations.com/MID16> last accessed 30 September 2024.

[54] Matterhorn by Court Innovations, <https://www.courtinnovations.com/> last accessed 30 September 2024.

[55] ibid.

[56] 'Resolve a Dispute Online with MI-Resolve' (Michigan Courts, One Court of Justice) <https://www.courts.michigan.gov/administration/offices/office-of-dispute-resolution/mi-resolve/> last accessed 30 September 2024.

[57] Matterhorn (n 54).

[58] 'MI-Resolve Family System (Michigan Courts, One Court of Justice) <https://www.courts.michigan.gov/administration/offices/office-of-dispute-resolution/mi-resolve/MIResolveFamily/> last accessed 30 September 2024.

[59] 'Friend of the Court: New Alternative Dispute Resolution (ADR) Policy' (Eaton County, 2020) <https://www.eatoncounty.org/224/Friend-of-the-Court> last accessed 30 September 2024.

[60] ibid.

[61] 61st District Court (n 51).

also may provide online portals for parties to request and establish online payment plans for citations, subject to court approval.[62] The key distinction in these cases, as opposed to MI-Resolve, is that qualified judges and law enforcement officers continue to make final decisions, applying the same criteria as if the case were heard in a traditional court setting.[63]

There is limited research regarding ODR in Michigan, including research focused on text-based systems discussed below and an external evaluation of family ODR in Ottawa County, Michigan. The Ottawa County program used text-based ODR. The findings indicated that text-based ODR can lead to a greater probability of agreement and higher party satisfaction in family cases.[64] Still, the report noted areas for improvement. For example, parties lacked understanding regarding how the ODR process worked and expected that there would be video. This observation has become prevalent with the expansion of Zoom and Teams in the courts. This problem highlights the importance of providing clear information and demonstration videos for ODR participants. Information must be thorough, but concise and understandable. A comparison between Zoom Dispute Resolution and MI-Resolve has been conducted, revealing that both options are effective and highly rated by users.[65] Still, it is essential that participants know what a process entails before they join that process. Also, the invitation to join an ODR process must make clear whether it is required or if there is a way to opt out. Accessibility is also often an issue, and ODR providers should furnish screen readers and voice activation functionalities to enhance accessibility for those who need this assistance.[66]

These are just a few examples of ODR in US courts and some initial research related to these projects. These examples provide background for the next sections—highlighting the need for deeper and varied research to inform more focused dispute system design and redesign in court technology development.

[62] 41B District Court (n 51).

[63] 'Online Case Review' (74th District Court) <https://cii2.courtinnovations.com/MID74> last accessed 30 September 2024.

[64] In this research, two surveys were conducted: one prior to receiving assistance on the matter (referred to as 'Survey 1') and another after exiting the ODR platform (referred to as 'Survey 2'). Survey 2 was administered to individuals for whom Family Court (FOC) caseworkers had inputted their contact details into the ODR platform. This survey was distributed shortly after the closure of their cases within the ODR platform, regardless of whether they had utilized the platform or not. The evaluation period extended from 2 November 2020 to 31 August 2021. Data regarding case outcomes was gathered and recorded up until 21 October 2021.

[65] Sharon L Pizzuti and Michael D Campbell, 'Evaluation of Two Statewide Virtual Dispute Resolution Services in Michigan' (Michigan Courts, March 2022) <https://www.courts.michigan.gov/49c110/siteassets/reports/odr/sji-evaluation-report-final-report.pdf> last accessed 30 September 2024; 'Independent Evaluation: MI-Resolve, Zoom Rated as Effective Tools for Dispute Resolution' (Michigan Courts, 6 June 2022) < https://www.courts.michigan.gov/news-releases/2022/june/independent-evaluation-mi-resolve,-zoom-rated-as-effective-tools-for-dispute-resolution/> last accessed 30 September 2024.

[66] Donna Shestowsky and Jennifer Shack, 'Online Dispute Resolution for Post-Judgment Family Law Cases: A Report to the Ottawa County, Michigan, Friend of the Court' (2022) <https://s3.amazonaws.com/aboutrsi/591e30fc6e181e166ffd2eb0/RSI-Evaluation-of-ODR-for-Post-Judgment-Family-Law-Cases--Michigan---FINAL.pdf> last accessed 30 September 2024. On the program's efficiency, those who engaged with ODR were notably more likely to achieve agreements compared to those who were offered ODR but chose not to utilize it. Furthermore, those who used ODR had a significantly higher agreement rate in comparison to those who opted for mediation or informal resolution instead of ODR, with percentages standing at 59.2 per cent versus 26.7 per cent.

C. Movements Toward Research

1. Pew Charitable Trust and Harvard

The NCSC and PEW Charitable Trust have funded research regarding ODR.[67] This began before the Covid-19 Pandemic, with a request for proposals and competitive selection process.[68] For example, PEW funded a project led by a team of researchers at Harvard. In a recent report, the Harvard team reported results that mainly noted the challenges of two randomized control trials (RCTs) they conducted to assess whether ODR improved A2J in the studied projects.[69] These RCTs were implemented in two courts, which the authors refer to as Court A and Court B.[70] In Court A, ODR was used for traffic cases and information about the court's ODR platform was provided on all traffic citation forms provided to individuals. When users registered for the ODR platform, they were randomized into two groups: one that received additional information on whether they could negotiate their charges and, if not, elect for alternative options such as payment plans, and the other group received no additional information.[71] Court B also used ODR for traffic cases. In Court B, all traffic citation forms provided to individuals included a web address that directed users to choose one of three options: plead guilty and pay the citation, use the ODR platform, or appear in court.[72] Individuals who were mainly self-represented litigabts (SRLs) who received these citations were then randomly separated into two groups. One group received a postcard encouraging them to use the ODR platform, and the other group did not receive a postcard.[73]

In Court A, only one person registered to use the ODR platform in the four-month study.[74] The authors noted that information about ODR registration was in small font, hidden in boilerplate language on the citation, and some individuals who attempted to use the platform were ineligible due to narrow eligibility guidelines.[75] Additionally, the citation included information about a scheduled hearing, likely leading to confusion regarding whether the ODR platform was available to individuals that could have used the platform.[76]

In the Court B study, researchers were not able to reach any conclusions regarding encouragement through the postcards. The ODR usage rate in the two groups was

[67] 'Online Dispute Resolution Faces Major Challenges—Survey' (Artificial Lawyer, 19 March 2019) <https://www.artificiallawyer.com/2019/03/19/online-dispute-resolution-faces-major-challenges-survey/> last accessed 30 September 2024. l

[68] 'Courts and Communities' (Pew Charitable Trusts) <https://www.pewtrusts.org/en/projects/courts-and-communities> accessed 30 September 2024; 'Outcome Evaluation for Online Dispute Resolution in State Courts' (Pew Charitable Trusts, 2019) < https://www.pewtrusts.org/-/media/assets/2019/04/2019-clsm-rfp-01-amended.pdf > last accessed 30 September 2024.

[69] Renee Danser et al, 'Online Dispute Resolution of Low-Level Court Proceedings: Two Broken Field Experiments, One Unexpected Result' (4 February 2023) 2–3.

[70] ibid 16–17.

[71] ibid 16–17.

[72] ibid 17.

[73] ibid 17.

[74] ibid 17–18.

[75] ibid 17–18.

[76] ibid 17–18.

72.5 per cent for the postcard group, as compared to 72.6 per cent for the no-postcard group. Researchers noted that the study faced significant hurdles because Court B moved in-person hearings online at the start of the study due to the COVID-19 pandemic shutdown. Also, Court B paid for the ODR vendor for the first 1,500 cases, after which Court B passed the cost of case processing to users. Still, it is unclear why the researchers did not alter the study considering hurdles or otherwise change course with these studies, although that may not have been possible with the courts studied.

The authors concluded by again stating that RCTs are essential in this area, although this study did not provide robust data. They also set forth recommendations for courts looking to implement ODR systems. First, they encouraged courts to evaluate the costs of implementing ODR systems in relation to the benefits of improving A2J through the use of ODR.[77] Second, the authors discussed how narrow eligibility requirements, lack of reminders, and hidden registration information reduce ODR utilization.[78] Third, the researchers recommended that courts create a project management team to oversee ODR deployment, although this increases the costs of an ODR system.[79] While these researchers continued to recommend RCTs, it appears that such studies can be very challenging in this area. It will be interesting to see whether RCTs will be used going forward and what study design lessons have been learned.

2. RSI Research in the US

Resolution Systems Institute (RSI) is a leading organization that conducts research and evaluates alternative dispute resolution systems for their effectiveness. RSI has published several evaluations and reports on dispute resolution that have been helpful to courts. For example, Jennifer Shack, the Director of Research at RSI, and Donna Shestowsky, a Professor of Law at the University of California, Davis evaluated an ODR program in Texas. This was an ODR program for debt and small claims cases that was meant to assist SRLs, as most debtors cannot afford an attorney. The pilot used a text-based stepped ODR platform that began with access to a platform on which parties could securely seek to negotiate a settlement agreement. If they were unable to reach an agreement through negotiation, they could pay $40 for an online mediator to assist them via text on the platform.[80]

The RSI/California, Davis, evaluation found that the program had a high satisfaction rate among participants, but a low participation rate among eligible cases.

[77] ibid 24.
[78] ibid 24.
[79] ibid 24.
[80] Donna Shestowsky and Jennifer Shack, *Online Dispute Resolution for Debt and Small Claims Cases: A Report on a Pilot Program in a Justice of the Peace Court in Collin County, Texas* (University of California, Davis and Resolution Systems Institute 2022).

Specifically, several key issues prevented ODR from being used by both parties in about 76 per cent of cases.[81] First, the process for using the ODR platform was dependent on the courts having email addresses for parties on both sides of the case.[82] This issue appeared to be the most common reason that cases with answers filed were not uploaded to ODR.[83] Second, litigant survey responses indicated that only about one in ten litigants even received information about the ODR program. The only way for litigants to receive information about the program was through physical mail, email, or a text from the court, which only happened after the defendant filed an answer that included this crucial contact information. Despite these issues, however, two out of three survey respondents who did not participate in ODR indicated interest in using ODR in the future.[84] Lack of information about the ODR program was a significant hurdle, and the text-based process may have turned off some individuals. While some enjoy the flexibility and safety of asynchronous discussions, others may struggle to express themselves in writing. This is especially true for those with lower literacy levels or limited English proficiency.

Additionally, RSI produced a report summarizing the findings from four focus groups conducted by RSI with self-represented litigants in small claims cases. The focus groups explored how courts can communicate effectively with litigants about ODR and encourage them to use it. As noted with respect to all ODR research to date, the need for more information about ODR stymies its use and efficacy. The RSI report highlighted the importance of considering diverse needs and offering court resources in various formats. The focus group discussions surfaced a lack of consensus among participants regarding the optimal means for receiving information about a lawsuit and how to proceed with ODR. For instance, out of the 26 participants, only half indicated a preference for receiving the initial lawsuit notice via mail. Six individuals favored receiving case notifications over the phone, five preferred text messages, and just one person expressed a preference for receiving information about their case through email. None of the parties expressed interest in instructional videos. The only real agreement was that the court's resources must be simple and easy to use, with attention to security.[85]

[81] 'Limited Participating Reduces Success of otherwise Promising Texas Pilot ODR Program, Evaluation Finds' (Just Court ADR, 31 May 2022) <https://blog.aboutrsi.org/2022/uncategorized/limited-participation-reduces-success-of-otherwise-promising-texas-pilot-odr-program-evaluation-finds/> last accessed 30 September 2024.

[82] ibid.

[83] ibid.

[84] ibid.

[85] Rachel Feinstein, 'Want Your Court Communications to Be Accessible? RSI Focus Groups Offer Insights' (Just Court ADR, 16 October 2023) <https://blog.aboutrsi.org/2023/research/want-your-court-communications-to-be-accessible-rsi-focus-groups-offer-insights/> last accessed 30 September 2024. RSI also has produced a comprehensive resource that covers the history, benefits, challenges, best practices, and examples of ODR. 'Online Dispute Resolution' (*Resolution Systems Institute*) <https://www.aboutrsi.org/special-topics/online-dispute-resolution> accessed 30 September 2024.See also 'Online Dispute Resolution' (*Resolution Systems Institute*) <https://s3.amazonaws.com/aboutrsi/59316376f8851827014cb4de/ODR-Special-Topic.pdf> last accessed 30 September 2024.

3. Comparison research of text vs. face-to-face processes

Many ODR programs are text-only, largely to allow for asynchronous discussions that foster flexibility because individuals can access the system and participate after hours and pursuant to individuals' own schedules. Also, some find asynchronous text to be easier and safer, out of the gaze of the opposing side.[86] Still, it is important to gather comparative research with video, as it seems intuitive that many would prefer video ODR. For example, researchers in Michigan examined Zoom dispute resolution and text-based MI-Resolve ODR from before the pandemic shutdown to later during the pandemic.[87] Some survey respondents recommended promoting MI-Resolve equally with in-person and Zoom mediation to promote optionality. In contrast, two respondents suggested that Michigan dispute resolution centers should attempt to get parties to use MI-Resolve first and then offer other mediation services if the dispute is not resolved.[88] At least one report suggests that text-based ODR in some contexts, such as traffic tickets, can help expand A2J by providing more flexibility than Zoom or in-person mediation.[89]

Additional research regarding text-based processes has suggested that text-only processes can mitigate and potentially eliminate biases that often accompany visual assessments of individuals, which inevitably occurs in face-to-face dispute resolution.[90] In particular, an international research team focused on Michigan's text-based interface for contesting or paying traffic tickets to further assess differences with face-to-face processes and outcomes. Researchers compared in-person and text-only processes in sets of traffic cases.[91] The final dataset included 5,232 cases: 2,713 face-to-face and 2,519 text-based proceedings.[92] The findings focused on differences based on age, gender, and race.[93] Findings indicated strong evidence that younger drivers pay higher fines, especially in face-to-face proceedings.[94] Older drivers also experienced more reductions of fines, which was true even in online proceedings—but to a lesser extent in online versus in-person proceedings.[95] In face-to-face proceedings, women received 'slightly lower' fines than men, and in text proceedings, women

[86] Jennifer Shack, 'Five Tips for Courts Considering Text-Based ODR Programs' (*ABA*, 30 March 2023) < https://www.americanbar.org/groups/dispute_resolution/resources/just-resolutions/2023-march/five-tips-courts-considering-text-based-odr-programs/?login&abajoin = true/> last accessed 30 September 2024.

[87] Pizzuti (n 65); Michigan Courts (n 65).

[88] ibid.

[89] 'Reimagining Our Courthouses: Report and Recommendations' (Michigan Justice for All Commission) <https://www.courts.michigan.gov/49f36c/siteassets/reports/special-initiatives/justice-for-all/draft-reimagining-courthouses-reportrecs-feedbacksessions.pdf> last accessed 30 September 2024.

[90] Prescott (n 49) 2033–34.

[91] Avital Mentovich et al, 'Are Litigation Outcome Disparities Inevitable? Courts, Technology, and the Future of Impartiality' (2020) 71 Ala L Rev 893, 944. One set of data was from face-to-face proceedings, and one from online proceedings. Because the study focuses on differences in the severity of punishment based on judge discretion, cases without judge discretion for punishment were excluded from the study. Default cases, cases with a not-guilty disposition, cases with a guilty disposition without fines ordered, and cases dismissed on technical grounds are also excluded.

[92] ibid 944.

[93] ibid 941.

[94] ibid 948. Age brackets are 36 and older and 35 and younger. ibid 949.

[95] ibid 948.

received 'fines that are almost identical to men'.[96] The data on the reduction in fines followed the same pattern.[97] In face-to-face proceedings, women were 'slightly more likely' to receive fine reduction; in online proceedings, 'there is no sign of a different tendency'.[98]

Findings with respect to race were perhaps the most interesting. In face-to-face hearings, black defendants received higher fines than in text-based processes, and this difference was statistically significant.[99] In text-based proceedings, the researchers estimated that black defendants received slightly lower fines than non-black drivers.[100] Fine reduction followed a similar pattern. In face-to-face hearings, black defendants were 'significantly less likely' to receive fine reductions.[101] In text-based hearings, the difference 'evaporates'.[102] The researchers noted that they were unable to control for all variables, including infraction history (which could have a serious effect on these values).[103] This research provides support for text-based processes to address and help lessen biases that occur when judges see defendants. Importantly, the text-based processes studied are very simple and accessible on a mobile device. The process requires very little narrative, with mainly 'click-through' options set up for simple traffic ticket disputes.

In sum, the research is still quite limited regarding ODR, both video and text-based processes. There is a need for more independent research, such as the user experience study conducted in Utah, and more in-depth research regarding outcomes in online versus in-person processes. Indeed, part of the battle is that we lack baseline research regarding in-person processes, making it difficult to do comparative studies of in-person versus online processes and outcomes. Furthermore, many of the studies to date were hindered by the pandemic shutdowns and life disruptions during that time. Even the Utah study is quite limited due to low participation rates, caused by pandemic shutdowns. Again, research is essential to revise programs with an aim toward addressing failures and expanding access to remedies and voice.

D. Getting Back to Basics to Design for Access to Justice Expansion

Given the background of ODR in the US and emerging research, we have reached a point in ODR development where it is important to reflect on what has and has not worked, while continuing to advocate for deeper research. Some jurisdictions have ended or paused their pilot ODR programs. That is the case in Ohio.[104] Leaders in Ohio ODR development are considering the next steps for ODR redesign, and it

[96] ibid 948.
[97] ibid 948.
[98] ibid 948.
[99] ibid 953. Roughly 4 per cent higher than the average fine. ibid.
[100] ibid 953.
[101] ibid 954.
[102] ibid 954–56.
[103] ibid 957.
[104] 'OH-Resolve' (Supreme Court of Ohio, 16 February 2024) <https://www.supremecourt.ohio.gov/courts/services-to-courts/dispute-resolution/oh-resolve/> last accessed 30 September 2024.

appears that New York may also be doing a reboot on their ODR program.[105] Their program is currently looking for a new ODR vendor and hopes to resume the ODR program by utilizing a new ODR vendor during 2024.[106] Still, any ODR redesign or '2.0' should be in accordance with solid research and dispute system design. What follows are concepts and design elements based on research to date and dispute system design principles that should guide the development and redesign of ODR systems that are aimed to expand access to voice, remedies, resolutions—and hopefully A2J.

1. User-centric and ethical systems

ODR systems must be user-centric/human-centric with attention to fairness. This means that systems should prioritize user needs through an intuitive and accessible interface design and should be in accordance with user research that considers the user/human experience on every level. This includes options like text resizing, audio controls, and screen reader compatibility for those with disabilities. These are key considerations for user-centric design. Relatedly, the language used should be clear, concise, and, in plain terms, easily understood by the average user. Allowing user customization, offering self-help resources, and providing on-demand human helpers can also improve the user experience.[107]

At the same time, procedural fairness in ODR requires giving parties adequate notice and a reasonable opportunity to present facts and arguments to an unbiased decision-maker. Some degree of transparency around the procedures, decision criteria, and neutrality assurances allows users to understand the process better and have confidence in the outcome. Strict rules around conflicts of interest and disclosures also help avoid bias. Indeed, ODR providers should establish and enforce strong ethical guidelines to govern participant conduct and business practices. This includes honesty, competence, confidentiality, and avoiding conflicts of interest. Providers must safeguard user data privacy and security. They should also proactively monitor for and prevent bias, fraud, deception, and other unethical behavior.

Adherence to ethical codes of conduct help ensure integrity across the dispute resolution process. Drawing inspiration from the International Council for Online Dispute Resolution (ICODR) ethical standards[108] and the American Bar Association (ABA) Dispute Resolution Section ODR Guidance,[109] a robust ODR system should prioritize principles such as impartiality, accessibility, and user empowerment.

[105] 'Online Dispute Resolution: What We've Learned and What We Need to Learn' (NYCourts.Gov, 12 August 2022) <https://www.nycourts.gov/LegacyPDFS/accesstojusticecommission/tc/2022/3AOnlineDisputeResolution.pdf> last accessed 30 September 2024.

[106] 'Courts & Justice' (Tyler Technologies) <https://www.tylertech.com/solutions/courts-public-safety/courts-justice> last accessed 30 September 2024. 'LA-ODR(TurboCourt)' (Los Angeles County Consumer & Business Affairs) <https://dcba.lacounty.gov/turbocourt/> last accessed 30 September 2024.

[107] Amy Schmitz and Heather S Kulp, 'Real Feedback from Real People: Emphasizing User-Centric Designs for Court ODR' (2020) 26(2) Dispute Resolution Magazine 6.

[108] 'Online Dispute Resolution Standards' (*ICODR*, 2017, updated 2022) <https://odr.info/wp-content/uploads/2022/05/NCTDR_and_ICODR_ODR_Standards_2022.pdf> last accessed 30 September 2024.

[109] David Larson, Amy Schmitz, and Alan Weinder, 'ABA ODR Guidance Has Been Adopted' (2023) 38 Ohio State Journal on Dispute Resolution 235.

Ethical ODR design involves crafting processes and interfaces that guarantee parties' equal access to information, fair treatment, and the ability to participate meaningfully in the resolution process. Adhering to confidentiality standards, protecting sensitive information, and ensuring the security of the ODR platform are vital elements in upholding ethical norms. Moreover, as further discussed later in this chapter, continuous monitoring and assessment should be embedded in the design to identify and address ethical concerns as they emerge, fostering a system that resolves disputes efficiently and upholds the highest standards of integrity and justice.

2. Dispute system design

Still, none of this matters if an ODR system is not effective. To effectively resolve disputes, ODR systems should be designed intentionally and thoughtfully. To do this, it is wise to begin with a system design framework, such as that created by Amsler, Martinez, and Smith, with six elements: goals, stakeholders, context and culture, structures and processes, resources, and accountability.[110] Specifying the system's goals is the most critical of the design elements: what does the designer seek to accomplish, and what disputes will be addressed? Goals can include efficiency, compliance, A2J, innovation, dispute prevention, reputation, and more, all of which are likely desirable. Articulating the priority goals will focus on the process choice and provide a metric for evaluating the system's effectiveness. In designing a Court ODR program, goals should align with the broader objectives of the justice system, such as enhancing A2J, expediting case resolution, and improving the overall efficiency of the legal process. Striking a balance between fairness and efficiency is crucial.

This balance is not easy. Again, we do not even take the time to articulate goals and measure effectiveness of in-person processes in court. Still, it is worthwhile to consider whether a court ODR program provides a more cost-effective alternative to traditional court proceedings. This includes consideration of the affordability of the process for individuals, including any fees, compared to the costs associated with traditional litigation (eg, legal representation, court filing fees, and travel expenses). Furthermore, goals should look at efficiency to enable faster resolution of disputes compared to traditional court processes.

Next is the identification of stakeholders, their interests, relationships, and relative power. Stakeholders include the people and organizations that create, host, use, and are affected by a system; ideally, they will be involved in the design from the start and share experiences as users. For example, court users, administrators, judges, and ODR providers may all be stakeholders who should be involved in the design and implementation of an ODR system. This means that designers must consider the demographic profile of users engaging with the ODR program, including diverse individuals and those that face barriers in accessing traditional court processes. This

[110] Janet Martinez, Lisa Blomgren Bingham, and Stephanie E Smith, *Dispute System Design: Preventing, Managing, and Resolving Conflict* (Stanford University Press 2020); 'Stephanie Smith and Janet Martinez, 'An Analytic Framework for Dispute System Design' (2009) 14 Harv Negot L Rev 123.

includes individuals with limited financial means, disabilities, or those residing in remote areas. Tailoring the system to meet the needs of the most vulnerable is essential.

Context and culture comprise the third element—context, meaning the circumstance or situation in which a system is designed, and culture, meaning the implicit assumptions and values held by the surrounding community that help define the dispute. Policymakers must consider procedural rules and societal expectations, especially with court ODR. The ODR system should complement existing court procedures, fostering a harmonious relationship between technology and tradition. The system must comply with rules and procedures in the jurisdiction.

Structures and processes are important with court ODR, especially, as designers must consider how the ODR process will work with the formal legal system. Policymakers also should look at the various process types, ranging from direct negotiation to third-party facilitation, mediation, arbitration, and court adjudication. As a process option, ODR offers an advantage in efficiency and accessibility in terms of timing outside of usual court hours. Mobile friendly ODR opens up the possibilities even further and may bring in new court users who are not comfortable with traditional processes. Still, as noted earlier, any system must comply with legal requirements. Designers also should consider the sequence of online procedures and integrating the ODR process with court enforcement. The challenge lies in ensuring that the ODR system maintains the integrity of legal procedures while promoting flexibility and efficiency.

Of course, resources are critical. Without resources to support design, implementation, and upkeep, any process will ultimately fail. This considers what financial, human, data, technological, information, and training resources are needed and available to support a system. Leadership should collaborate with other stakeholders to use resources wisely for system development, training, and ongoing support and maintenance. Allocating resources strategically ensures the sustainability of the ODR system and its ability to evolve in response to changing legal landscapes.

Finally, a system's accountability and success will depend on the degree of transparency around its operation and whether the system includes monitoring, learning, and evaluation components. Evaluation, such as the research noted above, enables courts to establish metrics on whether the system functions effectively in terms of participation, cost-benefit, quality neutrals, and user satisfaction. Establishing accountability mechanisms is crucial for maintaining public trust in the legal system. This involves clarifying the roles and responsibilities of all parties involved, from the developers of the ODR platform to the legal professionals utilizing it. Ensuring transparency, fairness, and adherence to ethical standards is imperative in upholding the credibility of the court ODR system.

This note on dispute system design is important as we enter this next phase of redesign for ODR in the US. It is important to start from the perspective of user-centric design and emphasize the importance of due process in court ODR. Still, it is difficult to deliver on these aspirations without a framework for analysis. Dispute system design principles help situate considerations and create a concrete methodology for design and redesign, as well as research to assist further revisions. Of course, courts often lack the resources or know-how for elaborate consideration of all these elements, but it is worthwhile to invest the time and resources necessary for proper design in order to avoid the costs of ODR system failures.

3. Research, revise, reimagine A2J

Moreover, court ODR design is never 'one and done.' There must be a continual cycle of research and redesign based on that research—aiming to reimagine A2J. This includes evaluations such as those noted above and outreach to determine what individuals want from ODR. In any redesign, efforts should begin with research regarding what worked and did not work in any ODR pilots. From the research above, for example, we have learned that courts must raise awareness about the availability of ODR as an option for dispute resolution, as well as assistance in using a process.

Furthermore, with a goal of enhancing A2J, programs must be built for the most vulnerable. Specifically, ODR programs should monitor the participation and outcomes of marginalized groups, including low-income individuals, racial and ethnic minorities, and individuals with disabilities, and analyze whether these groups benefit from the ODR program or if any disparities need to be addressed.

Continuous improvement is essential. Again, there must be mechanisms for ongoing evaluation and improvement of any ODR program. It is important to remember that assessing A2J is not easy, and there are varied definitions of 'justice', let alone A2J.[111] Bridging the A2J gap is a long-standing goal for courts that often feels unattainable. Barriers to access to justice include: monetary costs, language and framing, the complexity of proceedings, and psychological burdens. [112] The introduction of technology into the legal realm can be a tool for helping reduce barriers to justice.

The procedural justice model emphasizes the administration of legal proceedings rather than their outcomes. There are three interrelated elements of the model: 1) quality of interpersonal treatment (captures how parties feel authorities treat them); 2) quality of the procedure (parties' perception of the decision-making mechanism); and 3) significance of voice and participation (whether parties felt heard). At the end of the day, people tend to care more about courts treating them with respect than giving them a certain remedy or process.[113] Still, the focus should be on the most vulnerable individuals, who generally have the least and worst access to courts, remedies, and resolutions.[114] With this in mind, ODR 2.0 should go beyond communication portals to include online problem diagnosis and self-help tools, as well as technologies to promote online negotiation, mediation, arbitration, community courts, and variations thereof.[115]

[111] Avital Mentovich and JJ Prescott, 'Legitimacy and Online Proceedings: Procedural Justice, Access to Justice, and the Role of Income' (2023) 57(2) Law & Society Review 189.

[112] ibid.

[113] ibid.

[114] · Amy J Schmitz, 'Measuring "Access to Justice" in the Rush to Digitize' (2020) 88 Fordham L Rev 2381; Amy J Schmitz, 'Secret Consumer Scores and Segmentations: Separating Consumer "Haves" from "Have-Notes"' [2014] Michigan State L Rev 1411, 1411–74.

[115] Amy J Schmitz 'Drive-Thru Arbitration' (n 4).

The journey should not end with the first ODR design. It also should not end with old technologies. With a foundation in research, it is time to use AI to improve A2J with a healthy regard for addressing bias and inequality.[116] Lawyers and judges now use AI assistants throughout the world, and the most powerful and resource-rich law firms have their own AI programs that are getting smarter every day. It is time to build AI into processes for self-represented litigants in ODR programs geared to expand A2J.[117] We are learning that AI can be very user-friendly and may even empower individuals who otherwise lack voice.

It is not enough that ODR promises to open new low-cost avenues to remedies, as it saves the costs of travel and time that exist in traditional in-person processes.[118] Well-designed ODR has capacity to empower individuals through online 'wizards' for case diagnostics, along with easy means for quickly filling out forms and uploading related documents using a photo of a document. Of course, any such use of AI must be with caution and following ethical standards.[119] The use of AI in legal proceedings, such as helping individuals write pleadings or create documents, is a novel idea and can raise ethical concerns. It may even result in sanctions or penalties when used inappropriately.[120] Indeed, the use of AI deserves a more thorough discussion, which is left for another day.[121] Additionally, it will be discussed in other chapters of this book. Regardless, we cannot assume that all ODR projects are 'fair,' inclusive, and effective. It is essential that we ask whether these ODR projects are, in fact, promoting A2J and continue to research, revise, and reimagine A2J.

E. Conclusion

ODR in the courts of the US has entered its next wave, as courts end pilot projects and consider revisions and redesign for ODR. In some cases, courts are considering new providers after failed projects employing private ODR. ODR projects have been blooming throughout US courts since 2014, but not all projects have been successful. Indeed, we are at a critical time in which courts and policymakers must get back to basics and focus on creating systems that work for real people with real problems. Consideration of the user experience is essential, along with solid system design analysis. The symbiotic integration of design concepts and frameworks paves the way for effective design and continuous improvement through informed research. Designers

[116] Mary Anne Noone and Lola Akin Ojelabi, 'Ensuring Access to Justice in Mediation within the Civil Justice System' (2016) 40 Monash University L Rev 528.

[117] Amy J Schmitz and John Zeleznikow, 'Intelligent Legal Tech to Empower Self-Represented Litigants' (2022) 23 Columbia Science and Technology L Rev 142.

[118] Schmitz and Rule (n 3). See also Schmitz, 'Building on OArb Attributes' (n 3).

[119] ibid. See also Schmitz, 'A Blueprint for Online Dispute Resolution' (n 11); Schmitz, 'There's an "App" for That' (n 11). This article does not purport to specify all the ethical issues and considerations. That is left for another day due to space constraints.

[120] *Mata v Avianca, Inc*, No. 22-cv-1461, 2023 US Dist. LEXIS 108263, 2023 WL 4114965, at *1 (SDNY 22 June 2023) (finding 'bad faith on the part of [legal counsel] based upon acts of conscious avoidance and false and misleading statements to the Court' and imposing sanctions when counsel 'submitted non-existent judicial opinions with fake quotes and citations created by the artificial intelligence tool ChatGPT').

[121] This author is working on a forthcoming book that will explore AI in civil dispute resolution, including the courts.

must thoughtfully scrutinize and enhance programs over time, incorporating valuable insights from ongoing research to make iterative edits and redesigns.

The feedback loop of research and design is particularly crucial for promoting A2J, ensuring that ODR systems evolve in response to diverse user groups' changing needs and challenges. By emphasizing research-driven redesigns, we empower policymakers to not only create systems aligned with A2J principles initially but also to actively refine and optimize ODR systems as technology evolves. System design, informed by ongoing research and attention to ethics, becomes a powerful engine driving a fair and effective evolution of ODR systems.

Bibliography

'Alternative Dispute Resolution Services' (*Florida's 10th Judicial Circuit Court*) <https://www.jud10.flcourts.org/mediation>.

Butler S et al, 'The Utah Online Dispute Resolution Platform: A Usability Evaluation and Report' (Innovation for Justice Program, 8 September 2020) ii < https://law.arizona.edu/sites/default/files/i4J_Utah_ODR_Report.pdf >.

'Courts & Communities' (*Pew Charitable Trusts*) < https://www.pewtrusts.org/en/projects/courts-and-communities>.

'Courts & Justice' (*Tyler Technologies*) < https://www.tylertech.com/solutions/courts-public-safety/courts-justice>.

Danser R et al, 'Online Dispute Resolution of Low-Level Court Proceedings: Two Broken Field Experiments, One Unexpected Result' (4 February 2023) 2–3.

Email from Clayson Quigley, District Court Program Administrator in the Greater Salt Lake City area, in the Administrative Office of Utah Courts, to Andrew Johnson, Research Assistant to Professor Schmitz (9 August 2018).

Embley P, 'NCSC, Presentation at the First Int'l Forum on Online Courts.' US Courts and Online Dispute Resolution' (3 Dec 2018) 13 <https://assets.publishing.service.gov.uk/government/uploads/system/uploads/attachment_data/file/761379/US.pdf>.

Feinstein R, 'Want You Court Communications to Be Accessible? RSI Focus Groups Offer Insights' (Just Court ADR, 16 October 2023) < https://blog.aboutrsi.org/2023/research/want-your-court-communications-to-be-accessible-rsi-focus-groups-offer-insights/>.

'Friend of the Court: New Alternative Dispute Resolution (ADR) Policy' (*Eaton County*, 2020) < https://www.eatoncounty.org/224/Friend-of-the-Court>.

'Independent Evaluation: MI-Resolve, Zoom Rated as Effective Tools for Dispute Resolution' (*Michigan Courts,* 6 June 2022) <https://www.courts.michigan.gov/news-releases/2022/june/independent-evaluation-mi-resolve,-zoom-rated-as-effective-tools-for-dispute-resolution/>.

Katsh E and Rule C, 'What We Know and Need to now About Online Dispute Resolution' (2016) 67 SC L Rev. 329, 330.

Katsh E and Rabinovitch-Einy O, *Digital Justice: Technology and the Internet of Disputes* (OUP 2017) 1–25.

'LA-ODR(TurboCourt)' (*Los Angeles County Consumer & Business Affairs*) <https://dcba.lacounty.gov/turbocourt/>.

Larson D, Schmitz A, and Weinder A, 'ABA ODR Guidance Has Been Adopted' (2023) 38 Ohio State Journal on Dispute Resolution 235.

'Limited Participating Reduces Success of otherwise Promising Texas Pilot ODR Program, Evaluation Finds' (*Just Court ADR,* 31 May 2022) <https://blog.aboutrsi.org/2022/uncategorized/limited-participation-reduces-success-of-otherwise-promising-texas-pilot-odr-program-evaluation-finds/>.

Love Kourlis R. and Samnani R, 'A Court Compass for Litigants' (*IAALS*, May 2017) <https://iaals.du.edu/sites/default/files/documents/publications/court_compass_mapping_the_future.pdf>.

Martinez J, Blomgren Bingham L, and Smith S, *Dispute System Design: Preventing, Managing, and Resolving Conflict* (Stanford University Press, 2020).

Mata v Avianca, Inc, No. 22-cv-1461, 2023 US Dist. LEXIS 108263, 2023 WL 4114965, at *1 (SDNY June 22, 2023).

Matterhorn by Court Innovations, <https://www.courtinnovations.com/>.

Mentovich A et al, 'Are Litigation Outcome Disparities Inevitable? Courts, Technology, and the Future of Impartiality' (2020) 71 Ala L Re. 893, 944.

Mentovich A and Prescott J, 'Legitimacy and Online Proceedings: Procedural Justice, Access to Justice, and the Role of Income' (2023) 57(2) Law & Society Review 189.

'MI-Resolve Family System (Michigan Courts, One Court of Justice) < https://www.courts.michigan.gov/administration/offices/office-of-dispute-resolution/mi-resolve/MIResolveFamily/>.

Nevin J, 'Online Ticket Review Helps Make Courts More Accessible and Efficient' (Michigan Courts News Release, 8 June 2015) <https://www.courts.michigan.gov/49c6b5/siteassets/news-releases/online-ticket-review-news-release.pdf>.

New State Ice Co v Liebmann, 285 US 262, 311 (1932).

Noone M and Akin Ojelabi L, "Ensuring Access to Justice in Mediation within the Civil Justice System' (2016) 40 Monash University L Rev 528.

'NSCS/PEW Charitable Trusts ODR Project Announcement' (*NCTDR*, 10 July 2018) <https://odr.info/ncscpew-charitable-trusts-odr-project-announcement/>.

'OH-Resolve' (Supreme Court of Ohio, 16 February 2024) <https://www.supremecourt.ohio.gov/courts/services-to-courts/dispute-resolution/oh-resolve/>.

'Online Case Resolution' (*Eleventh Judicial Circuit of Florida*) <https://www.jud11.flcourts.org/About-the-Court/Court-Divisions/Traffic/Online-Case-Resolution>.

'Online Case Review' (8th *District Court*) <https://cii2.courtinnovations.com/MID08> accessed 30 September 2024.

'Online Case Review' (*61st District Court*) <https://cii2.courtinnovations.com/MID61> accessed 30 September 2024.

'Online Case Review' (*74th District Court*) <https://cii2.courtinnovations.com/MID74>.

'Online Dispute Resolution Faces Major Challenges – Survey' (*Artificial Lawyer*, 19 March 2019) < https://www.artificiallawyer.com/2019/03/19/online-dispute-resolution-faces-major-challenges-survey/>.

'Online Dispute Resolution' (*Resolution Systems Institute*) <https://www.aboutrsi.org/special-topics/online-dispute-resolution>.

'Online Dispute Resolution' (*Resolution Systems Institute*) <https://s3.amazonaws.com/aboutrsi/59316376f8851827014cb4de/ODR-Special-Topic.pdf>

'Online Dispute Resolution Standards' (*ICODR*, 2017, updated 2022) < https://odr.info/wp-content/uploads/2022/05/NCTDR_and_ICODR_ODR_Standards_2022.pdf>.

'Online Dispute Resolution Resources' (*Florida Courts*, 6 April 2023) https://www.flcourts.gov/Administration-Funding/Performance-Accountability/Online-Dispute-Resolution-Resources.

'Online Dispute Resolution Workgroup, 'Online Dispute Resolution Pilot Program Report' (*Florida Courts*, January 2021) <https://www.flcourts.gov/content/download/725954/file/Online%20Dispute%20Resolution%20Pilot%20Program%20Report%20-%20Final%20with%20Appendices.pdf> September.

'Online Dispute Resolution: What We've Learned and What We Need to Learn' (*NYCourts.Gov*, 12 August 2022) <https://www.nycourts.gov/LegacyPDFS/accesstojusticecommission/tc/2022/3AOnlineDisputeResolution.pdf>.

'Outcome Evaluation for Online Dispute Resolution in State Courts' (*Pew Charitable Trusts*, 2019) <https://www.pewtrusts.org/-/media/assets/2019/04/2019-clsm-rfp-01-amended.pdf>.

'Online Ticket Review/Online Warrant Resolution' (*16th District Court*) <https://cii2.courtinnovations.com/MID16> accessed 30 September 2024.

Matterhorn by Court Innovations, <https://www.courtinnovations.com/> accessed 30 September 2024.

'Online Review' (*41B District Court*) <https://cii2.courtinnovations.com/MID41B>.

Pizzuti S and Campbell M, 'Evaluation of Two Statewide Virtual Dispute Resolution Services in Michigan' (*Michigan Courts*, March 2022) <https://www.courts.michigan.gov/49c110/siteassets/reports/odr/sji-evaluation-report-final-report.pdf>.

Prescott J, 'Improving Access to Justice in State Courts with Platform Technology' (2017) 70 Vanderbildt L Rev 1993, 1994–96.

'Reimagining Our Courthouses: Report and Recommendations' (Michigan Justice for All Commission) <https://www.courts.michigan.gov/49f36c/siteassets/reports/special-initiatives/justice-for-all/draft-reimagining-courthouses-reportrecs-feedbacksessions.pdf>.

'Resolve a Dispute Online with MI-Resolve' (*Michigan Courts, One Court of Justice*) <https://www.courts.michigan.gov/administration/offices/office-of-dispute-resolution/mi-resolve/>.

Sandefur R, 'The Fulcrum Point of Equal Access to Justice: Legal and Nonlegal Institutions of Remedy' (2009) 42 Loyola of Los Angeles L Rev 949, 950–54.

Love Kourlis R and Samnani R, 'A Court Compass for Litigants' (*IAALS*, May 2017) <https://iaals.du.edu/sites/default/files/documents/publications/court_compass_mapping_the_future.pdf>.

Schmitz A, 'Building on OArb Attributes in Pursuit of Justice' in PiersvM and Aschauer C (eds), *Arbitration in the Digital Age: the Brave New World of Arbitration* (CUP 2018).

Schmitz A, '"Drive-Thru" Arbitration in the Digital Age: Empowering Consumers through Regulated ODR' (2010) 62 Baylor L Rev 178.

Schmitz A, 'Building Bridges to Remedies for Consumers in International eConflicts' (2012) 34 University of Arkansas Little Rock L Rev 779.

Schmitz A, 'Expanding Access to Remedies through E-Court Initiatives' (2019) 67 Buffalo L Rev 101.

Schmitz A, 'Expanding Access to Remedies, Voice, and Possible Justice in United States Court Online Dispute Resolution (ODR)' in Esteban de la Rosa F, Cortés P, and Marchal N (eds), *Digital Courts: Integrating Human and Artificial Intelligence* (OUP forthcoming).

Schmitz A, 'A Blueprint for Online Dispute Resolution System Design' (2018) 21 J Internet L 3.

Schmitz A, 'There's an "App" for That: Developing Online Dispute Resolution to Empower Economic Development' (2018) 32 Notre Dame JL, Ethics & Public Policy 1.

Schmitz A, 'Measuring "Access to Justice" in the Rush to Digitize' (2020) 88 Fordham L Rev 2381.

Schmitz A, 'Secret Consumer Scores and Segmentations: Separating Consumer "Haves" from "Have-Notes"' [2014] Michigan State L Rev 1411, 1411–74.

Schmitz A and Kulp H, 'Real Feedback from Real People: Emphasizing User-Centric Designs for Court ODR' (2020) 26(2) Dispute Resolution Magazine 6.

Schmitz A and Rule C, *The New Handshake: Online Dispute Resolution and the Future of Consumer Protection* (American Bar Association Section on Dispute Resolution 2017).

Schmitz A and Zeleznikow J, 'Intelligent Legal Tech to Empower Self-Represented Litigants' (2022) 23 Columbia Science and Technology L Rev 142.

Shack J, 'Five Tips for Courts Considering Text-Based ODR Programs' (ABA, 30 March 2023) < https://www.americanbar.org/groups/dispute_resolution/resources/just-resolutions/2023-march/five-tips-courts-considering-text-based-odr-programs/?login&abajoin = true/>.

Shestowsky D and Shack J, *Online Dispute Resolution for Debt and Small Claims Cases: A Report on a Pilot Program in a Justice of the Peace Court in Collin County, Texas* (University of California, Davis and Resolution Systems Institute 2022).

Shestowsky D and Shack J, 'Online Dispute Resolution for Post-Judgment Family Law Cases: A Report to the Ottawa County, Michigan, Friend of the Court' (2022) < https://s3.amazonaws.com/aboutrsi/591e30fc6e181e166ffd2eb0/RSI-Evaluation-of-ODR-for-Post-Judgment-Family-Law-Cases---Michigan---FINAL.pdf>.

Smith S and Martinez J, 'An Analytic Framework for Dispute System Design' (2009) 14 Harvard Negotiation L Rev 123.

Stiglich M, *Utah Online Dispute Resolution Pilot Project*, NCSC (December 2017) 1–3.

Susskind R, *Tomorrow's Lawyers: An Introduction to Your Future* (OUP 2013).

Utah Courts Recent Press Notifications. Aug. 13, 2020 'Utah Courts' <http://www.utcourts.gov/utc/news/2020/08/13/to-tackle-the-unmet-legal-needs-crisis-utah-supreme-court-unanimously-endorses-a-pilot-program-to-assess-changes-to-the-governance-of-the-practice-of-law/>.

7
Delivering Justice in the Digital Economy
Innovations in China's E-Courts

Alex Chung[*] and Ying Yu[**]

A. Introduction

China's digital economy has vastly expanded over the past decade. The rapid growth of China's digital economy and e-commerce, including domestic and international trade, has drastically increased the volume of internet-related disputes.[1] This trend

[*] Partner at Scopium and former Consumer Policy and Law Expert at UN Trade and Development.
[**] Distinguished Professor at Beijing Normal University's (BNU) Internet Institute and former Legal Officer at the United Nations.

[1] United Nations Conference on Trade and Development (UNCTAD), *Consumer trust in the digital economy: The case for online dispute resolution* (UNCTAD Research Paper No 72, UNCTAD/SER.RP/2021/15, last accessed November 2021).

Alex Chung and Ying Yu, *Delivering Justice in the Digital Economy* In: *Digitalization and Artificial Intelligence in Courts*. Edited by: Fernando Esteban de la Rosa, Pablo Cortés, and Nuria Marchal Escalona, Oxford University Press.
 DOI: 10.1093/9780198918752.003.0007

became particularly evident during the Covid-19 pandemic as the number of cases received by China's national public online dispute resolution (ODR) platform for consumers, '12315',[2] increased by ten-fold year-on-year since 2020.[3]

For ease of reference, such consumer ODR platforms—including business in-house consumer complaints-handling systems—are referred to as consumer dispute resolution (CDR) systems or platforms henceforth. The notion of CDR in this chapter combines both litigation and non-litigation methods of resolving consumer disputes.[4]

Although there exists a variety of ways in which Chinese consumers use non-litigation means of resolving disputes, such as in-house CDR mechanisms provided by ecommerce platforms as well as the CDR platforms provided by '12315' and the China Consumer Association,[5] litigation remains an important option for both consumers and micro, small, and medium-sized enterprises (MSMEs) alike.[6]

However, litigation in 'traditional' courts—namely court processes and proceedings involving in-person interaction—is increasingly recognized as no longer fit for purpose in the digital age. Some of the limitations that hinder the use of traditional courts when dealing with internet-related disputes include the following: the geographical distance or state borders between litigants and courts; the low monetary value of certain disputes, particularly e-commerce disputes; the time-consuming nature of court processes; the complexity of trial proceedings, particularly those concerning cross-border disputes; the psychological and emotional toll on the litigants; and the expensive fees involved.[7]

Recognizing these limitations, China has undertaken significant efforts to transform its judiciary to better serve the needs of the public and the demands of the digital economy. A series of initiatives have led to the establishment of a nationwide online litigation ecosystem focused on civil lawsuits. This judicial ecosystem, which contributes to the wider CDR landscape, enables litigants and judges to conduct the entire legal process online—from filing a lawsuit to undertaking negotiation, mediation, or hearings—through a single portal, also known as one-stop shop.[8]

[2] 'National Platform of Consumer Dispute Resolution' *State Administration for Market Regulation of the People's Republic of China* <http://36.110.229.139/> last accessed 14 October 2024.

[3] Ying Yu and Alex Chung, 'CDR: Catalyst for China's E-Commerce' in Xandra Kramer, Stefaan Voet, Lorenz Ködderitzsch, Magdalena Tulibacka, and Burkhard Hess (eds), *Delivering Justice: A Holistic and Multidisciplinary Approach: Liber Amicorum in Honour of Christopher Hodges* (Hart Publishing 2022) 227–44.

[4] For the rationale behind this manner of categorization, see page 230 in ibid.

[5] United Nations Conference on Trade and Development (UNCTAD), *Consumer Dispute Resolution in the World* (UNCTAD Report, UNCTAD/DITC/CPLP/2023/2, March 2024)(</IBT) 11.

[6] As defined in art 39 of the Consumer Rights and Interests Protection Law, the five CDR approaches are: 1) negotiate and settle with the business directly; 2) request mediation through a consumer association or other organizations established in accordance with the law; 3) lodge a complaint with the relevant administrative department; 4) seek arbitration based on the arbitration organization specified in the contract agreement; 5) bring a lawsuit before a people's court. For an analysis on CDR approaches 1 to 4, see pp 230–31 in ibid. In July 2024, the Chinese Government promulgated a set of regulations on the implementation of the aforementioned consumer law. For details, see arts 42 to 47 in Chapter V: Dispute Resolution: 'People's Republic of China Regulations for the Implementation of the Law on the Protection of Consumer Rights and Interests' (*The Government of the People's Republic of China,* 19 March 2024) <https://www.gov.cn/zhengce/content/202403/content_6940158.htm> last accessed 20 October 2024.

[7] United Nations Conference on Trade and Development, *Consumer trust in the digital economy: The case for online dispute resolution* (UNCTAD Research Paper No 72, UNCTAD/SER.RP/2021/15, November 2021).

[8] ibid.

In accordance with these initiatives, the Hangzhou Internet Court was launched in August 2017, followed by the Beijing Internet Court and the Guangzhou Internet Court in September 2018. These Courts have special jurisdiction over internet-related disputes and are primarily designed for mediation and hearings involving small claims and less complex claims.[9]

The three Internet Courts by default and by design conduct most of their hearings online; depending on the court, they also offer in-person services at the courts' physical location. For instance, the Hangzhou Internet Court provides mediation rooms for face-to-face mediation,[10] the Beijing Internet Court provides 'cabins' (enclosed booths) for in-person participation in online negotiation and online mediation,[11] and the Guangzhou Internet Court provides 'e-kiosks' (enclosed booths) for in-person participation in online mediation and virtual trial hearing.[12]

In addition to the three Internet Courts, many of the 3,500 + people's courts at all levels across China have been developing or have implemented online litigation and other online pre-litigation features.[13] These services are provided for criminal litigation and civil litigation[14] both through their individual court websites as well as via a mobile applet within a ubiquitously popular messenger application—WeChat—to be discussed in the following section.

For instance, the courts of Shanghai—China's most populous city—have heard 8,883 criminal cases online in 2020, representing 30.63 per cent of all criminal cases, as 'online court hearings for criminal cases have become common in Shanghai courts'.[15] People's courts also commonly feature 'operation manual' for users and litigants to learn how to participate in online pre-litigation activities, including online negotiation and online mediation, as well as online hearing.[16]

[9] 'Beijing Internet Court: Virtual court cabin' (17 September 2021) <https://english.bjinternetcourt.gov.cn/2021-09/17/c_408.htm> last accessed 13 October 2024.

[10] Yang Lin, 'Visual Law: China's Three Internet Courts' (2021) 2(3) SAS Journal 534.

[11] ibid 535. Trial judges can also use physical booths at the Beijing Internet Court to preside over online hearing. 'Beijing Internet Court: Virtual court cabin' (17 September 2021) <https://english.bjinternetcourt.gov.cn/2021-09/17/c_408.htm> last accessed 13 October 2024.

[12] Caixia Zou, 'Achievements and Prospects of Artificial Intelligence Judicature in China' (2022) 11(04) Chinese Studies 209.

[13] 'Digital advances herald judicial progress' *China Daily* (17 October 2024) <https://www.chinadaily.com.cn/a/202410/17/WS67105f23a310f1265a1c8041_1.html> <https://www.chinadaily.com.cn/a/202410/17/WS67105f23a310f1265a1c8041_2.html> <https://www.chinadaily.com.cn/a/202410/17/WS67105f23a310f1265a1c8041_3.html> <https://www.chinadaily.com.cn/a/202410/17/WS67105f23a310f1265a1c8041_4.html> <https://www.chinadaily.com.cn/a/202410/17/WS67105f23a310f1265a1c8041_5.html> last accessed 21 October 2024.

[14] 'How Online Criminal Litigation Works in China: The Case of Shanghai' (*China Justice Observer*, 5 November 2021) https://www.chinajusticeobserver.com/a/how-online-criminal-litigation-works-in-china-the-case-of-shanghai last accessed 21 October 2024.

[15] ibid.

[16] See the following websites from the Courts of Shanghai as an example: 'Shanghai Courts Litigation Service Network' <https://www.hshfy.sh.cn/shwfy/ssfww/> last accessed 21 October 2024. 'Shanghai Courts Litigation Service Network: Client-side download' <hshfy.sh.cn/shwfy/download/client_0/ > last accessed 21 October 2024. 'Shanghai Courts Litigation Service Network: Online negotiation manual' <https://www.hshfy.sh.cn/shwfy/download/viewpdf.jsp?lx = 6> last accessed 21 October 2024. 'Shanghai Courts Litigation Service Network: Online mediation manual' <https://www.hshfy.sh.cn/shwfy/download/viewpdf.jsp?lx = 1> last accessed 21 October 2024. 'Shanghai Courts Litigation Service Network: Online trial hearing manual' <https://www.hshfy.sh.cn/shwfy/download/viewpdf.jsp?lx = 0> last accessed 21 October 2024.

On a national level, statistics published by the SPC shows that in 2021, approximately 33.52 million cases were accepted by all courts across China, which is more than twice that of 2013 (14.22 million cases). Of those, 30.10 million cases were concluded and enforced.[17]

Breaking that down further, 11.44 million cases were filed online, a year-on-year increase of 8.94 per cent; 10.84 million cases were resolved through online mediation; and 1.27 million cases were resolved through online litigation, a year-on-year increase of 48.94 per cent.[18]

In other words, the total number of disputes resolved through both online litigation and online mediation in China in 2021 was approximately 12.11 million, which accounted for more than one-third (36.12 per cent) of all court cases nationwide.

While the Internet Courts of Beijing, Guangzhou, and Hangzhou only accounted for a portion of that one-third—since they were the early pilot projects upon which 3,500 other people's courts look to and/or model their online litigation systems—based on the aforementioned significant year-on-year increase in online litigation and mediation in 2021, this trend will likely continue, particularly after the SPC-issued 'Online Litigation Rules for People's Courts' took effect in 2021.[19]

The remainder of this chapter examines some of the solutions that have been implemented by these three e-Courts to reduce hurdles for litigants, with a view to enhancing the effectiveness and efficiency of pre-trial and proceedings-related processes. Some of these solutions involve digital innovations such as blockchain and artificial intelligence (AI), while other initiatives such as the publication of 'typical cases', decisions of public interest, and judicial recommendations are also discussed.

Before further taking stock of the technological and judicial innovations of these e-courts, the following discussion firstly provides an overview of the Chinese judiciary's initiatives in laying the groundwork for the development of a 'smart' judicial ecosystem.

B. Initiatives for China's 'Smart' Judicial Ecosystem

1. Directives from the Supreme People's Court of China

In establishing the three e-courts in the Chinese cities of Beijing, Guangzhou, and Hangzhou, a different set of challenges needed to be addressed along the way,

[17] 'In numbers: Achievements of China's courts in the last decade' The Supreme People's Court of the People's Republic of China (11 October 2022) <https://english.court.gov.cn/2022-10/11/c_818933.htm> last accessed 19 October 2024.

[18] 'Numbers in the SPC 2022 work report' The Supreme People's Court of the People's Republic of China (10 March 2022) <https://english.court.gov.cn/2022-03/10/c_761359.htm> last accessed 19 October 2024. 'Work Report of the Supreme People's Court of the People's Republic of China' The Supreme People's Court of the People's Republic of China (8 March 2022) <https://view.officeapps.live.com/op/view.aspx?src = https%3A%2F%2Fenglish.court.gov.cn%2Fpdf%2FWorkReportoftheSupremePeoplesCourtofthePeoplesRepublicofChina.docx&wdOrigin = BROWSELINK> last accessed 19 October 2024. '线上法院为你"云断案"' [Online Courts Deliver Judgments through Cloud Proceedings] *People's Daily* (15 June 2022) <http://paper.people.com.cn/rmrbhwb/html/2022-06/15/content_25923050.htm> last accessed 19 October 2024.

[19] Discussed in section B.3.

including how to: remotely and reliably authenticate the identity of litigants when accessing the e-court portal; ensure that the integrity of the digital evidence submitted to the e-court remains intact through robust security measures; enforce judgment in a timely manner if a litigant fails abide by the terms of the judicial or mediation outcome; optimize the efficiency of the e-court processes given the high volume of case filings; increase the transparency of the court processes and proceedings, including in high profile cases or cases of public interest; create mechanisms that feedback to regulators to proactively tackle emerging issues that have a systemic impact on the society.

To address these challenges and modernize the judicial system, the Supreme People's Court (SPC) of China promulgated a regulation on Internet Courts in September 2018, titled 'Provisions on Several Issues Concerning the Trial of Cases by Internet Courts'.[20] The regulation provides the legal basis for the establishment of e-courts and associated judicial platforms for case filing and other functions such as mediation hearings,[21] in accordance and compliance with China's Cybersecurity Law and other relevant data protection laws and regulations.[22] It also specifies the special internet-related jurisdiction of the three e-courts of Beijing, Guangzhou, and Hangzhou.[23] The regulation also allows litigants to submit digital evidence via a blockchain-enabled platform which is aimed at improving the way with which the court handles and uses digital evidence throughout the litigation process.[24]

Following the promulgation of the regulation, the three e-courts developed and launched their respective digital platforms in collaboration with a range of other public institutions and large e-commerce and business entities.[25] This development has important implications for litigation in China's bustling digital economy.

As litigation arising from the digital economy often involve disputes that have taken place online, litigants that are geographically distant from one another, and transaction or evidence that is in a digital format, it is crucial that the court have the capability to deal such cases in a way that conforms to the concepts of 'fairness' and 'justice'.[26]

[20] 'Provisions of the Supreme People's Court on Several Issues Concerning the Trial of Cases by Internet Courts' (*Gazette of the Supreme People's Court of the People's Republic of China*, September 6, 2018) <http://gongbao.court.gov.cn/Details/7e594961f195254a863d6cc90be5cd.html> last accessed 25 May 2024.

[21] Art 1, ibid.

[22] Art 5, ibid and 'Cybersecurity Law of the People's Republic of China' (*Peking University Law*, July 2016) <https://www.pkulaw.com/en_law/4dce14765f4265f1bdfb.html?way = textSlc#tiao_0> last accessed 25 May 2024.

[23] Art 2, 'Provisions of the Supreme People's Court on Several Issues Concerning the Trial of Cases by Internet Courts' (*Gazette of the Supreme People's Court of the People's Republic of China,* September 6, 2018) <http://gongbao.court.gov.cn/Details/7e594961f195254a863d6cc90be5cd.html> last accessed 25 May 2024.

[24] Blockchain can be defined as a type of distributed database, or distributed ledger, which records the transactions of multiple parties in a secure, immutable manner. There are three main types of blockchains: public, consortium, and private blockchains. The implementation of blockchain technology in Chinese courts has mainly occurred in consortium blockchains. Tian Lu, 'The Implementation of Blockchain Technologies in Chinese Courts' (2021) 4(1) JBPL 102, 103.

[25] 'Why are Chinese internet courts keen on blockchain technology' (*China Justice Observer*, 15 December 2019) <https://en.chinajusticeobserver.com/a/why-are-chinese-internet-courts-keen-on-blockchain-technology> last accessed 25 May 2024.

[26] For a detailed discussion on these notions in the context of the Chinese judiciary and policy environment, see Straton Papagianneas and Nino Junius, 'Fairness and justice through automation in China's smart court'. (2003) 51 Computer Law and Security Review 105897.

To this end and as part of the development of a nationwide Chinese 'smart' judicial ecosystem, blockchain-enabled and AI-powered portals and digital applications have been implemented by the courts. This has not only enhanced the ease and speed with which litigation is conducted but also significantly reduced financial costs and environmental impact that are associated with conventional courts.[27]

Prior to the establishment of the internet courts, litigants needed to adhere to the working hours of the court when filing paper documents and/or evidence and physically attend the court. This has often led to undue delays and inconvenience for all parties involved. internet courts, however, offer a seamless online litigation process that can be undertaken at the convenience of the parties—from case and evidence filing to negotiation, mediation or conciliation, and from trial proceedings to rendering decision and/or enforcement of judgment.[28]

By allowing litigants to asynchronously and remotely verify their identity, file case documents, and submit evidence through the court portal or application all within seconds to minutes, as well as participate in pre-trial processes or court hearing within days to weeks, the accessibility and efficiency of the entire litigation process has manifoldly increased, thereby contributing to the overall 'fairness' of the smart judicial ecosystem.[29] The result is a paperless, eco-friendly approach that has drastically reduced physical travel and carbon emissions.[30]

2. China Mobile Mini Court

To further the regulation's aim of creating a 'smart' judicial ecosystem and enhancing the convenience of and accessibility to litigation, the SPC launched the nationwide 'China Mobile Mini Court' (CMMC) mobile applet in August 2018. The CMMC applet interfaces with the People's Courts across China to facilitate with case filing and other related tasks online.[31] It is accessible only through, and interoperable with, the WeChat mobile application. WeChat is a messenger and payment mobile application that is used by the vast majority of the Chinese population.[32]

[27] '以高质量互联网司法护航中国式现代化' [High-Quality Internet Judiciary Safeguards Chinese-Style Modernization] (*China Court,* 29 October 2023) <https://www.chinacourt.org/article/detail/2023/10/id/7600832.shtml> last accessed 25 May 2024.

[28] '互联网法院：网络法治的中国智慧与方案-中国法院网' [Internet Courts: China's Wisdom and Solutions for Online Rule of Law] (*China Court*, 29 September 2024) <https://www.chinacourt.org/article/detail/2024/09/id/8136142.shtml> last accessed 19 October 2024.

[29] Straton Papagianneas and Nino Junius, 'Fairness and justice through automation in China's smart court.' (2003) 51:105897 Computer Law and Security Review.

[30] '以高质量互联网司法护航中国式现代化' [High-Quality Internet Judiciary Safeguards Chinese-Style Modernization] (*China Court,* 29 October 2023) <https://www.chinacourt.org/article/detail/2023/10/id/7600832.shtml> last accessed 25 May 2024.

[31] 'Improving the Cyber Legal System and Protecting the People's Legitimate Rights and Interests—The press conference of the State Council Information Office focused on the rule of law on the Internet to ensure high-quality development' (The Government of the People's Republic of China, 19 June 2024) <https://www.gov.cn/zhengce/202406/content_6958050.htm> last accessed 12 October 2024.

[32] Roughly 1.2 billion registered users and counting in China. 'Chinese Courts on Smart Phones' (*China Justice Observer*, 6 June 2021) <https://www.chinajusticeobserver.com/a/chinese-courts-on-smart-phones> last accessed 25 May 2024.

The CMMC applet accepts not only consumer and internet-related cases but also other types of cases, including personal injury and tort law.[33] The applet has more than 30 functions, including online case filing, case inquiries, online delivery, legal inquiry, enforcement application, and WeChat payment.[34] In September 2020, the SPC approved the blockchain feature on the applet which allows litigants to submit and store digital evidence using the applet during case filing.[35]

Since its launch, the CMMC applet has quickly attracted a large number of registered users and cases: by the end of 2020, the applet had 3,275,300 users and handled more than 2.2 million cases involving more than 2.1 million litigants. Of these, 72.6 per cent took less than 15 minutes for the litigant to file their case using the applet.[36]

3. Regulations on e-court, blockchain, and artificial intelligence

In June 2021, three years after the 'Provisions on Several Issues Concerning the Trial of Cases by Internet Courts' was promulgated, the SPC issued the 'Online Litigation Rules for People's Courts', which came into effect in August 2021. This set of rules contains 39 articles which apply to the SPC as well as over 3,500 lower courts throughout China. The rules set out, for the first time, the legal validity, basic principles, applicable scope, and applicable conditions of online litigation. They also provide guidance on how to conduct litigation activities online, including how to review the authenticity of blockchain evidence.[37]

To further strengthen the suite of digital technologies used in e-courts, the SPC released two opinion pieces on the application of blockchain and AI technologies in the judicial system in May 2022 and December 2022, respectively. The first document is titled 'Opinions of the Supreme People's Court on Strengthening Blockchain

[33] '"移动微法院"全国版试运行:极简化操作 无延时开庭 见证式执行' [Nationwide Trial Run of Mobile Micro Court: Streamlined Operations, Instant Hearings, Transparent Enforcement] *Xinhua News* (18 August 2018) <http://www.xinhuanet.com/politics/2018-08/18/c_1123288515.htm> last accessed 25 May 2024.

[34] For an analysis on the full range of functionalities of the applet and its envisioned benefits, see Changming Hu, '移动电子诉讼的司法实践及其限度——以中国"移动微法院"为例' [Judicial Practice and Limits of Mobile E-Litigation: The Case of China's 'Mobile Micro Court'] (2021) 2 China Applied Law 73–86.

[35] '移動微法院訴訟保全區塊鏈系統順利通過測評，獲最高法院認可' [Mobile Micro Court Litigation Preservation Blockchain System Successfully Passes Evaluation, Gains Supreme Court Approval] (*0x Information*, 2 September 2020) <https://0xzx.com/zh-tw/202009021058796300.html> last accessed 25 May 2024.

[36] Ying Yu and Alex Chung, 'CDR: Catalyst for China's E-Commerce' in Xandra Kramer, Stefaan Voet, Lorenz Ködderitzsch, Magdalena Tulibacka, and Burkhard Hess (eds), *Delivering Justice: A Holistic and Multidisciplinary Approach: Liber Amicorum in Honour of Christopher Hodges* (Hart Publishing 2022) 227–44.

[37] 'China: Supreme People's Court Issues Online Litigation Rules, Addressing Review of Blockchain Evidence' (US Library of Congress, 21 July 2021) <https://www.loc.gov/item/global-legal-monitor/2021-07-21/china-supreme-peoples-court-issues-online-litigation-rules-addressing-review-of-blockchain-evidence/> last accessed 25 May 2024.

Application in the Judicial Field',[38] and the second document is titled 'Opinions on Regulating and Strengthening the Judicial Application of Artificial Intelligence'.[39]

These documents set out the legal rules and standards for applying blockchain technology, including smart contracts,[40] and AI technology so that data can be better protected, processes can be optimized efficiently, and interconnectivity between collaborating institutions as well as trial hearing outcomes and enforcement can be enhanced. The goal is to develop, by 2025, an interconnected and fully operational judicial ecosystem that embody these technologies.

4. Internet Judicial Blockchain platform

Traditional litigation faced challenges with the use of digital evidence in many respects, including the storage of evidence, the susceptibility of evidence to tampering, and the expensive costs of notarization where the authentication of evidence is needed.

Blockchain is advantageous in this regard owing to its qualities of permanency, immutability, and transparency. Blockchain-enabled platform allows courts to securely accept, manage, store and transmit digital evidence in a transparent and trackable manner, as well as enabling judges to verify the evidence through a simple online process. This not only saves parties time and money by reducing the cost and stress of travelling and paper processes, but also provides for a more reliable and secure means of case filing.

Recognizing the benefits of having a centralized blockchain portal for digital evidence used in litigation and following the release of the two aforementioned regulations, the SPC launched an 'Internet Judicial Blockchain' platform.[41]

The platform is interconnected to more than 3,500 courts across China. This centrally administered platform ensures that every e-document served by any court in the country is blockchain-verified. In cases where the litigant is uncertain about the authenticity or authority of an e-document, the litigant can submit it to this central platform for verification.[42] According to the real time data published on its website,

[38] 'Opinions of the Supreme People's Court on Strengthening Blockchain Application in the Judicial Field' *China Daily* (25 May 2022) <https://www.chinadaily.com.cn/m/supremepeoplescourt/2022-05/25/content_37550749.htm> last accessed 12 October 2024.

[39] 'Opinions on Regulating and Strengthening the Judicial Application of Artificial Intelligence' (*China Court,* December 9, 2022) <https://www.chinacourt.org/law/detail/2022/12/id/150461.shtml> last accessed 12 October 2024.

[40] A smart contract can be understood as 'a set of computer codes that, when triggered, is capable of running automatically according to its prespecified functions'. In the context of judicial system, a smart contract does not represent the legal concept of a contract; instead, it is an enforcement tool. Tian Lu 'The Implementation of Blockchain Technologies in Chinese Courts' (2021) 4.1 JBPL 117.

[41] 'People's Courts of the People's Republic of China: Si Fa Lian' <https://sfl.court.gov.cn> last accessed 25 May 2024.

[42] '全国法院电子送达文书均已支持在线核验' [Electronic Service of Court Documents Nationwide Now Supports Online Verification] *Xinhua News* (14 March 2023) <http://www.news.cn/2023-03/14/c_1129431979.htm> last accessed 25 May 2024.

the blockchain-enabled platform has conducted approximately 127 million verification operations by May 2024.[43]

C. Internet Court Case Studies

1. The Beijing Internet Court

The Beijing Internet Court was launched in September 2018. Its jurisdiction spans various sectors of the digital economy and 11 types of B2B (business to business) and B2C (business to consumer) internet-related claims, including social media, e-commerce, technical services, mobile applications, online intellectual property rights (IPR), online education, and finance.[44] By late 2023, the Beijing Internet Court comprised of 45 judges and 190 enforcement officers.[45]

1.1. Operational statistics

From its inception in September 2018 until September 2023, the Beijing Internet Court had dealt with approximately 199,000 cases of which 187,000 were concluded. All case filings were submitted online, of which 99.90 per cent of the hearings took place virtually.[46] The majority of the cases involved disputes over copyright ownership, (online) infringement, and online sales contract, accounting for 71.57 per cent, 11.27 per cent and 8.65 per cent of all cases handled.[47]

During 2023, the court received nearly 25,000 new cases. The annual rate of case completion was 92.09 per cent, while the acceptance rate of first instance judgment by litigants was 89.84 per cent.[48]

[43] 'People's Courts of the People's Republic of China: Si Fa Lian' <https://sfl.court.gov.cn>last accessed 25 May 2024.

[44] 'Beijing Internet Court' <https://www.bjinternetcourt.gov.cn/> and <https://english.bjinternetcourt.gov.cn/2019-03/25/c_23.htm> last accessed 25 May 2024.

[45] ibid. '五年答卷！一图读懂《北京互联网法院审判工作白皮书》' [Five-Year Review! Key Insights from the Beijing Internet Court Trial Work White Paper at a Glance] (*Beijing Internet Court*, 9 October 2023) <https://mp.weixin.qq.com/s?__biz = MzU1NDk0NjE3MA==&mid = 2247511513&idx = 1&sn = 01a8bfbd860e957c9140c1fc37726f7a&chksm=> and '北京互联网法院：个人信息保护纠纷覆盖社交电商等多行业' [Beijing Internet Court: Personal Data Protection Disputes Span Social Media, E-Commerce and Multiple Industries] *Beijing China News* (2 November 2023) <https://www.bj.chinanews.com.cn/news/2023/1102/92564.html> last accessed 25 May 2024. Some examples of the claim types include the following: personal information protection disputes, such as information leaks that led to users falling prey to telecom fraud; online education applications that seek to unnecessarily obtain excessive personal information during registration; e-commerce platforms making excessive phone calls to customers and improperly using or disclosing personal information; office software accused of removing users from work groups without consent.

[46] '以高质量互联网司法护航中国式现代化" [High-Quality Internet Judiciary Safeguards Chinese-Style Modernization] (*China Court*, 29 October 2023) <https://www.chinacourt.org/article/detail/2023/10/id/7600832.shtml> last accessed 25 May 2024.

[47] '北京互联网法院5年受案19万余件 著作权权属、侵权纠纷占比超七成' [Beijing Internet Court Processes Over 190,000 Cases in Five Years, with Copyright Ownership and Infringement Disputes Accounting for Over 70%] (*Beijing Political and Legal Network*, 5 September 2023) <https://www.bj148.org/zf1/zfyw/202309/t20230905_1656406.html> last accessed 25 May 2024.

[48] '盘点2023丨14组数据！见证北京互联网法院这一年的精彩' [2023 in Review | 14 Key Data Points Showcasing a Year of Progress at Beijing Internet Court] (Beijing Internet Court, 23 January 2024) <https://mp.weixin.qq.com/s/BsXE42siEgK9Bp7coRZWcQ> last accessed 25 May 2024.

Statistics from 2022 showed that online hearings conducted over the Beijing Internet Court platform took on average 35 minutes to complete, while cases on average took 76 days to close. Prior to September 2022, the threshold for case fees for small claims was 50 RMB. In September 2022, a new policy came into effect stipulating that if the case was settled through online mediation during the pre-trial period, the service would be free of charge. However, if the case proceeded with an online trial, the litigant would be liable to pay 10 RMB[49] in hearing fees.[50]

1.2. Technological innovations

As part of its efforts to adhere to the principles of 'neutrality, openness, security, and controllability,' the Beijing Internet Court launched 'Tianping Lian,' a blockchain-based platform, in September 2018. It was established through a joint effort between 20 judicial institutions, which included the Beijing High Court, the Judicial Appraisal Centre, and the Notary Office, as well as industry organizations, financial institutions, and large e-commerce platforms.[51]

It is advantageous for various entities to be jointly involved in the development of blockchain platform, since the submissions made used during e-litigation—including litigant's verified identity information, contract and transaction record, digital evidence—often need to be shared between those entities in a simple, fast, and secure manner during court filing and online hearing. As many of the aforementioned entities' digital applications are already interoperable[52] with one another and becoming increasingly connected to a wider network of blockchain-powered network,[53] the efficiency and cost of the network is optimized for all members of China's judicial blockchain platforms.

The use of blockchain platform is necessary for ascertaining the authenticity and legality of e-submission before it is admitted as evidence by the court, since the court can use the blockchain record to verify that the e-evidence has not been altered or processed between when it was written onto the blockchain, and when it was presented in court as evidence. By ensuring that the chain of custody is intact, the use of blockchain in court helps to uphold the integrity and transparency of the judicial system.[54]

In the case of Tianping Blockchain, it is used for identity and access management as well as the submission, verification, and storage of electronic evidence during the

[49] Equivalent to approximately 1.40 USD or 1.10 GBP at the time of writing.

[50] Ying Yu, 'Digitalization' (Oxford University EU ADR Conference, 9–10 November 2022).

[51] Written as 天平链 in Chinese Mandarin, Tianping Blockchain can be translated as 'scale of justice chain'. 'Beijing Internet Court: Tian Ping Lian' <https://tpl.bjinternetcourt.gov.cn/tpl/> last accessed 25 May 2024.

[52] 'Chinese Courts on Smart Phones' (*China Justice Observer*, 6 June 2021) <https://www.chinajusticeobserver.com/a/chinese-courts-on-smart-phones> last accessed 25 May 2024. 'Guangzhou Internet Court: Judicial innovation' <https://gzinternetcourt.gov.cn/#/articleList?type = InnovationInitiative&titleType = judicialInnovation&apiType = routine> last accessed 14 October 2024.

[53] Including WeChat and Union Pay, two of the largest companies in China involved in the provision of messenger services and financial services, respectively. 'What is Blockchain and Why is WeChat and Union Pay using it?' (*HiredChina.com*, 24 October 2023) <https://www.hiredchina.com/articles/what-is-blockchain-and-why-is-wechat/> last accessed 19 October 2024.

[54] Zhuhao Wang, 'China's E-Justice Revolution' (2021) 105(1) Judicature https://judicature.duke.edu/articles/chinas-e-justice-revolution/ last accessed 25 May 2024.

application and review processes. It helps to ensure the security and integrity of the electronic evidence throughout the entire judicial process, and it improves the rate of acceptance for digital evidence submitted to the court. To ensure transparency, the data from the blockchain is published on its website in real time, including the number of data collected online, the number of online evidence validations, and the date and time of the corresponding block height, hash, and number of transactions.[55]

The Beijing Internet Court also integrated an online litigation service centre into its platform, which includes an AI-powered chatbot. This automated chatbot, which appears on screen in the form of an AI-generated virtual female judge, provides guidance to the litigant throughout the processes of online filing and evidence submission. The chatbot helps not only to answer frequently asked questions but also as an assistant to the human judge, by completing basic administrative and preparatory tasks, so that the human judge can focus on the trial proceedings.[56]

Also based on blockchain technology, the Beijing Internet Court spearheaded and uses judicial smart contract service, the first of its kind in China when it was introduced in 2018. When the Beijing Internet Court concluded an internet infringement case in October 2018 after the parties reached a mediation agreement, the Court employed smart contract technology for the first time by enabling automatic 'one-click case filing' if the defendant failed to comply with the contractually agreed obligations in due time. Whereas 'the traditional way of filing an enforcement case requires several steps such as manually completing multiple forms, re-examining deadlines and facts, and confirming the identification of each party,'[57] a smart contract programmes into a single click all necessary and relevant elements as well as time-consuming procedures involved. Once triggered upon clicking, the Court reviews the case to determine whether it should be transferred to the enforcement division.[58]

Therefore, smart contracts in judicial systems can increase the efficiency and effectiveness of the judicial procedure and reduce human interventions and potential for errors. This is further illustrated by the following discussion on recent 'typical cases' adjudicated by the Beijing Internet Court.

1.3. Evolving nature of disputes: 'Typical cases'

In early 2024, the Beijing Internet Court released a summary of the 'Top 10 Typical Cases of 2023'.[59] These cases, concluded between 2021 and 2023, were published to highlight adjudicative norms and practices with a view to improve the consistency and quality of adjudication.

The following are three selected cases concluded by the Beijing Internet Court:

[55] ibid.

[56] 'Beijing Internet court launches AI judge' *Xinhua News* (27 June 2019) <http://www.xinhuanet.com/english/2019-06/27/c_138178826.htm> last accessed 25 May 2024.

[57] Tian Lu, 'The Implementation of Blockchain Technologies in Chinese Courts' (2021) 4.1 JBPL 118.

[58] ibid.

[59] '北京互联网法院2023年度十大典型案件（上）' [Beijing Internet Court's Top 10 Landmark Cases of 2023 (Part I)] (*Beijing Internet Court*, 21 January 2024) <https://mp.weixin.qq.com/s/NcMpln1g5XGOzvwS2x6h_w> and '北京互联网法院2023年度十大典型案件（下）' [Beijing Internet Court's Top 10 Landmark Cases of 2023 (Part II)] (*Beijing Internet Court*, 22 January 2024) <https://mp.weixin.qq.com/s/Lh9QL7gSCZpBxdC_esHGBw> last accessed 25 May 2024.

1 A copyright infringement dispute involving AI-generated content online:[60] the defendant had used AI-generated digital pictures that the plaintiff had created, not only without obtaining expressed consent from the plaintiff but also cropped out the plaintiff's signature on the digital pictures. The court ruled in the plaintiff's favour, reasoning that although an AI software itself cannot become the author of a picture under China's Copyright Law, the plaintiff did go through a specific process to generate the pictures in question using an AI software. This included the prompts used to generate the characters and presentation methods as well as the parameters used to create the layout and composition of the pictures.[61] As such and under the Copyright Law, the pictures exhibit 'originality' that required intellectual input which belonged to the plaintiff as the author of the picture. Therefore, in the absence of evidence from the defendant to show that they had used a similar process as the plaintiff to generate the pictures in question, it was determined that the defendant had infringed on the plaintiff's copyrighted work, including the removal of the plaintiff's signature.
2 A libel case involving online content:[62] the defendant, a social media content creator, had published articles and videos online which defamed the plaintiff, a technology company, thereby causing reputational damage. Upon review of the published content by the court, it became clear that the derogatory terms used in the content referred to the plaintiff and did constitute reputational harm. The defendant was ordered by the court to delete their online content and cease such activities.
3. An injunction case against personal rights infringement online:[63] the defendant had conducted more than 40 live broadcast sessions during which he verbally attacked the plaintiff and disclosed the plaintiff's digital identity number. Upon examining the defendant's live broadcast content, the court determined that the plaintiff's accusations were accurate and credible, and ordered the defendant to cease publishing content that infringed upon the plaintiff's reputational and personal rights.

In each of these three examples, the plaintiffs would have been required to present digital evidence to support their claim, whether it was in the form of visual, audio, or video content, or a combination thereof. The use of blockchain technology during the sharing, verification, and storage of such digital evidence by the litigants and the court helped to ensure the security, transparency and integrity of the digital evidence throughout the e-litigation process.

Further, the use of smart contract technology in the judgment enforcement stage would have significantly reduced the complexity of the aforementioned enforcement processes, including identification verification, manual completion of multiple forms, document and deadline re-examination, and online payment of fees or fines. This not

[60] Beijing Internet Court [2023] Jing 0491 Min Chu 11279. The copyright case of 'AI Wensheng Diagram'.
[61] ibid.
[62] Beijing Internet Court [2021] Jing 0491 Min Chu 51722. A case on the protection of the reputation rights of private enterprises.
[63] Beijing Internet Court [2023] Jing 0491 Min Chu 3167. A personality rights injunction case.

only ensures that the e-litigation processes adhere to the principles of natural justice but also that substantive justice—in addition to procedural justice—is delivered in a timely manner.[64]

1.4. Evolving nature of disputes: Cross-border disputes

The Beijing Internet Court has handled over 160 cross-border cases involving e-commerce platforms over a five-year period. In some cases where cross-border e-commerce transaction is involved, the Beijing Internet Court invalidated the e-commerce platforms' terms and conditions that aimed to exclude the jurisdiction of Chinese courts.[65] This contributes to establishing standards for determining the validity of jurisdictional clauses in cross border transaction contracts, which effectively safeguarded the legitimate interests of Chinese consumers in cross-border e-commerce disputes.[66]

1.5. Evolving nature of disputes: Emerging issues

In April 2024, the Beijing Internet Court set a precedent for a novel type of dispute concerning a personal rights infringement case involving AI technology.[67]

In this case, a software company acquired the audio recording of the plaintiff's voice from a cultural media company that the plaintiff had worked with, processed her voice using AI technology, and subsequently sold it to an app operator for a profit, the latter of whom used the AI-processed voice in numerous audiobooks without the plaintiff's consent. It is worth noting that this case bears striking similarity to that of the recent high-profile incident involving actress Scarlett Johansson and OpenAI, the company behind ChatGPT.[68]

The court ruled that there are unique features which can be used to identify a natural person's voice, including voiceprint tone and frequency, and any alternation of the natural voice using AI technology does not void it of its legal protection, since in this case, the AI-processed voice can still elicit thoughts or emotions associated with the plaintiff and her personal identity.

For these reasons, the court ruled that the software company had infringed upon the plaintiff's legitimate rights, and that both the software company and the cultural media company were jointly responsible for compensating the plaintiff for economic losses; the app operator and the software company were also ordered to issue an apology to the plaintiff within seven days of the judgement.

[64] 'Beijing Internet Court: Tian Ping Lian' <https://tpl.bjinternetcourt.gov.cn/tpl/> last accessed 25 May 2024 and '我为群众办实事｜执行案款可"扫码支付"，当事人仅需三步即可完成执行案款交纳' [Serving the People | Enforcement Payments Now Available via QR Code, Completed in Just Three Steps] (*Beijing Internet Court*, 2 September 2021) <https://mp.weixin.qq.com/s?__biz = MzU1NDk0NjE3MA= =&mid = 2247497949&idx = 1&sn = a8d67bd596f93635ac24dd46a3331daa&chksm> last accessed 25 May 2024.

[65] 'Beijing Internet Court: Tian Ping Lian' <https://tpl.bjinternetcourt.gov.cn/tpl/> last accessed 25 May 2024.

[66] ibid.

[67] 'Court rules on China's first AI voice rights case, sounding alarm for industry' *Global Times* (23 April 2024) <https://www.globaltimes.cn/page/202404/1311121.shtml> last accessed 25 May 2024.

[68] See 'Scarlett Johansson says a ChatGPT voice is 'eerily similar' to hers and OpenAI is halting its use' (*MSN News*, May 2024) <https://www.msn.com/en-us/news/us/scarlett-johansson-says-a-chatgpt-voice-is-eerily-similar-to-hers-and-openai-is-halting-its-use/ar-BB1mJigd> last accessed 25 May 2024.

1.6. Judicial Innovations

Based on the types of claims the Beijing Internet Court had handled between 2018 and 2023, the Court developed a WeChat applet which was launched in August 2023. This tool, directly accessible through WeChat, serves as a repository of high-quality rulings that are accessible to registered users and the judges.[69]

The rulings are searchable by keyword in the repository. They are organized by four categories of adjudication rules: IPR, civil matters, commercial matters, and procedural matters. Under these four categories of rules, the rules are further classified into seven sub-categories of rules. Sixty-three rules were established and classified under these seven frameworks in the repository as of August 2023.[70]

This tool helps to raise public awareness and understanding about internet-related issues and disputes that one may encounter. It also serves as a reference point and judicial guidance for judges to promote consistency in the application of laws.[71] This is particularly important as new types of disputes continue to emerge in rapidly evolving digital economies and technology landscapes not only in China but around the world.

It is worth noting that the development and implementation of searchable databases of rulings, judgments, and cases is not limited to the Internet Courts but has been observed in People's Courts nationwide.[72]

Following around a decade of judicial reform focused on improving judicial accountability, monitoring, and supervision, People's Courts have been trialling various 'similar case' database search tools since the 2010s, including the provincial and municipal courts of Shanghai, Jiangsu, Zhejiang, Guizhou, Yunnan, Hainan, Guangzhou, and others.[73]

These tools are designed to assist presiding judges in their decision-making process during the judgment review stage by leveraging big data, AI, cloud computing, and machine learning technologies to analyse and extract information about comparable cases as well as make judgment and sentencing recommendations.[74] Overall,

[69] '上新了！北京互联网法院裁判规则库小程序上线' [New Release! Beijing Internet Court's Judgment Rules Database Mini-Program Goes Live] (*Beijing Internet Court,* 31 August 2023) https://mp.weixin.qq.com/s?__biz = MzU1NDk0NjE3MA==&mid = 2247510288&idx = 1&sn = 1924fef8d0eb2a8e48515e5a40afb3c4&chksm= last accessed 25 May 2024.

[70] ibid.

[71] ibid.

[72] Meng Yu and Guodong Du, 'Why Are Chinese Courts Turning to AI?' (*The Diplomat*, 19 January 2019) <https://thediplomat.com/2019/01/why-are-chinese-courts-turning-to-ai/> last accessed 30 November 2024.

[73] Haiyan Wang, 'AI and Administration of Justice in China,' (December 2023) National reports on Evidence through Artificial intelligence: Artificial Intelligence and Administration of Criminal Justice. Li Yao, 'Implementing Rule of Law Concept in the Digital Sphere: China's Experience,' (2023) 4/4 Legal Issues in the Digital Age. Felicity Bell, Lyria Bennett Moses, Michael Legg, Jake Silove, and Monika Zalnieriute, 'AI Decision-Making and the Courts' (June 2022 and December 2023) The Australasian Institute of Judicial Administration Incorporated.

[74] Haiyan Wang, 'AI and Administration of Justice in China,' (December 2023) National reports on Evidence through Artificial intelligence: Artificial Intelligence and Administration of Criminal Justice. Li Yao, 'Implementing Rule of Law Concept in the Digital Sphere: China's Experience,' (2023) 4/4 *Legal Issues in the Digital Age.* Felicity Bell, Lyria Bennett Moses, Michael Legg, Jake Silove, and Monika Zalnieriute, 'AI Decision-Making and the Courts' (June 2022 and December 2023) The Australasian Institute of Judicial Administration Incorporated.

such tools aim to regulate judicial discretion, encourage similar judgments for similar cases and help the court presidents to exercise monitoring and administrative powers.[75]

In July 2020, the SPC issued the 'Guiding Opinions Concerning Strengthening Search for Similar Cases to Unify the Application of Law'[76] (Guiding Opinions) to codify what has already been in practice for years. Although China is a civil law country, it can be argued that the requirement for presiding judges to consider precedent during the decision-making process is similar to *stare decisis*, even though the Guiding Opinions does not address this issue.[77]

In that regard and to ensure adjudicative consistency and predictability in the application of law with regard to similar cases, the Guiding Opinions require that prior to rendering judgement and in certain applicable situations where the relevant law is unclear, the presiding judge conducts a search of the SPC's database or other case databases.[78]

The search will include SPC guiding cases as well as the following types of cases, prioritizing those from the preceding three years: SPC typical cases and judgment or rulings of the SPC, and reference cases and effective judgments published by other people's courts, including high courts. The precedents are not binding but only meant for the judges to consider when rendering judgment.[79]

Some database search systems have incorporated 'deviation early warning' feature, whereby the AI-powered system will evaluate the judge's verdict based on the system's predetermined parameter values and algorithm to determine if there is significant divergence from similar cases in its database. If significant deviation is found, the system will produce a reminder to the judge and/or the court president so that further review of the verdict can be conducted.[80]

2. The Guangzhou Internet Court

Similar to the scope and structure of the Beijing Internet Court, the Guangzhou Internet Court was also launched in September 2018 and deals with the same 11 types

[75] Li Yao, 'Implementing Rule of Law Concept in the Digital Sphere: China's Experience,' (2023) 4/4 Legal Issues in the Digital Age, 126.

[76] 'Guiding Opinions on Strengthening Searches for Similar Cases to Unify the Application of Law (Provisional)' (*China Law Translate*, 27 July 2020) <https://www.chinalawtranslate.com/en/case-review/> last accessed 30 November 2024.

[77] Ray Worthy Campbell, 'Artificial Intelligence in the Courtroom: The Delivery of Justice in the Age of Machine Learning,' (2020) 18 Colo Tech LJ 323, Peking University School of Transnational Law Research Paper, 21.

[78] 'Supreme People's Court's new guidance on similar case search' (Supreme People's Court Monitor, 27 July 2020) https://supremepeoplescourtmonitor.com/2020/07/27/supreme-peoples-courts-new-guidance-on-similar-case-search/ last accessed 30 November 2024.

[79] ibid.

[80] Haiyan Wang, 'AI and Administration of Justice in China,' (December 2023) National reports on Evidence through Artificial intelligence: Artificial Intelligence and Administration of Criminal Justice, 21. Li Yao, 'Implementing Rule of Law Concept in the Digital Sphere: China's Experience,' (2023) 4/4 Legal Issues in the Digital Age, 126.

of B2B and B2C internet-related disputes.[81] It operates out of the Pazhou Greater Bay Area AI and Digital Economy Pilot Zone in Guangzhou, and comprises of 35 judges and 65 trial and administrative personnel.[82]

The services provided by the Guangzhou Internet Court platform is centred around the design of a speedy and user-friendly online one-stop shop for the entire litigation process, powered by 5G network. Various technologies are also incorporated into the platform design, including big data, AI, and blockchain.[83] The platform also has litigation service terminals that provides litigants with comprehensive administrative services.[84]

2.1. Non-litigation dispute resolution

In addition to e-litigation, the platform also offers non-litigation dispute resolution services, through the joint effort of 66 collaborating institutions and 489 mediators.[85] These services include voluntary conciliation and a wide range of mediation options such as mediation by appointment, remote mediation, asynchronous mediation, cross-border mediation, joint mediation, and mediation by external party.[86]

As many e-businesses are interoperable with the Guangzhou Internet Court, third-party business mediators from e-commerce platforms or online shops are at times invited to mediate disputes arising their own e-businesses. In such cases, the mediation is carried out with the judicial support of the Guangzhou Internet Court, while business mediators are encouraged to follow the mediation procedure of the Court.[87]

These online mediation processes allow the user to conduct all the steps from identity and document verification, consultation, assessment, mediation (via videoconference), confirmation, through to the service of documents all within the e-portal. To help the parties resolve their dispute effectively and efficiently, a team of judges is available to guide them through the various dispute resolution options available to them, including conciliation, mediation, or arbitration (in addition to litigation).[88]

2.2. Operational statistics

Since its establishment in September 2018 until August 2023, the Guangzhou Internet Court had dealt with approximately 210,000 cases of which 203,000 were concluded.

[81] The 11 types of disputes are identical to those dealt with by the Beijing Internet Court, including online shopping contract and product disputes, online financial loan disputes, disputes arising from administrative actions, online copyright and infringement disputes, online IPR disputes, domain name disputes, and public interest litigation. 'Guangzhou Internet Court: Brochure' https://gzinternetcourt.gov.cn/#/articleDetail?id = uzpj9c02270cfazd1q2csrc30mh80811&titleType = broadMutualDemeanor&type = GhElegantDemeanor&apiType = convincing last accessed 14 October 2024.

[82] ibid.

[83] ibid.

[84] ibid.

[85] Data ending in September 2022. '广州互联网法院四年结案18.4万宗，办案质效居全国前列' [Guangzhou Internet Court Concludes 184,000 Cases in Four Years, Ranking Among the Nation's Top in Case Quality and Efficiency] (*Guangdong Politics and Legal Network*, 29 September 2022) <https://www.gdzf.org.cn/wzsjb/znzf/content/post_120908.html> last accessed 25 May 2024.

[86] 'Guangzhou Internet Court: Judicial innovation' https://gzinternetcourt.gov.cn/#/articleList?type = InnovationInitiative&titleType = judicialInnovation&apiType = routine last accessed 14 October 2024.

[87] ibid.

[88] ibid.

The overall acceptance rate of first instance judgement by litigants was 97.99 per cent, while the rate of compliance and fulfilment of judgment ruling by litigants was 85.19 per cent.[89]

Data ending in 2022 showed that 99.88 per cent of all case filings were submitted online, and 99.76 per cent of the trials took place online.[90] The average duration of online trials was approximately 25 minutes, while the average time for a case to reach completion was 37 days. The rate of appeal was 1.63 per cent, as compared to 13.1 per cent for traditional courts recorded during the same period.[91]

By September 2022, the dispute resolution platform operated by the Guangzhou Internet Court had resolved nearly 58,000 disputes, or 31.52 per cent of all cases, through mediation, with an average duration of 29 days for case completion.[92]

2.3. Technological innovations: Smart credit and Internet Legal Chain

As part of its efforts to modernise traditional judicial processes, the Guangzhou Internet Court launched 'Legal Internet Chain', a blockchain-based platform.[93] The platform is used for electronic evidence verification to minimise the burden of proof, as well as litigation procedure management to improve the litigation experience. It is interoperable with major e-commerce platforms—such as Taobao, Tmall, JD.com, and Pinduoduo—and online shops so that litigants can collect digital evidence using the 'one-click evidence collection' feature.[94] By September 2022, 33 collaborating institutions were participating in this ecosystem.[95]

The Internet Legal Chain features smart case filing and batch submission of digital evidence for financial organizations and online businesses. Once the digital evidence is submitted, received, and verified, it can be transmitted and shared electronically

[89] '广州互联网法院激发司法治理新活力，助力市域社会治理现代化建设' [Guangzhou Internet Court Stimulates New Vitality in Judicial Governance and Contributes to the Modernization of Municipal Social Governance] (*Guangdong Politics and Legal Network*, last 10 August 2023) <https://www.gdzf.org.cn/zwgd/content/post_139755.html> last accessed 25 May 2024.

[90] '广州互联网法院四年结案18.4万宗，办案质效居全国前列' [Guangzhou Internet Court Concludes 184,000 Cases in Four Years, Ranking Among the Nation's Top in Case Quality and Efficiency] (*Guangdong Politics and Legal Network*, 29 September 2022) <https://www.gdzf.org.cn/wzsjb/znzf/content/post_120908.html> last accessed 25 May 2024.

[91] '景汉朝, '互联网法院的时代创新与中国贡献' [Jing Hanchao: Era-Defining Innovations and China's Contributions to Internet Courts] (*Legal Daily*, last 2 November 2023) <http://www.legaldaily.com.cn/xjpfzsx/content/content_8922364.html> last accessed 25 May 2024.

[92] Roughly 184,000 cases had been filed as of September 2022. '广州互联网法院四年结案18.4万宗，办案质效居全国前列' [Guangzhou Internet Court Concludes 184,000 Cases in Four Years, Ranking Among the Nation's Top in Case Quality and Efficiency] (*Guangdong Politics and Legal Network*, last accessed 29 September 2022) <https://www.gdzf.org.cn/wzsjb/znzf/content/post_120908.html> last accessed 25 May 2024.

[93] The platform is known as 'Wang Tong Fa Lian' or 网通法链 in Chinese Mandarin. 'Guangzhou Internet Court: Evidence' <http://bc.gzinternetcourt.gov.cn:9001/gzinternetcourt-evidence/index.html#/netcomchain> last accessed 25 May 2024.

[94] 'Guangzhou Internet Court: Judicial innovation' <https://gzinternetcourt.gov.cn/#/articleList?type = InnovationInitiative&titleType = judicialInnovation&apiType = routine> last accessed 14 October 2024. 'Guangzhou Internet Court: Evidence' <http://bc.gzinternetcourt.gov.cn:9001/gzinternetcourt-evidence/index.html#/netcomchain> last accessed 25 May 2024.

[95] '广州互联网法院四年结案18.4万宗，办案质效居全国前列' [Guangzhou Internet Court Concludes 184,000 Cases in Four Years, Ranking Among the Nation's Top in Case Quality and Efficiency] (*Guangdong Politics and Legal Network*, 29 September 2022) <https://www.gdzf.org.cn/wzsjb/znzf/content/post_120908.html> last accessed 25 May 2024.

among eight politico-legal organs including the Intermediate People's Court of Guangzhou. The Legal Internet Chain also regulates the conducts of third-party judicial service agencies by setting a suite of rules and standards, including rules explaining the Legal Internet Chain's underlying technology and standards for access and management as well as the technical specifications for the storage and use of digital data during evidence verification.[96]

Using smart technology, the Internet Legal Chain also pools information from collaborating organizations to enable the sharing of credit data relevant to the judicial processes, such as the credit and employment situations of individuals and businesses. Based on this data, an in-built smart credit assessment mechanism provides various types of analyses that can be used to support the enforcement stage of the judicial process.[97]

2.4. Technological innovations: Smart credit and smart enforcement

To ensure that litigants follow through with the obligations set out in the mediation outcome or court judgment, the Guangzhou Internet Court launched the 1) 'E-Chain Smart Enforcement' platform[98] and the 2) 'E-Chain Cloud Mirror' smart analysis system[99] in support of enforcement efforts.

1. The E-Chain Smart Enforcement platform enables enforcement proceedings to be carried out fully online. Its functions include identity verification of the parties, automatic retrieval of case details from written judgements, filing of enforcement case, affixture of the parties' signatures and/or stamps, and the parties' financial disclosure through the portal.

   The E-Chain Smart Enforcement platform's interoperability with other parties, including telecommunications operators, e-commerce platforms and online shops, enable it to track down debtor parties with a 60 per cent+ success rate. This coordination mechanism facilitates concerted enforcement efforts, such as the serving of court documents, discovery of hidden assets belonging to the debtor party, and sharing of information between the court and credit institutions to generate credit report for judicial purposes.[100]
2. The E-Chain Cloud Mirror system is a platform that combines the technologies of big data, AI and blockchain to facilitate the enforcement of judicial outcomes imposed by the Guangzhou Internet Court. By analysing and tracking the physical and economic activities of the debtor party, enforcement measures

[96] 'Guangzhou Internet Court: Judicial innovation' <https://gzinternetcourt.gov.cn/#/articleList?type = InnovationInitiative&titleType = judicialInnovation&apiType = routine> last accessed 14 October 2024. The Guangzhou Internet Court has produced two documents outlining these rules: 1) Guangzhou Internet Court Internet Legal Chain Electronic Data Evidence Preservation and Access Management Specifications; and 2) Technical Specifications for Electronic Data Preservation and Access of the Guangzhou Internet Court's Netcom Legal Chain. <http://bc.gzinternetcourt.gov.cn:9001/gzinternetcourt-evidence/index.html#/netcomchain> last accessed 25 May 2024.

[97] 'Guangzhou Internet Court: Judicial innovation' <https://gzinternetcourt.gov.cn/#/articleList?type = InnovationInitiative&titleType = judicialInnovation&apiType = routine> last accessed 14 October 2024.

[98] ibid.

[99] ibid.

[100] ibid.

> are tailored to suit the debtor party's situation in order to maximize the chances of successful enforcement.[101]

More specifically, the system mines and collects fragmented data on the debtor party's online financial transactions, analyses the data, and generates an overall picture, or 'behaviour profile' of the debtor party. The data collected are categorized into 'static data' derived from their existing assets, and 'dynamic behaviour' based on their online financial activities such as their consumption patterns including mobile payments and online shopping activities, income received, financial situation and credit rating, and potentially any hidden assets.

> In the case that the debtor party has refused to make the payment as obligated by their judgment ruling, the system assesses whether they actually have the financial means to do so using the aforementioned data. This assessment, using AI technology, produces a report that determines the debtor party's financial capability to make the repayment.
>
> Based on the outcome of the assessment and again using AI technology, the system makes proposals for targeted enforcement measures that are suited to the particular financial circumstances of the debtor party.[102]

2.5. Judicial innovations

Whereas the Beijing Internet Court released 'typical cases' as exemplary guidance for the public and the judges, the Guangzhou Internet Court regularly produces judicial recommendations following their rulings.[103]

These tailored recommendations aim to create a lasting impact from the rulings that help to proactively target the root causes of disputes in order to prevent similar disputes from arising. They cover various sectors including e-commerce transactions, online IPR protection, financial supervision, online lending, live streaming, platform governance, and information security.

The recommendations are selectively published in the news media and disseminated to a diverse set of recipients in a timely manner to prompt immediate remedial and preventative action. The recipients, encompassing over 80 entities, range from litigants to businesses and e-commerce platforms, as well as industry associations to sectoral regulators and administrative bodies.

By September 2023, the Guangzhou Internet Court has issued 98 judicial recommendations, of which 90 recommendations received feedback from, and were adopted

[101] ibid.

[102] On the last point, the system will constantly monitor for any potential hidden assets. For instance, in the case that an abnormally large transaction is observed or any other activities that could lead to suspicion of a transfer of property is detected, an alert is generated by the system for further investigation to determine any implications for the implementation of enforcement measures.

[103] '广州互联网法院：以"小切口"推动社会治理"大作为"' [Guangzhou Internet Court: Driving Major Social Governance Advancements Through Targeted Reforms] *Xinhua News Guangdong* (19 September 2023) <http://www.gd.xinhuanet.com/20230919/9266c757ad8645af8bb6517a07f8e80a/c.html> last accessed 25 May 2024.

by, the recipients. The adoption and implementation of these recommendations into practice have tangibly improved public safety in the digital sphere, as illustrated by the following case studies.[104]

1. In a lawsuit against an online gaming platform, a plaintiff claimed financial compensation for allowing his 11-year-old child to make approximately 39,000 RMB[105] worth of repeat in-game purchases on the plaintiff's mobile phone without his consent.[106]

   During the court facilitated mediation process, the court found that the authentication procedure was not functional but merely a formality, as the registered name on the account did not match the identification information submitted during the verification process.

   Following mediation, the gaming platform agreed to refund approximately 30,000 RMB to the plaintiff. The court also issued the following judicial recommendation to the gaming platform: improve the enforcement of its registration system based on real names; proactively identify and eliminate risks; and reinforce corporate social responsibility to protect minors.

   In response to the recommendation, the gaming platform took measures to ensure that strict verification of real-name information was implemented; accounts that had not complied with real-name registration were required to re-authenticate upon login; and users were required to complete real-name registration before accessing a game.
2. In a dispute over an online romance scam, the plaintiff filed a lawsuit against a dating app after matching with a scammer on the app who then proceeded to defraud the plaintiff of over 1 million[107] RMB using a Bitcoin investment scam.[108]

   The court found that while the dating platform did not commit the fraud, it did have a role to play in the plaintiff's losses due to, among other things, a lack of adequate identity verification process to protect its users. Consequently, the operator of the dating app was ordered to compensate the plaintiff for a portion of the losses.

   The court also issued a judicial recommendation to the platform, which led to an overhaul of their management practices, including strengthening the verification of member information and enhancing protective measures against online crime.

[104] ibid.

[105] Around 4,250 GBP or 5,400 USD at the time of writing.

[106] '广州互联网法院：以"小切口"推动社会治理"大作为"' [Guangzhou Internet Court: Driving Major Social Governance Advancements Through Targeted Reforms] *Xinhua News Guangdong* (19 September 2023) <http://www.gd.xinhuanet.com/20230919/9266c757ad8645af8bb6517a07f8e80a/c.html> last accessed 25 May 2024.

[107] Roughly equivalent to 109,000 GBP or 138,000 USD at the time of writing.

[108] '广州互联网法院：以"小切口"推动社会治理"大作为"' [Guangzhou Internet Court: Driving Major Social Governance Advancements Through Targeted Reforms] *Xinhua News Guangdong* (19 September 2023) http://www.gd.xinhuanet.com/20230919/9266c757ad8645af8bb6517a07f8e80a/c.html last accessed 25 May 2024.

3. In a case that led to the improvement of consumer rights protection, the plaintiff disputed the provenance of a luxury belt they had purchased through a cross-border e-commerce platform.[109]

   Although the court found that the platform was able to provide evidence confirming the authenticity of the belt, the lawsuit raised questions about the responsibility of e-commerce platform in providing clear information about the sources of its advertised products and any risks associated with making a purchase.

   Accordingly, the court issued a judicial recommendation to the platform, prompting it to adjust its policies concerning the provision of consumer information and transparency, including providing a channel for consumers to trace and verify the origin of the advertised products.
4. In a loan contract dispute, the court discovered that the small loan business's contract in question contained unclear and non-standard provisions regarding the collection of personal information.[110]

   After concluding the case, the court provided judicial recommendations directly to the local financial regulatory authority aimed at reducing similar disputes from arising in the first place. The recommendations focused on strengthening supervision and clarifying standards for collecting and using personal data.

   In response to the recommendations, the financial authority reformed its contract templates to better protect borrowers' privacy and developed training for online small loan businesses to prevent misuse and leakage of personal information.

These selected cases highlight how judicial recommendations have played a key role in not only resolving disputes but also in encouraging systemic improvements within digital platforms. Courts, particularly the Guangzhou Internet Court, have effectively influenced practices related to user verification, consumer protection, and data privacy. This has demonstratively led to multistakeholder collaborations between the court, the regulators, and industry actors, thereby fostering a concerted effort to better protect consumers' rights through co-regulation of the digital economy.[111] It also illustrates the potential for the judiciary to support broader societal goals such as enhancing public safety in the digital space.

For example, by requiring stricter identity verification processes or improving transparency in consumer transactions, judicial recommendations promote a safer and more trustworthy online environment. This integration of judicial guidance into operational practices reflects a growing alignment between the legal and regulatory frameworks governing digital platforms, with courts actively contributing to the development of best practices in areas such as data protection and corporate responsibility.

[109] ibid.
[110] ibid.
[111] ibid.

This shift toward a more proactive judicial role reflects the broader evolution of courts in the digital age. By issuing recommendations that address not just the legal dimensions of individual cases but also the underlying systemic issues, courts are helping to shape industry practices and enhance regulatory compliance.

3. The Hangzhou Internet Court

The Hangzhou Internet Court was established in August 2017. Its physical location and personnel, including 20 judges,[112] are based in Hangzhou City, home to China's e-commerce hub and the conglomerate Alibaba Group.

The Court has jurisdiction over 11 types of B2B and B2C internet-related disputes,[113] identical to those covered by the Internet Courts of Beijing and Guangzhou. It also offers a separate mediation platform for users that prefer to resolve their dispute via non-litigation options.[114]

3.1. Operational statistics

Between 2017 and 2023, the Hangzhou Internet Court had concluded more than 90,000 cases, averaging 39.2 days to complete a case—as compared to roughly twice as long for traditional courts to conclude a case. Around 98.5 per cent of the cases submitted to the Hangzhou Internet Court are filed through the online portal while, on average, it takes five minutes to submit a case. More than half of all trial proceedings take place asynchronously, and the average duration of the trial hearings is 28 minutes in length. The acceptance rate for court judgement is 99 per cent.[115]

3.2. Technological innovations

As the first virtual court specializing in online disputes, the Hangzhou Internet Court ushered in an era which witnessed a subsequent increase in the launch of e-courts in other parts of China. It is also the first court in China to admit evidence authenticated by blockchain technology.[116] In addition to enabling the court to authenticate litigant's identity and submitted evidence, the blockchain platform also allows digital content creators to submit their work through its blockchain portal. This helps to ensure that their work is copyrighted by timestamping its storage on the blockchain node. In the

[112] Data as of 2021. Zhuhao Wang, 'China's E-Justice Revolution' (2021) 105(1) Judicature <https://judicature.duke.edu/articles/chinas-e-justice-revolution/> last accessed 25 May 2024.

[113] Includes online shopping contract and product disputes, online financial loan disputes, disputes arising from administrative actions, online copyright and infringement disputes, online IPR disputes, domain name disputes, and public interest litigation. 'Hangzhou Internet Court' <https://www.netcourt.gov.cn/?lang = En> last accessed 25 May 2024.

[114] 'Hangzhou Internet Court: Tiao jie' <https://tiaojie.netcourt.gov.cn/> last accessed 25 May 2024.

[115] 'Hangzhou Internet Court' <https://www.netcourt.gov.cn/?lang = En> and '杭州互联网法院发布六周年改革创新成果' [Hangzhou Internet Court Releases Six-Year Reform and Innovation Achievements] (Hangzhou Chinese People's Political Consultative Conference, 3 August 2023) <https://www.hzzx.gov.cn/cshz/content/2023-08/03/content_8593083.htm> last accessed 25 May 2024.

[116] 'Hangzhou Internet Court: Evidence' <https://evidence.netcourt.gov.cn/#/page> and Zhuhao Wang, 'China's E-Justice Revolution' (2021) 105(1) Judicature <https://judicature.duke.edu/articles/chinas-e-justice-revolution/> last accessed 25 May 2024.

event of an online infringement dispute, the author of the work can easily authenticate their copyright and ownership.[117]

In June 2019, the Hangzhou Internet Court also launched its own 'AI assistant judge'—powered by 'Ali AI,' developed by Alibaba—the same month that the Beijing Internet Court launched its virtual judge.[118] However, instead of being limited to providing guidance and assisting with rudimentary tasks around case filing and evidence submission, the assistant judge for the Hangzhou Internet Court is capable of providing a human judge with its analysis of the disputed points and give recommendations for mediation resolution or judgment based on case law and legal provisions—all within a fraction of a second. This helps the human judge to save around two hours worth of time and effort at the outset in determining the direction of the trial or whether mediation is a viable option.[119]

3.3. Evolving nature of disputes: Cross-border disputes

As China's cross-border e-commerce continued to expand over the past decade, so has the volume of cross-border online disputes. To address this gap in judicial capacity and consumer rights protection, the Hangzhou Internet Court established China's first cross-border trade tribunal and platform in addition to its main platform for domestic disputes.[120]

Its cross-border dispute resolution platform is designed to enable litigants to log in to the platform in different places, round the clock at any time of the day or night. The platform can be used for both Chinese plaintiff against foreign defendant[121] and foreign plaintiff against Chinese defendant.[122] Litigants can participate from any country as there is no specified limitation in this regard.[123]

[117] 'Hangzhou Internet Court' <https://www.netcourt.gov.cn/?lang=En> and '杭州互联网法院发布六周年改革创新成果' [Hangzhou Internet Court Releases Six-Year Reform and Innovation Achievements] (Hangzhou Chinese People's Political Consultative Conference, 3 August 2023) <https://www.hzzx.gov.cn/cshz/content/2023-08/03/content_8593083.htm> last accessed 25 May 2024.

[118] Mei Zhu, '杭州互联网法院试点应用"AI助理法官"' [Hangzhou Internet Court Pilots 'AI Assistant Judge' Application] (*Baidu News Hangzhou*, 14 June 2019) <https://baijiahao.baidu.com/s?id=1636313472795379686&wfr=spider> last accessed 25 May 2024.

[119] Including reading the case file, querying the transaction dialogue records, refining the focus of the dispute, and finding the relevant legal provisions. ibid. For in-depth discussions on how such virtual judges function, see Nyu Wang and Michael Yuan Tian, '"Intelligent Justice": human-centered considerations in China's legal AI transformation' (2023) 3(2) AI Ethics, 349–354; and Ummey Sharaban Tahura and Niloufer Selvadurai, 'The use of artificial intelligence in judicial decision-making: the example of China' (2023) February, IJLET, 1–20.

[120] For the cross-border litigation platform's procedural flowcharts and its jurisdiction, the latter of which is categorized into seven types of disputes including cross-border e-commerce platform network service and unfair competition dispute, see 'Hangzhou Internet Court: Digital Trade Litigation Platform' <https://www.netcourt.gov.cn/pamir/foreign/app/home> last accessed 25 May 2024.

[121] '杭州互联网法院受理涉网知识产权案近3万件' [Hangzhou Internet Court Handles Nearly 30,000 Internet-Related Intellectual Property Cases] (*China News*, 24 April 2024) <https://www.chinanews.com.cn/cj/2024/04-24/10205414.shtml> last accessed 25 May 2024.

[122] 'Filing Lawsuits While Living Abroad: China's New Policy' (*China Justice Observer*, 7 March 2021) <https://www.chinajusticeobserver.com/a/filing-lawsuits-while-living-abroad-china-s-new-policy> last accessed 13 October 2024. 'How to Sue in Chinese Court Online While Living Abroad?' (*China Justice Observer*, 14 March 2021) <https://www.chinajusticeobserver.com/a/how-to-sue-in-chinese-court-online-while-living-abroad> last accessed 13 October 2024.

[123] 'Can I resolve cross-border online shopping disputes through the Chinese Internet Court: Inside China's Internet Courts Series -03' (*China Justice Observer*, 6 April 2019) <https://www.chinajusticeobserver.com/a/can-i-resolve-cross-border-online-shopping-disputes-through-the-chinese-internet-court> last accessed 13 October 2024.

Its capability of allowing trial hearings to be conducted asynchronously on its platform helps to overcome the physical and temporal barriers inherent to cross-border disputes due to the different countries and time zones involved.[124] Although online hearings shall be conducted in the languages of China pursuant to China's Civil Procedure Law, the Court can provide interpreter and/or translation services at the request of foreign litigants, the latter of whom would be required to cover the associated expenses.[125]

Since the Hangzhou Internet Court's first cross-border online dispute hearing involving a Singapore user and a Chinese e-commerce platform,[126] the Court has accepted more than 200 cross-border e-commerce cases by September 2022.[127] Cross-border consumer disputes concerning e-commerce platforms have been observed as one of the most prevalent types of cases adjudicated by the Court.

Despite this, the Court seldomly rules in favour of the consumer or plaintiff in such cases. An example is when customers of large e-commerce platforms such as Taobao or Tmall attempt to dispute the outcome of the platforms' in-house CDR mechanism—very rarely would the Court overrule the outcomes in favour of the consumer. Presumably, this would further promote the legitimacy and the use of e-commerce platforms' internal CDR mechanisms as the primary method for resolving disputes, whilst dissuading consumers from disputing its outcome.[128]

The Hangzhou Internet Court also experienced a high number of case withdrawal by plaintiffs, mainly due to plaintiffs' inability to accurately identify or locate the foreign defendant. Challenges faced by the Court involving cross-border e-commerce disputes included the costly and time-consuming nature of identity document verification; the judges' ability to determine the authenticity of identity and other evidentiary documents due to language barriers; and the complex nature of the application of cross-border e-commerce law.[129]

[124] '杭州互联网法院发布六周年改革创新成果' [Hangzhou Internet Court Releases Six-Year Reform and Innovation Achievements] (Hangzhou Chinese People's Political Consultative Conference, 3 August 2023) <https://www.hzzx.gov.cn/cshz/content/2023-08/03/content_8593083.htm> last accessed 25 May 2024.

[125] 'How Chinese Judges Deal with Foreign Litigants Who Don't Understand Chinese?' (*China Justice Observer*, 4 May 2019) <https://www.chinajusticeobserver.com/a/how-chinese-judges-deal-with-foreign-litigants-who-dont-understand-chinese> last accessed 13 October 2024.

[126] 'China opens first cross-border trade tribunal' (The Supreme People's Court of the People's Republic of China, 16 July 2020) <https://english.court.gov.cn/2020-07/16/c_768336.htm> last accessed 25 May 2024.

[127] 'Cross-border E-commerce Dispute Resolution in the Eyes of Chinese Courts' (*China Justice Observer*, 25 September 2022) <https://en.chinajusticeobserver.com/a/cross-border-e-commerce-dispute-resolution-in-the-eyes-of-chinese-courts> last accessed 25 May 2024.

[128] Zhang, Angela Huyue, *High Wire: How China Regulates Big Tech and Governs Its Economy* (OUP 2024) 207.

[129] 'Cross-border E-commerce Dispute Resolution in the Eyes of Chinese Courts' (*China Justice Observer*, 25 September 2022) <https://en.chinajusticeobserver.com/a/cross-border-e-commerce-dispute-resolution-in-the-eyes-of-chinese-courts> last accessed 25 May 2024. Presumably, the enforcement of Chinese civil judgments against foreign litigants would also pose a significant challenge for the Hangzhou Internet Court, as is the case for Chinese courts and plaintiffs in general. However, some progress has been made in recent years where for the first time in an increasing number of countries, the recognition and enforcement of Chinese civil judgments has occurred, including the Netherlands, New Zealand, and

Other notable types of disputes adjudicated by the cross-border platform of the Hangzhou Internet Court include online IPR infringement. In some cases, e-commerce platforms abroad have taken advantage of the ease with which the Court can be used to sue Chinese sellers in order to gain an unfair competitive advantage in the market. Product quality disputes is another category that has seen an increase in the volume of cases, including fake goods and quality defects for food products, infant products or other fast-moving consumer goods or household products.[130]

To address some of these issues, the Hangzhou Internet Court has taken steps to boost its capacity in accurately determining and verifying the identity of foreign defendants when serving them. It has also developed a set of internationally recognized and accepted online litigation procedural mechanisms for resolving cross border online disputes. In a recent online IPR dispute involving a famous gaming company, the Court for the first time served a foreign defendant through its cross-border platform, thereby setting a precedent and practice for effective identity authentication online.[131]

3.4. Evolving nature of disputes: 'Typical cases' and emerging issues

With the implementation of a similar practice as the Beijing Internet Court, the Hangzhou Internet Court also releases 10 'typical cases' annually which are of public interest for the purposes of awareness-raising and providing judicial guidance. In the 2024 edition, the 'Top 10 Typical Cases' centred on online IPR disputes.[132] One of the reasons for the emphasis on online IPR disputes is that over the past six years, the Hangzhou Internet Court has concluded nearly 30,000 online IPR cases, of which 85 per cent concerned copyright issues.[133]

As many online IPR disputes, including those listed among the 'Top 10 Typical Cases', involve novel case types, emerging issues and new business models, they are grouped together in the following discussion to illustrate the Court's innovative approaches to dealing with them.

Australia. See 'Dutch Court Recognizes a Chinese Judgement for the First Time' (*China Justice Observer*, 3 April 2020) <https://www.chinajusticeobserver.com/a/dutch-court-recognizes-a-chinese-judgement-for-the-first-time> last accessed 13 October 2024. 'New Zealand Court Recognizes a Chinese Judgment for the First Time' (*China Justice Observer*, 21 June 2020) <https://www.chinajusticeobserver.com/a/new-zealand-court-recognizes-a-chinese-judgment-for-the-first-time> last accessed 13 October 2024. 'The First Time Australia Recognizes Chinese Civil Settlement Statements' (*China Justice Observer*, 24 July 2022) <https://www.chinajusticeobserver.com/a/the-first-time-australia-recognizes-chinese-civil-settlement-statements> last accessed 13 October 2024. 'Enforcing Chinese Judgments' (*Transnational Litigation Blog*, 19 July 2022). <https://tlblog.org/enforcing-chinese-judgments/> last accessed 13 October 2024.

[130] See the sources cited in n 129.

[131] '杭州互联网法院受理涉网知识产权案近3万件' [Hangzhou Internet Court Handles Nearly 30,000 Internet-Related Intellectual Property Cases] (*China News*, 24 April 2024) <https://www.chinanews.com.cn/cj/2024/04-24/10205414.shtml> last accessed 25 May 2024.

[132] '杭州互联网法院网络知识产权十大典型案例发布，"虚拟数字人"等案入选' [Hangzhou Internet Court Releases Top 10 Landmark Cases on Online Intellectual Property, Including 'Virtual Digital Human' Cases] (Zhi Chan Li, 19 January 2024) <https://www.zhichanli.com/p/827454524> last accessed 25 May 2024.

[133] '抓取销售直播间数据 一科技公司被诉不正当竞争' [Tech Company Sued for Unfair Competition Over Scraping Sales Livestream Data] *Hangzhou News* (25 April 2024) <https://hznews.hangzhou.com.cn/jingji/content/2024-04/25/content_8720766.htm> last accessed 25 May 2024.

Among these cases, some focused on the determination of the legal attributes of audio-visual content generated through AI or human-computer interaction to better protect copyrighted original content.[134] Since some aspects of these emerging issues are discussed in the foregoing section on the Beijing Internet Court, similar cases from the Hangzhou Internet Court are omitted in the following discussion to focus on other precedents and novel issues.

1. In a dispute over online IPR infringement,[135] a Shenzhen-based company that enjoyed the copyright and property rights of a popular anime image filed a lawsuit against a Hangzhou-based metaverse platform, accusing it of failing to fulfil its duty of care as a non-fungible token (NFT)[136] trading platform. The accusation was based on the grounds that an NFT digital artwork of the said popular image—an exact replica of the original popular image, even including the watermark of the original creator—was sold by a seller on the platform for a profit, while both the seller and the platform made a financial profit from the transaction.

   The Court found that, among other reasons, since the defendant or metaverse platform was capable of reviewing the commodities traded on the platform for IPR infringement prior to being listed, and given that the platform had benefited financially from this particular transaction, it bore a duty of care to do so. This was especially the case as the plaintiff noted that NFT digital artwork was immutably and permanently recorded on the blockchain, thus making it impossible for the seller to edit it after the fact and easy for the platform to conduct its review had it wanted to do so.

   For these reasons, the court ruled in favour of the plaintiff and ordered the defendant to immediately delete the NFT digital artwork listed on the platform and compensate the plaintiff for its financial losses in the amount of 4,000 RMB. As this was the first NFT court case of its kind in China, the ruling set a precedent for adjudication in the future.
2. In this case,[137] the plaintiffs, a Zhejiang-based network technology company and a film production company, filed a lawsuit requesting that the Court affirm

[134] Some examples include the following cases: 'Judicial regulation of "virtual digital humans" in the form of rights aggregation'; 'Determination of the legal attributes of intelligent human-computer interaction generators'; 'Review and determination of "impersonation and song-washing" infringement in the digital age'; and 'Criteria for determining the originality of short video template works'. '杭州互联网法院网络知识产权十大典型案例发布，"虚拟数字人"等案入选' [Hangzhou Internet Court Releases Top 10 Landmark Cases on Online Intellectual Property, Including 'Virtual Digital Human' Cases] (*Zhi Chan Li*, 19 January 2024) https://www.zhichanli.com/p/827454524 last accessed 25 May 2024.

[135] ibid. Determination of the attributes of NFT digital works and the legal liability of their trading platforms. Hangzhou Internet Court [2022] Zhe 0192 Min Chu 1008. Hangzhou Intermediate People's Court [2022] Zhe 01 Min Zhong 5272.

[136] 'NFT' refers to a unique identifier that is recorded on a blockchain which is used to certify ownership and authenticity of digital artwork ensuring that it cannot be copied or changed, thus allowing it to be transferred, sold, and traded. See Michael D Murray, 'NFT Ownership and Copyrights' (2 July 2022), SSRN <https://papers.ssrn.com/sol3/papers.cfm?abstract_id = 4152468> last accessed 25 May 2024.

[137] '杭州互联网法院网络知识产权十大典型案例发布，"虚拟数字人"等案入选' [Hangzhou Internet Court Releases Top 10 Landmark Cases on Online Intellectual Property, Including 'Virtual Digital Human' Cases] (*Zhi Chan Li*, 19 January 2024) <https://www.zhichanli.com/p/827454524> last accessed 25 May 2024. Judicial determination of the relationship between online games and the adaptation of magical special effects films. Hangzhou Internet Court [2021] Zhe 0192 Min Chu 10369. Hangzhou Intermediate People's Court [2023] Zhe 01 Min Zhong 453.

that they did not infringe upon the IPR of an online game by broadcasting an online film. The reason was that an online game company, who was a creator of the popular said game, had approached the online platform warning it to cease broadcasting the said film, accusing the plaintiffs of IPR infringement due to the similarities between the film and the game.

The court found that while both the film and the game were audio-visual works, the dispute lay in whether the film infringed the adaptation right and information network dissemination right of the online game. The key was to determine whether the film used original content that could be linked to the online game. Having reviewed six aspects of the film and the game, the court determined that various audio-visual contents either had no basis for comparison or lacked similarity, and those parts that were similar could be seen as original expressions of audio-visual works protected by China's Copyright Law. In particular, the court noted that films and games had completely different picture composition, picture smoothness, lens experience, and audio-visual effects.

For these reasons, the court ruled in favour of the plaintiffs and ordered the defendant to financially compensate the plaintiffs in the amount of 200,000 RMB in reasonable expenses.

3. In a competition dispute,[138] the plaintiff—a video livestreaming platform—accused a Guangdong-based technology company of selling software that were used by third parties to capture user's personal data during livestreaming on the plaintiff's platform. The data collected included user identification number, account number, comments made by the user, and online gifts sent by the user.

 The plaintiff argued that such actions constitute unfair competition and infringed upon the legitimate rights and interests of the platform's registered users, including their privacy. As a result, the plaintiff received numerous complaints from their users—both viewers and content providers—about the issue.

 The defendant dismissed the accusations by counterarguing that it is only a seller of the software and not the developer; and that the livestream host had the right to enable the privacy protection feature in the online room and in the case that they chose not to, the data collection feature enabled by the software would be no more than the scraping of public data.

 Following this case and in early October 2024, the Hangzhou Internet Court released the 'Guidelines on Legal Risk Prevention for Intellectual Property Protection in the Live Streaming Industry' and presented notable cases showcasing the industry's growth.[139] These guidelines encourage live streaming operators, marketers, and streamers to produce original content and secure copyright protection through defined collaboration models. Additionally, the guidelines support the creation of innovative live streaming formats, safeguarding the

[138] '抓取销售直播间数据 一科技公司被诉不正当竞争' [Tech Company Sued for Unfair Competition Over Scraping Sales Livestream Data] *Hangzhou News* (25 April 2024) <https://hznews.hangzhou.com.cn/jingji/content/2024-04/25/content_8720766.htm> last accessed 25 May 2024.

[139] '关注！杭州互联网法院发布直播行业知识产权保护典型案例|互联网|法院|杭州市_新浪科技_新浪网' [Attention! Hangzhou Internet Court Releases Landmark Cases on Intellectual Property Protection in the Livestreaming Industry] (*Sina News*, 6 October 2024) <https://finance.sina.com.cn/tech/roll/2024-10-06/doc-incrrraw9111390.shtml> last accessed 19 October 2024.

commercial benefits and competitive advantages derived from these models under anti-unfair competition laws.

These case studies highlight the complex and intersecting issues concerning recent online IPR disputes before the Hangzhou Internet Court. As China's digital economy continue to evolve, so too will novel types of disputes and issues emerge that require the Court to adopt innovative adjudication procedures and rules to deal with them effectively and efficiently.

In reference to the aforementioned NFT dispute, having a blockchain repository of existing digital artworks, such as the one established by the Hangzhou Internet Court, can prove valuable should other similar online IPR infringement disputes arise and there is a need to quickly and accurately ascertain the ownership and/or copyright of any submitted digital artwork as evidence.

In other cases, the deliberation processes before judgments are rendered can be laborious and time-consuming, as they involve the review of complex case facts and numerous precedents and legislation around intersecting issues. As shown in the above-noted case studies two (film vs game) and three (livestreaming user data), it is particularly challenging to untangle and identify legal attributes of technical features and artistic expressions in emerging technologies such as generative AI and audio-visual works. In these examples, an AI-powered virtual judge, such as that implemented by the Hangzhou Internet Court, can greatly increase efficiency and reduce the workload of the presiding human judge.

D. Conclusion

In China, wholly online litigation is fast becoming the norm.[140] The increasing popularity and usage of e-courts in China owes, in part, to how it has helped consumers and MSMEs to overcome barriers posed by traditional, in-person litigation. As litigants gain awareness of the ease and convenience of e-courts, one should also expect to observe less dispute avoidance. For instance, recent cases illustrate successfully filed lawsuits in which 0.1 RMB[141] was disputed in one case[142] and an overseas defendant was served in the other.[143]

This fundamental shift from offline litigation to online litigation was brought forth by a judicial reform as part of a broader effort to adapt China's legal framework to the

[140] '以高质量互联网司法护航中国式现代化'' [High-Quality Internet Judiciary Safeguards Chinese-Style Modernization] (29 October 2023) <https://www.chinacourt.org/article/detail/2023/10/id/7600832.shtml> last accessed 25 May 2024.

[141] Equivalent to around 0.01 GBP or 0.01 USD.

[142] In a case from October 2020, the court ruled in favour of the plaintiff who disputed multiple charges of 0.1 RMB by a company to unsubscribe from its text message promotions. '"每日优鲜APP推送商业短信案"宣判 法院认定一毛钱短信退订费由平台负担' [Court Rules in 'Missfresh App Commercial SMS Case': Platform Liable for One-Cent Unsubscribe Fee] (*Beijing Internet Court,* 23 October 2020) <https://mp.weixin.qq.com/s/G5Nkupzb7tXVToXh53Hqwg> last accessed 25 May 2024.

[143] '杭州互联网法院受理涉网知识产权案近3万件' [Hangzhou Internet Court Handles Nearly 30,000 Internet-Related Intellectual Property Cases] (24 April 2024) <https://www.chinanews.com.cn/cj/2024/04-24/10205414.shtml> last accessed 25 May 2024.

demands of the digital era. The digital transformation of not only online courts but the development of an entire e-justice ecosystem involved—and continues to require—deep collaboration between the judiciary and various sectors of the digital economy, as highlighted in the discussion on the nationwide CMMC applet and the Internet Judicial Blockchain platform.

This resulted in a wide-ranging jurisdiction coverage by the Internet Courts which include disputes over e-commerce contracts, online services, online financial loans and small loans, online intellectual property, internet domain names, and online infringements of personal and property right. Further, product liability disputes due to defective products purchased via e-commerce platforms that harm personal or property rights, as well as public interest and administrative cases related to the digital economy also fall under within the purview of the internet courts.[144]

China's judiciary's comprehensive approach to modernizing its legal system includes directives from the SPC and the development of the CMMC applet. These initiatives have improved accessibility and convenience for litigants, having registered and processed millions of users and cases through the applet. China's Internet Judicial Blockchain platform, interconnected with over 3,500 courts, ensures the authenticity of e-documents and enhances cross-departmental collaboration. The SPC's ongoing efforts to integrate blockchain and AI technologies aim to develop a fully operational, interconnected judicial ecosystem by 2025.

While blockchain helps secure and authenticate digital evidence within China's courts, there may be challenges when dealing with cross-border cases where the recognition of blockchain-based evidence is not universally accepted. Many Western legal systems still rely on traditional methods for verifying evidence, and it may take time for these countries to fully embrace blockchain technologies in judicial processes.

The establishment of internet courts in Hangzhou, Beijing, and Guangzhou reflects significant advancements in judicial processes, emphasizing both dispute avoidance and efficiency. These courts exemplify best practices through proactive judicial recommendations that pre-empt disputes by encouraging improvements in digital platform verification systems and transparency. Additionally, blockchain technology ensures the authenticity of digital evidence, preventing future litigation by making records tamper-proof. The courts' round-the-clock online access enables faster dispute resolution, while their collaboration with industries helps streamline regulatory compliance.

This 'green' and efficient online litigation model, exemplified by the Beijing Internet Court, has reduced travel by 184 million kilometres between 2018 and 2023, thereby saving 22,000 tons in carbon emissions and amount of paper equivalent to the height of a 556-storey building or 550 trees.[145] These figures illustrate how legal innovation

[144] '最高人民法院关于互联网法院审理案件若干问题的规定' [Supreme People's Court Provisions on Key Issues in Internet Court Case Adjudication] (*China Court*, 8 September 2018)<https://www.chinacourt.org/article/detail/2018/09/id/3489797.shtml> last accessed 19 October 2024.

[145] '以高质量互联网司法护航中国式现代化' ' [High-Quality Internet Judiciary Safeguards Chinese-Style Modernization] (*China Court*, 29 October 2023) <https://www.chinacourt.org/article/detail/2023/10/id/7600832.shtml> and '盘点！北京互联网法院十大创新工作机制' [Review! Beijing Internet Court's Top 10 Innovative Working Mechanisms] (*Beijing Internet Court*, 2 October 2023) <https://mp.weixin.qq.com/s/IaHiYWmP2QMYrK_Emk-OzQ> last accessed 25 May 2024.

can contribute to both sustainability and judicial efficiency. Western legal systems could adopt similar strategies to reduce environmental footprint while advancing digital transformation.

By embracing technological advancements such as blockchain and AI, the e-courts of Beijing, Guangzhou, and Hangzhou have shown that they are capable of both handling voluminous caseload in an efficient and transparent way as well as delivering substantive justice through effective enforcement. The continued development of specialised judicial mechanisms, including adjudication rules and recommendations, which feedback to and improve the work of judges and regulators, will allow the governance bodies to keep pace with and promote healthy development of China's digital economy.

In conclusion, the judicial landscape in China has been transformed by the establishment of e-courts and associated digital tools, through the joint efforts of the Chinese Government, judiciary and industry actors. This has increased the accessibility, efficiency, and fairness of the justice system in the digital age, as illustrated through the aforementioned case statistics and outcomes.

This model of online litigation and integrated digital solutions can be useful for other nations looking to modernize their legal systems and address the complexities of the digital economy. Best practices such as the use of blockchain technology for securing evidence in China's Internet Courts could be useful for Western countries. However, challenges like balancing efficiency with data privacy laws, especially in regions with strict regulations,[146] will require thoughtful integration of such technologies.

Bibliography

0x Information, '移動微法院訴訟保全區塊鏈系統順利通過測評，獲最高法院認可' [Mobile Micro Court Litigation Preservation Blockchain System Successfully Passes Evaluation, Gains Supreme Court Approval] (*0x Information*, 2 September 2020), <https://0xzx.com/zh-tw/202009021058796300.htm>.

Beijing China News, '北京互联网法院：个人信息保护纠纷覆盖社交电商等多行业' [Beijing Internet Court: Personal Data Protection Disputes Span Social Media, E-Commerce and Multiple Industries] *Beijing China News* (2 November 2023), <https://www.bj.chinanews.com.cn/news/2023/1102/92564.html>.

Beijing Internet Court [2021] Jing 0491 Min Chu 51722. A case on the protection of the reputation rights of private enterprises.

Beijing Internet Court [2023] Jing 0491 Min Chu 11279. The copyright case of "AI Wensheng Diagram".

Beijing Internet Court [2023] Jing 0491 Min Chu 3167. A personality rights injunction case.

Beijing Internet Court: 'Tian Ping Lian', <https://tpl.bjinternetcourt.gov.cn/tpl/>.

Beijing Internet Court: 'Virtual court cabin' (17 September 2021), <https://english.bjinternetcourt.gov.cn/2021-09/17/c_408.htm>.

Beijing Internet Court <https://www.bjinternetcourt.gov.cn/> and <https://english.bjinternetcourt.gov.cn/2019-03/25/c_23.htm>.

Beijing Internet Court, '"每日优鲜APP推送商业短信案"宣判 法院认定一毛钱短信退订费由平台负担' [Court Rules in 'Missfresh App Commercial SMS Case': Platform Liable for One-Cent

146 Such as the European Union. See 'Data protection in the EU' (European Commission) <https://commission.europa.eu/law/law-topic/data-protection/data-protection-eu_en> last accessed 19 October 2024.

Unsubscribe Fee] (Beijing Internet Court, 23 October 2020), <https://mp.weixin.qq.com/s/G5NkupzB7tXVToXh53Hqwg>.

Beijing Internet Court, '上新了！北京互联网法院裁判规则库小程序上线' ' [New Release! Beijing Internet Court's Judgment Rules Database Mini-Program Goes Live] (Beijing Internet Court, 31 August 2023), <https://mp.weixin.qq.com/s?__biz=MzU1NDk0NjE3MA==&mid=2247510288&idx=1&sn=1924fef8d0eb2a8e48515e5a40afb3c4&chksm=>.

Beijing Internet Court, '五年答卷！一图读懂《北京互联网法院审判工作白皮书》' [Five-Year Review! Key Insights from the Beijing Internet Court Trial Work White Paper at a Glance] (Beijing Internet Court, 9 October 2023), <https://mp.weixin.qq.com/s?__biz=MzU1NDk0NjE3MA==&mid=2247511513&idx=1&sn=01a8bfbd860e957c9140c1fc37726f7a&chksm=>.

Beijing Internet Court ,'北京互联网法院2023年度十大典型案件（上）' [Beijing Internet Court's Top 10 Landmark Cases of 2023 (Part I)] (Beijing Internet Court, 21 January 2024), <https://mp.weixin.qq.com/s/NcMpln1g5XGOzvwS2x6h_w>.

Beijing Internet Court ,'北京互联网法院2023年度十大典型案件（下）' [Beijing Internet Court's Top 10 Landmark Cases of 2023 (Part II)] (Beijing Internet Court, 22 January 2024), <https://mp.weixin.qq.com/s/Lh9QL7gSCZpBxdC_esHGBw>.

Beijing Internet Court, '盘点！北京互联网法院十大创新工作机制' [Review! Beijing Internet Court's Top 10 Innovative Working Mechanisms] (Beijing Internet Court, 2 October 2023), <https://mp.weixin.qq.com/s/IaHiYWmP2QMYrK_Emk-OzQ>.

Beijing Internet Court, '盘点2023丨14组数据！见证北京互联网法院这一年的精彩' ' [2023丨202314组数据！见证北京互联网法院这一年的精彩' ' [in Review | 14组数据！见证北京互联网法院这一年的精彩' ' [] (Beijing Internet Court, 23 January 2024), <https://mp.weixin.qq.com/s/BsXE42siEgK9Bp7coRZWcQ>.

Beijing Political and Legal Network, '北京互联网法院5年受案19万余件 著作权权属、侵权纠纷占比超七成' ' [Beijing Internet Court Processes Over 190,000 Cases in Five Years, with Copyright Ownership and Infringement Disputes Accounting for Over 70%] (*Beijing Political and Legal Network*, 5 September 2023). Available at https://www.bj148.org/zf1/zfyw/202309/t20230905_1656406.html.

Bell F, Moses LB, Legg M, Silove J, and Zalnieriute M, 'AI Decision-Making and the Courts' (June 2022 and December 2023) The Australasian Institute of Judicial Administration Incorporated.

Campbell RW, 'Artificial Intelligence in the Courtroom: The Delivery of Justice in the Age of Machine Learning', (2020) 18 Colo Tech LJ 323 Peking University School of Transnational Law Research Paper.

China Court, 'Opinions on Regulating and Strengthening the Judicial Application of Artificial Intelligence'. (*China Court*, December 9, 2022) <https://www.chinacourt.org/law/detail/2022/12/id/150461.shtml>.

China Court, '互联网法院：网络法治的中国智慧与方案-中国法院网' [Internet Courts: China's Wisdom and Solutions for Online Rule of Law] (*China Court*, 29 September 2024), <https://www.chinacourt.org/article/detail/2024/09/id/8136142.shtml>.

China Court, '最高人民法院关于互联网法院审理案件若干问题的规定' [Supreme People's Court Provisions on Key Issues in Internet Court Case Adjudication] (*China Court*, 8 September 2018), <https://www.chinacourt.org/article/detail/2018/09/id/3489797.shtm>l.

China Court, '以高质量互联网司法护航中国式现代化'' [High-Quality Internet Judiciary Safeguards Chinese-Style Modernization] (*China Court*, 29 October 2023), <https://www.chinacourt.org/article/detail/2023/10/id/7600832.shtml>.

China Daily, 'Digital advances herald judicial progress' *China Daily* (17 October 2024), <https://www.chinadaily.com.cn/a/202410/17/WS67105f23a310f1265a1c8041_1.html>. <https://www.chinadaily.com.cn/a/202410/17/WS67105f23a310f1265a1c8041_2.html>. <https://www.chinadaily.com.cn/a/202410/17/WS67105f23a310f1265a1c8041_3.html>. <https://www.chinadaily.com.cn/a/202410/17/WS67105f23a310f1265a1c8041_4.html>. <https://www.chinadaily.com.cn/a/202410/17/WS67105f23a310f1265a1c8041_5.html>.

China Daily, 'Opinions of the Supreme People's Court on Strengthening Blockchain Application in the Judicial Field' (25 May 2022) <https://www.chinadaily.com.cn/m/supremepeoplescourt/2022-05/25/content_37550749.htm.

China Justice Observer, 'Can I resolve cross-border online shopping disputes through the Chinese Internet Court: Inside China's Internet Courts Series -03' (6 April 2019), <https://www.chinajusticeobserver.com/a/can-i-resolve-cross-border-online-shopping-disputes-through-the-chinese-internet-court>.

China Justice Observer, 'Dutch Court Recognizes a Chinese Judgement for the First Time' (3 April 2020), <https://www.chinajusticeobserver.com/a/dutch-court-recognizes-a-chinese-judgement-for-the-first-time>.

China Justice Observer, 'Filing Lawsuits While Living Abroad: China's New Policy' (7 March 2021), <https://www.chinajusticeobserver.com/a/filing-lawsuits-while-living-abroad-china-s-new-policy>.

China Justice Observer, 'How Chinese Judges Deal with Foreign Litigants Who Don't Understand Chinese?' (4 May 2019) <https://www.chinajusticeobserver.com/a/how-chinese-judges-deal-with-foreign-litigants-who-dont-understand-chinese>.

China Justice Observer, 'How Online Criminal Litigation Works in China: The Case of Shanghai' (5 November 2021) <https://www.chinajusticeobserver.com/a/how-online-criminal-litigation-works-in-china-the-case-of-shanghai>.

China Justice Observer, 'How to Sue in Chinese Court Online While Living Abroad?' (14 March 2021), <https://www.chinajusticeobserver.com/a/how-to-sue-in-chinese-court-online-while-living-abroad>.

China Justice Observer, 'New Zealand Court Recognizes a Chinese Judgment for the First Time' (21 June 2020), <https://www.chinajusticeobserver.com/a/new-zealand-court-recognizes-a-chinese-judgment-for-the-first-time>.

China Justice Observer, 'The First Time Australia Recognizes Chinese Civil Settlement Statements' (24 July 2022) <https://www.chinajusticeobserver.com/a/the-first-time-australia-recognizes-chinese-civil-settlement-statements>.

China Justice Observer, 'Chinese Courts on Smart Phones' (6 June 2021) <https://www.chinajusticeobserver.com/a/chinese-courts-on-smart-phones>.

China Justice Observer,'Cross-border E-commerce Dispute Resolution in the Eyes of Chinese Courts' (25 September 2022) <https://en.chinajusticeobserver.com/a/cross-border-e-commerce-dispute-resolution-in-the-eyes-of-chinese-courts>.

China Justice Observer, 'Why are Chinese internet courts keen on blockchain technology' (15 December 2019) <https://en.chinajusticeobserver.com/a/why-are-chinese-internet-courts-keen-on-blockchain-technology>.

China Law Translate, 'Guiding Opinions on Strengthening Searches for Similar Cases to Unify the Application of Law (Provisional)' (27 July 2020), <https://www.chinalawtranslate.com/en/case-review/>.

China News, '杭州互联网法院受理涉网知识产权案近3万件' [Hangzhou Internet Court Handles Nearly 30,000 Internet-Related Intellectual Property Cases] (24 April 2024), <https://www.chinanews.com.cn/cj/2024/04-24/10205414.shtml>.

European Commission, 'Data protection in the EU' (European Commission) <https://commission.europa.eu/law/law-topic/data-protection/data-protection-eu_en<.

Gazette of the Supreme People's Court of the People's Republic of China, 'Provisions of the Supreme People's Court on Several Issues Concerning the Trial of Cases by Internet Courts' (September 6, 2018) <http://gongbao.court.gov.cn/Details/7e594961f195254a863d6cc90be5cd.html>.

Global Times, 'Court rules on China's first AI voice rights case, sounding alarm for industry' (23 April 2024) <https://www.globaltimes.cn/page/202404/1311121.shtml>.

Government of the People's Republic of China, 'Improving the Cyber Legal System and Protecting the People's Legitimate Rights and Interests—The press conference of the State Council Information Office focused on the rule of law on the Internet to ensure high-quality development' (19 June 2024) <https://www.gov.cn/zhengce/202406/content_6958050.htm>.

Government of the People's Republic of China, 'People's Republic of China Regulations for the Implementation of the Law on the Protection of Consumer Rights and Interests' (19 March 2024) <https://www.gov.cn/zhengce/content/202403/content_6940158.htm>.

Guangdong Politics and Legal Network, '广州互联网法院四年结案18.4万宗，办案质效居全国前列' [Guangzhou Internet Court Concludes 184,000 Cases in Four Years, Ranking Among the

Nation's Top in Case Quality and Efficiency] (29 September 2022) <https://www.gdzf.org.cn/wzsjb/znzf/content/post_120908.html>.

Guangdong Politics and Legal Network, '广州互联网法院激发司法治理新活力，助力市域社会治理现代化建设' [Guangzhou Internet Court Stimulates New Vitality in Judicial Governance and Contributes to the Modernization of Municipal Social Governance'] (last 10 August 2023) <https://www.gdzf.org.cn/zwgd/content/post_139755.html>.

Guangzhou Internet Court, 'Guangzhou Internet Court: Brochure' <https://gzinternetcourt.gov.cn/#/articleDetail?id=uzpj9c02270cfazd1q2csrc30mh80811&titleType=broadMutualDemeanor&type=GhElegantDemeanor&apiType=convincing>.

Guangzhou Internet Court: Evidence' <http://bc.gzinternetcourt.gov.cn:9001/gzinternetcourt-evidence/index.html#/netcomchain>.

Guangzhou Internet Court: Judicial innovation' <https://gzinternetcourt.gov.cn/#/articleList?type=InnovationInitiative&titleType=judicialInnovation&apiType=routine>.

Hangzhou Chinese People's Political Consultative Conference, '杭州互联网法院发布六周年改革创新成果' [Hangzhou Internet Court Releases Six-Year Reform and Innovation Achievements] (3 August 2023) <https://www.hzzx.gov.cn/cshz/content/2023-08/03/content_8593083.htm>.

Hangzhou Intermediate People's Court [2022] Zhe 01 Min Zhong 5272.

Hangzhou Intermediate People's Court [2023] Zhe 01 Min Zhong 453.

Hangzhou Internet Court [2021] Zhe 0192 Min Chu 10369.

Hangzhou Internet Court [2022] Zhe 0192 Min Chu 1008.

Hangzhou Internet Court: 'Digital Trade Litigation Platform'. Available at <https://www.netcourt.gov.cn/pamir/foreign/app/home.>

Hangzhou Internet Court: 'Evidence'<https://evidence.netcourt.gov.cn/#/page>.

Hangzhou Internet Court: 'Tiao jie',<https://tiaojie.netcourt.gov.cn/>.

Hangzhou Internet Court <https://www.netcourt.gov.cn/?lang=En>.

Hangzhou News, '抓取销售直播间数据 一科技公司被诉不正当竞争' [Tech Company Sued for Unfair Competition Over Scraping Sales Livestream Data] (25 April 2024). Available at <https://hznews.hangzhou.com.cn/jingji/content/2024-04/25/content_8720766.htm>.

Hangzhou News, 'What is Blockchain and Why is WeChat and Union Pay using it?' (24 October 2023). <https://www.hiredchina.com/articles/what-is-blockchain-and-why-is-wechat/>.

Hu CM, '移动电子诉讼的司法实践及其限度——以中国"移动微法院"为例' '[Judicial Practice and Limits of Mobile E-Litigation: The Case of China's Mobile Micro Court]' (2021) 2 China Applied Law 73–86.

Judicature, 'China's E-Justice Revolution' (2021) 105(1) *Judicature* <https://judicature.duke.edu/articles/chinas-e-justice-revolution/>.

Legal Daily, '景汉朝, '互联网法院的时代创新与中国贡献' '[Jing Hanchao: Era-Defining Innovations and China's Contributions to Internet Courts]' (last 2 November 2023) <http://www.legaldaily.com.cn/xjpfzsx/content/content_8922364.html>.

Lin Y, 'Visual Law: China's Three Internet Courts' (2021) 2(3) SAS Journal 531–38.

Lu T, 'The Implementation of Blockchain Technologies in Chinese Courts' (2021) 4(1) JBPL 102–20.

MSN News, 'Scarlett Johansson says a ChatGPT voice is "eerily similar" to hers and OpenAI is halting its use' (*MSN News*, May 2024), https://www.msn.com/en-us/news/us/scarlett-johansson-says-a-chatgpt-voice-is-eerily-similar-to-hers-and-openai-is-halting-its-use/ar-BB1mJigd.

Murray MD, 'NFT Ownership and Copyrights' (2 July 2022). SSRN. Available at https://papers.ssrn.com/sol3/papers.cfm?abstract_id=4152468.

Papagianneas S and Junius N, 'Fairness and justice through automation in China's smart court'. (2003) 51 Computer Law and Security Review 105897.

Peking University Law, 'Cybersecurity Law of the People's Republic of China' (July 2016). Available at <https://www.pkulaw.com/en_law/4dce14765f4265f1bdfb.html?way=textSlc#tiao_0>.

People's Courts of the People's Republic of China: Si Fa Lian', <https://sfl.court.gov.cn>.

People's Daily, '线上法院为你"云断案"' ' [Online Courts Deliver Judgments through Cloud Proceedings] (15 June 2022), <http://paper.people.com.cn/rmrbhwb/html/2022-06/15/content_25923050.htm>.

Shanghai Courts Litigation Service Network: 'Client-side download' <hshfy.sh.cn/shwfy/download/client_0/>.

Shanghai Courts Litigation Service Network: 'Online mediation manual' <https://www.hshfy.sh.cn/shwfy/download/viewpdf.jsp?lx=1>.

Shanghai Courts Litigation Service Network: 'Online negotiation manual' <https://www.hshfy.sh.cn/shwfy/download/viewpdf.jsp?lx=6>.

Shanghai Courts Litigation Service Network: 'Online trial hearing manual' <https://www.hshfy.sh.cn/shwfy/download/viewpdf.jsp?lx=0>.

Shanghai Courts Litigation Service Network <https://www.hshfy.sh.cn/shwfy/ssfww/>.

Sina News, '关注！杭州互联网法院发布直播行业知识产权保护典型案例|互联网|法院|杭州市_新浪科技_新浪网' [Attention! Hangzhou Internet Court Releases Landmark Cases on Intellectual Property Protection in the Livestreaming Industry] (6 October 2024). Available at https://finance.sina.com.cn/tech/roll/2024-10-06/doc-incrrraw9111390.shtml.

State Administration for Market Regulation of the People's Republic of China, 'National Platform of Consumer Dispute Resolution' <http://36.110.229.139/>.

Supreme People's Court Monitor, 'Supreme People's Court's new guidance on similar case search'. (27 July 2020) <https://supremepeoplescourtmonitor.com/2020/07/27/supreme-peoples-courts-new-guidance-on-similar-case-search/>.

Supreme People's Court of the People's Republic of China, 'In numbers: Achievements of China's courts in the last decade' (11 October 2022) <https://english.court.gov.cn/2022-10/11/c_818933.htm>.

Supreme People's Court of the People's Republic of China, 'Numbers in the SPC 2022 work report' (10 March 2022) <https://english.court.gov.cn/2022-03/10/c_761359.htm>.

Supreme People's Court of the People's Republic of China, 'Work Report of the Supreme People's Court of the People's Republic of China' (8 March 2022) <https://view.officeapps.live.com/op/view.aspx?src=https%3A%2F%2Fenglish.court.gov.cn%2Fpdf%2FWorkReportoftheSupremePeoplesCourtofthePeoplesRepublicofChina.docx&wdOrigin=BROWSELINK>.

Tahura US and Selvadurai N, 'The Use of Artificial Intelligence in Judicial Decision-Making: The Example of China' (2023) International Journal of Law, Ethics, and Teechnology 1–20.

The Supreme People's Court of the People's Republic of China, 'China opens first cross-border trade tribunal' (16 July 2020) <https://english.court.gov.cn/2020-07/16/c_768336.htm>.

Transnational Litigation Blog, 'Enforcing Chinese Judgments' (19 July 2022) <https://tlblog.org/enforcing-chinese-judgments/>.

United Nations Conference on Trade and Development (UNCTAD), *Consumer Dispute Resolution in the World* (UNCTAD Report, UNCTAD/DITC/CPLP/2023/2, March 2024).

United Nations Conference on Trade and Development (UNCTAD), *Consumer Trust in the Digital Economy: The Case for Online Dispute Resolution* (UNCTAD Research Paper No 72, UNCTAD/SER.RP/2021/15).

US Library of Congress, 'China: Supreme People's Court Issues Online Litigation Rules, Addressing Review of Blockchain Evidence' (21 July 2021) <https://www.loc.gov/item/global-legal-monitor/2021-07-21/china-supreme-peoples-court-issues-online-litigation-rules-addressing-review-of-blockchain-evidence/>.

Wang HY, 'AI and Administration of Justice in China,' (December 2023) National reports on Evidence through Artificial intelligence: Artificial Intelligence and Administration of Criminal Justice.

Wang N and Tian MY, '"Intelligent Justice": human-centered considerations in China's legal AI transformation' (2023) 3(2) AI Ethics, 349–54.

Xinhua News Guangdong, '广州互联网法院：以"小切口"推动社会治理"大作为"' [Guangzhou Internet Court: Driving Major Social Governance Advancements Through Targeted Reforms] (19 September 2023) http://www.gd.xinhuanet.com/20230919/9266c757ad8645af8bb6517a07f8e80a/c.html.

Xinhua News, '"移动微法院"全国版试运行:极简化操作 无延时开庭 见证式执行' ' [Nationwide Trial Run of Mobile Micro Court: Streamlined Operations, Instant Hearings, Transparent Enforcement] (18 August 2018) <http://www.xinhuanet.com/politics/2018-08/18/c_1123288515.htm>.

Xinhua News, 'Beijing Internet Court Launches AI Judge' (27 June 2019) <http://www.xinhuanet.com/english/2019-06/27/c_138178826.htm>.

Xinhua News, '全国法院电子送达文书均已支持在线核验' ' [Electronic Service of Court Documents Nationwide Now Supports Online Verification] (14 March 2023) <http://www.news.cn/2023-03/14/c_1129431979.htm>.
Yao L, 'Implementing Rule of Law Concept in the Digital Sphere: China's Experience,' (2023) 4(4) Legal Issues in the Digital Age <https://doi.org/10.17323/2713-2749.2023.4.114.133>.
Yu M and Du GD, 'Why Are Chinese Courts Turning to AI?' (*The Diplomat*, 19 January 2019) <https://thediplomat.com/2019/01/why-are-chinese-courts-turning-to-ai>.
Yu Y, 'Digitalization' (Oxford University EU ADR Conference, 9–10 November 2022).
Yu Y and Chung A, 'CDR: Catalyst for China's E-Commerce' in Kramer X, Voet S, Ködderitzsch L, Tulibacka M, and Hess B (eds), *Delivering Justice: A Holistic and Multidisciplinary Approach: Liber Amicorum in Honour of Christopher Hodges* (Hart Publishing 2022) 227–44.
Zhang AH, *High Wire: How China Regulates Big Tech and Governs Its Economy* (OUP 2024).
Zhi Chan Li, '杭州互联网法院网络知识产权十大典型案例发布，"虚拟数字人"等案入选' [Hangzhou Internet Court Releases Top 10 Landmark Cases on Online Intellectual Property, Including 'Virtual Digital Human' Cases] (19 January 2024) <https://www.zhichanli.com/p/827454524>.
Zhu M, '杭州互联网法院试点应用"AI助理法官"' [Hangzhou Internet Court Pilots 'AI Assistant Judge' Application] (*Baidu News Hangzhou*, 14 June 2019) <https://baijiahao.baidu.com/s?id=1636313472795379686&wfr=spider>.
Zou CX, 'Achievements and Prospects of Artificial Intelligence Judicature in China' (2022) 11(4) Chinese Studies 197–227.

8

The Digitalization of the Pakistani Justice System

Challenges and Solutions

Nauman Reayat[*]

A. Introduction

The digitalization of the justice system is a global phenomenon. Digitalization generally refers to the processing of data using digital technologies, leading to fundamental changes in processes and the development of new models and innovations.[1] Digitalization of justice system may encompass various tools, including, but not limited to, the electronic communications (for submission of claims[2] and judicial service), case management systems, video conferencing, online dispute resolution

* Lecturer in Law, Leicester Law School, University of Leicester.

[1] SAP, 'Digitisation vs Digitalisation' <https://www.sap.com/uk/products/erp/digitization-vs-digitalization.html> last accessed 2 December 2024. See also Gartner, 'Digitalization' https://www.gartner.com/en/information-technology/glossary/digitalization> last accessed 2 December 2024.

[2] In the United Kingdom (UK), the term *claim* is commonly used for submissions and requests made by litigants to courts. However, similar processes are referred to differently in other countries. In Pakistan, *writ petition* refers to proceedings before provincial high courts, where the initiating party is known as the *petitioner* and the opposing parties as *respondents*. A *civil suit* refers to proceedings before civil courts, with the initiating party termed the *plaintiff* and the opposing parties as *defendants*.

Nauman Reayat, *The Digitalization of the Pakistani Justice System* In: *Digitalization and Artificial Intelligence in Courts*. Edited by: Fernando Esteban de la Rosa, Pablo Cortés, and Nuria Marchal Escalona, Oxford University Press.
 DOI: 10.1093/9780198918752.003.0008

(ODR) platforms or the online availability of the courts rulings. Each tool serves distinct objectives. The use of case management systems may help increase efficiency. Electronic communications and video conferencing between courts and litigants during legal proceedings can help overcome geographical barriers and reduce delays, also contributing to greater efficiency.[3] Additionally, the online availability of court rulings enhances the transparency of the judicial system. Without digitalization, legal processes can be inefficient and limit access to justice, especially for small claims and for those cases where it is not convenient for parties to meet face to face. Undeniably, the COVID-19 pandemic enhanced the importance of digitalization worldwide.[4]

The efficiency gains from the digitalization of the justice system may play a particularly significant role in low- and middle-income countries[5] with large populations and substantial backlogs of pending cases. As of February 2024, according to the Law and Justice Commission of Pakistan, 2.26 million cases were pending before Pakistan's lower and higher judiciary.[6] Nearly 3.7 million cases are pending before different courts in Bangladesh,[7] and 0.8 million are pending before different Sri Lankan courts,[8] even though the country's total population is only 21.8 million. Brazil has approximately 100 million pending cases.[9] Advancing the digitalization of the justice system can enable these countries to effectively address case backlogs and enhance overall efficiency.

Technologically advanced countries such as the United Kingdom, Australia, Canada, and the United States are rapidly digitalizing their justice systems, while low- and middle-income countries struggle to advance this process. In low- and middle-income countries, digitalization of the justice systems has largely been limited to uploading the status of pending cases and claims, along with important rulings, on court websites and occasional correspondence between courts and external actors via email, without achieving a significant increase in the efficiency. Most studies on the digitalization of courts focus on technologically advanced countries,[10] and few discuss the

[3] Anyu Lee, 'Online Dispute Resolution in China: today and Future' in Daniel Rainey, Ethan Katsh, and Mohamed S. Abdel Wahab (eds), *Online Dispute Resolution: Theory and Practice* (Eleven International Publishing 2021).

[4] Judith Townend and Paul Magrath, 'Remote Trial and Error: How Covid -19 Changed Public Access to Court Proceedings' (2021) 13 J of Media L 107.

[5] The World Bank uses the Gross National Income (GNI) per capita to classify countries into four income groups: low-income ($1,145 or less), lower-middle-income (between $1,146 and $4,515), upper-middle-income (between $4,516 and $14,005), and high-income (more than a GNI per capita of $14,005). For details see The World Bank, 'The World by Income and Region' <https://datatopics.worldbank.org/world-development-indicators/the-world-by-income-and-region.html> last accessed 22 December 2024.

[6] Staff Reporter, 'July–Dec 2023 Statistics Show 2.26 Million Cases Pending in Courts: Report' (*Dawn*, 16 February 2024) <www.dawn.com/news/1814586> last accessed 23 September 2024.

[7] UNB News, 'Nearly 3.7 Mln Cases Pending' (*United News of Bangladesh*, 16 July 2020). <www.unb.com.bd/category/Bangladesh/nearly-37-mln-cases-pending/54740> accessed 23 September 2024.

[8] Zulfick Farzan, '800,000 Pending Cases in Sri Lankan Courts' (*News 1st*, 31 December 2020) <www.newsfirst.lk/2020/12/31/800000-pending-cases-in-sri-lankan-courts> last accessed 23 September 2024.

[9] Richard Susskind, *Online Courts and the Future of Justice* (OUP 2019).

[10] ibid; Mavis Maclean and Bregje Dijksterhuis (eds), *Digital Family Justice: From Alternative Dispute Resolution to Online Dispute Resolution?* (Bloomsbury Publishing 2019); Eryn J Newman, Bethany Muir, and Nericia Brown, 'The Virtual Court: Implications for Eyewitnesses and Beyond' in Emily Pica, David Ross, and Joann Pozz (eds), *The Impact of Technology on the Criminal Justice System: A Psychological Overview* (Routledge 2024).

specific challenges of low- and middle-income countries.[11] Moreover, many studies do not explain how the digitalization of courts could advance in low- and middle-income countries and how this advancement will function in the context of these countries where communication between courts and litigants via email or other electronic means, such as Skype, Zoom, or telephone conferencing, as well as data organization and management, is typically not standard practice. This chapter seeks to answer the following questions: Why is digitalization limited in countries like Pakistan? What are the challenges facing the digitalization of the Pakistani justice system to reach a significant increase of the efficiency of the system, and how can these challenges be addressed?

The chapter examines the challenges of advancing the digitalization of the Pakistani justice system and proposes ways on how to improve it to contribute to speedy and inexpensive justice in general and a decrease in caseload. It argues that the digitalization of the justice system in Pakistan needs to go beyond the limited use of IT to decrease the need for the physical presence of judges, staff, lawyers, litigants, and the number of required hearings at any stage. The chapter proposes that Pakistan should establish a legal framework for the digitalization of its justice system, increase funding, ensure effective data organization and sharing among institutions, develop an integrated online hub for courts nationwide, introduce a software to assist judges with case processing and decision-making, and improve the stability of internet connectivity and security.

The study focuses on Pakistan for several reasons. First, Pakistan's legal system has many remnants of colonial rule, making it a reference case for authoritarian countries and those with colonial histories.[12] As explained later in this chapter, Pakistan is confronted with massive case backlogs and litigants with limited knowledge of the law, similar to challenges in other countries, such as India, Nigeria, Mexico, and Iraq. An in-depth analysis of the digitalization of the Pakistani justice system may provide insights that other countries can adopt to suit their requirements. This chapter has

[11] Liyuan Wang, 'Application of Information Technology in Judicial Field: The Development Model of Online Litigation in China' (2024) 52 CLS Rev 105936; Bich Thao Nguyen and Thanh Huong Ngo, 'Building Electronic Court in Vietnam: Recent Developments and Challenges' (2024) 16 Lex Humana 573; Panpan Zheng et al, 'Judicial Informatization and Digital Transformation: Evidence from the Establishment of the Internet Court' (2024) Applied Economics Letters 1.

[12] For details on the features Pakistan inherited from its colonial past and the nature of authoritarian regimes in the country, see: Osama Siddique, *Pakistan's Experience with the Formal Law: An Alien Justice* (CUP 2013). Authoritarian countries have political systems where power is concentrated in a leader, political party, or military group. They are categorized into three types: military regimes, single-party regimes, and personalist regimes. Military regimes are led by a group of officers, such as in Brazil (1964–1985) and Argentina (1976–1983). Single-party regimes are dominated by one political party, even if others exist. Personalist regimes revolve around a single leader who holds unchecked power, as seen with Rafael Trujillo's regime in Dominica (1930–1961), Saddam Hussain's regime (1979–2003) in Iraq, Muammar al-Gaddafi's regime (1969–2011) in Libya, and Idi Amin's regime (1971–1979) in Uganda. See the following for details on authoritarian countries: Barbara Geddes, 'What do we know about democratization after twenty years', Annual Review of Political Science (1999) 2(1) 115-144; Barbara Geddes 'Paradigms and sand castles: Theory building and research design in comparative politics' (University of Michigan Press 2023). In Pakistan, the military regimes of General Ayub Khan (1958–1969), General Yahya (1969–1971), General Zia ul Haq (1977–1988), and General Musharraf (1999–2008) were personalist in nature, with each army chief centralizing power and controlling decision-making across state institutions, including the judiciary.

some limitations that future research can explore. This study does not deal with the technical details of the digitalization of the justice system, such as software coding instructions, cybersecurity measures to ensure that the system is not vulnerable to cyberattacks and steps to safeguard data protection and management. The chapter is divided into four parts. The first section discusses international examples as examples of best practices in the digitalization of justice systems. For those unfamiliar with Pakistani jurisdiction, the second section provides a basic understanding of the country's legal system and investigates the status of the digitalization of the Pakistani justice system. The third section discusses challenges in the advancement of digitalization of the Pakistani justice system and makes proposals and recommendations for advancing the digitalization of courts in Pakistan. Lastly, the chapter provides the conclusions.

B. The Digitalization of Justice Systems Worldwide

Sourdin suggests the following different levels of the use of technology in the justice system: supportive, replacement and disruptive.[13] At the most rudimentary level of digitalization are the support tools, which assist, inform, or advise people involved in the justice system (eg locating justice services online and obtaining information about justice processes through the internet).[14] At the second level are the technological tools, which replace functions and activities that humans traditionally perform in person (eg videoconferencing, including internet-based group video calls, teleconferencing, and email correspondence).[15] At the most advanced level are disruptive technologies, which alter how legal professionals work and include using artificial intelligence (AI) tools by judges.

On the other hand, Reiling identified three distinct ways in which technology is used in courts.[16] The first involves the application of technology to processes that occur within the court itself. The second pertains to the back office: the use of technology in case administration, document production, and case management. The third relates to employing technology for communication with parties and the general public outside the court.

The digitalization of justice systems is not a simple 'yes or no' concept but rather a relative one. It tends to increase over time. For example, it progresses from replacing typewriters with computers in courtrooms, to informing the general public about court activities through websites, to the use of AI, and it may continue to evolve. Therefore, it is challenging to establish final standards for the digitalization of justice systems.

[13] Tania Sourdin, Bin Li, and Tony Burke, 'Just, Quick and Cheap? Civil Dispute Resolution and Technology' (2019) 17 Macquarie LJ 19; Tania Sourdin, 'Judge v Robot: Artificial Intelligence and Judicial Decision-Making' (2018) 41(4) UNSWLJ 1114.

[14] ibid.

[15] ibid.

[16] Dory Reiling, *Technology for Justice: How Information Technology Can Support Judicial Reform* (Leiden University Press 2009) 48.

Nonetheless, justice systems worldwide are rapidly progressing at the second level and slowly moving towards the advanced level referred to by Sourdin.[17] The digitalization of these systems involves all the types of technologies referred to by Reiling. For instance, online courts and tribunal services in the UK allow people to pay court fines, plead guilty to traffic offences, fill out applications, and submit documentary evidence in civil matters, such as divorce, claims, and benefits decisions.[18] The UK government has also introduced an online court called the Online Civil Money Claims.[19] Additionally, His Majesty's (HM) Courts and Tribunal Service, police, judiciary, and professional users in the UK share the same case management system known as the common platform. This system enables them to register for an account on this system, link themselves to defendants, and serve case materials and documents including preparation for effective trial form and initial details of the prosecution case on courts.[20]

The Ministry of Justice in the Netherlands owns an intranet for the courts known as JustitieNet (Justice Network). [21] There is a separate registration and management mechanism for cases in the administrative and civil courts, and the Public Ministry Registration has an online portal named Compas. Criminal courts receive relevant case data from this portal, and the concerned parties can register data in the system. The common assessments of allowances, such as alimony or child support, are performed by a system named Iudex Non-Aestimat.[22]

Many online applications have been developed to process cases submitted before Dutch courts. The JustWord application manages textual data in Microsoft Word format and merges data involving Word documents from the registration system.[23] Moreover, this application can recognize speech to prevent impersonation. The courts are connected to a shell called Rapsody, which extracts production and management information from the registration system.[24] Additionally, the courts use other online applications, such as PCSII and Porta Iuris, to collect and process data and deliver orders and decisions to the concerned parties.[25] PCSII is an application that assists the court in reporting its production by receiving information from Rapsody. Porta Iuris is a portal that facilitates' courts' access to European and national case law and legislation, the database for criminal sanctions and the Justex database for administrative justice.

The Civil Resolution Tribunal (CRT) in British Columbia, Canada, uses two applications to resolve disputes. The first is Solution Explorer, which diagnoses disputes

[17] Zbynek Loebl, *Designing Online Courts: The Future of Justice Is Open to All* (Wolters Kluwer 2019).

[18] HM Courts and Tribunal Service, 'Online Court and Tribunal Services for Professional Users and the Public' (*GOV.UK*, 13 July 2020) <www.gov.uk/guidance/online-court-and-tribunal-services-for-professional-users-and-the-public> last accessed 23 September 2024.

[19] GOV.UK, 'Make a Court Claim for Money' (2024) <www.gov.uk/make-court-claim-for-money/make-claim> last accessed 22 September 2024.

[20] GOV.UK, 'HMCTS Common Platform' (2024) <https://www.gov.uk/guidance/hmcts-common-platform-view-or-manage-a-case> last accessed 11 November 2024.

[21] Dory Reiling, 'Doing Justice with Information Technology' (2006) 15 I&CTL 189, 191.

[22] Ibid.

[23] ibid.

[24] ibid.

[25] ibid.

and provides necessary information. The second is a dispute resolution application that includes negotiation, facilitation, and adjudication to the parties involved.[26] These web forms record, organize and process data uploaded to online web forms. All relevant parties have access to these pages and can provide input.[27]

New South Wales (NSW) courts and tribunals have similarly moved towards online courts in Australia.[28] They have an online registry for the Federal Court of Australia or Federal Circuit and Family Court of Australia. While the United Kingdom is still expanding the digitalization of courts, the NSW judiciary, similar to the United States and Canada, has adopted the digitalization of courts more extensively. The online portal allows users to submit cases by filling out and uploading court forms and supporting documents and evidence.

The state of Victoria in Australia over 20 years ago already envisioned online courts in its report titled 'Technology and the Law'.[29] The report recommends integrating case registration and administration of all Victorian courts and tribunals, providing training for judges and administrators on using new technology, fostering international collaboration through a law and technology clearinghouse, establishing a department that can coordinate and implement a centralized mechanism for the introduction and use of technology, and developing standards and protocols for a justice information system based on best practices worldwide.[30] Electronic arbitration rooms comprising facilities for recording electronic evidence and statements through online chatrooms, webcasting, document imaging, and point-to-point data lining are functional in Sydney[31] and are used to resolve disputes.

The state of Michigan in the United States set up cyber courts where online tribunals resolve disputes exceeding US$25,000.[32] The jurisdiction is limited to the consumer and business sectors. The Community Justice and Tribunal System of Singapore provides two tools for settling disputes online: eNegotiation and eMediation.[33] The former is aimed at settling the dispute online on their own, whereas the latter settles the dispute online with the help of a court-appointed mediator.

The above examples illustrate digitalization in technologically advanced, high-income countries. These countries have the financial stability to afford the infrastructure required for digitalization and possess stable political and legal systems to

[26] Civil Resolution Tribunal, 'The CRT Process' <https://civilresolutionbc.ca/crt-process/> last accessed 23 September 2024.

[27] Civil Resolution Tribunal, 'What Kinds of Claims Can the CRT Take?' <https://civilresolutionbc.ca/help/what-kinds-of-claims-can-the-crt-take/> last accessed 22 September 2024.

[28] Federal Court of Australia, 'eCourtroom: Online Courtroom for Registered Users' <www.fedcourt.gov.au/online-services/ecourtroom> last accessed 24 September 2024.

[29] Eugene Clark and Cho George, 'Law and Technology: What Does the Future Hold for ADR?' (2001) 20(3) The Arbitrator and Mediator 23. Also cited in Padma Raman, 'Towards a 21st Century Legal System' (2000) Globalisation and Law Reform 76, 19–24.

[30] ibid.

[31] Eugene Clark, Cho George, and Arthur Hoyle, 'Online Dispute Resolution: Present Realities, Pressing Problems and Future Prospects' (2010) 17(1) Int Rev L 7; see also Clark and George (n 29).

[32] R Young, 'Cyber Courts: House Bill 6447' (Michigan Legislature, 3 December 2002) <www.legislature.mi.gov/documents/2001-2002/billanalysis/House/htm/2001-HLA-6447-a.htm> last accessed 11 September 2024.

[33] Singapore Courts, 'Settle a Tribunal or Protection from Harassment Dispute Online: eNegotiation or eMediation' (SG Courts, 3 April 2024) <www.judiciary.gov.sg/alternatives-to-trial/enegotiation-emediation> last accessed 24 September 2024.

advance it. Unsurprisingly, the wider literature on the digitalization of justice systems, including most of this book's chapters, focuses on the digitalization of justice systems in these countries. Much less research exists about low- and middle-income countries with a growing population of young people, increasing use of the internet and mobiles and unstable political and legal systems.

Low- and middle-income countries are also gradually digitalizing their justice systems. They are making slow progress at the second level of technology use and are gradually transitioning toward the third level described by Sourdin.[34] The digitalization of these systems incorporates all the types of technologies mentioned by Reiling.[35] However, they are unable to progress at the same pace as high-income countries. For example, e-courts have been established across different tiers of the Indian judiciary under the E-Courts Mission Mode Project to transform the judiciary and digitalize the administration of justice.[36] The second phase of this project includes providing hardware, software, and training to courts, which were not covered in the first phase. New services introduced in this phase include a cloud computing mechanism and a centralized judicial filing system. The courts are interconnected horizontally and vertically through a core-periphery computerized information system, with a national server at the core and state servers at the periphery. However, India is struggling to digitalize its justice system and has been unable to introduce facilities similar to CRT in Canada or small claim courts in England.

Besides, India might not be an ideal example to examine the limited digitalization of the justice system in low- and middle-income countries because it is politically and economically more stable[37] than other low- and middle-income countries. It is somewhat of an outlier, having advanced further than other neighboring countries. However, despite all economic and political challenges, other low- and middle-income countries continue digitalizing their justice system on a limited scale. For example, in Bangladesh, mass protests recently resulted in regime change and political breakdown.[38] Sri Lanka could not pay its national and international debts and declared bankruptcy.[39] Pakistan was a few steps away from default[40] and struggling to receive packages from the International Monetary Fund.[41] Yet, higher judiciaries in these countries have websites where people can see rulings and the status of pending

[34] Sourdin, Judge v Robot' (n 13).

[35] Reiling (n 16).

[36] The Supreme Court of India, 'E-Courts Mission Mode Project' ,<https://ecommitteesci.gov.in/project/brief-overview-of-e-courts-project/> last accessed 21 September 2024.

[37] BTI Transformation Index, 'India Country Report 2024' < https://bti-project.org/en/reports/country-report/IND#pos6> last accessed 23 December 2024.

[38] Anbarasan Ethirajan and Hannah Ritchie, 'What Sparked the Protests that Toppled Bangladesh's PM? (*BBC News*, 6 August 2024) <www.bbc.co.uk/news/articles/cq5xye1d285o> last accessed 24 September 2024.

[39] Bharatha Mallawarachi, 'Sri Lanka Reaches Deal on Debt Restructuring with Bilateral Creditors Including China and France' (*AP News*, 27 June 2024) <https://apnews.com/article/sri-lanka-economic-crisis-india-japan-china-503d8871e4b14c8bda9822b171f73b8d> last accessed 24 September 2024.

[40] Mahira Sarfraz, 'A Diary of (Near) Default: Pakistan's Journey to Avoid Insolvency in 2023' (*Dawn*, 30 December 2023) <www.dawn.com/news/1800599> last accessed 24 September 2024.

[41] Shahbaz Rana, 'Pakistan's Existential Economic Crisis' (United States Institute of Peace, 6 April 2023) <www.usip.org/publications/2023/04/pakistans-existential-economic-crisis> last accessed 24 September 2024.

cases. Nonetheless, the pace of digitalization in these countries is very slow when compared to most developed countries. So, what are the options available to them to advance the digitalization? Should they import applications and software from the mentioned countries, or should they take a piecemeal approach with different steps? To address these questions, the next two sections will examine the current state of digitalization in Pakistan, discuss the challenges it faces, and propose strategies to advance the digitalization of the Pakistani justice system.

C. The Current State of Digitalization in Pakistan's Justice System

There is no single path to the digitalization of justice systems. The momentum of this digitalization requires a clear understanding of the starting point to identify the next steps needed for digitalization to achieve its goal of improving the efficiency of the justice system. This section provides a basic understanding of Pakistan's legal system and investigates the current status of the digitalization of the Pakistani justice system.

Pakistan became independent and inherited the British colonial judicial system in 1947. Since then, it has enacted three constitutions: the 1956 Constitution, the 1962 Constitution and the 1973 Constitution. The judiciary in Pakistan has three tiers: the Supreme Court of Pakistan (SCP), provincial high courts and district judiciary. As the last court of authority, the SCP has original, appellate, contempt, and advisory jurisdictions under the 1973 Constitution of Pakistan. Its original jurisdiction has two parts: one related to federalism and the other to public interest and the enforcement of human rights. The SCP is empowered to decide on conflicts between the federal and provincial governments[42] and issues about public interest and human rights to ensure justice[43]. Rulings by the provincial high courts ultimately reach the appellate jurisdiction of the SCP.[44] The SCP and provincial high courts can issue contempt notices for not implementing their orders.[45]

According to the Law and Justice Commission of Pakistan's biannual report, in February 2024, 1.86 million cases were pending at the district level in Pakistan,[46] primarily due to announced and unannounced strikes of lawyers[47] and frivolous litigation.[48] Digitalizing the justice system is necessary to efficiently process the pending

[42] The Constitution of Pakistan 1973, art 184(1).
[43] ibid art 184 (3).
[44] ibid art 185.
[45] ibid art 204.
[46] Staff Reporter (n 6).
[47] Muhammad Sher Shah, 'Peshawar Solutions to Case Flow Management' in Kamal Ahmad, Christine Lao, and Kirsten Weisenberger (eds), *Law and Policy Reform at the Asian Development Bank: Report from the ADB Symposium on Challenges in Implementing Access to Justice Reforms* (Asian Development Bank 2005).
[48] Raza Ullah Shah, Shadi Ullah Khan, and Sumera Farid, 'Causes for Delay in Civil Justice in Lower Courts of Pakistan: A Review' (2014) 6 Pakistan J Crim 47; Muhammad Saeed, 'Assessing the Efficiency of the District Courts of Pakistan—Why Is Better Evaluation Needed?' (2020) 1(2) Amicus Curiae 418; Ibrahim Haroon, 'Reform of the Code of Civil Procedure' (2022) 13 Pakistan L Rev 1; Hafiz Muhammad Ihsan Zafeer, Hong Zue, and Samra Maqbool, 'Delaying Factors Regarding Civil Justice in Pakistan' (2020) 2 J Humanities and Social Science Studies 15.

cases and control the caseload, and various initiatives have been taken in Pakistan to achieve this goal.

The Law and Justice Commission of Pakistan was entrusted with implementing the Access to Justice Program, financed by the Asian Development Bank (ADB) in 2002 and aimed at introducing various tools and applications across the country. These tools and applications included case management, management information, IT training, e-court, video conferencing, case law management, accounts management, and files tracking systems.[49] Similarly, the National Judicial Policy of Pakistan 2009 provided a list of long-term measures, which included computerization and networking at all levels of judicial hierarchy, the introduction of specifically designed software to check and monitor the case flow, the measurement of the quantitative and qualitative output of judicial officers, and examination of witnesses through video link.[50]

While some of the above plans, such as the launch of websites of the SCP and high courts, SMS alerts of hearings, online access to reported judgments, case flow management system (CFMS), online cause lists, and video conferencing, have been achieved, others have not. For example, according to the Annual Report of SCP 2015–16, the CFMS became fully functional in the main registry of SCP in Islamabad and the branch registry of SCP in four provinces of Pakistan in 2015–16.[51] CFMS enables lawyers, litigants, and judges to see the status of cases, upcoming hearing dates and case history. All the branch registries have been connected to the central database, providing all registries access to the primary data repository and helping the main registry stay informed about the filing status of fresh cases in branch registries.[52]

Many higher and district courts in Pakistan have incorporated IT, and implemented CFMS and video conferencing technology for virtual hearings, enabling litigants and their counsels to appear in court from provincial branches.[53] However, not all district courts have their own websites, and those that do are not currently connected through a centralized online system. Litigants cannot connect to hearings from their houses or workplaces. Additionally, video conferencing facilities are not available equally to all litigants. The SCP has developed standard operating procedures (SOPs) that have laid down eligibility criteria for the provision of this facility.[54] These requirements include

[49] Asma Hamid, 'The Case of Smart Courts: Digital Transformation of Courts in Pakistan' (*RIAA Barker Gillette*, 15 April 2020) 1 <www.riaabarkergillette.com/pk/wp-content/uploads/2020/04/The-Case-for-Smart-Courts-RIAA-Barker-Gillette-PK.pdf> last accessed 24 September 2024.

[50] National Judicial (Policy Making) Committee, National Judicial Policy 2009 (rev edn, 2012) 45–46 <www.supremecourt.gov.pk/downloads_judgements/all_downloads/National_Judicial_Policy/NJP2009.pdf> last accessed 24 September 2024.

[51] Supreme Court of Pakistan, 'Annual Report June 2015–May 2016' (2016) 114 <www.supremecourt.gov.pk/downloads_judgements/all_downloads/annual_reports/SCP_Annual_Report_2015_2016_.pdf> last accessed 19 August 2024.

[52] ibid.

[53] The Peshawar High Court launched video conferencing in 2018. See Peshawar High Court, 'PHC Launches Video Conferencing Technology' (21 December 2018) <https://peshawarhighcourt.gov.pk/image_bank/Orders/Zoom%20Meeting%2021122018.pdf> last accessed 24 September 2024; see also Sindh High Court, 'SHC Launches Video Conference Facility for Litigants and Lawyers' (27 May 2023) <www.thenews.com.pk/print/1074221-shc-launches-videoconference-facility-for-litigants-and-lawyers> last accessed 19 August 2024.

[54] Supreme Court of Pakistan, 'Standard Operating Procedure (SOP) for Video Link Facility' (2024) www.supremecourt.gov.pk/downloads_judgements/press_release/SOPs_for_Video_Link_Request.pdf last accessed 24 September 2024.

the litigants filling out a video link form, sending a formal application/request to avail themselves of the video link facility to the office of the Deputy Registrar (Judicial) at least two days before the commencement of the hearing of the case and explaining sufficient, and valid/genuine and justifiable ground to avail access to the facility.[55] The High Court of Sindh has developed similar SOPs.[56]

Courts have set up information booths, conducted electronic indexing and e-filing, and provided access to legal information. For example, the Peshawar High Court has started communicating directly with litigants via SMS and email,[57] and the writ branch of the court seems to be sharing scanned copies of entire files with the parties concerned. A separate mobile number for the principal staff officer is also available on its website,[58] in addition to mechanisms for uploading case statuses[59] and cause lists[60] and checking court activities, judges' details,[61] and the court's organizational system.

The High Court of Sindh has launched a mobile application that provides litigants and lawyers access to the judicial system, developed an online system for submitting bail bonds and paying fines and fees and initiated a pilot project called eNotice. This project aims to replace traditional paper notices with electronic notices for litigants and lawyers through mobile phones or computers.[62] However, eNotice has not been fully implemented.

While the SCP and provincial high courts have organized some data by categorizing and classifying them into various categories within CFMS, this has been done in isolation or on different scales by separate courts and bodies. For example, these websites classify data by year, type of case, judge's name, and date.[63] However, they only provide data on cases that the judge of a particular court considers important, which is not a good professional practice. Furthermore, the categories are incomplete, as they do not include information about the petitioners and respondents, their backgrounds, the parties involved in the cases, and the number of hearings conducted for a case.

Following the footsteps of the higher judiciary, the district judiciary in Pakistan also moved towards providing online services.[64] Yet, most have not established online portals and do not match the pace of provincial high courts in IT use. Neither the high courts nor the district-level judiciary has progressed beyond email notifications

[55] ibid.

[56] Sindh High Court, 'Standard Operating Procedure (SOP) for Video Link Facility' (6 June 2023) <https://sindhhighcourt.gov.pk/news_notifications/source_files/Circular_SOP_VideoLink.pdf> last accessed 24 September 2024.

[57] 'Peshawar High Court' www.peshawarhighcourt.gov.pk last accessed 24 September 2024.

[58] ibid.

[59] Peshawar High Court, 'Sitting Judges in Peshawar High Court' (2024) <https://peshawarhighcourt.gov.pk/app/site/35/c/Sitting_Judges.html> last accessed 24 September 2024.

[60] Peshawar High Court, 'Current Causelist' (2024) <https://peshawarhighcourt.gov.pk/app/site/18/p/Current_Causelist.html> last accessed 24 September 2024.

[61] Peshawar High Court (n 59).

[62] Marvi Qazi, 'Infusing Digital Technology in Judicial Operations in Pakistan: A Critical Analysis of Global Best Practices and Local Initiatives' (11 April 2023) 4 <https://papers.ssrn.com/sol3/papers.cfm?abstract_id = 4378378> last accessed 24 September 2024.

[63] Peshawar High Court, 'Judgement Management System' < https://peshawarhighcourt.gov.pk/PHCCMS/reportedJudgments.php> last accessed 5 June 2025.

[64] District and Sessions Courts Peshawar https://sessionscourtpeshawar.gov.pk/public/app last accessed 19 June 2025; Swat District Courts <https://dsjswat.gov.pk/> last accessed 19 June 2025.

to citizens or uploading cause lists of cases, case statuses[65], important judgments, and judges' profiles[66].

Nonetheless, the Pakistani government took different initiatives to advance the digitalization of the justice system. It launched the 'E-Court Project' in 2019, followed by the implementation of online case hearings in high courts and district courts. The SCP started conducting online hearings of cases with judges sitting at the principal seat of the court situated in Islamabad and lawyers arguing from the Supreme Court branch registry in Karachi through video link from May 2019 onwards.[67] Recently, the court started the live coverage of SCP proceedings.[68]

A significant change in the use of online technology was seen during the COVID-19 pandemic. Some courts, such as the Islamabad High Court and the SCP, used technology during their proceedings. Infected judges conducted proceedings remotely from home to prevent the spread of COVID-19.[69] Similarly, witness statements were submitted, and counsels' arguments were recorded via video links. These practices extended to other provincial high courts and continued after the COVID-19 pandemic.[70] Such developments increased litigants' access to provincial high courts and the SCP and decreased inconvenience.

In November 2023, the Chief Justice of Pakistan reconstituted the National Judicial Automation Committee (NJAC), which, although it existed before, was not very active. NJAC is a sub-committee of the National Judicial Policy Making Committee of Pakistan (NJPMC).[71] The Judicial Commission of Pakistan acts as the secretariat of NJPMC. NJAC aims to automate and integrate the judiciary and introduce AI in the legal process and research.[72] The committee seeks to develop a national plan for using technology and AI in legal processes, work towards digitalizing the court's processes and records and introduce mobile applications to enhance access to justice. However, at the time of writing, the committee did not specify the steps to materialize the plan or discuss the nature and scope of the advancement of digitalization of courts in Pakistan.

The initiatives mentioned above only provided plans. Most of these plans (eg CFMS and mobile applications) focus on implementing previously introduced initiatives but do not envisage the advancement of digitalization of justice system. These plans do not involve steps leading to the establishment of online small claim courts similar to

[65] Ibid.

[66] Ibid.

[67] Supreme Court of Pakistan, 'E-Court System Successfully Launched in Supreme Court' (2024) <www.supremecourt.gov.pk/e-court-system-successfully-launched-in-supreme-court/> last accessed 13 August 2024.

[68] Asif Shahzad, 'Pakistan's Top Court Proceedings Shown Live on TV for the First Time' (*Reuters*, 18 September 2023) <www.reuters.com/world/asia-pacific/pakistans-top-court-proceedings-shown-live-tv-first-time-2023-09-18/> last accessed 24 September 2024. Live coverage is not a regular practice.

[69] Saqib Bashir, 'Judge Hears Cases Online from Quarantine' (*The Express Tribune,* 2 December 2020) <https://tribune.com.pk/story/2274308/judge-hears-cases-online-from-quarantine> last accessed 24 September 2024.

[70] Hasnaat Malik, 'The Case for Online Hearings' (*The Express Tribune,*11 April 2021) < https://tribune.com.pk/story/2294089/the-case-for-online-hearings > last accessed 20 June 2025

[71] Press Information Department, 'Digitalization of the Judiciary in Pakistan' (17 November 2023) https://pid.gov.pk/site/press_detail/23936 accessed 24 September 2024.

[72] ibid.

those in England or as discussed in Canada with the Civil Resolution Tribunal. Online submission of claims related to divorce or small claims is not available on any website of the lower judiciary. Additionally, high courts or the SCP do not accept online submissions of cases and applications. The focus is more on CFMS, such as uploading the status of submitted claims on court websites, and information management, including categorizing cases by year and area of law (eg, civil petitions or constitutional petitions). This is a repetition of long-term measures envisaged in the National Judicial Policy of 2009.[73]

The digitalization of courts in Pakistan is not progressing at the same pace as in the examples of developed countries discussed above. In view of the crushing number of pending cases, the Pakistani justice system needs rapid advancement of digitalization that can go beyond uploading the online status of pending cases, decisions, applications for copies of order sheets, and other court activities to courts' websites. Pakistan's justice system can borrow good digitalization practices from foreign countries to advance digitalization and process and decide cases quickly. However, the country faces several challenges and requires reforms, which are discussed in the next section.

D. Challenges and Proposals for a further Digitalization of the Pakistani Justice System

This section examines the various challenges facing the digitalization of the Pakistani justice system and proposes steps to address them. These challenges include, but are not limited to, the lack of a legal framework, limited funding, the absence of mechanisms for data organization and sharing, the need for an integrated data portal for the entire legal system, the lack of software to assist judges in decision-making, unstable and insecure internet connectivity, and the absence of litigation officers and skilled workforce within organizations. These challenges hinder the advancement of digitalization of the justice system in countries like Pakistan.

1. Institutionalization

The main challenge in advancing the digitalization of the Pakistani justice system is the absence of a legal framework. Any degree of advancement in the digitalization of the justice system is not sustainable without a legal framework. Currently, the nature and scope of digitalization of courts are not specified in laws related to legal processes (eg The Code of Civil Procedure (CPC), 1908[74] and Criminal Procedure Code, 1898[75]). Terms such as 'e-filing', 'e-hearing', 'e-records', and 'e-certification' are not present in the civil procedure code or criminal procedure code. Moreover, any special

[73] National Judicial (Policy Making) Committee (n 50)

[74] Ministry of Law and Justice, 'The Pakistan Code' <https://pakistancode.gov.pk/english/UY2FqaJw1-apaUY2Fqa-apeb-sg-jjjjjjjjjjjj> last accessed 14 June 2025

[75] Ministry of Law and Justice, 'The Pakistan Code' <https://pakistancode.gov.pk/english/UY2FqaJw1-apaUY2Fqa-apaUY2Npa5lp-sg-jjjjjjjjjjjj> last accessed 14 June 2025

statutes do not provide for the online submission of claims and their processing, rendering digitalization unprotected. The government and other stakeholders, such as judges, lawyers, and litigants, are not obliged to take steps towards the advancement of digitalization of justice system. Litigants cannot initiate any proceedings under the relevant provisions of the law to compel the government to automate the administration of courts.

Furthermore, alternate dispute resolutions are crucial for resolving disputes and controlling caseloads. Different laws regulate face-to-face dispute resolution in various provinces of Pakistan, such as the Alternate Dispute Resolution Act 2017,[76] Punjab Alternate Dispute Resolution Act 2020,[77] and Khyber Pakhtunkhwa Alternate Dispute Resolution Act 2020.[78] However, formal dispute resolution is not popular because people resolve disputes informally through social institutions.[79] Additionally, these laws do not provide for ODR, and there is currently no legislation or set of rules providing for ODR in Pakistan .[80]

The digitalization of the justice system can be vulnerable to data protection breaches without robust data security measures. These measures must include data storage, organization, and management in compliance with relevant laws, such as the UK Data Protection Act 2018.[81] Pakistan does not have any legislation that particularly regulates matters concerning the processing of personal data. The Prevention of Electronic Crimes Act 2016[82] is the only legislation that deals with electronic crimes and unauthorized access to personal data. However, it must protect data to develop people's trust in its legal system. People will not be comfortable with any advancement of digitalization if they are worried about the misuse of their data.

A way to address the above challenge is to introduce special laws that ensure data protection and data management and to include definitions of 'e-filing', 'e-hearing', 'e-records', and 'e-certification' in CPC 1908 [Pakistan]. In this regard, amendments may be required to various provisions of the CPC 1908. These provisions involve processes including but not limited to written service of orders and notices,[83] postage,[84] appearance of parties in civil courts through recognized agents or pleaders,[85] service

[76] Alternative Dispute Resolution Act 2017 [Pakistan] <www.na.gov.pk/uploads/documents/1495101925_486.pdf> last accessed 24 September 2024.

[77] Punjab Alternative Dispute Resolution Act 2019 [Pakistan] <http://punjablaws.gov.pk/laws/2739.html> last accessed 24 September 2024.

[78] Alternate Dispute Resolution Act 2020 [Pakistan], Government of Khyber Pakhtunkhwa, act no. XLVIII of 2020 <https://kp.gov.pk/uploads/2021/11/alternate-dispute-relolution-act-2020-XLVIII-GAZATTEED.pdf> last accessed 24 September 2024.

[79] See Naveed Ahmad Shinwari, 'Understanding the Informal Justice System: Opportunities and Possibilities for Legal Pluralism in Pakistan' (Community Appraisal & Motivation Programme 2015) <https://fid4sa-repository.ub.uni-heidelberg.de/3795/1/UnderstandingtheInformalJusticeSystem.pdf> last accessed 24 September 2024.

[80] Iqra Bano Sohail, 'Expediting Justice Through Online Dispute Resolution' (*The Express Tribune*, 23 March 2024) <https://tribune.com.pk/story/2460214/expediting-justice-through-online-dispute-resolution> last accessed 24 September 2024.

[81] See The Data Protection Act, <https://www.gov.uk/data-protection> last accessed 22 November 2024. The act controls how organizations, government, and businesses use personal information in UK.

[82] Prevention of Electronic Crimes Act 2016 [Pakistan] (*The Gazette of Pakistan*, 22 August 2016) <www.dataguidance.com/sites/default/files/pak104952.pdf> last accessed 24 September 2024.

[83] S. 142 of the CPC 1908.

[84] S. 143 of the CPC 1908.

[85] Order III Rule 1 of the CPC 1908..

of process by pleaders,[86] and agents,[87] acceptance of service by agents,[88] institution of suits,[89] framing of issues,[90] material propositions,[91] appearance of parties and the consequences of non-appearance,[92] examination of parties by the civil court,[93] summoning and attendance of witnesses,[94] payments into the civil court,[95] the commission to examine witnesses,[96] suits involving the government or public officers,[97] suits involving corporations,[98] suits involving firms,[99] the power to state cases for obtaining a court opinion,[100] summary procedures for negotiable instruments,[101] temporary injunctions and interlocutory orders,[102] referral of questions to the provincial high court,[103] miscellaneous matters,[104] and appeals to the SCP.[105] Similarly, amendments may be required to the Supreme Court Rules 1980,[106] the rules of each high court, and law of evidence in general,[107] particularly with respect to rules regarding the notice to produce,[108] the order of the production and examination of witnesses,[109] and the admissibility of evidence obtained through modern devices.[110] The aforementioned laws pertaining to dispute resolution need to be amended to incorporate provisions for ODR.

However, introducing new laws and amending existing ones cannot be effectively enforced without adequate funding. New laws create a demand for additional human and financial resources to ensure proper implementation. Without sufficient funding for online portals, new software, internet security measures, salaries for dedicated litigation officers, training programs, and skilled labor for data organization and sharing, as well as other online tools that are discussed below, the government of Pakistan will face significant challenges in implementing any proposals for the digitalization of its justice system. The challenge of inadequate funding is discussed in the next section.

[86] Order III Rule 5 of the CPC 1908.
[87] Order III Rule 3 of the CPC 1908.
[88] Order III Rule 6 of the CPC 1908.
[89] Order IV of the CPC 1908.
[90] Order IV Rule 1 of the CPC 1908..
[91] Order IV Rule 1 of the CPC 1908.
[92] Order IX of the CPC 1908.
[93] Order X of the CPC 1908.
[94] Order XVI of the CPC 1908.
[95] Order XXIV of the CPC 1908.
[96] Order XXVI of the CPC 1908.
[97] Order XXVII of the CPC 1908.
[98] Order XXIX of the CPC 1908.
[99] Order XXX of the CPC 1908..
[100] Order XXXVI of the CPC 1908.
[101] Order XXXVII of the CPC 1908.
[102] Order XXXIX of the CPC 1908..
[103] Order XLVI of the CPC 1908.
[104] Order XLVIII of the CPC 1908..
[105] Order XLV of the CPC 1908.
[106] Supreme Court of Pakistan, Supreme Court Rules 1980 (last amended 11 November 2017).
[107] Qanun-e-Shahadat Order 1984 [Pakistan], https://khalidzafar.com/wp-content/files_mf/1527158791QanuneShahadatOrder1984.pdf last accessed 19 December 2024.
[108] ibid art 77.
[109] ibid art 130.
[110] ibid art 164.

2. Funding

Innovation has its costs. The digitalization of the justice system is continuous and may incur huge costs. The concerned government of Pakistan, either provincial or federal, may not provide sufficient resources to hire more judges, ministerial staff and experts to train judges and staff.[111] Litigants may not have personal computers, tablets, or access to efficient internet, which are required to use online judicial services. The first-ever digital development index report in 2024 revealed that over half of Pakistan's population does not have access to the internet.[112] Providing litigants laptops or tablets on loan and creating online training videos about using the system may incur additional costs, which leads to another challenge of litigants' lack of knowledge about how judicial services are accessed online through electronic equipment.

Asian Development Bank (ADB) approved a 350 million USD package for Pakistan's Access to Justice Program in 2002.[113] Of this package, 24.76 million USD [114] were allocated to automating procedures in the country's justice system.[115] 'Automation of Federal Court and Tribunals' and 'National Judicial Automation Unit' are ongoing schemes of the Ministry of Law and Justice under the Public Sector Development Program in the annual budgets of the fiscal years 2023–24[116] and 2024–25.[117] The government allocated 5.71 million USD [118] in the annual budget 2023–24 and 5.1 million USD [119] in 2024–25 for the automation of federal courts/tribunals. The allocated amount is insufficient to introduce tools similar to those in technologically advanced countries and achieve the proposals discussed later in this chapter.

It is recommended that the government fund these required changes, including the hiring of dedicated litigation officers for departments that do not have one, maintaining technical staff to manage software and technical equipment, paying additional skilled staff to convert the current data electronically and organize the data, and providing general training to everyone in the government.[120] The interconnected challenges can be addressed by increasing funds for courts and tribunals to loan electronic equipment to litigants and run awareness programmes on online services.

111 Saima Tabassum et al, 'Evaluating the Impact of Strength of Judges on Dispensation of Justice in District Judiciary of Pakistan' (2021) 12 Int J Mgmt 266.

112 Ikram Junaidi, 'Over Half of Pakistan Does Not Have Access to Internet' (*Dawn*, 24 April 2024) <www.dawn.com/news/1829281> last accessed 24 September 2024.

113 Hamid (n 49).

114 This equals to 1,479 million Pakistani rupees @ 1 US Dollar = 59.72 Pakistani Rupees in 2002. See <https://fx.sauder.ubc.ca/etc/USDpages.pdf> last accessed for US Dollar to Pakistani Rupees conversion.

115 ibid.

116 Government of Pakistan, 'Public Sector Development Program 2023–24' (June 2023) <www.pc.gov.pk/uploads/archives/PSDP_2023-24.pdf> last accessed 24 September 2024.

117 Recorder Report, 'Ministry of Law and Justice: Rs1368.874m Earmarked for Development Schemes in PSDP' (*Business Recorder*, 13 June 2024) <www.brecorder.com/news/40308201> last accessed 24 September 2024.

118 This equals to 160 million Pakistani Rupees @ 1 US Dollar = 280 Pakistani Rupees in 2024. See <https://fx.sauder.ubc.ca/etc/USDpages.pdf> for US Dollar to Pakistani Rupees conversion.

119 This equals to 143 million Pakistan rupees @ 1 US Dollar = 278.31 Pakistani Rupees in 2024. See <https://fx.sauder.ubc.ca/etc/USDpages.pdf> for US Dollar to Pakistani Rupees conversion

120 These changes are discussed in greater detail later in this chapter.

The government can arrange funding by increasing allocated budgets in its annual budget or opening the project to national and international bidders. After examining and verifying their documents, the government can call for expressions of interest and invite interested parties to explain their road maps and invest further. Alternatively, the government can borrow money to finance the project.

Adequate funding is essential for the feasibility of any project, but fundamental steps are necessary to implement it effectively and make the most of the available resources. Any process of digitalization requires organized data and mechanisms to share that data across governmental organizations. This will enable all stakeholders to make digitalization accessible to the general public and achieve what is currently feasible in the digitalization process. The challenge of the lack of data organization and sharing is discussed in the next section.

3. Data organization and sharing

As the funds are insufficient to advance the justice system's digitalization, making the most of available funds and prioritizing the investment on key developments are equally important. A digital system cannot retrieve and process data and implement machine instructions if the data are unorganized. Data organization is an important aspect of any advancement of digitalization in the justice system, and data in Pakistan is currently neither complete nor accurate,[121] let alone organized, properly categorized, analyzed, or tagged.[122] Pakistan inherited a colonial state that deals with official communications mainly through documents and bureaucracy. Most data are still collected and maintained through written documents and are unavailable in electronic form. However, processing data on paper is challenging for digitalization. Introducing online tools and initiating training programmes cannot be effective without data organization and sharing.

Further, the digitalization process cannot advance quickly if data are not shared across government departments, courts at various levels, the National Database Registration Authority (NADRA) and different databases in an online network. This networking can facilitate information sharing, processing and authentication during legal processes.

Nonetheless, the Pakistani government has developed important databases comprising organized data. NADRA works under the Ministry of Interior and has personal data (names, family trees and marital statuses) about all citizens and registered residents. NADRA is connected to mobile companies and banks. Details of mobile service users and bank account holders are electronically verified with NADRA at the

[121] For details on the challenges of data collection in Pakistan see Asad Elahi, 'Challenges of Data Collection: with Special Regard to Developing Countries' https://www.pbs.gov.pk/sites/default/files/other/documents/Elahi%20Article%20-%20For%20FBS%20Homepage.pdf last accessed 18 December 2024.

[122] For details on unclear presentation of judicial data see Naadia Khadam, Saadia Zahoor, Sana Taha Gondal, and Salvat Kainat Tatari, 'Analytical Framework for Judicial Data Collection in Pakistan' (2019) 16 (2) Policy Perspectives 87–105 <https://www.jstor.org/stable/10.13169/polipers.16.2.0087> last accessed 20 December 2024.

time of mobile service[123] and bank account registration.[124] However, NADRA is not yet connected to the online system courts use.

Additionally, a nationwide computerized land record system based on a geographic information mechanism and subsequent court connection is unavailable. Most cases before the civil courts involve land disputes, and although steps towards the computerization of land records have been taken,[125] they are still administered using pre-colonial and colonial paper systems. The government has failed to achieve complete computerization.

If a computerized land record database is electronically connected to courts, the courts can retrieve information about disputed properties, including land, from this system. Computerized land records will show the status of a property and the steps required in connection to a court's decisions on a disputed property. Currently, court orders are sometimes not implemented for several years, leading to additional petitions for contempt of court and taking up more of the concerned courts' time. Connecting computerized land records to courts electronically will compel individuals and government departments to comply with judgments more promptly, as courts will be able to monitor the enforcement of their decisions online.

Pakistan also lacks a nationwide criminal record database, like the absence of computerized land records. England has a criminal database called the Police National Computer (PNC).[126] The PNC is a centralized system managed by the Home Office and used by the police and other law enforcement agencies across the UK. The absence of a nationwide criminal record database in Pakistan is another challenge in advancing the digitalization of the justice system. Pakistan has only established a forensic laboratory with a limited capacity to assess submitted evidence in the province of Punjab.[127]

Consequently, the state and the people depend on departments such as the prosecution and the police for information. Crimes are reported directly to the police stations, which register them mostly in print form. The records are kept at the stations, so the only way to verify information is to contact them.

If a case reaches the trial stage, the police station submits its report to the session court and the Department of Prosecution via a designated officer, who verifies the report and records statements before the court, if required over several hearings.[128]

[123] Khurram Ali Mehran, 'New System for Activation of SIM Launched' (Pakistan Telecommunication Authority, 1 February 2009) <www.pta.gov.pk/category/new-system-for-activation-of-sim-launched-343760439-2023-06-01> last accessed 24 September 2024.

[124] Khalid Hameed Shah, 'Biometric Verification for Banks Account Opening' (*Kiosk Solutions*, 2024) <www.kiosksolutions.com.pk/docs/Opening-of-Bank-Account.pdf> last accessed 24 September 2024.

[125] Muhammed Usman Qazi, 'Computerisation of Land Records in Pakistan: A Comparative Analysis of Two Projects from a Human Security Perspective' (*VNU*, 2006) <http://danida.vnu.edu.vn/cpis/files/Papers_on_CC/PIS/1.pdf> last accessed 19 April 2024.

[126] <https://hmicfrs.justiceinspectorates.gov.uk/glossary/police-national-computer/> last accessed 18 June 2025.>

[127] 'Punjab Forensic Science Agency' <https://pfsa.punjab.gov.pk/> last accessed 29 September 2024.

[128] For details on prosecution in Pakistan see Zubair Ahmad Ijaz, Shahzada Aamir Mushtaq, Allah Raaka, Asma Jabeen Khan and Shabnam Shahab, 'The Evolving Role of Prosecution in Pakistan's Criminal Justice System' (2024) The Critical Review of Social Sciences Studies 2(2) 210-229 < https://pdfs.semanticscholar.org/5287/027d009add485a2f42ea2a110a08fa2a4014.pdf> last accessed 21 June 2025

With a nationwide criminal database, the departments involved in criminal investigations can access information and communicate with each other quickly, preventing several hearings and delays during criminal proceedings.

Collecting accurate data, converting it into electronic form, and organizing it are the first steps toward implementing the digitization of the Pakistani justice system. I recommend that the government must electronically record and organize accurate data on individuals and cases from different departments for any online tools to achieve the desired results, and data from various government departments and courts should be better organized. All government departments and private organizations must collect personal data about the people working in their departments (e.g. name, date of birth, gender, domicile, and email address) and their activities. They must establish data organization and management and infrastructure mechanisms to classify the data under different categories and tags, such as date, time, place, nature of the case, statute, and statute sections.

Second, an exhaustive database of all previous decisions of the SCP and high courts should be established separately or within an integrated hub. If established independently, it must be connected to an integrated online hub (discussed below). These decisions must be codified according to multiple parameters, such as:

- Articles and statutes on which the decisions were based
- Legal principles and dictations laid down by the court in similar cases concerning either the:
    - o similar nature of the parties
    - o similar nature of the precedents quoted in the original petition
- Questions of law on which similar decisions were consistently made
- A general categorization, such as service cases, bail cases/criminal petitions, and possession of property cases
- The identities of the parties (for example, some government departments or bodies are often defendants, so their categorization is also necessary).

Pakistanlawsite.com[129] has developed a similar database where data is organized using the above parameters, but complete data has not been uploaded on the website. If one enters a statute or constitution section or specifies the court, a result is provided, but it is not always relevant, accurate and complete. Hence, the database needs further development and integration into the hub, as discussed below.

If public, private, and semi-government organizations are initially organizing data, data-sharing arrangements should be in place using an integrated hub to notify any

[129] Pakistanlawsite.com <www.pakistanlawsite.com> last accessed 24 September 2024. This website houses all the federal and provincial statutes and cases, including (but not limited to) taxation, service, copyright, state planning and labour laws. In addition, it covers all kinds of fiscal statutes and contains around 1,200 essays and other legal documents. It also contains all the journals published by Pakistan Legal Documents Publishers (All Pakistan Legal Decisions, Supreme Court Monthly Review, Civil Law Cases, Pakistan Criminal Law Journal, Pakistan Tax Decision, Pakistan Labour Cases, Corporate Law Decisions, Yearly Law Reporter, and Gilgit-Baltistan Law Reports).

individual or organization about a claim submission. If the claimant enters a name or address, the system can automatically record an individual's email and send a notice to the corresponding email address. This is discussed in the next section.

4. Integrated data portal for the entire legal system

The creation of databases alone is not sufficient to advance the digitalization of the justice system if they are not integrated into the online systems that Pakistani courts use. No integrated online portal exists in Pakistan that could connect all tiers of courts to all government departments or at least those with current databases available. Although provincial high courts and the SCP have CFMS functional on their websites, this only gives information about the previous and current status of cases and the next hearing fixed in that case. This does not enable litigants to submit their claims online and receive court instructions or allow courts to verify the details of litigants and the documents they submit to authorities issuing them. Courts have to conduct several hearings to wait for the responses, which could verify submissions and details submitted by the parties involved.

Like the English Common Platform,[130] Pakistan must create an integrated web portal or online hub for the judicial system. This portal must connect all tiers of the judiciary, including civil judges' courts, the judicial magistrate, and the SCP, to share data on cases that reach appellate jurisdiction or are remanded to the lower judiciary. It can also facilitate the communication of instructions and a consistent pattern of decision-making based on precedents. For example, the lower judiciary could utilize the latest decisions received through the integrated online hub in their rulings on relevant issues.

However, currently, only provincial high courts and SCP have websites that provide CFMS, while most district courts lack online portals and do not offer CFMS. Separate portals for the lower judiciary, provincial high courts, and SCP must be established before they can be interconnected through a unified portal. Litigants should be able to go directly to the relevant court's website and fill out forms, making the system user-friendly. Step-by-step online forms for small claims in some areas (eg divorce and damages) can be established, allowing the courts at different tiers to retain their autonomy.

However, in the end, machines only do what humans instruct them to do. Any online system requires clear instructions and commands from its creators to deliver the desired services to its users. These instructions and commands are embedded in software. The absence of appropriate software is a significant challenge to advancing the digitalization of the Pakistani justice system.

[130] HM Courts and Tribunals Service, 'Fact Sheet: Common Platform' (*GOV.UK*, 7 March 2024) www.gov.uk/government/publications/hmcts-reform-crime-fact-sheets/fact-sheet-common-platform last accessed 24 September 2024.

5. Software

A software able to run an integrated online portal and capable of receiving, storing, and processing electronic versions of claims and evidence and communicating with litigants and their counsels is not available in Pakistan. Pakistani courts have developed software to support CFMS and have not gone beyond that.

Various software applications are available in the market to assist decision-making. For example, Casedoc is a comprehensive, end-to-end court and justice software solution that helps legal bodies worldwide automate processes, monitor case activity and support decision-making.[131] Likewise, HM Courts and Tribunals Service has invested £6 million in developing software to combine scheduling and listing activities into a single tool as part of their over £1 billion reform programme.[132]

> Specific software that can present questions to litigants, assign tags, categorize submissions into different case types and retrieve data based on those tags and categorizations is required to run an online data hub, which might be difficult and costly to develop. Although Pakistan might not be in a position to develop this initiative, it might not need to create something from scratch, as systems with similar features working in different areas of governance are already available in the country and only need an upgrade. Notably, Pakistan Citizen Portal (PCP)[133] is a government-owned mobile application developed by the Prime Minister's Performance Delivery Unit and the National Information Technology Board.[134] It functions as a citizen-centric governance tool, enabling individuals to raise complaints, seek redressals, and provide suggestions to government authorities. Citizens can register on PCP using their mobile numbers and computerized national identity card numbers, submit grievances, and track their status through regular updates. To date, the platform has 4,033,290 registered users,[135] with 4,933,260 complaints submitted and 4,821,392 resolved.[136] Similar to PCP, the Pakistan Law Site[137] has tags and filters that, when activated, categorize submissions into different case types and provide data based on them. However, these systems work independently of online tools courts use for case management. The government may need to upgrade the features of the Pakistan Law Site, PCP, and the online systems currently used by courts, and integrate them into the proposed software.

[131] GoPro Consulting Ltd, 'Casedoc Court and Justice: Cloud Software Service' (*GOV.UK Digital Marketplace*) <www.applytosupply.digitalmarketplace.service.gov.uk/g-cloud/services/841557749624373> last accessed 24 September 2024.

[132] HM Courts and Tribunals Service, 'Investment of Up to £6m in New Listing Technology to Benefit Courts Users' (*GOV.UK*, 4 June 2020) <www.gov.uk/government/news/investment-of-up-to-6m-in-new-listing-technology-to-benefit-court-users> last accessed 24 September 2024.

[133] Prime Minister's Performance Delivery Unit, 'Pakistan Citizen's Portal: PCP' <https://citizenportal.gov.pk/> last accessed 24 September 2024.

[134] 'The National Information Technology Board' <www.nitb.gov.pk/> last accessed 24 September 2024.

[135] Prime Minister's Performance Delivery Unit (n 133).

[136] ibid.

[137] Pakistanlawsite.com (n 129).

By upgrading and integrating them into the proposed software, the integrated online hub would be able to provide extra services to its users. Claimants could register themselves on the integrated online hub and the software. Users could submit through the online system proposed above a) the claim, including their details and the nature of the dispute and the relevant laws and articles under which they are asking for remedy or relief; b) facts, c) grounds and d) arguments. These should be stored and linked to the previous judgments database (eg Pakistan Law Site). Relevant precedents retrieved from the Pakistan Law Site, connected to this hub, should appear for the knowledge of all concerned, and they could click any of the list of precedents if they wish to rely on them. This can be achieved by developing the PCP and Pakistan Law Site databases and connecting them to the integrated online hub through the proposed software.

The online form will have different categories to accommodate the relevant information, with every field having an option to upload evidence. Spaces for other details, such as the opposing party's name, address, contact number, and email address, will be included. If the opposing party is the government[138] or a government-affiliated body, then the address of the concerned litigation officer will already be in the stored list and can be selected by the claimant.

If the opposing party is a private individual or organization, then their basic data, such as their full name, address recorded in the NADRA[139] and subscriber identity module cards registered in their name, must be provided so that the system can automatically retrieve data from other organizations' databases under previous data sharing arrangements.

Once the online form is uploaded, the litigant can pay the court fee online using a credit or debit card. As soon as the submit button is clicked, an automatic reference number will be generated, with the names of all concerned parties and an option to include additional relevant persons in the future.

After submitting the documents and court fee, the judge and opposite parties should automatically receive emails and SMS. A separate notice regarding the relevant laws will be sent to the defendant's email address, the defendant's legal counsel and the section of the court that deals with the serving of notices, preventing a traditional cause of delay: failure to serve notice.

The defendant will have 15 working days to register if they have not already registered and can enter the reference number to access the case details in the hub. They can appoint their legal representative to submit a reply to the claimant or a claim similar to the claimants with an online form that allows them to record counter arguments and upload evidence. Laws relevant to their request for action can be selected from the items stored in the hub to draw out precedents from the database of judgments. When the defendant clicks the submit button, the claimant's legal representatives and the judge will receive the response.

Once the concerned parties upload the arguments, evidence, precedents, and other submissions and have examined the available material, they will be given 15–30 days

[138] As in England, parties in Pakistan can appear before tribunals without a lawyer, making this system more suitable for such a model.

[139] National Database and Registration Authority <www.nadra.gov.pk/> last accessed 24 September 2024.

to upload additional materials or record further explanations that they believe will strengthen their case. The uploaded information will be shared with the other parties, who can file replies and record more information and evidence. All concerned parties, along with their authorized legal representatives, will be able to view these developments and download files relevant to the case.

In this way, the time and effort expended by the litigant to visit the court for admission of cases before arguments is decreased. The others will receive an email and SMS whenever any concerned make additions. After 15–30 days, the case will be locked for all except the judge. When everything has been uploaded, the judge needs to make a decision and notify that to parties. The software's instruction code should collect personal information through registration, receive litigants' plaints and petitions, retrieve relevant information from other organizations and the hub, issue notices to the parties' addresses entered in the online form and assist decision-making by providing precedents, arguments and evidence. If the judge needs further information or wishes to put a query to parties they could do through the system or can conduct an online hearing if needed. If any party raises an issue (eg, impersonation or evidence tampering) that requires an in-person hearing, a date for a physical appearance to present arguments and decide on that issue may be scheduled.

An email and SMS alert containing that date will automatically be sent to the concerned parties. When the parties check the portal, they will find an option to request a date earlier or later than the one fixed by the judge. Their reasons will be recorded and visible to all parties. The opposite party will have the opportunity to record their objections. On the day of the physical hearing, the parties can examine the online file prepared by the court using the online portal. After the arguments have been heard, the court will decide on the case and record its judgment on the portal.

Some studies found maintaining access to the justice system when the courts adopted technology during the COVID-19 pandemic was difficult.[140] Most cases in the lower courts involve due process problems under normal circumstances, as recording statements, cross-examinations, submission of evidence, and other phases usually take time. The registration process allows initial contact with the claimant but not the witnesses and other stakeholders. This problem can be solved a) if the claimant provides the basic details of the respondents/defendants and witnesses, such as their email addresses and telephone numbers, so that automatic emails and SMS can be delivered to them and b) by linking NADRA to the integrated hub. NADRA stores mobile numbers and other details during the renewal or issuance of a national identity card. The process can be changed slightly to record a few more applicant details, such

[140] Nuffield Family Justice Observatory, *Remote Hearings in the Family Justice System: A Rapid Consultation* (May 2020) 15 <www.nuffieldfjo.org.uk/resource/remote-hearings-rapid-consultation> last accessed 24 September 2024; see also Alicia Summers and Sophia Gatowski, *Nevada Court Improvement Program Remote Hearing Study* (2020) 9 <https://nevadacurrent.com/wp-content/uploads/2022/01/21-17924.pdf> last accessed 24 September 2024; California Commission on Access to Justice, *Remote Hearings and Access to Justice During COVID-19 and Beyond* (18 May 2020) 13–14 <www.ncjfcj.org/wp-content/uploads/2020/06/2020-Remote-Hearings-Guide.pdf> last accessed 24 September 2024; Pew Research Center, 'Internet, Broadband Fact Sheet' (31 January 2024) <www.pewresearch.org/internet/fact-sheet/internet-broadband/> last accessed 21 May 2024; Alicia L Bannon and Douglas Keith, 'Remote Court: Principles for Virtual Proceedings During the COVID-19 Pandemic and Beyond' (2021) 115 Northwestern U L Rev 1875, 1891.

as email address. The proposed software must include timers that require litigants to respond accordingly so that the system can generate results.

A nationwide integrated data portal and appropriate software will not enable the government of Pakistan to achieve optimal digitalization of its justice system if internet connectivity remains limited or unstable, and online systems are not secure. Stakeholders may lose trust in a digitalized system and refrain from using it. The challenges of limited or unstable internet connectivity and inadequate online security in Pakistan are discussed in the next section

6. Online connectivity and security issues

Pakistan has a poor track record of protection against cyberattacks. The SCP's website was hacked in 2011.[141] The Federal Board of Revenue operates Pakistan's largest data center and contains citizens' personal and tax data. However, this was also hacked in August 2021.[142] Additionally, a software glitch may corrupt the flow of code, and the whole digitalized justice system may crash, undermining trust in digital services. People may not trust an unsecured digital system and stop subscribing. The government of Pakistan will need to employ sophisticated programming codes for the software mentioned above and enhance online security measures, such as firewalls and antimalware mechanisms, to safeguard the online integrated hub from cyberattacks.

Furthermore, as discussed above, over half of Pakistan's population does not have access to the internet. Connection problems and delays in transmitting audio-visual (AV) data over the internet may also occur if the courts opt for live streaming, which occurred at the NSW Supreme Court.[143] Limited bandwidth can cause parties to turn off their videos, making them feel unheard and unseen when giving testimony.[144] The government of Pakistan can resolve connectivity issues and AV interruptions by increasing internet bandwidth and providing backup communication lines. Additionally, separate channels can be provided for the public to view court proceedings. This will require significant time and investment, but the government can implement it gradually in stages.

Although the proposed solutions may incur significant initial financial costs, including additional expenses for enhanced cybersecurity protocols, they will help prevent hackers from intruding on ongoing cases, corrupting case materials, and will stabilize the service. A free, fair, open and competitive tendering process can secure reasonable prices for online servers, software, and hardware from international bidders.

141 BBC, 'Pakistan Supreme Court Website Hacked' (*BBC News*, 27 September 2011) <www.bbc.co.uk/news/world-south-asia-15073132> last accessed 24 September 2024.

142 Shahbaz Rana, 'Neglect Caused FBR Cyber-Attack' (*The Express Tribune*, 22 August 2021) <https://tribune.com.pk/story/2316604/neglect-caused-fbr-cyber-attack> last accessed 24 September 2024.

143 Michael Legg, 'The COVID-19 Pandemic, the Courts and Online Hearings: Maintaining Open Justice, Procedural Fairness and Impartiality' (2021) 49 Federal L Rev 161.

144 Elizabeth G Thornburg, 'Observing Online Courts: Lessons from the Pandemic' (2020) SSRN Electronic Journal 193 <http://dx.doi.org/10.2139/ssrn.3696594> last accessed 24 September 2024

7. Appointment of litigation officers

Managing an integrated online portal (if established) would be challenging at first without a dedicated litigation officer in government departments. Every department and organization must have a dedicated litigation officer. A dedicated officer or focal person would be essential to access the portal, consult relevant authorities based on the information uploaded, gather responses and necessary documents, and submit the response on behalf of the department. As discussed above, this would require training of all individuals involved in digitalization.

The litigation officer should have a dedicated official email stored in the integrated online hub so that if any complaint or mention of a department's name is fed into the hub, the litigation officer will receive an automated email, after which there are several possible scenarios. First, a complaint can be lodged directly against the concerned department, and the litigation officer or assigned focal person can initiate the second stage. With the name of the department referred to by the complainant as a matter of evidence or a witness, the concerned litigation officer will verify the situation in the context of the parent department referred to by the claimant.

Second, the claim could rely on submitted documents, which an authority of that department will issue. The litigation officer of that department could communicate with the concerned authority to verify such documents and then upload them to the hub in the relevant section of an online form. A claimant can either mention the name of that organization in their statement of reliance on evidence from the organization or submit their claim against any government organization or autonomous body.

However, advancing the digitalization of the Pakistani justice system is not feasible without individuals possessing the necessary skills, such as data collection, organization, and management. Moreover, the implementation of the proposed measures would be ineffective if the intended beneficiaries of digitalization lack an understanding of how to use online tools and their importance. At present, many individuals involved in the Pakistani justice system have limited familiarity with technology and online tools.[145] This challenge is discussed in the next section.

8. Skilled workforce

As mentioned earlier, data must be available in electronic form to be processed by a digital system. However, collecting accurate data, converting it from print to electronic format, and organizing it will require skilled labour with the appropriate data management skills. The project may require recruiting extra staff to develop and expedite the process of an expedited thematic codification and categorization of decisions. Technical staff qualified to use and maintain this technology must be hired.

Additionally, although the courts have access to computers and electronic equipment, judges, lawyers, and professional support staff may have limited knowledge of online tools in the justice system.[146] This is not unique to Pakistan. It has been

145 Qazi (n 62) 5.
146 ibid.

argued that a limited understanding of digitalization prevented the UK public from harnessing the full potential of digitalization, thus impacting socio-economic inequality.[147] Limited IT skills of court staff and litigants and a lack of clear procedures made online prosecution in criminal proceedings in some countries, such as Indonesia, difficult.[148]

Any advancement in the digitalization of the justice system will require judges, lawyers, court staff, and litigants to improve their skills in using online tools and training from skilled instructors who charge for their time and service. The biggest challenges are helping litigants in Pakistan become familiar with the digitalization of the justice system and educating them about their potential.

This problem can be addressed in Pakistan with short- and long-term plans. In the short run, experts can hold training sessions at the Federal Judicial Academy (FJA) and provincial judicial academies. A contract between the software company and federal and provincial judicial academies should be made to train officers annually or when new judges are appointed. This will enhance the judges' familiarity, awareness, and knowledge about the technology and its optimum use before performing their court duties. In the long run, the Government of Pakistan could work closely with the Higher Education Commission of Pakistan and provincial governments to revise law college curricula, and the topic of digitalization of the justice system will be introduced, which will comprise practical training sessions.

As proposed in this chapter, advancing digitalization of Pakistani justice system will take time, and its complete implementation in some legal issues may not be possible. The online processing of data and evidence to reach a decision may be possible in civil cases but might not be feasible in criminal cases, where the examination of evidence and the recording of statements are standard procedures. The best way forward is to advance the digitalization of the justice system by first implementing the proposed measures in a specific area, such as small claims or family courts. Based on the results, these proposals can then be expanded to other fields of law or types of courts. Alternatively, one could follow Susskind's suggestion that the most feasible approach is to carefully initiate pilot projects, analyze their results, and gradually build and improve online justice systems based on the insights gained, rather than attempting to achieve completion in a single step.[149]

The above analysis offers insights into digitalization of justice systems in other low- and middle-income countries, such as Nigeria[150], Bangladesh[151], Sri

[147] Vanessa Long, 'Online Courts: Re-Assessing Inequality in the "Remote" Courtroom' (2021) 11 Excursions 77-102.

[148] Ardito Yudho Pratomo, Umar Ma'ruf, and Aryani Witasari, 'Implementation of Criminal Action Prosecution Online in Realizing Principle of Fast Prosecution, Simple and Low Cost' (2021) 4(2) Journal Daulat Hukum 132.

[149] Susskind (n 9) 109.

[150] See Olufunmilayo Arewa and Ayodeji Fakolade, 'Digitalization, Fragmentation, and Justice in Nigeria' in Markus Ludwigs, José Hernán Muriel Ciceri, Annika Velling, (eds.) *Digitalization as a Challenge for Justice and Administration* (Wurzberg University Press 2023) for details on the challenges facing the digitalization of the Nigerian justice system, which are similar to those discussed in this chapter.

[151] See the following for details on the challenges facing the digitalization of the justice system of Bangladesh, which are similar to those discussed in this chapter: Raisul Sourav, 'Bangladesh and the quest for a digitised judiciary' (The Daily Star 21 March 2025) <https://www.thedailystar.net/law-our-rights/news/bangladesh-and-the-quest-digitised-judiciary-3853801> last accessed 20 June 2025; Mohammad

Lanka[152], Egypt[153], Iraq[154], and Mexico[155]. These countries have different legal and political systems. Some are federal states with civil or common law systems, while others are unitary states with common law or hybrid (combination of civil and common law) systems. While some features of legal and political systems, such as court hierarchies in federal and unitary states, may differ others are broad patterns in every legal system. For example, a claimant has to apply to initiate proceedings against their opponent. The courts have to allow the opposite side to submit a response and defend itself. Stages such as evidence submission, cross-examination, and arguments exist in every legal system but have different formats and timeframes. Arguably, the challenges facing digitalization and steps involved in the process proposed in this chapter may not work in all legal and political contexts. However, they face similar challenges: large populations, unstable political, legal and economic systems, limited access to justice for minorities, massive case backlogs and decreasing public trust in the justice system. These challenges shape the context in which they need to introduce similar solutions some of which have been proposed above.

Therefore, the legal and political systems of low- and middle-income countries should not stop them from working on the proposals discussed in this chapter and

Ikbal Hasan and Fahmida Johura Rupa, 'Digitalization of Bangladesh Judiciary and Access to Justice' (2021) Asian Journal of Social Sciences and Legal Studies 3(3) 49-58. https://doi.org/10.34104/ajssls.021.049058

Muhammad Abu Taher and Siti Zaharan Jamaluddin, 'Enhancing access to justice through e-judiciary in Bangladesh: A study' (2022) UUM Journal of Legal Studies 13(2) 317-344 <https://doi.org/10.32890/uumjls2022.13.2.13> accessed 20 June 2025 for details on challenges facing digitalization of the Bangladeshi justice system which are similar to those discussed in this chapter.

152 See Parajwal Bhattarai and Sujit Kumar Chaudhary 'Digital Justice in Nepal: A South Asian perspective on Legal-Tech Reforms, Global Benchmarks and Transformative Policy Pathways' International Journal of Trends in Emerging Research and Development (2025) 3(2) 11-16 for comparison of digitalization of justice system of Nepal, Pakistan, India, Bangladesh, and Sri Lanka. Digitalization of justice system in these countries face similar challenges.

153 The Economic Court of Egypt is an exception, as it is more advanced in terms of digitalization. Apart from this court, the digitalization of the justice system in Egypt faces challenges similar to those discussed in this chapter. See 'Link Development Digitalizes Egypt's Ministry of Justice, Economic Courts, with Microsoft Dynamics' <https://linkdevelopment.com/app/uploads/2021/05/MOJ-Economic_Courts-Case-Study.pdfaccessed 20 June 2025 for details on digitalization of the Ministry of Justice, Economic Court. See the following for details on the challenges facing the digitalization of the Egyptian justice system, which are similar to those discussed in this chapter: Moustafa Ahmad Kamal Mahmoud Ahmad, 'The Challenges and Aspirations of the Digital Transformation of the State Council of Egypt' [Master's Thesis, the American University in Cairo]. (AUC Knowledge Fountain 2021). https://fount.aucegypt.edu/etds/1637; Karem Aboelazm, 'The Role of Digital Transformation in Improving the Judicial System in the Egyptian Council of State An Applied Study from a Comparative Perspective', Journal of Law and Emerging Technologies, 2(1), (2022), 11-50

154 See the following for details on the challenges facing the digitalization of the Iraqi justice system, which are similar to those discussed in this chapter: Alaa Hussein Ali, Tarek Abdulaziz Omar, Hanah Saleh Alkhrbeet, Saeed Hameed Aldulaimi, Mohammed Marwan Abdeldayem and Mohammed, 'Digital Transformation of Legal Frameworks of Judicial Procedures: A Comparative Study In Hamdan', R.K. (eds) Tech Fusion in Business and Society (Springer 2025) https://doi.org/10.1007/978-3-031-84636-6_41.

155 See the following for details on the challenges facing the digitalization of the Mexican justice system, which are similar to those discussed in this chapter.

Mexico: Guidelines for Technological Transformation in the Administration of Justice <https://publikationen.freiheit.digital/en/liberale-menschenrechtsarbeit/2022/mexiko> last accessed 20 June 2025; Laurence Pantin and Sandra Escamilla (20 January 2023) Digital Justice in Mexico: the balance one year after the start of pandemic <https://www.mexicoevalua.org/digital-justice-in-mexico-the-balance-one-year-after-the-start-of-the-pandemic/> last accessed 20 June 2025

adapting them to suit their systems. Large-scale advancement of digitalization in low- and middle-income countries may take years and enormous financial resources, but at the same time, it is needed and can bring cost savings in the long term. The demand for the digitalization of the justice system in these countries is considerable due to their rapidly growing populations, and the legal system has to adapt and respond to this demand. These countries could consider licencing tools currently used by Western countries discussed above as these would be available at much lower cost than developing them from scratch.

E. Conclusion

The digitalization of the justice system is a global phenomenon. As of 2024, countries like the US, the UK, and Canada are rapidly digitalizing their justice systems, helping courts improve their performance and people's access to justice. However, digitalization is slow in many low- and middle-income countries, where legal and political systems are unstable, populations are huge and economies are struggling. Pakistan is a good case study for these countries because it is a postcolonial, common-law, and politically and economically unstable country.

As in other populous low- and middle-income countries, the courts in Pakistan take considerable time to decide cases. Decision delays are caused by factors including but not limited to lawyers' strikes and frivolous litigation. Digitalizing the justice system will enable courts to handle small claims or frivolous applications online. This will eliminate the need for people to visit courts for hearings on such cases, thereby contributing to a reduction in the number of hearings overall. These reasons highlight the need to advance the digitalization of the justice system, moving beyond efficient websites and merely displaying case statuses online.

There are multiple challenges in the digitalization of the Pakistani justice system, including insufficient funding, data insecurity, absence of computerized land records and a nationwide criminal database, and interruptions to online communication. This chapter has made proposals to address the above challenges and for advancing the digitalization of the Pakistani justice system. An increase in government funds is recommended to improve litigants' access to equipment required for digitalization of justice system. Connectivity issues can be resolved by providing multiple users with alternative or separate channels. All government departments and courts at different levels must be connected through online servers, and a database comprising decisions of superior courts and higher courts must be developed. An online portal for various tiers of the judiciary is required, where litigants, including claimants and defendants, can upload their arguments, evidence and prayers, and the legal statutes under which they seek relief. Judges will supervise this virtual portal and fix dates for physical hearings for final arguments. Ultimately, the judges will decide cases and upload them to the portal.

Implementing these proposals could reduce the number of initial hearings held for case admissions and the issuance of notices. Courts would not need separate hearings for serving notices to parties, as summons and notices would be delivered electronically. Given the growing global population, the challenges of delayed and costly justice, and the increasing number of online users, the digitalization of the justice system is an inevitable step forward.

Bibliography

'National Judicial Data Grid,' <https://njdg.ecourts.gov.in/njdg_v3/>.

'Peshawar High Court, <www.peshawarhighcourt.gov.pk>.

'Punjab Forensic Science Agency',<https://pfsa.punjab.gov.pk/>.

'The National Information Technology Board' <www.nitb.gov.pk/>.

Aboelazm K 'The Role of Digital Transformation in Improving the Judicial System in the Egyptian Council of State: An Applied Study from a Comparative Perspective', Journal of Law and Emerging Technologies, 2(1), (2022), 11-50

Ahmad M A K M 'The Challenges and Aspirations of the Digital Transformation of the State Council of Egypt' [Master's Thesis, the American University in Cairo]. (AUC Knowledge Fountain 2021) <https://fount.aucegypt.edu/etds/1637>.

Alam MS, 'Problems of Delay and Backlog Cases' (*The Daily Star*, 25 February 2010) <https://archive.thedailystar.net/suppliments/2010/02/ds19/segment3/delay.html>.

Ali A H , Omar T A , Alkhrbeet H S, Aldulaimi S H, Abdeldayem M M, Mohammed, M N 'Digital Transformation of Legal Frameworks of Judicial Procedures: A Comparative Study In Hamdan', R.K. (eds) Tech Fusion in Business and Society (Springer 2025) <https://doi.org/10.1007/978-3-031-84636-6_41>

Alternate Dispute Resolution Act 2020 [Pakistan], Government of Khyber Pakhtunkhwa, act no. XLVIII of 2020 <https://kp.gov.pk/uploads/2021/11/alternate-dispute-relolution-act-2020-XLVIII-GAZATTEED.pdf >.

Alternative Dispute Resolution Act 2017 [Pakistan] <www.na.gov.pk/uploads/documents/1495101925_486.pdf>.

Arewa O and Fakolade A, 'Digitalization, Fragmentation, and Justice in Nigeria' in Markus Ludwigs, José Hernán Muriel Ciceri, Annika Velling, (eds.) *Digitalization as a Challenge for Justice and Administration* (Wurzberg University Press 2023)

Bannon AL and Keith D, 'Remote Court: Principles for Virtual Proceedings During the COVID-19 Pandemic and Beyond' (2021) 115 Northwestern U L Rev 1875.

Bashir S, 'Judge Hears Cases Online from Quarantine' (*The Express Tribune,* 2 December 2020) <https://tribune.com.pk/story/2274308/judge-hears-cases-online-from-quarantine>.

BBC, 'Pakistan Supreme Court Website Hacked' (*BBC News,* 27 September 2011) www.bbc.co.uk/news/world-south-asia-15073132.

Bhattarai P and Chaudhary S K'Digital Justice in Nepal: A South Asian perspective on Legal-Tech Reforms, Global Benchmarks and Transformative Policy Pathways' International Journal of Trends in Emerging Research and Development (2025) 3(2) 11-16

Briggs LJ, 'Civil Courts Structure Review: Interim Report' (Judiciary of England and Wales, 2015), <https://www.judiciary.uk/wp-content/uploads/2016/01/ccsr-interim-report-dec-15-final1.pdf>.

BTI Transformation Index, 'India Country Report 2024', <https://bti-project.org/en/reports/country-report/IND#pos6>.

California Commission on Access to Justice, *Remote Hearings and Access to Justice During COVID-19 and Beyond* (18 May 2020) <www.ncjfcj.org/wp-content/uploads/2020/06/2020-Remote-Hearings-Guide.pdf>.

Civil Resolution Tribunal, 'The CRT Process' <https://civilresolutionbc.ca/crt-process/>.

Civil Resolution Tribunal, 'What Kinds of Claims Can the CRT Take?' <https://civilresolutionbc.ca/help/what-kinds-of-claims-can-the-crt-take/>.

Clark E and George C, 'Law and Technology: What Does the Future Hold for ADR?' (2001) 20(2) The Arbitrator and Mediator 1.

Clark E, George C, and Hoyle A, 'Online Dispute Resolution: Present Realities, Pressing Problems and Future Prospects' (2010) 17(1) Int Rev L 7.

Code of Civil Procedure 1908 [Pakistan] <https://pakistancode.gov.pk/english/UY2FqaJw1-apaUY2Fqa-apeb-sg-jjjjjjjjjjjjj>Constitution of Pakistan 1973.

District and Sessions Courts Peshawar <https://sessionscourtpeshawar.gov.pk/public/app>

eCommittee, Supreme Court of India, 'eCourts Mission Mode Project' <https://ecommitteesci.gov.in/project/brief-overview-of-e-courts-project/>.

Elahi A., 'Challenges of Data Collection: with Special Regard to Developing Countries' <https://www.pbs.gov.pk/sites/default/files/other/documents/Elahi%20Article%20-%20For%20FBS%20Homepage.pdf>.

eCourts Services, 'E-Courts: About Us' (*District and Taluka Courts of India*) <https://services.ecourts.gov.in/ecourtindia_v6/?p=about_us&app_token=5e58210dc369e7b05b149ab8b527288f49186e5acc725d6807ece33a027948da> accessed 24 September 2024.

Esteban De la Rosa F and Zeleznikow J, 'Making Intelligent Online Dispute Resolution Tools Available to Self-Represented Litigants in the Public Justice System: Towards an Ethical Use of the AI Technology in the Administration of Justice' in *ICAIL '21: Proceedings of the Eighteenth International Conference on Artificial Intelligence and Law* (Association for Computing Machinery 2021) <https://doi.org/10.1145/3462757.3466077> accessed 24 September 2024.

Ethirajan A and Ritchie H, 'What Sparked the Protests that Toppled Bangladesh's PM? (*BBC News*, 6 August 2024) <www.bbc.co.uk/news/articles/cq5xye1d285o>.

Farzan Z, '800,000 Pending Cases in Sri Lankan Courts' (*News 1st*, 31 December 2020) <www.newsfirst.lk/2020/12/31/800000-pending-cases-in-sri-lankan-courts>.

Federal Court of Australia, 'eCourtroom: Online Courtroom for Registered Users' <www.fedcourt.gov.au/online-services/ecourtroom>.

Gartner, 'Digitalization' <https://www.gartner.com/en/information-technology/glossary/digitalization>.

Geddes B, 'What do we know about democratization after twenty years' (1999) Annual Review of Political Science 2(1) 115-144.

Geddes B, 'Paradigms and sand castles: Theory building and research design in comparative politics'(University of Michigan Press 2003)

GoPro Consulting Ltd, 'Casedoc Court and Justice: Cloud Software Service' (*GOV.UK Digital Marketplace*) <www.applytosupply.digitalmarketplace.service.gov.uk/g-cloud/services/841557749624373>.

GOV.UK, 'Make a Court Claim for Money' (2024) <www.gov.uk/make-court-claim-for-money/make-claim>.

Government of Pakistan, 'Public Sector Development Program 2023–24' (June 2023) <www.pc.gov.pk/uploads/archives/PSDP_2023-24.pdf>.

Hamid A, 'The Case of Smart Courts: Digital Transformation of Courts in Pakistan' (*RIAA Barker Gillette* 15 April 2020) <www.riaabarkergillette.com/pk/wp-content/uploads/2020/04/The-Case-for-Smart-Courts-RIAA-Barker-Gillette-PK.pdf>.

Haroon I, 'Reform of the Code of Civil Procedure' (2022) 13 Pakistan L Rev 1

Hasan M I and Rupa F J 'Digitalization of Bangladesh Judiciary and Access to Justice' (2021) Asian Journal of Social Sciences and Legal Studies 3(3) 49-58 <https://doi.org/10.34104/ajssls.021.049058>

HM Courts and Tribunal Service, 'Online Court and Tribunal Services for Professional Users and the Public' (*GOV.UK*, 13 July 2020) <www.gov.uk/guidance/online-court-and-tribunal-services-for-professional-users-and-the-public> accessed 23 September 2024.

HM Courts and Tribunal Service, 'Fact Sheet: Common Platform' (*GOV.UK*, 7 March 2024) <www.gov.uk/government/publications/hmcts-reform-crime-fact-sheets/fact-sheet-common-platform>.

HM Courts and Tribunals Service, 'Investment of Up to £6m in New Listing Technology to Benefit Courts Users' (*GOV.UK*, 4 June 2020) <www.gov.uk/government/news/investment-of-up-to-6m-in-new-listing-technology-to-benefit-court-users>.

Hussain F, 'The Judicial System of Pakistan' (Supreme Court of Pakistan, 2015) <www.supremecourt.gov.pk/downloads_judgements/all_downloads/Judicial_System_of_Pakistan/thejudicialsystemofPakistan.pdf>.

Iqbal S, 'AI in Pakistan Courts of Law' (International Bar Association, 1 June 2023) <www.ibanet.org/AI-in-Pakistani-courts-of-law>.

Ijaz Z A, Mushtaq S A, Raaka A, Khan A J and Shahab S, 'The Evolving Role of Prosecution in Pakistan's Criminal Justice System' (2024) The Critical Review of Social Sciences Studies 2(2) 210-229 < https://pdfs.semanticscholar.org/5287/027d009add485a2f42ea2a110a08fa2a4014.pdf>

Peshawar High Court, 'Judgement Management System' < https://peshawarhighcourt.gov.pk/PHCCMS/reportedJudgments.php>

Junaidi I, 'Over Half of Pakistan Does Not Have Access to Internet' (*Dawn*, 24 April 2024) <www.dawn.com/news/1829281>.

Katsh E, 'Online Dispute Resolution: Some Implications for the Emergence of Law in Cyberspace' (2007) 21 IRLCT 97.

Khadam N, Saadia Z, Sana TG, and Salvat KT, 'Analytical Framework for Judicial Data Collection in Pakistan' (2019) 16 (2) Policy Perspectives 87–105 <https://www.jstor.org/stable/10.13169/polipers.16.2.0087>.

Khalil F, 'A Vision for Digitizing Judicial Processes and Integrating Artificial Intelligence in Pakistan's Judiciary: Enhancing Efficiency and Upholding Judicial Integrity' (2024) Intl J L Ethics Tech 3.

Khan FS and Khan SR, *A Benchmark Study on Law-and-Order and the Dispensation of Justice in the Context of Power Devolution* (Sustainable Development Policy Institute 2003).

Lapper R, 'Access to Justice in Canada: The First On-line Court' (Commonwealth Lawyers Association 2020) <www.commonwealthlawyers.com/cla/access-to-justice-in-canada-the-first-on-line-court/>.

Law and Justice Commission of Pakistan, 'Consolidate Statement Showing Pendency' (2021) <http://ljcp.gov.pk/nljcp/assets/dist/news_pdf/courts.pdf>.

Lee A, 'Online Dispute Resolution in China: today and Future', in Rainey D, Katsh E, and Wahab MSA (eds), *Online Dispute Resolution: Theory and Practice* (Eleven International Publishing 2021).

Legg M, 'The COVID-19 Pandemic, the Courts and Online Hearings: Maintaining Open Justice, Procedural Fairness and Impartiality' (2021) 49 Federal L Rev 161.

'Link Development Digitalizes Egypt's Ministry of Justice, Economic Courts, with Microsoft Dynamics' <https://linkdevelopment.com/app/uploads/2021/05/MOJ-Economic_Courts-Case-Study.pdf>

Loebl Z, *Designing Online Courts: The Future of Justice Is Open to All* (Wolters Kluwer 2019).

Long V, 'Online Courts: Re-Assessing Inequality in the "Remote" Courtroom' (2021) 11 Excursions 77102.

Maclean M and Dijksterhuis B (eds), *Digital Family Justice: From Alternative Dispute Resolution to Online Dispute Resolution?* (Bloomsbury Publishing 2019).

Mallawarachi B, 'Sri Lanka Reaches Deal on Debt Restructuring with Bilateral Creditors Including China and France' (*AP News,* 27 June 2024) <https://apnews.com/article/sri-lanka-economic-crisis-india-japan-china-503d8871e4b14c8bda9822b171f73b8d> .

Malik H, 'The Case for Online Hearings' (*The Express Tribune,* 11 April 2021) < https://tribune.com.pk/story/2294089/the-case-for-online-hearings >.

Mehran KA, 'New System for Activation of SIM Launched' (Pakistan Telecommunication Authority, 1 February 2009) <www.pta.gov.pk/category/new-system-for-activation-of-sim-launched-343760439-2023-06-01>.

Mexico: Guidelines for Technological Transformation in the Administration of Justice <https://publikationen.freiheit.digital/en/liberale-menschenrechtsarbeit/2022/mexiko>

Ministry of Law and Justice, 'The Pakistan Code' <https://pakistancode.gov.pk/english/UY2FqaJw1-apaUY2Fqa-apeb-sg-jjjjjjjjjjjj>

Ministry of Law and Justice, 'The Pakistan Code' <https://pakistancode.gov.pk/english/UY2FqaJw1-apaUY2Fqa-apaUY2Npa5lp-sg-jjjjjjjjjjjj> last accessed 14 June 2025

National Database and Registration Authority <www.nadra.gov.pk/> accessed 24 September 2024.

National Judicial (Policy Making) Committee, National Judicial Policy 2009 (rev edn, 2012) 45–46 <www.supremecourt.gov.pk/downloads_judgements/all_downloads/National_Judicial_Policy/NJP2009.pdf>.

Nawaz CH, 'Delay Reduction with Effective Court Management' (Federal Judicial Academy Pakistan) <www.fja.gov.pk/files/articles/DELAYREDUCTIONWITHEFFECTIVECOURTMANAGEMENT.pdf>.

Nayab D, 'Estimating the Middle Class in Pakistan' (2011) 50(1) Pakistan Development Rev 1.

Newman EJ, Muir B, and Brown N, 'The Virtual Court: Implications for Eyewitnesses and Beyond' in Pica E, Ross D, and Pozz J (eds), *The Impact of Technology on the Criminal Justice System: A Psychological Overview* (Routledge 2024).

Nguyen BT and Ngo TH, 'Building Electronic Court in Vietnam: Recent Developments and Challenges' (2024) 16 Lex Humana 573.

Nuffield Family Justice Observatory, *Remote Hearings in the Family Justice System: A Rapid Consultation* (May 2020) 15 <www.nuffieldfjo.org.uk/resource/remote-hearings-rapid-consultation>.

Pakistanlawsite.com <www.pakistanlawsite.com>

Pantin L and Escamilla S (20 January 2023) Digital Justice in Mexico: the balance one year after the start of pandemic <https://www.mexicoevalua.org/digital-justice-in-mexico-the-balance-one-year-after-the-start-of-the-pandemic/>

Peshawar High Court, 'Current Causelist' (2024) <https://peshawarhighcourt.gov.pk/app/site/18/p/Current_Causelist.html>

Peshawar High Court, 'PHC Launches Video Conferencing Technology' (21 December 2018) https://peshawarhighcourt.gov.pk/image_bank/Orders/Zoom%20Meeting%2021122018.pdf.

Peshawar High Court, 'Sitting Judges in Peshawar High Court' (2024) <https://peshawarhighcourt.gov.pk/app/site/35/c/Sitting_Judges.html>.

Pew Research Center, 'Internet, Broadband Fact Sheet' (31 January 2024) <www.pewresearch.org/internet/fact-sheet/internet-broadband/>.

Pratomo AY, Ma'ruf U,.and Witasari A, 'Implementation of Criminal Action Prosecution Online in Realizing Principle of Fast Prosecution, Simple and Low Cost' (2021) 4(2) Jurnal Daulut Hukam 132.

Press Information Department, 'Digitalization of the Judiciary in Pakistan' (17 November 2023) <https://pid.gov.pk/site/press_detail/23936>.

Prevention of Electronic Crimes Act 2016 [Pakistan] (The Gazette of Pakistan, 22 August 2016) <www.dataguidance.com/sites/default/files/pak104952.pdf>.

Prime Minister's Performance Delivery Unit, 'Pakistan Citizen's Portal: PCP' <https://citizenportal.gov.pk/>,

Punjab Alternative Dispute Resolution Act 2019 [Pakistan] <http://punjablaws.gov.pk/laws/2739.html>.

Qanun-e-Shahadat Order 1984 [Pakistan] <https://khalidzafar.com/wp-content/files_mf/1527158791QanuneShahadatOrder1984.pdf>.

Qazi MU, 'Computerisation of Land Records in Pakistan: A Comparative Analysis of Two Projects from a Human Security Perspective' (*VNU*, 2006) <http://danida.vnu.edu.vn/cpis/files/Papers_on_CC/PIS/1.pdf>.

Qazi M, 'Infusing Digital Technology in Judicial Operations in Pakistan: A Critical Analysis of Global Best Practices and Local Initiatives' (11 April 2023) <https://papers.ssrn.com/sol3/papers.cfm?abstract_id=4378378>.

Raman P, 'Towards a 21st Century Legal System' (2000) Globalisation and Law Reform 76, 19-24 < https://www.austlii.edu.au/au/journals/ALRCRefJl/2000/4.pdf>.

Rana S, 'Pakistan's Existential Economic Crisis' (United States Institute of Peace, 6 April 2023) <www.usip.org/publications/2023/04/pakistans-existential-economic-crisis>.

Recorder Report, 'Ministry of Law and Justice: Rs1368.874m Earmarked for Development Schemes in PSDP' (*Business Recorder,* 13 June 2024) <www.brecorder.com/news/40308201>

Rehman QUA, 'Pakistan Digital Resolution: Enhancing Efficiency, Transparency and Accessibility in the Judicial System' (*Jurist News*, 13 July 2024) <www.jurist.org/features/2024/07/13/pakistans-digital-revolution-enhancing-efficiency-transparency-and-accessibility-in-the-judicial-system/>.

Rehman S and Imran A, 'Pakistan: Data Protection Overview' (*OneTrust DataGuidance*, July 2024) <www.dataguidance.com/notes/pakistan-data-protection-overview.

Reiling D, 'Doing Justice with Information Technology' (2006) 15 I&CTL 189.

Reiling D, *Technology for Justice: How Information Technology Can Support Judicial Reform* (Leiden University Press 2009).

Rossner M, Tait D, and McCurdy M, 'Justice Reimagined: Challenges and Opportunities with Implementing Virtual Courts' (2022) 33 CICJ 94.

Rusakova EP and Frolova EE, 'Procedural Aspects of Proof in China's Internet Courts: Opportunities for Receiving BRICS Jurisdiction' in Popkova EG and Sergi BS (eds), *Modern Global Economic System: Evolutional Development vs Revolutionary Leap* (Lecture Notes in Networks and Systems 198, Springer 2021).

SAP, 'Digitisation vs Digitalisation' <https://www.sap.com/uk/products/erp/digitization-vs-digitalization.html>.

Saeed M, 'Assessing the Efficiency of the District Courts of Pakistan—Why Is Better Evaluation Needed? (2020) 1(2) Amicus Curiae 418.

Sarfraz M, 'A Diary of (Near) Default: Pakistan's Journey to Avoid Insolvency in 2023' (*Dawn*, 30 December 2023) <www.dawn.com/news/1800599.

Shah KH, 'Biometric Verification for Banks Account Opening' (*Kiosk Solutions*, 2024) <www.kiosksolutions.com.pk/docs/Opening-of-Bank-Account.pdf>.

Shah MS, 'Peshawar Solutions to Case Flow Management' in Ahmad K, Lao C, and Weisenberger K (eds), *Law and Policy Reform at the Asian Development Bank: Report from the ADB Symposium on Challenges in Implementing Access to Justice Reforms* (Asian Development Bank 2005).

Shah RU, Khan SU, and Farid S, 'Causes for Delay in Civil Justice in Lower Courts of Pakistan: A Review' (2014) 6 Pakistan J Crim 47.

Shahbaz Rana, 'Neglect Caused FBR Cyber-Attack' (*The Express Tribune*, 22 August 2021) <https://tribune.com.pk/story/2316604/neglect-caused-fbr-cyber-attack>.

Shahzad A., 'Pakistan's Top Court Proceedings Shown Live on TV for the First Time' (*Reuters*, 18 September 2023) <www.reuters.com/world/asia-pacific/pakistans-top-court-proceedings-shown-live-tv-first-time-2023-09-18/>.

Shinwari NA, *Understanding the Informal Justice System: Opportunities and Possibilities for Legal Pluralism in Pakistan* (Community Appraisal & Motivation Programme 2015) <https://fid4sa-repository.ub.uni-heidelberg.de/3795/1/UnderstandingtheInformalJusticeSystem.pdf>.

Siddique O, *Pakistan's Experience with the Formal Law: An Alien Justice* (CUP 2013)

Sindh High Court, 'SHC Launches Video Conference Facility for Litigants and Lawyers' (27 May 2023) <www.thenews.com.pk/print/1074221-shc-launches-videoconference-facility-for-litigants-and-lawyers>.

Sindh High Court, 'Standard Operating Procedure (SOP) for Video Link Facility' (6 June 2023) <https://sindhhighcourt.gov.pk/news_notifications/source_files/Circular_SOP_VideoLink.pdf>.

Singapore Courts, 'Settle a Tribunal or Protection from Harassment Dispute Online: eNegotiation or eMediation' (SG Courts, 3 April 2024) <www.judiciary.gov.sg/alternatives-to-trial/enegotiation-emediation>.

Sohail IB, 'Expediting Justice Through Online Dispute Resolution' (*The Express Tribune*, 23 March 2024) <https://tribune.com.pk/story/2460214/expediting-justice-through-online-dispute-resolution>.

Sourdin T, 'Judge v Robot: Artificial Intelligence and Judicial Decision-Making' (2018) 41(4) UNSWLJ 1114.

Sourdin T, Li B, and Burke T, 'Just, Quick and Cheap? Civil Dispute Resolution and Technology' (2019) 17 Macquarie LJ 19.

Sourav R, 'Bangladesh and the quest for a digitised judiciary' (The Daily Star 21 March 2025) <https://www.thedailystar.net/law-our-rights/news/bangladesh-and-the-quest-digitised-judiciary-3853801> last accessed 20 June 2025

Staff Reporter, 'July–Dec 2023 Statistics Show 2.26 Million Cases Pending in Courts: Report' (*Dawn*, 16 February 2024) <www.dawn.com/news/1814586>.

Sturge G, 'Court Statistics for England and Wales' (House of Commons Library, 13 September 2024) <https://commonslibrary.parliament.uk/research-briefings/cbp-8372/>.

Summers A and Gatowski S, *Nevada Court Improvement Program Remote Hearing Study* (2020) <https://nevadacurrent.com/wp-content/uploads/2022/01/21-17924.pdf.

Supreme Court of Pakistan, 'Annual Report June 2015–May 2016' (2016) <www.supremecourt.gov.pk/downloads_judgements/all_downloads/annual_reports/SCP_Annual_Report_2015_2016_.pdf> .

Supreme Court of Pakistan, 'E-Court System Successfully Launched in Supreme Court' (2024) <www.supremecourt.gov.pk/e-court-system-successfully-launched-in-supreme-court/>.

Supreme Court of Pakistan, 'Standard Operating Procedure (SOP) for Video Link Facility' (2024) <www.supremecourt.gov.pk/downloads_judgements/press_release/SOPs_for_Video_Link_Request.pdf>.

Supreme Court of Pakistan, Supreme Court Rules 1980 (last amended 11 November 2017).

Susskind R, *Online Courts and the Future of Justice* (OUP 2019).

Swat District Courts <https://dsjswat.gov.pk/>.

The Supreme Court of India, 'E-Courts Mission Mode Project' <https://ecommitteesci.gov.in/project/brief-overview-of-e-courts-project/>.

The World Bank, 'The World by Income and Region' <https://datatopics.worldbank.org/world-development-indicators/the-world-by-income-and-region.html>.

Tabassum S et al, 'Evaluating the Impact of Strength of Judges on Dispensation of Justice in District Judiciary of Pakistan' (2021) 12 Int J Mgmt 266.

Taher M A and Jamaluddin S Z 'Enhancing access to justice through e-judiciary in Bangladesh: A study' (2022) UUM Journal of Legal Studies 13(2) 317-344 <https://doi.org/10.32890/uumjls2022.13.2.13> accessed 20 June 2025

Thornburg EG, 'Observing Online Courts: Lessons from the Pandemic' (2020) SSRN Electronic Journal 193 <http://dx.doi.org/10.2139/ssrn.3696594>.

Townend J and Paul M, 'Remote Trial and Error: How Covid-19 Changed Public Access to Court Proceedings' Journal of Media Law (2021) 107–21.

UN Women Pakistan, *National Report on the Status of Women in Pakistan, 2023: A Summary*, (2023) <https://pakistan.unwomen.org/sites/default/files/2023-07/summary_-nrsw-inl_final.pdf>.

UNB News, 'Nearly 3.7 Mln Cases Pending' (*United News of Bangladesh*, 16 July 2020) <www.unb.com.bd/category/Bangladesh/nearly-37-mln-cases-pending/54740>.

United States Courts, 'Judicial Caseload Indicators: Federal Judicial Caseload Statistics 2023' <www.uscourts.gov/judicial-caseload-indicators-federal-judicial-caseload-statistics-2023>.

Wang L, 'Application of Information Technology in Judicial Field: The Development Model of Online Litigation in China' (2024) 52 CLS Rev 105936.

Young R, 'Cyber Courts: House Bill 6447' (Michigan Legislature, 3 December 2002) <www.legislature.mi.gov/documents/2001-2002/billanalysis/House/htm/2001-HLA-6447-a.htm>.

Zafeer HMI, Zue H, and Maqbool S, 'Delaying Factors Regarding Civil Justice in Pakistan' (2020) 2 J Humanities and Social Science Studies 15.

Zheng P et al, 'Judicial Informatization and Digital Transformation: Evidence from the Establishment of the Internet Court' (2024) Applied Economics Letters 1.

9

Facilitation of Digital Access to Justice in Cross-Border Environments

The New System of European Judicial Cooperation in Civil Matters

*Nuria Marchal Escalona**

A. Introduction

Digital transformation is a crucial step in improving access to justice, efficiency, quality, and transparency of the judicial systems of the Member States of the European Union (EU), as emphasized in the Commission's Communication published on 2 December

* Professor in Private International Law (nmarchal@ugr.es). Member of the Research Unit of Excellence 'Digital Society: Security and Protection of Rights' of the University of Granada. This research has been generously supported by the Spanish Ministry of research, innovation, and universities, within the project TED2021-131127B-100 'Building the foundations for an efficient, legal and guarantee-based digitalization of alternative dispute resolution systems for consumer disputes through technological platforms'.

Nuria Marchal Escalona, *Facilitation of Digital Access to Justice in Cross-Border Environments* In: *Digitalization and Artificial Intelligence in Courts*. Edited by: Fernando Esteban de la Rosa, Pablo Cortés, and Nuria Marchal Escalona, Oxford University Press. DOI: 10.1093/9780198918752.003.0009

2020 on 'The Digitalization of Justice in the EU: A Range of Opportunities'.[1] The use of technological tools in proceedings where the claimant and defendant reside or are domiciled in different Member States can contribute to facilitating access to justice, reducing processing time, and saving costs.[2] In this regard, technological solutions adapted to the cross-border environment are required, as well as a regulatory framework that increases efficiency, accessibility, and the protection of fundamental rights. As stated in the European Declaration on Digital Rights and Principles (Recital 7[3]), the challenge is to develop a digital justice model that strengthens the human dimension and respects individuals' fundamental rights. Europe aspires to achieve a sustainable,[4] prosperous, and human-centred digital future.[5] The goal is to digitalize the human and humanize the digital.[6]

However, this task is complex. The implementation of new technologies in the judicial field must be designed in a way that respects fundamental rights, ensuring access to justice for all individuals, as stipulated in Article 6.1 of the European Convention on Human Rights (ECHR[7]), Article 47 of the Charter of Fundamental Rights of the EU (CFR[8]), and Article 24 of the Spanish Constitution (CE). This is particularly relevant for vulnerable individuals such as persons with disabilities, in line with the provisions of the UN Convention on the Rights of Persons with Disabilities.[9] Furthermore, the protection of personal data must be guaranteed. The exchange of information between authorities must comply with strict cybersecurity standards and respect key principles, such as legality, transparency, data minimization, and confidentiality. Data may only be used for the specific purposes for which they are transmitted, and irrelevant data must be immediately deleted in accordance with the General Data Protection Regulation (GDPR[10]), Regulation 2018/1725,[11] and the other related data

[1] <https://eur-lex.europa.eu/legal-content/ES/ALL/?uri = CELEX%3A52020DC0710> last accessed 20 September 2024.

[2] Fernando Esteban de la Rosa, 'Obligaciones, derechos y garantías frente a las brechas digitales en la vertebración de la justicia en línea' in JF Rodríguez Ayuso, *Nuevos retos en materia de derechos digitales en un contexto de pandemia: perspectiva multidisciplinar* (Thomson Reuters/Aranzadi 2022) 439–70.

[3] On 15 December 2022, the Presidents of the Council of the EU, the European Parliament, and the Commission signed the European Declaration on Digital Rights and Principles for the Digital Decade, <https://digital-strategy.ec.europa.eu/es/library/european-declaration-digital-rights-and-principles> last accessed 20 September 2024.

[4] Each e-Justice service should be implemented and operated in a sustainable way, meaning that its economic, environmental, and social impact can be predicted and sustained in the long term. See European Union, European e-Justice Strategy 2024–2028 [2025] OJ C437.

[5] See OECD, 'Recommendation on Access to Justice and People-Centred Justice Systems', [2023]. <https://legalinstruments.oecd.org/en/instruments/OECD-LEGAL-0498> last accessed 20 September 2024; Antonio Lazari, 'La protección de los derechos digitales: Una cuestión identitaria europea', (2024) 1, 16, Cuadernos de Derecho Transnacional, 295–318, 316.

[6] See Chapter 1.

[7] Convention for the Protection of Human Rights and Fundamental Freedoms, made in Rome on 4 November 1950, and amended by Additional Protocols No 3 and No 5, of 6 May 6 1963, and 20 January 1966 (BOE núm 243, de 10 de octubre de 1979).

[8] [2000] OJ C364/1.

[9] *BOE* núm 96, de 21 de abril de 2008.

[10] Regulation (EU) No 2016/679 of the European Parliament and of the Council, of 27 April 2016, on the protection of natural persons with regard to the processing of personal data and on the free movement of such data, and repealing Directive 95/46/EC [2016] OJ L119/1.

[11] Regulation (EU) No 2018/1725 of the European Parliament and of the Council, of 23 October 2018, on the protection of natural persons with regard to the processing of personal data by the institutions,

protection regulations.[12] Ensuring the legal acceptance and probative value of electronic documents has become a key aspect of justice. It is also essential to have tools that ensure rapid, secure, and direct communication, guaranteeing the authenticity of the content, correct identification of the participants, and integrity of the information.[13] In this regard, Regulation (EU) 910/2014 (eIDAS Regulation[14])[15] plays a fundamental role.[16]

Numerous regulatory instruments have been adopted to date under Article 81(2) of the Treaty on the Functioning of the European Union (TFEU).[17] The COVID-19 pandemic has accelerated the search for more efficient justice. The 'dematerialization' of European proceedings—the European order for payment[18] and small claims[19,20] and the implementation of the European Online Dispute Resolution (ODR) Platform are the first steps taken by the European legislator in this direction. In the last decade, efforts have intensified to provide a favourable regulatory framework to facilitate the digitalization of justice in cooperation. To this end, the regulation on the obtaining of evidence,[21] the regulation on the service of documents abroad,[22] and the Digitalization Regulation[23] have been adopted. These instruments have represented a

bodies, offices, and agencies of the Union, and on the free movement of such data, and repealing Regulation (EC) No 45/2001 and Decision No 1247/2002/EC [2018] OJ L295/39.

[12] Directive 2002/58/EC of the European Parliament and of the Council of 12 July 2002, concerning the processing of personal data and the protection of privacy in the electronic communications sector [2002] OJ L201/37.

[13] Fernando Esteban de la Rosa et al, *Justicia Digital, Guía para el diálogo sobre el diseño y uso eficiente, de calidad y ético de herramientas tecnológicas en la justicia civil* 39. <https://hdl.handle.net/10481/76835> last accessed 20 September 2024.

[14] Regulation (EU) No 910/2014 of the European Parliament and of the Council of 23 July 2014, on electronic identification and trust services for electronic transactions in the internal market, and repealing Directive 1999/93/EC [2014] OJ L257/73.

[15] See Chapter 4.

[16] Gabriela Fierbințeanu and Vasile Nemes, 'Digital tools for judicial cooperation across the EU—the benefits of digital technologies in judicial proceedings' (2022) XXXIX Lex et Scientia 1–9; Marco Velicogna, 'Justice Systems and ICT: What can be learned from Europe?' (2007) Utrecht L Rev 129.

[17] [2010] OJ C83/47.

[18] Regulation (EC) No 1896/2006 of the European Parliament and of the Council of 12 December, 2006, establishing a European Order for Payment Procedure [2006] OJ L391/1.

[19] Regulation (EC) No 861/2007 of the European Parliament and of the Council of 11 July 2007, establishing a European Small Claims Procedure [2007] OJ L199/1.

[20] Both Regulations were amended by Regulation (EU) No 2915/2421 of the European Parliament and of the Council of 16 December 2015 [2015] OJ L341/ [2015] OJ L341/1.

[21] Regulation (EU) No 2020/1783 of the European Parliament and of the Council of 25 November 2020, on cooperation between the courts of the Member States in the field of the obtaining of evidence in civil or commercial matters (Obtaining of Evidence) (Consolidated version)–RETE 2020 [2020]–OJ L405/1.

[22] Regulation (EU) No 2020/1784 of the European Parliament and of the Council of 25 November 2020, concerning the service and transfer of judicial and extrajudicial documents in the Member States in civil or commercial matters (Service and Transfer of Documents) (Consolidated version)–Service of Documents Regulation–[2020] OJ L 405/40.This Regulation is binding on all EU Member States, including Denmark. See Nuria Marchal Escalona, 'La digitalización de la notificación en el espacio judicial europeo' in Mercedes Llorente Sánchez-Arjona and Sonia Calaza López (dirs), *Digitalización de la Justicia: Prevención, Investigación y enjuiciamiento* (Thomson Reuters/Aranzadi 2022), 387–415; Vincent Richard, 'A refonte du règlement sur la notification des actes judiciaires et extrajudiciaires' (2021) 2 Revue critique de droit international *privé* 349–60.

[23] Regulation (EU) No 2023/2844 on the digitalization of judicial cooperation and access to justice in cross-border civil, commercial, and criminal matters, amending certain legal acts in the field of judicial

significant step forward in defining the European model of judicial cooperation digitalization in civil matters and in creating European infrastructure aimed at serving this purpose. However, we are still in the process of implementing the European digital system, which, owing to its complexity, requires a phased implementation for its definitive launch.

The European model is characterized by not offering exhaustive regulation, needing to be complemented by the procedural rules of the Member States, which have unevenly integrated information and communication technologies (ICT) into their judicial systems. This disparity is one of the main weaknesses of the European regulatory system and one of the greatest obstacles to the effective implementation of the digital route in cross-border proceedings and to the construction of a common European procedural law.

The objective of this chapter is to review the innovations of the European system to assess how they address the promise of facilitating access to justice that digitalization offers and to what extent the adopted model serves as an example to be followed in other regional contexts. The chapter analyses the elements of building the new European digital system for judicial cooperation in civil matters and contains proposals for improvement as well as recommendations for guiding future developments. Owing to the specificity of its regulation, one chapter particularly addresses the practice of taking evidence via videoconference.[24]

B. Tools and Infrastructure that Facilitate European Judicial Cooperation and Access to Justice for Citizens in Cross-Border Proceedings

The new European system is based on three technological pillars: The decentralized computer system, e-Codex, and an electronic access point, each with specific functions. It also contemplates, in certain cases and within established limits, the use of electronic tools provided in the procedural systems of different Member States, both for direct notification to the recipient[25] and for holding remote hearings.[26] However, there are significant differences in how each Member State has integrated ICT into their judicial systems.

1. The decentralized computer system and the e-CODEX platform

As a tool to facilitate the direct, reliable, and secure electronic exchange of information between judicial authorities and to promote and accelerate cross-border judicial

cooperation (Digitalization Regulation), as well as the accompanying Directive (EU) 2023/2844 [2023] OJ L2023/2844.

24 See Chapter 10.
25 Service of Documents Regulation, Art 19.
26 Digitalization Regulation, Art 5.

cooperation, the European legislator has provided for the use of a decentralized computer system. Given that Member States already have systems for communication among authorities, the European legislator's initiative has been to make a leap by fostering the interconnection and interoperability of national systems. This system can be defined as a network of national computer systems and interoperable access points that operate under the individual responsibility and management of each Member State, and allow secure and reliable cross-border information exchange between national computer systems.

Digital connectivity and interoperability between national judicial systems is facilitated by *e-Justice Communication via On-line Data Exchange* (e-CODEX, digital connectivity and interoperability between national judicial systems is facilitated by e-CODEX, called the 'Justice Digital Exchange System ('JUDEX'), which is currently managed by the European Agency eu-LISA[27]).[28] This system is regulated by Regulation (EU) 2022/850 (e-CODEX Regulation[29]) and consists of two logical support elements (software): a gateway for exchanging messages with other gateways and a connector which offers a range of functionalities related to the exchange of messages between national computer systems. Currently, the gateway is based on a component of the 'Connecting Europe' Mechanism maintained by the Commission known as 'eDelivery', while the management of the connector is handled by the entity that manages the e-CODEX system.[30] The connector provides functions, such as verifying electronic signatures through a security library and sending acknowledgements of receipt. With the e-CODEX Regulation, this platform becomes part of European law, linking all Member States, except Denmark, as in accordance with Articles 1 and 2 of Protocol 22 annexed to the Treaty on European Union and the TFEU

The implementation of the decentralized computer system is somewhat complex, as it also requires Member States to use, a 'reference application software' to be developed by the Commission, instead of their own national systems.[31] This program must be designed according to accessibility requirements and must provide high levels of cybersecurity and data protection. Additionally, its configuration must facilitate the reuse or improvement of the existing national infrastructure.

The described system constitutes an important step towards a more modern, accessible, and efficient justice system in the EU. It is intended to become an indispensable tool to build trust in the internal market and stimulate Member States' judicial systems to incorporate new technologies at the domestic level. Its functioning presupposes

[27] See Rafal Manko, 'Computerised system for communication in cross-border judicial proceedings (e-CODEX)', EPRS, European Parliament (2021). <https://www.europarl.europa.eu/thinktank/en/document/EPRS_BRI(2021)690667> last accessed 15 June 2024. See Marco Velicogna, 'Coming to Terms with Complexity Overload in Transborder e-Justice: The e-Codex Platform' in Francesco Contini and Giovan Francesco Lanzara (eds), *The Circulation of Agencyin E-Justice: Interoperability and Infrastructures for European Transborder Judicial Proceedings* (Springer 2014) 309–30.

[28] Art 2(2) of the Service of Documents Regulation and Art 2(3) of the Digitalization Regulation.

[29] Regulation (EU) of the European Parliament and of the Council of 30 May 2022, regarding a computerized system for the cross-border electronic exchange of data in the field of judicial cooperation in civil and criminal matters (e-Codex system), which amends Regulation (EU) 2018/1726 [2022] OJ L150/1.

[30] Recital 11 of the e-CODEX Regulation.

[31] Recital 12 of the Service of Documents Regulation and Recital 21 of the Digitalization Regulation.

that the EU provides technical and financial support to countries with less digital infrastructure to ensure that they can access the benefits of the system. Furthermore, a flexible and scalable design is required to adapt to future technological advancements along with a long-term maintenance plan. Although this system aims to be secure, concerns persist regarding its vulnerability to cyberattacks. To ensure that this tool has a positive impact on access to justice, Member States must allocate sufficient resources to improve the skills and digital literacy of judicial officials, so that the lack of digital skills does not become an obstacle to using the decentralized computer system.

2. The European electronic access point

The EU seeks to make courts and judicial services more accessible to citizens. To this end, it has created the 'European e-Justice Portal',[32] which can be defined as a portal accessible to both natural and legal persons, as well as their representatives, throughout the EU, and is connected to an interoperable access point within the decentralized computer system.[33] Its objective is to provide citizens with a single entry point to access information, submit documents, and carry out judicial procedures between Member States, simplifying procedures and ensuring interoperability between national systems, to make judicial services more accessible, efficient, and secure.

Once implemented, this access point will,[34] become a key tool for the implementation of e-Justice within the EU, enabling natural and legal persons as well as their representatives to file claims, make requests, send and receive procedural information, communicate with competent authorities, and receive judicial document notifications and services. However, its scope is limited, as its use is restricted to certain procedures[35]. Its implementation faces several challenges related to interoperability, language barriers, digital inequality, and a lack of trust in the systems.[36]

[32] Digitalization Regulation, Art 4.

[33] ibid Art 2 (4).

[34] According to Art 26(3) of the Digitalization Regulation, Art 4 shall apply from the first day of the month following the two-year period from the date of entry into force of the corresponding implementing acts referred to in Art 10(2).

[35] According Art 4 (2), the European electronic access point may be used for electronic communication between natural or legal persons or their representatives and competent authorities in the following instances: (a) procedures provided for in Regulations (EC) No 1896/2006, (EC) No 861/2007 and (EU) No 655/2014; (b) procedures provided for in Regulation (EC) No 805/2004; (c) proceedings for recognition, a declaration of enforceability or refusal of recognition provided for in Regulations (EU) No 650/2012, (EU) No 1215/2012 (39), and (EU) No 606/2013 of the European Parliament and of the Council and Council Regulations (EC) No 4/2009, (EU) 2016/1103 (40), (EU) 2016/1104 (41), and (EU) 2019/1111; (d) procedures related to the issuance, rectification and withdrawal of: (i) extracts provided for in Regulation (EC) No 4/2009, (ii) the European Successions Certificate and the attestations provided for in Regulation (EU) No 650/2012 (iii) certificates provided for in Regulation (EU) No 1215/2012, (iv) certificates provided for in Regulation (EU) No 606/2013, (v) attestations provided for in Regulation (EU) 2016/1103, (vi) attestations provided for in Regulation (EU) 2016/1104, (vii) certificates provided for in Regulation (EU) 2019/1111; (e) the lodging of a claim by a foreign creditor in insolvency proceedings under Art 53 of Regulation (EU) 2015/848; (f) communication between natural or legal persons or their representatives with the Central Authorities under Regulation (EC) No 4/2009 and Regulation (EU) 2019/1111 or the competent authorities under Ch IV of Directive 2003/8/EC.

[36] To support Member States in this task, the Council recently adopted an e-Justice Strategy 2024–2028. The strategy not only describes the principles and objectives for the development of e-Justice over the next five years. It also sets out the actions that Member States and the EU should take to achieve these objectives.

3. State computer tools

Electronic tools are increasingly being integrated into national judicial systems, and the EU has sought to leverage them to strengthen cross-border judicial cooperation. For this reason, national tools are part of the European system. The European legislators have authorized their use for the international service of documents[37] and for holding remote hearings.[38] However, their application varies among Member States owing to differences in technological development, legal traditions, and available resources, resulting in uneven implementation, which is likely to continue because of the lack of a unified European legal framework. Therefore, Member States needs to invest in digital infrastructure, training, and legal harmonization to prevent digitalization from creating new inequalities in access to justice in cross-border proceedings. However, the functionality of these electronic tools is conditioned upon the fulfilment of a series of requirements, among which the explicit consent of the parties stands out.

C. The Digitalization of Judicial Cooperation in Civil Matters: The Regime of Specific Aspects

1. Electronic communications between competent authorities through the decentralized computer system

The decentralized IT system is intended to enable direct communication transmission between competent authorities, facilitate the interconnection and interoperability of national systems, and improve cooperation in cross-border procedures. To ensure security during transmissions, it establishes the use of trust services, e-IDAS.[39]

This system performs different functions under these two Regulations. Under the Notification Regulation, the system aims to facilitate communication between authorities to transmit judicial documents to other EU Member States for notification and delivery to recipients. The key components of this communication mechanism are, on the one hand, the transmitting and receiving bodies of cooperation requests, and, on the other hand, the central authority in each Member State.[40]

In the Digitalization Regulation, the objective is to facilitate communication between the competent authorities of different Member States, as well as between a national competent authority and an EU body or agency, in cross-border matters outlined and listed in Annex I.[41] However, it is important to note that in matters

[37] Service of Documents Regulation, Art 19.

[38] Digitalization Regulation, Art 5.

[39] Art 5(3) of the Service Documents Regulation and Art 7 of the Digitalization Regulation.

[40] See Marta Requejo Isidro, 'Means of Communication to be Used by Transmitting Agencies, Receiving Agencies and Central Bodies' in Apostolos Anthimos and Marta Requejo Isidro (eds), *The European Service Regulation: A Commentary* (Edward Elgar Publishing 2023) 71–75; Guillermo Palao Moreno, 'El Reglamento (UE) núm. 2020/1784 y su contribución al impulso de la digitalización de la cooperación judicial en materia civil y mercantil en la Unión Europea' (2024) 21 Actualidad Jurídica Iberoamericana 190–223.

[41] The legal acts included within its scope of application are: (1) Council Directive 2003/8/EC of 27 January 2003 to improve access to justice in cross-border disputes by establishing minimum common rules relating to legal aid for such disputes; (2) Regulation (EC) No 805/2004 of the European Parliament

related to maintenance obligations, the decentralized system is compatible with the software developed in this area by the Hague Conference on Private International Law: iSupport,[42] which enhances the effectiveness and efficiency of the transnational enforcement of maintenance obligations, reducing costs and delays.

We are aware that the implementation of this system will require significant multi-level efforts, particularly in technical and organizational areas, which explains why it is not yet operational. As set out in Article 37(2) of the of the Service of Documents Regulation, this system will come into force on the first day of the month following the three-year period after the entry into force of the corresponding implementing regulation. According to the approved regulation,[43] this date will be 1 May 2025.

However, one of the greatest challenges is ensuring that each country's IT systems are compatible and can communicate efficiently with one another while maintaining high standards of security and efficiency. To achieve full success, continuous cooperation between Member States, strengthening the digital infrastructure, and support for training are essential.

This system will be operational in all Member States, except Denmark, because it is not part of the e-CODEX Regulation. However, the Commission Implementing Regulation (EU) 2024/1570,[44] allows Denmark to participate in the decentralized IT system if it adapts its domestic legislation to incorporate certain provisions of

and of the Council of 21 April 2004 creating a European Enforcement Order for uncontested claims; (3) Regulation (EC) No 1896/2006 of the European Parliament and of the Council of 12 December 2006 creating a European order for payment procedure; (4) Regulation (EC) No 861/2007 of the European Parliament and of the Council of 11 July 2007 establishing a European Small Claims Procedure; (5) Council Regulation (EC) No 4/2009 of 18 December 2008 on jurisdiction, applicable law, recognition and enforcement of decisions and cooperation in matters relating to maintenance obligations; (6) Regulation (EU) No 650/2012 of the European Parliament and of the Council of 4 July 2012 on jurisdiction, applicable law, recognition and enforcement of decisions and acceptance and enforcement of authentic instruments in matters of succession and on the creation of a European Certificate of Succession; (7) Regulation (EU) No 1215/2012 of the European Parliament and of the Council of 12 December 2012 on jurisdiction and the recognition and enforcement of judgments in civil and commercial matters (recast); (8) Regulation (EU) No 606/2013 of the European Parliament and of the Council of 12 June 2013 on mutual recognition of protection measures in civil matters; (9) Regulation (EU) No 655/2014 of the European Parliament and of the Council of 15 May 2014 establishing a European Account Preservation Order procedure to facilitate cross-border debt recovery in civil and commercial matters; (10) Regulation (EU) 2015/848 of the European Parliament and of the Council of 20 May 2015 on insolvency proceedings; (11) Council Regulation (EU) 2016/1103 of 24 June 2016 implementing enhanced cooperation in the area of jurisdiction, applicable law and the recognition and enforcement of decisions in matters of matrimonial property regimes; (12) Council Regulation (EU) 2016/1104 of 24 June 2016 implementing enhanced cooperation in the area of jurisdiction, applicable law and the recognition and enforcement of decisions in matters of the property consequences of registered partnerships; (13) Council Regulation (EU) 2019/1111 of 25 June 2019 on jurisdiction, the recognition and enforcement of decisions in matrimonial matters and the matters of parental responsibility, and on international child abduction.

[42] Theoduloz, Santiago and Villegas Candela, 'iSupport como herramienta modelo para el acceso a la justicia en el ámbito del derecho internacional privado', Facultad de Derecho de la Universidad Católica de Uruguay, (2021) 24 128 143.

[43] Commission Implementing Regulation (EU) 2022/423 of 14 March 2022 laying down the technical specifications, measures and other requirements for the implementation of the decentralized IT system referred to in Regulation (EU) 2020/1784 of the European Parliament and of the Council [2022] OJ L87/9. This Regulation has been subsequently amended by the Implementing Regulation (EU) 2024/1570. However, this amendment has in no way affected the date of its application.

[44] [2024] OJ 1570.

the of the Service of Documents Regulation [Articles 8, 9, 11(3), (4), and (6), 12, 14, 15(1), and (3), and Article 20], thus ensuring the proper functioning of the system. Denmark is expected to join the system and participate in the implementation of the Digitalization Regulations.

1.1. The 'digital by default' principle

The 'digital by default' principle is key to ensuring the successful implementation of the decentralized system among EU Member States.[45] Once operational, the decentralized system will become a mandatory and preferred system over any other communication method currently in place between competent authorities.

The proclamation of this principle in judicial document notification has significant implications, as it introduces a hierarchy that did not previously exist among the various notification methods established under the Notification Regulation (such as postal and consular). Thus, the decentralized system will become the preferred and exclusive notification method within the EU, thereby altering the previous doctrine of the Court of Justice of the European Union (CJEU), which considered all communication methods as alternatives without any hierarchy between them. This marks a shift from the previous approach to the new Regulation's framework. [46]

However, the European legislator acknowledges that digitalization is not a panacea. While the decentralized system will be the preferred communication method between authorities, other methods will be allowed when their use is not possible or convenient, particularly when direct communication is required between judicial bodies under certain regulations, as is the case with Regulations (EU) 2015/848[47] and (EU) 2019/1111.[48] In such cases, authorities may resort to other means of communication. The transmission must be carried out via the most appropriate alternative means, whether through other secure electronic methods or by postal service.[49]

1.2. The 'functional equivalence' principle

The principle of 'functional equivalence' is fundamental to the operability of the decentralized IT system within the EU.[50] This principle ensures that electronic documents hold the same legal value as paper documents, provided that they meet security, authenticity, and reliability requirements. This guarantees that electronically

[45] Embracing a 'digital by default' approach will streamline processes, reduce paperwork, and enhance the overall efficiency of legal proceedings. Digitalizing legal services will pave the way for a more accessible and user-friendly justice system, benefiting both legal professionals and the general public. See European Union, *European e-Justice Strategy* 2024–2028.

[46] See ECJ Case 473-04 *Plumex v Young Sports NV* (9 February 2006).

[47] Regulation (EU) 2015/848 of the European Parliament and of the Council of 20 May 2015 on insolvency proceedings [2015] OJ L141/19.

[48] Council Regulation of 25 June 2019 on jurisdiction, recognition and enforcement of judgments in matrimonial matters and in matters of parental responsibility, and on international child abduction [2019] OJ L178/1.

[49] Recital 15 of the Service of Documents Regulation and Recital 24 of the Digitalization Regulation.

[50] See Burkhard Hess, 'Article 6. Legal effects of electronic documents' in Apostolos Anthimos y Marta Requejo Isidro, *The European Service Regulation: A Commentary* (Edward Elgar Publishing 2023) 76, 78; Guillermo Palao Moreno, (n 40) 212.

transmitted documents are considered equivalent to traditional documents in terms of legal effectiveness without affecting their admissibility as evidence under national law. Thus, it is prohibited to deny the legal effects of electronic documents or to consider them inadmissible solely because of their digital format. [51]

2. Digital submission and communication in cross-border cases via the European access point

The Digitalization Regulation aims to facilitate access to justice through a European electronic access point, allowing citizens to submit digital documents, consult court records, communicate with competent authorities, and receive notifications. The electronic documents transmitted through this system have full legal effects.[52]

One of its key functions is the possibility of citizens or their representatives communicating with the competent authorities. For this, they must provide consent, either specific to each procedure or general for multiple procedures. While the regulation promotes people-centred digital transformation, it has been criticized for not ensuring fully informed consent, as it only sets requirements regarding format, language, and representation in accordance with EU law and national law. [53]

The European electronic access point is a key initiative for e-Justice in the EU intended to facilitate access to justice and improve judicial cooperation. Once operational, it will be hosted on the European e-Justice portal, similar to existing systems in countries such as Estonia (KIS2 system),[54] the Netherlands (eNCC system),[55] and Spain (Lex-Net).[56] Despite its potential to enhance accessibility, efficiency, and sustainability in cross-border civil justice, its scope is limited, as evidenced by its focus only on the procedures outlined. This limitation is surprising, as it does not enable the handling of cross-border family laws, succession, or property-related cases.

The success of the European electronic access point depends on overcoming several key challenges. To be effective, it must be available in all official EU languages and build trust among users who may have concerns about data security and the reliability of electronic procedures. Additionally, access depends on the availability of technology and the internet, which can lead to inequalities. The complexity of judicial procedures and the lack of experience with electronic platforms can be additional barriers. Although the system may be intuitive, some users require further training. Performance issues may also occur if many users access the system simultaneously, and the system can become obsolete if it is not properly updated.

For digital transformation to be beneficial for all, it is crucial to address these challenges. Therefore, it is a sound decision for the European Commission to manage, develop, maintain, and secure the system as well as provide free assistance to users.

[51] Art 6 of the Service of Documents Regulation and Art 8 of the Digitalization Regulation.
[52] Art 8.
[53] Art 4 (4).
[54] <https://www.rik.ee/en/international/court-information-system> last accessed 15 June 2024.
[55] <https://www.rechtspraak.nl/English/NCC/Pages/eNCC.aspx> last accessed 15 June 2024.
[56] <https://lexnetjusticia.gob.es> last accessed 15 June 2024.

This assistance includes guidance on how to submit applications, legal requirements, and the procedures of each Member State as well as information on how to access legal assistance in other EU countries, particularly in cross-border cases.

Ultimately, the success of the system depends on comprehensive management that combines security, digital inclusion, and information dissemination. The digital transformation of justice must therefore include the digital empowerment of and capacity-building among users.[57] The Digitalization Regulation, following the framework of the eIDAS Regulation, introduces trust services and addresses digital gaps by offering citizens the option to choose between electronic communication and alternative methods. These alternatives aim to protect vulnerable individuals such as those with limited digital skills or restricted access to technology. This concern is well known in comparative law, where systems that initially enabled electronic submission have allowed submissions through other means, as seen in the Netherlands, Germany, and Estonia.[58] However, this option only applies to individuals, excluding legal entities that are required to use electronic means exclusively, as is the case in the Spanish procedural system.[59] Nevertheless, if citizens do not understand how to participate or lack confidence in the system, its adoption will be limited, regardless of how secure or inclusive the access point is. Citizens must be aware of its existence and understand the opportunities it offers. Therefore, it is crucial to strengthen outreach and training for the legal communities involved. Moreover, the European legislators should anticipate solutions to address potential technical difficulties and exceptional situations in which electronic delivery may not be possible.

3. Judicial notification by electronic means

Electronic notification improves the efficiency, speed, and security of communication between judicial authorities and document recipients. A key achievement of the regulatory framework for digitalizing justice has been the regulation of digital judicial notification, both to the recipient's address (Art 19 of the Service of Documents Regulation) and through the European electronic access point (Art 24 of the Digitalization Regulation). The success of this method is supported by complementary European legislation such as the eIDAS Regulation and data protection regulations, which ensure, with the necessary precautions, the authentication of the parties and the protection of the recipient's personal data.

3.1. Direct electronic notification to the recipient's address

Direct electronic notification allows judicial documents to be sent and received electronically between courts and recipients, improving the efficiency and reducing the costs of the process. The new European framework enables direct electronic

[57] Recital 30 European e-Justice Strategy 2024–2028.

[58] Esteban de la Rosa (n 2) 447–48.

[59] Art 32 of Royal Decree-Law 6/2023 (BOE núm 303, de 20 de diciembre de 2023).

notification to the recipient's address in another Member State, provided that the established requirements are met (Art 19).[60]

Electronic notification is a communication channel already familiar to some national procedural systems within the EU (eg Spain,[61] France,[62] Belgium,[63] Estonia,[64] Hungary,[65] Italy,[66] and Germany[67]).[68] This innovative form of notification, operational from 1 July 2022 represents the pinnacle of agility and speed in the transmission of cross-border notifications. It combines the immediacy provided by electronic means with the direct nature of the process, as both the judicial authority sending the notification to another EU Member State and the recipient receiving it are key participants. Owing to its speed, in principle, it is the recommended notification method. However, its feasibility presents the challenge of ensuring the fundamental requirements of justice.

For the European Court of Human Rights (ECHR), it is indisputable that the use of electronic notification is compatible with fundamental rights, as evidenced by the decision in the case *Stichting Landgoed Steenbergen and others v Netherlands*,[69] provided that: 1) The medium is accessible, and 2) there is a balance between the interests at stake (§ 47). In the case of *Zavodnik v Slovenia*,[70] the Court found a violation of the right to effective judicial protection because the medium of notification did not meet

[60] Art 74(1)(c) of the UNIDROIT Model Rules on Civil Procedure also refers to this type of notification. <https://www.europeanlawinstitute.eu/fileadmin/user_upload/p_eli/Publications/Reglas-en-espan__ol-2022-28-junio.pdf> last accessed 15 June 2024.

[61] According to Art 155(1) of the Civil Procedure Act (CPA), as amended by Art 103.24 of Royal Decree-Law 6/2023 of 19 December 2023 approving urgent measures for the implementation of the Recovery, Transformation and Resilience Plan in the areas of the Judiciary, the Civil Service, Local Government and Patronage (2023) (Real Decreto-ley 6/2023, de 19 de diciembre, por el que se aprueban medidas urgentes para la ejecución del Plan de Recuperación, Transformación y Resiliencia en materia de servicio público de justicia, función pública, régimen local y mecenazgo) (SPA)—BOE núm. 303, de 20 de diciembre de 2023–), the acts of communication shall be carried out through electronic means (according to Art 152 of the Civil Procedure Act) whenever: a) the intervening party is required to use electronic systems; b) when, without being required, they have contractually committed to using such systems; and c) when, without being obligated, they choose to use these means.

[62] Art 653 of Code de procédure civile. <https://www.legifrance.gouv.fr/codes/id/LEGISCTA000006135900/> last accessed 15 June 2024.

[63] Art 332 of Code judiciaire. <https://www.ejustice.just.fgov.be/cgi_loi/change_lg_2.pl?language=fr&nm = 1967101052&la=> last accessed 15 June 2024.

[64] Art 311 of Code of Civil Procedure. https://www.riigiteataja.ee/en/eli/513122013001/consolide> last accessed 15 June 2024.

[65] See s 9(1) of Law 222 of 2015 on the General Regulation of Electronic Administration and Fiduciary Services (E-Administration Act). <https://njt.hu/jogszabaly/en/2015-222-00-00> last accessed 15 June 2024.

[66] See Mauricio Reale, 'La posta elettronica certificata e le sue applicazioni nel mondo della giustizia comunicazioni e notifiche telematiche di cancelleria', <https://www.cortedicassazione.it/cassazione-resources/resources/cms/documents/relazione_Maurizio_Reale.pdf > last accessed 15 June 2024.

[67] Lawyers are required to receive electronic communications as of 1 January 2018, <https://www.brak.de/fuer-anwaelte/bea-das-besondere-elektronische-anwaltspostfach/> last accessed 15 June 2024.

[68] For a comparative legal analysis see Fernando Gascón Inchausti, 'Electronic service of documents. National and international aspects' in Miklós Kengyel and Zoltán Nemessányi (eds), *Electronic Technology and Civil Procedure: new paths to justice form around the world* (Springer 2012) 137–80.

[69] Grand Chamber, no 19732/17, ECHR 2021. App no 19732/17 (ECHR, 16 February 2021) by (ECHR, 16 February 2021).

[70] Grand Chamber no 53723/13, ECHR 2015. App no 53723/13 (ECHR, 21 May 2015) by (ECHR, 21 May 2015).

the accessibility requirement, leading to a lack of effective knowledge of legal proceedings by the defendant.[71]

Despite this, it is undeniable that the use of this medium presents a series of weaknesses, partly linked to the functioning of email, which advises against its use for judicial notifications, particularly for the notification of initial summons. In such cases, the impact on this right may be undeniable as it can hinder the defendant's awareness of the start of the process, preventing them from effectively exercising their rights. Nevertheless, the European legislator has not restricted the use of this method for the notification of the document initiating the process. It is well known that, while the COVID-19 pandemic accelerated the use of digital tools across all Member States, the level of digital development has not been the same in all of them.[72] It is intended to facilitate the use of electronic means, even for the notification of the initial summons, if this possibility is contemplated in national procedural law. Thus, this provision provides legal coverage only for practices that exist at the national level, as is the case in Italian law (Art 149 of the Italian Code of Civil Procedure).[73] However, given the low level of security offered by this communication medium, the European legislators should adopt more protective regulations. They can opt for a multichannel approach, where electronic notifications are complemented by other communication methods such as postal mail. This hybrid solution ensures that those without internet access receive notifications. Some argue that given the potential impact on effective judicial protection, email should generally only be used as a means of sending notices. Notices are the key tools for improving communication and ensuring security.[74] Therefore, it is worth highlighting the statement made by the Hungarian government which establishes a five-day deadline for the receipt of documents notified or transferred via a secure messaging system. Thus, if the recipients neither collect the mail within this period nor reject it, they will receive a second notice on the first business day following the expiration of five days.[75]

A direct electronic judicial notification to the recipient residing in another Member State is subject to the fulfilment of a series of requirements:

A) The first requirement for the use of electronic means in judicial notifications is that these means must be available at the national level in the Member State in which the procedure is taking place (*lex fori regit processum*). Despite advances made by the EU, the regime of civil judicial cooperation has not created a common European procedural system. The Regulation on Service of Documents partially harmonises electronic judicial notification in the European space but respects national procedural rules, which continue to apply to determine whether a judicial document can be notified

[71] Nuria Marchal Escalona, 'La notificación electrónica en el Espacio Judicial Europeo: Retos y problemas' (2023) 15 2 Cuadernos de derecho transnacional, 743–44.

[72] See Commission, 'The 2023 EU Justice Scoreboard' (Communication) COM(2023) <https://commission.europa.eu/strategy-and-policy/policies/justice-and-fundamental-rights/upholding-rule-law/eu-justice-scoreboard_en> last accessed 17 November 2024.

[73] *<https://www.gazzettaufficiale.it/atto/serie_generale/caricaArticolo?art.progressivo = 0&art.idArticolo = 149&art.versione = 3&art.codiceRedazionale = 040*U1443&art.dataPubblicazioneGazzetta = 1940-10-28&art.idGruppo = 21&art.idSottoArticolo> last accessed 17 November 2024.

[74] For an in-depth analysis of this issue and potential, see Esteban de la Rosa et al (n 13) 42–43.

[75] <https://e-justice.europa.eu/39433/ES/service_of_documents_official_transmission_of_legal_documents?HUNGARY&member = 1> last accessed 15 June 2024.

electronically and, if so, by which means. Furthermore, it is up to the State in which the recipient is domiciled to determine the conditions under which digital notification is accepted.[76]

Article 19 of the Service of Documents Regulation does not limit the electronic means for notifying judicial documents to another State, allowing the use of email, SMS,[77] telephone,[78] fax, WhatsApp, social media,[79] or other applications provided that they are accepted in the Member State where the process is taking place. The only condition is that the medium must be operational within the forum. To determine the permitted means in each State, it is necessary to consult the specific declarations made by Member States regarding the application of the regulation. An analysis of these declarations reveals that, in some States, electronic notification is not operational, as is the case in Ireland,[80] Croatia,[81] Poland,[82] Sweden,[83] Romania,[84] Latvia,[85] Luxembourg,[86] Malta,[87] Portugal,[88] and Finland;[89] Spain has declared that the provision relating to electronic notification does not apply, which is surprising given that this method is operational at the national level, according to Article 103.24 of Royal Decree-Law 6/2023.[90] This implies that Spanish judicial authorities cannot send judicial documents to recipients abroad via electronic notification. However, recipients

[76] Art 19(2)(b) of the Regulation.

[77] This method of notification is used by the Internet Courts in the cities of Hangzhou, Beijing, and Guangzhou. See Fang Xuhui, 'Recent Development of Internet Courts in China' (2018) 5 1–2 Intl J on Online Dispute Resolution 49–55. Moreover, in Saudi Arabia, women are notified via text message (SMS) about any change in their marital status, such as a divorce or the reactivation of their single status. <https://www.elmundo.es/internacional/2019/01/08/5c33483bfdddff51a28b461f.html> last accessed 15 November 2024.

[78] As is the case, for example, in Denmark. See *Study on the service of documents. Comparative legal analysis of the relevant. Laws and practices of the Member States Final Report*, p 48 available at <https://www.mpravde.gov.rs/files/Analiza%20Evropske%20Komisije%20u%20vezi%20sa%20dostavljanjem%20dokumenata.pdf> last accessed 15 November 2024.

[79] As is the case in the US: *Baidoo v BloodDzraku* (5 NYS 3d 309 (NY Sup Ct 2015) <https://www.casebriefs.com/blog/law/civil-procedure/civil-procedure-keyed-to-glannon/baidoo-v-blood-dzraku/> and *FTC v PCcare247, Inc* (2013), last accessed 13 November 2024.

[80] <https://e-justice.europa.eu/38580/ES/serving_documents_recast?IRELAND&member = 1> last accessed 15 June 2024.

[81] <https://e-justice.europa.eu/38580/ES/serving_documents_recast?CROATIA&member = 1> last accessed 15 June 2024.

[82] <https://e-justice.europa.eu/38580/ES/serving_documents_recast?POLAND&member = 1> last accessed 15 June 2024.

[83] <https://e-justice.europa.eu/38580/EN/serving_documents_recast?SWEDEN&member = 1> last accessed 15 June 2024.

[84] <https://e-justice.europa.eu/38580/ES/serving_documents_recast?ROMANIA&member = 1> last accessed 15 June 2024.

[85] <https://e-justice.europa.eu/38580/ES/serving_documents_recast?LATVIA&member = 1 last accessed 15 June 2024.

[86] <https://e-justice.europa.eu/38580/ES/serving_documents_recast?LUXEMBOURG&member = 1> last accessed 15 June 2024.

[87] <https://e-justice.europa.eu/38580/ES/serving_documents_recast?MALTA&member = 1> last accessed 15 June 2024.

[88] <https://e-justice.europa.eu/38580/ES/serving_documents_recast?PORTUGAL&member = 1> last accessed 15 June 2024.

[89] <https://e-justice.europa.eu/38580/ES/serving_documents_recast?FINLAND&member = 1> last accessed 15 June 2024.

[90] Available at https://e-justice.europa.eu/38580/EN/serving_documents_recast?SPAIN&clang = en last accessed 15 June 2024.

domiciled in Spain can receive electronic judicial documents from other EU countries without additional requirements when the notification is carried out under Article 19(1)(b) of the Regulation.

In some EU Member States, such as the Czech Republic,[91] Hungary,[92] the Netherlands,[93] Belgium,[94] France,[95] and Germany,[96] only email is permitted for electronic notifications. However, other countries such as Slovakia restrict their use, allowing electronic notification in general, except in cases where personal notification is required.[97] This diversity in the acceptance and scope of electronic notification highlights the lack of a fully harmonized common European procedural regime.

Currently, the only electronic medium uniformly accepted for direct judicial notification in the EU is email, except in Germany, where the use of fax is allowed for certain trusted professionals. Other electronic means such as social media are not feasible because of the lack of guarantees regarding their authenticity and integrity, which are essential for meeting security requirements and the right to effective judicial protection.[98] Not all electronic media meet the basic requirements of ensuring the authenticity and integrity of what is sent and not all are compatible with the right to effective judicial protection.

B) The second requirement for electronic notification is that it be sent to a recipient with a known email address. According to Article 19 of the Service of Documents Regulation, the recipient is responsible for providing this information, because the use of electronic means is conditioned on the recipient's prior (express or general) consent. A notification sent to an email address designated for those required to interact electronically with the Administration of Justice, as in the Spanish system (Art 32 of Royal Decree-Law 6/2023), would not be valid as consent legitimizes the use of this notification method.

C) For the electronic notification to be valid, it is essential that the recipient gives their express, free, and voluntary consent. This consent is a fundamental requirement and must be adapted to national procedural systems, as in Spanish law, where electronic notification is mandatory for certain individuals. According to Article 19 of the Service of Documents Regulation, such consent may be granted in two ways: a) Generally, for the notification of documents in the context of various judicial procedures, in which

[91] <https://e-justice.europa.eu/39433/ES/service_of_documents_official_transmission_of_legal_documents?CZECHIA&member = 1.> last accessed 15 June 2024.

[92] https://e-justice.europa.eu/39433/ES/service_of_documents_official_transmission_of_legal_documents?HUNGARY&member = 1.

[93] <https://e-justice.europa.eu/39433/ES/service_of_documents_official_transmission_of_legal_documents?NETHERLANDS&member = 1> last accessed 15 June 2024.

[94] <https://e-justice.europa.eu/38580/ES/serving_documents_recast?BELGIUM&member = 1> last accessed 15 June 2024.

[95] <https://e-justice.europa.eu/38580/ES/serving_documents_recast?FRANCE&member = 1> last accessed 15 June 2024.

[96] <https://e-justice.europa.eu/39433/ES/service_of_documents_official_transmission_of_legal_documents?GERMANY&member = 1> last accessed 15 June 2024.

[97] Law number 160/2015 del *Civilný sporový poriadok*) and Law number 161/2015 *Civilný mimosporový poriadok* (Ley de jurisdicción civil voluntaria), <https://e-justice.europa.eu/38580/ES/serving_documents_recast?SLOVAKIA&member = 1> last accessed 15 June 2024.

[98] M.ª Luisa Villamarín López, 'Influencia de los estándares europeos en el régimen procesal español de notificaciones' in Fernando Gascón Inchausti and Pilar Peiteado Mariscal (dirs), *Estándares europeos y proceso civil. Hacia un proceso civil convergente con Europa* (Atelier 2022) 213–14.

case the documents must be sent and received electronically through qualified electronic delivery services, as per the eIDAS Regulation [Art 19(1)(a)]; or b) for a specific procedure, without the need for the use of qualified electronic delivery services, as long as proof of receipt of the document is provided, which may be confirmed by the recipient through an electronically signed acknowledgement of receipt[99] or by sending an email from the address provided by the recipient [Art 19(1)(b)]. In the second case, Member States may impose additional conditions to ensure the security of the transmission, as in Estonia.[100] In the first case, there is a greater risk of vulnerability for the recipient, as they are required to exercise excessive diligence, and technical failures may occur in the electronic means such as email.[101]

The requirement for this condition highlights the European legislator's commitment to establishing a notification method centred on the individual. However, its regulation is insufficient as it does not guarantee that the recipient is fully aware of the implications of electronic notification, which can affect their right to defence. Therefore, the European legislator should establish more detailed regulations, ensuring that consent is only valid if granted after receiving clear information in a language understandable to the recipient, and ensuring that the recipient is duly informed each time this method of notification is used.[102]

D) Finally, electronic judicial notification must guarantee high levels of authenticity, accuracy, and reliability, ensuring traceability of the transmission, receipt, content integrity, and identity of the parties. To build trust in the system, the digitalization of notifications must employ secure authentication systems.[103] In this regard, Article 19.1(a) requires that this process be subject to the general legal framework of the eIDAS Regulation. However, this requirement is mitigated when the recipient provides consent for a specific procedure, as in those cases, only an acknowledgement of the receipt is required along with the effective receipt date of the notification [Art 19.1(b)] of the Service of Documents Regulation. In such cases, the additional requirements imposed by Member States for the reception of these notifications must also be met.

However, despite the benefits of this method, the European regulatory framework remains insufficient. The legislator should foresee measures to prevent the digital

[99] Recital 33 of the Service of Documents.

[100] In accordance with Estonian law, a procedural document is considered to have been notified or transferred to the recipient by email if the recipient confirms its receipt. Such confirmation must indicate the date of receipt of the document and bear the signature of the recipient or their representative. The electronic confirmation must include the digital signature of the sender or be transmitted in another secure manner that allows for the identification of the sender and indicates when it was sent, unless the court has no reason to doubt that the unsigned confirmation was sent by the recipient or their representative. The electronic confirmation may be sent to the court by email if the recipient's email address is known to the court and if it can be presumed that no unauthorized person has access to it, and also if the court has already transmitted documents to that email address in the context of the same case or if the party has independently provided their email address to the court. The confirmation must be sent to the court without delay. Courts may impose sanctions on a party or their representative for failing to comply with this obligation. <https://e-justice.europa.eu/38580/ES/serving_documents_recast?ESTONIA&member = 1>last accessed 15 June 2024.

[101] Fernando Esteban de la Rosa (n 2) 440.

[102] Nuria Marchal Escalona (n 71) 751–753.

[103] See Modernización de los sistemas judiciales en la UE. Preguntas y respuestas, available at:< https://ec.europa.eu/commission/presscorner/detail/eS/qanda_20_2247 last accessed 20 June 2024.

divide and technological discrimination, ensuring that all citizens can exercise their procedural rights without relying on access to digital technologies. The exclusion of individuals without access to, or familiarity with, technology can violate their right to effective judicial protection. Therefore, it is essential to provide an alternative means of notification to those who cannot or do not wish to use the electronic system. Furthermore, Member States should promote access to electronic devices through grants or loans for those who cannot afford them.

3.2. Notification via the European Electronic Access Point

The objective of the Digitalization Regulation is to improve judicial cooperation within the European judicial area, both qualitatively and quantitatively. To this end, the European legislators have strengthened the Notification Regulation, allowing judicial notifications to be made through the European e-Justice Portal. In this regard, Article 24.3 of the Digitalization Regulation introduces Article 19 bis into the Service of Documents Regulation, which allows judicial notification of individuals with a known address in another Member State via this access point.

The use of secure portals for judicial electronic notifications offers clear advantages such as access to various devices, secure authentication, and signing processes, and compliance with confidentiality and data protection standards.[104] However, its implementation is subject to two requirements: a) Knowing the recipient's address in another Member State and b) the recipient having provided explicit consent during the procedure. This requirement for specific consent ensures compatibility with the right to effective judicial protection, as it prevents notifications from being made that initiate judicial proceedings.

It is an electronic notification tool that confirms that the recipient has received the notification, thereby ensuring the necessary authentication conditions. Although it does not use qualified delivery services in line with the eIDAS Regulation, it requires the recipient to confirm receipt, which is essential for building trust and preventing unfairness in legal processes. However, the tool has shortcomings as it does not clearly regulate the explicit and informed consent of recipients to receive electronic notifications. This highlights the need for more detailed regulation by the European legislator, particularly regarding how and under what conditions this consent should be given (eg in what language and in what form).

However, this tool has several limitations. If the content is not presented understandably, or if the platforms are not intuitive, recipients may not understand the content or know how to act in the legal process. Moreover, individuals without access to necessary technologies face inequality that jeopardizes their right to access the judicial system. To address these issues, awareness campaigns and training programs have been proposed to ensure that platforms are compatible with assistive technologies for people with disabilities. Furthermore, an online assistance service, such as a phone or chat line, is necessary to help users resolve issues related to access to European access point.

[104] Fernando Esteban de la Rosa et al (n 13) 42–43.

Nevertheless, this electronic notification system plays a secondary role in the notification of judicial documents abroad once the decentralized system becomes fully operational, as anticipated.

4. The holding of oral hearings via videoconference

The holding of hearings via videoconference has been key to the digitalization of justice driven by the COVID-19 pandemic.[105] This model allows courts to conduct remote hearings, overcoming geographical barriers and improving their efficiency. It is particularly beneficial in cross-border proceedings, and the European legislator has promoted it as a tool to ensure access to justice and reduce physical and logistical barriers.

The Regulation establishes the optional use of videoconferencing or other means of communication (Art 5 of the Digitalization Regulation), respecting the parties' right to interact in person with the Administration of Justice, which aligns with the objective of centring the digitalization process on human beings. Although it only partially harmonizes the conditions for conducting electronic hearings in cross-border cases, it does not provide a complete common regulation, meaning that its implementation depends on national procedural systems.

To address the technological challenges of the digitalization of justice, particularly in the conduct of oral hearings via videoconference or other electronic means, it is crucial to meet various technical and regulatory requirements that ensure both the efficiency of the system and the protection of the rights of the parties involved.[106] Specifically, it is necessary to address the following four elements:

a) Availability, adequacy, and accessibility of technological means

Whatever electronic means are used for this purpose must be available in the procedural systems of the states involved [Art 5.1(a)]. Regrettably, the legislator has not anticipated the principle of mutual assistance established by the Regulation on the obtaining of evidence (Art 12.4, final part). However, a hearing by electronic means should not be denied solely because national rules do not regulate the use of remote communication technologies. Instead, the most appropriate national rules should be applied.[107]

The procedure to initiate and hold hearings via videoconference or other remote communication technologies must be governed by the law of the member state in which the procedure takes place; that is, the member state that organises the procedure. In practice, this is where we encounter the greatest challenges and heterogeneous applications, depending on the provisions of each national legal system. Nevertheless, the competent authorities must select the most appropriate technology.[108] For instance, a

[105] See AA.VV., in Bart Krans and Anna Nylund (eds), *Civil Courts Coping with Covid-19* (Eleven International Publishing 2021).

[106] See María José Fernández-Fígares Morales, *Audiencias telemáticas en la justicia. Presente y futuro* (Tirant Lo Blanch 2021).

[107] Recital 22.

[108] Art 5.1° c) y Recital 35.

mere telephone call should not be considered suitable technology for conducting oral hearings.[109]

European regulations do not ignore the need to ensure that participants can access videoconference hearings. To this end, the Regulation requires judicial authorities to send participants a link that allows them to join the videoconference and receive technical assistance. For example, they must provide instructions on the software to be used and, if necessary, arrange a technical test before the hearing. Moreover, these tools should not leave vulnerable individuals behind. Therefore, competent authorities must ensure that these individuals, particularly those with disabilities, have access to videoconference hearings, considering their specific needs.[110] This requirement should be viewed positively, as it aligns with the need to minimize the digital divide. However, efforts must be made to resolve technological and accessibility challenges to ensure that these practices do not undermine the rights of those involved in judicial proceedings.

b) Technical requirements

A key element of the telematic conduct of a procedural act is an adequate technical system for capturing, reproducing, and recording sounds and images that offer security.[111] The technical methods used must be secure and reliable. They should allow competent authorities to authenticate the identity of the individuals to be questioned and ensure proper visual, auditory, and verbal interactions among all the participants in the hearing. To this end, the *Guide on Videoconferencing in Cross-Border Judicial Procedures* establishes common rules for its use, thus contributing to the harmonization of judicial procedures among EU Member States.[112] It addresses the organizational, technical, and legal aspects related to the implementation of videoconferencing, including the use of appropriate equipment in hearing rooms and witnesses, as well as the use of mobile devices to facilitate remote participation.[113] This guide provides a solid and detailed framework in this area, although its compliance depends on its practical implementation in courts and adaptation of national judicial systems to the technological and regulatory requirements of the EU.

The quality of the connection is crucial for the smooth running of oral hearings via videoconference. Connectivity issues such as interruptions or signal loss can disrupt the normal course of the hearing and ultimately violate the procedural rights of the parties involved. Additionally, interruptions or technical issues during transmission may arise, which can affect the judicial process, thereby delaying or complicating interactions between parties and judges.[114] This underscores the importance of a reliable, high-quality technological infrastructure to ensure the integrity and smooth flow of virtual hearings.[115]

[109] Recital 32.
[110] Recital 38.
[111] Esteban de la Rosa et al (n 13) 96.
[112] https://www.consilium.europa.eu/media/30590/qc3012963esc.pdf last accessed 13 November 2024.
[113] ibid.
[114] Javier García Sanz and Javier González Guimaraes-da Silva, 'Las «vistas telemáticas» en el proceso civil español: visión comparada, regulación y cuestiones prácticas que suscita su celebración' (2020) 9659, Diario La Ley. < https://diariolaley.laleynext.es/Content/Documento.aspx?params = H4sIAAAAAAAEAMtMSbF1CTEAAmNDIwMTC7Wy1KLizPw827DM9NS8klQAYoIO6SAAAAA=WKE> last accessed 7 November 2024.
[115] ibid.

c) Respect for fundamental rights

The technology used in oral hearings via videoconference must ensure compliance with the fundamental principles of judicial proceedings, such as the right to defence and the equality of the parties. Videoconferencing or any other electronic means must not compromise the parties' right to be heard or to present their defences. Lawyers must communicate confidentially with their clients during hearings, which requires the use of secure platforms that allow private consultations. Additionally, the lack of physical contact between the parties can influence the judge's perception of witness testimony; therefore, additional measures must be implemented to ensure the impartiality and integrity of the hearing.[116]

To this end, judicial authorities must ensure all parties have adequate access to videoconferences or offer options such as physical presence. Furthermore, the court must have the necessary technical expertise to manage the videoconference, ensuring the quality of the image and sound for the proper evaluation of testimonies and evidence. The right to interpretation must not be affected by using such technologies.

This requirement presents the challenge of having suitable equipment and infrastructure that guarantee the necessary security standards, [117] enabling both the judge and other judicial officials and legal professionals to perform their functions effectively. Videoconferences must be conducted in controlled and secure environments, with access restricted to the parties participating in the hearing. There must also be a clear protocol for interrupting or suspending the videoconference in case of technical problems, ensuring that the rights of the parties are not violated. Systems must have robust security protocols to protect the confidentiality of communication and prevent any type of interception or alteration. Access to videoconference must be controlled and limited to authorized individuals (judges, lawyers, prosecutors, parties, witnesses, etc) to prevent leaks or unauthorized access.

Regarding the handling of personal data during hearings, such data must be managed in accordance with the data minimization principle of the GDPR, collecting only information that is strictly necessary for the hearing. Recordings must be securely stored and access should be restricted to judicial purposes, with the express consent of those involved. Furthermore, data must be retained only for as long as necessary and must be securely deleted once the judicial process is concluded.

d) Technological Humanism

The regulation emphasizes the importance of hearing the parties' opinions on the use of technologies in judicial procedures (Art [5.1(b)], aligning with the European legislator's objective of centring digital transformation on the well-being of citizens. To this end, the competent authorities must choose an appropriate method for gathering opinions in accordance with domestic procedural law. Furthermore, when the recording of hearings is required under the national law of the Member State where

[116] See Judgment of the Federal Court of Australia of 15 April (*Capic v Ford Motor Company of Australia Limited (Adjournment)* [2020] FCA 486), <https://www.arbitrators.co.za/wp-content/uploads/2020/07/A-CASE-IN-POINT_Capic-v-Ford-Motor-Company-of-Australia-Limited-.pdf> last accessed 10 November 2024.

[117] ibid 51.

the hearing takes place, it is essential to inform the parties about this practice and their right to object to the recording, thus ensuring greater transparency and respect for the rights of those involved. [118]

D. Conclusions

For decades, the EU has been developing a digitalization strategy to exercise its competencies to balance the efficiency of international judicial cooperation with the safeguarding of procedural rights and access to justice. This approach can serve as a model for countries outside the EU, particularly for those seeking to modernize their judicial systems and enhance their efficiency.

The current legal framework offers great potential to adapt judicial cooperation within the EU to the digital age, promoting sustainable and people-centred justice that empowers both citizens and businesses while ensuring that technology benefits cross-border processes without undermining fundamental rights. Key regulations such as the eIDAS Regulation and data protection legislation are crucial for ensuring secure digital communication that respects citizens' rights. However, these advances are limited by the referral to the national law of the Member States, which leads to heterogeneous applications depending on each national legal system, thereby reducing their practical effectiveness and harmonisation capacity. To prevent digitalization from increasing inequalities in access to justice, countries must invest in digital infrastructure and training for judicial officers and citizens. Proper preparation for the use of these technologies contributes to faster, more efficient, and transparent justice. The exclusion of Denmark from the e-Codex and Digitalization Regulations also does not contribute positively, creating disparities in the progress of judicial digitalization among Member States and negatively impacting citizens and areas of freedom, security, and justice in Europe. It would be desirable for Denmark to join these efforts to digitalize cross-border justice within the EU.

To successfully achieve full digitalization of cross-border European justice, it is essential to have appropriate infrastructure and technical equipment that facilitate the interoperability of communications. In this regard, the technological pillars supporting the new European system are the decentralized computer system, e-Codex, and electronic points, each of which serves a specific function in the digitalization process.

The implementation of the European decentralized system based on the e-Codex represents a key advancement in the digitalization of cross-border justice, facilitating connectivity and communication among judicial authorities within the EU. However, this process requires a coordinated multilevel effort, particularly in technical and organizational terms. The pillars of this system are the principles of 'digital by default' and 'functional equivalence'. One of the expected benefits of the e-Codex is that it not only improves the efficiency of cross-border justice but also promotes the modernization of national judicial systems, accelerating the adoption of new technologies. Its success faces challenges, such as interoperability between systems, data protection,

[118] Recital 36 of the Digitalization Regulation.

and user training. To overcome these obstacles, continuous cooperation among Member States, strengthening digital infrastructure, and ongoing training of judicial staff are crucial, with an inclusive approach to avoid deepening inequalities between EU countries. However, the European legislators acknowledge that this system is not a panacea. Alternative channels may be employed if the communication channel is not feasible or suitable.

The European e-Justice Portal plays a key role in the EU's strategy to modernize and enhance the efficiency of the cross-border judicial system. It facilitates electronic access to judicial information, the submission of documents, and communication with judicial authorities, and enables the notification of judicial documents. This advancement represents a significant step towards the efficiency of cross-border procedures without compromising citizens' rights. However, its scope is limited because it applies only to certain procedures and does not bind to all Member States. Furthermore, it faces challenges such as language barriers, digital inequality, and a lack of trust in electronic systems. Its effectiveness depends on overcoming these obstacles and ensuring that all users, including those with limited technological skills, benefit from it. It is essential to promote awareness among citizens, ensure the necessary digital competencies, and implement solutions for vulnerable individuals, such as those with disabilities, using assistive technologies.

Along with this infrastructure, national IT tools form part of the European regulatory framework. The European legislator has authorized their use for international notifications and the holding of oral hearings, while respecting the existing culture and digital practices of each Member State but always within the limits and conditions established.

Although electronic notification presents numerous advantages, its proper implementation, compatible with the right to effective judicial protection, would require the incorporation of additional safeguards, particularly concerning the notification of the claim. A multichannel approach would be desirable, combining electronic notification with other methods, such as postal mail, to ensure that individuals without internet access also receive notifications. Furthermore, informed consent should be more thoroughly regulated to ensure that recipients understand how and in which language they provide informed consent. These measures would protect citizens' rights and optimise the use of technologies in the judicial field. It is crucial that Member States promote digital inclusion, improve internet access, and provide subsidies for the acquisition of devices.

The implementation of videoconferencing and other electronic means for oral hearings present significant opportunities and challenges. For its successful implementation, it is necessary to ensure that the technical aspects align with the fundamental rights of the participants and that all parties involved are well-prepared for its use. The Guide on videoconferencing in cross-border judicial proceedings is a key resource for facilitating the digitalization of justice within the EU. Although it provides a solid and detailed framework, its compliance depends on practical implementation in courts and the adaptation of national judicial systems to European technological and regulatory requirements. Courts must ensure equitable and secure use of technology and minimize technical risks and issues related to unequal access. One of the main challenges is ensuring that the right to interpretation—the right of individuals to understand and be understood during legal or official proceedings—is not compromised by the use of technology.

Bibliography

AA VV, in Krans B and Nylund A (eds), *Civil Courts Coping with Covid-19* (Eleven International Publishing 2021).

Aguilar Moreno M, 'La cooperación judicial civil en la Unión Europea: el llamado principio Digital by Default' in Martínez Velencoso LM and Plaza Penadés J, *Retos normativos del Mercado Único Digital Europeo* (Tirant lo Blanch 2022), 25.

Barei B, 'Le notificazioni nello spazio giuridico europeo dopo il Regolamento (UE) 2020/1784' (2022) 2 Riv.dir.int.priv.proc. 531.

Bueno de Mata F, 'Interoperabilidad de sistemas de gestión procesal y debido proceso: experiencias a nivel nacional y europeo para alcanzar una verdadera digitalización de la justicia' in Sánchez-Arjona ML and Calaza López S (eds), *Digitalización de la Justicia: Prevención, Investigación y enjuiciamiento* (Thomson Reuters/Aranzadi 2022), 151–76.

Hess B, 'Article 6. Legal effects of electronic documents', in Anthimos A and Requejo Isisdro M, The European Service Regulation: A Commentary (Edward Elgar Publishing 2023) 76.

Cernada Badía R, L*a notificación judicial electrónica: garantía del derecho a la tutela judicial efectiva y retos que plantea a la administración de la Justicia en España*, Tesis doctoral (Valencia 2016), <https://roderic.uv.es/bitstream/handle/10550/57638/TESIS%20DOCTORAL%20ROSA%20CERNADA%20BADIA.pdf?sequence=1&isAllowed=y>.

Commission, 'The 2023 EU Justice Scoreboard' (Communication) COM (2023) 309.

Comisión Europea, Modernización de los sistemas judiciales en la UE. Preguntas y respuestas. Comunicación sobre la digitalización de la justicia en la Unión Europea <https://ec.europa.eu/commission/presscorner/detail/es/qanda_20_2247>.

Cortés P, 'El acceso a la justicia del consumidor inglés a través de las comunicaciones electrónicas' in Esteban de la Rosa F (dir) and Moreno Cordero G and Olariu C (coords), *Justicia Digital Mercado y Resolución de Litigios de Consumo. Innovación en el diseño del Acceso a la Justicia* (Thomsom Reuters/Aranzadi 2022) 89–117.

De Asís Pulido M, 'La incidencia de las nuevas tecnologías en el derecho al debido proceso' (2020) 6(2) Ius et Sicentia 186–99.

Díaz-Silveira Santos C, 'El apoyo europeo a las redes iberoamericanas de cooperación judicial a la espera de los acuerdos de asociación subregionales entre la Unión Europea y América Latina y el Caribe' (2008) 2 Revista Electrónica Iberoamericana 79–92.

Directrices para la Resolución de litigios en línea en los procedimientos judiciales civiles y administrativos aprobadas el 16 de junio de 2021 por el Comité de ministros del Consejo de Europa <https://rm.coe.int/publication-guidelines-andexplanatory-memoreandum-odr-mechanisms-in-c/1680a4214e>.

EP, Council and Commission, European Declaration on Digital Rights and Principles for the Digital Decade, OJEU 23/01/2023 C23/1.

Esteban de la Rosa F, 'Obligaciones, derechos y garantías frente a las brechas digitales en la vertebración de la justicia en línea' in Rodríguez Ayuso JF, *Nuevos retos en materia de derechos digitales en un contexto de pandemia: perspectiva multidisciplinar* (Thomson Reuters/Aranzadi 2022) 439–70.

Esteban de la Rosa F et al, *Guía Justicia Digital. Guíía para el diálogo sobre el diseño y uso eficiente, de calidad y ético de herramientas tecnológicas en la justicia civil,* 2022. <https://hdl.handle.net/10481/76835>.

Fernández-Fígares Morales MªJ, *Audiencias telemáticas en la justicia. Presente y futuro* (Tirant Lo Blanch 2021).

Fierbințeanu G and Nemes V, 'Digital tools for judicial cooperation across the EU– the benefits of digital technologies in judicial proceedings' (2022) XXXIX Lex et Scientia 1–9.

Fontestad Portalés L, 'Evolución y avances en materia de cooperación judicial internacional a través de las transmisiones electrónicas' in Sánchez-Arjona MLvand Calaza López S (dirs), *Digitalización de la Justicia: Prevención, Investigación y enjuiciamiento* (Thomson Reuters/Aranzadi 2022) 239.

García Sanz J and González Guimaraes-da Silva J, 'Las «vistas telemáticas» en el proceso civil español: visión comparada, regulación y cuestiones prácticas que suscita su celebración' (2020) 9659, Diario La Ley <https://diariolaley.laleynext.es/Content/Documento.aspx?params=H4sIAAAAAAAEAMtMSbF1CTEAAmNDIwMTC7Wy1KLizPw827DM9NS8klQAYoIO6SAAAAA=WKE>.

Gascón Inchausti F, 'Electronic service of documents. National and international aspects' in Kengyel M and Nemessányi Z (eds), *Electronic Technology and Civil Procedure: New Paths to Justice Form around the World* (Springer 2012) 137–80.

Guía sobre videoconferencias en procedimientos judiciales transfronterizos <https://www.consilium.europa.eu/es/documents-publications/publications/guide-videoconferencing-cross-border-proceedings/>.

Illamola Dausà M, 'EU-LISA. 'The new model of operational management of the various EU databases' (2015) 111 Revista CIDOB d'Afers Internacionals 105–26.

Kramer XE, 'Access to Justice and Technology: Transforming the Face of Cross-Border Civil Litigation and Adjudication' in Benyekhlef K, Bailey J, Burkell J, and Gelinas F (eds), *e-Access to Justice* (University of Ottawa Press 2016) 351–75.

Kramer XE, 'Digitising Access to Justice: The Next Steps in the Digitalisation of Judicial Cooperation in Europe' (2022) 56 Revista General de Derecho Europeo 1–9.

Kondring, J, 'International Service by WhatsApp: Reflections on the Hague Service Convention and the 1928 Anglo-German Convention in Judgement and Recognition Proceedings' (2022) 6 IPRax, 577–85.

Lupo G and Bailey J, 'Designing and Implementing e-Justice Systems: Some Lessons Learned from EU and Canadian Examples' (2014) Laws, 353–87.

Manko R, 'Computerised system for communication in cross-border judicial proceedings (e-CODEX)', EPRS, European Parliament (2021) <https://www.europarl.europa.eu/thinktank/en/document/EPRS_BRI(2021)690667>.

Marchal Escalona N, 'La digitalización de la notificación en el espacio judicial europeo' in Sánchez-Arjona ML and Calaza López S (dirs), *Digitalización de la Justicia: Prevención, Investigación y enjuiciamiento* (Thomson Reuters/Aranzadi 2022) 387–415.

Marchal Escalona N, 'El nuevo marco europeo sobre notificación y obtención de pruebas en el extranjero: hacia un espacio judicial europeo digitalizado' (2022) 74(1) Revista española de derecho internacional 155–79.

Marchal Escalona N, 'La notificación electrónica en el Espacio Judicial Europeo: Retos y problemas' (2023) 2 Cuadernos de Derecho transnacional 736–66.

Martín González M, 'La definitiva tecnificación de las comunicaciones judiciales dirigidas al justiciable' in Sánchez-Arjona ML and Calaza López S (dirs), *Digitalización de la Justicia: Prevención, Investigación y enjuiciamiento* (Thomson Reuters/Aranzadi 2022) 446–47.

Moreno García L, 'Las notificaciones procesales por medios electrónicos a la luz de la reciente doctrina Constitucional' in Conde Fuentes J and Serrano Hoyo G (dirs), *La Justicia digital en España y en la Unión Europea* (Atelier 2019) 61–70.

OECD, 'Recommendation on Access to Justice and People-Centred Justice Systems', [2023] <https://legalinstruments.oecd.org/en/instruments/OECD-LEGAL-0498>.

Palao Moreno G, 'El Reglamento (UE) núm. 2020/1784 y su contribución al impulso de la digitalización de la cooperación judicial en materia civil y mercantil en la Unión Europea' (2024) 21 Actualidad Jurídica Iberoamericana 190–223.

Peréz Daudi V, 'La justicia civil ante el reto de las TIC' in Conde Fuentes J and Serrano Hoyo G (dirs), *La justicia digital en España y la Unión Europea* (Atelier 2019) 95–97.

Reale M, 'La posta elettronica certificata e le sue applicazioni nel mondo della giustizia comunicazioni e notifiche telematiche di cancelleria', <https://www.cortedicassazione.it/cassazione-resources/resources/cms/documents/relazione_Maurizio_Reale.pdf>.

Requejo Isidro M, 'Article 5. *Means of communication to be used by transmitting agencies, receiving agencies and central bodies*, in Anthimos A y Requejo Isidro M (eds), *The European Service Regulation*: A Commentary (Edward Elgar Publishing 2023) 71–75.

Richard V, 'A refonte du règlement sur la notification des actes judiciaires et extrajudiciaires' (2021) 2 Revue critique de droit international privé 349–60.

Richter J, 'Cross-border service of writs of summons according to the revised EU Service Regulation' (2022) 5 IPRax 433–41.

Theoduloz S and Villegas C, 'iSupport como herramienta modelo para el acceso a la justicia en el ámbito del derecho internacional privado' *Facultad de Derecho de la Universidad Católica de Uruguay*, (2021) 24 128–43.

Velicogna M, 'Justice Systems and ICT: What can be learned from Europe?' 2007 Utrecht L Rev 129–47.

Velicogna M, 'Coming to Terms with Complexity Overload in Transborder e-Justice: The e-Codex Platform' in Contini F and Francesco Lanzara G (eds), *The Circulation of Agencyin E-Justice: Interoperability and Infrastructures for European Transborder Judicial Proceedings* (Springer 2014) 309–30.

Villamarín López Mª L, 'Influencia de los estándares europeos en el régimen procesal español de notificaciones', in Gascón Inchausti F and Peiteado Mariscal P (dirs), *Estándares europeos y proceso civil. Hacia un proceso civil convergente con Europa* (Atelier 2022) 213–14.

Xuhui F, 'Recent Development of Internet Courts in China' (2018) 5 (1–2) International Journal on Online Dispute Resolution 49–55.

10

The Framework for Evidence-Taking under the Policy of European Judicial Cooperation on Civil Matters

María José Fernández-Fígares Morales[*]

A. Integrating Videoconferencing for the Taking of Evidence During European Judicial Cooperation in Civil Matters

The health crisis caused by the Covid-19 pandemic majorly impacted the technological progress of the judiciary as it accelerated its digitalization, raising the challenge

* Full Professor of Procedural Law. University of Granada.

María José Fernández-Fígares Morales, *The Framework for Evidence-Taking under the Policy of European Judicial Cooperation on Civil Matters* In: *Digitalization and Artificial Intelligence in Courts*. Edited by: Fernando Esteban de la Rosa, Pablo Cortés, and Nuria Marchal Escalona, Oxford University Press.
DOI: 10.1093/9780198918752.003.0010

of transforming the physical judiciary into an electronic form.[1] The increased use of videoconferencing has made it possible to configure this digital medium, which is ideal for conducting acts of international judicial cooperation in civil matters, particularly for judicial activities in Europe. Indeed, one of the defining elements of the European Union (EU) is the creation of a European area of justice, which is articulated in regulations based on Article 81 of the Treaty on the Functioning of the EU. This includes the adoption of measures aimed at ensuring effective judicial protection and cooperation in the gathering of evidence.[2] One of the EU objectives in the field of judicial cooperation in civil matters is to guarantee citizens easy and effective access to civil justice for the resolution of cross-border disputes and to simplify the instruments of cross-border cooperation between national civil courts. As the European Commission pointed out in its Communication of 2 December 2020, the use of videoconferencing 'significantly reduces the need for costly and time-consuming travel and can facilitate the conduct of proceedings'.[3]

The use of videoconferencing is particularly suitable for the taking of evidence when it has to be obtained on the territory of a Member State other than that of the court ordering the taking of evidence. The European cooperation framework has sought to overcome the limitations imposed by the rules of general international law on territorial sovereignty to facilitate cross-border evidence gathering and thus parties' access to evidence.[4] However, as we shall see, this objective has not been fully realized owing to the exceptional nature of the Danish case. The possibility for the courts of a Member State to 'exercise their national jurisdiction beyond the frontiers of their State' was already provided for in the previous Regulation (EC) 1206/2001,[5] on the taking of evidence ('RETE 2001').[6] Moreover, the favourable effect of the introduction of videoconferencing on the taking of evidence in the field of European judicial cooperation in civil matters should be highlighted. For example, in Spain in 1991 when this regulation was applied, 159 requests were received, 160 were resolved, and 34 remained pending. This represents an increase compared to the previous year (2020), when 89 requests were received, 93 were resolved, and 36 remained pending,[7] and is good news from the perspective of procedural efficiency.

[1] Sonia Calaza López, *El impacto de la oportunidad sobre los principios procesales clásicos: Estudios y diálogos* (Extrajudicial &Judicial Tech Iustel 2021) 41.

[2] Treaty on the Functioning of the European Union of 25 March 1957 [2010] OJ C83/47.

[3] Commission, 'Digitalisation of justice in the European Union A toolbox of opportunities' (Communication) COM (2020) 710 final.

[4] Luigi Fumagalli, 'Problemi vecchi e nuovi nella cooperazione per l'assunzione delle prove all'estero in materia civile: la rifusione della disciplina nell'Unione Europea' [2021] 4 Rivista di diritto internazionale privato e processuale 848.

[5] Council Regulation (EC) 1206/2001 of 28 May 2001 on cooperation between the courts of the Member States in the taking of evidence in civil or commercial matters [2001] OJ L174/1.

[6] Begoña Vidal Fernández, 'Obtención de pruebas' in Mar Jimeno Bulnes (eds), *La cooperación judicial civil y penal en el ámbito de la Unión Europea: instrumentos procesales* (Bosch 2007) 202.

[7] Consejo General del Poder Judicial, 'Los instrumentos de reconocimiento y ejecución de documentos judiciales y de auxilio judicial internacional en el orden civil a la luz de la Estadística Judicial 2021' [2022] Boletín de Información Estadística 5. Open access: <www.poderjudicial.es/cgpj/es/Temas/Estadistica-Judicial/Estudios-e-Informes/Datos-de-Justicia> last accessed 23 October 2024.

The new European regime contained in Regulation (EU) 2020/1783 on judicial cooperation in civil matters on the taking of evidence ('RETE 2020') aims to better meet the requirements of immediacy, speed, and flexibility that these procedures demand.[8] To this end, the new regulation allows the requesting court of a Member State, subject to certain conditions, to take evidence directly by means of videoconferencing or other telecommunications technology, where the taking of evidence consists of a hearing or examination of a witness, a person who is a party to the proceedings, or an expert who is located in another Member State.

The implementation of the new European framework for the taking of evidence through videoconferences is not without challenges. The first relates to the interoperability of the system used. Ensuring the interconnection of the programs or platforms used to carry out audiovisual communication in proceedings is a crucial issue to avoid obstacles that would hinder the effective use of the resource. Thus, it is necessary to evaluate the steps that the forthcoming implementation of the decentralized platform provides for in European regulations encompassing this area. An additional difficulty is posed by the lack of common procedural rules in EU Member States on the use of videoconferencing for the collection of evidence. Accordingly, it is necessary to evaluate the results of the coordination between legislation introduced by the new regulation in terms of achieving the necessary balance between efficiency and guaranteeing the rights involved in this practice of taking evidence at a distance. Videoconferencing must also comply with general European data protection legislation. Various issues, including the form of access and identification in videoconferences, the protection of information about videoconferences, and the security or confidentiality of data, must be adequately defined in the cross-border environment. Furthermore, there is the general challenge of achieving human incorporation of videoconferencing as a means of evidence in a manner that simultaneously contributes to the empowerment of the persons to be interrogated. To address this challenge, personal perceptions and psychological reactions to technology in the legal and technical configuration of this phenomenon should be considered. These issues affect the values that the EU defends and wants to promote through the European Declaration on Digital Rights and Principles, which aims to create a safe digital space characterised by inclusion and accessibility.[9] This study examines the European regime for the taking of evidence in civil and commercial matters by video conference consisting of the hearing of the parties, the examination of witnesses, experts, etc, in the context of judicial cooperation among EU Member States to assess whether the coordination provided for in recent European legislation, especially RETE 2020, is sufficient to meet the challenges posed and to suggest areas for improvement.

[8] Parliament and of the Council Regulation (EU) 2020/1783, of 25 November 2020 on cooperation between the courts of the Member States in the taking of evidence in civil or commercial matters (taking of evidence) [2020] OJ L405/1.

[9] European Declaration on Digital Rights and Principles for the Digital Decade [2023] OJ C 23/1.

B. Legal and Technological Requirements For The Use Of Videoconferencing for the Taking of Evidence During European Judicial Cooperation in Civil Matters

1. Guaranteeing the rights of defence through European coordination regulation

The European Court of Human Rights has ruled that the use of videoconferencing in trials is permissible if two conditions are met: (1) a legitimate purpose is pursued, and (2) the rights of defence are respected.[10] According to RETE 2020, the procedures for obtaining, preserving, and presenting evidence must ensure respect for the rights of defence (Recital 30), procedural rights (Recital 31), and the right to privacy, confidentiality, and data protection (Recital 32). Article 32 of Regulation 2020/1784 on notifications[11] confirms the protection of the principles of equal access to justice.

The principle of non-discrimination is a fundamental principle of the EU and a necessary condition for the realization of freedom, security, and justice, as set out in Article 67 of the TFEU,[12] of which cross-border investigative cooperation is a direct manifestation. Furthermore, access to civil justice is guaranteed by Article 47 of the Charter of Fundamental Rights of the European Union (ECFR)[13] and Article 6(1) of the European Convention on Human Rights (ECHR).[14] [15] From these two provisions, we derive the minimum and indispensable elements for the proper exercise of justice based on the concept of a *fair trial.*

The concept of a *fair trial* includes the *right of defence.* As has already been stated, this right 'guarantees the parties the opportunity to argue their respective claims and to refute the grounds which the opposing party may have put forward in support of their claims without it being necessary for an effective argumentative controversy to take place de facto between the litigants, which, for one reason or another, may not take place'.[16] Owing to technical limitations, a videoconference restricts one of these powers, infringing the aforementioned right.

It is the policy of the EU that the division of the EU into separate Member States should not affect the exercise of individuals' rights before judicial authorities. Moreover, the rules of the private international law of Member States generally link international judicial cooperation with the right to an effective remedy. Such a link is established 'by establishing in this context a clear approximation aimed at protecting'

[10] *Marcello Viola v Italia* (2006) App no 77633/16 ECtHR, 5 October 2006.

[11] Regulation (EU) 2020/1784 of the European Parliament and of the Council of 25 November 2020 on the service in the Member States of judicial and extrajudicial documents in civil or commercial matters (service of documents) [2020] OJ L405/40.

[12] Treaty on the Functioning of the European Union [2010] OJ C83/47.

[13] Charter of Fundamental Rights of the European Union [2000] OJ C364/1.

[14] Convention for the Protection of Human Rights and Fundamental Freedoms of 4 November 1950 [1950].

[15] See <www.coe.int/en/web/human-rights-convention> last accessed 23 October 2024.

[16] Joan Picó i Junoy, 'Derecho a la defensa', in Joan Picó i Junoy (eds), *Las garantías constitucionales del proceso* (Boch 2012) 121.

and respecting 'the rights and legitimate interests of individuals'.[17] Similarly, evidentiary assistance is part of the right to evidence, as it is 'that which the parties possess, consisting in the use of the means of evidence necessary to form the conviction of the judicial body about what is discussed in the process, and therefore all relevant evidence requested, in accordance with the legal requirements, must be admitted and practised'.[18] An audiovisual format has advantages when applied to international judicial cooperation, as it 'significantly reduces the need for costly travel and facilitates the conduct of proceedings'.[19]

On the other hand, it has been stated that 'the right of citizens to enjoy the protection of the courts acquires a particular peculiarity when the conflict has an international dimension, inasmuch as its guarantee could be limited; for this reason, this fundamental right is reinforced at European level'.[20] It is perhaps for this reason that the role assigned to the use of audiovisual telematics for the purpose of obtaining personal evidence has acquired particular importance in the field of international judicial cooperation and, more specifically, in the EU. For example, RETE 2020 envisages its use in overcoming physical barriers across borders. According to the regulation, 'the full potential of modern communications technology, such as videoconferencing, which is an important means of simplifying and speeding up the taking of evidence, is not currently being exploited'.

The European regime of Judicial Cooperation in Civil Matters on the use of videoconferencing for the taking of evidence does not aim to create a complete and common European procedural regime but rather to achieve coordination so as to allow the use of videoconferencing for the taking of evidence, in which the procedural systems of Member States will continue to apply with respect to various issues. For this reason, the regulation of a specific regime for the taking of evidence via videoconference is not entirely uniform. The general criterion for the taking of evidence through videoconferencing is the application of the national procedural rules of the competent court. The national rules of each Member State decide issues such as the requirement of judicial presence during the virtual acquisition of evidence, the more/less explicit level of specific requirements for the format and quality of retransmission, and the necessary possibility of bilateral communication during retransmission. There are also differences in the national treatment of the recognition of the rights of defence and its implications for remote practices. This right implies that parties or their representatives may participate and intervene in remote practice to defend their respective interests during the proceedings. In this respect, the coordination of RETE 2020 in Recital 18 is intended to facilitate the effective exercise of the rights of defence by providing that the parties should be able to be present when evidence is taken, if the law of the Member

[17] Albert Font i Segura, 'Artículo 3. Principio General favorable de cooperación', in Fernando Pedro Méndez González and Guillermo Palao Moreno (eds), *Comentarios a la Ley de Cooperación Jurídica Internacional en materia civil* (Tirant Lo Blanch 2017) 77.

[18] Joan Picó i Junoy, *Las garantías constitucionales del proceso* (2nd edn, Bosch 2012) 177.

[19] José Ramón De Blas Javaloyas and Carmen María García Mirete, 'El futuro de la cooperación judicial civil en la Unión Europea. Una perspectiva' [2022] Actualidad Civil 1.

[20] María Dolores Ramírez Benavente, 'La obtención de prueba en la unión europea: evolución y análisis del Reglamento (UE) 2020/1783 relativo a la cooperación entre los órganos jurisdiccionales de los estados miembros en el ámbito de la obtención de pruebas en materia civil o mercantil' [2021] Revista General de Derecho Europeo 1.

State of the requesting court so provides, in order to be able to follow the proceedings in a manner comparable to the situation if the evidence had been taken in the Member State of the requesting court. However, the requesting court should determine the conditions under which they may participate in accordance with national law.

2. Technological requirements arising from the protection of safeguards and rights

The lack of homogeneity in national procedural rules must translate into a need for technological equipment that can meet any requirements that may arise. The necessary equipment must be available for evidentiary videoconferences to be conducted in accordance with all national procedural rules. In the absence of such equipment and to avoid infringing on procedural rights, videoconferencing should be excluded in the taking of evidence.

When a videoconference is used as evidence, it is essential to demand the highest technological quality, secure interface requirements, a solid system of identification of the remote interlocutors, a means of ensuring testimony remains untainted, and a visual and organizational configuration of the presentation that is as faithful as possible to the apparent and formal aspects of hearings in a regime of physical presence. Only in this way will it be possible to speak of genuine presence; from then on, the level of protection of procedural guarantees will no longer be subject to the drift of technical constraints and will be solely in the hands of the competent court, as is the case with hearings in the regime of physical presence. For our part, we maintain the need for technology with improved functionality compared to traditional videoconferencing technology.

In order for videoconferencing to be used successfully for the taking of evidence during European judicial cooperation, the technology used must, in our view and according to a previous study we conducted, be able to support both high-quality images and sound, which must be synchronized and provided without time delay with a continuous and uninterrupted connection. The technology must also allow easy identification of the persons involved in the written image and ensure the quality of their interventions. Furthermore, it must enable bilateral and simultaneous communication, guaranteeing the continuity of the audiovisual channel without interruptions, and allow visual, audio, and verbal interaction between two persons or groups of persons. It must also provide opportunities to question or contradict other parties and to exercise one's respective rights of defence. The rights to privacy, dignity, and data protection must be respected during the signal flow, which should allow the complete recording of the event as a means of documenting it. In addition, a remotely questioned person should provide evidence in a manner that is subject to judicial control and has the appearance of formality, such as conducting the proceedings in the room of a competent judicial body or at a secure access point with identical judicial precautions and symbols.[21] Some procedural laws allow the court to authorize the taking of

[21] María José Fernández-Fígares Morales, *Audiencias Telemáticas en la Justicia. Presente y futuro* (Tirant Lo Blanch 2021) 136.

evidence 'from anywhere'. This is the case in Spain, owing to the recent introduction of Article 137 bis.3 LEC:[22] the only requirement is the mandatory consent of the judicial authority, which must take into account the circumstances of the case and ensure the means are available to accurately identify the intervener in accordance with the provisions of the law. Concerning this alternative method of connection, it should be noted that the use of home equipment gives rise to a great deal of uncertainty regarding the general quality of the connection, and, more importantly, the effective monitoring or control of the evidence by the court, since there may be disloyal practices on the part of the person questioned such as receiving instructions or synchronous dictation from a third party of the answers to be given by the person questioned during their testimony.[23]

In addition, it is advisable to install a panoramic or mobile camera that covers a wide field of vision and leaves no blind spots at the place where the testimony is taken in order to ensure that the judge has technical control over the proceedings at all times to effectively control the process. The Council of the European Union's 2013 Guide to Videoconferencing in Cross-Border Proceedings defines what the image should look like as follows: 'In cross-border videoconferencing, it is expected that the screen can be used for three different levels' [24] and, in all cases, 'the judge must have the technical capacity to direct the conduct of the proceedings'.[25]

The aforementioned technical requirements are intended to ensure that the judge has direct access to the evidence. Such direct judicial control ensures that the same principles, guarantees, and procedural rights are respected in an oral environment with a physical presence. In this respect, the European Commission warns that the use of videoconferencing must not infringe on the right to a fair trial or the rights of defence, including the right to be present at the trial, to communicate confidentially with counsel, to question witnesses, and to challenge evidence.[26] Moreover, when the control of the videoconferencing is assumed by the requesting authority, which is competent to decide the case, direct assessment through the virtual channel optimizes compliance with the requirements derived from the principle of immediacy. It has been affirmed that the complete telematic implementation—the entire procedure—'could jeopardise the rights and guarantees concerned, which should be sacrificed only in exceptional cases and when the physical presence of the declarant is materially

[22] See Article 137 bis.3º of the Civil Procedure Act (2000) (Ley 1/2000, de 7 de enero, de Enjuiciamiento Civil) (SPA), in the version given by Royal Decree-Law 6/2023 of 19 December approving urgent measures for the implementation of the Recovery, Transformation and Resilience Plan in the areas of the Judiciary, the Civil Service, Local Government and Patronage (2023) (Real Decreto-ley 6/2023, de 19 de diciembre, por el que se aprueban medidas urgentes para la ejecución del Plan de Recuperación, Transformación y Resiliencia en materia de servicio público de justicia, función pública, régimen local y mecenazgo) (SPA).

[23] Fernández-Fígares Morales (n 21) 63.

[24] Council of the European Union, General Secretariat of the Council, *Guide on videoconferencing in cross-border proceedings* (European e-justice Publications Office 2013) 18 <https://data.europa.eu/doi/10.2860/76243 > last accessed 23 October 2024.

[25] Javier García Sanz and Javier González Guimaraes-Da Silva, 'Las `vistas telemáticas` en el proceso civil español: visión comparada, regulación y cuestiones prácticas que suscita su celebración' [2020] Diario La Ley 16.

[26] Commission, 'Digitalisation of justice in the European Union A toolbox of opportunities' (Communication) COM (2020) 710 final.

impossible'.[27] However, these concerns about videoconferencing lose their relevance in the field of judicial cooperation in matters of evidence. This is because we are addressing specific evidentiary acts where legal authorization allows for overcoming the lack of immediacy in the traditional mutual legal assistance system. By using videoconferencing, the evidence source is brought closer to the judge, effectively extending jurisdiction beyond the court's physical territory. For this reason, some legal systems, such as that of Spain, openly allow the use of videoconferencing in evidentiary proceedings in which persons outside the territorial limits of the court, whether national or transnational, have to testify. This means is prioritized over traditional mutual legal assistance, which is relegated to a residual means owing to its lack of immediacy.[28]

C. The Regime for the Taking of Evidence during European Judicial Cooperation in Civil Matters

1. Bodies, empowered countries and acts covered for the issuing and receiving requests: typology of letters rogatory

When dealing with cross-border requests for evidence, the focus is on the 'requesting court' and the 'requested court'. Both must belong to the countries participating in the regulation; that is, EU Member States, with the exception of Denmark. Since Denmark has maintained its previous position on the new regulation with regard to other instruments of judicial cooperation in civil matters, it does not participate in this regulation and is not bound by it (Recital 38). As a result, two systems of judicial cooperation coexist between EU Member States: 1) that which applies in relations between the States where the regulation applies, and 2) that which applies in relations between each of these States and Denmark and, in particular, the 1970 Hague Convention on the Taking of Evidence Abroad in Civil and Commercial Matters.[29] [30]

According to RETE 2020, the term 'court' covers not only courts but also other authorities of the Member States notified to the Commission under a monitoring system established by the regulation itself; that is, Article 31(3). However, relevant authorities must fulfil the following conditions: 1) exercise judicial functions, 2) act by delegation of powers from a judicial authority or be under the control of such an authority, and 3) be competent under national law to take evidence for judicial proceedings in civil or commercial matters. It follows from the above requirements that administrative bodies are excluded from such considerations, and, for the same reason, arbitral tribunals are not directly eligible for such assistance.[31] Therefore, a request for a witness

[27] María Elena Laro González, 'Una justicia eficiente y digital para una administración de justicia obsoleta' in Mercedes Llorente Sánchez-Arjona and Sonia Calaza López (eds), *Digitalización de la Justicia: Prevención, investigación y enjuiciamiento* (Thomson Reuters Aranzadi 2022) 322.

[28] Civil Procedure Act (SPA), arts 129 and 177.

[29] Convention on the taking of evidence abroad in civil or commercial matters of 18 March 1970.

[30] See <https://www.hcch.net/en/instruments/conventions/full-text/?cid = 82> last accessed 23 October de 2024.

[31] Stefano Signorin, 'La digitalizzazione della cooperazione giudiziaria in materia civile e commerciale nell'Unione Europea: L'assunzione transfrontaliera delle prove nel prisma della piattaforma informatica decentrata e-CODEX' [2024] 1 Cuadernos de Derecho Transnacional 606.

statement made in the context of administrative disciplinary proceedings or in the course of arbitral proceedings is inadmissible.

A more controversial question is whether injunctions issued by judicial authorities in the execution of assistance given to an arbitral tribunal are legitimate injunctions. The doctrine has different opinions for [32] and against.[33] In our opinion, such injunctions should be admitted as Article 1 of RETE 2020 does not impose any restrictions in this respect, referring in general terms to 'proceedings already instituted or intended to be instituted' (Art 1(2)), without mentioning that these must be proceedings for trial or decision by the requesting authority itself. In any case, it is necessary to consider arbitrators' prior recognition by the national law of judicial assistance in the taking of evidence. In Spanish law, for example, this is provided for in Law 60/2003 of 23 December 2003 on Arbitration, in Article 33 (Recognition and regime of judicial assistance in the taking of evidence) in relation to Article 8.2 (judicial competence to assist the arbitrators in the taking of evidence).

Regarding the status of the proceedings in which the requests originate, they must be based on judicial proceedings already instituted or to be instituted, as in the case of possible preliminary proceedings (Art 1(2)), that have taken place after this regulation came into force: 1 July 2022. The direct taking of evidence—from the requesting authority to the person questioned—which may take place through the use of videoconferencing, includes, in particular, the taking of a statement or questioning of a person present in another Member State (Art 20(1)). With regard to the concept of 'evidence-gathering measures', the question arises as to whether pre-trial measures and, more generally, measures which, in addition to their evidentiary function, have an exploratory purpose, such as the so-called 'fishing expedition', are covered by this concept.[34] In any event, the concept of an evidentiary act should be understood in a broad sense, so as to cover any judicial measure to obtain material for the sole purpose of gathering evidence, regardless of whether it is provided for in the procedural systems of Member States. The rationale behind this approach is that RETE 2020 proposes a paradigm of quasi-free investigative activity to consider the different evidentiary procedural modalities in the national laws of Member States.[35]

The cooperation between the judicial authorities of the EU Member States provided for in the RETE 2020 envisages two ways in which evidence may be taken on a transnational basis: a) a court of an EU Member State may request the competent court of another Member State take evidence and b) evidence may be taken directly in another Member State (Art 1(1)). Each of these is discussed below.

[32] Ángel Marcos Gómez Aguilera, 'La práctica de pruebas en materia civil y mercantil en la Unión Europea: el Reglamento (CE) 1206/2001' [2020] Revista de Derecho VLex 198.

[33] Signorin (n 31) 606.

[34] Ibid 607.

[35] Nicolo Trocker, 'Il regolamento (CE) n. 1206/2001 del Consiglio, del 28 maggio 2001, relativo alla cooperazione fra le autorità giudiziarie degli Stati membri nel settore dell'assunzione delle prove in materia civile e commerciale' in Michele Taruffo and Vicenzo Varano (eds), *Manuale di diritto processuale civile europeo* (Giappichelli 2011) 285.

2. Indirect taking of evidence: the use of videoconferencing by the requested judicial body

The possibility of requesting that the court of another Member State take evidence is maintained in RETE 2020. To this end, each Member State must draw up a list of competent courts and their respective territorial jurisdictions or special assignments for the taking of evidence in civil or commercial matters falling within the scope of the regulation (Art 3). This list and any amendments to it must be communicated by Member States to the Commission, which will make this information available electronically, particularly through the European e-justice portal (Art 31). Regarding the use of audiovisual means by the requested authority, RETE 2020 gives preference to the technology indicated by the requesting authority (ie videoconferencing or teleconferencing). If such a use is incompatible with national law or if the requested court cannot use it because of major practical difficulties, the requested court must inform the requesting court. If the reason for refusing enforcement by such technical means is the unavailability of the technology in the requesting or requested court, the requesting or requested court may make it available through mutual agreement (Art 12 (4)).

The requested body is obliged to execute the request as soon as possible and within 90 days of receipt of the request (Art 12(1)). The procedure for executing a request is governed by the national law of the requested body (Art 12(2)); however, RETE 2020 allows the issuing authority to include a request for the execution of a reference to a special procedure provided by its own national law. The executing authority must comply with this request unless it is incompatible with national law or impossible due to major practical difficulties, in which case the requesting authority must be informed (Art 12(3)). However, technological obstacles can be overcome. The regulation provides that if the requested authority does not have the appropriate technical means, these may be provided by the requesting authority through mutual agreement (Art 12), which is consistent with the principles of speed and efficiency.

Regarding the presence and participation of the parties or their representatives during the taking of evidence, RETE 2020 is subject to possible provisions of the law of the Member States of the requesting court. The requesting court is required to mention this in its request in Form A, and subsequent transmission of such a request is permitted (Arts 13(1) and (2)). Once the request has been made, the requested authority determines the conditions under which it may participate (Art 13(3)); however, it must follow the general rules on the execution of a request laid down in Article 12 of the regulation itself. Notably, the requested body is responsible for informing the parties and, where appropriate, their representatives of the time and place where the taking of evidence will take place and, where appropriate, of the conditions under which they may participate in the taking of evidence (Art 13(4)). Irrespective of the initiative of the parties as to their presence in the taking of evidence, the executing authority also has the power to invite the parties to attend or participate if such a provision exists in its national law (Art 13(5)). It is worth mentioning that the recent Regulation 2023/2844, known as the European Digitalization Regulation,[36] contains

[36] European Parliament and of the Council Regulation (EU) 2023/2844 of 13 December 2023 on the digitalization of judicial cooperation and access to justice in cross-border civil, commercial and criminal matters and amending certain acts in the field of judicial cooperation [2023] OJ L2023/2844.

more precise rules on the possibility of parties participating in hearings by videoconference or other means of remote communication in civil, commercial, and criminal matters when one of the parties or their representative is present in another Member State (Art 5.1).

3. Direct taking of evidence: the use of videoconferencing by the requesting judicial body

RETE 2001, which preceded the current rules, provided for the direct taking of evidence by the requesting court. However, this had to be done by a member of the judicial staff or another person, such as an expert, appointed in accordance with the law of the Member State of the requesting court. Moreover, the rules did not provide the possibility of connecting via videoconference. Under the previous system, the judge who provided the judgment did not have direct access to the source in these cases. What was provided for, by case law, was the possibility of the requesting court hearing the person questioned who was resident in another State directly, but this required their physical presence. For example, the Court of Justice of the European Union (First Chamber), in its judgment of 6 September 2012, adopted this practice, which consisted of the person questioned appearing 'at the seat of the court in the State hearing the case'.[37] Doctrine confirms this possibility.[38] Moreover, in its judgement of 21 February 2013, the Court of Justice of the European Union (First Chamber) opened its eyes to other systems of access to evidentiary sources, stressing the need to strengthen the possibilities for cross-border gathering of evidence that underpin the rules on judicial cooperation without preventing judicial authorities from using other mechanisms—hitherto not provided for—that are simpler, more effective, and quicker in light of the circumstances.[39] This is also the line taken up by the existing doctrine.[40]

In this context, the current regulation, adopted in the wake of RETE 2020, promotes efficiency and immediacy by allowing the use of videoconferencing for the direct taking of evidence. It allows a court in one Member State to ask a court in another Member State to facilitate the taking of evidence in person by video conference. However, this possibility is limited to the taking of evidence or the hearing of a witness, party to the proceedings, or expert present in another Member State (Art 20(1)). The only condition of this regulation is that audiovisual technology is available to the court, and that the court, with regard to the specific circumstances of the case, considers the use of such an application appropriate (Art 20(1)). Videoconferencing may

[37] Case C-170/11 *Lippens v Kortekaas* [2012] ECR 28.

[38] Francisco de Paula Puig Blanes, 'Juicios telemáticos entre distintos países de la Unión Europea' [2021] Diario La Ley 1.

[39] Case C-332/11 *ProRail BV v Xpedys NV* [2013] ECR 42.

[40] Aleš Galič, 'Open issues concerning the non-mandatory character of the Cross-Border Taking of Evidence Regulation' [2017] 3 Era Forum 213.

also be used to hear a child in matrimonial or family matters in accordance with the provisions of Regulation (EU) 2019/1111.[41]

Under the system implemented by RETE 2020, the court retains its rightful place in the litigation process and is the interlocutor who can now directly witness the sources of evidence telematically through its own senses. This is a major step towards the direct assessment of evidence, which avoids the biases inherent in the use of traditional assistance provided through the intervention of the necessary courts and written results.

It is of great importance that this form of videoconferencing for the direct taking of evidence is not coercive but voluntary (Art 19(2)), a clear distinction in relation to the effectiveness of a videoconference carried out by the requested authority with respect to persons within its own territorial jurisdiction, which has binding effects. This characterization is based on the link between state sovereignty and jurisdiction, from which it follows that only judicial bodies vested with jurisdiction in accordance with state regulations can exercise their functions in a coercive manner.[42] In our view, this difference in treatment is inappropriate as it leaves the provision of the requested evidence to the will of the person questioned, which, in turn, may affect the proper development of the principle of procedural effectiveness. Indeed, if the person from whom the remote evidence is to be taken refuses to testify directly before the requesting authority, the latter will have no choice but to request European judicial cooperation once again, but this time, with a view to the requested authority taking the evidence. In our view, this alternative system, involving the personal taking of evidence by the requested authority following the instructions of the requested authority, is not good news for compliance with the principle of immediacy, even if it is carried out by videoconference, fully recorded, and subsequently made available to the requesting authority as it involves moving the source of evidence away from the decision-making body. It should be noted that the immediacy of the court to the evidence made possible by the use of videoconferencing results in the protection of the right to effective judicial protection and, in particular, the protection of the right to trial without undue delay, which is in line with the requirements of Article 6(1) of the ECHR. This practice optimizes the effectiveness of the principle of procedural economy,[43] favours compliance with the principle of concentration,[44] and, in short, is a driving force for the principle of procedural speed. According to the doctrine, these latter principles aim to achieve the maximum amount of procedural activity with the minimum amount of means. Videoconferencing contributes to this concentration and speed by avoiding the possible suspension of oral proceedings as this tool makes it possible to avoid failure due to, for example, the inability to travel to court.[45]

[41] Council Regulation (EU) 2019/1111 of 25 June 2019 on jurisdiction, the recognition and enforcement of decisions in matrimonial matters and the matters of parental responsibility, and on international child abduction (recast) [2019] OJ L178/1.

[42] Jaime Guasp Delgado, *Comentarios a la Ley de Enjuiciamiento Civil*, I (Aranzadi 2011) 11.

[43] Enrique Jiménez Asenjo, 'Economía Procesal', *Nueva Enciclopedia Jurídica Seix* (1974) 897.

[44] Niceto Alcalá-Zamora y Castillo, 'La teoría de las crisis del proceso, aplicada al proceso penal' [1951] Revista de Derecho Procesal 375.

[45] María Jesús Pesqueira Zamora, *La suspensión de los juicios orales especial atención a sus causas y tratamiento procesal* (Bosch 2015) 52.

As has been pointed out, 'immediacy is a means of ensuring that the judge always intervenes directly in the judicial process'. Moreover, with regard to oral acts, 'the judge must be present at all of them, especially those involving the taking of evidence, insofar as they are relevant to the exercise of jurisdiction, normally to the passing of sentence', so that 'the judge cannot pass sentence on the basis of what he has been told, but on the basis of what he himself has seen'. Directness implies that the judge actively participates in the proceedings, especially in the testimonies of the persons asking for clarifications that help them to form their judgment.[46] This principle provides what is known as a *guarantee of correctness*, which function is to avoid the risks of inappropriate evaluation of evidence caused by the use of an intermediary between the evidence and the evaluator.

In this sense, from the point of view of the theory of social communication, it should be noted that it is necessary to ensure that the judge or tribunal in the evidentiary practice intervenes in such a way that they directly perceive, through their own senses, the progress of the same. This precaution prevents the introduction of bias that could arise from the use of intermediaries. It has been said that 'prudential judgement necessarily implies objective knowledge of the relevant facts'.[47] Moreover, it is precisely this objective knowledge that is fostered by the direct assessment of the source of evidence.

For these reasons, it is possible to propose, as a more satisfactory arrangement than the current one, conciliatory solutions aimed at achieving simultaneous compliance with the requirements of the principle of national competence and those arising from the principle of immediacy. This can be achieved through joint actions involving the presence of staff from the requesting and requested authorities. The provision of assistance in the form of direct videoconferences has already been provided for in Article 20(2), although it only refers to assistance in practical aspects. The proposed formula makes it possible to harmonize respect for sovereignty and jurisdiction and, above all, to optimize the guarantee of immediacy.

The introduction of videoconferencing has brought about a conceptual revolution, even at the terminology level, to the extent that the standard of immediacy is *direct appreciation* by the court. However, it is now possible to distinguish between physical and virtual presence in two forms of immediacy. During international judicial cooperation in the taking of evidence, the use of direct videoconferencing (directed by the requesting authority) has brought us closer to the concept of immediacy as we are moving from no direct assessment to direct assessment via videoconferencing.

However, it should be noted that recent studies assessing the perceptions of those involved in online hearings based on surveys suggest uncertainty about the appropriateness of using videoconferencing in all scenarios. For example, when gathering information on the impact of telehearings, we found a report on remote hearings during COVID-19 in the UK in 2021 showing that this is not always the preferred resource as more than one-third of the judges (36 per cent) said they preferred face-to-face hearings, while 45 per cent said they preferred face-to-face or remote hearings, depending

[46] Jordi Nieva Fenoll, *Derecho Procesal I. Introducción* (Tirant Lo Blanch 2019) 157.

[47] Ignacio Sancho Gargallo, *La incidencia de los sesgos cognitivos en el enjuiciamiento* (Tirant Lo Blanch 2024) 19.

on the circumstances detailed in the study itself.[48] The authors also concluded that, unlike users of the public justice system, (eg witnesses, experts) who find the use of teleconferencing for court hearings acceptable, 'judges and other legal professionals consider that the most complex acts and those that can change people's lives ... are less appropriate to be dealt with at a distance'.[49] The study also found that judges in civil and family courts were more likely to report that remote hearings negatively impacted their health and well-being more than judges in other jurisdictions. This indicates that legal representatives working in courts were less likely to express a preference for remote hearings.[50] In addition, judges and other professionals have reported that remote hearings do not work well for public service users who require interpreters.[51] Another aspect evaluated was communication with legal representatives during remote hearings. This was a concern for some users, particularly vulnerable people. In addition, some judges are concerned that remote hearings are not sufficiently formal and do not convey the seriousness of the proceedings.[52]

4. Practical aspects of the use of videoconferencing for taking evidence

One of the areas in which European coordination is crucial concerns the modalities for the production of documents during the taking of evidence via videoconferences. On this point, there are reports on the use of videoconferencing that note complaints about the impossibility of having 'a system for the parties to examine the documents provided by electronic means, deficiencies which it is hoped will be remedied during the current exercise'.[53] The regulation merely states that the court must provide the parties and their legal representatives with instructions concerning the procedure for the production of documents or other materials when the taking of evidence or the performance of a hearing is conducted by videoconference or other appropriate telecommunications technology (Recital (23) of RETE 2020). We are of the opinion that the submission of documents by the parties to the court and to other parties should take place at the times determined by the procedural law applicable to the case and, where appropriate, at the oral hearing, if so determined. It is, therefore, necessary to provide 'advanced technology' to ensure the immediate uploading, delivery, and viewing by the court and the parties during the oral proceedings by means of videoconferencing if the acts performed so require.[54]

It is worth noting the value that RETE 2020 places on reaching a consensus among the requesting, central, and requested courts on 'practicalities'. However, this legal term can be vague and confusing. Therefore, we must distinguish between purely

[48] Janet Clark, *Evaluation of remote hearings during the Covid 19 pandemic* (Research report HM Courts & Tribunal Service United Kingdom 2021) 67.
[49] ibid 90.
[50] ibid 92.
[51] ibid 94.
[52] ibid 96.
[53] Tribunal Superior de Justicia de Asturias, *Memoria Judicial 2022* (Portal del poder Judicial de España, 2023) 31. Open access: <https://www.poderjudicial.es/cgpj/es/Poder-Judicial/Tribunales-Superiores-de-Justicia/TSJ-Asturias/Actividad-del-TSJ-Asturias/Memoria-Judicial/> last accessed 23 de October 2024.
[54] Fernández-Fígares Morales (n 21) 136.

organizational matters and aspects of evidence practice. When RETE 2020 speaks of 'practical aspects', it is, in fact, referring to purely organizational matters, since it alludes to purely logistical management or the means to be used (Art 20(2)). Hence, without wishing to be exhaustive, aspects such as the references of the case, names of the intervening bodies, technical data of the requesting party, preferred form of connection, preferred date and time of connection, need for an interpreter, mention of whether the practice is to be recorded, and other similar information are included under this heading (Arts 12(4) and (20) and Form). Another practical aspect is the need to assist the requesting judicial authority in finding an interpreter for taking evidence through videoconferencing (Consideration (22) and Art 20(2), second paragraph).

Moreover, as regards the details of the taking of evidence, issues such as the questioning of assistants, the admissibility or inadmissibility of the questions asked, the powers of the court to withdraw a question or to put forward questions to the person being questioned, and the need to require a prior oath or affirmation from the person being questioned are all aspects that govern the taking of evidence as a procedural act and are therefore not the 'practical aspects' referred to in RETE 2020, as these are determined by the procedural rules of the requesting State in the case of direct evidence.[55]

As far as the 'practical'—or rather organizational—aspects are concerned, RETE 2020 provides for a Form N on technical aspects related to the implementation of a videoconference or the use of other telecommunication technologies, which is required to request the use of such a tool. RETE 2020 provides the necessary assistance to the requesting court to find an interpreter at the request of the requesting court (Art 20(2)). This is a welcome provision as in certain cases it is not easy to find a suitable professional. The *Guide to Videoconferencing in Cross-Border Proceedings* makes this point, recognizing that 'the witness may not be used to working with interpreters and the feeling of distance may make interpretation difficult. For the interpreters, it may be useful for the judge to coordinate the order in which the participants speak', if they also opt for consecutive rather than simultaneous interpretation and pays particular attention to his preparatory tasks.[56]

However, the issues of access and identification of participants in videoconferences are also relevant. In this regard, Regulation 910/2014 of the European Parliament and of the Council of 23 July 2014 on electronic identification and trust services for electronic transactions in the internal market has incorporated new and useful possibilities for the digital justice system. For example, they have raised possibility of incorporating facial biometrics systems, but these 'face the need to incorporate high-level security elements in order to exclude fraudulent uses (masks, photographs, avatars) that could lead to identity theft'. In addition, its use 'raises reliability issues, both for the data and for the system used to collect and recognise it, and errors may occur in the form of false positives (eg twin brothers) or false negatives (eg a person not recognised because of new features due to age)'. For this reason, it is a system which, in

[55] Miguel Bueno Benedí, *Videoconferencia y juicios telemáticos* (La Ley 2023) 250.

[56] Council of the European Union, General Secretariat of the Council, *Guide to Videoconferencing in Cross-border Proceedings*, 11.

the field of the administration of justice, 'should not be used autonomously but only in a complementary way, leaving open the entry of subsidiary systems'.[57] An example of this type of proposal is the experimental implementation of a dual verification system—documentary and biometric—aimed at carrying out the appearance *apud acta* in the courts of the Canary Islands (Spain).[58]

D. The European Model for the Transmission of Requests for Evidence in the Field of European Judicial Cooperation in Civil Matters: A Decentralized System

Article 2 of RETE 2001 provides that the requesting court's request for the taking of evidence—including evidence to be taken by videoconference—by the competent court of another Member State (ie the requested court) should be transmitted directly, but Article 6 of RETE 2001 provides only a general mandate that the request 'shall be transmitted by the swiftest means accepted by the requested Member State'.

RETE 2020 maintains the requirement of direct transmission of requests of its predecessor, RETE 2001, and to this end, establishes a list of bodies and their respective competencies (Art 3), which is a major step forward. However, the real innovation introduced by the latest RETE 2020 is the mandate for the implementation of a decentralized computerized system in the context of international mutual legal assistance subject to compliance with safeguards. Thus, requests and communications are to be transmitted via a secure and reliable decentralized IT system that must fully and properly respect fundamental rights and freedoms. This decentralized computer system was designed as an interoperable solution called e-CODEX (Art 7 of the regulation).

As a necessary complement to RETE 2020, Regulation (EU) 2022/850 of 30 May 2022,[59] regulating a computerized system for the electronic cross-border exchange of data in the field of judicial cooperation in civil and criminal matters (the e-CODEX system) has been adopted as a necessary complement to RETE 2020. This regulation allows the community stamp to be affixed to the e-CODEX system. However, it should be noted that Denmark does not participate in this regulation and is not bound by it nor subject to its application. Denmark's refusal to do so has had an adverse effect on the desired European unity in that it has created a 'two-speed' Europe, given the disparity in the level of legal assistance between EU Member States.

The e-Justice Communication via Online Data Exchange (e-CODEX) is a constellation of access points in Member States, interconnected by common electronic protocols and standardized digital forms. Ideally, e-CODEX will not require costly

[57] Fernando Esteban de la Rosa (ed), *Justicia Digital, Guía para el diálogo sobre el diseño y uso eficiente, da calidad y ético de herramientas tecnológicas en la justicia civil* (Fundación Cotec 2022) 33.

[58] See <http://www.gobiernodecanarias.org/platino/servicios/SFB/> last accessed 23 October 2024.

[59] Regulation (EU) 2022/850 of the European Parliament and of the Council of 30 May 2022 on a computerized system for the cross-border electronic exchange of data in the area of judicial cooperation in civil and criminal matters (e-CODEX system), and amending Regulation (EU) 2018/1726 (Text with EEA relevance) [2022] OJ L150.

modifications or replacement of existing national back-end information systems.[60] Thus, it can be seen as a crucial measure representing a methodology that will significantly speed up the processing of such requests, leading to better compliance with the principles of procedural economy and efficiency and providing solutions to the obstacles to interconnection and interoperability.

It should also be noted that although RETE 2020 will enter into force on 1 July 2022 (Art 35), the provisions concerning the establishment of a decentralized IT system for the communication of data between institutions will apply from a later date. Specifically, according to Article 35(3), the provisions on 'the transmission of requests and other communications' will apply 'from the first day of the month following the expiry of a period of three years after the date of entry into force of the implementing acts referred to in Article 25'. The latter provision states that these acts will be adopted on 23 March 2022; hence, the date of application is to be 1 April 2025. However, the official EU website states that the date of application in this case will be 1 May 2025, which does not correspond to the criterion set out in the regulation.[61] In the meantime, as provided for in Article 34.1 of RETE 2020, a *vacatio legis* is established, during which the traditional means of sending applications and other communications; that is, those provided for in Article 6 of Regulation (EC) No 1206/2001, will continue to apply.

On the other hand, with regard to the reference software provided for in RETE 2020, it is noteworthy that although it states that Member States must be able to use it instead of a national computer system—as stated in Recital 9 and Article 27—it does not explicitly mention that this software, known as background or *back-end* software, includes, in particular, the technical resources essential for conducting telematic hearings. Indeed, the wording of the abovementioned recital seems to refer in general terms to interoperability in the 'exchange of information'. In fact, the direct use of personal evidence by the requesting court by means of videoconferencing is subject to the condition that this technology is available to the requested court and that the latter considers the use of this technology to be appropriate with regard to the specific circumstances of the case and the proper conduct of the proceedings. The requested court may even impose certain necessary conditions and refuse the direct taking of evidence if doing so would be contrary to the fundamental principle of the law of that Member State (Recital 21).

This regulation leads us to the conclusion that, given the possible existence of obstacles on the part of the courts of the Member States with regard to audiovisual technology, this could lead, for example, to the abolition of direct evidence collection—a potentially unfavourable outcome. The solution could be to provide a common platform adequately equipped for remote audiovisual communication to which all courts within the scope of RETE 2020 would have access.

[60] Francesco Contini and Giovani Francesco Lanzara, *Building interoperability for European civil proceedings online* (CLUEB 2013) 107.

[61] See <https://e-justice.europa.eu/38581/ES/taking_evidence_recast> last accessed 23 October 2024.

E. The Challenge of Adequate Data Protection Treatment in the Videoconferencing Evidence Regime of European Judicial Cooperation in Civil Matters

The reference software established by RETE 2020 must comply with the requirements and principles of data protection in accordance with EU and national law (Recital 9). In addition, the regulation stresses the importance of having an effective means of obtaining, preserving, and presenting evidence, taking due account of the rights of defence and the need to protect confidential information (Recital 32). Therefore, promoting the use of modern technologies is important. It is also essential to ensure that this regulation is implemented in accordance with the EU data protection law and that it respects the right to privacy, as enshrined in the Charter of Fundamental Rights of the EU. Moreover, any processing of personal data under the regulation must be carried out in accordance with Directive 2002/58/EC of the European Parliament and Council.[62]

It should be added that Article 30(2) of RETE 2020 requires competent authorities, as data controllers, to erase collected personal data that are inadequate or irrelevant. The gathered data should be limited to what is necessary in relation to the purposes for which they are processed, and personal data should only be processed under Regulation 2020 for the specific purposes specified therein.

In any case, reference should be made to the *Guidelines of the European Data Protection Supervisor 3/2019* with regard to data processing,[63] which sets out the following criteria: 1) only data necessary for identification should be collected and only for the minimum time necessary for identification; 2) further use of such data for incompatible secondary purposes should be prevented and safeguards should be put in place; 3) data should be processed and, where appropriate, stored in a secure digital environment to ensure data integrity, confidentiality, and availability are maintained; and 4) raw data (eg images) and data whose retention is not justified should be deleted as soon as possible. This is in line with the data protection principle of minimization.[64]

With regard to the protection of data confidentiality, the following measures should be taken: 1) Access to court files, which includes access to the recording of telematic hearings, should be associated with high-level active security measures; 2) Access should be granted only to legitimate parties or professionals representing or assisting them; and 3) The appropriate configuration of European Electronic Justice (EEJ) access requires the establishment of levels of access authorization and specifications on whether access is granted as an interested party, as an interested party with a legitimate interest, as a lawyer, as an advocate, as a judge, or as a member of the judiciary.

[62] European Parliament and of the Council Directive 2002/58/EC of 12 July 2002 concerning the processing of personal data and the protection of privacy in the electronic communications sector (Directive on privacy and electronic communications) [2002] OJ L201/37.

[63] The European Data Protection Board, *Guidelines 3/2019 on processing of personal data through video devices* (The European Data Protection Board 2020) 15.

[64] The European Data Protection Board and the European Data Protection Supervisor, *Joint Opinion 5/2021 on the proposal for a Regulation of the European Parliament and of the Council laying down harmonised rules on artificial intelligence (Artificial Intelligence Act)* (The European Data Protection Board and the European Data Protection Supervisor 2021).

The technological system must establish different access routes for each subject, differentiate the documents that can be accessed, and identify the users and the type of information they handle and to which they have access; 4) In view of the scope of the access, the authorization should be granted by the judge; 5) Access must be granted by requiring the electronic web authentication of the user; 6) In cases where it is not possible to use an authentication system, there must be an alternative procedure, such as requesting a copy of the file; 7) Access and authentication criteria should be adequately published and comprehensible; 8) When users access information on court files, they must be informed of the need to keep information confidential as it relates to other persons; 9) The user should be informed that access is being granted to protected data for which there is an obligation of confidentiality. This information should be marked as read at the time of access; and 10) The use of watermarks, anti-copying systems, or personalized versions of documents is recommended in order to identify the person who has made the unauthorized disclosure of information.[65]

With regard to data security, it is advisable that in the case of outsourcing videoconferencing systems, appropriate protective measures be included in the supply contracts, such as those that prevent the leakage of personal data outside the secure digital environment of the telematic link or specific electronic communication. Sufficiently visible warnings should also be included and addressed to the parties accessing the environment of the telematic link or electronic communication that instruct them not to share or transmit the personal data they access to third parties outside of the dispute. This measure can be reinforced in accordance with the principle of *privacy by design* by requiring each interested party to prove that they have read and understood the aforementioned warning.[66] This issue is the subject of another chapter of this work.

F. Conclusions

Within the EU, efforts are being made to establish a system for overcoming intra-community borders when taking evidence in civil and commercial matters. In fact, prior coordination has already been envisaged, particularly regarding the use of videoconferencing for these purposes. For example, RETE 2001 already provides for the taking of evidence by videoconference, but exclusively in the situation of the requested judicial body taking evidence at the request of the requesting party and only under certain conditions. The current system has the disadvantage of being indirect when it comes to taking personal evidence because the recipient of the evidence is a judicial body other than the one that has to decide the case and can only see the result through audiovisual recording. The COVID-19 pandemic has led to the use of videoconferencing in judicial proceedings and its recognition as an extremely useful tool, particularly for taking evidence from parties, witnesses, or experts in international judicial cooperation in civil or commercial courts.

It is worth highlighting that RETE 2020 has led to innovations in how judicial bodies hear the testimony of parties, witnesses, or experts directly from persons

[65] Esteban de la Rosa (n 57) 36.
[66] ibid 73.

located beyond the borders of the requesting body but within the territory of almost all EU Member States. Direct videoconferencing represents a real advance over the previous system by bringing the sentencing court closer to the source of the evidence, a contact that is favourable for the effective protection of the principle of immediacy. However, respect for national sovereignty and jurisdiction means that direct videoconferences retain limited effectiveness owing to their voluntary nature for the addressee, who resides in an EU Member State other than the one that took the initiative. To overcome this disadvantage, the judicial authority for the requested State of evidence should be present alongside the requesting authority.

In any event, both indirect and direct videoconferencing have provided a basis for progress in procedural efficiency in so far as this tool can accelerate the procedures for obtaining evidence between Member States. Moreover, its cross-border utility facilitates the protection of parties' right to effective defence and, in particular, their right to access evidence. The references in these regulations that indicate national legislation should regulate the specific way in which each evidentiary practice is to be developed must be understood in the sense that these practices are also subject to European legislation on procedural guarantees to be observed in the performance of evidentiary practice. Furthermore, in general, any virtual evidentiary hearing must meet certain functional and technological configuration requirements to achieve practical and legal equivalence with physical hearing conditions.

Regarding the form of transmission of requests for the taking of evidence, including videoconferencing, between EU judicial bodies within the scope of the regulation, we maintain that this is directly covered by the current RETE 2020. In addition, this regulation goes much further than its predecessor by providing for the implementation of a decentralized IT system linked to guarantees, fundamental rights, and freedoms. It is based on an interoperable solution, e-CODEX, which, when it becomes available (likely from 1 May 2025), will significantly speed up the processing of such requests and provide solutions to the obstacles to interconnection. However, the regulation does not specifically mention whether this platform will include an appropriate technical resource for the remote collection of audiovisual evidence with access to all judicial bodies corresponding to the regulated area.

With regard to the territorial scope of this regulation, it should be stressed that the exclusion of Denmark from this regulation regarding cooperation in the taking of evidence and participation in the e-CODEX platform does not correspond to the spirit of inspiration of the EU, nor does it contribute to the efficiency of the procedural systems throughout its territory, which has led to regulatory and effective dysfunctionality in view of the parallel and two-speed coexistence of these practices within the EU.

Concerning the data protection applicable to this type of videoconferencing, RETE 2020 includes the abovementioned reference software, which replaces the respective national ones. Specifically, the regulation presents the e-CODEX platform as a flagship and establishes a reference to comply with the requirements and principles of data protection, as provided for by EU and national law. In particular, it states that these procedures must comply with the requirements set out in Regulations (EU) 2018/1725 and (EU) 2016/679. Data protection must also be respected in accordance with Directive 2002/58/EC of the European Parliament and of the Council.

RETE 2020 requires the restriction or deletion of certain inappropriate data and the use of such data only for the purposes for which they were collected. Regarding the treatment of data, we must also refer to the Guidelines of the European Data Protection Supervisor 3/2019, which are restrictive and secure. With regard to privacy protections, a number of additional measures should be adopted such as those relating to access to court records and the establishment of authorization levels and electronic user authentication.

With regard to the identification of participants, which is not addressed by RETE 2020, we highlight the unreliability of systems based on facial biometrics, which is left open by Regulation 910/2014. These systems should be complementary and not stand-alone because facial biometrics should be complemented with additional verification methods to improve reliability and security, as sole reliance on them can lead to inaccuracies and privacy vulnerabilities. Furthermore, in the case of outsourced systems, appropriate safeguards must be included in supply contracts as well as implementation measures to prevent data leakage. Visible warnings should also be included in line with privacy by design, wherein all data subjects are required to demonstrate that they have read and understood the warning.

Bibliography

Aguilera Morales M, 'La cooperación judicial civil en la Unión Europea: el llamado principio digital by default' in Martínez Velencoso LM, and Plaza Penadés J (eds), *Retos normativos del mercado único digital europeo* (Tirant lo Blanch 2022).

Alcalá-Zamora y Castillo N, 'La teoría de las crisis del proceso, aplicada al proceso penal' [1951] Revista de Derecho Procesal.

Bueno Benedí M, *Videoconferencia y juicios telemáticos* (La Ley 2023).

Calaza López S, *El impacto de la oportunidad sobre los principios procesales clásicos: Estudios y diálogos* (Extrajudicial & Judicial Tech Iustel 2021).

Clark J, *Evaluation of remote hearings during the Covid 19 pandemic* (Research Report HM Courts & Tribunal Service United Kingdom 2021).

Consejo General del poder Judicial, 'Los instrumentos de reconocimiento y ejecución de documentos judiciales y de auxilio judicial internacional en el orden civil a la luz de la Estadística Judicial 2021' [2022] Boletín de Información Estadística 5.

Contini F and Lanzara GF, *Building Interoperability for European Civil Proceedings Online* (CLUEB 2013).

Council of the European Union, General Secretariat of the Council, *Guide on videoconferencing in cross-border proceedings* (European e-justice Publications Office 2013).

De Blas Javaloyas JR and García Mirete CM, 'El futuro de la cooperación judicial civil en la Unión Europea. Una perspectiva' [2022] Actualidad Civil.

Esteban de la Rosa F (ed), *Justicia Digital, Guía para el diálogo sobre el diseño y uso eficiente, da calidad y ético de herramientas tecnológicas en la justicia civil* (Fundación Cotec 2022).

Fernández-Fígares Morales MJ, *Audiencias Telemáticas en la Justicia. Presente y futuro* (Tirant Lo Blanch 2021).

Font i Segura A, 'Artículo 3. Principio General favorable de cooperación' in Méndez González FP y Moreno GP (eds), *Comentarios a la Ley de Cooperación Jurídica Internacional en materia civil* (Tirant Lo Blanch 2017).

Fumagalli L, 'Problemi vecchi e nuovi nella cooperazione per l'assunzione delle prove all'estero in materia civile: la rifusione della disciplina nell'Unione Europea' [2021] Rivista di diritto internazionale privato e processuale.

Galič A, 'Open issues concerning the non-mandatory character of the Cross-Border Taking of Evidence Regulation' [2017] 3 Era Forum.
García Sanz J and González Guimaraes-Da Silva J, 'Las 'vistas telemáticas' en el proceso civil español: visión comparada, regulación y cuestiones prácticas que suscita su celebración' [2020] Diario La Ley.
Gómez Aguilera AM, 'La práctica de pruebas en materia civil y mercantil en la Unión Europea: el reglamento (CE) 1206/2001' [2020] Revista de Derecho VLex.
Guasp Delgado J, *Comentarios a la Ley de Enjuiciamiento Civil, I* (Aranzadi 2011).
Jiménez Asenjo E, 'Economía Procesal', *Nueva Enciclopedia Jurídica Seix* (1974).
Laro González ME, 'Una justicia eficiente y digital para una administración de justicia obsoleta' in Sánchez-Arjona MLand Calaza López S (eds), *Digitalización de la Justicia: Prevención, investigación y enjuiciamiento* (Thomson Reuters Aranzadi 2022).
Nieva Fenoll J, *Derecho Procesal I. Introducción* (Tirant Lo Blanch 2019).
Pesqueira Zamora MJ, *La suspensión de los juicios orales especial atención a sus causas y tratamiento procesal* (Bosch 2015).
Picó i Junoy J, *Las garantías constitucionales del proceso* (Boch 2012).
Puig Blanes FP, 'Juicios telemáticos entre distintos países de la Unión Europea' [2021] Diario La Ley.
Ramírez Benavente MD, 'La obtención de prueba en la Unión Europea: evolución y análisis del reglamento (UE) 2020/1783 relativo a la cooperación entre los órganos jurisdiccionales de los estados miembros en el ámbito de la obtención de pruebas en materia civil o mercantil' [2021] Revista General de Derecho Europeo.
Sancho Gargallo I, *La incidencia de los sesgos cognitivos en el enjuiciamiento* (Tirant Lo Blanch 2024).
Signorin S, 'La digitalizzazione della cooperazione giudiziaria in materia civile e commerciale nell'Unione Europea: L'assunzione transfrontaliera delle prove nel prisma della piattaforma informatica decentrata e-CODEX' [2024] 1 Cuadernos de Derecho Transnacional.
Sourdin T and Zeleznikow J, 'Courts, Mediation and COVID-19' [2020] Australian Business L Rev.
The European Data Protection Board and the European Data Protection Supervisor, *Joint Opinion 5/2021 on the proposal for a Regulation of the European Parliament and of the Council laying down harmonised rules on artificial intelligence (Artificial Intelligence Act)* (The European Data Protection Board and the European Data Protection Supervisor 2021).
The European Data Protection Board, *Guidelines 3/2019 on processing of personal data through video devices* (The European Data Protection Board 2020).
Tribunal Superior de Justicia de Asturias, *Memoria Judicial 2022* (Portal del Poder Judicial de España 2023).
Trocker N, 'Il regolamento (CE) n. 1206/2001 del Consiglio, del 28 maggio 2001, relativo alla cooperazione fra le autorità giudiziarie degli Stati membri nel settore dell'assunzione delle prove in materia civile e commerciale' in Taruffo M and Varano V (eds), *Manuale di diritto processuale civile Europeo* (Giappichelli 2011).
Vidal Fernández B, 'Obtención de pruebas' in Jimeno Bulnes M (ed), *La cooperación judicial civil y penal en el ámbito de la Unión Europea: instrumentos procesales* (Bosch 2007).

PART III

THE RISE OF AI IN DIGITAL COURTS

11

Human Rights-Compliant Artificial Intelligence

Regulatory Frameworks for Upholding Democracy and the Rule of Law in the Digital Age

Ozana Olariu and John Zeleznikow***

A. Introduction

Whilst Artificial Intelligence (AI) is rapidly transforming various aspects of human life, presenting unprecedented opportunities and challenges for society, it is not a new phenomenon.[1] Early research in AI focused upon expert systems (ES), which are computer programs 'capable of functioning at the standard of (and sometimes even at a higher standard than) human experts in given fields'. In the rule-based ES approach,

* Ozana Olariu is a Lecturer of Public International Law and International Relations at School of Law, University of Granada, Spain.

** John Zeleznikow is a Professor of Law and Technology at the Latrobe University, Australia. The authors thank the chapter reviewers for their thoughtful comments and insights.

[1] The term AI was first developed at the Dartmouth Conference in the northern hemisphere summer of 1956. See Roberto Cordeschi, 'AI Turns Fifty: Revisiting its Origins' (2007) 21(4–5) Applied Artificial Intelligence 259–79.

Ozana Olariu and John Zeleznikow, *Human Rights-Compliant Artificial Intelligence* In: *Digitalization and Artificial Intelligence in Courts*. Edited by: Fernando Esteban de la Rosa, Pablo Cortés, and Nuria Marchal Escalona, Oxford University Press.
 DOI: 10.1093/9780198918752.003.0011

the knowledge of a specific domain is represented as a collection of rules of the form IF <condition(s)> THEN <action/conclusion>. Such expert systems were widely used in the 1980s and the 1990s. They are still heavily used today: particularly in the British Columbia Civil Resolution Tribunal[2] and the Rechtwijzer System.[3] Both these systems are well described in Schmitz and Zeleznikow (2021).[4] An important misuse of rule-based AI was the Robodebt system, which is discussed later in the chapter. Rule-based systems can provide knowledge that is incorrect, when the rules are poorly designed by human software developers.

Machine learning is that subsection of learning in which the artificial intelligencesystem attempts to automatically learn patterns. These learned patterns can then be harnessed to automate tasks. Machine learning can only be applied if sufficient suitable data are available. When using Machine Learning, software developers do not in general input human knowledge. Rather, the software attempts to learn from data. If the data chosen for the training set is inaccurate or biased, then poor conclusions will be drawn. Thus, evaluation of the efficiency and justice of AI systems occurs very differently depending on whether the AI being used is rule-based or uses machine learning. A large language model is a machine learning model that is trained to generate text that is like human language. It is called 'large' because it is trained on a large dataset and can generate highly realistic and coherent text. The development of computer hardware has allowed us to process such large data.

Generative AI is an umbrella term to describe machine learning solutions trained on massive amounts of data to produce output based on user prompts. ChatGPT is a large language model (LLM) which is specialized for natural language processing. It produces various forms of text-based output.[5]

While AI Systems offer the potential to enhance human well-being, productivity, and innovation, they also raise significant concerns regarding their impact on human rights, democracy, and the rule of law,[6] particularly regarding access to justice and the digitalization of the judicial system. Access to justice is a basic principle of the rule of law. In the absence of access to justice, people are unable to have their voices heard, exercise their rights, or challenge discrimination.

The pervasive nature of AI systems necessitates a robust regulatory framework that ensures these technologies are developed and deployed in a manner that respects, protects, and fulfils human rights, democratic values, and the principles of the rule of law. Furthermore, AI can also enable a better access to digital justice, as well as significantly contribute to alleviating the work of courts and tribunals, as well as online dispute mechanisms. Learning software and algorithms powered by advanced

[2] Shannon Salter and Darin Thompson, 'Public-centred Civil Justice Redesign: A Case Study of the British Columbia Civil Resolution Tribunal' (2016) 3 McGill J Disp Resol 113–53.

[3] Laura Kistemaker, 'Rechtwijzer and uitelkaar. nl. dutch experiences with odr for divorce' (2021) 59.2 Family Court Rev 232, 243.

[4] Amy Schmitz and John Zeleznikow, 'Intelligent Legal Tech to Empower Self-represented Litigants' (2021) 23 Colum Sci & Tech L Rev 142, 191.

[5] See Henrik Skaug Sætra, 'Generative AI: Here to Stay, but for Good?' Technology in Society (2023) 75 102372.

[6] David Leslie et al, 'AI, Human Rights, Democracy, and the Rule of Law—A Primer' (Council of Europe 2021) <https://edoc.coe.int/en/artificial-intelligence/10206-artificial-intelligence-human-rights-democracy-and-the-rule-of-law-a-primer.html> last accessed 20 December 2024.

technologies should not operate oblivious of the human contexts and should be designed to achieve human-defined goals, in full respect of the human dignity as a core value of the international society and the international human rights standards. Furthermore, the design of AI systems, their functioning and supervision must respect international human rights standards and prevent the use of harmful human biases. Thus, in addition to evaluating the technical aspects of AI, accountability requires a thorough assessment of potential benefits and harms for particularly vulnerable individuals or groups, such as women, children, the LGBTY community, persons belonging to national, ethnical or linguistic minorities, amongst others. Unjust biases, for instance, can emerge when AI systems generate discriminatory predictions or treat specific demographic groups differently, without justification. Assessing the potential harm of AI systems is further complicated by the opacity of some AI technologies, some of which are often built using data, specialized knowledge, or as large language models and can be challenging to interpret or explain due to their technical complexity and intellectual property protections.

To examine the human rights implications of AI systems, it is vital to consider the broad networks of human rights treaties, adopted both at global, as well as regional level. Beyond these legal frameworks, AI also raises additional concerns related to democracy and the rule of law.[7] A comprehensive assessment of the risks and opportunities presented by AI systems enables us to identify where existing rights and freedoms offer necessary safeguards, where further clarification of these rights is needed, and where new rights and freedoms must be tailored to address the novel challenges and opportunities posed by all forms of AI, whether they be rule-based reasoning, case-based reasoning, or machine learning. The deployment of AI, particularly in critical areas such as the criminal justice system, has the potential to undermine the liberty and justice of individuals.[8] The intricacy and lack of transparency in machine learning[9] systems can certainly hinder the right to a fair trial, which includes the right to equality in presenting evidence as well as the right to a reasoned decision. Machine learning systems do not automatically provide explanations.[10] Overall, it can

[7] On the triangular relationship between human rights, democracy, and the rule of law, see Tanja A Börzel and Thomas Risse, 'Human Rights, Rule of Law, and Democracy' in *Effective Governance Under Anarchy: Institutions, Legitimacy, and Social Trust in Areas of Limited Statehood* (CUP 2021) 18. On the rule of law specifically, see Luis M Hinojosa Martínez and Carmen Pérez Bernárdez, *Enhancing the Rule of Law in the European Union's External Action* (Edward Elgar Publishing 2023). For the specific relation between democracy and AI, see Andreas Jungherr, 'Artificial Intelligence and Democracy: A Conceptual Framework' (2023) 9(3) Social Media + Society <https://doi.org/10.1177/20563051231186353> last accessed 12 January 2025; Jelena Cupać, Hendrink Schopmans, and Tuncer-Ebetürk, 'Democratization in the Age of Artificial Intelligence: Introduction to the Special Issue' (2024) 31(5) Democratization 899 https://doi.org/10.1080/13510347.2024.2338852 last accessed 9 December 2024.

[8] See Jeroen Temperman and Alberto Quintavalla (eds), *AI and Human Rights* (online edn, OUP 2023) <https://doi.org/10.1093/law/9780192882486.001.0001> last accessed 9 December 2024; Caroline Gans-Combe, 'Automated Justice: Issues, Benefits and Risks in the Use of AI and Its Algorithms in Access to Justice and Law Enforcement' in *Ethics, Integrity, and Policymaking: The Value of the Case Study* (Springer Nature Link 2022) 175.

[9] Rule-Based systems are transparent because the user can check the rule being used. Similarly, case-based reasoning is also transparent because one matches the closest case(s). Machine learning, being primarily statistical, lacks transparency.

[10] John Zeleznikow, 'The benefits and dangers of using machine learning to support making legal predictions' (2023) 13.4 Wiley Interdisciplinary Reviews: Data Mining and Knowledge Discovery 1, 21.

ultimately hinder access to justice and negatively impact the rule of law.[11] There are major problems when courts make automated decisions based on algorithms. While AI's application in this context can help mitigate arbitrariness and discriminatory actions, the involvement of AI in judicial decisions may have adverse effects on the rule-making process and the decisional independence of the judiciary.[12] Consequently, it is imperative that judicial actors possess a sufficient understanding of the AI System they employ to ensure accountability for decisions made with its assistance.

This chapter examines the emerging regulatory framework for human rights-compliant AI and explores potential venues to enhance human rights promotion in the digital world. It analyses the key principles that underpin a human rights-based approach to AI governance and discusses the mechanisms necessary for effective implementation. The chapter argues that embedding human rights norms, democratic values, and the principles of the rule of law into the development and deployment of AI systems is essential to mitigate the risks associated with these technologies and to ensure that they are used for the benefit of all. It is in this context in which this chapter considers how the use of AI systems can comply with human rights principles.

B. Regulatory Frameworks

Addressing AI's legal challenges could involve a multi-faceted approach: (1) modernizing existing treaties through additional protocols; (2) adopting new comprehensive international treaties specific to AI; and (3) relying on evolutionary interpretation techniques within courts to incorporate digital rights into pre-existing legal frameworks.[13] While new treaties offer legal certainty and a level playing field, they risk being overly rigid or slow to adopt, especially at the global level where consensus is difficult. Conversely, a framework convention that establishes broad principles with minimal state obligations could offer short-term flexibility, but risk delaying the adoption of more stringent binding rules. The overburdening of international courts tasked with updating the content of human rights provisions highlights the need for clear, binding international AI regulations to ensure systematic and uniform compliance. Soft law instruments, such as non-binding declarations and recommendations, provide initial guidance for States and private actors, facilitating consensus-building and laying the groundwork for future binding treaties. These instruments are adaptable to regional and socio-cultural specificities, making them a practical interim solution. Additionally, comparative domestic laws and best practices can inspire international action, contributing to a toolbox of regulatory models and strategies for assessing

[11] Lucy William, 'Access to Justice and the Rule of Law' (2020) 40(2) OJLS 377 < https://doi.org/10.1093/ojls/gqaa012> last accessed 17 October 2022.

[12] Council of Europe, European Ethical Charter on the Use of Artificial Intelligence in Judicial Systems and their Environment (2018) <https://www.coe.int/en/web/cepej/cepej-european-ethical-charter-on-the-use-of-artificial-intelligence-ai-in-judicial-systems-and-their-environment> last accessed 20 December 2024.

[13] The interpretation of human rights instruments as 'living documents', as established in Art 31 of the Vienna Convention on the Law of Treaties and the jurisprudence of the European Court of Human Rights, enables the application of traditional rights to contemporary digital contexts.

AI's human rights impact. Such tools would encourage a universal culture of human rights-respecting AI systems, ultimately enhancing the rule of law and democratic governance.

Given the multilevel regulation of human rights and fundamental freedoms, the imperative to regulate AI governance[14] rises accordingly both at global, regional, and national level. The current regulatory efforts have significantly focused on the general risk of using AI such as the European Union's AI Act (EU AI Act'),[15] or setting a principled approach as was the case of the Council of Europe's AI Framework Convention, as well as the general approach adopted at a global level. There are other noteworthy precedents and soft law mechanisms both at global and regional level that spearheaded the AI regulatory spree. All in all, achieving a balanced and comprehensive AI governance system requires a combination of binding treaties, soft law instruments, and domestic best practices. This integrated approach will ensure AI systems operate responsibly, advance societal well-being, and uphold human dignity, rights, and democratic values on a global scale.

1. Global level

1.1. United Nations

The United Nations (UN), while not directly establishing binding AI legal instruments, plays a crucial role in guiding the international community towards responsible and ethical AI development and use.[16] Its efforts focus on fostering dialogue, sharing best practices, and developing guidelines aligning with universal values and principles, particularly in human rights,[17] equity, transparency, and sustainability. Several UN initiatives contribute to shaping the global approach to AI. The UN Secretary-General's High-Level Panel on Digital Cooperation, in its 2019 report 'The Age of Digital Interdependence', recognized AI's potential to both accelerate progress

[14] For the concept of AI governance, see Allan Dafoe, 'AI Governance: A Research Agenda' (Centre for the Governance of AI Future of Humanity Institute, University of Oxford 2018) 5; James Butcher and Irakli Beridze, 'What is the State of AI Governance Globally?' (2019) 164 RUSI J 88.

[15] See Future of Life Institute, 'The AI Act: What is the EU AI Act?', The AI Act, (Web page) <https://artificialintelligenceact.eu/> last accessed 17 October 2022.

[16] Margarita Robles Carrillo, 'Artificial Intelligence: From Ethics to Law' (2020) 44(6) Telecommunications Policy 101937.

[17] See Universal Declaration of Human Rights (adopted 10 December 1948 UNGA Res 217 A(III)); International Covenant on Civil and Political Rights (adopted 16 December 1966, entered into force 23 March 1976) 999 UNTS 171; International Covenant on Economic, Social and Cultural Rights (adopted 16 December 1966, entered into force 3 January 1976) 993 UNTS 3; International Convention on the Elimination of All Forms of Racial Discrimination (adopted 21 December 1965, entered into force 4 January 1969) 660 UNTS 195; Convention on the Elimination of All Forms of Discrimination against Women (adopted 18 December 1979, entered into force 3 September 1981) 1249 UNTS 13; Convention against Torture and Other Cruel, Inhuman or Degrading Treatment or Punishment (adopted 10 December 1984, entered into force 26 June 1987) 1465 UNTS 85; Convention on the Rights of the Child (adopted 20 November 1989, entered into force 2 September 1990) 1577 UNTS 3; International Convention on the Protection of the Rights of All Migrant Workers and Members of Their Families (adopted 18 December 1990, entered into force 1 July 2003) 2220 UNTS 3; Convention on the Rights of Persons with Disabilities (adopted 13 December 2006, entered into force 3 May 2008) 2515 UNTS 3; International Convention for the Protection of All Persons from Enforced Disappearance (adopted 20 December 2006, entered into force 23 December 2010) 2716 UNTS 3.

towards the Sustainable Development Goals (SDGs) and pose risks to human rights.[18] The UN's role is further emphasized in UN General Assembly Resolution A/RES/78/265, 'Seizing the opportunities of safe, secure and trustworthy AI systems for sustainable development', adopted by consensus in March 2024.[19] This resolution stresses that human rights and fundamental freedoms must be respected throughout the AI lifecycle,[20] and calls upon AI that is human-centric, reliable, explainable, ethical, inclusive, in full respect, promotion and protection of human rights and international law, privacy preserving, sustainable development oriented, and responsible—have the potential to accelerate and enable progress towards the achievement of all 17 Sustainable Development Goals and sustainable development in its three dimensions—economic, social, and environmental—in a balanced and integrated manner; promote digital transformation; promote peace; overcome digital divides between and within countries; and promote and protect the enjoyment of human rights and fundamental freedoms for all, while keeping the human person at the centre. It also calls upon member states to refrain from using AI systems that cannot comply with international human rights law or pose undue risks to human rights enjoyment.[21] The resolution encourages collaborative transdisciplinary approaches involving AI, ethics, law, philosophy, and social sciences to craft ethical frameworks and standards for AI-powered decision-making tools. The UN's commitment is further demonstrated by the appointment of a UN Envoy on Technology,[22] whose role progressively encompasses AI and its relationship with human rights and the SDGs. Other UN initiatives include the UN Inter-Agency Committee on Bioethics,[23] which examines the ethical implications of AI in areas like healthcare; the AI for Good initiative,[24] which promotes dialogue and partnership to identify practical AI applications for accelerating progress towards the SDGs; and UN Global Pulse,[25] an innovation initiative leveraging big data and AI for sustainable development and humanitarian action. Furthermore, the UN hosts expert group meetings and forums to discuss AI's impact on human rights, privacy,

[18] UN Secretary-General's High-level Panel on Digital Cooperation, The Age of Digital Interdependence: Report of the UN Secretary-General's High-level Panel on Digital Cooperation (2019) <https://www.un.org/en/pdfs/DigitalCooperation-report.pdf> last accessed 30 November 2023. Also see Office of the High Commissioner for Human Rights, A HRIA of Digital Activities—Introduction (OHCHR 2020) UN Educational, Scientific and Cultural Organization, Recommendation on the Ethics of AI (UNESCO 2021).

[19] UN General Assembly, Seizing the opportunities of safe, secure, and trustworthy AI systems for sustainable development, UNGA Res 78/265 (21 March 2024) UN Doc A/RES/78/265.

[20] ibid para. 5. According to its preamble, life cycle includes the stages: pre-design, design, development, evaluation, testing, deployment, use, sale, procurement, operation, and decommissioning. See, for more details, Martina Šmuclerová, Král Luboš and Jan Drchal, 'AI Life Cycle and Human Rights: Risks and Remedies' in Jeroen Temperman and Alberto Quintavalla (eds), *AI and Human Rights* (online edn, OUP 2023) <https://doi.org/10.1093/law/9780192882486.003.0002> last accessed 16 December 2024.

[21] UNGA Res 78/265 (n 19) Preamble.

[22] See the Office of the Secretary General´s Envoy on Technology, <https://www.un.org/techenvoy/> last accessed 16 December 2023.

[23] See the UN Inter-Agency Committee on Bioethics, <https://www.unesco.org/en/ethics-science-technology/uniacb> last accessed 16 December 2023.

[24] See AI Skills Coalition, <https://aiforgood.itu.int/> last accessed 16 December 2023.

[25] See the UN Global Pulse,< https://www.unglobalpulse.org/> last accessed 26 December 2024.

security, and ethical challenges. Outcomes from these meetings shape policy recommendations and guide member states in their national AI regulation efforts.[26]

1.2. Organisation for Economic Co-operation and Development

The Organisation for Economic Co-operation and Development (OECD) has spearheaded AI governance standard setting and established comprehensive, human rights-based, and innovative principles through the 2019 OECD Council Recommendation on AI.[27] These principles advocate for the sustainable use of AI, emphasizing its benefits for both people and the planet while grounding its application and design in human-centered values, human rights, the Rule of Law and democratic principles. Central to this framework is the imperative for transparency, enabling citizens to understand, contribute and, when necessary, challenge AI outcomes.[28] This non-binding recommendation further encourages its adherents to incorporate these principles into domestic policies and international cooperation, with particular attention to the needs of businesses, and be applicable in the larger context of sustainable development and fight against climate change.

2. Regional level

Neither of the regional human rights instruments, given their time of adoption, respond to the challenges of a growing digital society.[29] Regional courts and tribunals, however, have been faced with examining complaints related to digital human rights and the impact of technology on human rights, specifically the right to a fair trial and the right to privacy.[30] Global attempts have been unable to regulate AI according to Human Rights Principles. In the European context, great strides have been jointly

[26] UN Special Rapporteur on freedom of opinion and expression <https://www.ohchr.org/en/special-procedures/sr-freedom-of-opinion-and-expression> last accessed 28 June 2021; UN, Our Common Agenda: Report of the Secretary-General, 2021. A Global Digital Compact—an Open, Free and Secure Digital Future for All, May 2023.

[27] OECD Principles on AI' (OECD) <https://www.oecd.org/going-digital/ai/principles/> last accessed 28 June 2021.

[28] 'Recommendation of the Council on AI' (OECD Legal Instruments, 21 May 2019) <https://legalinstruments.oecd.org/en/instruments/OECD-LEGAL-0449> last accessed 28 June 2021.

[29] European Convention for the Protection of Human Rights and Fundamental Freedoms (adopted 4 November 1950, entered into force 3 September 1953) ETS No 5; European Social Charter (adopted 18 October 1961, entered into force 26 February 1965) ETS No 35; American Convention on Human Rights (adopted 22 November 1969, entered into force 18 July 1978) OAS Treaty Series No 36; African Charter on Human and Peoples' Rights (adopted 27 June 1981, entered into force 21 October 1986) 1520 UNTS 217; Arab Charter on Human Rights (adopted 22 May 2004, entered into force 15 March 2008) reprinted in 12 IHRR 893 (2005); ASEAN Human Rights Declaration (adopted 18 November 2012) ASEAN Document Series on Human Rights.

[30] See, for instance, *Glukhin v Russia* App no 11519/20 (ECtHR, 4 July 2023), involving the use of facial recognition technology by law enforcement to track down and arrest an individual who participated in a peaceful solo protest. *S and Marper v United Kingdom* [GC], nos 30562/04 and 30566/04, ECHR 2008, concerned the retention of DNA profiles and fingerprints in the UK. They raised concerns about individuals' right to privacy; or *Yüksel Yalçınkaya v Türkiye* [GC], no 15669/20 (ECtHR, 26 September 2023), a case concerning the use of data obtained from the encrypted messaging application ByLock as primary evidence to convict the applicant of membership in a terrorist organization.

made by the EU as well as the Council of Europe (CoE) to adopt binding instruments that regulate the lifecycle of AI systems.

2.1. The European two-fold approach to human rights and AI

Europe is at the forefront of regulating AI with a two-pronged approach, aiming to foster innovation while safeguarding fundamental rights. This analysis will examine two key instruments: the AI Act and the CoE Framework Convention on AI, Human Rights, Democracy and the Rule of Law (CoE AI Convention).[31] It will delve into their intersections, critiques, and potential pitfalls from a human-centric perspective, highlighting the EU's commitment to ensuring that technology serves humanity. The AI Act and the CoE AI Convention, despite their differing approaches, share common goals and complement each other.

2.1.1. The EU and the AI Act: a risk-based approach

The EU Act aims to regulate 'high risk' AI and legally limit AI that poses too hazardous an outcome while concurrently enabling investment and innovation in AI and promoting international cooperation.[32] The AI Act has received academic acclaim for this identification of AI systems as 'high risk',[33] but should be also strongly criticized for failing to deliver progress from a human-rights-centric perspective.[34] Despite the comprehensive framework established by the AI Act, significant issues persist regarding the requirements for high-risk systems. Of particular concern is a loophole that allows providers to unilaterally determine that their AI system does not fall within the high-risk category, even when it is explicitly classified as such under the Act.

Annex III of the AI Act deals with the concept of 'high risk' AI. However, it provides far too much leeway for states to qualify AI systems as 'high risk'. These deficiencies in the legislation present a substantial threat to the human rights of EU citizens, particularly those belonging to marginalized communities. Such gaps undermine foundational values of diversity, inclusivity, and equality, contradicting the principles the Act seeks to uphold. Moreover, there is an urgent need for more robust safeguards and clearly defined guidelines to ensure that the AI Act achieves an optimal balance between fostering technological innovation and safeguarding human rights and environmental sustainability. Providers can bypass these obligations simply by registering their own assessment, effectively rendering the requirements inapplicable to their systems. Furthermore, although national and EU authorities retain the ability to review and investigate these assessments, the effectiveness of such oversight remains

[31] Council of Europe: Committee of Ministers, Council of Europe Framework Convention on Artificial Intelligence and Human Rights, Democracy and the Rule of Law, CETS No 25, 17 May 2024.

[32] Josh Meltzer & Aaron Tielemans, 'The EU AI Act: Next steps and issues for building international cooperation' (Policy Brief, May 2022).

[33] Sónia Moreira and Patrícia Borges, 'AI and jurisdictional decisions: is the Robot-Judge imminent?' (Draft chapter, Law and Society Association Conference, 13–16 July 2022).

[34] Clarke et al, 'Submission of Feedback to the European Commission's Proposal for a Regulation laying down harmonised rules on AI', Feedback from: University of Cambridge (Leverhulme Centre for the Future of Intelligence and Centre for the Study of Existential Risk (Feedback form, August 2021) <https://ec.europa.eu/info/law/better-regulation/have-your-say/initiatives/12527-Artificial-intelligence-ethical-and-legal-requirements/F2665626_en> last accessed 24 April 2024.

uncertain due to potential resource limitations. Under European data protection law, individuals have the right to decline automated decisions not authorized by law, thereby asserting their entitlement to a human review of such decisions. Similarly, the Digital Services Act and the Consumer ADR Directive ensure users can request human oversight when decisions are made by automated systems. However, practical challenges arise, as the volume of automated decisions often exceeds the capacity for comprehensive human review. In many cases, humans may simply approve AI-generated outcomes without meaningful scrutiny. This precedent raises questions about the capacity of regulatory bodies to enforce the AI Act effectively. The AI Act's emphasis on risk mitigation and proportionality aims to balance innovation with the protection of fundamental rights. Nevertheless, although it has a good backbone, it certainly lacks teeth.

2.1.2. The CoE and the Framework Convention on AI, Human Rights, Democracy and the Rule of Law: a principle-based approach

After nearly two years of work, on 5 September 2024, the CoE adopted the Framework Convention on Artificial Intelligence, Human Rights, Democracy, and the Rule of Law, with ten initial signatories, including Andorra, Georgia, Iceland, Israel, Moldova, Norway, San Marino, the United Kingdom, the United States, and the European Union. This landmark treaty is the world's first legally binding international agreement on AI, emphasizing the protection of human rights, democratic values, and the rule of law in the AI landscape. It takes a broad, principle-based approach and has no enforcement mechanism. Unlike the AI Act, the AI Convention does not specify risk categories or prohibited systems. Instead, it provides high-level obligations and a framework for risk assessment, requiring signatory states to translate these principles into domestic law. This approach allows for flexibility in implementation, catering to diverse legal systems and cultural contexts.

2.1.3. Critiques and potential pitfalls of the European approach

Despite their strengths, both instruments face critiques and potential pitfalls. Concerns remain regarding the clarity of definitions and potential loopholes, particularly regarding the exclusion of AI systems used for military and national security purposes. The ambiguous definition of 'national security' in both instruments creates loopholes, allowing AI systems which can pose risks, to evade regulation under this broad category. This threatens to undermine safeguards against AI misuse in surveillance and law enforcement contexts. It could lead to the development and deployment of AI systems with significant human rights implications outside the scope of the regulation. The effectiveness of the AI Act hinges on robust enforcement mechanisms. Insufficient resources or lack of political will could undermine its impact. The AI Act's primary focus on market regulation, while essential, could potentially overshadow the broader societal impacts of AI, such as its implications for democracy, social justice, and equality.

The CoE AI Convention's most important flaw is its very format. Operating as a framework convention, it lacks specific obligations: the Convention's principle-based approach, while flexible, is likely to lead to inconsistencies in implementation across signatory states, resulting in a multilevel protection for human rights amongst state parties. Furthermore, it is highly dependent on adequate domestic implementation: The Convention's effectiveness relies heavily on signatory states translating their principles into concrete domestic law and enforcement mechanisms. Judging from previous examples, although a huge milestone has been achieved within the CoE, delays or inadequate implementation could weaken the impact of this one-of-a-kind treaty. The Convention does not provide for direct individual complaints to the European Court of Human Rights, nor does it create autonomous enforcement mechanisms, limiting its enforcement potential and effectively undermining the positive progress otherwise achieved.

All in all, the European two-fold approach to AI regulation, though not without challenges, marks a significant step towards ensuring that AI development is grounded in human rights. By promoting a human-centric perspective, the EU seeks to harness the transformative potential of AI while safeguarding fundamental freedoms for all. The same impulse has been projected in the remainder of the regional human rights systems, albeit unable to boast the same level of achievement.

2.2. Inter-American human rights system

The Inter-American human rights system provides a robust framework for the protection of human rights, democracy, and the rule of law in Latin America. It is based on the American Convention on Human Rights (ACHR) and the Protocol of San Salvador,[35] and overseen by the Inter-American Commission on Human Rights (IACHR) and the Inter-American Court of Human Rights. Most Latin American states are parties to the ACHR and are therefore bound by its provisions, in particular bound to respect, protect, and fulfil human rights.[36] The IACHR and the Court have developed a rich body of jurisprudence that has helped to define the scope of human rights in the region and the obligations of states to protect them. The Inter-American system recognizes that AI governance must be grounded in human rights.[37] This means that AI systems must be designed and used in a way that respects human dignity, autonomy, and equality.[38] States have a duty to ensure that AI systems do not discriminate against individuals or groups, and that they are used in a transparent and accountable manner. The IACHR has emphasized the need for a human-centred approach to AI governance, which places individuals at the core of AI advancements.[39]

[35] American Convention on Human Rights (adopted 22 November 1969, entered into force 18 July 1978) 1144 UNTS 123; Protocol of San Salvador (Additional Protocol to the American Convention on Human Rights in the Area of Economic, Social and Cultural Rights) (adopted 17 November 1988, entered into force 16 November 1999) 32 ILAM 541.

[36] Veridiana Alimonti and Rafaela Cavalcanti; de Alcântara, 'Inter-American Standards and State Use of AI for Rights-Affecting Determinations in Latin America: Appendix' (Electronic Frontier Foundation, October 2024).

[37] Maria Pilar Llorens, 'Crossing Routes: AI Governance and Human Rights in Latin America' (2023) 31 CEBRI-Journal 83.

[38] Francisco Javier Sempere, 'El Sistema Del Consejo De Europa Y La Gobernanza De La Inteligencia Artificial' in Francisco Javier Sempere (ed), *Comentarios al Reglamento Europeo de Inteligencia Artificial* (Aranzadi, 2024).

[39] Llorens (n 37).

2.3. African human rights system

The burgeoning field of AI presents both opportunities and challenges for Africa. While AI promises economic and social progress, the lack of robust, context-specific AI governance frameworks raises significant human rights concerns. The limited development of state-led AI regulation in Africa, as noted by Effoduh, underscores the urgency of establishing comprehensive legal safeguards to prevent potential abuses related to privacy, discrimination, and freedom of expression.[40] These risks are particularly pertinent given existing inequalities and vulnerabilities across the continent.

The African Commission on Human and Peoples' Rights (ACHPR) acknowledging the potential negative impacts of AI on human rights, adopted Resolution 473 of 25 February 2021.[41] This Resolution calls upon African states to ensure AI development adheres to the ACHPR's core principles, which encompass human dignity, privacy, equality, non-discrimination, and accountability. This highlights a critical need for human rights-centred AI regulation in Africa, placing the well-being and rights of individuals and communities at the forefront. However, the effectiveness of such regulations is contingent on strong enforcement mechanisms, which, as Abe and Eurallyah point out, remain a challenge in many African states due to 'weak enforcement capabilities and corruption'.[42]

The development of comprehensive and contextually relevant AI regulations is essential for Africa. This requires further research and policy initiatives that balance human rights protection with responsible innovation and technological advancement.

3. Domestic level

Without the aim of being exhaustive, this section briefly examines two countries at the forefront of AI regulation: Australia and Canada.

In Australia, much of the concern arose from the Robodebt debacle, a major flaw in the use of legal expert systems in Australia.[43] Robodebt was an automated decision-making system designed to automatically match an income reported to Centrelink with the income declared to the Australian Taxation Office in order to identify people who are being paid benefits to which they may not be entitled. From the initial rollout of the OCI system, it came under sustained public criticism because numerous people complained to the Commonwealth Ombudsman's office that the debts were incurred incorrectly. In November 2019, Deanna Amato successfully challenged Centrelink in the Federal Court, which ordered that the alleged debt demanded by Centrelink was invalid because the averaged ATO income was not capable of satisfying a decision-maker that Ms Amato owed a debt within the scope of ss 1222A(a) and 1223(1) of the

[40] BO Effoduh, 'Designing an African Framework for the Governance of AI' in C Ncube and O Kolawole (eds), *AI and the Law in Africa* (Juta 2023).

[41] African Commission on Human and Peoples' Rights, 'Resolution 473 (EXT.OS/XXXI) on the Right to Freedom of Information and Expression on the Internet in Africa' (25 February 2021).

[42] O Abe and AJ Eurallyah, 'Regulating AI through a Human Rights-Based Approach in Africa' (2022) 14 African J L Studies 425–48.

[43] Adam Grayca and Adam B Masters, 'Bureaucratic Bastardry: Robodebt/debt Recovery, AI and the Stigmatisation of Citizens by Machines and Systems'. Intl J of Public Policy 16.5–6 (2022) 333–44.

Social Security Act 1991. What can be learnt from Robodebt is not how unreliable AI is, but rather, that the success of digital transformation relies on the awareness, acceptance, and readiness of the public to engage with the digitalized process. There needs to be recognition and understanding that automated systems are most appropriate for dealing with prescriptive rules and, in most government decisions, there is a need for the exercise of discretion.

There is a great deal of value in being able to automate the easy, routine parts of the decision to free up human arbiters to deal with the discretionary aspects of a decision-making process. But it is important to recognize that the exercise of human discretion is critical in a just society and must not be eliminated—even if this is only implemented in the appeals process.

It is also important to recognize that computers are not magic. If the policy or law is bad, all that automated decision-making will do will enable the faster application of bad laws or bad policy, and at a larger scale. A transparent, traceable decision will still deliver an unjust decision if it is the implementation of an unjust law.

The Australian Government has remarked that, following its consultations, it considers the current regulatory system to be unfit for purpose to respond to the distinct risks posed by AI. Therefore, it has released a proposals chapter for introducing mandatory guardrails for AI in 'high risk' settings[44] as well as a Voluntary AI Safety Standard[45] following its consultations on safe and responsible AI. In the proposals chapter, feedback is sought on:

1. **Defining high-risk AI**—the proposed principles for determining high-risk AI settings and their potential application to general-purpose AI (GPAI) models.
2. **Mandatory guardrails** applying across the AI supply chain and throughout the AI lifecycle—10 guardrails proposed for AI systems in high-risk settings to reduce the likelihood of harms occurring from the development and deployment of AI systems.[46] These preventative measures require developers and deployers of AI in high-risk settings to take steps to ensure their products are safe, including in relation to:
   a. *testing* during development and in deployment to ensure systems perform as intended and meet appropriate performance metrics.
   b. *transparency* about how AI products are developed and used with end-users, other actors in the AI supply chain and relevant authorities.

[44] Australian Government Department of Industry, Science and Resources, 'Proposals Paper for Introducing Mandatory Guardrails for AI in High-Risk Settings' (September 2024) <https://storage.googleapis.com/converlens-au-industry/industry/p/prj2f6f02ebfe6a8190c7bdc/page/proposals_ chapter_for_introducing_mandatory_guardrails_for_ai_in_high_risk_settings.pdf> last accessed 15 December 2024.

[45] Australian Government Department of Industry, Science and Resources, 'Voluntary AI Safety Standard' (August 2024) <https://www.industry.gov.au/sites/default/files/2024-09/voluntary-ai-safety-standard.pdf> last accessed 15 December 2024.

[46] The proposals chapter establishes the following guardrails:

1. Establish, implement, and publish an accountability process including governance, internal capability, and a strategy for regulatory compliance.
2. Establish and implement a risk management process to identify and mitigate risks.
3. Protect AI systems and implement data governance measures to manage data quality and provenance.

   c. *accountability* for governing and managing the risks associated with AI systems; and
3. **Regulatory options to mandate guardrails**—this section considers three options for implementing the proposed mandatory guardrails:
   a. Option 1 –Domain specific approach– adapting existing regulatory frameworks to include the proposed mandatory guardrails.
   b. Option 2 –Framework approach– introducing framework legislation, with associated amendments to existing legislation, or
   c. Option 3 –Whole of economy approach– introducing a new cross-economy AI Act.

The Australian government has attempted to spearhead the protection of the digital rights of children by limiting children under 16 from using social media.[47] The ban, which will not take effect for at least 12 months and could see technology companies heavily fined in case of infringement. Decision on implementation will be made later by Australia's communications minister, who will seek advice from the eSafety Commissioner—an internet regulator who will enforce the rules.[48]

Canada's first comprehensive AI legislation, the AI and Data Act (AIDA) is still in development at the time of writing, with AIDA being under review in the Canadian House of Commons as part of Bill C-27.[49] In the meantime, voluntary guidelines are in place, and provincial and international efforts are progressing. It is important for businesses to stay informed and prepared for future regulatory changes. The Canadian Government has developed a document on the use of Generative AI. It states:

> Public servants must not input personal information into publicly available online generative AI tools. Doing so would constitute an unlawful disclosure of the information because the supplier might store a copy of the information. Public servants may, however, input personal information into generative AI systems that are controlled or configured by the government when the appropriate privacy and security controls

4. Test AI models and systems to evaluate model performance and monitor the system once deployed.
5. Enable human control or intervention in an AI system to achieve meaningful human oversight.
6. Inform end-users regarding AI-enabled decisions, interactions with AI and AI-generated content.
7. Establish processes for people impacted by AI systems to challenge use or outcomes.
8. Be transparent with other organizations across the AI supply chain about data, models, and systems to help them effectively address risks.
9. Keep and maintain records to allow third parties to assess compliance with guardrails.
10. Engage your stakeholders and evaluate their needs and circumstances, with a focus on safety, diversity, inclusion, and fairness.

[47] Online Safety Amendment (Social Media Minimum Age) Bill 2024 <https://www.aph.gov.au/Parliamentary_Business/Bills_Legislation/bd/bd2425/25bd39> last accessed 15 December 2024.

[48] BBC News 'Australia approves social media ban on under-16s' (London, 20 December 2024) <https //www.bbc.com/news/articles/c89vjj0lxx9o> last accessed 15 December 2024.

[49] See Government of Canada, 'Artificial Intelligence and Data Act (AIDA)—Companion Document' (June 2022) <https://www.justice.gc.ca/eng/csj-sjc/pl/charter-charte/c27_1.htm> last accessed 15 December 2024.

are in place. When using a generative AI tool controlled by the institution, employees are responsible for following all privacy and protection of personal information requirements as they are for any other system.[50]

C. Human Rights and Fundamental Freedoms Particularly Affected by AI

AI systems can contradict rights derived from human rights. Generative AI including large language models like ChatGPT as well as image or video generators such as DALL-E or Midjourney can also contradict rights derived from human rights.[51]

The UN Guiding Principles for Business & Human Rights published a Taxonomy of Human Rights Risks Connected to Generative AI noting that 'content created using deep learning models (ie generative AI), may pose serious risks to human rights,'[52] given that '[m]any users will find it difficult to distinguish which content is synthetic and what is genuine'.[53]

The taxonomy 'demonstrates how the most significant harms to people related to generative AI are in fact impacts on internationally agreed human rights', by relating generative AI to a list of rights enshrined in binding Human Rights law. Each right is accompanied by a summary of how generative AI might contradict this right, the citation of relevant Human Rights Instruments, as well as meta level examples.[54]

Without aiming to be exhaustive, this chapter shall only flesh out two noteworthy examples of potential human rights violations by AI systems. The right to a fair trial, potentially violated through the use of opaque algorithms in criminal justice, or the right to privacy, particularly endangered by AI used for surveillance and profiling. Although core human rights issues negatively impacted by AI will not be examined here, the focus will instead be on two examples that demonstrate how AI systems can also undermine the rule of law and democracy.

[50] Government of Canada, 'Guide on the Use of Generative Artificial Intelligence' (15 October 2024) <https://www.canada.ca/en/government/system/digital-government/digital-government-innovations/responsible-use-ai/guide-use-generative-ai.html> last accessed 15 December 2024.

[51] See Emmanuel Vargas Penagos, 'ChatGPT, can you solve the content moderation dilemma?' (2024) 32(1) Intl J L & Information Technology eaae028 >https://doi.org/10.1093/ijlit/eaae028> last accessed 16 December 2024.

[52] UN Human Rights Office of the High Commissioner, 'Taxonomy of Human Rights Risks Connected to Generative AI' (2023) <https://www.ohchr.org/sites/default/files/documents/issues/business/b-tech/taxonomy-GenAI-Human-Rights-Harms.pdf> last accessed 16 December 2024.

[53] A Spitale et al, 'Comprehensive annotation of RNA modification pathways reveals regulatory roles in stress adaptation and cell differentiation' (2023) Science Advances https://www.science.org/doi/pdf/10.1126/sciadv.adh1850 last accessed 13 June 2025.

[54] The taxonomy uses the following rights and freedoms: freedom from Physical and Psychological Harm, Right to Equality Before the Law and to Protection against Discrimination, Right to Privacy, Right to Own Property, Freedom of Thought, Religion, Conscience and Opinion, Freedom of Expression and Access to Information, Right to Work and to Gain a Living, Rights of the Child, Rights to Culture, Art and Science, references relevant Human Rights instruments, and cites risk examples.

1. Right to non-discrimination

The utilization of AI in automated decision-making processes carries the inherent risk of perpetuating and amplifying existing societal biases and discriminatory practices, thereby potentially infringing upon the fundamental right to non-discrimination. This right, enshrined in international human rights law, extends beyond the mere prohibition of differential treatment based on protected characteristics. It encompasses a broad spectrum of rights, including but not limited to equal access to employment, healthcare, education, and financial services. It is important to note that this right is intersectional, meaning that individuals may experience discrimination based on multiple grounds, such as gender,[55] biases in financial services,[56] biases in large language models such as ChatGPT, Google Bard, or LLMs when translating[57] or when producing recommendation letters,[58] or socio-economic bias when scoring student performances,[59] thus also infringing the right to education.

2. Freedom of opinion and expression and undermining democracy and the rule of law

Data-driven technologies can affect the right of individuals to give opinions and express their beliefs.[60] As seen with Cambridge Analytica, algorithms have the potential to affect elections and other forms of political participation and to suppress or censor certain types of speech. The UN General Assembly Report on the Promotion and Protection of the Right to Freedom of Opinion and Expression discusses the potential

[55] Fabian Lütz, 'AI and Gender-Based Discrimination' in Jeroen Temperman and Alberto Quintavalla (eds), *AI and Human Rights* (online edn, OUP 2023) <https://doi.org/10.1093/law/9780192882486.003.0014> last accessed 16 December 2024.

[56] Karen Mills, 'Gender Bias Complaints Against Apple Card Signal a Dark Side to Fintech' (Harvard Business School, 12 November 2019) <https://www.library.hbs.edu/working-knowledge/gender-bias-complaints-against-apple-card-signal-a-dark-side-to-fintech> last accessed 16 December 2024.

[57] See, for instance, when Google Translate was prompted to translate a Turkish text—a language that does not have gender-specific pronouns, ie no 'he' or 'she' —it created stereotypical gender pairings of the previously gender neutral pronouns: men were paired with roles such as doctor or engineer whilst women were a nurse or cook; available at <https://qz.com/1141122/google-translates-gender-bias-pairs-he-with-hardworking-and-she-with-lazy-and-other-examples> last accessed 16 December 2024. For proposals on how to reduce gender bias, see Danielle Saunders and Bill Byrne, 'Reducing Gender Bias in Neural Machine Translation as a Domain Adaptation Problem' ACL 2020. arXiv:2004.04498.

[58] See, eg, Yixin Wan, George Pu, Jiao Sun, Aparna Garimella, Kai-Wei Chang, and Nanyun Peng, 'Kelly Is a Warm Person, Joseph Is a Role Model: Gender Biases in LLM-Generated Reference Letters' (2023) Findings of the Association for Computational Linguistics: EMNLP 2023, 3730–48 (Association for Computational Linguistics, Singapore). ChatGPT and Alpeca were instructed to write recommendation letters for male and female applicants (Wan et al, 2023). They revealed a strong gender bias in how the applicants were described which could lead to the 'sabotage of the application success rate for female applicants'.

[59] For more information on a Biased GCSE Scoring Algorithm see D Kolkman and G van Maanen, 'Algorithmic Models Through a Representational Lens' (2024) The Information Society 1–18 shttps://doi.org/10.1080/01972243.2024.2398046> last accessed 16 December 2024.

[60] Report of the Special Rapporteur on the Promotion and Protection of the Right to Freedom of Opinion and Expression: Note by the Secretariat (UN Human Rights Council, 2018).

of AI systems to diminish the ability of individuals to freely form and express opinions, listing various mechanisms. Automated content curation algorithms determine what users see on social media,[61] often promoting sponsored, shocking, or novel content while excluding critical social or political stories. This lack of transparency leaves users unaware of the impact of AI on their information consumption. Additionally, the increasing personalization of online content creates echo chambers, where individuals are primarily exposed to views aligning with their own. This reinforces biases, reduces tolerance for differing opinions, and erodes shared societal understanding. Furthermore, Generative AI has the potential to create deep fakes that can be used to develop and spread mis- and disinformation. This is considered by the World Economic Forum as the top risk of the misuse of AI over the next two years, capable of widening the 'societal and political divides'.[62] This is especially risky due to the large number of elections in 2024 and 2025. The report suggests that deepfakes targeting political opponents could trigger civil unrest while also prompting government-imposed censorship and restrictions on the free flow of information, thereby undermining the right to freedom of opinion and expression.

D. Human Rights-Centric AI Criteria

Previous contributions to the present volume have addressed people-centred digitalization, primarily within the access to justice discourse. The European Declaration on Digital Rights coined the people-centric perspective, noting that '[p]eople are at the centre of the digital transformation' and technology 'empower them to pursue their aspirations, in full security and respect for their fundamental rights'[63] and the OECD Recommendations, specifically on Access to Justice place people at the heart of digital transformation. This means that technology should serve people and empower them, while respecting their fundamental rights and providing access to justice.

This chapter takes a much broader approach and aims to develop a roadmap for human rights-centric AI governance. A human rights-based approach to AI governance is paramount to mitigate the risks associated with these powerful technologies and to harness their potential for the betterment of humanity. This approach entails embedding human rights principles into all stages of the AI life cycle, from design and development to deployment and use.[64] The above-mentioned CoE's Framework Convention on AI, Human Rights, Democracy and the Rule of Law, adopted in 2024, is a landmark achievement in this regard. The Convention provides a comprehensive legal framework for AI governance, grounded in the CoE's already established

[61] Wang HC, Chen CC, and Li TW, 'Automatic Content Curation of News Events' (2022) 81 Multimedia Tools and Applications 10445 <https://doi.org/10.1007/s11042-022-12224-4> last accessed 16 December 2024.

[62] World Economic Forum, Global Risks Report 2024 (World Economic Forum, 2024) <https://www.weforum.org/publications/global-risks-report-2024/> last accessed 24 November 2024.

[63] OJEU 23/01/2023 C23/1.

[64] Noemi Nagy, '"Humanity's New Frontier": Human Rights Implications of AI and New Technologies' (2023) 64(2) Hungarian J L Studies 236; Kate Jones, 'AI Governance and Human Rights: Resetting the Relationship' (Chatham House, January 2023).

standards on human rights, democracy, and the rule of law, aiming to ensure that AI systems are developed and used in a manner that upholds these fundamental values.[65]

Considering the multiple multifaceted instruments adopted worldwide, the key principles that should guide the development and implementation of human rights-compliant AI systems should stem from the fundamental respect for human dignity and used in such a way that the inherent worth and autonomy of all individuals is respected,[66] regardless of their gender, sexual orientation, religion, political affiliation, ideology, etc. The principle of non-discrimination and equality of opportunity should guide the entire lifecycle of AI systems, thus contributing to the diminishing of existing inequalities, discriminatory practices or inherent biases, and promoting fairness and equality amongst its users.[67]

Furthermore, the decision-making processes of AI systems should be transparent and accessible to those affected by their decisions. Individuals should have the right to know how decisions are made and to challenge those decisions when necessary.[68] Individuals should also participate in the design process,.[69] Moreover, there should be clear lines of accountability for the development, deployment, and use of AI systems. Mechanisms should be developed to identify states that fail to abide by their due diligence obligations and safeguard individuals from the adverse effects of AI, which can occur because of failure to regulate appropriately or to provide for adequate redress mechanisms, or failure to implement effective enforcement mechanisms in such cases where human rights violations occur.[70] The development and deployment of AI systems should also be guided by the precautionary principle that potential risks and negative impacts should be carefully assessed and mitigated before deployment.[71] In addition, AI system's lifecycle should contribute towards sustainable development and the achievement of sustainable development goals and the 2030 Agenda.

A human rights-compliant AI system must be properly monitored throughout its entire lifecycle, and any breach of human rights must be properly and promptly addressed. A human rights approach to AI governance thus requires effective implementation mechanisms. These mechanisms respond to the different phases in the process of creation of AI systems. As conducting human rights due diligence is a requirement according to the UNGPs,[72] Human Rights Impact Assessments (HRIAs), whilst not mandatory according to the current global regulatory framework, can be

[65] Eileen Donahoe, Megan MacDuffee Metzger, 'AI and Human Rights' (2019) 30 Journal of Democracy 115.

[66] CoE, Explanatory Report CETS 225 AI (5 September 2024).

[67] Sue AnneTeo, 'Human Dignity and AI: Mapping the Contours and Utility of Human Dignity in Addressing Challenges Presented by AI' (2023) 15 Law, Innovation and Technology 241.

[68] CoE, Framework Convention on AI, Human Rights, Democracy, and the Rule of Law, CETS 225 (5 September 2024), Art 10.

[69] Fernando Delgado, Stephen Yang, Michael Madaio, and Qian Yang, 'The Participatory Turn in AI Design: Theoretical Foundations and the Current State of Practice' (arXiv, 3 October 2023) <https://doi.org/10.48550/arXiv.2310.00907 > last accessed 16 December 2024.

[70] CoE, Framework Convention on AI (n 68) art 8.

[71] ibid, Art 9.

[72] UN Human Rights Council, Guiding Principles on Business and Human Rights: Implementing the UN 'Protect, Respect and Remedy' Framework (UNHRC, 2011) A/HRC/17/31.

an important tool to assess the potential impact of AI systems on human rights before and during their deployment.[73]

The Committee on Economic, Social and Cultural Rights, in its 2017 General Comment No 24 on State Obligations under International Covenant on Economic, Social and Cultural Rights in the Context of Business Activities recognizes that:

> the obligation to protect entails a positive duty to adopt a legal framework requiring business entities to exercise human rights due diligence in order to identify, prevent and mitigate the risks of violations of Covenant rights and States should adopt measures such as imposing due diligence requirements to prevent abuses of Covenant rights in a business entity's supply chain and by subcontractors, suppliers, franchisees, or other business partners.

The UNGPs, which function as a soft law framework, have spurred a range of legislative efforts at the national level aimed at converting the human rights due diligence guidelines outlined in the UNGPs into binding legal requirements. There is growing legislative momentum worldwide among governments, particularly in Europe, to mandate companies to undertake human rights and environmental due diligence.[74] The CoE Framework Convention requires State Parties to 'adopt or maintain' certain measures to address the risks of AI.[75] Article 4 of the Framework Convention mandates that parties take stock of their existing human rights frameworks and mechanisms to ensure they are sufficient and effective in responding to the evolving AI landscape. Article 15 introduces a requirement for iterative risk and impact assessments for AI systems that could significantly impact human rights. democracy, and the rule of law, leading to the establishment of prevention and mitigation measures. Article 16 elaborates on the content of these assessments, requiring consideration of factors such as severity, probability, duration, and reversibility of risks and impacts. It also mandates considering the perspective of affected individuals and groups, as well as engaging relevant stakeholders, including technical experts and civil society. Article 19 reinforces the importance of international human rights law as the benchmark for assessing the potential impact of AI systems. This provision underscores the need for grounding HRIAs in established human rights standards and principles. Volker Türk, UN High Commissioner for Human Rights, formerly supported Fundamental Rights Impact Assessments (FRIAs) to be included expressly in the AI Act.[76] Although the AI Act does not explicitly use the term HRIA or FRIA, it does include provisions for impact assessments, particularly for high-risk AI systems, that encompass human

[73] ibid, Guiding Principle 17; Commissioner for Human Rights, Unboxing AI: 10 Steps to Protect Human Rights (2019).

[74] See: the French Duty of Vigilance Law 2017; German Act on Corporate Due Diligence Obligations in Supply Chain 2021; Norwegian Transparency Act 2021; and the EU Corporate Sustainability Due Diligence Directive 2024.

[75] CoE, Framework Convention on AI (n 68) Art 1, para 2.

[76] Volker Türk, UN High Commissioner for Human Rights, 'Open Letter from the UN High Commissioner for Human Rights to EU institutions on the EU AI Act ("AI Act")' (OHCHR, 8 November 2023) <https://www.ohchr.org/en/statements/2023/11/open-letter-united-nations-high-commissioner-human-rights-european-union-institutions> last accessed 16 November 2023.

rights,[77] data quality, and transparency. This assessment should consider potential harms to fundamental rights and lead to mitigation measures.

HRIAs must have a well delineated scope. These HRIAs should be regulated domestically and conducted by both public authorities and private sector actors. A HRIA is required to understand the level of risk of the system. This type of algorithmic audit focuses on assessing AI systems, mainly around detecting malfunctions or biased outputs and should be conducted at the outset (ie when defining the objective, before any resources were invested), throughout the lifecycle, and certainly before the system is deployed.[78] A system's risk can range from little to no impact to moderate to high and very high impact and should be completed by a multidisciplinary team at the beginning of the design phase to measure the impact that decisions will have across a broad range of factors and potential effects on society. These include the rights, economic interests, and health and well-being of individuals or communities, with a specific focus on vulnerable groups of persons, with the goal of preventing potentially increasing inequalities, the ongoing sustainability of an ecosystem and the duration and reversibility of the impacts the AI system may have.

HRIA should be publicly released in an accessible language. The Framework Convention acknowledges the diversity of legal systems and regulatory traditions of its potential signatories, providing flexibility in implementing specific provisions related to HRIAs, allowing states to adapt their approach to conducting and regulating HRIAs according to their domestic legal frameworks and national AI strategies. Several countries and Research Centres have developed comprehensive HRIA guidelines easily exportable to other jurisdictions, in the light of the CoE Commissioners' recommendations[79] and the Framework Convention.[80] The Danish Institute for Human Rights has already developed guidance and a toolbox for conducting HRIAs of digital activities, which have been used by businesses and public sector actors to assess human rights impacts. These resources provide practical guidance and support

[77] Regulation (EU) 2024/1689 of the European Parliament and the Council of 13 March 2024 laying down harmonized rules on AI (AI Act) and amending certain Union legislative acts (AI Act), [2024] OJ L135/31.See Art 6: defines rules for classifying AI systems as high-risk, including those used in law enforcement, border control, and employment, which often have significant implications for human rights. Art 9: mandates that providers of high-risk AI systems conduct conformity assessments that include a risk management system. This system should address risks to health, safety and fundamental rights throughout the AI system's lifecycle. Art 9(2)(a) specifically requires the 'identification and analysis of the known and the reasonably foreseeable risks that the high-risk AI system can pose to the health, safety or fundamental rights' when used as intended. This aligns with the core objective of HRIAs. Art 10: focuses on data quality for high-risk systems, requiring datasets to be relevant, representative, free from errors, and with appropriate statistical properties. This provision helps mitigate potential biases in AI systems, which could lead to discriminatory outcomes and human rights violations. Art 13: requires providers of high-risk AI systems to provide clear and comprehensive documentation, including information on the system's purpose, intended use, and potential risks. This transparency aims to facilitate scrutiny and accountability, enabling stakeholders to assess the system's impact on human rights. Art 81: allows for deployers (those using high-risk AI systems) to conduct impact assessments before deploying a system particularly if relevant factors have changed.

[78] Danaë Metaxa et al, 'Auditing Algorithms' (2021) 14 Foundations and Trends® in Human-Computer Interaction 272.

[79] CoE Commissioner for Human Rights, Follow-up Recommendation to 'Unboxing AI' (2019) 5.

[80] CoE, Framework Convention on AI, Human Rights, Democracy, and the Rule of Law, CETS 225 (5 September 2024), Art 20.

for organisations seeking to implement HRIAs. The Netherlands is the first country to introduce mandatory HRIAs for public institutions using algorithms to make decisions about individuals.[81] This pioneering legislation underscores the growing recognition of HRIAs as a crucial tool for AI governance. HRIAs are an essential tool for ensuring the responsible and ethical development of AI. By identifying and mitigating potential human rights impacts, HRIAs can help to build more just, equitable, and human-centred AI systems. As AI continues to evolve and become increasingly integrated into our lives, the importance of HRIAs will only grow.

Algorithmic Impact Assessments (AIAs) evaluating specific algorithms within AI systems for potential bias, fairness, and unintended consequences are also paramount. These assessments should be conducted systematically and rigorously, explicitly considering human rights impacts. Ensuring that algorithms are designed and trained on unbiased data sets, and that their outputs do not perpetuate or exacerbate existing inequalities, is crucial for upholding the right to non-discrimination and ensuring that AI systems promote fairness and justice.

Public consultations: all stakeholders, including civil society organizations, academia, experts, and specific sectors should be meaningfully consulted in the development and implementation of AI regulations and policies.[82]

Independent monitoring mechanisms: Independent bodies should be established to monitor and oversee the development and use of AI systems to ensure compliance with human rights standards.[83] The potentially global AI human rights treaty sheds a bit of light on this aspect as well. A dedicated follow-up mechanism, the Conference of the Parties, will monitor the implementation of the Framework Convention.[84] This body will assess state compliance with their obligations, including those related to HRIAs, and issue recommendations to ensure the convention's effectiveness.

Effective remedies: Individuals whose rights are violated by AI systems should have access to effective judicial and non-judicial remedies,[85] both at domestic and international level.

User-centred design is an iterative process in which designers focus on the users and their needs in each phase of the design process. According to Tim Brown,[86] human-centric design focuses on users' experiences to develop solutions that are both experimental and iterative. Such design principles are necessary so that non-expert users can appropriately use AI software. Richard Buchanan explicitly claimed human rights and human dignity as the first principle of user-centred design.[87] Margaret Hagan

[81] Council of Europe, Commissioner for Human Rights, *Follow-Up Recommendation on the 2019 Report: Human Rights by Design—Future Generations Matter* (2022) <https://rm.coe.int/follow-up-recommendation-on-the-2019-report-human-rights-by-design-fut/1680ab2279> last accessed 27 December 2024.

[82] CoE, Framework Convention on AI, Human Rights, Democracy, and the Rule of Law, CETS 225 (5 September 2024), Art 13.

[83] Danish Institute for Human Rights, Guidance on HRIA of Digital Activities (2020).

[84] CoE, Framework Convention on AI, Human Rights, Democracy, and the Rule of Law, CETS 225 (5 September 2024), Art 23.

[85] Commissioner for Human Rights, Follow-up Recommendation on AI, and Human Rights (2023), CommHR (2023)15.

[86] Tim Brown, 'Design Thinking' (2008) 86(6) Harv Bus Rev 84.

[87] Richard Buchanan, 'Human Dignity and Human Rights: Thoughts on the Principles of Human-Centered Design' (2001) 17(3) Design Issues 35, 36–37 <https://doi.org/10.1162/07479360175035178>.

advocates for a human-centric design approach to the design and implementation of AI systems to enhance the pursuit of access to justice. She argues people with unmet legal needs require more robust and user-friendly digital tools. [88]

E. Conclusions

The establishment of a robust, human rights-centred AI regulatory framework must build upon existing international human rights standards while incorporating effective enforcement and monitoring mechanisms. Such a framework should ensure that AI not only avoids infringing upon human rights and freedoms but also actively contributes to their realization. To achieve this, core human rights principles must be translated into actionable legal measures and implementation strategies. While the AI Convention represents a notable step toward legally binding state obligations, it currently serves as a guideline for integrating principles into national AI policies. Similarly, the AI Act, though a pioneering comprehensive legal framework, adopts a risk-based approach that grants states considerable flexibility, without fleshing out sufficiently detailed guidelines, thus allowing circumvention of certain contentious provisions. National legislation should complement these frameworks by enacting targeted laws that address algorithmic bias, data protection, and the use of AI in sensitive areas such as law enforcement, healthcare, and social services. Ideally, proactive states will exceed international minimum standards and drive forward a human rights-focused AI governance agenda.

Meaningful stakeholder engagement is critical to this process. Collaboration with civil society organizations, human rights experts, and affected communities ensures that diverse perspectives are included, risks are identified, and mitigation strategies are timely and effective. HRIAs should be mandatory throughout the AI lifecycle, particularly for high-risk systems. While the UN Guiding Principles outline due diligence for companies, groundbreaking AI regulations must impose direct obligations on businesses to respect human rights. AI developers and deployers should embed human rights considerations into design processes, data governance, and risk management strategies.

Effective oversight and enforcement are equally essential. Independent oversight bodies—at international, regional, and national levels—should monitor AI systems, investigate human rights complaints, audit compliance, and impose penalties for violations. Leveraging AI in the functioning of these oversight bodies can enhance transparency and empower individuals to understand and challenge decisions that affect their rights, including access to training data and decision-making logic.

Fostering digital literacy is key to empowering individuals to engage with AI systems, understand associated risks, and challenge biased outcomes. Providing accessible resources, such as plain-language explanations and mechanisms to report

[88] Margaret D Hagan, 'A Human-Centered Design Approach to Access to Justice: Generating New Prototypes and Hypotheses for Interventions to Make Courts User-Friendly'(2018) 6 Ind J & Soc Equal. 199, 200.

algorithmic harm, will enable public participation in AI governance and accountability processes.

Finally, international cooperation is vital to addressing the global challenges posed by AI and ensuring consistent human rights standards across borders. Public–private collaborations, including shared principles, best practices, and technical standards, can support a unified approach to AI governance. The EU, as a global regulatory leader, is well-positioned to champion ethical AI standards, promote regulatory convergence, and aid capacity-building efforts in developing nations. By implementing a comprehensive approach that embeds human rights considerations throughout all stages of AI development and governance, we can unlock the transformative benefits of this technology while mitigating the risks of algorithmic bias. Neglecting to do so may deepen existing inequalities, weaken public trust in democratic institutions, and undermine the very foundations of human rights protection.

Bibliography

Abe O and Eurallyah AJ, 'Regulating AI through a Human Rights-Based Approach in Africa' (2022) 14 African Journal of Legal Studies 425–48.

Alimonti V and Cavalcanti de Alcântara R, 'Inter-American Standards and State Use of AI for Rights-Affecting Determinations in Latin America: Appendix' (Electronic Frontier Foundation, October 2024).

Börzel TA and Risse T, 'Human Rights, Rule of Law, and Democracy' in *Effective Governance Under Anarchy: Institutions, Legitimacy, and Social Trust in Areas of Limited Statehood* (CUP 2021) 18.

Buchanan R, 'Human Dignity and Human Rights: Thoughts on the Principles of Human-Centred Design' (2001) 17(3) Design Issues 35 <https://doi.org/10.1162/074793601750357178>.

Clarke et al, 'Submission of Feedback to the European Commission's Proposal for a Regulation Laying Down Harmonised Rules on AI', Feedback from: University of Cambridge (Leverhulme Centre for the Future of Intelligence and Centre for the Study of Existential Risk, August 2021) <https://ec.europa.eu/info/law/better-regulation/have-your-say/initiatives/12527-Artificial-intelligence-ethical-and-legal-requirements/F2665626>.

Cordeschi R, 'AI Turns Fifty: Revisiting Its Origins' (2007) 21(4–5) Applied AI 259.

Cupać J, Schopmans H, and Tuncer-Ebetürk İ, 'Democratization in the Age of Artificial Intelligence: Introduction to the Special Issue' (2024) 31(5) Democratization 899 <https://doi.org/10.1080/13510347.2024.2338852>.

Delgado F, Yang S, Madaio M, and Yang Q, 'The Participatory Turn in AI Design: Theoretical Foundations and the Current State of Practice' (arXiv, 3 October 2023) <https://doi.org/10.48550/arXiv.2310.00907>.

Donahoe E and Metzger MM, 'AI and Human Rights' (2019) 30 Journal of Democracy 115.

Dafoe A, 'AI Governance: A Research Agenda' (Centre for the Governance of AI, Future of Humanity Institute, University of Oxford 2018).

Fournier-Tomalty E., *AI Governance and Human Rights: Resetting the Relationship* (Chatham House 2023).

Gans-Combe C, 'Automated Justice: Issues, Benefits and Risks in the Use of AI and Its Algorithms in Access to Justice and Law Enforcement' in *Ethics, Integrity, and Policymaking: The Value of the Case Study* (2022).

Graycar A and Masters A, 'Bureaucratic Bastardry: Robodebt/Debt Recovery, AI and the Stigmatisation of Citizens by Machines and Systems' (2022) International Journal of Public Policy 16.5–6 333.

Hagan MD, 'A Human-Centered Design Approach to Access to Justice: Generating New Prototypes and Hypotheses for Interventions to Make Courts User-Friendly' (2018) 6 Ind J & Soc Equal 199.

Hinojosa Martínez LM and Pérez Bernárdez C, *Enhancing the Rule of Law in the European Union's External Action* (Edward Elgar Publishing 2023).

Jungherr A, 'Artificial Intelligence and Democracy: A Conceptual Framework' (2023) 9(3) Social Media + Society <https://doi.org/10.1177/20563051231186353>

Kistemaker L, 'Rechtwijzer and uitelkaar. nl. dutch experiences with odr for divorce' (2021) 59(2) Family Court Review 232, 243.

Kolkman D and van Maanen G, 'Algorithmic Models Through a Representational Lens' (2024) The Information Society 1–18 <https://doi.org/10.1080/01972243.2024.2398046>.

Leslie D, Burr C, Aitken M, Cowls J, Katell M, and Briggs M, *AI, Human Rights, Democracy, and the Rule of Law—A Primer* (CoE, 2021).

Llorens MP, 'Crossing Routes: AI Governance and Human Rights in Latin America' (2023) 31 *CEBRI–Journal* 83.

Lütz F, 'AI and Gender-Based Discrimination' in Temperman J and Quintavalla A (eds), *AI and Human Rights* (online edn, OUP 2023) <https://doi.org/10.1093/law/9780192882486.003.0014>.

Marchenko AY and Entin ML, 'Artificial Intelligence and Human Rights: What Is the EU's Approach?' (2022) 3 Vestnik MGIMO Universiteta 43.

Mijatović D, *Human Rights by Design: Future-Proofing Human Rights Protection in the Era of AI* (CoE 2023).

Mills K, 'Gender Bias Complaints Against Apple Card Signal a Dark Side to Fintech' (Harvard Business School, 12 November 2019) <https://www.library.hbs.edu/working-knowledge/gender-bias-complaints-against-apple-card-signal-a-dark-side-to-fintech>.

Moreira S and Borges P, 'AI and Jurisdictional Decisions: Is the Robot-Judge Imminent?' (Draft chapter, Law and Society Association Conference, 13–16 July 2022).

Oostveen AM et al, *A Human Rights Impact Assessment of Digital Activities* (Berenschot 2021).

Palmerini E et al, 'Global Governance of Artificial Intelligence: The Council of Europe's Human Rights Perspective' (2023) 20 Law, Innovation and Technology 233.

Salter S and Thompson D, 'Public-centred Civil Justice Redesign: A Case Study of the British Columbia Civil Resolution Tribunal' (2016) 3 McGill J Disp Resol 113.

Schmitz A and Zeleznikow J, 'Intelligent Legal Tech to Empower Self-represented Litigants' (2021) 23 Colum Sci & Tech L Rev 142.

Sætra HS, 'Generative AI: Here to Stay, but for Good?' (2023) 75 Technology in Society 102372.

Sempere FJ, 'El Sistema Del Consejo De Europa Y La Gobernanza De La Inteligencia Artificial' in Sempere FJ (ed), *Comentarios al Reglamento Europeo de Inteligencia Artificial* (Aranzadi 2024).

Temperman J and Quintavalla A (eds), *AI and Human Rights* (online edn, OUP 2023) <https://doi.org/10.1093/law/9780192882486.001.0001>.

Türk V, 'Open Letter from the UN High Commissioner for Human Rights to EU Institutions on the EU AI Act ("AI Act")' (OHCHR, 8 November 2023) <https://www.ohchr.org/en/statements/2023/11/open-letter-united-nations-high-commissioner-human-rights-european-union-institutions>.

US Department of State, *Risk Management Profile for AI and Human Rights* (State Department 2024).

Wan Y, Pu G, Sun J, Garimella A, Chang KW, and Peng N, 'Kelly Is a Warm Person, Joseph Is a Role Model: Gender Biases in LLM-Generated Reference Letters' *Findings of the Association for Computational Linguistics: EMNLP 2023* (December 2023) 3730.

William L, Access to Justice and the Rule of Law (2020) 40 (2) OJLS 377 <https://doi.org/10.1093/ojls/gqaa012>.

Zeleznikow J, 'The benefits and dangers of using machine learning to support making legal predictions' (2023) 13(4) Wiley Interdisciplinary Reviews: Data Mining and Knowledge Discovery 1.

12
Governance of AI in the Judicial System

*Javier Valls-Prieto**

A. Introduction

The judicial system is vast and diverse, with a multitude of legal orders and actors, from public to private representation. This presents vast opportunities for the use of artificial intelligence (AI) systems at different levels, from the search for jurisprudence and the drafting of a contract to the automatic resolution of conflicts and the prediction of the recidivism of an offender.[1] Hence, when we speak about AI use in justice, we face an undefined object because it depends on two dynamic variables—the technology to be applied (an expert system, a generative AI, a predictive system or a language processing system) and the context in which it will be used (a small claims process, a conflict resolution system, a civil or administrative process or a criminal process).

The use of these intelligent tools in the justice system impacts fundamental rights. Raso et al identified a series of rights that may be affected in risk assessment to determine pre-trial detention, sentencing or the granting of parole, including freedom, process equality, the right to life, the right to security, the right to a fair trial, the right to the presumption of innocence and the right to privacy.[2] The use of these AI-based

* Professor of Criminal Law, Law Faculty, University of Granada. This research has been supported by the Spanish Ministry of Research, Innovation and Universities, within the project GOIA *La gobernaza de la inteligencia artificial basada en la ciudadanía* TED2021-129402B-C22.

[1] European Commission for the Efficiency of Justice (CEPEJ), 'European Ethical Charter on the Use of Artificial Intelligence in Judicial Systems and Their Environment' (Council of Europe 2018).

[2] Filippo Raso et al, 'Artificial Intelligence & Human Rights: Opportunities & Risks' <https://dash.harvard.edu/handle/1/38021439> last accessed 17 May 2021.

Javier Valls-Prieto, *Governance of AI in the Judicial System* In: *Digitalization and Artificial Intelligence in Courts*.
Edited by: Fernando Esteban de la Rosa, Pablo Cortés, and Nuria Marchal Escalona, Oxford University Press.
 DOI: 10.1093/9780198918752.003.0012

systems in the third branch of the State is relevant and can alter the conception of the powers of the State and the rights of citizens in a democratic system.

Technology continues to develop at great speed and the justice system cannot be left aside in its implementation. As an administrative body, the State must provide services to citizens who demand their right to be able to settle disputes orderly before the courts. The State must ensure that justice is equal and the rights of the parties are respected.

However, the challenges posed by AI implementation in the justice system are more legal-ethical than technological and plenty.

B. Artificial Intelligence in the Judicial System and the Ethical Principles

AI utilization in judicial decisions is a well-established practice in France where a system has been developed over several years for ensuring legal certainty in judicial decisions. To carry out this huge task, the first requirement is the datafication of judgments, which was attempted with the Digital Republic Act[3] to publish the most relevant judgments.[4] However, this project has been tempered in some points, such as, from a technical perspective, the lack of coordination in the collection of the main judgments of different levels of courts and the failure to achieve an automatic system that guarantees sentence anonymity. From a legal perspective, there are additional considerations, such as the potential for legal decisions to be influenced by the underlying logic. This raises the question of whether judges should be required to provide detailed explanations for their decisions. Another concern is that, in cases where the rule is not designed for the resolution of a specific case, it may differ from the approach taken by higher courts. This could result in inconsistency in the application of existing jurisprudence. Therefore, all judgments must be written using a consistent and logical approach.[5]

In civil, commercial, and administrative justice, AI can be useful to reduce uncertainty in the resolution that the judge will give before going to trial. Attorneys will be able to provide clients with an estimation of the likelihood of obtaining a favourable ruling. Law firms will be able to avoid unnecessary expenditures in lawsuits with minimal potential for favourable outcomes.[6] Furthermore, it allows justice managers to improve the flow of new procedures, allowing better management and reduced costs. The current system of using scales for damage awards, divorces, etc can be improved with probabilistic systems,[7] and small claims can be solved through online alternative dispute resolution systems. There are self-service systems for conducting compliance

[3] Law No. 2016-1321 of October 7, 2016, for a Digital Republic.
[4] ibid 18.
[5] European Commission for the Efficiency of Justice (CEPEJ) (n 1) 19.
[6] Michael Mills, 'Artificial Intelligence in Law: The State of Play 2016' (Legal Executive Institute, 23 February 2016) <https://www.legalexecutiveinstitute.com/artificial-intelligence-in-law-the-state-of-play-2016-part-1/> last accessed 1 June 2021.
[7] European Commission for the Efficiency of Justice (CEPEJ) (n 1) 31.

programmes, such as Neota Logic,[8] which applies a hybrid system of platforms that combines expert systems with other AI techniques, such as natural language processing and machine learning, to provide fact- and context-based answers for compliance, regulatory and legal issues. For example, Compliance HR[9] helps HR managers evaluate an external contractor, overtime pay, and other labour law issues, and Global Risk Solutions Service[10] helps conduct anti-corruption compliance programmes while respecting authorities' regulations. Similar AI techniques are being used in the lifecycle of a contract, from its creation to execution or termination.

AI implementation in the penal system is more complicated. The use of AI systems in the fight against crime ranges from prevention and the evaluation of the danger levels of the subjects[11] to the determination of the possibility of recidivism. The two main risks faced due to AI in this legal area are that they directly affect the most important fundamental rights of individuals (life and liberty) and the discriminatory decisions that the intelligent system may take.

1. Council of Europe ethical approach

The Council of Europe (CoE) created five ethical principles in 2018 that must be met during AI use in the justice system,[12] coinciding with the document of the European Commission (EC) on ethical principles in AI of the high-level experts group (HLEG). The five principles are:

1) Principle of respect for fundamental rights
2) Principle of non-discrimination
3) Principle of quality and security
4) Principle of transparency, impartiality and fairness
5) Principle of 'under user control'

The first principle cannot be strictly considered an ethical principle. It is more of a legal obligation. It states, 'The processing of judicial decisions and data must serve clear purposes, in full compliance with the fundamental rights guaranteed by the European Convention on Human Rights (ECHR) and the Convention on the Protection of Personal Data'. The principal idea is not to undermine the guarantees of the right of access to a judge and the right to a fair trial under Article 6 of the ECHR. It implies respect for the principles of the rule of law and the independence of judges in judicial decision-making. It suggests that these systems could be used and implemented from the beginning of a human-rights-by-design approach.[13] This human-rights approach

[8] 'Legal Operations Archives' (*Neota*) <https://neota.com/tag/legal-operations/> last accessed 23 April 2024.
[9] 'Home' (*ComplianceHR*) <https://compliancehr.com/> last accessed 23 April 2024.
[10] 'GRS_Bridge[SM] – Global Risk Solutions, Inc' <https://www.globalrisksolutions.com/technology1-2/grs_bridge/> last accessed 23 April 2024.
[11] Carlos María Romeo Casabona, 'Riesgo, Procedimientos Actuariales Basados En La Inteligencia Artificial y Medidas de Seguridad' (2018) 13 REDS 167 ff.
[12] European Commission for the Efficiency of Justice (CEPEJ) (n 1) 7–13.
[13] ibid 8.

is recognized in the HLEG guidelines for AI (AI HLEG);[14] however, it is not considered an ethical principle in itself. It must be considered as a duty of the rule of law in a democratic judicial system.

The second principle is an ethical one. AI use can reinforce the racial, ethical, and socio-economic prejudices against individuals or groups that a society may have.[15] The CoE's report emphasizes two phases that deserve extra care—the development and the deployment of these systems.[16] Its recommendation expresses the possibility of using intelligent systems to combat such discrimination.

The third principle focuses on collaboration with experts in law and social sciences to ensure the quality of the decisions made by AI. The models must allow decisions to be stored and executed in secure environments.

The fourth principle of transparency, impartiality, and fairness should be respected over the intellectual property of the system to comply with the openness of the justice system. Justice in a democracy depends on the transparency of sentences and the open arguments of the judges and courts. If the general public is unable to comprehend the rationale behind a decision, it could result in a permanent breach of trust.

The fifth principle is about using these technologies whilst keeping the control of the professionals in the administration of justice. User autonomy must be increased and professionals should be able to review judicial decisions and the data used to produce a result. The users must be informed in clear and understandable language whether or not the solutions offered by the intelligence tools are binding. This principle is more about maintaining transparency than about human oversight.

2. European Commission ethical principles

The EC's HLEG launched ethical guidelines for AI, comprising seven principles for AI use with the intent to implement them in practice.[17] The CoE principles are analogous to those of the HLEG; however, they are more comprehensive and provide greater clarity regarding citizens' expectations. If we compare the most important guidelines about AI use worldwide, we would observe that the HLEG includes all the other approaches to the topic.[18] Hence, these guidelines can be regarded as a standard:

1) Principle of human agency and oversight.
2) Principle of robustness and safety.
3) Principle of accuracy of the system.
4) Principle of transparency.

[14] High-Level Expert Group on Artificial Intelligence, 'Ethics Guidelines for Thrustworthy AI' <https://digital-strategy.ec.europa.eu/en/library/ethics-guidelines-trustworthy-ai> last accessed 23 April 2024.

[15] Virginia Eubanks, *Automating Inequality: How High-Tech Tools Profile, Police, and Punish the Poor* (First edn, St Martin's Press 2017) passim.

[16] European Commission for the Efficiency of Justice (CEPEJ) (n 1) 9.

[17] Nathalie A Smuha, 'The EU Approach to Ethics Guidelines for Trustworthy Artificial Intelligence' (2019) 20 Computer L Rev Intl 97, 101.

[18] Jessica Fjeld et al, 'Principled Artificial Intelligence: Mapping Consensus in Ethical and Rights-Based Approaches to Principles for artificial intelligence' [2020] SSRN Electronic Journal 20 <https://www.ssrn.com/abstract = 3518482> last accessed 24 March 2023.

5) Principle of diversity, non-discrimination and fairness.
6) Principle of trustworthy concept
7) Principle of accountability

The guidelines have three pillars requiring AI systems to be: 1) lawful (respect for human rights), 2) ethical (ethical principles and values) and 3) robust (from technical and social perspectives).[19] The first pillar is encompassed by the first principle of CoE. The rest of the pillars conform to the ethical values, as are received in the document, constituting the seven principles.

The first principle of human agency and oversight means that persons should be able to make informed decisions autonomously.[20] AI systems should support individuals in making better choices, in this case, legal professionals, and judges must keep their autonomy and independence. Regarding oversight, the principle helps in ensuring that an AI system does not undermine human autonomy or cause adverse effects.[21] This includes control over the system, the decisions made and the governance protocol.

The second principle of robustness and safety is more technical. AI systems should be developed with a preventative approach to avoid unintentional and unexpected harm. This principle plays an important role in the implementation of AI in the judicial system because of the sensitive nature of the data and the high interest in the cases. Administrative and civil jurisdiction is as important as criminal matters. The resilience to external attacks is crucial for the right functioning of the justice system where a lack of security could result in personal damages and hamper the credibility of the third power of the State. The safety measures should depend on AI use. Thus, for instance, developing a claim assistant tool would require fewer security and safety measures than an automatic resolution system or a predicting parole tool for convicts.

The third principle of the accuracy of the system is of great importance in the judicial system. The system does not need to be infallible; however, the use of an AI system that affects human lives must ensure a high accuracy level. One of the major problems with AI use in the legal system is data use. In general, AI systems must guarantee privacy and data protection throughout the lifecycle of cases. In particular, legal professionals dealing with sensitive personal data must guarantee a high level of data governance. The data set includes the names of the parties, financial information, information about relatives and information about third parties. It further includes personal information that should be confidential.[22] In the judicial system, the data used must be of good quality and, if provided from third-party databases, it should not have social biases, inaccuracies, errors, and mistakes.[23] Data access must be restricted to the persons involved in the process because of privacy and security reasons.

The fourth principle of transparency must be held by three key factors—traceability, that is, the need to document the datasets, data gathering, and the algorithms used to

[19] High-Level Expert Group on Artificial Intelligence (n 14) 5.
[20] ibid 16.
[21] Ibid 16.
[22] European Commission for the Efficiency of Justice (CEPEJ) (n 1) 20.
[23] High-Level Expert Group on Artificial Intelligence (n 14) 17.

ensure traceability that permit system audit and explainability, that is, the system has the capability, functionality or features to do what needs to be done.[24] Hence, the decisions made by the AI system should be comprehensible and traceable by humans. Citizens have the right to demand a suitable explanation of the AI system's decision-making process. Moreover, they have the right to know in advance that they are going to interact with AI systems.

The fifth principle of diversity, non-discrimination and fairness ensures equal access through inclusive design processes and equal treatment. Bias is a human phenomenon and it is represented in the data set used for training and operation. This could lead to discrimination against certain groups or people, directly or indirectly, and increase with an amplification outcome from the use of intelligent systems. One of the solutions to deal with this problem is to let stakeholders participate in the entire process of implementing AI systems.

The sixth principle of the trustworthy concept is about societal and environmental well-being. The topic of common good is rarely addressed concerning AI. Sustainability and environmentally friendly should be adopted as there should be minimal energy use in the development, deployment and use. The implementation of AI systems can both enhance and deteriorate social skills, affecting people's physical and mental well-being. Thus, the systems should be monitored carefully regarding these aspects. Their impact on institutions, democracy and society is quite high. Thus, the use of intelligent systems within the judicial system, as a branch of the State, must be developed with special care.

The seventh principle of accountability means that the auditability of the systems entails the assessment of algorithms, data, and design processes. Reporting of negative impacts of its use in justice must be ensured with information about identification, assessment, documentation and minimisation of the negative impacts. In the event of negative impacts, mechanisms should be put in place to offer adequate redress, in particular, for vulnerable persons or groups.

3. The three ethical principles linked to democracy

As we have seen, the five principles of the CoE are covered by the HLEG principles; hence, the AI used in the judicial system that complies with the former principles can be considered to comply with the latter too.

If we consider that these principles must be implemented in a democratic society, we have to focus, following Erman and Furendal, on three of them.[25] 'Transparency' is tied, in several public documents about ethics in AI, to participation, dialogue, and principles of democracy. It promotes freedom and autonomy by not reducing the knowledge and options for citizens. Although justice is not a political debate, citizens should know about the public laws and sentences, the judge or the tribunal members

[24] Scott Thiebes, Sebastian Lins, and Ali Sunyaev, 'Trustworthy Artificial Intelligence' (2021) 31 Electronic Markets 447, 455.

[25] Eva Erman and Markus Furendal, 'The Global Governance of Artificial Intelligence: Some Normative Concerns' (2022) 9 Moral Philosophy and Politics 267, 273.

and, in case of AI use in the resolution of cases, if this technology has been used and the criteria followed in decision-making. Hence, fairness and justice are understood as equity and impartiality, non-biases and non-discriminatory procedures.[26]

Another issue is 'access to AI systems' to obtain correct, complete, and diverse data to avoid misuse of AI in decision-making approaches.[27] Finally, 'accountability and responsibility' set who is responsible for the actions and decisions of AI systems. In our case, developers and stakeholders involved in the judicial process, including lawyers, judges, and police forces, have responsibility for AI use to solve judicial cases.

The remaining principles focus on technical aspects. While they are not less important, as the judicial system is one of the three powers in a democracy, the use of AI in the judicial system must focus on respecting democratic values.

C. Human Rights Impacts

The first approach to the impact on fundamental rights (considering those of the Universal Declaration of Human Rights, the International Convention on Civil and Political Rights and the International Convention on Economic, Social and Cultural Rights) was out by the Berkman Klein Centre, which focused on six areas—the judicial system, the financial system, health, content moderation, human resources, and education. This selection serves as a reference for political, civil, economic, social, and cultural rights. An analysis of the rights affected is achieved by an analysis limited to certain sectors.[28]

They start with the justice system where the impact on fundamental rights is important. Since the justice system in a democratic state is an institution that can restrict or limit fundamental rights, the use of smart systems has a large impact on rights. The negative impact, according to this study, would affect the right to a fair public hearing, the right to be presumed innocent until proven guilty—the inherent nature and complexity and the inscrutability of the results—and the right to privacy—the need for large amounts of data creating a problem for privacy. On a neutral level, it has positive and negative impacts depending on its use. Regarding the principle of equality before the law and non-discrimination, the system can avoid human discrimination; however, by design or result interpretation, it can generate biases in some groups of citizens. Regarding the right to life, liberty and personal safety, lower-risk cases can benefit from faster sentences and shorter penalties and society can benefit from effective justice with faster resolutions. Regarding the right not to be arbitrarily arrested, detained, or expelled, algorithms can classify certain individuals as high risk, providing the possibility of pre-/post-trial arrests.[29]

An example of these situations, we examine the Correctional Offender Management Profiling for Alternative Sanctions (COMPAS) with automatic justice systems. The

[26] ibid 274.
[27] Thilo Hagendorff, 'The Ethics of artificial intelligence Ethics: An Evaluation of Guidelines' (2020) 30 Minds and Machines 99, 102.
[28] Raso et al (n 2) 19.
[29] ibid 20.

European Union (EU) Agency for Fundamental Rights has carried out a report based on more than 100 interviews with people from the public and private sectors, related to AI in Europe, to understand their consideration regarding the impact of AI use on fundamental rights in four areas—social assistance, crime prediction, health services, and personalized advertising.[30]

The report starts with the Charter of Fundamental Rights of the EU as a framework for analysis, the Treaties of the EU where more rights and principles can be found in addition to the Charter and secondary legislation. An example of the rights included in the Treaties is the right to non-discrimination, which is included in the Charter (Arts 20 and 21), the EU Treaty and the Treaties on the Functioning of the EU (Arts 2 and 10, respectively) and secondary law (Directives 2000/78/EC, 2000/43/EC, 2004/113/EC and 2006/54/EC), achieving greater determination.

The analysis provided a selection of affected rights, such as human dignity, privacy and data protection, equality and non-discrimination, access to justice, the right to social security and social assistance, those related to consumers and the right of citizens to good administration.[31]

Article 1 of the Charter places human dignity as one of the pillars of the EU, which implies that any AI development must be subservient to humans. This is in line with most of the ethical guidelines. Furthermore, Article 2 stipulates the right to life and Article 3 the integrity of persons. Harmful use of AI must be avoided to prevent the violation of these rights. Moreover, it covers more extreme cases in the protection of rights. It must be understood that people must not be subjected to AI use without their knowledge and express consent.[32]

The right to privacy and data protection, contained in Articles 7 and 8 of the Charter, are at the centre of the discussion about data-driven AI systems. This information can indirectly affect the rights of freedom of expression and information (Article 11), the right of association (Article 12) due to the importance it can have in connection with political ideas when this association refers to trade unions, political parties or religious freedom (Article 10).[33]

Articles 20 and 21 of the Charter set the rights to equality and non-discrimination. Discrimination is understood as the less favourable treatment of a person with respect to the treatment that another person receives or would receive in the same situation. This includes the treatment of vulnerable groups, such as racial, ethnic, gender, religious, minors (Art 24), the elderly (Art 25) and persons with disabilities (Art 26). The latter groups are of particular interest in cases of AI use in care and medicine.

The principle of effective judicial protection (Art 47) can be affected by intelligent systems when they do not determine whether or not to accept a certain request or when the final decision in a certain case is taken by an intelligent system. The opacity of the system makes the citizen suspicious of the decisions as he/she cannot understand the justification of the judicial decision.[34]

[30] European Union Agency for Human Rights, 'Getting the Future Right. Artificial Intelligence and Fundamental Rights' (Publications Office of the European Union 2020) 1.

[31] ibid 60 ff.

[32] ibid 60.

[33] ibid 61.

[34] ibid 78.

The right to social security and social assistance is a social right enshrined in Art 34 of the Charter. It does not set a minimum limit of assistance but must be understood as a limit when restricting the current state of social intervention by the States. It affects non-discrimination based on nationality, within the freedom of movement within the Union, in matters of labour rights and pensions to be received after years of contribution, regardless of nationality.[35]

Consumer protection is not a right enshrined in the Charter; however, the Agency's report takes it into account as a result of Art 169 of the Treaty on the Functioning of the EU (TFEU), which is of particular importance in the marketing techniques used by certain companies through AI or the surveillance of markets that affect the freedom of consumers, manipulating their decisions or prices through user profiles.[36]

The right to good administration (Art 41) refers to the right of the administered party to access the data handled by the administration and the obligation to justify the decision taken concerning the citizen. In both cases, the incidence of the use of intelligent systems by the administration can seriously endanger this right.[37]

Another study of interest is the one carried out within the European SHERPA project on the ethical dimensions of intelligent information systems from a European perspective. The rights affected by intelligent systems include the right to education, privacy, non-discrimination, democracy, freedom of expression and thought, security, health and the right to environment.[38]

Kuriakose and Iyer analyse the differences between existing human rights (extended to the digital sphere) and new digital rights.[39] The former included the right to equality and the right to work and the latter included the right to privacy and the right to non-discrimination.[40] Their analysis highlights the emergence of new values that must be taken into account when interpreting rights, such as establishing the limitations on the final deduction of data, explanation of the correlation of data, traceability (the possibility of identifying the source and the path of the data), the accountability or level of trust of the data and transparency (the disclosure of the process by which the deduction is produced).

The doctrine focused on the study of how AI affects specific rights in specific areas. One of the difficulties of the study of the rights affected by AI is that it varies greatly from the field in which it is applied. As seen previously in Raso et al, depending on the scope of the application, the rights affected can vary substantially. Thus, the scope of application, such as education or health, constitutes the fundamental rights. Furthermore, the use of intelligent systems to protect or improve the application of a right may cause collateral damage, endangering others.

So far, we have focused on the general studies of the impact on fundamental rights. We will now devote a portion of our discussion to the doctrine that has developed in

[35] ibid 79.

[36] ibid 80.

[37] ibid 81.

[38] Andreas Andreou, Stephanie Laulhe-Shaelou and Doris Schroeder, *Current Human Rights Frameworks* (Project SHERPA 2019).

[39] Francis Kuriakose and Deepa Iyer, 'Human Rights in the Big Data World' (Centre of Governance & Human Rights (CGHR) 2018) 15 https://papers.ssrn.com/sol3/papers.cfm?abstract_id = 3246969.

[40] ibid 17.

greater depth, with more detailed studies conducted on specific sectors. These include surveillance, trade, public administration, the health system, and labour.

In recent years, the proliferation of automated mass surveillance systems has taken place in two areas—law enforcement agencies and companies for personalized advertising. In both cases, privacy is strongly at risk. However, in police surveillance, the rights affected range from discriminatory treatment based on race, ethnicity, gender, or place of origin to the lack of a fair trial, impacting the rights of evaluation of evidence, respect for the principle of innocence or the right of defence of the accused on an equal footing.[41] A similar situation occurs with the use of automatic facial recognition systems, which affects the right to privacy provided in Article 8 of the European Convention on Human Rights. In a public space, the right to privacy of individuals may be undermined; however, this should not be replicated in a system that collects and stores biometric data. Without questioning the effectiveness of facial recognition systems, with failure rates of as high as 93 per cent,[42] it impacts the right of presumption of innocence of individuals. Furthermore, in use by law enforcement, the use of crime prediction systems using AI systems is particularly interesting. The transfer of statistical systems based on personality and social environment studies impacts the principle of non-discrimination and the presumption of innocence of individuals.

D. Governance of Artificial Intelligence

What is governance in the field of AI? This is not an easy question to answer. In the last two years, scholars have debated about an appropriate answer. It is not easy to design a government plan for AI[43] that covers all its uses in judicial systems. In the first approach to the governance of AI, it was clear that it is a multidisciplinary field[44] and focused on three pillars—ethics, standardization, and norms[45]—to avoid and mitigate risks.[46] All of these make a matrix of variables that make governance complicated. As noticed before, different uses of different AI technologies require different ways of control, including notices, ethics guidelines, international standards, and regulations. It is due to this complexity that some authors have to advocate a hybrid system to govern AI use.[47] Self-regulation based on ethical guidelines is a good starting point; however, we need a hard law regulation, similar to the General Data Protection Regulation (GDPR) or the Regulation (EU) 2024/1689 of the European Parliament

[41] Eleni Kosta, 'Algorithmic State Surveillance: Challenging the Notion of Agency in Human Rights' (2020) 16 Regulation & Governance 212, 216 ff.

[42] Damien Gayle, 'Met Police Deploy Live Facial Recognition Technology' (*the Guardian*, 11 February 2020) <http://www.theguardian.com/uk-news/2020/feb/11/met-police-deploy-live-facial-recognition-technology> last accessed 17 May 2021.

[43] Roxana Radu, 'Steering the Governance of Artificial Intelligence: National Strategies in Perspective' (2021) 40 Policy and Society 178, 182.

[44] Stefan Larsson, 'On the Governance of Artificial Intelligence through Ethics Guidelines' (2020) 7 Asian J L & Society 437, 449.

[45] Corinne Cath, 'Governing Artificial Intelligence: Ethical, Legal and Technical Opportunities and Challenges' (2018) 376 Philosophical Transactions of the Royal Society A: Mathematical, Physical and Engineering Sciences 20180080, 5.

[46] Araz Taeihagh, 'Governance of Artificial Intelligence' (2021) 40 Policy and Society 137, 143.

[47] Radu (n 43) 183; Taeihagh (n 46) 146.

and of the Council of 13 June 2024 laying down harmonized rules on artificial intelligence (AI Act).[48] This hybrid system has two goals.[49] First is identifying the risk related to AI use in the judicial system in a proactive manner, with different stakeholders, raising awareness and opening a public debate. Second is the flexibility of the solutions because of technological innovation and because the citizens are involved in the process. Hence, it is crucial to assess the risks with multiple stakeholders during the life cycle of the process.

Although ethical principles are important, the legal approach is critical.[50] For the implementation of intelligent systems in the justice system, apart from respecting fundamental rights and appropriate procedural laws, it must comply with the new regulations on AI. Regardless of its wording, in one way or another, it will affect the fundamental rights that protect citizens before the action of justice, therefore, will be considered as high risk because all the uses relating to law enforcement are considered such.[51] Thus, these systems need a governance plan and human rights impact assessment.[52]

The governance of AI systems must take into account three starting points—what particular technology will be defined, what artefact will be used and what application will it have.[53] Clarifying these points can assist the government make a risk plan in the field of justice.

The first step is to create an analysis based on the different phases of AI use. We must start with data gathering. In this phase, we should assess the human rights that will be impacted by data collection, such as privacy rights. Taking into account the fact that for a judicial procedural real data from real cases must be provided, the use of sensitive data and personal data is included in this use. Tackling the challenges is not a big issue if the data comes from judicial databases; however, in the end, prediction systems need data from third parties to work. Thus, there is a security issue because the system can be fed with fake data, consciously or unconsciously, and that can affect the outcomes.

Another aspect of data gathering is the kind of data and dataset that will enrich the system. This is important because the precedent data, which will train the system, may not match the present situation, that is, the data is old, and may be biased.

This was seen in the most talked about case of COMPAS. COMPAS was used by the Wisconsin Court to determine, in part, the sentencing of cases. The system works with a statistical system that includes static and dynamic information collected through a

[48] Regulation (EU) 2024/1689 of the European Parliament and of the Council of 13 June 2024 laying down harmonized rules on artificial intelligence and amending Regulations (EC) No 300/2008, (EU) No 167/2013, (EU) No 168/2013, (EU) 2018/858, (EU) 2018/1139 and (EU) 2019/2144 and Directives 2014/90/EU, (EU) 2016/797 and (EU) 2020/1828 (Artificial Intelligence Act) [2024] OJ L 1689/1.

[49] Taeihagh (n 46) 146.

[50] Roos de Jong, Linda Kool and Rinie van Erst, 'This Is How We Put artificial intelligence into Practice Based on European Values' (Rathenau Instituut 2019) 13.

[51] Point 6 of the Annex III of the Regulation of the European Parliament and of the Council laying down harmonized rules on artificial intelligence (Artificial Intelligence Act) and amending certain Union legislative acts.

[52] Regulation (EU) 2024/1689 of the European Parliament and of the Council of 13 June 2024 laying down harmonized rules on artificial intelligence (n 48).

[53] Philip AE Brey, 'Anticipatory Ethics for Emerging Technologies' (2012) 6 NanoEthics 1, 7–8.

137-question questionnaire, criminal records, such as age, zip code, criminal or family history,[54] and the defendant's answers to questions, such as 'Does a hungry person has the right to steal?' or 'How old were you when your parents separated?' The COMPAS hit rate is around 70 per cent in determining whether a person can have alternative systems to prison.

However, as ProPublica's research showed, the system had a bias against black inidividuals. Thus, a person of colour, for a crime similar to that committed by a white person, is more likely to be considered high risk while a white person would be considered low risk.[55] It further indicates that in cases of violent crime, the COMPAS programme was only 20 per cent accurate.

The problem lies in two types of errors—false positives and false negatives.[56] In the case of COMPAS positives, black individuals were twice as likely to be punished than whites, while in false negatives white offenders were labelled as less dangerous than black offenders.[57] The main problem with this discrimination is that people embed their biases in the algorithms[58] during data selection and result interpretation. Seven criminological factors form the 137 questions, including financial, educational, or vocational deficits and the skills to attain them, contact with antisocial or pro-criminal groups and dysfunctional family/marital relationships. As Meredith Broussard points out, these factors are outcomes of poverty.[59] The problem is not whether to use data-driven algorithmic systems instead of lifelong judges, instead how to do it properly, which implies an important reflection on AI use that must be within the ethical codes. Judges have biases and prejudices; however, there are no studies on their level of accuracy or bias; hence, it is taken for granted.[60]

The second step is data processing. In this phase, we observe an impact on privacy and discrimination problems and security rights. The security measures of the system have to be implemented to avoid external attacks or the feeding of false information. The main problem is the explainability of the programme's decision-making, called the 'black box issue'. To avoid this situation, an assessment should be carried out at two crucial points—before starting to design the device and before launching it to the public. This will provide a record of whether adequate measures have been taken to mitigate known and, in some cases, unknown risks. By monitoring the performance of the intelligent systems, it will be possible to determine the relationship between decision-making and accidents.

For such situations, the AI Act provides governance guidelines for AI systems in the public sector that are considered high-risk. Thus, Annex III of the agreement for an AI Act[61] regulates six uses of AI in justices considered as high risk. These include the use

[54] Katherine Freeman, 'Algorithmic Injustice: How the Wisconsin Supreme Court Failed to Protect Due Process Rights in State v Loomis' (2016) 18(5) North Carolina JL & Tech 75.

[55] Julia Angwin et al, 'Machine Bias' (*ProPublica*, 2016) <https://www.propublica.org/article/machine-bias-risk-assessments-in-criminal-sentencing> last accessed 6 May 2024.

[56] Hannah Fry, *Hello World: How to Be Human in the Age of the Machine* (Black Swan 2019) 72.

[57] Angwin et al (n 55).

[58] Meredith Broussard, *Artificial Unintelligence: How Computers Misunderstand the World* (The MIT Press 2018) 156.

[59] ibid.

[60] Fry (n 56) 90–91.

[61] Regulation (EU) 2024/1689 of the European Parliament and of the Council of 13 June 2024 laying down harmonized rules on artificial intelligence (n 48).

of AI on behalf of law enforcement authorities or by Union institutions, agencies and offices of bodies:

a) in support of law enforcement authorities or on their behalf to assess the risk of a natural person to become a victim of criminal offences
b) in support of law enforcement authorities as polygraphs and similar tools
c) in support of law enforcement authorities to evaluate the reliability of evidence in the course of investigation or prosecution of criminal offences
d) in support of law enforcement authorities to evaluate the reliability of evidence in the course of investigation or prosecution of criminal offences
e) in support of law enforcement authorities for assessing the risk of a natural person offending or re-offending, not solely based on profiling of natural persons as referred to in Article 3(4) of Directive (EU) 2016/680 or to assess personality traits and characteristics or past criminal behaviour of natural persons or groups
f) in support of law enforcement authorities for profiling of natural persons as referred to in Article 3(4) of Directive (EU) 2016/680 in the course of detection, investigation or prosecution of criminal offences.

Although the use of AI systems in the judicial system has several possibilities and risks, the AI Act focuses only on criminal jurisdiction because of the example mentioned before and the importance of the rights to freedom and non-discrimination.

This mandatory governance of high-risk AI uses means that we need to clarify some questions before starting. First, a group of multidisciplinary stakeholders should be identified, including computer engineers, philosophers of technology, and legal experts, along with judges, lawyers, citizens, and other legal professionals.

Second, clarify the technology to be used and its purpose. As mentioned, multiple technologies can be used in the legal system based on the purpose. With this analysis, the goal is to assess the human rights and ethical principles at risk. There is no preference; however, it is important to know what can happen when the technology is implemented. The feared events should be analysed, considering their impact on the citizens' rights in a judicial trial, and threats and vulnerabilities should be identified to create a risk map.

It is crucial to create a plan to mitigate and eliminate the risks associated with the use of technology. The measures should be implemented in the system and assessed to evaluate their effectiveness. A human rights risk report should be created and reviewed, at least annually, to approach by design.

E. Conclusions

The judicial system cannot exempt technological innovations in its daily work. However, there are different uses and use intensities. The use of AI systems when drafting legal texts, such as lawsuits, complaints, or judgments, to speed up processes, does not have to be a problematic issue. The same applies to case law search engines in law firms or courts. However, there are cases in which the rights to a fair trial, the presumption of innocence, or the possibility of being heard in a judicial process may be seriously affected.

It is this negative impact on the judicial rights of citizens, which can be tremendously detrimental in the resolution of disputes and jeopardize the application of justice in a democratic system. The use of data without respecting the privacy of the subjects while maintaining the publicity of judicial decisions, the indirect discrimination of certain sectors of the population that will be excluded from the judicial system for not being able to use these tools, not respecting their rights as a minority group or the right to be heard in a procedure are risks that are occurring in several examples of AI use in the justice system.

Therefore, the new regulation of the AI Act imposes human rights impact assessment with the use of high-risk intelligent systems in the public sector and for private companies performing tasks for the public sector. The main risk lies in the use of these predictive tools in the criminal justice system; hence, these uses are categorized as high-risk, requiring an impact assessment to mitigate or eliminate the risks. Although Annex III clarifies its use as a high-risk factor in the application of criminal justice, Recital 61 of the AI Act generalizes it to civil and administrative justice.

Our proposed assessment system creates a systematic process to bring the tenets of the AI Act within a system of evaluation and analysis that will reduce existing risks. For all other uses, impact assessments are not mandatory, but recommended. As pointed out, three of the ethical principles of the HLEG guideline are directly related to democratic principles and values, therefore, the impact assessment will be necessary for almost all uses in the judicial system, beyond the criminal justice system.

AI governance systems are based on a hybrid system of self-regulation (ethical principles) and hard law (the human rights enshrined in legislation and the new regulation of AI). Hence, governance systems must have a specific, ad hoc application of the technology and intended use. Simultaneously, they must have a broad scope in reducing risks to citizens' rights. Hence, the rest of the ethical principles must be respected. The three principles for the respect of democratic values are undoubtedly important. However, the rest are designed to respect fundamental rights, such as human life and dignity, privacy, social rights that achieve a common good and respect for the environment.

By maintaining the enlightened values of respect for fundamental rights in a democratic system, it will be possible to use powerful tools, such as intelligent systems, in a manner that justice continues to be legitimized.

Bibliography

'AI Act' <https://data.consilium.europa.eu/doc/document/ST-5662-2024-INIT/en/pdf%E2%80%A6>.

Andreou A, Laulhe-Shaelou S, and Schroeder D, *Current Human Rights Frameworks* (Proyecto SHERPA 2019).

Angwin J et al, 'Machine Bias' (*ProPublica*, 2016) <https://www.propublica.org/article/machine-bias-risk-assessments-in-criminal-sentencing>.

Brey PAE, 'Anticipatory Ethics for Emerging Technologies' (2012) 6 NanoEthics 1.

Broussard M, *Artificial Unintelligence: How Computers Misunderstand the World* (The MIT Press 2018).

Cath C, 'Governing Artificial Intelligence: Ethical, Legal and Technical Opportunities and Challenges' in (2018) 376 Philosophical Transactions of the Royal Society A: Mathematical, Physical and Engineering Sciences 20180080.

De Jong R, Kool L, and van Erst R, 'This Is How We Put AI into Practice Based on European Values' (Rathenau Instituut 2019).

Erman E and Furendal M, 'The Global Governance of Artificial Intelligence: Some Normative Concerns' (2022) 9 Moral Philosophy and Politics 267.

Eubanks V, *Automating Inequality: How High-Tech Tools Profile, Police, and Punish the Poor* (First edn, St Martin's Press 2017).

European Commission for the Efficiency of Justice (CEPEJ), 'European Ethical Charter on the Use of Artificial Intelligence in Judicial Systems and Their Environment' (Council of Europe 2018).

European Parliament, 'Artificial Intelligence Act: Deal on Comprehensive Rules for Trustworthy AI|News|European Parliament' (9 December 2023) <https://www.europarl.europa.eu/news/en/press-room/20231206IPR15699/artificial-intelligence-act-deal-on-comprehensive-rules-for-trustworthy-ai>.

European Union Agency for Human Rights, 'Getting the Future Right. Artificial Intelligence and Fundamental Rights' (Publications Office of the European Union 2020).

Fjeld J et al, 'Principled Artificial Intelligence: Mapping Consensus in Ethical and Rights-Based Approaches to Principles for AI' [2020] SSRN Electronic Journal <https://www.ssrn.com/abstract=3518482>.

Freeman K, 'Algorithmic Injustice: How the Wisconsin Supreme Court Failed to Protect Due Process Rights in State v Loomis' (2016) 18(5) North Carolina JL & Tech 75.

Fry H, *Hello World: How to Be Human in the Age of the Machine* (Black Swan 2019).

Gayle D, 'Met Police Deploy Live Facial Recognition Technology' (*The Guardian*, 11 February 2020) <http://www.theguardian.com/uk-news/2020/feb/11/met-police-deploy-live-facial-recognition-technology>.

'GRS_Bridge^{SM} – Global Risk Solutions, Inc' <https://www.globalrisksolutions.com/technology1-2/grs_bridge/>.

Hagendorff T, 'The Ethics of AI Ethics: An Evaluation of Guidelines' (2020) 30 Minds and Machines 99.

High-Level Expert Group on Artificial Intelligence, 'Ethics Guidelines for Trustworthy AI' <https://digital-strategy.ec.europa.eu/en/library/ethics-guidelines-trustworthy-ai>.

'Home' (ComplianceHR) <https://compliancehr.com/>.

Kosta E, 'Algorithmic State Surveillance: Challenging the Notion of Agency in Human Rights' (2020) 16 Regulation & Governance 212.

Kuriakose F and Iyer D, 'Human Rights in the Big Data World' (Centre of Governance & Human Rights (CGHR) 2018) <https://papers.ssrn.com/sol3/papers.cfm?abstract_id=3246969>.

Larsson S, 'On the Governance of Artificial Intelligence through Ethics Guidelines' (2020) 7 Asian Journal of Law and Society 437.

'Legal Operations Archives' (*Neota*) <https://neota.com/tag/legal-operations/> accessed 23 April 2024.

Mills M, 'Artificial Intelligence in Law: The State of Play 2016' (Legal Executive Institute, 23 February 2016) <https://www.legalexecutiveinstitute.com/artificial-intelligence-in-law-the-state-of-play-2016-part-1/>.

Radu R, 'Steering the Governance of Artificial Intelligence: National Strategies in Perspective' (2021) 40 Policy and Society 178.

Raso F et al, 'Artificial Intelligence & Human Rights: Opportunities & Risks' <https://dash.harvard.edu/handle/1/38021439>.

Romeo Casabona CM., 'Riesgo, Procedimientos Actuariales Basados En La Inteligencia Artificial y Medidas de Seguridad' (2018) 13 Revista de Derecho, Empresa y Sociedad (REDS) 39.

Smuha NA., 'The EU Approach to Ethics Guidelines for Trustworthy Artificial Intelligence' (2019) 20 Computer L Rev Intl 97.

Taeihagh A, 'Governance of Artificial Intelligence' (2021) 40 Policy and Society 137.

Thiebes S, Lins S, and Sunyaev A, 'Trustworthy Artificial Intelligence' (2021) 31 Electronic Markets 447.

13

Artificial Intelligence Systems Processing Judicial Decisions and Legal Data Under the EU Legal Framework

Roberta Montinaro[*]

A. Introduction

Legal scholars have long been exploring the potential benefits of using innovative technologies in the legal sector.

A field of research has emerged for this purpose, called 'jurimetrics'.[1] The American researcher who coined this term claimed that 'jurimetrics promises to cut windows in the house of law', in order to suggest that behind this field of research there is a quest for transparency, predictability, accessibility, and efficiency of both the administration of justice and the provision of legal services. Such a view rests on two (questionable) assumptions: on the one hand, that the law can be confined to a mere calculus of precedents, on the other hand, that entrusting judicial tasks to powerful machines can lead to greater objectivity and efficiency in the administration of justice. In a nutshell,

* Professor of Private Law at the Department of Humanities and Social Sciences of the University of Naples L'Orientale (rmontinaro@unior.it). Jean Monnet Professor and Scientific Coordinator of the Jean Monnet Centre of Excellence 'AI-CoDED (Artificial Intelligence and Communication in a Digitalised European Democracy)'.

[1] Lee Loevinger, 'Jurimetrics: Science and Prediction in the Field of Law' (1961) Minnesota L Rev 255–75 <https://www.core.ac.uk/reader/217207250> last accessed 21 June 2024. Loevinger explored the use of computers for the purposes of legal data storage and retrieval, analysis of complex evidence, predictive justice, and analysis and drafting of legal documents of all kinds.

Roberta Montinaro, *Artificial Intelligence Systems Processing Judicial Decisions and Legal Data Under the EU Legal Framework* In: *Digitalization and Artificial Intelligence in Courts*. Edited by: Fernando Esteban de la Rosa, Pablo Cortés, and Nuria Marchal Escalona, Oxford University Press. © Roberta Montinaro 2025. DOI: 10.1093/9780198918752.003.0013

this theory heralds that the use of mathematical methodologies shows the potential of giving rise to a veritable 'revolution' in the field of law.[2]

Over time, jurimetrics has evolved to become Legal analytics,[3] a broad term that denotes the deployment of Artificial Intelligence (hereinafter 'AI') systems to carry out a vast array of legal tasks, including the analysis of judicial decisions and legal data. For example, Legal analytics can be used by the judiciary, as well as by law firms and legal practitioners in general, to predict the outcome of a case, to assess relevant case law, to assist in legal reasoning, and to retrieve and manage legal information. The use of AI for such tasks can bring several benefits[4], but also raises ethical and legal concerns, as highlighted by a copious academic literature.[5]

To understand the benefits that AI can bring in this sector while at the same time acknowledging the ensuing risks, it is crucial to unveil the fallacy of the myths surrounding AI in general and its use in the legal field in particular: the myth of the 'objectivity of data', as well as the one of the 'infallibility of AI'.

In a broad sense, AI is a type of software capable of producing certain outputs on the basis of input data fed into the system. When machine learning techniques are applied, computer software automatically analyses data and identify correlations between the data (pattern recognition) to give rise to the sequence (the model) to be used to draw certain conclusions (outputs). The data used for this purpose is far from objective, being on the contrary the result of choices and activities (collection, labelling, etc) made by humans.[6] Such activities may be influenced by economic interests or individual opinions and may conflict with legal principles and legally protected interests. Moreover, AI systems are not infallible; on the contrary, they could lead to inaccurate or biased outputs due to a number of factors, such as a deficiency in the required quantity and quality of the data employed, flaws of the model created (its lack of robustness, security), etc. Every AI system has its own higher or lower performance capability, which deployers and end users may ignore, as well as they may be unable to

[2] See in this respect, Perry Mayer, 'The Use of Jurimetrics in Legal Research' (1966) 1 The Canadian Bar Rev 1–16.

[3] Giuseppe Contissa and Giovanni Sartor, 'AI to Serve the Efficiency and the Quality of Justice', Council of Europe (2018), <https://www.rm.coe.int/giuseppe-contissa-presentation-study-session-artificial-intelligence-2/16808b7586> last accessed 26 November 2024.

[4] Caroline Gans-Combe, 'Automated Justice: Issues, Benefits and Risks in the Use of Artificial Intelligence and its Algorithms in Access to Justice and Law Enforcement' in Dónal O'Mathúna and Ron Iphofen (eds), *Ethics, Integrity and Policymaking. The Value of the Case Study* (Springer 2022) 175–94: 'LegalTech advocates keep repeating that by automating certain tasks, AI would lighten the daily lives of judges and lawyers by relieving them of certain administrative constraints. Judges could also rely on AI for decision support, while lawyers would refine their strategies thanks to the case analyses proposed by AI. As for litigants, the creation of databases from court decisions would give them access to a real legal library. They could see the cost of their proceedings fall due to simplified management, and the time taken to appear in court would decrease'.

[5] Richard M Re and Alicia Solow-Niederman, 'Developing Artificially Intelligent Justice' (2019) 22 Stanford Technology L Rev 242–89 <https://www.law.stanford.edu/wp-content/uploads/2019/08/Re-Solow-Niederman_20190808.pdf> last accessed 27 November. See also Dijana Spajosevic, Ashwin Ittoo, Emmanuel de Kerchove et al, *Study on the use of innovative technologies in the justice field* (European Commission 2020) <https://doi.org/10.2838/585101> last accessed 9 October 2024.

[6] Gregory Bateson, *From Versailles to cybernetics. Steps to an Ecology of Mind* (University of Chicago Press 2000) 477.

interpret its outputs, particularly when an AI system is complex in its operation and is characterized by a high level of technical and legal opacity.

In this context, the aim of sections B and C of this chapter is to examine the legal framework that governs the use of AI systems by the judiciary and by legal practitioners.

More recently, a dramatic increase in the technical capabilities of Large Language Models, ie advanced artificial intelligence systems capable of processing and generating legal language (hereinafter referred to as 'LLMs'), has resulted into previously unexplored issues relating to the employments of such tools in the legal sector. These issues, on the one hand, are due to the characteristics of these instruments, on the other hand, originate from the fact that they have become easily accessible by judges, legal practitioners, and the general public.[7] They will form the subject matter of section D.

B. Ai Systems Intended to Assist Judges and Legal Professionals in Fulfilling Their Tasks: The Eu Legal Framework

AI is not allowed to replace entirely human decision-making,[8] since a 'prescriptive approach' to the use of AI is at odds with the legal framework of the EU[9] and the Council of Europe.[10]

What is legally permissible is setting up an «enhanced (human) justice» regime, whereby AI systems are deployed in support of a vast array of activities, some merely instrumental to the administration of justice, while other pertaining to the core of the tasks of legal professionals, such as conducting legal research, analyzing previous decisions and documents, writing briefs and contracts, etc.[11] It can also be argued that, since recent technological advances have made this technology very effective, its deployment in the legal field fits perfectly with the public interest of enhancing the efficiency and accessibility of the administration of justice.

However, the establishment of an AI-enhanced human justice appears feasible provided that, first of all, the way in which AI systems are deployed does not undermine

[7] Harry Surden, 'ChatGPT, AI Large Language Models, and Law' (2024) Fordham L Rev 1941–70.

[8] AI systems used in the legal sphere can be conceived as 'predictive' tools when they are intended, for instance, to predict legal rulings; or as 'prescriptive' tools when they are meant to replace human decision-making in whole or in part. Regarding Alternative dispute resolution (ADR), see Art 5(2)(c) of the Proposal for a Directive amending Directive 2013/11/EU on alternative dispute resolution for consumer disputes, as well as Directives (EU) 2015/2302, (EU) 2019/2161 and (EU) 2020/1828 <https://www./commission.europa.eu/publications/revision-adr-directive-all-documents_en> last accessed 20 December 2024, which ensures the right for the revision of an automated procedure by a natural person.

[9] See Art 47 'right to an effective remedy and a fair trial' of the Charter of Fundamental Rights of the European Union [2000] OJ C364/01.

[10] See Art 6 of the European Convention on Human Rights (hereinafter 'ECtHR') < https://www. coe.int/en/web/human-rights-convention/> last accessed 26 November 2024. For an overview of the work done in relation to AI in the different pillars of the Council of Europe, see Ad hoc Committee on Artificial Intelligence ('CAHAI') <https://www. coe.int/en/ web/artificial-intelligence/cahai> last accessed 26 November 2024.

[11] For examples of AI systems and products deployed in the legal domain see <https://www. cotec.es/proyectos-cpt/guia-para-la-justicia-digital/> 23–24, last accessed 26 November 2024.

the 'right to a fair trial' under Article 6 of the European Convention on Human Rights (hereinafter 'ECtHR') which covers the sub-principles of adversarial proceedings, equality of arms, impartiality, and independence of the judiciary). To this end, some scholars who have analysed the use of legal analytics applications hold that judges and legal professionals shall become aware of what uses of AI are in line with this principle.[12]

This starts by clarifying the normative value of AI outputs when AI is used to predict the outcome of legal cases. These outputs are in fact mere statistical data and cannot be regarded as irrefutable factual or legal arguments. As such, they must be disclosed with respect to their origin as information created by AI systems. They shall also be subject to verification and evaluated in light of other arguments.[13]

Recognizing the value of AI outputs under the law helps to clarify certain questions. For instance, according to Article 6 ECtHR AI systems deployed to assist a judge in adversarial proceedings must be amenable to justification and scrutiny, so as to allow the parties to verify how they were obtained, to comment on them, etc. This implies a number of requirements and obligations, not only for the judiciary, but also for those who provide AI systems to be used for such purposes (for instance, providers shall design and build AI systems that are interpretable by judges, etc.).

It is also imperative to build and deploy AI systems which do not pose a risk for the fundamental rights at stake, particularly by ensuring that the data which is used to train the AI system, or its algorithm, is not biased or flawed.

In addition, legal and judicial professionals currently have access to LLMs that are not tailored to the legal sector. However, this technology can mimic legal reasoning and generate text without any guarantee of accuracy. This could, inter alia, affect the quality of the provision of justice and legal services, as will be discussed in Section D below. At the European level, the Regulation of the European Parliament and of the Council laying down harmonized rules on the placing on the market, the putting into service, and the use of artificial intelligence in the Union (Artificial Intelligence Act, hereinafter 'AI Act')[14] distinguishes between AI systems intended for purely ancillary administrative activities and AI systems designed to 'assist judicial authorities in research, interpretation of facts and the law, and application of the law to a concrete set of facts' (see Art 6 (2) and Annex III (8) AI Act). Only the latter are considered high-risk AI systems between these two use cases. However, as simple as it may seem at first sight, this distinction involves some 'grey areas'. For example, the automated allocation of cases to judges based on their complexity, despite counting as an administrative activity under Art 6 (2) and Annex III (8) AI Act may pose risks of errors and biases.[15]

[12] See Geneviève Vanderstichele, 'The normative value of Legal Analytics—Is there a case for statistical precedent?' (August, 30 2019) 1–69 <doi.org/10.2139/ssrn.3474878> last accessed 26 November 2024.

[13] Vilte Kristina Steponenaite, Peggy Valcke, 'Judicial analytics on trial: An assessment of legal analytics in judicial systems in light of the right to a fair trial' (2020) 27 (6) Maastricht J of Eur & Comp L 759–773, 762 <doi.org/10.1177/1023263X20981472> last accessed 26 November 2024.

[14] Regulation (EU) No. 2024/1689 of the European Parliament and of the Council of 13 June 2024 laying down harmonized rules on artificial intelligence and amending Regulations (EC) No 300/2008, (EU) No 167/2013, (EU) No 168/2013, (EU) 2018/858, (EU) 2018/1139 and (EU) 2019/2144 and Directives 2014/90/EU, (EU) 2016/797 and (EU) 2020/1828 (Artificial Intelligence Act) [2024] OJ L1689/1.

[15] Sebastian Felix Schwemer, Letizia Tomada, and Tommaso Pasini, 'Legal AI systems in the EU's proposed Artificial Intelligence Act' in *Proceedings of the Second International Workshop on AI and Intelligent Assistance for Legal Professionals in the Digital Workplace* (LegalAIIA 2021), held in conjunction with

More generally, AI applications that do not fall within the narrow scope of high-risk AI systems under the AI Act may raise challenges to the right to a fair trial and, in particular, to the independence of the judiciary. For example, argument-mining software, which aims to extract information about the main arguments on which a particular judgment is based, is not a high-risk system because it does not require the application of the law to a concrete set of facts. Nevertheless, it is capable of influencing the decision-making process of judges and legal practitioners who could passively rely on it without exercising critical scrutiny. In a nutshell, precluding the use of AI as a replacement for judicial authorities is not a panacea for all problems. There is unanimous consensus that also employing AI systems as a supporting tool for tasks falling within the legal domain must be surrounded by constraints and safeguards in order to avoid any harm to legally protected interests and the rule of law (see later on in this section, as well as in sections C and D).

For example, with regard to forms of so-called 'predictive justice', some authors claim that a well-known effect of predictions is to shape the behaviour of those whose activities are being measured, with the consequence that predictions may take on a *de facto* 'normative' value.[16] As it has been argued, the term 'prediction' is misleading, since AI systems can only establish statistical correlations (which could be 'false' or 'spurious') between data. The tasks these systems perform merely consist in anticipating the probability of a decision or in evaluating past decisions (in order to extract some relevant information, eg on certain driving factors). Nevertheless, they may limit the judge's autonomy when the latter relies unduly on AI outputs without an adequate understanding of them or without the ability to critically review them.

According to research conducted by experts in economics and social psychology, when AI systems serve as 'decisional aides' to human decision makers, cognitive biases can arise. The propensity of algorithms to learn and hence perpetuate bias and stereotypes from the data used to train them (so called 'algorithmic biases') is a well-known issue.[17] On the contrary, the risks stemming from biases affecting human decision-makers processing information obtained from (automated systems and, in particular, from) AI systems is a less explored phenomenon. Cognitive biases can be of two types: i) automation biases, ie decision-makers tend to over-trust AI outputs, which are considered more reliable than human advice; ii) confirmation biases, ie decision-makers are inclined to selectively search for information and interpret the information retrieved in the light of their pre-existing opinions, beliefs, etc. This attitude seems to be reinforced when they interact with LLMs outputs.[18] A risk of unintended

ICAIL 2021 (June 21, 2021) <https://www.//papers.ssrn.com/sol3/papers.cfm?abstract_id = 3871099> last accessed 20 June 2024.

[16] Mirelle Hildebrandt, 'Law as computation in the era of artificial intelligence. Speaking law to the power of statistics' (2017) 68 University of Toronto LJ 1–16, 12 <doi10.3138/utlj.2017-0044>: 'predictions impact the behaviour they supposedly predict' last accessed 27 November 2024.

[17] See Ignacio N Cofone, 'AI and Judicial Decision-Making' in Florian Martin-Bariteau and Teresa Scassa (eds), Artificial Intelligence and the Law in Canada (LexisNexis 2021) 1–15, 9 <https://ssrn.com/abstract = 3733951> last accessed 27 November 2024.

[18] Saar Alon Barkat and Madalina Busuioc, 'Human-AI Interactions in Public Sector Decision Making: "Automation Bias" and "Selective Adherence" to Algorithmic Advice' (2022) XX J of Public Administration Research and Theory 1–17.

delegation of decision-making to AI exists when deployers do not really understand or lack the power to deviate from the outputs of the AI system.

In the field of alternative dispute resolution ('ADR') the employment of AI is advocated and sometimes also encouraged by law (see Art 21 (3) (d) of the (EU) Regulation No 2022/2065 of the European Parliament and of the Council of 19 October 2022 on a Single Market for Digital Services and amending Directive 2000/31/EC (Digital Services Act 'DSA').[19] Forms of combination of ADR and AI have been developed, for instance, for automated dispute diagnosis, ie AI models that, on the basis of a series of questions, draw up proposals for resolving a given dispute.[20] In such cases, inter alia, the impartiality and reliability of the outputs, as well as their transparency, must be guaranteed. These uses may be considered lawful provided that are surrounded by safeguards, such as deploying such systems with the presence of a trained third party (eg a lawyer or mediator).[21] As noted in section C, AI systems intended to be used by ADR bodies for such purposes should also be considered as high risk, if the results of ADR procedures produce legal effects for the parties, in accordance with Article 6 (2), Annex III (8 and recital 61 AI Act).

Online dispute resolution ('ODR') is a further field where deployment of AI can bring benefits. However, ODR Bots or similar technical tools must be utilized in such way that end-users are aware that the processing of their dispute is carried out in an entirely automated way, without the involvement of a mediator or arbitrator. In this vein, Article 50 AI Act establishes a transparency obligation for deployers of AI systems intended to interact directly with natural persons, without prejudice to further, more specific obligations. Among them there are those stemming from the EU Unfair Commercial Practices Directive 2005/29/EC (hereinafter 'UCPD'[22]), such as the duty to inform users of ODR services, who qualify as consumers, in a clear and non-misleading manner that the 'online court' is in reality a machine performing

[19] (EU) Regulation No 2022/2065 of the European Parliament and of the Council of 19 October 2022 on a Single Market for Digital Services and amending Directive 2000/31/EC (Digital Services Act 'DSA') [2022] OJ L277/1. In accordance with Art 21(1) of the DSA, recipients of digital services have the right to choose an out-of-court dispute settlement body for the settlement of disputes which have previously been dealt with by the internal complaints system that is mandatory under Art 20 of the DSA. Art 21(3)(d) of the DSA clarifies that the out-of-court dispute settlement body to which the parties may refer the dispute must be certified by the Digital Services Coordinator. One of the conditions set by the DSA for the release of the certification is that the out-of-court dispute settlement body uses electronic communication tools, which may include the application of AI systems. See Mateja Durovic and Franciszek Lech, 'Legal Tech and ADR' in Larry A Di Matteo, André Janssen, Pietro Ortolani, et al (eds), *Lawyering in the Digital Age* (Cambridge: CUP 2023) 99–115, highlighting, inter alia, issues of transparency, explainability and access to justice.

[20] See, for example, AirHepl <https://www.airhelp.com/it/?utm_source = google&utm_medium = cpc&utm_campaign = 12654525826&gad_source = 1&gclid = Cj0KCQiAgJa6BhCOARIsAMiL7V_4FLfYuG8PKoi1NsuxQ65SqhwAONwNRpERGI3hPwZA-4acxfKmiIwaAgKCEALw_wcB> last accessed 26 November 2024.

[21] See European Commission for the Efficiency of Justice (CEPEJ), 'In-depth study on the use of AI in judicial systems' 65 <https://www.coe.int/en/web/cepej/cepej-european-ethical-charter-on-the-use-of-artificial-intelligence-ai-in-judicial-systems-and-their-environment> last accessed 28 November 2024.

[22] Directive 2005/29/EC of the European Parliament and of the Council of 11 May 2005 concerning unfair business-to-consumer commercial practices in the internal market and amending Council Directive 84/450/EEC, Directives 97/7/EC, 98/27/EC and 2002/65/EC of the European Parliament and of the Council and Regulation (EC) No 2006/2004 of the European Parliament and of the Council ('Unfair Commercial Practices Directive') [2005] OJ L149/22.

an automated task and that it may produce inaccurate results. Moreover, the parties must, on the one hand, retain the right to disagree with the advice provided by the AI system, on the other hand, be granted the right to access a fair trial and an effective remedy according to Articles 6 and 13 of the ECtHR. In turn, this requires that the outputs of AI systems are understandable and verifiable by both those who employ them and the impacted persons, as already explained in this section (see earlier in this chapter).

Constraints to the way AI systems are used for ADR/ODR purposes also arise from Article 22 Regulation (EU) 2016/679 (General Data Protection Regulation, 'GDPR')[23] on solely automated decision-making, when applicable. In this respect, it is worth noting that, under EU law, in such instances, a decision based on a decision-support system may nevertheless count as a purely automated decision, as stated by a recent decision of the European Court of Justice delivered in the case *Shufa Holding*.[24]

The AI Act has added a further layer of rules setting out transparency and interpretability requirements, which, however, are only applicable to AI systems used for alternative dispute resolution purposes which qualify as high-risk systems in accordance with Article 6 (2) and Annex III (8) and recital 61 of the AI Act (see also section C).

Lastly, AI applications offer a number of opportunities, but also pose severe risks in the field of legal services, where lawyers and law firms are active alongside other entities, such as Legal Tech platforms,[25] in offering legal advice or legal information, also to consumers.

When lawyers deploy AI applications in order to perform their tasks, quality and fairness of the legal service must be ensured (particularly when predictive analytics tools are deployed[26]), according, inter alia, to Member States' legal services regulations and deontological rules.

Whether it is allowed to use a particular AI application in a specific case depends on a number of factors, such as the technical capabilities of that application, the type of legal service in question, and the nature and severity of the risks involved. All these factors must be taken into account in light of the rules of conduct that legal professionals must observe under the applicable legal services legislation.

[23] Regulation (EU) 2016/679 of the European Parliament and of the Council of 27 April 2016 on the protection of individuals with regard to the processing of personal data and on the free movement of such data, and repealing Directive 95/46/EC (General Data Protection Regulation), [2016] OJ L119/1.

[24] ECJ Case C-634/21 *OQ v Land Hessen* (7 December 2023). See Peter Davis and Sebastian Felix Schwemer, 'Rethinking Decisions under Article 22 GDPR. Implications for Semi-Automated Legal Decision-Making' in *Proceedings of the Second International Workshop on AI and Intelligent Assistance for Legal Professionals in the Digital Workplace* (LegalAIIA 2023), held in conjunction with ICAIL 2023 (June 2023) 1 <http://dx.doi.org/10.2139/ssrn.4478107> last accessed 28 November 2024.

[25] See examples in <https://dashboard.hiil.org/the-gamechangers/online-information-advice-and-representation/> last accessed 28 November 2024. See in this regard Martin Ebers, 'Legal Tech and EU Consumer Law' in Larry A Di Matteo, André Janssen, Pietro Ortolani et al (eds), *Lawyering in the Digital Age* (CUP 2023) 195–219, 203.

[26] Florian Moslein and Maximilian Horn, 'Emerging Rules on Artificial Intelligence. Trojan Horses of Ethics in the Realm of Law' in Larry A Di Matteo, André Janssen, Pietro Ortolani, et al (eds), *Lawyering in the Digital Age* (CUP 2023), 77–95, 93.

Legal advice is tailored to the needs of the individual customer and represents a restricted service in many jurisdictions.[27] On the contrary, providing legal information is not subject to this limitation, since legal information is generic and does not entail analysis of a specific set of facts nor advising to take a certain course of action on the basis of the law. And yet, the way sophisticated technologies, such as LLMs (eg ChatGPT), work and the fact that they have already been embedded in publicly accessible services, make this distinction somewhat outdated. In fact, LLMs, on the one hand, blur the boundaries with the provision of legal advice, given that, via the promptings, they are sometimes given facts and asked by users to subsume them into law provisions. On the other hand, they pose risks for the recipients of legal information that are not comparable to those arising from other sources of legal information (eg a website), since the responses LLMs provide appear to be accurate, engendering trust in their reliability. In short, when asked, these AI systems are able to provide tailored or bespoke advice that goes beyond the provision of legal information. The problem is that this information may be inaccurate, without the consumers being aware of such a risk (see section D).

In view of these considerations, in 2019 the European Commission for the Efficiency of Justice (CEPEJ) adopted the *European ethical Charter on the use of Artificial Intelligence in judicial systems and their environment*,[28] a set of ethical principles which are designed to guide lawmakers, the judiciary and legal professionals of Member States, which can be summarized as follows:

a) ensuring that the design and implementation of artificial intelligence tools and services are compatible with fundamental rights;
b) preventing any discrimination between individuals or groups of individuals;
c) ensuring quality of data and security of data processing: with regard to the processing of judicial decisions and legal data, this entails using certified sources of data alongside models conceived in a multi-disciplinary manner, in a secure technological environment
d) upholding the principles of transparency, impartiality and fairness: this requires making data processing methods accessible and understandable, as well as authorizing external audits;
e) embracing also by design the principle 'under user control': which means precluding that a prescriptive approach might prevail among deployers by ensuring that the latter retain control of their choices.

Ethical principles and non-binding guidelines are not a sufficient guarantee that these objectives are fulfilled.

Hence, the Council of Europe Framework Convention on Artificial Intelligence and Human Rights, Democracy and the Rule of Law of 17 May 2024 ('CoE Convention'),[29] mandates that the Parties to the Convention adopt or maintain measures that seek to

[27] See the Italian 'Legge professionale forense', 31 dicembre 2012 n. 247 <https://www.consiglionazionaleforense.it/documents/20182/51913/Legge + 247-2012+-+Testo + aggiornato+al + 18+luglio + 2020/c8146804-2291-4c3e-b49f-f1c41a53bec0> last accessed 26 November 2024.

[28] Available at: <https://www.coe.int/en/web/cepej/cepej-european-ethical-charter-on-the-use-of-artificial-intelligence-ai-in-judicial-systems-and-their-environment> last accessed 26 November 2024.

[29] Avalaible at: <https://rm.coe.int/1680afae3c> last accessed 26 November 2024.

ensure that AI systems are not used to undermine the integrity, independence, and effectiveness of democratic institutions and processes, including the principle of the separation of powers, respect for judicial independence and access to justice' (Art 5 (1)). The accompanying document explains that

> In implementing its obligations to protect democratic institutions and processes under Article 5, Parties may wish to focus, for example, on the risks of artificial intelligence systems to: . . . g) respect for the rule of law (generally encompassing the principles of legality, legal certainty and non-arbitrariness) and the principle of access to justice and its proper administration; and h) respect for the principle of judicial independence.

Moreover, the CoE Convention mandates the Parties to adopt or maintain appropriate legislative, administrative, or other measures to prevent AI systems from negatively impacting fundamental rights, democracy, and the rule of law (Art 1 (2) CoE Convention).

Deployment and development of AI systems used in the legal field do not occur in a 'legal void'.

Alongside the data protection legal framework, which applies whenever a processing of personal data takes place, at European and national level, tort law sets out as incentives for a responsible development and deployment of AI systems in the legal domain. For instance, reliance on AI outputs by human judges may lead to errors and harms to legally protected interests which must be compensated under tort law, provided that certain conditions established by the applicable legal regimes of the Member States are met.

In the same vein, duties of professional care for legal practitioners using AI systems arise from national provisions and deontological rules concerning the regulation of legal services. Duties of diligence, competence, confidentiality, transparency, etc are broad and flexible enough to adapt to the specificities and risks of AI. These duties comprise, for instance: i) choosing an adequate AI application, in view of the intended use and in light of the ensuing risks and limitations (duty of competence); ii) supervising the operation of the systems in order to assess their reliability etc., depending on the functions the system is meant to perform, as well as the accuracy and quality of AI systems (duty of verification/supervision); iii) duty to disclose the deployment of such systems and any related risks.

Under the majority of jurisdictions, the provision of legal services cannot be de facto delegated to AI systems. Hence, relying even partially on the outputs of LLMs does not meet the standard of care.

It is therefore imperative that legal professionals who employ these tools remain able to critically analyse, interpret and review their outputs, in order to be able to depart from them, so as to retain their autonomy of judgment.

Duties of professional care arising from deontological rules define liability of legal professionals for damages resulting from the use of AI systems. In fact, these rules, although non-binding, in many jurisdictions are regarded as secondary sources of law or otherwise play at least an indirect role in the assessment of legal malpractice. Accordingly, the breach of such rules is relevant in contractual or tort liability claims. For instance, if an AI system produces inaccurate outputs, legal professionals who bear the duty to verify them can be held liable for any harm caused by using that information.

Manufacturers of AI systems can also be held liable under fault or strict liability regimes, such as liability for defective products. Liability for lack of conformity of an AI system with the supply contract may also arise in the relationship between the provider of the system and its buyer/deployer (be it the judiciary or a law firm) under member States' contract laws.

It is worth highlighting that, in principle, any injured party can claim compensation from AI systems' providers for damage arising from the use of incorrect, biased or erroneous output under the applicable tort law. To that end, such a party should: first be aware that an LLM was used; then prove the provider's fault and/or the causal link between the output of the LLM and the damage.

As to EU law, under the revised Product Liability Directive (Directive (EU) 2024/2853 on liability for defective products[30]) a software such as an AI system constitutes a product or a component of a product. Moreover, the injured party must prove the defect in the product and the causal link between defect and damage, but not the fault of the producer. The burden of proving these factors is simplified, as the plaintiff may resort to a number of presumptions provided for therein. For example, there is a presumption of defect when the claimant demonstrates that the damage was caused by an obvious malfunction of the product during reasonably foreseeable use or under ordinary circumstances. However, this Directive ensures the right to compensation only to natural persons who suffer damage caused by a defective product. It also guarantees compensation only for the types of damage provided for in Article 6, while for all other cases it refers to national law.

Moreover, both the action for damages and the availability of such presumptions require transparency as to the use of an AI system and its functioning (the data used or the software, etc). This could be a critical issue. It is unlikely that an injured party, such as a lawyer's client or a citizen accessing the justice system, who is unaware that an AI system has been used by the lawyer or judge, will invoke the right to compensation against the manufacturer under Directive (EU) 2024/2853 (see section D regarding duties of transparency resting on deployers of AI systems used in the legal field).

C. AI Systems Intended for Use in the Legal Sector Seen from the Point of View of the AI Act

In order to foster both responsible development and deployment of AI systems, the EU lawmaker has enacted a series of harmonized rules and principles within the AI Act.

The AI Act has established as a principle that 'The use of AI tools can support the decision-making power of judges or judicial independence, but should not replace it: the final decision-making must remain a human-driven activity' (Recital 61), in line with the CEPEJ Principles above mentioned.

[30] Directive (EU) 2024/2853 of the European Parliament and of the Council of 23 October 2024 on liability for defective products and repealing Council Directive 85/374/EEC [2024] OJ L2853/1.

Accordingly, the Regulation distinguishes between those systems 'intended to be used by a judicial authority or on its behalf to assist judicial authorities in researching and interpreting facts and the law and in applying the law to a concrete set of facts' and systems 'intended for purely ancillary administrative activities that do not affect the actual administration of justice in individual cases, such as anonymization or pseudonymization of judicial decisions, documents or data, communication between personnel, administrative tasks' (Art 6 (2) and Annex III (8) AI Act).[31] Only the former category of systems qualifies as high-risk, in view of the 'risks of potential biases, errors and opacity' they entail (Recital 61).

However, this definition does not to cover AI systems used by legal practitioners, nor those employed for the provision of legal advice or legal information via an API to end-users (by law firms or legal tech platforms). Only AI systems developed and marketed for being used by the judiciary would fulfil the requirement and thus be considered high-risk. In addition, according to a literary interpretation, in order to fall within this definition, an AI system must be cumulatively intended for assisting in researching and interpreting facts and the law, as well as for applying them to a concrete case. Hence, the scope of the definition encompasses systems that use methodologies of predictive justice, while those designed only for information retrieval and case law search are not included therein,[32] even when they are used by judicial authorities.

On the contrary, according to Article 6(2) (2) and Annex III (8) AI Act and recital 61, alternative dispute resolution bodies must be considered to act on behalf of the judicial authority, but only when alternative dispute resolution proceedings lead to legal effects for the parties.[33]

Providers and deployers of legal AI systems that fall within the scope of Article 6 (2) and Annex III (8) of the AI Act are required to comply with the whole set of accountability, transparency, and impact assessment requirements set forth in the AI Act.

Mitigation of risks related to the accuracy of the outputs and the occurrence of bias in these systems is pursued by establishing data quality and data governance requirements, as well as documentation and disclosure obligations.

According to Article 10 (1), AI systems which make use of machine learning techniques shall be developed on the basis of training, validation, and testing data sets that meet certain criteria. The data should be relevant, sufficiently representative, free of errors and complete in view of the intended purpose (art. 10 (3)). Deployers, to the extent that they exercise control over the input data, shall also ensure that the data is relevant and representative in view of the intended purpose.

In addition, data sets must be dealt with by adopting appropriate data governance and management practices. Such practices shall concern, among other things: i)

[31] See Annex III (8) (a) AI Act: 'AI systems intended to be used by a judicial authority or on their behalf to assist a judicial authority in researching and interpreting facts and the law and in applying the law to a concrete set of facts, or to be used in a similar way in alternative dispute resolution'.

[32] Susan Nevelow Mart, 'The Algorithm as a Human Artifact: Implications for Legal {Re}Search' (26 October 2016) 1–50 <https://www.ssrn.com/abstract = 2859720 > last accessed 28 November 2024.

[33] See Recital 61 AI Act: 'AI systems intended to be used by alternative dispute resolution bodies for those purposes should also be considered to be high-risk when the outcomes of the alternative dispute resolution proceedings produce legal effects for the parties'.

examination in view of possible biases that are likely to affect the health and safety of persons, have a negative impact on fundamental rights or lead to discrimination prohibited under Union law, especially where data outputs influence inputs for future operations' and (ii) appropriate measures to detect, prevent, and mitigate possible biases identified by providers (Art 10 (2) AI Act).

A duty to ensure an adequate level of accuracy and robustness and to disclose the relevant accuracy metrics (Art 15 AI Act) is imposed on providers. Such systems must be built to be immune from errors, faults or inconsistencies, such as those that may arise when a system uses its own biased outputs as input data for future predictions (self-fulfilling prophecy).

Gaining knowledge about the sources, nature, and characteristics of the data used, as well as about the accuracy of the model, should help to contrast the false myths referred to above, that of 'data neutrality' and the 'infallibility of AI'. In this vein, data quality measures and accuracy metrics must be disclosed according to the documentation and transparency requirements set out in the AI Act.

Documentation duties are provided for by Article 11 and annex IV AI Act for providers of high-risks systems, who shall draw up a detailed description of the AI system and of the process for its development including: *a)* architecture and design specifications; b) information about the data used and its main characteristics (their provenance, scope, etc) as well as about the training methodologies and techniques.

Mandating to disclose such elements is meant to counter the opacity of high-risk AI systems and to enable oversight by accessing the mandatory documentation.[34]

As already noted, in the field of Legal AI, it is vital to ensure that deployers retain their ability to interpret the outputs of AI systems and to depart from them when appropriate.[35]

In light of this, under the AI Act, high-risk AI systems shall be designed and developed in such a way to ensure that their operation is sufficiently transparent to enable deployers to interpret a system's output and use it appropriately (Art 13 (1) AI Act) and shall be accompanied by instructions for use that include information that is relevant, accessible, and comprehensible to them.

It is important to note that the type and degree of transparency and interpretability required is dependent on the obligations of deployers, as laid down in the Regulation and other national or EU laws—that is, if deployers are judicial authorities, the obligations to exercise control over the functioning of a system and to understand its operation must be taken into account when it comes to determining the level of transparency and interpretability that a system shall ensure. In this vein, the subject matter of the information to be supplied covers characteristics, capabilities, and limitations of performance of the AI system, its level of accuracy, including accuracy metrics, information on the data used, as well as any information needed 'to enable deployers to interpret the output of the high-risk AI system and use it appropriately' (Art 13 (3) (b)

[34] Indeed, supervision of such systems is entrusted to market surveillance authorities who 'should have effective investigative and corrective powers, including at least the power to obtain access to all personal data that are being processed and to all information necessary for the performance of its tasks' (Recital 159 AI Act).

[35] On the concept of meaningful human intervention see <https://digibug.ugr.es/handle/10481/82089> last accessed 26 November 2024.

AI Act). All this information must be tailored to the intended purpose of the AI system and, as mentioned, is instrumental to enabling supervision by the deployer.

In the same way, it is mandated that high-risk AI systems are designed and developed in a manner that allows 'effective oversight' by natural persons. This level of human oversight must be built into the system (according to a by design approach) or implemented by providers or deployers. Among the many human oversight measures that are mandatory some are of interest for the purposes of the present analysis: i) measures aiming at ensuring that natural persons are aware of the relevant capabilities and limitations of the high-risk AI system and capable of duly monitoring its operation; ii) measures aiming at enabling them to decide, in any particular situation, not to use the system or otherwise to ignore or override the output of the high-risk system; and iii) measures to counter the tendency of natural persons to automatically or excessively rely on the output produced by a high-risk AI system. The former two kinds of measures are meant to preserve the autonomy and self-determination of deployers, while human oversight measures of the latter type are specifically aimed at counteracting the cognitive biases which may occur when AI systems are intended to provide information or recommendations for decisions to be taken by natural persons (see Art 14 (4) (b).

Moreover, providers of high-risk systems are obliged to put in place a risk management system under Article 9 (2) (a) (d) AI Act. The risk management system aims at: i) 'the identification and analysis of the known and the reasonably foreseeable risks that the high-risk AI system can pose to health, safety or fundamental rights' and ii) the adoption of 'appropriate and targeted risk management measures designed to address the risks identified', 'through the development or design of the high-risk AI system, or the provision of adequate technical information (Art 9 (3) AI Act)'.

When it comes to AI systems intended for use by the judiciary, risks for the fundamental rights and the rule of law could be identified, depending on the intended purpose for which they are employed. The assessment of the existence of such a risk and its severity is a variable dependent on several, factors, like 'the technical knowledge, experience, education, the training to be expected by the deployer, and the presumable context in which the system is intended to be used' (Art 9 (5) AI Act).

In addition, deployers of high-risk AI systems are required to use such systems and implement human supervision in accordance with the instructions for use accompanying the systems. Moreover, those deployers who are bodies governed by public law, or private entities providing public services and employ high-risk AI system referred to in Article 6 (2), are mandated to perform a fundamental rights impact assessment (Art 27 AI Act)[36] and accordingly to set out appropriate mitigation measures. These duties apply to judicial authorities that employ AI systems to assist them in researching, interpreting and applying the law to a set of concrete facts. Among the mitigation measures just mentioned, judicial authorities could be required to employ tools

[36] On the specificities of this kind of risk assessments, see Alessandro Mantelero, 'The Fundamental Rights Impact Assessment (FRIA) in the AI Act: roots, legal obligations and key elements for a model template' (2024) 54 Computer L & Security Rev 106020 <https://doi.org/10.1016/j.clsr.2024.106020> last accessed 28 November 2024.

that ensure model interpretability, bias detection, and performance monitoring, etc, so that the supervision of AI systems can span throughout the AI lifecycle.

However, it should also be borne in mind that the AI Act merely sets out minimum safety standards, without prejudice to additional obligations arising from other Union or national law (Art 29 (2) AI Act).

D. Uses of LLMs in the Legal Domain

LLMs (such as ChatGPT, Gemini, Co-Pilot, Perplexity, etc) are deep learning models that are pretrained using vast amounts of data. This enables them to learn probability relationships between words or group of words and to generate coherent language in response to users' prompts.

Uses of LLMs in the legal domain include: i) search and retrieval of legal text and legal information; ii) legal documents generation; and iii) natural language understanding, which comprises, inter alia, semantic search, legal text classification, argument mining,[37] and legal judgment prediction, ie predicting the adjudication of a given case on the basis of previous legal cases with similar facts[38] with a view to provide decisional support for judges and legal practitioners. Understanding LLMs technical capabilities as well as their limitations and the risks arising from their deployment in the legal field is key to envisage the implications under EU law.

If we consider the current state of the art, compared to other machine learning AI systems, LLMs are not simply bigger models, trained on more data, they present the following technical capabilities:

a. can operate outside of the context of the things they were trained to do (hence, are capable of generalization and can be deployed for several diverse tasks);
b. show the ability to solve problems and thus to engage in reasoning about law and facts. This is due to a deep learning methodology called 'transformer', coupled with some significant advances such as 'instruction fine tuning' (ie LLMs are trained to follow instructions and answer questions) and reinforcement learning (a methodology under which humans or AI systems rate manually or automatically an LLM's answers).
c. can not only recognize patterns of letters, but also 'understand' the underlying meaning of the words, thanks to methodologies such as 'word vectors';
d. are capable of in context learning, ie the ability of LLMs to read and analyse the information included in a prompt. Recent advancements have enabled LLMs to

[37] On the use of LLMs for abstractive summarization of legal documents see Santosh T.y.s.s., Mahmoud Aly, and Matthias Grabmair, 'LexAbSumm: Aspect-based Summarization of Legal Decisions' <https://arxiv.org/html/2404.00594v1> last accessed 28 November 2024. Regarding argument mining see Ivan Habernal, Daniel Faber, Nicoletta Recchia et al., 'Mining legal arguments in court decisions' (2023) Artificial Intelligence and Law 1–39 <https://arxiv.org/abs/2208.06178> last accessed 28 November 2024.

[38] See Jinquy Lai, Wensheng Gan, Jiayang Wu, Zhenlian Qi, and Philip S Yu, 'Large Language Models in Law: A Survey' (2024) 5 AI Open 181 <https://doi.org/10.1016/j.aiopen.2024.09.002Get rights and content> last accessed 28 November 2024.

process long portions of text within the context window. Context length is crucial, since the more context is provided to a LLM, the better it performs.[39]

In a nutshell, LLMs' technical capabilities make them promising tools for the legal domain. However, they also show several limitations and pose risks to the rule of law, proper administration of justice, and judicial independence.

Indeed, LLMs cannot understand legal language in ways comparable to human understanding. They only produce statistical outputs. Despite their sophistication and tremendous improvements in their technical capabilities, they may produce irrelevant or inaccurate outputs or even invent untrue but plausible information (so-called 'legal hallucinations').[40]

LLMs are based on processes of digitization of legal text: to make them read, interpret etc legal language, words must be turned into computer-readable data. Legal language differs from everyday language for the number of technical terms, the careful precision, as well as for the interconnected and evolving nature of legal concepts. Moreover, the forms of legal argumentation are manifold and diverse. Much of the richness of information in the legal language and legal argumentation may be lost during the process of translating legal text into data amenable to computational analysis. Hence, LLMs could make relevant information, such as case law and doctrinal work, 'disappear' (ie information may be disregarded despite being relevant in a specific case).[41]

It follows that LLMs performance is dependent on the quality of the data (more than quantity) as well as of the chosen software design processes. Therefore, it is crucial to rely on reputable sources of legal text to train these models, as well as to adopt adequate methodologies for their design and development (eg ensuring that the team of developers also comprises experts in law and legal argumentation theory).

Some emerging technical solutions can improve the quality of the data, such as using domain specific data to finetune LLMs and adjusting the parameters,[42] so that they learn how to master legal language, or using exclusively specialized data sets to pre-train LLMs. In fact, LLMs pretrained on non-domain specific data are fine-tuned for coherence more than accuracy.

Furthermore, the accuracy of LLM's outputs is dependent on how the prompting is carried out. If not properly interrogated, LLMs can produce outputs that lack relevance, accuracy or consist in legal hallucinations—for example, in the task of information retrieval and extraction, the way prompts are devised dramatically influences the reliability of the outputs. Proper legal education and training for legal professionals are needed, so that they can act as 'skillful interrogators' when dealing with LLMs.

[39] Harry Surden (n 7)1941.

[40] Eliza Mik, 'Caveat Lector: Large Language Models in Legal Practice' (2024) 4 The Chinese University of Honk Kong Faculty of Law Research Paper 1-60.

[41] On semantic searches in the legal domain see Andrew Dang, 'Unlocking the Power of Semantic Searches in the Legal Domain' (4 October 2023) <https://www.ailawlibrarians.com/2023/10/04/semantic-search-in-law/> last accessed 27 November 2024.

[42] Ilias Chalkidis, Ion Androutsopoulos, and Nikolaos Aletras, 'Neural legal judgment prediction in English' in *Proceedings of the 57th Annual Meeting of the Association for Computational Linguistics*. 57th Annual Meeting of the Association for Computational Linguistics (2019) 4317–23 <https://www.aclweb.org/anthology/P19-1424.pdf> last accessed 27 November 2024.

A relatively new field of research has emerged: 'Legal Prompt Engineering'[43] concerning adequate prompting practices and methodologies. One promising approach is 'Prompt augmentation', ie a technique consisting in including more information in the context window.

A further methodology is called chain-of-thought prompting, ie, not only seeking an answer but also requiring the model to explain its steps to arrive at that answer. This approach improves the accuracy and interpretability of model outputs, particularly in complex reasoning tasks. Automatic prompts augmentation via RAG ('retrieval augmented generation') is a technical feature that automatically adds relevant content to an LLM's context window and hence helps to enhance its performance.

LLMs are also complex 'black box' AI systems, while their application in the legal field demands that their outputs are justifiable and generated in conformity with pre-established and identifiable norms and legal reasoning.[44] Moreover, legal professionals using LLMs need to be able to verify the outputs, to preserve their independence and fulfil the duties of diligence resting upon them.[45] Methodologies to make LLMs explicable in the legal sphere and their output verifiable are already available.[46] However, they require to be translated into technical features of LLMs.[47] For instance, source reference is a solution which enables a model to trace back and show the inputs (eg the legal sources).

Lastly, LLMs can pose severe risks to data protection, confidentiality, and intellectual property rights of third parties.

For instance, privileged and private information included in the prompts could be integrated into the system and/or used for LLMs training, if allowed by their design and terms of service.

Dialogue-based LLMs are designed to be anthropomorphic. This feature may exacerbate the problem of cognitive biases above-mentioned and affect the autonomy of its users. In fact, those interacting with them could underestimate the above-mentioned drawbacks, ie lack of accuracy of outputs and 'legal hallucinations'. To overcome this risk, transparency with regard to accuracy of LLMs outputs is crucial, eg providing information on an LLM's ability to produce legally correct answers, on how well it performs in identifying relevant legal sources, etc.

[43] See Dietrich Trautmann, Alina Petrova, and Frank Schilder, 'Legal Prompt Engineering for Multilingual Legal Judgement Prediction'(December, 5 2022) 1–7 < https://arxiv.org/pdf/2212.02199 > last accessed 27 November 2024): 'Legal prompt engineering is the process of creating, evaluating, and recommending prompts for LLMs deployed for legal tasks'.

[44] Karen McGregor Richmond, Satya M Muddamsetty, Thomas Gammeltoft-Hansen, et al, 'Explainable AI and Law: An Evidential Survey' (2024) 3(1) Digital Society 1–33 <https://link.springer.com/article/10.1007/s44206-023-00081-z> last accessed 27 November 2024.

[45] See the case of *Mata v Avianca, Inc* 678 F. Supp. 3d 443 (S.D.N.Y. 2023) which highlights the dangers of relying on AI-generated legal content without proper verification. In this case, a lawyer representing Roberto Mata in a personal injury lawsuit against Avianca used ChatGPT to draft a legal brief. The brief cited numerous court cases that were later found to have been 'fabricated' by ChatGPT. The lawyer admitted to using ChatGPT for legal research without prior verification, assuming it provided accurate information.

[46] The deployment of AI in the legal field has led to the development of a sub-domain of explainability, ie justification of AI outcomes, which differs from AI explanation, consisting, on the contrary, in understanding how the AI system produced its outputs.

[47] Hahoyan Luo and Lucia Specia, 'From Understanding to Utilization: A Survey on Explainability for Large Language Models' (23 January 2024) 1–13 <https://www.arxiv.org/abs/2401.12874> last accessed 27 November 2024.

As noted above, at the EU and national level regulations are already in force which are addressed to both providers and deployers of AI systems, including LLMs.

These regulations appear adequate to promote the responsible use of AI in the legal sector. However, they lack incentives for the providers of such AI systems to market products and services that meet the needs and address the risks inherent in the sector.

Starting with the rules governing how LLMs are deployed, we find that the emergence of LLMs and their increased deployment by legal professionals has led to the adoption of ad hoc deontological rules at supranational level, that are intended to complement and clarify national rules on the provision of legal services so as to ensure that AI in general and LLMs in particular are employed in accordance with the principles of the sector (eg the duties of care, competence, confidentiality, transparency, etc, mentioned in section B).

Examples of such rules are the European Bars Federation's Guidelines 'European Lawyers in the era of ChatGPT'[48] and the Guidelines issued by the CEPEJ Working Group on Cyberjustice and Artificial Intelligence: 'Use of Gen AI by judicial professionals in a work-related context'.[49] Both are meant to specify and adapt existing ethical norms, bringing more clarity about the ways legal and judicial professionals are expected to deal with LLMs.

Some of the guidelines released by the European Bars Federation, which are only addressed to law firms and legal practitioners in general, are of great significance:

- 'Understand LLMs' and 'Acknowledge limitations/risks' (No 1 and 2): these rules relate to the duty of diligence and competence of legal professionals, which entail gaining an understanding of LLMs capabilities and learning how to responsibly use them. They can be read as including a duty to deploy domain specific LLM's instead of general LLMs, as well as a duty to become proficient in legal prompting.
- 'Complement legal expertise' (No 4) implies a duty to use LLMs as 'legal assistants': legal professionals should preserve their own autonomy and independence including by verifying their outputs and exercising supervision on how they are employed;
- 'Inform clients and assume responsibility' (No 7) entails a duty of transparency which encompasses as well disclosing the use of LLMs for a given task, its purposes, limitations and the safeguards adopted to mitigate them. Therefore, information cannot shift part of the liability onto the clients;
- 'Maintain attorney-client privilege' (No 5) requires to only adopt tools that guarantee confidentiality and to verify LLMs terms of service. Hence a duty to refrain from using a given LLMs when the terms of service are not accessible or clear cut in this respect arises from this guideline;

[48] European Bars Federation, *European Lawyers in the era of ChatGPT* (June 2023), <https://www.fbe.org/wp-content/uploads/2023/06/European-lawyers-in-the-era-of-ChatGPT-FBE-Guidelines-on-how-lawyers-should-take-advantage-of-the-opportunities-offered-by-large-language-models-and-gene-kcpia.pdf> last accessed 26 November 2024.

[49] CEPEJ Working Group on Cyberjustice and Artificial Intelligence, *Use of Gen AI by judicial professionals in a work-related context* (February 2024) <https://www.coe.int/en/web/cepej/-/information-note-on-the-use-of-generative-artificial-intelligence-ai-by-judicial-professionals-in-a-work-related-context> last accessed 28 November 2024.

- 'Ensure data protection and privacy' (No 6) obliges to employ only tools that guarantee compliance with data protection law.

The aforementioned CEPEJ Working Group on Cyberjustice and Artificial Intelligence's Guidelines 'Use of Gen AI by judicial professionals in a work-related context' also emphasize the importance of the duty to verify the results of LLMs and the duty of transparency. Regarding the first aspect, it is suggested that legal professionals in general 'always' verify the correctness of the answers of an LLM. The fulfilment of the duty of transparency on the part of legal professionals allows the affected parties to be informed of the use of LLMs, which otherwise risks being kept 'under the radar'.

It is worth noting that some jurisdictions are moving towards regulating AI, including LLMs, by adopting ad hoc hard law provisions on the use of AI systems in the administration of justice and in the provision of legal services.

For instance, according to the Italian draft Bill on artificial intelligence of 23 April 2024, 'Artificial intelligence systems shall be used exclusively for the purposes of managing and simplification of judicial work as well as for case law and legal literature retrieval (Art 14 (1))'.[50] It is also made clear therein that all decisions concerning the interpretation of the law, the assessment of facts and doctrinal and jurisprudential research are reserved to the judge (Art14 (2)). Moreover, under the Bill, the use of artificial intelligence systems for the provision of legal services is permitted only if it is carried out in accordance with the principle that legal practice must be predominantly based on human knowledge and expertise (Art 12). The latter must always form the backbone of any legal service provision, which can only be enhanced by the adoption of AI systems. Accordingly, legal practitioners shall take full responsibility for the tools they use by exercising supervision, verifying AI outputs, etc. The bill also requires that legal practitioners inform their clients about the use of AI systems in plain and easily understandable language.

However, Member States are granted the competence to regulate the use of AI systems, but are not allowed to introduce rules and restrictions regarding the placing on the market of AI systems, as this power lies with the European Union and was exercised by adopting the aforementioned AI Act.

As already mentioned, according to the AI Act, LLMs qualify as high-risk AI systems only when: i) they are deployed by the judiciary or on its behalf or by ADR bodies in procedures having legal effects for the parties and ii) are intended to be used to 'assist' them in researching and interpreting facts and the law *and* in applying the law to a concrete set of facts (Art 6 (2) and Annex III (8) AI Act).

If the above-mentioned conditions are met, providers of LLMs must comply with the stringent requirements on data governance, transparency and human oversight set out in the AI Act.

For instance, under Article 10 (3) AI Act 'Training, validation and testing data sets shall be relevant, sufficiently representative, and to the best extent possible, free of errors and complete in view of the intended purpose'. Accordingly, providers must

[50] Atto Senato n 1146, XIX Legislatura <https://www.senato.it/leg/19/BGT/Schede/Ddliter/dossier/58262_dossier.htm> last accessed 26 November 2024.

ensure that the data used to train LLMs intended for such uses comply with those requirements.

At the same time, Article 13 (1) AI Act states that 'High-risk AI systems shall be designed and developed in such a way as to ensure that their operation is sufficiently transparent to enable deployers to interpret a system's output and use it appropriately'. Hence, LLMs which qualify as high-risk systems must be made interpretable by design.

Moreover, according to Article 14 (1) AI Act, 'High-risk AI systems shall be designed and developed in such a way, including with appropriate human-machine interface tools, that they can be effectively overseen by natural persons'. For this purpose, deployers shall be made aware of the capabilities and limitations of a given LLM, as well as of the risks related to cognitive biases. In addition, they shall be enabled to correctly interpret the high-risk AI system's output, thanks to the interpretation tools and methods available.

On the contrary, as already discussed above, the AI Act fails to promote the accountability of providers of LLMs which do not fall within the narrow category of high-risk AI systems. This gap in the legal framework can hardly be filled by tort law for the reasons already explained (see section B).

This is both a cause for concern and an obstacle to the meaningful use of such tools in the legal field.

In that regard, it is worth highlighting that some of the above-mentioned duties of professional care resting on judicial and legal professionals can be fully complied with only if LLMs providers disclose information to deployers and/or if they develop LLMs in such a way to enable compliance. For instance, to fulfil the duty to choose an adequate LLM for a given legal task, deployers should be made aware of its capabilities and limitations. This in turn presupposes that accuracy metrics and/or information on characteristics of the data used to train LLMs are disclosed by providers in an easily understandable way. In the same vein, to assess the correctness of the outputs generated by an LLM, it is necessary to understand the reasoning behind it, as well as to know the legal sources on which they are based. This is only feasible if its provider has adopted a 'by design' approach.

Incentives for LLMs providers to design tools which are in line with legal and ethical requirements may come from market dynamics. Indeed, the risk of incurring liability for failing to fulfil the duties of professional care could prompt legal professionals to demand that LLMs are built in such a way to comply with existing legal-ethical constraints. For instance, the fact that legal professionals demand that LLMs meet explainability requirements should lead providers to design tools that ensure the explainability of the outputs, etc.

Contractual liability between provider and deployer of an LLM for lack of conformity with the supply contract may also serve this purpose. This kind of liability may arise if providers guarantee that the technology is reliable and suitable for a given legal task ('performance claims' of LLMs), without also explaining their limitations and risks. In view of the purpose for which an LLM is intended, a lack of conformity may arise if the LLM's training data are incomplete or otherwise lack the necessary qualities and if the supplier has not taken measures to minimize distortions or inaccuracies, etc.

LLMs supply contracts could provide instruments for the allocation of liability arising from the use of LLM, e.g. by including indemnification clauses and guarantees regarding the accuracy and soundness of a given LLM.

To achieve this policy objective, however, it is crucial to ensure competition in the market of LLMs designed for legal uses. This enables legal professionals to exercise an actual free choice and verify the terms of services (to assess if they comply with ethical–legal standards, with data protection rules etc.).

This could also help to ensure that LLM providers do not unilaterally impose contract terms limiting or excluding liability for damages resulting from errors due to defects in the design and development of LLMs.

Lastly, in order to retain the benefits of the use of these models while mitigating their risks, as required by the CoE Convention, a number of policy measures could prove useful. Such measures could comprise the creation of a 'public infrastructure' through the development of open access LLMs intended for use by the judiciary and legal professionals and, to this end, the establishment of forms of cooperation between public institutions and the private sector.

E. Conclusions

This chapter examined the use of AI systems for processing judicial decisions and legal data from the perspective of the EU legal framework. It also considered the potential and limitations of LLMs when used for such purposes. The analysis paid particular attention to the European AI Act and the Council of Europe Framework Convention on Artificial Intelligence and Human Rights, Democracy and the Rule of Law.

The AI Act fails to incentivize the responsible development of AI systems, including LLMs, for the legal sector. Indeed, according to the AI Act, the latter qualify as high-risk AI systems only when: i) are deployed by the judiciary or on its behalf or by ADR bodies in procedures having legal effects for the parties and ii) are intended to be used to 'assist' them in researching and interpreting facts and the law *and* in applying the law to a concrete set of facts (Art 6 (2) and Annex III (8) AI Act).

The EU product liability regime only partially fills this gap. Indeed, the revised Product Liability Directive only guarantees the right to compensation to natural persons who have suffered damage caused by a defective product and limits compensation to the types of damage provided for in Article 6, referring to national law for all other cases. Furthermore, both the right to compensation and the availability of the presumptions of defect and causal link set out therein require transparency about the use of an AI system and at least its basic functioning (the data or software used, etc). This may be a critical point. It is unlikely that an injured party, such as a lawyer's client or a citizen accessing the justice system, who is unaware that an AI system has been used by the lawyer or judge, will invoke the right to compensation against the manufacturer under Directive (EU) 2024/2853.

Accordingly, the governance of the majority of AI systems used in the legal sector remains entrusted to soft law instruments and hard law bodies in force at national levels, which address the deployment of AI systems.

The emergence of LLMs and their increased deployment by legal professionals has led to the adoption of *ad hoc* deontological rules at supranational level, which are intended to complement and clarify national rules on the provision of legal services so as to ensure that AI systems in general and LLMs in particular are employed in accordance with the principles of the sector (e.g. the duties of care, competence, confidentiality, transparency, etc).

At the same supranational level, soft law norms have been adopted which are addressed to legal professionals in general, including judges, with the aim of updating their duties of professional diligence.

Some of the above duties of professional care that fall to legal and judicial professionals can only be fully met if LLM providers disclose information to deployers and/or develop LLMs in such a way as to enable compliance. For example, in order to fulfil the duty to select an appropriate LLM for a given legal task, deployers should be made aware of its capabilities and limitations. This in turn requires that accuracy metrics and/or information about the characteristics of the data used to train LLMs be disclosed by providers in an easily understandable manner. Similarly, in order to assess the accuracy of the outputs produced by an LLM, it is necessary to understand the reasoning behind them and the legal sources on which they are based. This is only possible if the provider has adopted a 'by design' approach.

In short, the analysis has shown that, as a result, there is insufficient accountability among those who develop and provide AI systems for the legal sector.

This raises the question of whether the current legal framework is in line with the Council of Europe's Framework Convention on Artificial Intelligence, which requires Parties to adopt or maintain in force appropriate legislative, administrative or other measures to ensure that fundamental rights and the rule of law are not undermined by the development and deployment of AI systems.

Some incentives for LLMs providers to design tools that comply with legal and ethical requirements may come from market dynamics. Indeed, the risk of incurring liability for failing to meet professional standards of care may lead legal professionals to demand that LLMs are designed to satisfy existing legal and ethical constraints. For example, the fact that legal professionals demand that LLMs meet explainability requirements should lead providers to design tools that ensure the explainability of the outputs, etc.

Contractual liability between the provider and the user of an LLM for failure to comply with the supply contract may also serve this purpose.

In addition, in order to preserve the benefits of the use of these models while mitigating their risks, as required by the CoE Convention, a number of policy measures could prove useful. Such measures could include the creation of a 'public infrastructure' through the development of open access LLMs for use by the judiciary and legal practitioners and, to this end, the establishment of forms of cooperation between public institutions and the private sector.

Bibliography

Alon-Barat S and Busuioc M, 'Human-AI Interactions in Public Sector Decision Making: "Automation Bias" and "Selective Adherence" to Algorithmic Advice' (2022) XX *Journal of Public Administration Research and Theory* 1–17.

Bateson G, *From Versailles to Cybernetics: Steps to an Ecology of Mind* (Jason Aronson Inc. 1972) 477–85.

Chalkidis I, Androutsopoulos I, and Aletras N, 'Neural Legal Judgment Prediction in English', *Proceedings of the 57th Annual Meeting of the Association for Computational Linguistics*, 57th Annual Meeting of the Association for Computational Linguistics (2019) 4317–23 <https://www.aclweb.org/anthology/P19-1424.pdf>.

Contissa G and Sartor G, 'AI to Serve the Efficiency and the Quality of Justice', Council of Europe (2018) <https://rm.coe.int/giuseppe-contissa-presentation-study-session-artificial-intelligence-2/16808b7586>.

Dang A, 'Unlocking the Power of Semantic Searches in the Legal Domain' (4 October 2023) <https://www.ailawlibrarians.com/2023/10/04/semantic-search-in-law/>.

Davis PAE and Schwemer SF, 'Rethinking Decisions under Article 22 GDPR. Implications for Semi-Automated Legal Decision-Making',Proceedings of the Second International Workshop on AI and Intelligent Assistance for Legal Professionals in the Digital Workplace (LegalAIIA 2023), held in conjunction with ICAIL 2023 (June 2023) 1–9 <http://dx.doi.org/10.2139/ssrn.4478107>.

Durovic M and Lech F, 'Legal Tech and ADR' in LA Di Matteo, A Janssen, P Ortolani, F De Elizalde, M Cannarsa, and M Durovic (eds), *Lawyering in the Digital Age* (CUP 2023) 99–121.

Ebers M, 'Legal Tech and EU Consumer Law' in LA Di Matteo, A Janssen, P Ortolani, F De Elizalde, M Cannarsa, and M Durovic (eds), *Lawyering in the Digital Age* (CUP 2023) 195–219.

Gans-Combe C, 'Automated Justice: Issues, Benefits and Risks in the Use of Artificial Intelligence and its Algorithms' in Dónal O'Mathúna and Ron Iphofen (eds), *Access to Justice and Law Enforcement Ethics, Integrity and Policymaking: The Value of the Case Study* (Springer 2022) 175–94.

Habernal I, Faber D, Recchia N, Bretthauer S, Gurevych I, Spiecker genannt Döhmann I, and Burchard C, 'Mining Legal Arguments in Court Decisions' (2023) *Artificial Intelligence and Law* 1–38, <https://arxiv.org/abs/2208.06178>.

Hildebrandt M, 'Law as computation in the era of artificial intelligence. Speaking law to the power of statistics' (2917) 68 University of Toronto LJ 12–35 <doi 10.3138/utlj.2017-0044>.

Lai J, Gan W, Wu J, Qi Z, and Yu PS, 'Large Language Models in Law: A Survey' (2024) 5 AI Open 181 <https://doi.org/10.1016/j.aiopen.2024.09.002Get rights and content>.

Loevinger L, 'Jurimetrics: Science and Prediction in the Field of Law' (1961) Minnesota L Rev 255–75 <https://core.ac.uk/reader/217207250>.

Mayer P, 'The Use of Jurimetrics in Legal Research' (1966) 1 The Canadian Bar Rev 1–24.

Mantelero A, 'The Fundamental Rights Impact Assessment (FRIA) in the AI Act: roots, legal obligations and key elements for a model template' (2024) 54 Computer L & Security Rev 106020 <https://doi.org/10.1016/j.clsr.2024.106020>.

McGregor Richmond K, Muddamsetty SM, Gammeltoft-Hansen T, Palmer Olsen H, and Moeslund TB, 'Explainable AI and Law: An Evidential Survey' (2024) 3 (1) Digital Society 1–33.

Mik E, 'Caveat Lector: Large Language Models in Legal Practice' The Chinese University of Honk Kong Faculty of Law Research Paper No. 2024-04 <https://papers.ssrn.com/sol3/papers.cfm?abstract_id=4757452>.

Moslein F and Horn M, 'Emerging Rules on Artificial Intelligence. Trojan Horses of Ethics in the Realm of Law' in Di Matteo LA, Janssen A, Ortolani P, de Elizalde F, Cannarsa M, and Durovic M (eds), *Lawyering in the Digital Age* (CUP 2023) 77–95.

Nevelow Mart S, 'The Algorithm as a Human Artifact: Implications for Legal {Re}Search' (October 26, 2016) <https://ssrn.com/abstract=2859720 or http://dx.doi.org/10.2139/ssrn.2859720>.

Re RM and Solow-Niederman A, 'Developing Artificially Intelligent Justice' (2019) 22 Stanford Technology L Rev 242–89 <https://ssrn.com/abstract=3390854>.

Santosh TYSS, Mahmoud A, and Grabmair M, 'LexAbSumm: Aspect-based Summarization of Legal Decisions' <https://arxiv.org/html/2404.00594v1>.

Schwemer SF, Tomada L, and Pasini T, 'Legal AI systems in the EU's proposed Artificial Intelligence Act' Proceedings of the Second International Workshop on AI and Intelligent Assistance for Legal Professionals in the Digital Workplace (LegalAIIA 2021), held in conjunction with ICAIL 2021 (Sao Paulo, Brazil, 21 June 2021) <https://papers.ssrn.com/sol3/papers.cfm?abstract_id=3871099>.

Steponenaite VK and Valcke P, 'Judicial analytics on trial: An assessment of legal analytics in judicial systems in light of the right to a fair trial' (2020) 27(6) Maastricht Journal of European and Comparative Law 759–73, 762 <https://doi.org/10.1177/1023263X20981472>.

Surden H, 'ChatGPT, AI Large Language Models, and Law' (2024) Fordham L Rev 1941–72.

Trautmann D, Petrova A, and Schilder F, 'Legal Prompt Engineering for Multilingual Legal Judgement Prediction' (5 December 2022) <https://arxiv.org/pdf/2212.02199)>.

Vanderstichele G, 'The Normative Value of Legal Analytics: Is There a Case for Statistical Precedent?' (30 August 2019) <http://dx.doi.org/10.2139/ssrn.3474878>.

14

The Integration of Artificial Intelligence in the Digitalization Process of the Administration of Justice

John Zeleznikow[*]

A. Introduction

Over the past fifty years, there have been many significant movements that have significantly affected the way justice is administered. These changes include:

- The increasing use of Alternative Dispute Resolution (ADR);
- In Common Law countries, the rise of the number of litigants representing themselves in courts without the assistance of a lawyer—so called pro-se or self-represented litigants (SRL);
- The development of the World Wide Web; and
- The rising use of Artificial Intelligence (AI)

These movements, both human and technical are slowly altering the way in which justice is administered. The recent advancements in generative AI are likely to significantly alter legal processes. In this paper we indicate what changes have occurred and

* Research Unit of Excellence Digital Society: Security and Protection of Rights, University of Granada, Spain and Law and Technology Group, Law School, La Trobe University, Australia. E-mail: J.Zeleznikow@latrobe.edu.au.

John Zeleznikow, *The Integration of Artificial Intelligence in the Digitalization Process of the Administration of Justice*
In: *Digitalization and Artificial Intelligence in Courts*. Edited by: Fernando Esteban de la Rosa, Pablo Cortés, and Nuria Marchal Escalona, Oxford University Press. © John Zeleznikow 2025. DOI: 10.1093/9780198918752.003.0014

hypothesize about how technology might influence future justice systems. Our focus is more upon how litigants, rather than the judiciary, might use AI.

We focus upon how nonlegal professionals might be able to navigate the judicial system. We spend some time examining their needs and capabilities. We also consider both research prototypes and systems in current use that assist self-represented litigants.

We do need to emphasize that proponents argue that the use of AI will enable legal systems to be more effective and efficient. There have been few claims that the use of AI will make the system more just.[1]

B. The Vanishing American Trial, the Increasing Use of Alternative Dispute Resolution and the Rise of Self-represented Litigants

The 1970s saw a significant movement examining alternatives to litigation. This trend was heavily influenced by the *National Conference on the Causes of Popular Dissatisfaction with the Administration of Justice*, which took place in Minneapolis, Minnesota from 7–9 April 1976.[2] At this conference, the then US Chief Justice Warren Burger encouraged the exploration and use of informal dispute resolution processes. Soon afterwards, Mnookin and Kornhauser introduced the notion that commercial and civil disputes are resolved in the shadow of the law.[3] Bibas has claimed that some scholars (but not himself) treat plea-bargaining as simply another case of bargaining in the shadow of a trial.[4] He notes that

> the conventional wisdom is that litigants bargain towards settlement in the shadow of expected trial outcomes. In this model, rational parties forecast the expected trial outcome and strike bargains that leave both sides better off by splitting the saved costs of trial. . . . This shadow of trial model now dominates the literature on civil settlements.[5]

Fisher and Ury developed the notion of principled negotiation.[6] Principled negotiation promotes deciding issues on their merits rather than through a haggling process focused on what each side says it will and will not do. Amongst the features of

[1] Richard M Re and Alicia Solow-Niederman, 'Developing Artificially Intelligent Justice' (2019) 22 Stan Tech L Rev 242.

[2] Also known as the Pound conference <https://ncsc.contentdm.oclc.org/digital/collection/ctadmin/id/1245/> last accessed 19 March 2024. The conference took its title from a paper presented by Roscce Pound at the same location in 1906.

[3] Robert Mnookin and Lewis Kornhauser, 'Bargaining in the Shadow of the Law: The Case of Divorce' (1979) 88 Yale LJ 950.

[4] Stephanos Bibas, 'Plea Bargaining Outside the Shadow of the Trial' (2004) 117 Harv L Rev 2464, 2547 and Stephanos Bibas, 'Transparency and Participation in Criminal Procedure' (2006) 81 NYU L Rev 911, 966.

[5] Bibas, 'Plea Bargaining' (n 4) and Bibas, 'Transparency and Participation' (n 4).

[6] Roger Fisher and Willian Ury, *Getting to YES: Negotiating Agreement Without Giving* (Haughton Mifflin 1981).

principled negotiation is knowing your *BATNA* (*B*est *A*lternative *T*o a *N*egotiated *A*greement). The reason you negotiate with someone is to produce better results than would otherwise occur. If you are unaware of what results you could obtain if the negotiations are unsuccessful, you run the risk of entering into an agreement that you would be better off rejecting; or rejecting an agreement you would be better off entering into. Knowing your BATNA gives you an idea of the outcome of the disputation process and is very useful in computing outcomes. It is an important tool for reality testing.[7] There are many examples where Artificial Intelligence can be used to help us better assess appropriate BATNAs.[8]

Empirical research by Marc Galanter of the University of Wisconsin at Madison concluded that the number of trials in the United States, whether federal or state, civil or criminal, jury or bench, is declining.[9] As we shall see later, this is also the case in England, Canada, and Australia.[10] The shrinking number of trials is especially important because virtually everything else in the legal world is growing, including the number of lawyers, plethora of cases, expenditure on legal services, and amount of regulation.[11] For example, in the United States there has been an increase in legal activity among those with the most power and money.[12] Moreover, while trials in courts are in decline, 'trial-like events' such as arbitrations outside the courts are on a sharp rise.[13] In 2011, Peter Murray estimated that in the United States, the percentage of civil disputes that are actually decided by court adjudication is probably less than 2 per cent, indicating that 98 per cent are ending in settlement or dismissal.[14] The US National Center on State Courts, claimed that in 2018, 72 per cent of domestic relations (family law) cases have at least one unrepresented party.[15] In some states, as many as 80 per cent to 90 per cent of litigants were unrepresented in civil issues such as custody and family law cases, even though their opponent may have a lawyer.[16] Cortes claims that about 2 per cent of cases that are lodged in English courts end up

[7] Peter T Coleman, Morton Deutsch, and Eric C Marcus (eds), *The Handbook of Conflict Resolution: Theory and Practice* (John Wiley & Sons 2014).

[8] Arno R Lodder and John Zeleznikow, *Enhanced Dispute Resolution through the Use of Information Technology* (CUP 2010).

[9] For discussions about the number of US trials see Marc Galanter, 'The Hundred-Year Decline of Trials and the Thirty Years War' (2005) 57 Stan L Rev 1255–74. See also Jeffrey Q Smith and Grant R MacQueen, 'Going, Going. But not Quite Gone: Trials Continue to Decline in Federal and State Courts. Does it Matter?' (2017) 101 Judicature 26, 28 (indicating that the number of jury trials completed in US district courts had an almost annual linear decline from 6,893 in 2000 to 3,647 in 2016).

[10] For a discussion of the situation in England see Pablo Cortés, 'Embedding alternative dispute resolution in the civil justice system: a taxonomy for ADR referrals and a digital pathway to increase the uptake of ADR' (2023) 43.2 Legal Studies 312, 330.

[11] Galanter (n 9).

[12] Marc Galanter, 'The Vanishing Trial: An Examination of Trials and Related Matters in Federal and State Courts' (2004) 1 J Empirical Legal Stud 459, 460.

[13] Marc Galanter and Angela M Frozena, 'A Grin without a Cat: The Continuing Decline & Displacement of Trials in American Courts' (2014) 143 Daedalus 115, 126.

[14] Peter Murray, 'The Privatisation of Civil Justice' (2011) 85 Admin L J 490, 494.

[15] These arguments are made in National Center for State Courts, *The Landscape of Domestic Relations Cases in State Courts* 20 (2018), <https://www.ncsc.org/__data/assets/pdf_file/0018/18522/fji-landscape-report.pdf> last accessed 23 April 2024.

[16] Jessica K Steinberg, 'Demand Side Reform in the Poor People's Court' (2015) 47 Conn L Rev 741, 749.

in trial, but out of the 100 per cent lodged, around 80 per cent are undefended claims. Hence, out of the defended cases, around a quarter or less move to trial.[17]

Rabeea Assy claims that 'In common law jurisdictions, litigants are free to choose whether to procure legal representation or litigate in person'. He argues that the problem with self-representation is that it is usually ineffective for the self-represented litigant, and it is inefficient for the courts, which have to deal with litigants who do not know procedure, violate rules, and waste time with pointless and sometimes incoherent arguments. [18]

But this is not the case in civil law domains. European legal systems already prohibit self-representation beyond small claims, and therefore mandatory legal representation of the sort Assy proposes is not simply a theorist's hypothetical.[19] Nations with a civil law tradition, by contrast, adhere to what Americans call an 'inquisitorial' model in which judges are called upon to take a more active investigative role with the goal of achieving substantive justice. In an inquisitorial system, the judge actively supervises the gathering of evidence; the judge is therefore not a passive decision-maker.[20] Legal representation in civil law domains ensures that the inquisitorial judge will not be biased.

While perhaps a majority of countries recognize a right to legal aid to defend severe criminal charges, the constitutions of only a handful of countries—among them Italy, the Netherlands, Portugal, Spain, and South Africa—contain provisions explicitly extending this right to civil cases.[21] In several other countries, notably Switzerland and Germany, the highest court has held that constitutional equal protection or due process provisions—expressed in language similar to the comparable clauses in the US Constitution—guarantee indigent litigants in civil cases the right to free counsel.[22]

Julie Macfarlane and others at University of Windsor in Ontario tracked the SRL phenomenon in Ontario, Canada in five surveys over ten years 2011–21.

The authors, in the 2019 edition pondered why there were no SRLs under the age of 25. They speculated that it is possible that individuals under the age of 25 are less often engaged in family and civil disputes; it is also possible that they are choosing to resolve these disputes outside of the traditional legal process, for example, by using online mechanisms such as Online Dispute Resolution.[23]

In 2019, 65 per cent of intake form respondents indicated that they were the plaintiff or petitioner, while 34 per cent indicated they were the defendant or respondent. In 2021 the respective figures were 63.4 per cent and 36.6 per cent respectively. This

[17] cf Cortés (n 10).

[18] Rabeea Assy, *Injustice in Person: the Right to Self-representation* (OUP USA 2015).

[19] David Luban, 'Self-Representation, Access to Justice, and the Quality of Counsel: A Comment on Rabeea Assy's Injustice in Person: The Right of Self-Representation' (2018) 17 Jrslm. Rev Legal Stud 46.

[20] Sande L Buhai, 'Access to Justice for Unrepresentated Litigants: A Comparative Perspective' (2008) 42 Loy LAL Rev 979.

[21] See Symposium, Access to Justice: Does It Exist in Civil Cases? (2004) 17 Geo J Legal Ethics 455, 459 (discussing Italy, the Netherlands, and South Africa).

[22] Buhai (n 20).

[23] Julie Macfarlane and Megan Campbell, 'Self-Represented Litigants & Legal Doctrines of "Vexatiousness"—An Interim Report from The National Self-Represented Litigants Project', (2019) <https://scholar.uwindsor.ca/cgi/viewcontent.cgi?article = 1000&context = lawnsrlppubs> last accessed 14 April 2024.

approximately 2:1 plaintiff–defendant split is largely consistent with ratios observed in their previous data collection periods.

In 2021, Macfarlane and Sullivan reported that nearly 91 per cent of respondents indicated that the other party in their case was represented by counsel. This figure has consistently increased over the years —in 2013, 75 per cent of respondents indicated that the other side was represented; in 2017, the same figure was 86 per cent; and in 2018–19 it was 90 per cent. The vast majority of self-represented litigants in the sample were involved in cases where the other side was represented by counsel for at least part of the process.[24]

Respondents demonstrated a high level of educational attainment. In 2021, 43.9 per cent of self-represented litigants indicated having a university degree or equivalent professional qualification, and a further 22.3 per cent a college diploma. 15.4 per cent of respondents indicated 'Other,' with some specifying that they had some university education but ultimately did not complete or had not yet completed their degree or diploma program. These results are largely consistent with previous reports: in 2018–19, 46 per cent of respondents held a university or professional degree and 22 per cent a college diploma;11 in 2017, these figures sat at 47 per cent and 22 per cent respectively;12 and in 2013, at 50 per cent and 23 per cent respectively.

The majority of SRLs in the sample continued to report lower income levels (below $C50,000 per annum). Most respondents (50.8 per cent) reported their annual income as being under $C30,000, with an additional 16 per cent reporting their incomes as falling between $C30,000 and $C50,000 annually. 6.6 per cent of respondents indicated that they make over $C100,000 annually, which is consistent with data collected in previous years. 8 per cent of respondents in both 2018–19 and 2017 reported earning over $C100,000 per annum,14 and 6 per cent in both 2015–16 and 2013. Of the 2019–2021 respondents who reported earning more than $C100,000 annually (n = 17), 71.4 per cent stated that they had worked with a lawyer at a prior stage in their case. This is slightly lower than in 2018–19, at which time 84 per cent reported having worked with a lawyer at some point.

As was the case in previous reports, there is a significant gap between those eligible for Legal Aid and those who can afford some legal services while self-representing themselves. Although not all the high learning SRLs clarified why they chose to self-represent, previous expenditures on lawyers and debt load were mentioned by at least one respondent in the qualitative portion of the Intake Form, with the respondent stating that five years of paying for legal representation had effectively drained their savings. This suggests that the vast majority of SRLs in Canada, including high-earning SRLs, face difficulties affording legal services for the entirety of their case, especially if it is protracted. As noted in the 2018–19 report, this socioeconomic data is consistent with other studies having collected data on SRL income, which indicate that most people self-represent themselves because they can neither afford to pay for legal services, nor qualify for Legal Aid. The underlying trend is that many people who

[24] Kail Scarrow, Brandon Fragomeni, and Julie Macfarlane, 'Tracking the Trends of the Self-Represented Litigant Phenomenon: Data from the National Self-Represented Litigants Project, 2018/2019' (2020), <https://scholar.uwindsor.ca/cgi/viewcontent.cgi?article = 1011&context = lawnsrlppubs> last accessed 14 April 2024.

Table 14.1 Cases in which SRLs were involved in Ontario, Canada

Year of Report	per cent family law matters	per cent civil matters
2013	66.6	33.4
2017	53.0	47.0
2018–19	38.0	62.0
2021	42.2	57.8

are now self-representing themselves began with a lawyer representing them, but at some point, became unable to expend any more funds on legal assistance.[25]

Table 14.1 indicates the type of cases in which SRLs were involved. It is derived from data in the Macfarlane and Sullivan paper.[26]

We are seeing a trend where SRLs are engaging more and more in civil matters.

The authors of the report claim that their socioeconomic data is consistent with other studies that have collected data on SRL income. For example, respondents in a 2018 Northern Ireland study (Litigants in Person in Northern Ireland: Barriers to Legal Participation) found that the main reason people self-represent is because they could not afford to pay for legal services and did not qualify for legal aid. They described themselves as being 'caught in the middle'. Of those who responded, 68 per cent stated they had worked with a lawyer at some point during their current case. This is exactly the same percentage as reported in the 2017 Intake Report. It is higher than the 2013 Study figure of 53 per cent but shows the same trend.

Traditionally, the existence of SRLs has been much higher in common law countries where the judicial system is adversarial, than in civil law countries where judges are inquisitorial. In most civil matters in Australia, the loser pays the winner's costs, whereas in US each party pays their own costs regardless of the outcome of the trial. Even in common law countries there are domains of law when judges have been taking more investigative approaches. For example, in Australia, courts will assist applicants facing domestic abuse, and not having legal support, to obtain Domestic Violence Orders. Australian Family Court Judges, acting in the paramount interests of children, regularly refer litigants and their children to psychological and counselling services to provide independent professional advice to the courts.[27]

The rise of SRLs has many negatives, especially in the domestic violence domain. In Australia, Kaye, Wangmann, and Booth claimed 'Being a victim of family violence added a complex layer to self-representation.'[28] This experience framed and shaped

[25] Julie Macfarlane and Charlotte Sullivan, 'Tracking the Trends of the Self-Represented Litigant Phenomenon: Data from the National Self-Represented Litigants Project, 2019–2021' (2021) https://scholar.uwindsor.ca/lawnsrlppubs/12 report 10-2021 last viewed 15 June 2025.

[26] ibid.

[27] Under the adversarial Australian legal system, litigants regularly provide the testimony of their own expert witnesses to support the litigants' claims.

[28] See Miranda Kaye, Jane Wangmann, and Tracy Booth, '"No straight lines": Self-represented litigants in family law proceedings involving allegations about family violence' (2020) <https://www.anrows.org.au/publication/no-straight-lines-self-represented-litigants-in-family-law-proceedings-involving-allegations-about-family-violence/> last accessed 14 April 2024.

the issues that were the subject of the litigation, and the environment in which the parties were litigating. Several victims of violence who represented themselves not only continued to experience violence after separation, but this also took place in the court precinct; it was manifested in the courtroom and the nature of the litigation was often experienced as legal systems abuse. Without the buffer of a lawyer, SRLs faced this violence directly. Victims who were SRLs generally struggled to adequately document their experience of family violence in their affidavits, and experienced considerable pressure to settle for unsafe or unsatisfactory outcomes. When a SRL was an alleged perpetrator, the court system could be used as a tool to continue abuse, for example through numerous applications in multiple jurisdictions, prolonging court proceedings, refusing to settle and bringing proceedings after final orders.

These problems have led commentators to argue that all domestic abuse victims should be represented.[29] But such action would require a large financial commitment.

Early in the twenty-first century, AI and legal researchers started to wonder whether AI might be able to gainfully support SRLs. We now discuss this issue!

C. Artificial Intelligence in the Legal System

Artificial Intelligence (AI) is based on the assumption that the process of human thought can be mechanised. Ramon Lull in thirteenth century Spain developed several *logical machines* devoted to the production of knowledge by logical means. The golem, a man created out of clay who protects the Jewish ghettos of Prague from pogroms was discussed in the sixteenth century. Leibniz, Hobbes, and Descartes explored the possibility that all rational thought could be made as systematic as algebra or geometry. In the twentieth century, the study of mathematical logic (in particular Russell and Whitehead) provided the essential breakthrough that made artificial intelligence seem plausible.

The Turing test, originally called the imitation game by Alan Turing in 1950, is a test of a machine's ability to exhibit intelligent behaviour equivalent to, or indistinguishable from, that of a human. Turing proposed that a human evaluator would judge natural language conversations between a human and a machine designed to generate human-like responses. The evaluator would be aware that one of the two partners in conversation was a machine, and all participants would be separated from one another. The conversation would be limited to a text-only channel, such as a computer keyboard and screen, so the result would not depend on the machine's ability to render words as speech. If the evaluator could not reliably tell the machine from the human, the machine would be said to have passed the test. The test results would not depend on the machine's ability to give correct answers to questions, only on how closely its answers resembled those a human would give.[30] In many ways ChatGPT

[29] See Shazia Choudhry and Jonathan Herring, 'A Human Right to Legal Aid?—The Implications of Changes to the Legal Aid Scheme for Victims of Domestic Abuse' (2017) 39(2) Journal of Social Welfare and Family Law 152–67.

[30] See Alan Turing, 'Computing Machinery and Intelligence' (1950) 236 Mind 433, 460.

has already met this test for AI. In section F of this chapter, we discuss the operation of ChatGPT.

In 1955, John McCarthy (Dartmouth College) organized a group to clarify and develop ideas about thinking machines. He picked the name ***'Artificial Intelligence'*** for the new field.

One of the most promising areas of early research in AI was Expert Systems (ES). ESs are computer programs 'capable of functioning at the standard of (and sometimes even at a higher standard than) human experts in given fields. A number of ESs exist in the legal domain and deal with such disparate areas as the law of tax, trade secrets, chattel recovery, workers' compensation, and social security, to name but a few. In the rule-based ES approach, the knowledge of a specific legal domain is represented as a collection of rules of the form

IF <condition(s)> THEN <action/conclusion>

For example, consider the domain of driving offences, in Victoria, Australia. Drivers can lose their licence either by being drunk whilst driving or exceeding a specified number of points in a given time. More specifically, probationary drivers (those who have held a driver's licence for less than three years) are not permitted to have even a trace of any alcohol in their blood. Other drivers must have a blood alcohol level not exceeding 0.05 per cent. Probationary drivers cannot lose more than 5 points in 3 years, whilst other drivers cannot lose more than 12 points in 3 years.

This knowledge can be modelled by the following rules:

(a) IF drive(X) & (blood_alcohol(X) > .05) & (license(X) >= 36) THEN licence_loss(X);
(b) IF drive(X) & (blood_alcohol(X) > .00) & (license(X)< 36) THEN licence_loss (x)
(c) IF drive(X) & (loses_points(X) > 12) & (license(X) >= 36) THEN licence_loss(X);
(d) IF drive(X) & (loses_points(X) > 5) & (license(X) < 36) THEN licence_loss(X);

Until the late 1980s, LESs were largely confined to 'rule-based' systems. That is, most were comprised of a series of rules placed into a computer understandable form. These rules may be sections from an Act, the 'codification' of common law rules, or some other readily explicable system of rules. The computer stored these rules in a form of database called the rule base. Another part of the LES processed these rules and derived an answer from the rules when given a fact situation. This processor was commonly called the 'inference engine'. The fundamental problem with such a system is that it needs an explicable series of rules to process.

LESs have been fruitfully used for compliance issues and road traffic and administrative rules. Until recently, the principal use of AI for aiding those making decisions has been in areas of statutory interpretation, including the burgeoning rules as code movement.

Today when most people think of AI, they do not think of rule-based systems. Rather they think of machines using large amounts of data to provide advice and make decisions. But we need to reflect upon the situation that most useful tools have been rule-based, especially when considering compliance. Algorithms that are written in the statute books and applied mechanically by human administrators are the paper equivalents of allowing a computer to make the decisions.[31] By the late 1980s researchers in AI and law realized that to allow interpretation of rules and deal with discretion, AI and Law systems must deal with cases: even in civil law domains.

Open-textured problems are those problems that cannot be structured as rules in the form of: If <conditions> then <action> and which require some legal knowledge on the part of the user. For example:

- IF the person is under 18 THEN the person does not have the ability to sign legal documents
- IF the person is mentally incapacitated THEN the person does not have the ability to sign legal documents

The first rule does not require legal knowledge, the second does. The second rule is open textured.[32] Thus, we need more than rules to interpret law.

In the mid-late 1980s, AI researchers developed case-based reasoning to allow users to reason from past cases and experience. Case-based reasoning is the process of using previous experience to analyse or solve a new problem, explain why previous experiences are or are not similar to the present problem, and adapting past solutions to meet the requirements of the present problem. Case-based reasoning can also be used in integration with rule-based systems. Machine learning is that subsection of learning in which the artificial intelligence system attempts to automatically learn patterns. These learned patterns can then be harnessed to automate tasks. Machine learning can only be applied if sufficient suitable data are available. Machine learning is having an important impact on prediction, the automated examination of legal documents, and the analysis of legal contexts. The primary use of machine learning to support decision-making in legal domains has been in criminal detection, financial domains, and sentencing. Its use in these areas has led to concerns that the inappropriate use of AI leads to biased decision-making. This requires us to examine concerns about governance and ethics. Ethical concerns can be minimized by providing enhanced explanation, choosing appropriate data to be used, appropriately cleaning that data, and having human reviews of any decisions.[33]

D. Using Online Dispute Resolution to Enhance Access to Justice

As early as 2000, the National Center for State Courts (US) in partnership with the Illinois Institute of Technology's Institute of Design and the Chicago-Kent College of Law launched a research project to examine court processes and recommended modifications to eliminate or reduce procedural barriers to access for self-represented

[31] See Donald H Berman and Carole D Hafner, 'The potential of artificial intelligence to help solve the crisis in our legal system' (1989) 32.8 Communications of the ACM 928–38.

[32] The term open textured was introduced by Hart in Herbert Lionel Adolphus Hart, 'Positivism and the Separation of Law and Morals' (1958) 71 Harvard L Rev 593.

[33] John Zeleznikow, 'The benefits and dangers of using machine learning to support making legal predictions' (2023) 13.4 Wiley Interdisciplinary Reviews: Data Mining and Knowledge Discovery 1, 21.

litigants. The project had three major tasks: (1) to identify major barriers to access to justice that self-represented litigants encounter due to court procedures and administrative requirements; (2) to employ system design methodology to redesign court processes to remove those barriers; and (3) to translate the conceptual model for the redesigned court system into an internet-based prototype for implementation in the courts.[34]

At the same time, the recently deceased Karl Branting claimed that 'domestic abuse victims were particularly likely to have few resources and little opportunity to obtain the services of a lawyer'.[35] He stated that the growth of the consumer movement had increased the trend for self-represented litigation. Indeed, the growing availability of books, document kits, and computerized forms, and the increasing availability of legal materials on the internet, have enhanced opportunities for SRLs.

Branting had a JD from Georgetown University and a PhD in Artificial Intelligence from University of Texas at Austin. In the academic year 2000–01 he was a United States Supreme Court Fellow at the Administrative Office of US Courts. In this role he worked with the Idaho Supreme Court Technology Committee to develop a demonstration project to evaluate the applicability of AI to judicial administration. The committee considered developing sentencing, pre-trial release, child support, and protection order applications (In Idaho, a protection order is a document issued by a civil court that orders the person who is abusing or stalking an individual to stop doing so. If the person violates this order, they will be criminally punished by the court).[36] The committee ultimately selected protection order application assistance because the inability to offer advice to pro se protection order applicants was distressing to staff in Idaho courts. The Technology Committee felt that this distress could be alleviated by making personal computers with an advisory program available in district court lobbies. This allowed protection order applicants to obtain answers to many of their questions about whether they satisfied the requirements for a protection order; and to draft a petition. It relieved court staff of the painful choice between providing unauthorized legal advice and ignoring the needs of domestic violence victims.[37] In the US, unlike Australia, courts were reluctant to advise domestic abuse victims claiming that in future, the courts might be required to rule upon a domestic violence application. Much more recently, Singapore is using Generative AI to assist SRLs with small claims tribunal cases.[38]

At the same conference as Branting introduced his work on Protection Order Advisors, I claimed that there were an increasing number of litigants who were forced to represent themselves in court. This need caused major disruptions in the

[34] Charles L Owen, Ronald W Staud, and Edward B Pedwell, *Access to Justice: Meeting the Needs of Self-Represented Litigants* (Pearson Custom Pub 2002).

[35] Karl L Branting, '*Advisory Systems for Pro Se Litigants*' (2001) Proc of the 8th Int'l Conf on AI and Law 139.

[36] See Idaho Legal Aid Services, the meaning of a civil protection order, available at <https://www.idaholegalaid.org/files/What%20is%20a%20civil%20protection%20order.pdf> last accessed 14 April 2024.

[37] ibid.

[38] See Lydia Lam, 'Generative AI being tested for use in Singapore Courts, starting with small claims tribunal', available at <https://www.channelnewsasia.com/singapore/artificial-intelligence-court-small-claims-singapore-chatgpt-3801756> last accessed 15 April 2024.

judicial system and raised issues of access to justice. I argued that important support for unrepresented litigants could be provided by the construction of web-based legal decision support systems. At Melbourne's La Trobe University, our research team constructed web-based legal decision support systems in the domains of family law and eligibility for legal aid.[39]

According to Staudt discussing the Illinois Legal Needs Study, the justice system failed to meet the legal needs of the state's neediest justice customers.[40] The Access to Justice: Meeting the Needs of Self-Represented Litigants: A Consumer Based Approach project (Meeting the Needs Project) successfully identified the major barriers to access to justice for self-represented litigants including barriers to web-based document preparation. A key insight was that users need to be guided through processes that are foreign to them. The simple act of filling out forms raises unique challenges that the many self-represented litigants have trouble overcoming. Without a very simple front end, a user unfamiliar with web conventions would be unable to use online form systems. To be effective, guided interviews for self-represented litigants must be very simple.

Traditionally, all forms of dispute resolution relied on face-to-face communications. Recently, various forms of technology have been used to enhance negotiation. The use of technology can enhance efficiency and efficacy, but not necessarily justice. The decade of the 1990s saw the commercial development of the Internet and initial proposals for online dispute resolution (ODR). ODR was seen as the merger of ADR and Information Technology, or as Lodder and Zeleznikow say, 'whilst there is no generally accepted definition of Online Dispute Resolution (ODR), *we can think of it as using the Internet to perform Alternative Dispute Resolution (ADR)*'.[41] Increasingly, ODR has been seen to include online courts. Whilst mediation between two parties involves a third party (the mediator) ODR has a fourth party (the technology).[42]

Much of this early research was developed by legal academics rather than by information technology developers. These researchers saw the potential of ODR to resolve disputes that originated on the internet.[43] For example, the Fifth International Workshop on Online Dispute Resolution in Florence, Italy in December 2008[44] discussed much ODR research but few examples, and the examples discussed were for the Chamber of Arbitration of Milan and the Dutch Legal Aid Board. The Sixth International Workshop on Online Dispute Resolution, held in Liverpool, UK in December 2010,[45] also discussed substantial ODR research but only one example,

[39] John Zeleznikow, 'Using Web-Based Legal Decision Support Systems to Improve Access to Justice' (2002) 11(1) Information & Communications Technology Law 15, 33.

[40] This report was conducted by Kent Law School, the law school of Illinois Institute of Technology.

[41] Arno R Lodder and John Zeleznikow, *Enhanced Dispute Resolution Through the Use of Information Technology* (CUP 2010).

[42] Arno R Lodder and John Zeleznikow, 'Developing an online dispute resolution environment: Dialogue tools and negotiation support systems in a three-step model' (2005) 10 Harv Negot L Rev 287.

[43] See Ethan Katsh, 'Dispute Resolution in Cyberspace' (1995) 28 Conn L Rev 953.

[44] Marta Poblet (ed), *Expanding the Horizons of ODR: Proceedings of the 5th International Workshop on Online Dispute Resolution* <http://ftp.informatik.rwth-aachen.de/Publications/CEUR-WS/Vol-430/Proceedings.pdf> last accessed 20 March 2024.

[45] Marta Poblet, Brooke Abrahams, and John Zeleznikow, Proceedings of the 6th International Workshop on Online Dispute Resolution 2010, Liverpool, UK, 15 December 2010. CEUR Workshop Proceedings 684, CEUR-WS.org 2010 <https://ceur-ws.org/Vol-684/ODR2010proceedings.pdf> last accessed 20 March 2024.

again that of the Chamber of Arbitration of Milan was presented. And even the research article did not focus upon the courts.

It was not until the second decade of the twenty-first century that ODR was widely used for conflicts that were not internet based. By then Katsh and Rabinovich-Ein had investigated the use of ODR beyond e-commerce,[46] whilst Zeleznikow discussed the use of intelligent ODR to support self-represented litigants.[47]

The telephone was for some time the primary medium which supported people to negotiate.[48] It allowed people to communicate who cannot or should not meet in the same room, whether owing to the parties being physically far apart or to the existence of previously violent situations, such as the existence of domestic violence. In England all small claims going to English courts now must go to mandatory telephone mediation.[49] Today, information technology offers parties different levels of interactivity immediacy, and media richness. There are many different platforms through which parties can communicate: through text; through voice; and through real-time video. In the third option, disputants can see each other and where necessary, an arbitrator or mediator.

Sourdin and Zeleznikow claim that the emergence of the Covid-19 virus as a pandemic has emphasized the importance of the need for the development of ODR Systems.[50] Sadly, citizens of most countries were forced into isolation, and disputants were no longer meeting face-to-face. Nevertheless, it was essential that the justice system continue to operate in those circumstances—especially so for urgent cases such as bail applications, domestic violence orders, and family disputes. Four years later, most systems currently being used, such as IMMEDIATION,[51] MODRON,[52] and Our Family Wizard[53] only offer case management and communication support. They do not provide reality testing, have decision and trade-off support, or document drafting facilities.

Whilst many states and countries are piloting ODR, very few currently have widely functioning systems. For example, the Supreme Court of Ohio has initiated an ODR pilot project focused on mediating foreclosure, small claims, domestic, and eviction matters.

[46] Ethan Katsh and Orna Rabinovich-Ein, *Digital Justice: Technology and the Internet of Disputes* (OUP 2017).

[47] John Zeleznikow, 'The Challenges of Using Online Dispute Resolution to Support Self-represented Litigants' (2020) 23(7) J Int Law 3, 14.

[48] Mark Thomson, 'Alternative modes of delivery for family dispute resolution: The Telephone Dispute Resolution Service and the online FDR project' (2011) 17(3) Journal of Family Studies 253, 257.

[49] Pablo Cortés, 'Embedding alternative dispute resolution in the civil justice system: a taxonomy for ADR referrals and a digital pathway to increase the uptake of ADR' (2023) 43 Legal Studies 312, 330.

[50] Tania Sourdin and Jonh Zeleznikow, 'Courts, Mediation and COVID-19' (2020) 48(2) Australian Bus L Rev 138, 158.

[51] Available at <https://www.immediation.com/> last accessed 11 April 2020.

[52] See the website of MODRON available at https://www.modron.com last accessed 11 April 2020.

[53] See Allan E Barsky, 'The ethics of app-assisted family mediation' (2021) 34(1) Conflict Resolution Quarterly 31, 42.

During the past decade we finally have seen ODR being used in justice systems. Two such examples are the Canadian British Columbia Civil Resolution Tribunal (BC CRT)[54] and the Dutch Rechtwijzer System.[55]

The Dutch platform Rechtwijzer was designed to support separating couples to negotiate. Couples pay €100 to access the system. It commences by asking each partner for personal information such as their age, education, and income, as well as their priorities in the dispute, such as whether they want the children to live with only one parent or part time with each and other relevant preferences. The Rechwijzer platform has 1) a diagnosis phase; 2) an intake phase for the initiating party; and 3) an intake phase for the responding party. Following the completion of the intake process, the parties are encouraged to commence working on agreements on those issues that occur in every separation. These may include 1) future communication channels; 2) issues related to child welfare; 3) property issues (including housing, money, and debts); and 4) child support and spousal maintenance.

The prevalent dispute resolution model in Rechtwijzer is integrative negotiation. The platform uses algorithms to find points of agreement, and then proposes solutions. In the situation where the solutions proposed by the Rechtwijzer system are not accepted by the couple, the disputants are encouraged to request a mediator (this step costs an additional €360) or ask for a binding decision to be made by an adjudicator. Until the step where adjudication is requested, the use of the Rechtwijzer system is voluntary and non-binding. The initial goal of the Rechtwijzer developers was to have the system as self-financing, primarily through user contributions. Sadly, this did not occur, primarily for commercial reasons unrelated to the quality of the system.

In 2017, the collaborators behind Rechtwijzer dissolved the platform because of the difficulties in making the service financially viable. In its wake, some of the team members behind Rechtwijzer formed Justice42, a platform that offers similar services to a more targeted population in the Netherlands. While the platform represents a scaled-back version of the original service, it is intended to achieve the same goals and address the same values.[56]

The BC CRT is the most important and widely available ODR system. The system diagnoses the dispute and provides legal information and tools such as customized letter templates. If the initial provision of advice through the rule-based Solution Explorer (essentially advice about BATNAs and Bargaining in the Shadow of the Law) does not resolve the conflict, applicants can use the BC CRT to support dispute resolution.[57] Once the user has submitted the appropriate application forms and the application has been accepted, the disputants can enter a secure and confidential

[54] See the website of the Civil Resolution Tribunal at <https://civilresolutionbc.ca/#:~:text = The%20 CRT%20is%20Canada's%20first,collaborative%20approach%20to%20resolving%20disputes> last accessed 20 March 2024.

[55] See the website of Rechtwijzer at <https://rechtwijzer.nl> last accessed 20 March 2024.

[56] See Laura Kistemaker, 'Rechtwijzer and uitelkaar. nl. dutch experiences with odr for divorce' (2021) 59(2) Family Court Rev 232, 243.

[57] See Shannon Salter and Darin 'Thompson, 'Public-centered civil justice redesign: a case study of the British Columbia civil resolution tribunal' (2026) 3 McGill J Disp Resol 113.

negotiation platform, where the disputants can attempt, without external help, to resolve the dispute.

If this action fails, a facilitator or mediator can be employed to help resolve the conflict. When desirable, agreements can be turned into enforceable orders. If mediation, negotiation, or facilitation does not resolve the dispute, an independent member of the BC CRT will make a ruling about the case.

Currently, the BC CRT deals with the following five categories of cases: housing, motor injuries, owners' corporation disputes, small claims and cooperative associations and societies.[58] For these five domains, potential litigants are restricted to only using the CRT. Paper-based solutions are unavailable. This can potentially lead to major problems for the digitally disadvantaged. To deal with this dilemma, potential litigants can receive assistance in accessing the internet. We believe that the major reason for the significant success of the CRT is that the provincial British Columbia government has decreed that the BC CRT is the only forum in which residents can attempt to resolve those disputes listed above. Since 6 March 2023 British Columbia residents can use the CRT to make a claim for *an intimate image protection order*—to make someone delete the image or stop them from sharing or threatening to share it.[59]

The goal of BC CRT is to provide dispute resolution services that are timely, flexible, accessible, affordable, and efficient.[60] They encourage a collaborative approach to resolving disputes without the need to hire a lawyer or attend a court. But there is no discussion in their mission statement about fairness or justice!

In 2019, researchers at Thompson Rivers University's Faculty of Law in Kamloops BC conducted a qualitative survey of user experiences with the BC CRT.[61] The study found that most survey participants were satisfied with the CRT and found its resources helpful. It helped them solved their legal problems and save money. They found being able to access this information online and contact a remote platform at all times to be convenient, especially in consideration of work and other responsibilities. For some survey participants, the CRT provided proportional justice where they would not have otherwise had viable recourse. While some found the CRT process confusing and difficult to navigate, and some also criticized the CRT as a justice institution, the majority of survey participants who had experiences coping with legal problems (including in the traditional courts) found the CRT to be an improvement.

[58] The primary legislation underpinning the British Columbia Civil Resolution Tribunal is Civil Resolution Tribunal Act [sbc 2012] chapter 25. See <https://www.bclaws.gov.bc.ca/civix/document/id/complete/statreg/12025_01> last accessed 15 April 2024.

[59] See the information provided by the Civil Resolution Tribunal at the following website<https://civilresolutionbc.ca/solution-explorer/intimate-images/> last accessed 18 March 2024.

[60] See the information provided by the Civil Resolution Tribunal at the following website <https://civilresolutionbc.ca/about-the-crt/> last accessed 18 March 2024.

[61] See Katie Sykes, Rebecca Dickson, Sarah Ewart, Candice Foulkes, and Marina Landry, 'Civil Revolution: User Experiences with British Columbia's Online Court' (2020) 1 Windsor Yearbook of Access to Justice 161, 188.

E. Incorporating Artificial Intelligence into Dispute Resolution Systems

Both AI and game theory have been widely used to provide ADR advice.[62] Schoop et al note that '*Negotiation support* approaches do not automate the negotiation process but provide IT support for complex negotiations, leaving the control over the negotiation process with the human negotiators.'[63]

AI was used in the design of computer software to assist humans to enhance their negotiation skills. In this first generation of such tools, whether they used templates, rule-based reasoning, case-based reasoning, machine learning, or hybrids of these processes, the systems were developed in an ad hoc manner. And the systems operated in many diverse domains. There was no generic theory to help develop such systems.

Only over the past decade have we seen the development of intelligent ODR systems that are available in the marketplace. During this period there has been an increased emphasis on user-focused design because it has been realized that systems need to be developed for users who are not professionals.

Many of the first support systems were template based. Whilst they did not explicitly use AI, the systems did at that time provide important intelligent advice and support. Their primary focus was about how close disputants were to a negotiated settlement. By informing users of the issues in dispute and a measure of the level of the disagreement, they provided important negotiation advice.

In the early 1980s, the Rand Corporation used AI to develop two settlement-oriented decision support systems.[64] PERSUADER integrated case-based reasoning and game theory to provide negotiation support to assist with the resolution of US labour disputes.[65] Mediator used case retrieval and adaptation to generate enhanced resolutions to international disputes.[66]

The Split-Up system used machine learning to provide advice about the distribution of marital property following separation in Australian family law.[67]

Brams and Taylor used decision theory and game theoretic techniques to develop the Adjusted Winner algorithm.[68] The algorithm uses a two-party point allocation

[62] See eg John Zeleznikow, 'Using artificial intelligence to provide intelligent dispute resolution support' (2021) 30(4) Group Decision and Negotiation 789, 812.

[63] See Mareike Schoop, Aida Jertila, and Thomas List, 'Negoisst: a negotiation support system for electronic business-to-business negotiations in e-commerce' (2003) 47(3) Data & Knowledge Engineering 37, 401.

[64] The RAND systems are described in Donald Arthur Waterman and Mark A Peterson, *Models of Legal Decisionmaking: Research Design and Methods* (1981) 2717, no 1 (Rand Corporation, the Institute for Civil Justice); Donald Arthur Waterman, Jody Paul, and Mark Peterson, 'Expert systems for legal decision-making' (1986) 4 Expert Systems 3, 212, 226; Dean Schlobohm and Donald Arthur Waterman, 'Explanation for an expert system that performs estate planning' (1987) Proceedings of the 1st international conference on artificial intelligence and law 18–27.

[65] See Katia P Sycara, 'Machine learning for intelligent support of conflict resolution' (1993) 10(2) Decision Support Systems 121, 136.

[66] See Janet L Kolodner and Robert L Simpson, 'The Mediator: Analysis of an early case-based problem solver' (1989) 13(4) Cognitive Science 507, 549.

[67] See Andrew Stranieri, John Zeleznikow, Mark Gawler, and Bryn Lewis, 'A hybrid rule–neural approach for the automation of legal reasoning in the discretionary domain of family law in Australia' (1999) 7(2) Artificial Intelligence and Law 153, 183.

[68] See Steven J Brams and Alan D Taylor, *Fair Division: From Cake-cutting to Dispute Resolution* (CUP 1996).

procedure which distributes items or issues to disputants based on the premise of allocating items to those individuals who value the issue more highly. The principles behind the Adjusted Winner algorithm were the basis of the Family Winner system.[69]

Just as US Family Courts have advocated the use of Our Family Wizard, The Australian Family Court system has similarly, but unofficially, adopted an app (MyMob) designed to help separated families manage daily life. Judges prefer families to use the app because it fosters positive communication.[70]

In comparing dispute resolution processes, I contrasted Australian family dispute resolution processes with efforts to resolve the Israeli–Palestinian dispute:[71] I used our Asset Divider system designed to provide negotiation advice to separated disputing couples to advise about the Israel–Palestinian dispute.[72] From a historic examination of the Israel–Palestinian dispute, we decided that the following were major issues of dispute, and hence now discuss how these issues effect the protagonists: security, recognition of Israel as a Jewish state, autonomy, Jerusalem, right of return, the maintenance of nuclear weapons by Iran, dismantlement of settlements, and removal of the fence as a barrier between Israel and the Palestinian Territories. [73] For each of the eight issues I entered values indicating the Israeli and Palestinian positions. For each party, the sum of the issue values had to be 100.

The system suggested trade-off allocations—the party that wanted an issue most was offered it, and compensation was given to the other party. As a result, it was recommended that: (1) Israel recognizes a Palestinian state, with East Jerusalem as its capital; (2) the Israelis dismantle the current security fence; (3) The Israelis evacuate those smaller settlements in Judea and Samaria that are not within a close proximity to existing Israeli borders. So that such a solution would be acceptable to Israel it was recommended that: (4) The Palestinians would need to recognize the State of Israel and encourage other Arab states to do likewise; (5) The Palestinians would need to forgo any right of return to Israel (for which they would be adequately compensated) and (6) The Palestinians would need to make significant efforts to ensure that no anti-Israel violence emanated from Israeli territories. In addition, the system suggested that it would be desirable for the Palestinians to encourage the Iranian government not to develop nuclear weapons and not to make belligerent statements against Israel.

Interestingly enough, the solution I proposed is similar to the successful Camp David Accords between Israel and Egypt in 1978, where Israel gave up territory for recognition and security. I did not use the Camp David Accords as a model for the process. But they too involved interest-based negotiation and have endured for over

[69] See Emilia Bellucci and John Zeleznikow, 'Developing Negotiation Decision Support Systems that support mediators: a case study of the Family Winner system' (2005) 13 Artificial Intelligence and Law 233, 271.

[70] See the information provided by the Sydney Morning Herald at the following website: <https://www.smh.com.au/technology/judges-mandate-app-for-separated-parents-20190906-p52op7.html> last accessed 18 February 2020.

[71] See John Zeleznikow, 'Comparing the Israel–Palestinian dispute to Australian family mediation' (2014) 23 Group Decision and Negotiation 1301.

[72] See Brooke Abrahams, Emilia Bellucci, and John Zeleznikow, 'Incorporating fairness into development of an integrated multi-agent online dispute resolution environment' (2012) 21 Group Decision and Negotiation 3.

[73] See Steve Mock, Amer Obeidi, and John Zeleznikow, 'A brief outline of the Israel–Palestinian conflict' (2014) 23 Group Decision and Negotiation 1245, 1262.

45 years. Clearly a solution that involves the transfer of land in return for recognition and security is a logical one. However, whilst the Camp David Accords have endured, the then Egyptian President Anwar Sadat, who signed the Accords was assassinated by an Egyptian in 1981. And the Israeli Prime Minister Yitzhak Rabin, who signed the Oslo Accords in 1993, was assassinated by an Israeli in 1995. Clearly, any peace partner is at peril from dissidents on his own side! The reason such a solution, which is not novel, has not been adopted is that the disputing parties have a long history of distrust. And the events of 7 October 2023 in Southern Israel and the subsequent deaths in Gaza and Lebanon have exponentially increased the level of distrust between the combatants.[74]

There is no generic SRL. SRLs need guidelines about how to navigate legal processes. Many SRLs turn to ODR to resolve disputes related to debt, employment, family relationships, and a wide spectrum of other life problems. If non-professional SRLs hope to use ODR software with success, then such software must be user-friendly.

Thus, Margaret Hagan at the Stanford University Law School has advocated for a user-centric design approach to access to justice in ODR.[75] Human-centric design focuses on users' experiences to develop solutions that are both experimental and iterative.[76] Hagan's research into how judicial systems can serve non-professional SRLs identifies seven key recommendations for courts and Self Help Centers to focus on when making their systems more usable and efficient:

1. Courts must coordinate Navigable Pathways, which help people understand the whole sequence of events that will face them during their legal processes and more effectively assist them through that process.
2. People need more robust and user-friendly tools to navigate through the court.
3. People need warm and efficient welcome experiences to encourage them to follow through with the procedures.
4. Paperwork should be redesigned to be more visually clear, prioritized, and manageable.
5. Pre-court appearances—the development of more online court tools that can help people prep for their court visits and get their tasks done correctly.
6. Better workstations and materials in courts to prepare litigants for their appearances.
7. The court system needs to develop a culture of usability, testing, and feedback.[77]

Unless ODR systems are user-centric, they will not be used.

The State of Utah is piloting the use of ODR in small claims cases at 37 select courts throughout the state.[78] Currently it only involves online negotiation. An examination

[74] See the information provided by Reuters at <https://www.reuters.com/world/middle-east/major-events-during-100-days-war-between-israel-hamas-2024-01-14/> last accessed 15 April 2024.

[75] See Margaret D Hagan, 'A Human-Centered Design Approach to Access to Justice: Generating New Prototypes and Hypotheses for Interventions to Make Courts User-Friendly' (2018) 6 Ind J & Soc Equal 199, 200.

[76] See Tim Brown, 'Design Thinking' (2008) Harv Bus Rev 84.

[77] See Hagan (n 75) 201. For an example of a Self Help Center, see San Francisco Superior Court, Access Center, <https://sf.courts.ca.gov/self-help> last accessed 23 April 2024 and

[78] <https://www.utcourts.gov/en/self-help/case-categories/consumer/small-claims/odr.html#accordion-9c46f5da5a-item-08dc58f161> last accessed 22 March 2024.

of the usability of Utah's ODR program by researchers at the University of Arizona provides additional support for the need for a user-centric design approach.[79] Based on an analysis focused on functionality, usability, accessibility, and comprehension issues, the report makes five overall recommendations for improvement: (1) ease the transition from paper to platform, (2) streamline the registration process, (3) simplify document sharing and review, (4) improve ODR information and help, and (5) clarify legal information and user options.[80] These final two points are incredibly important, especially for SRLs. The system provides for online mediation and does not provide advice. [81] At the time of the publication of the Utah ODR evaluation, AI was not being used. The research team recommended integrating an AI chatbot or similar functionality within the ODR Facilitator chat feature. It is suggested that when users enter certain words, the chatbot would offer related help pages In addition, if chatbot-driven help pages cannot address a user's question, the ODR platform could notify the ODR Facilitator that they should join the chat. [82]

Providing user-centric design also means that the system should provide what the users need. This is particularly so for SRLs who have very limited legal knowledge. Thus, it is insufficient that the system merely be easy to use.

F. The Courts and Generative Artificial Intelligence

Samuel Dahan and David Liang argue that the digital transformation toward remote justice in response to the COVID-19 pandemic was not a paradigm shift. They claim that the COVID-19 pandemic merely exacerbated what was already an access to justice problem. [83] Jean-Francois Roberge and Veronique Fraser argue that an optimal ODR platform, from a commercial standpoint, should provide guides and flowcharts, an adaptive question and answer interface, transparent ethical commitments, outcome predictions, an expedited procedure leading to an enforceable outcome, a proportional cost model, a mediation process, and a range of communications.[84] They claim that the commercial world could learn from the technology in family law ODR.

Elisabeth Wilson Evered and John Zeleznikow discuss online family dispute resolution in detail. Because family law cases discourage adversarial conflict, are numerous and require negotiation, they are well-suited to the use of ODR. Current

[79] See Stacy Butler, Sarah Mauet, Christopher L Griffin, and Mackenzie Pish, 'The Utah Online Dispute Resolution Platform: A Usability Evaluation and Report', Arizona Legal Studies Discussion Paper (2020) 21-06 available at https://papers.ssrn.com/sol3/papers.cfm?abstract_id = 3696105 last accessed 23 April 2024.

[80] ibid.

[81] See <https://www.slc.gov/courts/small-claims/> last accessed 15 April 2024.

[82] See Butler et al (n 79).

[83] See Samuel Dahan and David Liang, 'The Case for AI-Powered Legal Aid' (2021) 46 Queen's LJ 415.

[84] See Jean-Francois Roberge and Veronique Fraser, 'Access to Commercial Justice: A Roadmap for Online Dispute Resolution (ODR) Design for Small and Medium-Sized Businesses (SMEs) Disputes', (2019) 35 Ohio St J Disp Resol 1, 11–12.

family law ODR systems that they discuss include: Coparenter, [85] Our Family Wizard, [86] Split-Up,[87] Our Family Winner,[88] Amica,[89] and Adieu. [90]

CoParenter is an online service that helps separated, divorced, and never-married parents make and manage co-parenting responsibilities, create court-ready parenting and holiday plans, resolve disputes, and make more informed, child-centric decisions that save them time and money and keep parents out of court. Integrated ODR facilitates online negotiation and mediation and adds means for collaboration among various parties over a long period of time. Whilst CoParenter advertises two uses of AI for parents: creating parenting plans and using IDR technology to predict and prevent common conflicts when parents are communicating with one another, it appears to be a 'rule-based' system set up to take parents step-by-step through the process of creating a plan, asking them yes or no questions about what they want to do next, their children's names, and other relevant information.[91]

Split Up provides advice to separating partners about reaching agreements on the division of their assets.[92] A predictive algorithm using neural networks and rules[93]can be used to determine a party's BATNA.[94] The system used 103 commonplace (or unreported) family court cases to develop predictives analytics for how future assets would be divided between couples in the event of a divorce. Couples input shared costs, performed labour, division of household duties, future job prospects, and more.[95] Amica[96] is a recently developed digital solution for Australian separating couples. Amica includes a machine learning algorithm that suggests division of former couples' total marital assets. Both Amica and Rechtwijzer were based upon the Split Up system.

Our Family Wizard offers tools to parents for scheduling, tracking, reimbursement requests and payments, communication, and creating logs of the communication[97]. Like CoParenter, Our Family Wizard emphasizes effective communication.

[85] See the information provided by coParenter at <https://coparenter.com> last accessed 15 April 2024.

[86] See the information provided by OurFamilyWizard at <https://www.ourfamilywizard.com last accessed 15 April 2024.

[87] See Stranieri et al (n 67) 183.

[88] See Emilia Bellucci and John Zeleznikow, 'Developing Negotiation Decision Support Systems that support mediators: a case study of the FamilyWinner system' (2005) 13 Artificial Intelligence and Law 233–71.

[89] See the information provided by Amica at <https://www.amica.gov.au> last accessed 15 April 2024. Portable and the Legal Services Commission of South Australia designed and developed Amica, a digital solution for Australian separating couples. Amica includes a machine learning algorithm that suggests division of former couples' total marital assets. Professor Zeleznikow was a consultant to the development of the Amica system, which emulates the Split Up system, especially in the way it integrates rule-based reasoning and machine learning to advise upon the distribution of assets following divorce in Australia.

[90] See the information provided by adieu.ai at <https://www.adieu.ai> last accessed 15 April 2024.

[91] ibid.

[92] See Stranieri et al (n 67) 183.

[93] Neural networks are a form of machine learning.

[94] John Zeleznikow and Emilia Bellucci, 'Family-Winner: Integrating Game Theory and Heuristics to Provide Negotiation Support' (2003) Proc of the 16th Int'l Conf on L Knowledge Based Systems 21, 23.

[95] See John Zeleznikow, *Computer Divorce*, YouTube (26 April 2020) <https://www.youtube.com/watch?v = u7A3H4lUjzM> for a useful video about the operation of the Split Up system.

[96] Details about AMICA are available at <https://www.amica.gov.au/> last accessed 20 July 2020.

[97] Our Family Wizard can be viewed at <https://www.ourfamilywizard.com/> last accessed 17 July 2021.

Family Winner[98] is a family law support system that uses a variety of AI and game theory techniques[99] developed by John Nash[100] to help structure the mediation process and give parties an idea of possible trade-offs. Family Winner requires users to input what issues are in dispute, how important each issue is, and how the issues relate to one another. The system then creates graphical trade-off maps and assigns values to each issue. Parties can then settle based on how the map presents the issues and their values and resulting allocations. If the parties do not agree with the proposed allocations, the system asks the parties to break down the issues further in order to identify the least contentious issues until they find sub-issues on which the parties can agree. Then, the system mathematically calculates which issue to give to each party, in order to maximize value and satisfaction to clients.

SRLs need advice about processes and likely resolutions of their dispute. Amy Schmitz and John Zeleznikow have developed a model of requirements for ODR systems which would prove useful for SRLs.[101] These include case management, triaging, advisory tools, communication tools, decision support tools, and agreement (or document drafting) technologies. Of these, judges would greatly appreciate document drafting systems. Advisory tools (such as for sentencing) can also be useful. But do current systems provide such tools? Schmitz and Zeleznikow[102] surveyed a list of 59 ODR providers maintained by the US National Center for Technology and Dispute Resolution (NCTDR) in Amherst, MA.[103] Not surprisingly almost all (55) provided communication tools. When most people think of ODR, their focus is upon communication. Three-quarters (44) provided case management. Other tools are less common: seventeen for advisory tools, nine for decision support tools and a minimal four for triaging and five for document drafting. Most advisory tools and decision support tools use AI, whilst all document drafting tools use AI.

When Schmitz and Zeleznikow introduced their model in 2021, computer scientists had conducted much research in automated negotiation.[104] The study of generative AI[105] and large language models[106] is much more recent. Grossman et al argue that

[98] See Emilia Bellucci and John Zeleznikow, 'Developing Negotiation Decision Support Systems that support mediators: a case study of the Family Winner system' (2005) 13 Artificial Intelligence and Law 233, 271.

[99] 'Game theory is a branch of applied mathematics that provides advice about the optimal distribution of resources. In the case of a negotiation, the goal of game theory is to develop the best outcome related to the choices each person has made'. Arno R Lodder and John Zeleznikow, *Enhanced Dispute Resolution Through the Use of Information Technology* (CUP 2010).

[100] See John Nash, 'Two-person Cooperative Games' (1953) Econometrica: Journal of the Econometric Society 128, 140.

[101] See Amy Schmitz and John Zeleznikow, 'Intelligent Legal Tech to Empower Self-Represented Litigants' (2021) 23 Colum Sci & Tech L Rev 142.

[102] ibid.

[103] The Provider List, NCTDR, is available at <http://odr.info/provider-list/> last accessed 27 March 2024.

[104] See for example, Nicholas R Jennings, Peyman Faratin, Alessio R Lomuscio, Simon Parsons, Carles Sierra, and Michael Wooldridge, 'Automated Negotiation: Prospects, Methods and Challenges', (2001) 10(2) International Journal of Group Decision and Negotiation 199, 215.

[105] See Erik Brynjolfsson, Danielle Li, and Lindsey R Raymond, 'Generative AI at Work' (2023) No w31161. National Bureau of Economic Research <https://www.nber.org/papers/w31161> last accessed 27 March 2024; Maura Grossman, Paul W Grimm, Dan Brown, and Molly Xu, 'The GPT Judge: Justice in a Generative AI World' (2023) 23 Duke Law & Technology Review 1.

[106] See Yupeng Chang, Xu Wang, Jindong Wang, Yuan Wu, Linyi Yang, Kaijie Zhu, Hao Chen, Xiaoyuan Yi, Cunxiang Wang, Yidong Wang, Wei Ye, Yue Zhang, Yi Chang, Philip S Yu, Qiang Yang, and Xing Xie, 'A Survey on Evaluation of Large Language Models' (2023) Cornell University 1.

generative AI is a specific subset of AI used to create new content, or to replicate an artistic style, by training on existing data taken from massive data sources—primarily the internet—in response to a user's prompt.[107] They believe that the speedy development of generative AI has shocked the public because of how well it fares on creative tasks like writing poetry and drawing images, and how well it can create synthesized content mimicking the work of real people. Another big change has been the remarkable fluency with language that current AI models demonstrate.

Until recently large language models (LLMs) would routinely 'forget' basic parts of the conversations they were having with human partners or would incomprehensibly 'babble' in the middle of answering a question. Now, these models are so adept with language that they can comfortably produce sentences indistinguishable from their human-authored counterparts and can 'recall' earlier parts of a conversation with ease. With these advances, it is likely that the provision of document drafting facilities by ODR systems will become routine.

In March 2023, the then latest version of ChatGPT aced the Arizona bar exam with score nearing 90th percentile.[108] The potential to use Generative AI is large for both litigants (whether represented by a lawyer or a SRL) and the judiciary. Each has different needs. Litigants want advice to present feasible arguments that comply with court processes and help with trade-offs.

A UK Court of Appeal Judge Lord Justice Birss used an AI chatbot to write part of a judgment.[109] This was the first known such use by a British judge. Globally, the judiciary would like ranges for sentencing and document drafting to help with decision-making. The problem with using automated document drafting is whether the information supplied is relevant and accurate and the conclusions drawn from the information is valid. To achieve this goal, it is essential for users to evaluate the quality of the advice being offered. And of course, legal professionals and academics are far more skilled in accurately evaluating advice than are SRLs. But even lawyers inappropriately using Generative AI. For example, in New York, a lawyer is facing a court hearing after his firm used AI tool ChatGPT for legal research. A judge said the court was faced with an 'unprecedented circumstance' after a filing was found to reference example legal cases that did not exist. The lawyer who used the tool had failed to check whether its content was valid.[110]

In her PhD at La Trobe University, under the supervision of John Zeleznikow, Jean Hall developed a process for evaluating legal knowledge-based systems based upon the Context Criteria Contingency-guidelines Framework.[111]

[107] See Grossman et al (n 105) 34.

[108] See the information at ABAJOURNAL, available at <https://www.abajournal.com/web/article/latest-version-of-chatgpt-aces-the-bar-exam-with-score-in-90th-percentile> last accessed 15 April 2024.

[109] See the information at The Guardian: <https://www.theguardian.com/technology/2023/sep/15/court-of-appeal-judge-praises-jolly-useful-chatgpt-after-asking-it-for-legal-summary> last accessed 16 April 2024.

[110] See the information at BBC: <https://www.bbc.com/news/world-us-canada-65735769> last accessed 16 April 2024.

[111] See Maria Jean J Hall, Richard Hall, and John Zeleznikow, 'A process for evaluating legal knowledge-based systems based upon the context criteria contingency-guidelines framework' (2003) Proceedings of the 9th international conference on Artificial intelligence and law 274, 283; Maria Jean J Hall, 'An Adaptive, Subsumptive Evaluation Framework for Intelligent Legal Systems', PhD thesis, La Trobe University, Faculty of Science Technology and Engineering, Bundoora, VIC, 3086, Australia, Jan 2005.

We can thus conclude that AI is most appropriately used in the judicial system to provide decision support rather than developing automated decision-making systems. AI is very useful for efficiency and effectiveness. The challenge when trying to use AI to enhance fairness in the justice system is that AI (or at least machine learning) uses past cases. Past cases repeat previous injustices and do not create new paradigms.[112] Thus the use of fully automated AI systems using past cases will not lead to the elimination of undesirable law.

There has been much focus upon whether AI can replace judges. Zeleznikow says that robot judges are not likely to provide valuable decisions in all but a few non-discretionary statutory domains! However, AI can provide very helpful tools for both judges and litigants, especially for the enforcement of arbitral awards or debts when no defence has been entered.[113] As Tania Sourdin states, 'AI programs that can produce a decision based on information input could be used to assist human judges, rather than replace them. These systems could produce a draft judgment based on the system's determined outcome. A human judge could then use this draft judgment to produce their own reasons, allowing for human oversight over the computer program, and enabling discretionary or social considerations to be made that may be beyond the capacity of the computer program'.[114]

G. Conclusion

As we have seen in our discussion, there have been many research prototypes that attempt to incorporate AI into the judicial system, especially in providing Access to Justice for SRLs. But except for the British Columbia Civil Resolution Tribunal (BC CRT) few are widely used, nor do they use AI. And even the AI in the BC CRT is the rule-based Solution Explorer.

We have discussed the machine learning Split Up system, which was used in Australia circa 2000. Recently, the Australian Government has developed the Amica system, based on the Split Up system,

But changes are afoot. With the recent focus upon generative AI, there is both excitement and concern about how AI is used in the judicial system. Generative AI and in particular ChatGPT have the ability to provide both lawyers and non-professionals with advice regarding the judicial system. We have seen how self-represented litigants, especially when using ODR, can receive important advice about processes and potential outcomes. Successful use of such tools will enhance access to justice for SRLs. But the rise of generative AI will also lead to many problems especially as to whether the advice is valid and whether it is being appropriately used.

[112] See John Zeleznikow, 'The benefits and dangers of using machine learning to support making legal predictions' (2023) *Wiley Interdisciplinary Reviews: Data Mining and Knowledge Discovery* 13.4 e1505.

[113] See John Zeleznikow, 'Can Artificial Intelligence and Online Dispute Resolution Enhance Efficiency and Effectiveness in Courts' (2026) 8 Intl J Court Administration 30.

[114] Tania Sourdin, 'Judge v Robot? Artificial Intelligence and Judicial Decision-Making' (2018) 41(4) University of New South Wales LJ 1114, 1133.

Bibliography

Abrahams B, Bellucci E, and Zeleznikow J, 'Incorporating fairness into development of an integrated multi-agent online dispute resolution environment' (2012) 21 Group Decision and Negotiation 3.
Assy R, *Injustice in Person: the Right to Self-Representation* (OUP 2015).
Barsky AE, 'The Ethics of App-Assisted Family Mediation' (2021) 34(1) Conflict Resolution Quarterly 31, 42.
Bellucci E and Zeleznikow J, 'Developing Negotiation Decision Support Systems that Support Mediators: A Case Study of the Family Winner System' (2005) 13 Artificial Intelligence and Law 233.
Berman DH and Hafner CD, 'The Potential of Artificial Intelligence to Help Solve the Crisis in Our Legal System' (1989) 32(8) Communications of the ACM 928.
Bibas S, 'Plea Bargaining Outside the Shadow of the Trial' (2004) 117 Harv L Rev 2464, 2547.
Bibas S, 'Transparency and Participation in Criminal Procedure' (2006) 81 NY University L Rev 911, 966.
Brams Steven J and Taylor Alan D, *Fair Division: From Cake-Cutting to Dispute Resolution* (CUP 1996).
Branting KL, '*Advisory Systems for Pro Se* Litigants' (2001) Proc of the 8th Int'l Conf on AI and Law 139, 146.
Brown T, 'Design Thinking' (2008) 86(6) Harv Bus Rev 84.
Buhai SL, 'Access to Justice for Unrepresented Litigants: A Comparative Perspective' (2008) 42 Loy LAL Rev 979.
Brynjolfsson E, Danielle L, and Raymond Lindsey R, 'Generative AI at Work' No w31161, National Bureau of Economic Research.
Chang Y, Wang X, Wang J, Wu, Y, Yang L, Zhu K, Chen H, Yi X, Wang C, Wang Wei Y, Zhang Y, Chang Y, Yu PS, Yang Q, and Xie X, 'A Survey on Evaluation of Large Language Models' (2023) Cornell University 1–45.
Choudhry S and Herring J, 'A human right to legal aid?–The implications of changes to the legal aid scheme for victims of domestic abuse' (2017) 39.2 *Journal of social welfare and family law* 152–167.
Coleman PT, Deutsch M, and Marcus EC (eds), *The Handbook of Conflict Resolution: Theory and Practice* (John Wiley & Sons 2014).
Cortés P 'Embedding Alternative Dispute Resolution in the Civil Justice System: A Taxonomy for ADR Referrals and a Digital Pathway to Increase the Uptake of ADR' (2023) 43(2) Legal Studies 312.
Dahan S and Liang D, 'The Case for AI-Powered Legal Aid' (2021) 46 Queen's LJ 415.
Fisher R and Ury W, *Getting to YES: Negotiating Agreement Without Giving* (Haughton Mifflin 1981).
Galanter M, 'The Hundred-Year Decline of Trials and the Thirty Years War' (2005) 57 Stan L Rev 1255–74.
Galanter M, 'The Vanishing Trial: An Examination of Trials and Related Matters in Federal and State Courts' (2004) 1 J Empirical Legal Stud 459.
Galanter M and Frozena AM, 'A Grin without a Cat: The Continuing Decline & Displacement of Trials in American Courts' (2014) 143 Daedalus 115.
Grossman M, Grimm PW, Brown D and Xu M, ' The GPTJudge: Justice in a Generative AI World' (2023) 23(1) Duke Law & Technology Rev 1.
Hagan MD, 'A Human-Centered Design Approach to Access to Justice: Generating New Prototypes and Hypotheses for Interventions to Make Courts User-Friendly' (2018) 6 Ind J & Soc Equal 199.
Hall MJ, Hall R, and Zeleznikow J, 'A process for evaluating legal knowledge-based systems based upon the context criteria contingency-guidelines framework' (2003) Proceedings of the 9th international conference on Artificial intelligence and law.
Hart HLA 'Positivism and the Separation of Law and Morals' (1958) 71 Harv L Rev 593.
Jennings NR, Faratin P, Lomuscio AR, Parsons S, Sierra C, and Wooldridge M, 'Automated Negotiation: Prospects, Methods and Challenges' (2001) 10(2) Intl J of Group Decision and Negotiation 199.
Katsh E, 'Dispute Resolution in Cyberspace' (1995) 28 Conn L Rev 953.

Katsh E and Rabinovich-Einy O, *Digital Justice: Technology and the Internet of Disputes* (OUP 2017).
Kaye M, Wangmann J, and Booth T '"No straight lines": Self-represented litigants in family law proceedings involving allegations about family violence' (2020) <https://www.anrows.org.au/publication/no-straight-lines-self-represented-litigants-in-family-law-proceedings-involving-allegations-about-family-violence/>.
Kistemaker L, 'Rechtwijzer and uitelkaar. nl. dutch experiences with odr for divorce' (2021) 59(2) Family Court Rev 232.
Kolodner JL and Simpson RL, 'The Mediator: Analysis of an Early Case-based Problem Solver' (1989) 13(4) Cognitive Science 507.
Lodder AR and Zeleznikow J, *Enhanced Dispute Resolution Through the Use of Information Technology* (CUP 2010).
Lodder AR and Zeleznikow J, 'Developing an Online Dispute Resolution Environment: Dialogue Tools and Negotiation Support Systems in a Three-Step Model' (2005) Harv Negot L Rev 10 287.
Luban D, 'Self-Representation, Access to Justice, and the Quality of Counsel: A Comment on Rabeea Assy's Injustice in Person: The Right of Self-Representation' (2018) 17 Jrslm Rev Legal Stud 46.
Macfarlane J and Campbell M, 'Self-Represented Litigants & Legal Doctrines of "Vexatiousness"—An Interim Report from The National Self-Represented Litigants Project' (2019) <https://scholar.uwindsor.ca/cgi/viewcontent.cgi?article=1000&context=lawnsrlppubs>.
Mnookin R and Kornhauser L, 'Bargaining in the Shadow of the Law: The Case of Divorce' (1979) 88 Yale LJ 950.
Re RM and Solow-Niederman A, 'Developing Artificially Intelligent Justice' (2019) 22 Stan Tech L Rev 242.
Mock S, Obeidi A, and Zeleznikow J, 'A Brief Outline of the Israel–Palestinian Conflict' (2014) 23 Group Decision and Negotiation 1245.
Murray P, 'The Privatisation of Civil Justice' (2011) 85(8) Admin LJ 490.
Nash J, 'Two-person Cooperative Games' (1953) Econometrica: Journal of the Econometric Society 128.
Owen CL, Staud RW, and Pedwell EB, *Access to Justice: Meeting the Needs of Self-Represented Litigants* (Pearson Custom Pub 2002).
Poblet M (ed), Expanding the Horizons of ODR: Proceedings of the 5th International Workshop on Online Dispute Resolution <http://ftp.informatik.rwth-aachen.de/Publications/CEUR-WS/Vol-430/Proceedings.pdf>.
Poblet M, Abrahams B, and Zeleznikow J, Proceedings of the 6th International Workshop on Online Dispute Resolution 2010, Liverpool, United Kingdom, 15 December 2010, CEUR Workshop Proceedings 684, CEUR-WS.org 2010 <https://ceur-ws.org/Vol-684/ODR2010proceedings.pdf>.
Roberge JF and Fraser V, 'Access to Commercial Justice: A Roadmap for Online Dispute Resolution (ODR) Design for Small and Medium-Sized Businesses (SMEs) Disputes, (2019) 35 Ohio St J on Disp Resol 1.
Salter S and Thompson D, 'Public-Centred Civil Justice Redesign: A Case Study of the British Columbia Civil Resolution Tribunal' (2016) 3 McGill J Disp Resol 113.
Scarrow K, Fragomeni B, and Macfarlane J, 'Tracking the Trends of the Self-Represented Litigant Phenomenon: Data from the National Self-Represented Litigants Project, 2018/2019' (2020) <https://scholar.uwindsor.ca/cgi/viewcontent.cgi?article=1011&context=lawnsrlppubs>.
Schlobohm D, Waterman DA, 'Explanation for an expert system that performs estate planning' in Proceedings of the 1st international conference on artificial intelligence and law, (1987) 18.
Schoop M, Jertila A, and List T, 'Negoisst: a negotiation support system for electronic business-to-business negotiations in e-commerce' (2003) 47(3) Data & Knowledge Engineering 371.
Smith JQ and MacQueen Grant R, 'Going, Going. But not Quite Gone: Trials Continue to Decline in Federal and State Courts. Does it Matter?' (2017) 101 Judicature 26, 28.
Schmitz A. and Zeleznikow, J. 'Intelligent legal tech to empower self-represented litigants' (2021) 23 Colum. Sci. & Tech. L. Rev. 142,191.
Sourdin T, 'Judge v Robot? Artificial Intelligence and Judicial Decision-Making' (2018) 41, no. 4 University of New South Wales LJ 1114.
Sourdin T and Zeleznikow J, 'Courts, Mediation and COVID-19' (2020) 48(2) Australian Business L Rev 138.

Stacy B, Mauet S, Griffin Ch.L, and Pish M, 'The Utah Online Dispute Resolution Platform: A Usability Evaluation and Report' Arizona Legal Studies Discussion Paper 21-06 (2020) available at <https://papers.ssrn.com/sol3/papers.cfm?abstract_id=3696105>.

Steinber JK, 'Demand Side Reform in the Poor People's Court' (2015) 47 Conn L Rev 741.

Stranieri A, Zeleznikow J, Gawler M, and Lewis B, 'A hybrid rule–neural approach for the automation of legal reasoning in the discretionary domain of family law in Australia' (1999) 7(2) Artificial Intelligence and Law 153.

Sycara KP, 'Machine Learning for Intelligent Support of Conflict Resolution' (1993) 10(2) Decision Support Systems 121.

Sykes K, Dickson R, Ewart S, Foulkes C, and Landry M, 'Civil Revolution: User Experiences with British Columbia's Online Court' (2020) 1 *Windsor Yearbook of Access to Justice* 161.

Thomson M, 'Alternative modes of delivery for family dispute resolution: The Telephone Dispute Resolution Service and the Online FDR Project1' (2011) 3 Journal of Family Studies 17 253.

Turing A, 'Computing Machinery and Intelligence' (1950) 236 Mind 433.

Waterman DA and Peterson MA, *Models of Legal Decisionmaking: Research Design and Methods* (1981) 2717, no 1 (Rand Corporation, the Institute for Civil Justice).

Waterman DA, Paul J, and Peterson M, 'Expert Systems for Legal Decision-Making Expert' (1986) 3(4) Expert Systems 212, 226.

Zeleznikow J, *Computer Divorce*, YouTube (26 April 2020) <https://www.youtube.com/watch?v=u7A3H4lUjzM>.

Zeleznikow J, 'The benefits and dangers of using machine learning to support making legal predictions' (2023) 13(4) Wiley Interdisciplinary Reviews: Data Mining and Knowledge Discovery 1.

Zeleznikow J, 'Using web-based legal decision support systems to improve access to justice' (2002) 11(1) Information & Communications Technology Law 15.

Zeleznikow J, 'The challenges of using online dispute resolution to support self-represented litigants' (2020) 23(7) J Int L 3.

Zeleznikow J, 'Using artificial intelligence to provide intelligent dispute resolution support' (2021) 30(4) Group Decision and Negotiation 789.

Zeleznikow J, 'Comparing the Israel–Palestinian dispute to Australian family mediation' (2014) 23 Group Decision and Negotiation 1301.

Zeleznikow J, 'Can artificial intelligence and online dispute resolution enhance efficiency and effectiveness in courts' (2017) 8 International Journal Court Administration 30.

15

Courthouse AI and Access to Justice in the United States

David Freeman Engstrom, *Ayelet Sela***, and *Natalie Knowlton****

A. Introduction

Nearly two-and-a-half decades into the twenty-first century, American courts seem to have finally settled into digitalization. COVID is an important part of the story. As the world went into lock-down, many courts launched their first experiments with remote hearings, and online dispute resolution (ODR) reached critical mass,[1] providing some of the first empirical evidence on the merits and demerits of new digital fora work.[2] Courts also leapt forward with digital self-help tools designed to reach

* LSVF Professor of Law and Co-Director, Deborah L. Rhode Center on the Legal Profession, Stanford Law School.

** Lecturer (Assistant Professor) at the Faculty of Law, Bar Ilan University and Civil Justice and Innovation Fellow, Deborah L. Rhode Center on the Legal Profession, Stanford Law School.

*** Associate Director of Legal Innovation, Deborah L Rhode Center on the Legal Profession, Stanford Law School.

[1] David Freeman Engstrom and RJ Vogt, 'The New Judicial Governance: Courts, Data, and the Future of Civil Justice' (2023) 72 DePaul L Rev 171, 171.

[2] Avital Mentovich, JJ Prescott, and Orna Rabinovich-Einy, 'Are Litigation Outcome Disparities Inevitable? Courts, Technology, and the Future of Impartiality' (2019) 71 Alabama L Rev 893; Victor D Quintanilla et al, 'Accessing Justice with Zoom: Experiences and Outcomes in Online Civil Courts' (2023)

David Freeman Engstrom, Ayelet Sela, and Natalie Knowlton, *Courthouse AI and Access to Justice in the United States* In: *Digitalization and Artificial Intelligence in Courts*. Edited by: Fernando Esteban de la Rosa, Pablo Cortés, and Nuria Marchal Escalona, Oxford University Press.
DOI: 10.1093/9780198918752.003.0015

litigants directly, such as legal information portals, chatbots, and document assembly tools. More important than any particular technology, however, courts shook loose some of the inertia that had long prevailed, toning innovation muscles that had long atrophied, if they had developed at all. As Bridget McCormack, then Chief Justice of the Michigan Supreme Court, put it, COVID was 'not the change we wanted, but it was the change we needed.'[3]

Now two further and powerful forces are bearing down on American courts, yielding yet more efforts to rethink how they perform some of their most vital work. First is mounting concern about access to justice. In something like three-quarters of the roughly 20 million civil cases filed in American courts each year, at least one side lacks a lawyer.[4] And these tend to be small but consequential cases. They are evictions, debt collections, and certain types of family law, particularly child support enforcement actions and domestic violence protective order petitions.[5] Many and even most, depending on case type, pit an institutional plaintiff (a bank, a credit card company, a debt buyer, a corporate or municipal landlord, or the government), nearly always with a lawyer, against an individual defendant without one.[6] Such large, systemic gaps in access to legal services limit who can defend their rights, magnifying disparities based on income, education, race, ethnicity, and gender.[7]

Second are the recent and stunning advances in artificial intelligence (AI), particularly generative AI, which have brought virtually every stage of the litigation life cycle within automation's sights.[8] Indeed, recent estimates suggest that nearly half of legal tasks can be automated,[9] as indicated by continuing growth in the 'legal-tech' marketplace.[10] Some of this growth can be attributed to rapid advances in the capabilities of

<https://www.repository.law.indiana.edu/cgi/viewcontent.cgi?article = 4087&context = facpub> last accessed 18 April 2024; Jennifer Shack and Donna Shestowsky, 'Access to Justice: Lessons for Designing Text-Based Court-Connected ODR Programs' (2023) 29 Dispute Resolution Magazine 29.

3 Justin P Hicks, 'Technology Brought "Much-Needed Change" to Judicial System, Michigan Supreme Court Chief Justice Tells Congress' (*MLive*, 25 June 2020) <https://www.mlive.com/public-interest/2020/06/technology-brought-much-needed-change-to-judicial-system-michigan-supreme-court-chief-justice-tells-congress.html> last accessed 6 June 2024.

4 Paula Hannaford-Agor, Scott Graves, and Shelly Spacek Miller, 'The Landscape of Civil Litigation in State Courts' (National Center for State Courts 2015) https://www.ncsc.org/__data/assets/pdf_file/0020/13376/civiljusticereport-2015.pdf last accessed 18 April 2024.

5 ibid.

6 ibid; Daniel Wilf-Townsend, 'Assembly-Line Plaintiffs' (2021) 135 Harvard L Rev 1704.

7 Victor D Quintanilla, Rachel A Allen, and Edward R Hirt, 'The Signaling Effect of Pro Se Status Symposium: Access to Justice' (2017) 42 Law & Social Inquiry 1091.

8 Lyria Bennett Moses et al, 'AI Decision-Making and the Courts: A Guide for Judges, Tribunal Members and Court Administrators (2023 Update)' (2023) <https://aija.org.au/wp-content/uploads/woocommerce_uploads/2022/06/AI-DECISION-MAKING-AND-THE-COURTS_Report_V5-2022-06-20-1lzkls.pdf> last accessed 20 March 2024; Colleen Chien et al, 'How Generative AI Can Help Address the Access to Justice Gap Through the Courts' (4 January 2024) <https://papers.ssrn.com/abstract = 4683309> last accessed 21 March 2024; Cary Coglianese and Lavi M Ben Dor, 'AI in Adjudication and Administration' (2020) 86 Brooklyn L Rev 791; David Freeman Engstrom and Jonah B Gelbach, 'Legal Tech, Civil Procedure, and the Future of Adversarialism' (2020) 169 University of Pennsylvania L Rev 1001.

9 Jan Hatzius et al, 'The Potentially Large Effects of Artificial Intelligence on Economic Growth' (26 March 2023) <https://www.gspublishing.com/content/research/en/reports/2023/03/27/d64e052b-0f6e-45d7-967b-d7be35fabd16.html> last accessed 8 March 2024.

10 Statista, 'Legal Tech Market Size Worldwide 2021-2027' (*Statista*, 2022) <https://www.statista.com/statistics/1155852/legal-tech-market-revenue-worldwide/> last accessed 3 April 2024.

natural language processing (NLP) algorithms and large language models (LLMs), such as OpenAI's GPT and Google's Gemini. These developments have made it possible to automate even higher-order legal cognitions, opening new technological vistas and powering new ways to realize the vision of 'law as data'.[11]

Nowhere, however, does AI's promise feel more significant or more urgent than in its capacity to narrow the justice gap, whether by serving millions of self-represented litigants (SRLs) directly or by empowering courts to adjudicate the crush of cases in more efficient, more effective, and fairer ways. To begin, AI-based technologies portend a new era of more efficient and effective court administration. From screening complaints for compliance with procedural rules to triaging cases into appropriate procedural and case management tracks,[12] AI allows courts to do more with less, blunting decades of stagnating budgets even as dockets have swelled. Perhaps more importantly, the new generative AI systems hold enormous access-widening potential because of their ability to perform two critical tasks that are necessary to serve SRLs directly. First is *translation*: Generative AI tools are a leap forward in converting legalese into plain language[13]—an essential ingredient of any litigant-facing system. Just as significant, generative AI can perform *mapping*, parsing lay-narratives—an individual's plain-language explanation of a legal problem—and then mapping them to legal ontologies[14] and procedural steps. Given the rate at which generative AI technologies are advancing, it is almost impossible *not* to think about the potential for these tools to offer millions of SRLs, in an unmediated, 'direct-to-consumer' way, actionable advice on options and outcomes—the core of what lawyers do.

This chapter wades into this complex landscape and argues that whether courts can realize AI's enormous access-to-justice potential will be a vital, and even fundamental, question for the American civil justice system in the years to come. The answer to that question, however, is hardly obvious. For starters, a still-nascent academic literature around courts and AI is not much help. Optimistic accounts too often move directly to thought experiments involving robojudges and robolawyers,[15] while pessimistic accounts drill down on AI's well-known perils, emphasizing its ability to perpetuate error, bias, and inequity.[16] Only rarely have scholars begun teasing out the numerous

[11] Michael A Livermore et al, 'Law Search in the Age of the Algorithm' (2020) 2020 Michigan State L Rev 1183, 2019–20.

[12] Joint Technology Committee, 'Introduction to AI for Courts (Version 2.0)' (National Center for State Courts 2024) <https://www.ncsc.org/__data/assets/pdf_file/0027/98910/JTC-AI-paper-update-3.5.24.pdf> last accessed 29 April 2024; National Center for State Courts, 'Impact of AI in the Courts (Webinar)' (19 October 2023) <https://vimeo.com/875960451> last accessed 5 May 2024.

[13] Colleen Chien and Miriam Kim, 'Generative AI and Legal Aid: Results from a Field Study and 100 Use Cases to Bridge the Access to Justice Gap' (14 March 2024) <https://papers.ssrn.com/abstract = 4733061> last accessed 21 March 2024; Aubrie Souza and Zach Zarnow, 'Court Chatbots' (National Center for State Courts 2024) <https://www.ncsc.org/__data/assets/pdf_file/0032/97187/Court-Chatbots.pdf> last accessed 22 May 2024.

[14] Hannes Westermann et al, 'Bridging the Gap: Mapping Layperson Narratives to Legal Issues with Language Models', *Proceedings of the 6th Workshop on Automated Semantic Analysis of Information in Legal Text co-located with the 19th International Conference on Artificial Intelligence and Law (ICAIL 2023), Braga, Portugal* (2023) <https://ceur-ws.org/Vol-3441/paper5.pdf> last accessed 24 May 2024.

[15] Benjamin Minhao Chen, Alexander Stremitzer, and Kevin Tobia, 'Having Your Day in Robot Court' (2022) 36 Harvard Journal of Law & Technology (Harvard JOLT) 127; Tania Sourdin, 'Judges, Technology and Artificial Intelligence: The Artificial Judge', *Judges, Technology and Artificial Intelligence* (Edward Elgar Publishing 2021); Eugene Volokh, 'Chief Justice Robots' (2018) 68 Duke LJ 1135.

[16] Bennett Moses et al (n 8) 30–40.

barriers, both technical and non-technical, that can stymie court innovation in between these two extremes.[17]

Yet identifying and understanding these barriers is critically important as AI sweeps into courts. Organizations the world over have learned that there is a yawning gap between touting AI's potential and ground-level implementation of effective and trustworthy systems.[18] There is also good reason to believe that courts face particular versions of these more general challenges. Indeed, court efforts to harness AI will run up against the famously decentralized structure of American courts, their near-total lack of technical capacity, and, despite perpetual hype, AI's technical limitations, particularly when it comes to performing legal analytics and serving court users directly. Perhaps most fundamental of all, fully leveraging AI's potential may require American courts to revisit their core institutional commitments to neutrality, impartiality, and adversarialism,[19] particularly regarding their relationship and obligations to SRLs.[20] Rather than look ahead to an as-yet-uncertain future or dwell on AI's well-known perils, the pages that follow instead aim to enrich the debate about courthouse AI by identifying and then elaborating the key challenges that will shape AI's incorporation into American courts as the civil justice system enters a new chapter.

The rest of this chapter proceeds as follows. Setion B offers a mostly descriptive overview of 'courthouse AI'—the myriad ways AI is already plugging into court operations. Section C turns to challenges, aiming to capture the dense and often interrelated institutional, technical, and legal-cultural barriers that stand in the way of effective and trustworthy courthouse AI. Section D steps back and considers the wider implications of our analysis, tracing out some of the different futures that current efforts to institutionalize courthouse AI allow us to glimpse.

B. Courthouse AI: A Menu

This section offers a bird's-eye view of the myriad ways American courts have begun to incorporate AI into the administration of civil justice. We focus on six broad use cases that span the litigation life-cycle: (i) document management and docketing; (ii) procedural screening; (iii) case triage and docket analytics; (iv) litigant self-help; (v) ODR; and (vi) judicial decision support. However, any such overview comes with caveats. The rapid pace at which court-relevant AI technologies, applications,

[17] John Morison and Adam Harkens, 'Re-Engineering Justice? Robot Judges, Computerised Courts and (Semi) Automated Legal Decision-Making' (2019) 39 Legal Studies 618; Nicolas Vermeys, 'The Computer As the Court: How Will Artificial Intelligence Affect Judicial Processes?' in Xandra Kramer et al (eds), *New Pathways to Civil Justice in Europe* (Springer 2021).

[18] David Freeman Engstrom et al, 'Government by Algorithm: Artificial Intelligence in Federal Administrative Agencies' (2020) <https://law.stanford.edu/wp-content/uploads/2020/02/ACUS-AI-Report.pdf> last accessed 6 June 2024; Kurt Glaze et al, 'Artificial Intelligence for Adjudication: The Social Security Administration and AI Governance' in Justin B Bullock et al (eds), *The Oxford Handbook of AI Governance* (OUP 2022).

[19] Engstrom and Gelbach (n 8).

[20] Amy J Schmitz, 'Expanding Access to Remedies through E-Court Initiatives' (2019) 67 Buffalo L Rev 89; Richard Zorza, 'The Access to Justice "Sorting Hat": Towards a System of Triage and Intake That Maximizes Access and Outcomes' (2011) 89 Denver University L Rev 859.

and business models are emerging renders any review of the state-of-the-art a moving target.[21] Moreover, courthouse AI tools, as with 'legal tech' more generally, rely on multiple methodologies, from simple 'expert systems' and other forms of symbolic AI to the newest LLM-based generative AI systems, and they are intended for different users, including court administrators, judges, lawyers, and litigants themselves.[22] In a highly dynamic area, our aim is to offer a useful framework for describing the core administrative and judicial tasks where AI has either already begun to gain a foothold in court operations or holds significant potential to transform them.

1. Document management and docketing

AI tools can automate many administrative and clerical case processing tasks, turning court clerks into 'reviewers' rather than 'doers.' Courts have begun to adopt document analysis AI tools—for example, in Palm Beach County, Florida, the court uses AI-powered software to classify e-filed documents, extract information from tagged fields, and docket the information in the case management system.[23] After initial testing on three high-volume, low-risk case types, the Court expanded this automation to more complex cases. Currently, it automatically dockets nearly a third of all e-filed documents, with a lower reported error rate compared to human clerks.[24] The Court subjects 15 per cent of all filings to human review, whether they were manually or automatically docketed, thereby enabling iterative updates of the software to reduce automated docketing mistakes.[25] Courts can use similar technologies to resolve a host of data quality issues within case management systems as well as to automate other tasks, such as scheduling.[26]

2. Procedural screening and compliance

A second and related form of courthouse AI automates procedural screens and audits to achieve compliance with pleading or other legal requirements.[27] In particular, courts have begun to build into their filing and case management systems new automated document review capabilities that have long powered tools used elsewhere in legal tech.[28] They are deploying those new review capabilities to audit forms and pleadings to detect procedural non-compliance and data errors and facilitate their correction.[29] Procedural screening systems hold particular promise in high-volume

[21] Bennett Moses et al (n 8).
[22] Engstrom and Gelbach (n 8).
[23] Joint Technology Committee (n 12) 9–11.
[24] ibid.
[25] Joint Technology Committee (n 12).
[26] National Center for State Courts, 'Webinar' (n 12).
[27] David Freeman Engstrom, Daniel Bernal, and Aviv Caspi, 'Compliance Courts' [2024] Working Paper.
[28] Steve Lohr, 'A.I. Is Doing Legal Work. But It Won't Replace Lawyers, Yet.' *The New York Times* (19 March 2017) <https://www.nytimes.com/2017/03/19/technology/lawyers-artificial-intelligence.html> last accessed 8 December 2023.
[29] Daniel Willian Granado, 'Artificial Intelligence Applied To The Legal Proceedings: The Brazilian Experience' (2019) 5 Revue Internationale de droit des données et du numérique 103.

dockets, characterized by pro se litigants and significant adversarial asymmetries.[30] Many jurisdictions have imposed case-specific pleading rules requiring certifications or the attachment of affirmative evidence that would not otherwise be required under conventional pleading rules, such as a requirement that debt collection plaintiffs provide affirmative proof of the chain of title of the debt, or that eviction plaintiffs certify compliance with relevant parts of the housing code.[31] In high-volume dockets, procedural screening thus doubles for the lawyer-driven, adversarial contestation that would normally surface those problems but often do not[32]—a controversial shift in courts' role that we return to below. As AI's capabilities continue to advance, it is plausible that AI can be used for even more complex procedural screening tasks, such as automatically alerting the court to claims that appear to have run the statute of limitations or sit outside the court's jurisdiction.[33]

3. Case triage and docket analytics

A third emerging type of courthouse AI leverages advanced analytics to sort and sift cases in support of new case triage and docket analytics practices. The use of AI is particularly relevant to a family of innovations commonly referred to as the 'pathways' approach. In recent years, courts battling a crush of cases in high-volume dockets have begun to experiment with new approaches, allocating cases to tracks based on identifiable case features such as case complexity, litigant characteristics, and remedies sought.[34] Different cases and litigants, the thinking goes, bring varying needs that shape the type of tasks that courts are required to perform to administer them, and the associated judicial, staff, and facility resources they demand.

While 'differentiated case management' is hardly new,[35] its potential has been limited by the need for manual triage by overburdened court staff. AI can significantly increase the feasibility of implementing consistent and largescale triage practices. AI also paves the way for more nuanced, tailored triaging by increasing the number and type of variables that can be considered in the procedural allocation process, such as litigants' language proficiency or capacity to complete litigation tasks (e.g., finalizing pleading, presenting evidence).[36] Finally, automation raises the possibility of a

[30] Engstrom, Bernal, and Caspi (n 27); Jessica K Steinberg, 'Adversary Breakdown and Judicial Role Confusion in Small Case Civil Justice' (2016) 2016 Brigham Young U L Rev 899.

[31] DeAnna Baumle, 'State Laws Governing Debt Collection Lawsuits' (Center for Public Health Law Research, Temple University Beasley School of Law 2024) <https://phlr.org/sites/default/files/uploaded_images/PEW%20Debt%20Collection%20Policy%20Brief_Feb2024.pdf> last accessed 5 June 2024.

[32] Engstrom, Bernal, and Caspi (n 27); Peter A Holland, 'Junk Justice: A Statistical Analysis of 4,400 Lawsuits Filed by Debt Buyers' (2013) 26 Loyola Consumer L Rev 179; Claire Johnson Raba and Dalié Jiménez, 'Pay to Plead: Finding Unfairness and Abusive Practices in California Debt Collection Cases' (24 October 2023) <https://papers.ssrn.com/abstract = 4611756> last accessed 29 May 2024.

[33] Engstrom, Bernal, and Caspi (n 27).

[34] Thomas M Clarke and Victor E Flango, 'Case Triage for the 21st Century' (National Center for State Courts 2012) <https://ncfsc-web.squiz.cloud/__data/assets/pdf_file/0017/18161/clarke-and-flango.pdf> last accessed 2 June 2024; Carolyn Kuhl and William F Highberger, 'Toward Fairer, Quicker, Cheaper Litigation: A Unified Theory of Case Management' (2023) 107 Judicature 34; Zorza (n 20).

[35] Clarke and Flango (n 34) 146.

[36] Zorza (n 20) 878.

more dynamic allocation process that extends beyond initial filing, taking account of changes in case circumstances that might require reallocation to a different pathway. To cite just one example beyond the US context, Brazil's Supreme Federal Court uses AI-enabled triaging in the VICTOR Project to help allocate judicial attention in its severely congested docket. The system identifies whether appeals meet the admission criteria to the Court of having 'general repercussion,' and sorts those that do into the most common themes to inform their allocation to judges.[37]

Case triage is closely related to another AI-powered type of court tech: docket analytics. These tools can be applied to the court's historic case data to glean insights about processing patterns that can improve court administration. For example, docket analytics can inform the development and fine-tuning of case triage models by testing the efficacy of allocation decisions, adjusting the weights assigned to each factor, or detecting procedural pathways that fail to ensure procedural or distributive justice. Courts can also use AI to identify pro se cases that have not received sufficient judicial attention and then optimize the triage allocation system to increase the odds that cases will be heard by a judge.[38] Finally, AI-powered docket diagnostics can help courts discover and analyse problematic procedural patterns in order to address them with policy interventions. One court used AI to analyse 15 years of traffic ticket cases, which revealed that 'women were less likely to be cited than men for the same infraction and, when cited, were more likely to be offered a plea deal.'[39] Going forward, advanced AI may pave the way for other innovative forms of docket analytics, such as predicting the causes of default judgments and designing procedural innovations to reduce them.

4. Litigant self-help tools

Litigant self-help tools are a fourth emerging form of courthouse AI, with significant potential to remake the court's relationship to its users. Over the past decade, particularly post-COVID, courts have begun to incorporate AI-powered functionalities into their litigant self-help service offerings, including litigant portals, standalone guided interviews, chatbots, and document assembly tools.

Courts have launched chatbots to provide SRLs with an interactive 'live chat' experience. Examples include Arizona's 'Gavel' chatbot, Florida's 'SANDI', and Fulton County Georgia's 'Maggie Magistrate'.[40] For the moment, these tools remain rule-based AI systems that are able to answer only basic information queries, such as how to request a fee waiver, participate in a remote hearing, or ask for an interpreter. However, powered with new LLM-based capabilities, court chatbots will likely soon enable SRLs to engage with them in plain-language free-text questions.[41]

[37] Ricardo Vieira de Carvalho Fernandes et al, 'The VICTOR Project: Applying Artificial Intelligence to Brazils Supreme Federal Court', *Research Handbook on Big Data Law* (Edward Elgar Publishing 2021) Granado (n 28) 104.

[38] Ryan W Copus, 'Statistical Precedent: Allocating Judicial Attention' (2020) 73 Vanderbilt L Rev 605, 661.

[39] Joint Technology Committee (n 12) 11.

[40] Souza and Zarnow (n 13) 15–16, 19.

[41] ibid 7–9, 15–16, 19.

Guided interviews are software tools that elicit information from SRLs and use it to automatically generate a ready-to-file form or document. Packaging expert systems behind a user-friendly interface, guided interviews take users through a series of plain-language questions and answers intended to mimic an interactive session with a legal helper. The preprogramed workflow essentially automates basic legal reasoning.[42] The structured nature of the interaction, plain language, and click-through user interface can facilitate SRLs' effective participation, by hand-holding users through the process and preventing common procedural mistakes.[43] Though often designed by third-party technology providers such as LawHelp Interactive, Tyler Technologies, and A2J Author that use document automation software such as HotDocs, Docassemble, and Gavel,[44] court-hosted document assembly tools are an increasingly pervasive part of court websites and portals.[45]

Here, too, recent advances in LLMs hold great potential to support SRLs by improving the interactivity of chatbots and, as noted previously, allowing for plain-text narrative inquiries.[46] In the future, courts may launch a fully integrated digital courthouse front door that elicits from a court user a plain-language description of a civil legal problem and then provides a mix of legal information, referrals to appropriate legal help, and routing to needed document preparation and electronic filing services.

5. ODR and Next-Gen ODR

Closely related to self-help tools yet distinct in important ways are ODR platforms. Pioneered by e-commerce giants eBay and PayPal to resolve disputes by platform users,[47] ODR platforms have since spread to courts and tribunals as a means to increase both access to justice and efficiency in public dispute processing.[48] Currently, most court-connected ODR systems in US state courts are part legal-help desk and part bargaining space.[49] They offer litigants the option to explore the issues in dispute and consider settlement options through a structured, asynchronous, text-based

[42] Michael Legg and Felicity Bell, 'Artificial Intelligence and the Legal Profession: Becoming the AI-Enhanced Lawyer' (2019) 38 U Tasmania L Rev 34, 39.

[43] Filing Fairness Project, 'Filing Fairness Toolkit: Simplifying Court Filing for All' (2023) <https://filingfairnessproject.law.stanford.edu/wp-content/uploads/2023/11/SLS_FilingFairnessProject_FF.pdf> last accessed 19 May 2024; Ayelet Sela, 'Streamlining Justice: How Online Courts Can Resolve the Challenges of Pro Se Litigation' (2016) 26 Cornell JL & Public Policy 331; Ayelet Sela, 'E-Nudging Justice: The Role of Digital Choice Architecture in Online Courts' (2019) 2019 Journal of Dispute Resolution 127.

[44] Quinten Steenhuis and David Colarusso, 'Digital Curb Cuts: Towards an Inclusive Open Forms Ecosystem COVID & the Practice of Law: Impacts of Legal Technology Symposium Issue' (2020) 54 Akron L Rev 773, 776–85.

[45] Filing Fairness Project (n 43).

[46] Souza and Zarnow (n 13); Westermann et al (n 14).

[47] Colin Rule, 'Making Peace on eBay: Resolving Disputes in the World's Largest Marketplace' (2008) Fall 2008 ACResolution Magazine 8.

[48] Maximilian A Bulinski and JJ Prescott, 'Online Case Resolution Systems: Enhancing Access, Fairness, Accuracy, and Efficiency' (2016) 21 Michigan Journal of Race & Law 205; Schmitz (n 20); Sela, 'Streamlining Justice' (n 43).

[49] Engstrom and Vogt (n 1) 183.

negotiation process, with some systems providing the option of a human mediator via the platform.[50]

Currently, US state courts provide litigants only limited court-connected ODR options in a discrete set of case types, including landlord-tenant, family and custody, debt collection, limited and unlimited civil disputes, and small claims.[51] However, the number of ODR programs in American courts grew significantly during and after COVID—a trend that is likely to continue.[52] Moreover, much of the ODR offered in US courts is a standalone, largely voluntary procedural component, a design choice that seems to have contributed to the low uptake of ODR.[53] Instituting better 'traffic rules'[54] to determine which cases can or must go to ODR will increase procedural certainty and potentially also its uptake.

In their current guise, most court-connected ODR platforms do not take full advantage of advanced forms of AI, using only expert system-based issue diagnosis, pleading, and procedural navigation via guided interviews. However, with further advances in AI, courts may be able to do more.[55] Private ODR systems have long demonstrated the potential of using AI to help disputants refine preferences, apply applicable rules, develop negotiation strategies, calculate trade-offs, generate resolution options, and even determine the final outcome.[56] As discussed below, American courts may not be able to offer all these functionalities without first amending legal service regulations and moving case processing into a fully integrated digital court platform. However, it is possible to think of a future in which they support at least some of them, bringing significant benefits to access to justice and court administration. For instance, commentators have proposed various ways in which fully digital courts could combine advanced docket analytics, triage, dispute resolution, and processing capabilities into a single, remade package.[57] With robust analytics and access to past case data on both the ODR platform and adjudicatory proceedings, advanced systems can even present disputants with predictive analytics pertaining to various aspects of their

[50] Shack and Shestowsky (n 2).

[51] Deno Himonas, 'Utah's Online Dispute Resolution Program Transcripts' (2017) 122 Dickinson L Rev [i]; Tyler Technologies, 'Online Dispute Resolution: Empower Citizens to Resolve Their Own Disputes Online, Anywhere, Anytime—With Proven Technology' <https://www.tylertech.com/Portals/0/OpenContent/Files/4080/Modria-Brochure.pdf>; Mentovich, Prescott, and Rabinovich-Einy (n 2).

[52] Engstrom and Vogt (n 1) 171.

[53] Renee Danser et al, 'Online Dispute Resolution of Low-Level Court Proceedings: Two Broken Field Experiments, One Unexpected Result' (4 February 2023) <https://papers.ssrn.com/abstract = 4375081> last accessed 24 October 2023; Donna Shestowsky and Jennifer Shack, 'Online Dispute Resolution for Debt and Small Claims Cases: A Report on a Pilot Program in a Justice of the Peace Court in Collin County, Texas'.

[54] David Freeman Engstrom, 'Digital Civil Procedure Symposium: "Civil Procedure, Judicial Administration, and the Future of the Field: A Festschrift in Honor of Professor Stephen B Burbank"' (2021) 23 U Penn J of Constit L 2178, 2196.

[55] JJ Prescott, 'Using ODR Platforms to Level the Playing Field: Improving Pro Se Litigation through ODR Design' in David Freeman Engstrom (ed), *Legal Tech and the Future of Civil Justice* (CUP 2023).

[56] Ayelet Sela, 'Can Computers Be Fair: How Automated and Human-Powered Online Dispute Resolution Affect Procedural Justice in Mediation and Arbitration' (2018) 33 Ohio State J on Dispute Resolution 91, 100.

[57] M Ethan Katsh and Orna Rabinovich-Einy, *Digital Justice: Technology and the Internet of Disputes* (OUP 2017) 36–38, 46; Orna Rabinovich-Einy, 'The Past, Present, and Future of Online Dispute Resolution' (2021) 74 CLP 125; John Zeleznikow, 'Can Artificial Intelligence and Online Dispute Resolution Enhance Efficiency and Effectiveness in Courts Academic Articles' (2017) 8 Intl J for Court Administration 30.

case, including a prediction as to how similar bargaining parties settled their cases and what would be the expected outcome in court if the case were litigated all the way to a judgment.[58] We return to these possibilities, and their collision with legal and court-cultural norms, below.

6. Judge work product tools

A final type of courthouse AI comprises tools that support the work of judges. Early versions of these tools provided algorithmic decision support—for instance, criminal risk assessment tools, such as COMPAS, that model risk factors of an arrestee or defendant and inform judicial decisions on bail, sentencing, and parole.[59] More recently, advancements in analytics, NLP, and LLMs have created new avenues for using AI to support a wider variety of judicial tasks. Many of the underlying applications are already in use by lawyers, who drive the market for litigation technology with significant investments.[60]

Judicial AI has begun to take several forms. The quality of automated legal content summarization has improved tremendously over the past few years,[61] enabling judges to summarize case materials such as briefs and exhibits. Another clear use case is legal research. Innovations in data analytics and NLP have enabled new techniques for discovering relevant legal materials and synthesizing them—a core chambers task. The transformation of legal research with AI is facilitated by the incorporation of these tools in the product suite of incumbents such as LexisNexis and Thomson Reuters (Westlaw)—through a series of start-up acquisitions. These revamped products enable users to discover legal materials through 'conversational search' (chat); summarize and analyse both corralled legal materials and external documents that were loaded into the platforms; generate legal memos and documents; and perform legal analytics to synthesize trends relating to previous cases, judges, parties, and areas of law.[62]

AI-powered document analysis capabilities can assist judges in core judicial tasks such as evaluating pleadings, identifying questions for oral argument, and informing decision-making. For example, AI-powered tools can review briefs, reporting on questionable cited caselaw and identifying caselaw or even arguments that were omitted.[63] LLMs can also provide judges a running start in drafting opinions, and

[58] Engstrom and Vogt (n 1) 100, 184; Zeleznikow (n 57) 34, 37.

[59] Julia Dressel and Hany Farid, 'The Accuracy, Fairness, and Limits of Predicting Recidivism' (2018) 4 Science Advances eaao5580; Morison and Harkens (n 17) 625–26.

[60] Engstrom and Gelbach (n 8); Megan Ma et al, 'Generative AI Legal Landscape 2024' (*Stanford Law School*, 6 March 2024) <https://law.stanford.edu/publications/generative-ai-legal-landscape-2024-2/> last accessed 3 April 2024.

[61] Huihui Xu and Kevin Ashley, 'A Question-Answering Approach to Evaluating Legal Summaries', *Legal Knowledge and Information Systems* (IOS Press 2023) <https://ebooks.iospress.nl/doi/10.3233/FAIA230977> last accessed 5 June 2024.

[62] Ethan Beberness, 'Inside Lexis+ AI: LexisNexis' Latest Research Tool' [2024] *Above the Law* <https://abovethelaw.com/2024/01/inside-lexis-ai-lexisnexis-latest-research-tool/> last accessed 5 June 2024; Rhys Dipshan, 'Lex Machina Launches Litigation Footprint, Tripling Its Legal Analytics Coverage' [2024] *Law.com* <https://www.law.com/legaltechnews/2024/03/20/lex-machina-launches-litigation-footprint-tripling-its-legal-analytics-coverage/> last accessed 5 June 2024.

[63] Engstrom and Vogt (n 1) 200–01.

further advances in analytics will make possible tools that not only draft but also propose case or motion decisions themselves.[64] For example, some litigation analytics services claim they can predict whether certain motions will be granted or denied with 85 per cent accuracy.[65] However, as we discuss below, many obstacles stand in the way, particularly norms of judicial independence and concerns about how software might shape the ultimate work product of a judge who uses (and supervises) it.

Outside the US, courts are experimenting with implementing these and other AI-powered decisional tools. So are mass adjudicatory agencies, such as the Social Security Administration.[66] China has probably gone the furthest in its adoption of court AI. The 'smart courts' initiative enables courts to experiment with integrating AI into adjudication in a variety of ways, including by using software that 'reviews evidence, suggests outcomes, checks the consistency of judgments, and makes recommendations on how to decide cases'.[67] One particularly interesting application in Chinese courts alerts judges when their judgment falls outside the program's predicted range of case outcomes.[68] In addition to overcoming normative barriers, the 'smart courts' initiative has been made possible by making large amounts of court data publicly available, including court decisions, court work reports, and live-streamed hearings.[69]

C. Barriers to Courthouse AI

Can courts deliver on the promise of section B's catalogue of use cases? This section sketches the mix of institutional, technical, and legal-cultural challenges that stand in the way of robust courthouse AI. We treat four such challenges. The first is institutional: the American commitment to federalism has wrought an inter- and intra-jurisdictional patchwork of technology and data infrastructures that deprives American courts of the scale and standardization needed to build truly potent courthouse AI. The second and third are technical limits: American courts, like so many courts elsewhere, lack the technical capacity needed to develop or oversee new AI-based tools, and, in any event, even powerful new forms of generative AI may not be powerful *enough* to perform subtle adjudicatory tasks or serve millions of SRLs in reliable and user-friendly ways. The fourth is a mix of legal and cultural: Many promising forms of courthouse AI will run up against the legal prohibition on unauthorized practice of law, or UPL, which applies to courthouse personnel as much as to other legal services providers, as well as more diffuse, but no less formidable, norms around neutrality and impartiality.

[64] Chien et al (n 8) 9.

[65] Sarah Martinson, 'Quinn Emanuel Adopts AI Litigation Analytics Tool Pre/Dicta' [2024] *Law360* <https://www.law360.com/pulse/articles/1836960/quinn-emanuel-adopts-ai-litigation-analytics-tool-pre-dicta> last accessed 5 June 2024.

[66] Engstrom et al (n 18); Glaze et al (n 18).

[67] Rachel E Stern et al, 'Automating Fairness? Artificial Intelligence in the Chinese Courts' (2020) 59 Columbia J Transnat L 515, 518, 525–27.

[68] ibid 542.

[69] ibid 521–24.

1. Court data and the patchwork challenge

A significant challenge for courthouse AI is access to sufficiently large quantities of data to satisfy the big data needs of machine learning algorithms. Despite recent digitalization efforts, court data have always been, relatively speaking, 'small data' compared to the internet-scale data that has driven much of the AI revolution.[70] Two underlying features of American courts contribute to courthouse AI's big data challenge: an *inter*-jurisdictional patchwork of technology systems and data infrastructures that results from America's distinctive approach to federalism; and an *intra*-jurisdictional patchwork of disconnected data systems, born of the ad hoc, incremental, and procurement-driven nature of much recent court digitalization.

The inter-jurisdictional challenge is the easier of the two patchwork problems to grasp. When one looks across the roughly 15,000 local court jurisdictions in the US, one sees a patchwork of technology systems and data infrastructures, not to mention differences in procedural and substantive law.[71] The resulting technological and legal Babel sharply limits the amount of usable data available to power courthouse AI. A popular conception is that courts are data monopolists that sit atop mountains of data. The reality is starkly different. Variation in available claims and defences, the procedures used to adjudicate them, and differences in the basic data fields that populate case management systems create an unusable morass of data. This feature of the American legal system limits AI architects' ability to aggregate data from different courts to create data pools that can support data-hungry AI applications.[72]

In principle, many courts, particularly medium-to-large municipal ones, could make effective use of their own local data for at least some forms of courthouse AI. After all, each court has a repository of structured data and a curated and ever-growing corpus of case documents. Even small-scale but high-quality data can be useful for some AI training purposes.[73] In reality, however, the usability of these data is further limited by what is often an intra-jurisdictional patchwork of data infrastructures.[74] The result is that court data are notoriously 'incomplete, inaccurate, dirty, and disorganized,'[75] rendering courts a 'data- and information-poor environment'.[76]

[70] Engstrom and Vogt (n 1) 191; Joint Technology Committee, 'Big Data: What State Courts Should Know' (National Center for State Courts 2014) <https://www.ncsc.org/__data/assets/pdf_file/0028/17938/big-data-1-0-1-23-2015-final.pdf>; AD (Dory) Reiling, 'Courts and Artificial Intelligence' (2020) 11 8, 8; Vermeys (n 17) 65–66.

[71] Coglianese and Dor (n 8) 794.

[72] David Colarusso and Erika J Rickard, 'Speaking the Same Language: Data Standards and Disruptive Technologies in the Administration of Justice' (2017) 50 Suffolk U L Rev 387; Engstrom and Vogt (n 1).

[73] Joint Technology Committee (n 70).

[74] Charlotte S Alexander and Mohammad Javad Feizollahi, 'On Dragons, Caves, Teeth, and Claws: Legal Analytics and the Problem of Court Data Access', *Computational Legal Studies* (Edward Elgar Publishing 2020); Claire Johnson Raba, 'Low-Income Litigants in the Sandbox: Court Record Data and the Legal Technology A2J Market' (24 February 2022) <https://papers.ssrn.com/abstract = 4069023> last accessed 16 April 2024.

[75] Tanina Rostain and Amy O'Hara, 'The Civil Justice Data Gap' in David Freeman Engstrom (ed), *Legal Tech and the Future of Civil Justice* (CUP 2023) 370.

[76] Charlotte S Alexander and Lauren Sudeall, 'Creating a People-First Court Data Framework' (2023) 58 Harvard Civil Rights-Civil Liberties L Rev 731, 737.

While there are many causes of this problem, perhaps the most salient is that many US courts do not have a programmatic data collection and data governance strategy to ensure their data are accurate, reliable, and usable.[77] Instead, court data collection tends to be operational, built around case management needs, rather than systematic and analytics oriented. In most courts, surprisingly little effort is devoted to achieving even basic trackability that connects court processes or programs, including sources of legal help, to case outcomes. This problem has been exacerbated as courts have digitalized, typically by incrementally grafting new applications onto existing legacy systems and business practices via an ad hoc and procurement-driven process.[78] As a result, even within a given court, many courts are a patchwork of multiple, disconnected systems that track and store data in inconsistent ways. Worse, even courts that have integrated their core e-filing and case management systems may still employ stand-alone self-help systems such as chatbots,[79] electronic document automation tools,[80] ODR platforms,[81] and systems for remote hearings.[82] The lack of data harmonization even within jurisdictions limits courts' ability to pursue data-driven innovations, including courthouse AI.

To overcome both versions of the patchwork problem, courts seeking to build robust courthouse AI must commit to comprehensive data standardization.[83] A first step in this direction is the National Center for State Courts' call for the adoption of 'National Open Court Data Standards (NODS)'.[84] Some states have followed suit with data-standards projects of their own.[85] These standards set rules by which court data are described and recorded to ensure consistency and facilitate data comparisons across courts.[86] However, NODS is not enough to solve the dual patchwork problem, as it is limited both in its scope and rate of adoption. NODS covers only select system data features that serve research and reporting purposes, and, at last count, only a handful of courts had adopted the standards.[87] Even widespread adoption would be, at best, a partial solution, as the legal Babel created by American federalism—variation in substantive and procedural law—would remain.

77 Courts Statistics Project CSP, 'Data Governance Policy Guide' (National Center for State Courts 2019) <https://www.courtstatistics.org/__data/assets/pdf_file/0031/23899/data-governance-final.pdf> last accessed 20 May 2024.

78 Colarusso and Rickard (n 72) 402.

79 Souza and Zarnow (n 13).

80 Filing Fairness Project (n 43); Steenhuis and Colarusso (n 44).

81 David Allen Larson, 'Designing and Implementing a State Court ODR System: From Disappointment to Celebration' (2019) 2019 Journal of Dispute Resolution 77; JJ Prescott, 'Using ODR Platforms to Level the Playing Field: Improving Pro Se Litigation through ODR Design' in David Freeman Engstrom (ed), *Legal Tech and the Future of Civil Justice* (CUP 2023); Schmitz (n 20).

82 National Center for State Courts, 'Remote Proceeding Toolkit' (2024) <https://www.ncsc.org/__data/assets/pdf_file/0027/82377/Remote-Proceeding-Toolkit-Final.pdf>.

83 Colarusso and Rickard (n 70); Engstrom and Vogt (n 1); Filing Fairness Project (n 43).

84 National Center for State Courts, 'National Open Court Data Standards (NODS' (2020) <https://www.ncsc.org/__data/assets/pdf_file/0014/34025/NODS-User-Guide.pdf> last accessed 30 May 2024.

85 Judicial Council of California, 'Tactical Plan for Technology—2023–2024' (2023) https://www.courts.ca.gov/documents/jctc-Court-Technology-Tactical-Plan.pdf last accessed 5 June 2024.

86 ibid.

87 National Center for State Courts, 'Trends in State Courts 2022' (2022) 106 <https://www.ncsc.org/__data/assets/pdf_file/0024/80358/Trends-2022.pdf> last accessed 30 May 2024.

2. The problem of immature AI

A second salient problem facing courthouse AI may seem counter-intuitive in the current era of AI hype and reports of human-level performance of LLMs on various tasks.[88] Despite the steady drumbeat of claims about the latest AI advance, a critically important question hangs over all of legal tech, whether court-hosted, lawyer-driven, or consumer-directed: Just how good can new AI-powered legal-tech tools get, and what will it take to make them truly effective and reliable?

Answering questions about AI's technical trajectory is a risky business. AI's capabilities are rapidly evolving and will surely remain so. One study that explored the ability of Open AI's GPT models to take the American Uniform Bar Examination found that GPT-4's performance increased by 26 per cent compared to GPT-3.5, demonstrating the swift advancements in LLM capabilities.[89] Moreover, evaluating the quality of AI in the legal domain, perhaps more so than other domains, requires accounting for the particular legal area, task, user, and AI technology being deployed[90] and the development of tailored evaluation benchmarks.[91] In the legal domain, it is particularly important to account for the risk level of tasks and for the expertise of the user. Compared to SRLs, lawyers and judges are arguably better-positioned to identify and mitigate instances of error-prone AI performance on legal tasks.

Two types of AI quality challenges are most relevant to the future of courthouse AI. First is the accuracy of LLM-based legal question-answer (Q/A) applications and drafting tools that provide a wide array of legal information and even advice to court users. Chief among the concerns is that LLM-powered tools are prone to 'hallucinations'—instances where generative AI tools present false, fabricated, inaccurate, or biased responses to prompts, often with misleading confidence.[92] The study of hallucinations in legal contexts is still in its infancy. The most rigorous study to date of legal Q/A settings suggests that hallucinations are alarmingly prevalent among general LLM-powered tools, occurring between 69 and 88 per cent of the time, depending on the tool used.[93] Performance was worse in local legal settings, as opposed to, say, US

[88] Ray Perrault and Jack Clark, 'Artificial Intelligence Index Report 2024' (Stanford University Human-Centered Artifical Intelligence 2024) 3, 85–89 <https://policycommons.net/artifacts/12089781/hai_ai-index-report-2024/12983534/> last accessed 6 June 2024.

[89] Daniel Martin Katz et al, 'GPT-4 Passes the Bar Exam' (15 March 2023) <https://papers.ssrn.com/abstract = 4389233.> last accessed 15 April 2024.

[90] Margaret Hagan, 'Towards Human-Centered Standards for Legal Help AI' (25 September 2023) <https://papers.ssrn.com/abstract = 4582745> last accessed 2 June 2024; Sayash Kapoor, Peter Henderson and Arvind Narayanan, 'Promises and Pitfalls of Artificial Intelligence for Legal Applications' (2024) 2 Journal of Cross-disciplinary Research in Computational Law <https://journalcrcl.org/crcl/article/view/62> last accessed 21 May 2024.

[91] Rohan Bhambhoria et al, 'Evaluating AI for Law: Bridging the Gap with Open-Source Solutions' (arXiv, 18 April 2024) <http://arxiv.org/abs/2404.12349> last accessed 4 May 2024; Matthew Dahl et al, 'Large Legal Fictions: Profiling Legal Hallucinations in Large Language Models' (arXiv, 2 January 2024) <http://arxiv.org/abs/2401.01301> last accessed 3 April 2024.

[92] Bhambhoria et al (n 91); Chien et al (n 8); Dahl et al (n 91).

[93] Dahl et al (n 91).

Supreme Court case law,[94] a clear problem for tools that seek to serve SRLs in high-volume dockets such as eviction or debt. Moreover, a recent study found that even the bespoke legal AI tools of LexisNexis and Thomson Reuters (Westlaw) still produce incomplete information and hallucinate at an alarming rate.[95] Finally, the risks for SRLs are further exacerbated by the sensitivity of LLMs' performance in Q/A tasks to the wording of questions (prompts), especially when they involve reasoning,[96] since SRLs are likely less skilled than legal professionals at legal 'prompt engineering'.[97]

Quality concerns also dog case-outcome prediction engines. The ability to predict case outcomes is the holy grail of legal tech, as it is a central component of lawyering. It is also the aspirational heart of key parts of the courthouse AI toolkit, including judicial decision support systems and self-help tools, from simple court portals to ODR 2.0. However, there is good reason to doubt whether AI-based case-outcome prediction will function at anything like human levels for the foreseeable future. Legal analytics are dizzyingly complex. As anyone with legal training knows, legal case outcomes turn on a mix of textual, analogical, evidentiary, and teleological arguments. Projecting case outcomes is a uniquely difficult prediction task that tests even the most advanced generative AI systems. The lack of consistent structure in court pleadings, papers, and especially judicial opinions adds further methodological complexities,[98] and bias concerns remain ever-present.[99] For all these reasons, case-outcome prediction, at least for the moment, can reliably replace human judgment only in narrow, technocratic, and self-contained areas of law, substantially limiting the reach of courthouse AI.

To be sure, the challenges of immature AI do not afflict all forms of courthouse AI equally. As section B noted, important swathes of courthouse AI will be devoted, not to direct-to-consumer applications, but to screening tools that automate procedural compliance or triage tools that can route cases to right-sized procedural and case management tracks. Such tools hold substantial potential to increase access to justice by more effectively allocating scarce court resources among tasks. But immature AI, and the distinct possibility that even significant further advances in generative AI may not suffice to support robust, direct-to-consumer tools, may drain courthouse AI of much of its access-to-justice potential. Even generative AI's vaunted capabilities leave significant questions about whether AI-based tools can ever serve more than a fraction of the justice needs of the millions of people who currently go without meaningful legal help.

[94] ibid.

[95] Varun Magesh et al, 'Hallucination-Free? Assessing the Reliability of Leading AI Legal Research Tools' (6 June 2024) <https://dho.stanford.edu/wp-content/uploads/Legal_RAG_Hallucinations.pdf> last accessed 6 June 2024.

[96] Perrault and Clark (n 88) 148–50.

[97] Noam Kolt, 'Predicting Consumer Contracts' (2022) 37 Berkeley Technology LJ 71, 104, 107–09.

[98] Nikolaos Aletras et al, 'Predicting Judicial Decisions of the European Court of Human Rights: A Natural Language Processing Perspective' (2016) 2 PeerJ Computer Science e93; Frank Pasquale and Glyn Cashwell, 'Prediction, Persuasion, and the Jurisprudence of Behaviourism Artificial Intelligence, Technology, and the Law' (2018) 68 University of Toronto LJ 63.

[99] Sandra G Mayson, 'Bias in, Bias Out' (2018) 128 Yale LJ 2218; Morison and Harkens (n 17).

3. The problem of court technical capacity

The problem of insufficient court technical capacity picks up where weak AI leaves off. Court information technology (IT) departments lack both the bandwidth and know-how to implement and scrutinize cutting edge AI-powered solutions. Many courts *do* have robust IT departments; even smaller court systems generally have in-house technologists nowadays. But they already face a dizzying array of demands managing court IT systems, integrating with third-party systems, and managing (and reporting on) data from these systems (see section A). The design and oversight of useful and trustworthy AI tools that can supplement the front and back end of court operations quickly stretches court technical capacity to the breaking point. Indeed, staff availability for integration and maintenance of technology initiatives and the costs of hiring and training personnel are a frequently cited consideration in court technology planning.[100]

Due to pervasive limits on the bandwidth, expertise, and budget of court IT departments, much of the technological infrastructure powering courts is sourced from private vendors via procurement. But even then, few vendor solutions are set-it-and-forget-it: internal court IT staff usually need to directly service them or work with the vendor to do so.

Generative AI raises particular problems here. Some off-the-shelf tools, whether open source or vendor-sourced, might suffice for specific tasks, such as summarization and text simplification.[101] But many of the generative AI-based research, analysis, simplification, and wayfinding tools that courts might deploy for direct-to-consumer use will require in-house work to customize.[102] Specifically, court staff will need to identify and curate jurisdiction-specific rules, procedures, and information to build into out-of-the-box solutions. Then, courts will need to thoroughly test these systems, *especially* those that are consumer facing—yet another drain on already-stretched courts.

Finally, vetting AI vendors and their software solutions necessitates considerable in-house resources and expertise, accounting for an ever-expanding list of considerations, such as training data, security and compliance, privacy, and errors. As more options hit the market, the procurement process will become even more time-consuming.

4. Legal-cultural barriers

A final and formidable set of barriers stands in the way of court-hosted, AI-powered self-help tools: deeply embedded norms of court neutrality and impartiality, which sit in increasingly sharp tension with growing court efforts, both digital and

[100] Judicial Council of California (n 85).

[101] Chien and Kim (n 13).

[102] Bhambhoria et al (n 89); McKinsey & Company, 'How Generative AI Can Help Global Governments' (07 2023) <https://www.mckinsey.com/industries/public-sector/our-insights/unlocking-the-potential-of-generative-ai-three-key-questions-for-government-agencies> last accessed 15 April 2024.

non-digital, to provide assistance to millions of SRLs who must otherwise navigate the system alone.

Part of this tension arises from regulatory prohibitions on the unauthorized practice of law, or UPL. Those rules vary by jurisdiction, and they are also famously vague in their construction, but they are roughly united in prohibiting any form of legal help that crosses the line from generalized information to tailored advice.[103] Importantly, courts and court staff, no less than legal services providers out in the world, must be careful not to cross that line.[104]

UPL's prohibition on assistance that strays across the information/advice line plainly implicates new AI-based forms of legal help. Automated tools that courts might seek to deploy to help SRLs fill out forms must operate within the bounds of the *scrivener exception* to UPL. This exception is very strict, and even design decisions in the software development phase can spark an enforcement action, as evidenced by litigation involving LegalZoom, Upsolve, and other legal-tech providers.[105] While even relatively simple tech tools could benefit SRLs with tasks such as calculating filing deadlines and due dates or selecting the appropriate forms for their case type, in most state courts, such forms of assistance are also forbidden. Finally, UPL rules may place particular limits on new self-help applications powered by generative AI, draining them of much of their access-to-justice potential. After all, and as noted previously, generative AI's great access-to-justice promise is its ability to convert an SRL's plain-language description of a civil legal problem into tailored, actionable advice, bringing it directly within UPL's heartland.

The other source of tension between maintaining court neutrality and providing effective assistance to SRLs is not hard-edged UPL rules but rather more diffuse legal-cultural norms. The most relevant is a set of institutional scripts coded into courts' DNA that extend from the bedrock American commitment to adversarialism and the idea that justice is best advanced by a party-driven clash of proof before a passive, neutral decision-maker.[106] As a result, even were UPL rules to be relaxed to make room for more robust forms of court-hosted self-help tools, a diffuse, but no less powerful, set of norms around neutrality, impartiality, and adversarialism and the ingrained role orientation of judges and court staff might still stand in the way.

None of this, of course, is set in stone. Open questions abound as to where exactly UPL's information/advice line sits when it comes to digital self-help tools, which are too new to have produced anything approaching mature bodies of law or regulation.[107] Moreover, a movement is afoot throughout the US to relax UPL rules to make room for alternative legal services providers.[108] Liberalization would presumptively

[103] Benjamin H Barton, 'The Lawyer's Monopoly—What Goes and What Stays' (2013) 82 Fordham L Rev 3067; Bruce A Green, 'Should State Trial Courts Become Laboratories of UPL Reform?' (2024) 92 Fordham L Rev 1285.

[104] David Freeman Engstrom, 'Courthouse UPL' [2024] Working Paper.

[105] Benjamin H Barton and Deborah L Rhode, 'Access to Justice and Routine Legal Services: New Technologies Meet Bar Regulators' (2018) 70 Hastings LJ 955; *In re Peterson* [2022] US Bankruptcy Court, D Md Case 19-24045.

[106] Stephan Landsman, *The Adversary System: A Description and Defense* (American Enterprise Institute 1984) 2.

[107] Engstrom (n 104).

[108] Barton and Rhode (n 105); Green (n 103).

extend to courts and their staff as well. Court culture is also changeable—and, indeed, American courts have substantially shifted their orientation toward SRLs in recent decades in response to mounting concern about pro se litigants and access to justice. Court staff, in addition to performing traditional administrative duties, have been asked to deliver services directly to the public.[109] Judges, too, have been encouraged—or mandated, depending on one's read of the US Supreme Court's 2011 decision in *Turner v Rogers*[110]—to play a more active role in developing the factual record or eliciting legal claims and defences during hearings involving SRLs.[111]

Time will tell if further such shifts are in store, whether of the legal-regulatory or court-cultural sort. The success or failure of current efforts to move both will fundamentally shape the future of courthouse AI as the civil justice system enters it next chapter.

D. Implications for The Future of Courthouse AI

To this point, we have identified a formidable set of barriers that will profoundly shape, and may well stymie, courthouse AI. This section steps back and considers three wider implications of our analysis and how each will shape courthouse AI's trajectory into the future.

1. The Catch-22 of courthouse AI tools for SRLs in high-volume dockets

An initial implication spans two of the challenges outlined above: Courthouse AI faces a catch-22 born of the data challenges that result from the inter-jurisdictional patchwork problem and the limited capacities and heightened needs of SRLs.

On the one hand, high-volume dockets—the crush of debt collection actions, evictions, home foreclosures, and child support actions that overwhelm the American civil justice system—seem the most promising context in which to develop litigant-facing courthouse AI. In particular, these dockets, given their staggering volume, provide the largest data pool with which to power AI-based tools. Indeed, large, municipal courts, and even some medium-sized ones, may have sufficient data from high-volume dockets to train, validate, and iterate on tools, performing the ongoing task customization that is central to building effective and trustworthy forms of courthouse AI. By contrast, data quantity quickly thins in lower-volume dockets—for instance, more complex and varied commercial disputes—and, at the same time, the

[109] Carolyn Kuhl, 'What Can Reformers of Legal Services Learn from Court Efforts to Assist Self-Represented Litigants?' in David Freeman Engstrom and Nora Freeman Engstrom (eds), *Rethinking the Lawyer's Monopoly: Access to Justice and the Future of Legal Services* (CUP 2004).

[110] *Turner v Rogers, et al* [2011] US Supreme Court 10-10, 564 US 431.

[111] Anna E Carpenter, 'Active Judging and Access to Justice' (2017) 93 Notre Dame L Rev 647; John Greacen and Michael Houlberg, 'Ensuring the Right to Be Heard: Guidance for Trial Judges in Cases Involving Self-Represented Litigants' (IAALS 2019) <https://iaals.du.edu/sites/default/files/documents/publications/ensuring_the_right_to_be_heard_guidance_for_trial_judges.pdf> last accessed 6 June 2024.

jurisdictional patchwork of data standards and procedural and substantive law defeat collaborative efforts to pool data across courts.

On the other hand, it is precisely the data-rich, high-volume dockets where fully automated, unmediated, direct-to-consumer courthouse AI may prove *least* effective at meeting court users' needs. Many of the SRLs who disproportionately populate high-volume dockets have limited capacities, whether technical or otherwise,[112] sharply limiting their ability to use even relatively robust and user-friendly legal-tech tools. Other SRLs may be technically *capable* of using legal tech, but will still require substantial human hand-holding and assistance, at least in some parts of the process. As a result, litigant-facing, direct-to-consumer tools may only be able to reach a portion, and perhaps only a small portion, of SRLs facing civil legal problems.

These competing dynamics raise hard questions about where courts (and also policymakers, foundations, and academics who wish to ease access-to-justice concerns) should spend their limited real and political capital going forward. Should courts focus their energies on building litigant-facing forms of courthouse AI that serve court users directly? Or should courts instead focus on building technology that extends the reach of existing legal services providers and helpers, such as legal aid groups, in serving SRLs—what Tanina Rostain has called 'trusted intermediaries'?[113] While the answer may vary by case type, typical court user, and the types of tasks the AI tools are used for,[114] the harsh reality is that the catch-22 created by data availability and limited litigant capacity may place a ceiling on courthouse AI's ability to narrow the justice gap. Courthouse AI's future will depend on courts' ability to see where that is the case and where it is not.

2. Courts' make-or-buy choice

A second and related implication facing courts as they consider how best to leverage potent courthouse AI is whether they should develop new technology tools on their own (*create*); procure technology from third-party vendors and then incorporate it into the court's core systems (*integrate*); or foster a robust legal-tech ecosystem where third-party vendors can serve court stakeholders (*facilitate*). These options define the contours of the tech-forward courts' unique version of a 'make or buy' dilemma.[115]

On the one hand, courts can 'make' new legal services for SRLs by developing court-hosted versions of the digital self-help tools (and supporting backend services) catalogued previously. Much of this, as noted above, will involve transitioning courts' analogue self-help services into new digitalized forms, including chatbots and other interactive Q/A systems, form-filling and form-filing tools, and ODR, particularly the next-gen AI-fuelled ODR. When 'making' these services, courts are likely to *create* tools where their design is straightforward and requires limited technical capacities

[112] Hannah EM Lieberman and Paula Hannaford-Agor, 'Meeting the Challenges of High-Volume Civil Dockets' (National Center for State Courts 2016) 91 <https://www.ncsc.org/__data/assets/pdf_file/0027/25578/meeting-the-challenges.pdf> last accessed 22 May 2024.

[113] Tanina Rostain, 'Techno-Optimism & Access to the Legal System' (2019) 148 Daedalus 93, 93.

[114] Hagan (n 90); Kapoor, Henderson, and Narayanan (n 90).

[115] Engstrom and Vogt (n 1) 180.

(eg simple chatbots or document assembly tools relying on no-code software). Where more advanced technologies are involved, however, courts are more likely to *integrate* and customize technology developed by external vendors. This is certainly the case with LLM-powered tools. Enterprising courts may even combine some or all of these things in a fully integrated, end-to-end digital courthouse front door, where court users can come, input a plain-language description of a problem, and get back actionable information and advice, be routed to other appropriate forms of legal help, or access needed form-filling and e-filing tools. 'Make' describes well this chapter's focus on courthouse AI.

As an alternative, courts can, in effect, 'buy' assistance for SRLs from third-party legal services providers by *facilitating* the ability of those providers to access court data and connect to court technology systems. Such facilitation can take the form of providing APIs that permit legal tech providers to readily connect to court systems, adopting common data standards and technology integration protocols,[116] and lowering barriers to e-filing.[117] In other words, 'buy'-side measures focus on making it easier for third-party legal services providers to serve SRLs who currently go without meaningful legal assistance. The aim is to foster a robust legal-tech ecosystem that serves most or all segments of the market.

Neither 'make' nor 'buy' is without challenges. As already noted at length, innovative new forms of courthouse AI may be stymied by the inter- and intra-jurisdictional patchwork of technology systems and data infrastructures in a decentralized American system, courts' woeful lack of technical capacity, and the limits of even potent new forms of generative AI to serve most SRLs in an unmediated, direct-to-consumer way. Each of these barriers, we have argued, may place significant brakes on court-hosted forms of innovation and limit their impact.

'Buy' has plenty of challenges of its own. The patchwork of technology and data systems that limit the 'make' choice will also narrow courts' ability to foster a robust ecosystem of third-party legal-tech providers by defeating the scale those providers need to serve customers who may only need services once and have limited ability to pay for them.[118] The uniquely challenging market economics of serving moderate- and low-income Americans may simply be too much to support a truly robust marketplace of reduced-fee providers. Add to that the usual rules that say that only lawyers can practice law (UPL) and own (or capitalize) law firms (Rule 5.4)—and a robust legal-tech marketplace may simply not materialize, particularly in the part of the system where access concerns are most acute.[119]

That said, the deep challenges facing courthouse AI in US state courts may ultimately nudge a system already afflicted by substantial inertia toward 'buy' over 'make.' Cultural, technical, and, for some use cases, regulatory constraints may simply prove too powerful, leading courts to prefer facilitating third-party legal services rather than court-hosted ones. The future of courthouse AI, and its ability to narrow the justice

[116] Judicial Council of California (n 85).
[117] Filing Fairness Project (n 43).
[118] David Freeman Engstrom and Jess Lu, 'The Puzzle of Anemic "Legal Tech" and the Future of Legal Services' in David Freeman Engstrom and Nora Freeman Engstrom (eds), *Rethinking the Lawyer's Monopoly: Access to Justice and the Future of Legal Services* (CUP 2024).
[119] Barton and Rhode (n 105).

gap, will turn in significant part on the ability of courts to understand where 'buy' is the best or even, because of regulatory constraints, the *only* choice, and where it is merely the path of least resistance.

3. Half loaves and full loaves in courthouse AI

A third and final implication requires us to work outward and think more broadly about how the challenges facing courthouse AI might shape its future trajectory.

From the current vantage, at least two broad innovation paths seem possible. To this point, the path that many or even most courts have taken has been opportunistic and disconnected from process improvements. As with any technology, poorly architected courthouse AI can merely reinforce underlying process inefficiencies and injustices.[120] Automate a bad process, the saying goes, and you still have a bad process. The result has been a slow, crippling innovation process, with semi-functional court portals that are separated from document assembly tools that are separated from e-filing platforms that are separated from the hearings process. In most courts, including many that are considered highly innovative and forward-leaning, siloed and segmented innovations touching only one part of the process have mostly ruled the day. Half loaves abound.

A second path is more promising—a full loaf—but is also harder to achieve. It is perhaps best reflected in efforts such as British Columbia's Civil Resolution Tribunal (CRT), an end-to-end effort to rearchitect the civil adjudicatory process, with a fully integrated platform with a suite of self-help and alternative dispute resolution services embedded in it.[121] The CRT takes users through an asynchronous, text-based stepped workflow that hand-holds them through the entire court process. Users first engage in a guided interview—the 'Solution Explorer'—to diagnose and inform themselves about their legal issues. If they decide to pursue a claim with the tribunal, the details of their exploration are seamlessly transferred into a claim that is filed on the CRT platform. The parties can then exchange information and negotiate on the platform through a structured ODR process, and, if necessary, ask the help of a human case-officer in facilitating an agreement or preparing for a hearing. If no agreement is reached, the parties are directed to remote adjudication via written submissions, telephone, or videoconferencing. However, at the adjudicator's discretion, the hearing may take place in-person.[122] The integrated, end-to-end CRT model has spread to other courts, including England and Wales.[123]

Glimpsing these two paths reveals a crucial question that will overhang efforts to build courthouse AI: Should we be working within existing legal services delivery channels to leverage AI in improving access to law and justice? Or should we be 'reimagining' the future of justice,[124] reconstructing the legal system's architecture

[120] Drew Simshaw, 'Access to A.I. Justice: Avoiding an Inequitable Two-Tiered System of Legal Services' (2022) 24 Yale J L & Tech 150.

[121] Shannon Salter and Darin Thompson, 'Public-Centered Civil Justice Redesign: A Case Study of the British Columbia Civil Resolution Tribunal' (2016) 3 McGill J Disp Res 113.

[122] Sela, 'E-Nudging Justice' (n 43) 134–35.

[123] Pablo Cortes, 'The English Online Court' (2022) 9 Intl J Online Disp Res 138, 140.

[124] Richard Susskind, *Online Courts and the Future of Justice* (OUP 2021).

to leverage AI in ways that are not currently envisaged or allowed? And how might we redesign law and law practice to ensure that our systems can evolve alongside the evolving capabilities of AI and needs of the public?

While any public bureaucracy may already be heavily biased toward the first, half-loaf, risk-averse path, all is not lost. A wide range of concrete policy measures could help courts to overcome current barriers to AI adoption. As noted above, promising proposals include improving the accessibility of court data, bridging the gap between legal process design and digital process design, creating innovative regulatory structures for legal-tech applications, and developing new normative and governance models for the role that courts play in resolving these disputes. This chapter has sought to surface challenges, not to warn court leaders away from courthouse AI but rather to help stimulate a conversation about possible solutions.

E. Conclusion

American courts are confronting the many challenges of the access-to-justice crisis, particularly in high-volume dockets dominated by institutional plaintiffs and self-represented defendants. Increasingly sophisticated AI tools present a promising opportunity to reimagine both how courts function internally and how they deliver the most effective service to their users. From automating administrative tasks such as docketing and document management to introducing innovative self-help tools and ODR platforms, AI has the potential to alleviate burdens on both courts and litigants.

However, realizing this potential is far from straightforward. Courts must navigate significant technical, institutional, and legal-cultural barriers. The decentralized structure of American courts, the fragmented state of their technological infrastructure, and concerns about AI's maturity—especially in direct-to-consumer applications—pose significant hurdles. In addition, courts must grapple with the tension between providing meaningful assistance to litigants and adhering to the constraints of judicial neutrality and UPL rules.

Ultimately, the future of courthouse AI will depend on courts' ability to commit to fundamental procedural and technological innovation. While incremental improvements, such as automating administrative processes and language translation services, can yield immediate benefits, unlocking AI's full potential may require courts to rethink deeply entrenched norms and structures, taking bolder steps toward procedural innovation, upgrading and integration of technology systems, and standardization of data infrastructures. Simply automating existing court processes does not guarantee improved accessibility; courts ought to commit to user-centred design of new procedures and technological tools, while accounting for variations in the needs and capabilities of different users. Ongoing evaluation and oversight of new AI technologies—whether developed in-house or procured externally—will be crucial for courts to ensure these tools are effective and equitable.

What is clear is that AI is not a panacea for the access-to-justice crisis. While it offers significant promise, it cannot address broader systemic issues such as poverty, institutional distrust, and socioeconomic disparities. Even if the challenges outlined in this chapter are overcome, AI tools must be complemented by human support services, particularly for SRLs who have technological constraints. A human-in-the-loop approach can ensure that courthouse AI is accessible, understandable, and genuinely helpful and provides a vital alternative for those who may struggle to effectively utilize AI tools.

Like many other public institutions, American courts sit at a crossroads as access concerns mount and advanced AI sweeps into the legal system. This chapter has offered an account of the possibilities and the limits at that intersection. The choices courts make in the coming years will determine whether AI becomes a transformative force that narrows the justice gap or merely reinforces existing inequalities and inefficiencies.

Bibliography

Aletras N et al, 'Predicting Judicial Decisions of the European Court of Human Rights: A Natural Language Processing Perspective' (2016) 2 PeerJ Computer Science e93.

Alexander CS and Feizollahi MJ, 'On Dragons, Caves, Teeth, and Claws: Legal Analytics and the Problem of Court Data Access', *Computational Legal Studies* (Edward Elgar Publishing 2020) https://www.elgaronline.com/edcollchap/edcoll/9781788977449/9781788977449.00010.xml.

Alexander CS and Sudeall L, 'Creating a People-First Court Data Framework' (2023) 58 Harvard Civil Rights–Civil Liberties L Rev 731.

Barton BH, 'The Lawyer's Monopoly—What Goes and What Stays' (2013) 82 Fordham L Rev 3067.

Barton BH and Rhode DL, 'Access to Justice and Routine Legal Services: New Technologies Meet Bar Regulators' (2018) 70 Hastings LJ 955.

Baumle D, 'State Laws Governing Debt Collection Lawsuits' (Center for Public Health Law Research, Temple University Beasley School of Law 2024) <https://phlr.org/sites/default/files/uploaded_images/PEW%20Debt%20Collection%20Policy%20Brief_Feb2024.pdf>.

Beberness E, 'Inside Lexis+ AI: LexisNexis' Latest Research Tool' [2024] *Above the Law* <https://abovethelaw.com/2024/01/inside-lexis-ai-lexisnexis-latest-research-tool/>.

Bennett Moses L et al, 'AI Decision-Making and the Courts: A Guide for Judges, Tribunal Members and Court Administrators (2023 Update)' (2023) <https://aija.org.au/wp-content/uploads/woocommerce_uploads/2022/06/AI-DECISION-MAKING-AND-THE-COURTS_Report_V5-2022-06-20-1lzkls.pdf>.

Bhambhoria R et al, 'Evaluating AI for Law: Bridging the Gap with Open-Source Solutions' (arXiv, 18 April 2024) <http://arxiv.org/abs/2404.12349>.

Bulinski MA and Prescott JJ, 'Online Case Resolution Systems: Enhancing Access, Fairness, Accuracy, and Efficiency' (2016) 21 Michigan Journal of Race & Law 205.

Carpenter AE, 'Active Judging and Access to Justice' (2017) 93 Notre Dame L Rev 647.

Chen BM, Stremitzer A, and Tobia K, 'Having Your Day in Robot Court' (2022) 36 Harv J L & Tech (Harvard JOLT) 127.

Chien C et al, 'How Generative AI Can Help Address the Access to Justice Gap Through the Courts' (4 January 2024) <https://papers.ssrn.com/abstract = 4683309>.

Chien C and Kim M, 'Generative AI and Legal Aid: Results from a Field Study and 100 Use Cases to Bridge the Access to Justice Gap' (14 March 2024) <https://papers.ssrn.com/abstract = 4733061>.

Clarke TM and Flango VE., 'Case Triage for the 21st Century' (National Center for State Courts 2012) <https://ncfsc-web.squiz.cloud/__data/assets/pdf_file/0017/18161/clarke-and-flango.pdf> .

Coglianese C and Dor LMB, 'AI in Adjudication and Administration' (2020) 86 Brooklyn L Rev 791.

Colarusso D and Rickard EJ, 'Speaking the Same Language: Data Standards and Disruptive Technologies in the Administration of Justice' (2017) 50 Suffolk University L Rev 387.

Copus RW, 'Statistical Precedent: Allocating Judicial Attention' (2020) 73 Vanderbilt L Rev 605.

Cortés P, 'The English Online Court' (2022) 9 Intl J Online Disp Res 138

CSP CSP, 'Data Governance Policy Guide' (National Center for State Courts 2019) https://www.courtstatistics.org/__data/assets/pdf_file/0031/23899/data-governance-final.pdf.

Dahl M et al, 'Large Legal Fictions: Profiling Legal Hallucinations in Large Language Models' (arXiv, 2 January 2024) <http://arxiv.org/abs/2401.01301>.

Danser R et al, 'Online Dispute Resolution of Low-Level Court Proceedings: Two Broken Field Experiments, One Unexpected Result' (4 February 2023) <https://papers.ssrn.com/abstract = 4375081> accessed 24 October 2023.

Dipshan R, 'Lex Machina Launches Litigation Footprint, Tripling Its Legal Analytics Coverage' [2024] *Law.com* <https://www.law.com/legaltechnews/2024/03/20/lex-machina-launches-litigation-footprint-tripling-its-legal-analytics-coverage/>.

Dressel J and Farid H, 'The Accuracy, Fairness, and Limits of Predicting Recidivism' (2018) 4 Science Advances eaao5580.

Engstrom DF, 'Digital Civil Procedure Symposium: "Civil Procedure, Judicial Administration, and the Future of the Field: A Festschrift in Honor of Professor Stephen B. Burbank"' (2021) 23 U Penn J Constit L 2178.

Engstrom DF, 'Courthouse UPL' [2024] Working Paper.

Engstrom DF, 'Government by Algorithm: Artificial Intelligence in Federal Administrative Agencies' (2020) <https://law.stanford.edu/wp-content/uploads/2020/02/ACUS-AI-Report.pdf> .

Engstrom DF, Bernal D and Caspi A, 'Compliance Courts' [2024] Working Paper.

Engstrom DF and Gelbach JB, 'Legal Tech, Civil Procedure, and the Future of Adversarialism' (2020) 169 University of Pennsylvania L Rev 1001.

Engstrom DF and Lu J, 'The Puzzle of Anemic "Legal Tech" and the Future of Legal Services' in Engstrom DF and Engstrom NF (eds), *Rethinking the Lawyer's Monopoly: Access to Justice and the Future of Legal Services* (CUP 2024).

Engstrom DF and Vogt RJ, 'The New Judicial Governance: Courts, Data, and the Future of Civil Justice' (2023) 72 DePaul L Rev 171.

Fernandes RV de C et al, 'The VICTOR Project: Applying Artificial Intelligence to Brazils Supreme Federal Court', *Research Handbook on Big Data Law* (Edward Elgar Publishing 2021) <https://www.elgaronline.com/edcollchap/edcoll/9781788972819/9781788972819.00021.xml>

Filing Fairness Project, 'Filing Fairness Toolkit: Simplifying Court Filing for All' (2023) <https://filingfairnessproject.law.stanford.edu/wp-content/uploads/2023/11/SLS_FilingFairnessProject_FF.pdf>

Glaze K et al, 'Artificial Intelligence for Adjudication: The Social Security Administration and AI Governance' in Bullock JB et al (eds), *The Oxford Handbook of AI Governance* (OUP 2022)

Granado DW, 'Artificial Intelligence Applied To The Legal Proceedings: The Brazilian Experience' (2019) 5 Revue Internationale de droit des données et du numérique 103

Greacen J and Houlberg M, 'Ensuring the Right to Be Heard: Guidance for Trial Judges in Cases Involving Self-Represented Litigants' (IAALS 2019) <https://iaals.du.edu/sites/default/files/documents/publications/ensuring_the_right_to_be_heard_guidance_for_trial_judges.pdf>

Green BA, 'Should State Trial Courts Become Laboratories of UPL Reform?' (2024) 92 Fordham L Rev 1285

Hagan M, 'Towards Human-Centered Standards for Legal Help AI' (25 September 2023) <https://papers.ssrn.com/abstract = 4582745> accessed 2 June 2024

Hannaford-Agor P, Graves S, and Spacek Miller S, 'The Landscape of Civil Litigation in State Courts' (National Center for State Courts 2015) <https://www.ncsc.org/__data/assets/pdf_file/0020/13376/civiljusticereport-2015.pdf> .

Hatzius J et al, 'The Potentially Large Effects of Artificial Intelligence on Economic Growth' (26 March 2023) <https://www.gspublishing.com/content/research/en/reports/2023/03/27/d64e052b-0f6e-45d7-967b-d7be35fabd16.html>

Hicks JP, 'Technology Brought "Much-Needed Change" to Judicial System, Michigan Supreme Court Chief Justice Tells Congress' (*MLive*, 25 June 2020) <https://www.mlive.com/public-interest/2020/06/technology-brought-much-needed-change-to-judicial-system-michigan-supreme-court-chief-justice-tells-congress.html>

Himonas D, 'Utah's Online Dispute Resolution Program Transcripts' (2017) 122 Dickinson L Rev [i]

Holland PA, 'Junk Justice: A Statistical Analysis of 4,400 Lawsuits Filed by Debt Buyers' (2013) 26 Loyola Consumer L Rev 179.

Johnson Raba C, 'Low-Income Litigants in the Sandbox: Court Record Data and the Legal Technology A2J Market' (24 February 2022) <https://papers.ssrn.com/abstract = 4069023>

Johnson Raba C and Jiménez D, 'Pay to Plead: Finding Unfairness and Abusive Practices in California Debt Collection Cases' (24 October 2023) <https://papers.ssrn.com/abstract = 4611756>

Joint Technology Committee, 'Big Data: What State Courts Should Know' (National Center for State Courts 2014) <https://www.ncsc.org/__data/assets/pdf_file/0028/17938/big-data-1-0-1-23-2015-final.pdf>

Joint Technology Committee, 'Introduction to AI for Courts (Version 2.0)' (National Center for State Courts 2024) <https://www.ncsc.org/__data/assets/pdf_file/0027/98910/JTC-AI-paper-update-3.5.24.pdf>

Judicial Council of California, 'Tactical Plan for Technology–2023–2024' (2023) <https://www.courts.ca.gov/documents/jctc-Court-Technology-Tactical-Plan.pdf>

Kapoor S, Henderson P, and Narayanan A, 'Promises and Pitfalls of Artificial Intelligence for Legal Applications' (2024) 2 Journal of Cross-disciplinary Research in Computational Law <https://journalcrcl.org/crcl/article/view/62> accessed 21 May 2024.

Katsh ME and Rabinovich-Einy O, *Digital Justice: Technology and the Internet of Disputes* (OUP 2017)

Katz DM et al, 'GPT-4 Passes the Bar Exam' (15 March 2023) <https://papers.ssrn.com/abstract = 4389233>.

Kolt N, 'Predicting Consumer Contracts' (2022) 37 Berkeley Technology LJ 71

Kuhl C, 'What Can Reformers of Legal Services Learn from Court Efforts to Assist Self-Represented Litigants?' in Engstrom DF and Engstrom NF (eds), *Rethinking the Lawyer's Monopoly: Access to Justice and the Future of Legal Services* (CUP 2004)

Kuhl C and Highberger WF, 'Toward Fairer, Quicker, Cheaper Litigation: A Unified Theory of Case Management' (2023) 107 Judicature 34

Landsman S, *The Adversary System: A Description and Defense* (American Enterprise Institute] 1984)

Larson DA, 'Designing and Implementing a State Court ODR System: From Disappointment to Celebration' (2019) 2019 J Disp Res 77

Legg M and Bell F, 'Artificial Intelligence and the Legal Profession: Becoming the AI-Enhanced Lawyer' (2019) 38 U Tasmania L Rev 34

Lieberman HEM and Hannaford-Agor P, 'Meeting the Challenges of High-Volume Civil Dockets' (National Center for State Courts 2016) <https://www.ncsc.org/__data/assets/pdf_file/0027/25578/meeting-the-challenges.pdf>

Livermore MA, et al, 'Law Search in the Age of the Algorithm' (2020) 2020 Michigan State L Rev 1183

Lohr S, 'A.I. Is Doing Legal Work. But It Won't Replace Lawyers, Yet' *The New York Times* (19 March 2017) <https://www.nytimes.com/2017/03/19/technology/lawyers-artificial-intelligence.html>

Ma M, et al, 'Generative AI Legal Landscape 2024' (*Stanford Law School*, 6 March 2024) <https://law.stanford.edu/publications/generative-ai-legal-landscape-2024-2/>

Magesh V et al, 'Hallucination-Free? Assessing the Reliability of Leading AI Legal Research Tools' (6 June 2024) <https://dho.stanford.edu/wp-content/uploads/Legal_RAG_Hallucinations.pdf>

Martinson S, 'Quinn Emanuel Adopts AI Litigation Analytics Tool Pre/Dicta' [2024] *Law360* <https://www.law360.com/pulse/articles/1836960/quinn-emanuel-adopts-ai-litigation-analytics-tool-pre-dicta>

Mayson SG, 'Bias in, Bias Out' (2018) 128 Yale LJ 2218

McKinsey & Company, 'How Generative AI Can Help Global Governments' (07 2023) <https://www.mckinsey.com/industries/public-sector/our-insights/unlocking-the-potential-of-generative-ai-three-key-questions-for-government-agencies>

Mentovich A, Prescott JJ, and Rabinovich-Einy O, 'Are Litigation Outcome Disparities Inevitable? Courts, Technology, and the Future of Impartiality' (2019) 71 Alabama L Rev 893

Morison J and Harkens A, 'Re-Engineering Justice? Robot Judges, Computerised Courts and (Semi) Automated Legal Decision-Making' (2019) 39 Legal Studies 618

National Center for State Courts, 'National Open Court Data Standards (NODS' (2020) <https://www.ncsc.org/__data/assets/pdf_file/0014/34025/NODS-User-Guide.pdf>

National Center for State Courts, 'Trends in State Courts 2022' (2022) <https://www.ncsc.org/__data/assets/pdf_file/0024/80358/Trends-2022.pdf>

National Center for State Courts, 'Impact of AI in the Courts (Webinar)' (19 October 2023) <https://vimeo.com/875960451> accessed 5 May 2024

National Center for State Courts, 'Remote Proceeding Toolkit' (2024) <https://www.ncsc.org/__data/assets/pdf_file/0027/82377/Remote-Proceeding-Toolkit-Final.pdf>

Pasquale F and Cashwell G, 'Prediction, Persuasion, and the Jurisprudence of Behaviourism Artificial Intelligence, Technology, and the Law' (2018) 68 U Toronto LJ 63.

Perrault R, and Clark J, 'Artificial Intelligence Index Report 2024' (Stanford University Human-Centered Artifical Intelligence 2024) <https://policycommons.net/artifacts/12089781/hai_ai-index-report-2024/12983534/>

Prescott JJ, 'Using ODR Platforms to Level the Playing Field: Improving Pro Se Litigation through ODR Design' in Engstrom DF (ed), *Legal Tech and the Future of Civil Justice* (CUP 2023)

Quintanilla VD et al, 'Accessing Justice with Zoom: Experiences and Outcomes in Online Civil Courts' (2023) <https://www.repository.law.indiana.edu/cgi/viewcontent.cgi?article = 4087&context = facpub>

Quintanilla VD, Allen RA, and Hirt ER, 'The Signaling Effect of Pro Se Status Symposium: Access to Justice' (2017) 42 Law & Social Inquiry 1091

Rabinovich-Einy O, 'The Past, Present, and Future of Online Dispute Resolution' (2021) 74 CLP 125.

Reiling AD (Dory), 'Courts and Artificial Intelligence' (2020) 11(2) Intl J for Court Administration 8.

Rostain T, 'Techno-Optimism & Access to the Legal System' (2019) 148 Daedalus 93.

Rostain T and O'Hara A, 'The Civil Justice Data Gap' in Engstrom DF (ed), *Legal Tech and the Future of Civil Justice* (CUP 2023).

Rule C, 'Making Peace on eBay: Resolving Disputes in the World's Largest Marketplace' (2008) Fall 2008 ACResolution Magazine 8.

Salter S and Thompson D, 'Public-Centered Civil Justice Redesign: A Case Study of the British Columbia Civil Resolution Tribunal' (2016) 3 McGill J Disp Res 113.

Schmitz AJ, 'Expanding Access to Remedies through E-Court Initiatives' (2019) 67 Buffalo L Rev 89.

Sela A, 'Streamlining Justice: How Online Courts Can Resolve the Challenges of Pro Se Litigation' (2016) 26 Cornell JL & Public Policy 331

Sela A, 'Can Computers Be Fair: How Automated and Human-Powered Online Dispute Resolution Affect Procedural Justice in Mediation and Arbitration' (2018) 33 Ohio State J Disp Res 91.

Sela A, 'E-Nudging Justice: The Role of Digital Choice Architecture in Online Courts' (2019) 2019 J Disp Res 127

Shack J and Shestowsky D, 'Access to Justice: Lessons for Designing Text-Based Court-Connected ODR Programs' (2023) 29 Dispute Resolution Magazine 29

Shestowsky D and Shack J, 'Online Dispute Resolution for Debt and Small Claims Cases: A Report on a Pilot Program in a Justice of the Peace Court in Collin County, Texas'

Simshaw D, 'Access to A.I. Justice: Avoiding an Inequitable Two-Tiered System of Legal Services' (2022) 24 Yale JL & Tech 150.

Sourdin T, 'Judges, Technology and Artificial Intelligence: The Artificial Judge', *Judges, Technology and Artificial Intelligence* (Edward Elgar Publishing 2021) <https://china.elgaronline.com/monobook/9781788978255.xml>.

Souza A and Zarnow Z, 'Court Chatbots' (National Center for State Courts 2024) <https://www.ncsc.org/__data/assets/pdf_file/0032/97187/Court-Chatbots.pdf>.

Statista, 'Legal Tech Market Size Worldwide 2021–2027' (*Statista*, 2022) <https://www.statista.com/statistics/1155852/legal-tech-market-revenue-worldwide/>.

Steenhuis Q and Colarusso ., 'Digital Curb Cuts: Towards an Inclusive Open Forms Ecosystem COVID & the Practice of Law: Impacts of Legal Technology Symposium Issue' (2020) 54 Akron L Rev 773.

Steinberg JK., 'Adversary Breakdown and Judicial Role Confusion in Small Case Civil Justice'. (2016) 2016 Brigham Young University L Rev 899.

Stern RE. et al, 'Automating Fairness? Artificial Intelligence in the Chinese Courts' (2020) 59 Columbia J Transnat L 515.

Susskind R., *Online Courts and the Future of Justice* (Oxford University Press 2021).

Tyler Technologies, 'Online Dispute Resolution: Empower Citizens to Resolve Their Own Disputes Online, Anywhere, Anytime — With Proven Technology'. <https://www.tylertech.com/Portals/0/OpenContent/Files/4080/Modria-Brochure.pdf>.

Vermeys N., 'The Computer As the Court: How Will Artificial Intelligence Affect Judicial Processes?' in Xandra Kramer et al (eds), *New Pathways to Civil Justice in Europe* (Springer 2021).

Volokh E, 'Chief Justice Robots' (2018) 68 Duke LJ 1135.

Westermann H et al, 'Bridging the Gap: Mapping Layperson Narratives to Legal Issues with Language Models', *Proceedings of the 6th Workshop on Automated Semantic Analysis of Information in Legal Text co-located with the 19th International Conference on Artificial Intelligence and Law (ICAIL 2023), Braga, Portugal* (2023) <https://ceur-ws.org/Vol-3441/paper5.pdf>.

Wilf-Townsend D, 'Assembly-Line Plaintiffs' (2021) 135 Harv L Rev 1704.

Xu H and Ashley K, 'A Question-Answering Approach to Evaluating Legal Summaries', *Legal Knowledge and Information Systems* (IOS Press 2023) <https://ebooks.iospress.nl/doi/10.3233/FAIA230977>.

Zeleznikow J, 'Can Artificial Intelligence and Online Dispute Resolution Enhance Efficiency and Effectiveness in Courts Academic Articles' (2017) 8 Intl J Court Admin 30.

Zorza R, 'The Access to Justice "Sorting Hat": Towards a System of Triage and Intake That Maximizes Access and Outcomes' (2011) 89 Denver University L Rev 859.

In re Peterson [2022] US Bankruptcy Court, D Md Case 19- 24045.

Turner v Rogers, et al [2011] US Supreme Court 10-10, 564 US 431.

16
Judging the Robot Judge

*Tania Sourdin and Ella Sourdin Brown**

A. Scope of Judicial Use of AI

There are many ways in which AI can be connected to judicial processes. Apart from the clear benefits of supportive AI that may assist a judicial officer to manage evidence and understand issues, there are replacement and more disruptive forms of AI that can transform the work of a human judge and result in a reduction in judicial tasks or the replacement of a judge altogether. To some extent, the likelihood of the judicial role being either 'supplemented' or replaced by a form of AI has increased partly because of the capacity to develop software that mimics human intelligence or at least appears to do so. Generative AI (a subcategory of AI), for example, offers much potential in the legal and advisory area and can also be used in the judicial decision making process. Perhaps even more significantly, open-source developer platforms such as GitHub[1] offer significant opportunities to develop tailored software that enable human approaches to be more effectively mimicked (for example, by including emotional and empathic responses via sentiment analysis and using more sophisticated agentic AI). However, these forms of AI can result in inaccurate, biased outcomes and raise significant issues relating to cyber security and protection of confidential information. In addition, generative forms of AI are really focused on probability distribution and when used by judges as a supportive tool to write decisions, may appear to be coherent, reliable, and 'human' whilst failing to address novelty or the need for

* Tania Sourdin is a Professor Emerita at the School of Law and Justice, University of Newcastle, Australia. Ella Sourdin Brown is a legal researcher and law graduate. The authors thank the Chapter reviewers for their thoughtful comments and insights. This work draws upon Tania Sourdin, *Judges, Technology and Artificial Intelligence: The Artificial Judge* (Edward Elgar Publishing 2021) with kind permission.

[1] GitHub, Let's build from here [online] <https://github.com/> last accessed 7 June 2025.

Tania Sourdin and Ella Sourdin Brown, *Judging the Robot Judge* In: *Digitalization and Artificial Intelligence in Courts*. Edited by: Fernando Esteban de la Rosa, Pablo Cortés, and Nuria Marchal Escalona, Oxford University Press.
 DOI: 10.1093/9780198918752.003.0016

innovation in the law. Their conclusions lack the depth and insight which comes from a human judge's knowledge and experience, resulting in shallow reasoning and unjust outcomes.

The 'law as code' movement also offers some opportunities for both litigants and judges. On one level, translating law into code is a process where algorithmic outputs could amount to an advisory or even a judicial decision and this approach may support a better and more comprehensive understanding of the impact of legislation and even case law. However, much of the law is beset by ambiguities because of the legislative drafting process and because the translation of complex human issues into data can be inaccurate and inappropriate. More sophisticated forms of AI that result from both machine learning and the development of neural networks may address some of these issues, however may still fail to deliver 'human' justice even when coded to respond with some type of empathy. [2]

At the core of AI processes that could be used to support or supplant judges, liminal and often ambiguous data is intended to be translated into literal data.[3] Some might argue that human judges perform this function while hearing a court case. For example, judges and their potential struggles with uncertainty and at times nebulous claims are at the heart of most democratic systems . This supports a human approach to justice. Therefore, it is perhaps not surprising that the judicial use of AI raises a plethora of ethical concerns and such considerations differ depending on the context in which the technology is used .[4] Although, AI may be both more effective and more efficient than human intelligence in certain circumstances that are discussed later in this Chapter, , there are still numerous issues arising from its use in the judicial sphere. Issues can be linked to the lack of output integrity and reliability as well as substantive issues related to explainability, governance, and democratic approaches (that can be connected to the pervasive control of 'big tech').

Despite these limitations, there is some appetite for Judge AI. In general, it is thought that as AI is transforming a range of human functions and tasks and there is scope for AI in a range of decision-making domains.[5] Increasingly both governments and industry (including insurers) are using automated decision-making processes.[6] In addition, there is some ongoing experimentation occurring across courts with predictive systems. For example, it was found in the US that an AI model could predict the outcome of a Supreme Court case in more than two-thirds of instances (70.2 per

[2] See C Montemayor, J Halpern, and A Fairweather, 'In principle obstacles for empathic AI: why we can't replace human empathy in healthcare' (2022) 37(4) AI & Soc 1353 <doi: 10.1007/s00146-021-01230-z> Epub 2021 May 26. PMID: 34054228; PMCID: PMC8149918. See also Jocelyn Maclure, 'AI, Explainability and Public Reason: The Argument from the Limitations of the Human Mind' (2021) Minds and Machines 13.

[3] This task involves significant challenges, given the inherently subjective and interpretive nature of many legal judgments, which must account for nuances of law, precedent, and human behaviours.

[4] See Milena Heinsech et al, 'Death Sentencing by Zoom: An Actor-Network Theory Analysis' (2020) 46(1) Alternative LJ 13.

[5] In addition, as noted in Tania Sourdin, *Judges, Technology and Artificial Intelligence: The Artificial Judge* (Edward Elgar Publishing 2021). The use of AI by judges may assist in case management, communication, allocation of case work and tasks, and the organization of material.

[6] See for example, Australian Research Council, Automated Decision Making in NSW (March 2024) [online] <https://www.ombo.nsw.gov.au/__data/assets/pdf_file/0007/145096/Research-Report-ADMS.pdf> last accessed 20 March 2024.

cent at a case level, and 71.9 per cent at individual judges' level).[7] While these statistics are encouraging, it could be suggested that far higher levels of accuracy should be obtained in the judicial setting before Judge AI could be considered.[8] It is in this context that this chapter considers the areas of law that the literature has deemed to be more (or less) amenable to the use of AI before considering broader issues concerning big tech, AI, and the judicial role.

B. Areas of Delineation

A review of the literature reveals three broad areas of law where judicial use of AI is arguably less appropriate: criminal, family and aberrant (or novel) matters.[9] There are also distinct areas of judicial activity where AI use may be more acceptable when AI is supporting judges. For example, when creating chronologies, summarizing material or using specialized generative AI tools to research particular issues. Initially, in this Chapter clear contextual areas of delineation are discussed.

1. Criminal law matters

In the criminal legal sphere, some commentators have argued that the use of AI is inappropriate as the outcome of these matters often has a significant impact on individual freedom.[10] For example, Zalnieruite and Bell argue that decisions in the criminal context that involve constraints on civil liberty 'should remain with humans'.[11] Plesničar and Stubbs support this contention, and have stated that certain procedures in criminal law are inappropriate for automation as there is 'too high an impact upon society and upon the human rights of individuals'.[12] Also in support, McKay has argued that the criminal law sphere is traditionally a 'human institution' that resolves 'human transgression in a communal fashion'.[13] She notes that the preservation of the 'communal' element of criminal justice is a persuasive argument against the use of AI. In recent times there has been a shift towards participatory justice in the resolution of

[7] Daniel Katz, Michael Bommarito, and Josh Blackman, 'A general approach for predicting the behaviour of the Supreme Court of the United States' (2017) 12(4) PLOS One 1.

[8] Notably, higher levels of accuracy have been recorded in respect of the European Court of Human Rights at 79 per cent. See Nikolaos Aletras, Dimitrios Tsarapatsanis, Daniel Preoţiuc-Pietro, Vasileios Lampos, 'Predicting Judicial Decisions of the European Court of Human Rights: a Natural Language Processing Perspective' (2016) 2(2) PeerJ Computer Science 93.

[9] There are some that do not delineate in this way. Susskind for example, considers that it is possible that should a form of Judge AI be shown to be 95 per cent accurate, then that could become the official determination—see Richard Susskind, *Online Courts and The Future of Justice* (OUP 2020) ch 27.

[10] Monika Zalnieriute and Felicity Bell, 'Technology and Judicial Role' in Gabrielle Appleby and Andrew Lynch (eds), *The Judge, the Judiciary and the Court: Individual, Collegial and Institutional Judicial Dynamics in Australia* (CUP 2021).

[11] ibid.

[12] Mojca Plesničar and Katja Stubbs, 'Subjectivity, Algorithms and the Courtroom' in Aleš Završnik (ed), *Big Data, Crime and Social Control* (Routledge 2018).

[13] Carolyn McKay, 'Predicting Risk in Criminal Procedure: Actuarial Tools, Algorithms, AI and Judicial Decision-Making' (2019) University of Sydney Law School Research Paper No 19/67.

criminal matters.[14] Both participation and restorative justice initiatives would likely be hindered if AI dealt with those affected by an offence. Conversely, it can be argued that the judicial use of AI in criminal law may be appropriate in circumstances where the 'decision' being made does not relate to a question of fact.[15] For example, Zalnieruite and Bell have noted that one area of judicial decision-making where AI has been deployed relates to sentencing decisions.[16] Indeed courts in China have developed supportive Judge AI systems that are able to monitor whether a human judge's sentencing decision is 'reasonable'.[17] Stobbs et al have similarly noted that sentencing law and practice is particularly receptive to AI 'because most of the relevant facts are established prior to or following a relatively short plea hearing'.[18] In this sense it is arguable that the 'human' element of judging is retained by having the adjudicator (and possibly a jury) first consider the unique factual matrix of the case, which may be beyond the capacity of an AI program.[19] There are some very simplistic supportive AI tools that have relied upon humans determining inputs. These have been criticized as biased in the past, however, have nevertheless been accepted by Courts despite these issues.[20]

2. Family legal disputes

Another area of law where the use of AI is arguably less suitable is in resolving family law disputes. High level of emotions can accompany family disputes.[21] Research by Barbas reveals that divorce is a 'stressful life event' that often leads to 'lower levels of wellbeing for all individuals involved'.[22] As a result, many commentators have argued that the empathetic abilities of a human judge are required to resolve such matters. For example, Bell has contends that parties to a family law dispute often need their

[14] See Centre for Innovative Justice, 'Innovative Justice Responses to Sexual Offending— Pathways to Better Outcomes for Victims, Offenders and the Community' (Report, May 2014).

[15] Zalnieruite and Bell (n 10); Justice Glenn Martin, 'How Far Has Technology Invaded the Criminal Justice System?' (Australia and New Zealand Education Law Association, Legal Studies Teachers' Conference, Brisbane, 11 May 2018).

[16] Zalnieruite and Bell (n 10).

[17] Meng Yu and Guondong Du, 'Why Are Chinese Courts Turning to AI?' (*The Diplomat*, 19 January 2019) <https://thediplomat.com/2019/01/why-are-chinese-courts-turning-to-ai/> accessed 10 October 2020. See also Li Zhonghao and Jiang Hao, 'Anhui R & D Case Guide Project and Trial' (*People's Court Daily*, 21 June 2016) <http://rmfyb.chinacourt.org/paper/html/2016-06/21/content_113216.htm> last accessed 15 March 2021.

[18] Nigel Stobbs, Dan Hunter, and Mirko Bagaric, 'Can Sentencing Be Enhanced by the Use of Artificial Intelligence' (2017) 41 Criminal LJ 261.

[19] For example, in regard to the use of *COMPAS* in the US, Zalnieruite and Bell have argued: 'a judge must still consider a defendant's arguments as to why other factors might impact the risk that he or she poses. As judicial decisions affect the freedom and lives of individuals, the use of algorithms to automate elements of them is particularly controversial': Zalnieruite and Bell (n 10). See also Denny Chin, 'Sentencing: A Role for Empathy' (2012) 160 University of Pennsylvania L Rev 1561, 1581.

[20] See the well-known case of State v Loomis, 881 N.W.2d 749 (Wis. 2016).

[21] See Kathleen Corcoran, 'Psychological and Emotional Aspects of Divorce' (*Mediate.com*, June 1997) <www.mediate.com/articles/psych.cfm> last accessed 7 June 2025.

[22] Sarah Barbas, 'Exploring the Experience of Separation in Australia: Perspectives from Formerly Married and Cohabiting Parents' (DPhil thesis, Edith Cowan University 2017).

matter to be considered on more than a mere 'mechanistic' level.[23] Similarly, a study by Macfarlane found that self-represented litigants desired 'human contact and support' when preparing to deal with their dispute.[24] This is of particular importance considering that the number of self-represented litigants in most Family Courts, including the Family Court of Australia has 'grown sharply' in recent years.[25]

Indeed, the need for human adjudication is particularly important in cases involving significant disputes relating to children. For example, in Australia, judges are required under the *Family Law Act 1975* (Cth) to have regard to the 'best interests' of the child when making a parenting order for separating or divorcing parties.[26] However, for want of effective processing,[27] there is a question about - whether AI would have the capacity to engage in this multifaceted task? Notably, research by Smyth and Fehlberg has established that separating parents typically consider automated options to be an inadequate substitute for human interaction.[28] Nevertheless, there may be an argument that the 'impartial' ability of an AI system to weigh the facts without being emotionally swayed could generate more 'just' outcomes.

AI may also not be appropriate for use in family law matters on a technical level. For AI systems that are based on machine learning to make accurate predictions or decisions, they need to be trained with a 'suitable amount of sample data.[29] However, Bell has highlighted that this is a particular issue in family law proceedings as most matters 'do not proceed to final hearing and judgment'.[30] Bell has cautioned that this could result in decisions being made based on 'outlier' data resulting in biased decisions.[31] The lack of generalizable data undoubtedly increases the risk of an erroneous or unjust decisions being made. Indeed, Surden has similarly warned against the use of AI 'where the sample size of previous cases is not large enough for the computer program to discover patterns and create effective generalizations'.[32] In addition to the perceived lack of generalizable data, the authors note that there are certain aspects of family law that are likely incapable of digitization. Significant questions arise as to how discretionary judgments related to non-quantifiable elements such as domestic violence or power imbalances that may be subject to societal and other changes could be 'built into' an AI system. There is evidence that consideration of such matters was

[23] Felicity Bell, 'Family Law, Access to Justice, and Automation' (2019) 19 Macquarie LJ 103, 131–32.

[24] Julie Macfarlane, 'The National Self-Represented Litigants Project: Identifying and Meeting the Needs of Self-Represented Litigants' (Report, May 2013) 67.

[25] Family Court of Australia, '2017–18 Family Court of Australia Annual Report' (Report, Family Court of Australia 2018) 7.

[26] Family Law Act 1975 (Cth) s 61DA (1).

[27] See Leandro Minku, 'Will AI Ever Understand Human Emotions?' (Blog Post, The Conversation 10 January 2017) <https://theconversation.com/will-ai-ever-understand-human-emotions-70960> last accessed 20 March 2024.

[28] Belinda Smyth and Bruce Fehlberg, 'Australian Post-Separation Parenting on the Smartphone: What's 'App-ening?' (2019) 41(1) Journal of Social Welfare and Family Law 53, 62. For an in-depth discussion of these issues, see Tania Sourdin et al, 'COVID-19, Technology and Family Dispute Resolution' (2020) 30(4) Australasian Dispute Resolution Journal 240.

[29] Harry Surden, 'Machine Learning and Law' (2014) 89 Washington L Rev 87, 105–06.

[30] Bell (n 23) 118.

[31] ibid.

[32] Surden (n 30) 105–06.

particularly important in the context of COVID-19, as lockdown restrictions led to an increase in familial tensions.[33]

While family law may represent a less appropriate domain for the judicial use of AI, particularly in relation to non-quantifiable elements, family law matters concerning quantifiable elements may be more amenable to the judicial use of AI. One early potential example of judicial use of AI in such matters has been demonstrated by an AI software called 'Split Up'. This software that was implemented by the Family Court of Australia some time ago as part of a trial process. Itis designed to predict the asset distribution of separated or divorced couples seeking court settlement orders.[34] Without overriding the authority of the presiding judge to determine the distribution of assets, 'Split Up' has the potential to increase the administrative efficiency of the Family Court of Australia by assisting the judiciary with a readily accessible blueprint for the apportionment of assets. Swift legal measures designed to ease administrative backlog in the judiciary are especially relevant when considering jurisdictions with significant backlogs.[35] While there remains a gap in the literature discerning the accuracy (or success or failure) of this supportive Judge AI software, it must also be noted that the accuracy of 'Split Up' is limited by the fact that each prediction is restricted to the assessment of only the most valuable assets in dispute.[36]

3. Novel legal matters

The literature also exposes a delineation regarding the use of AI in hard or 'aberrant' cases. Aberrant cases are those which are novel or involve a higher degree of complexity (either high levels of task complexity, behavioural complexity, or both) than typical cases of the kind. For example, a contractual dispute may be aberrant where it involves debate about the enforceability of a 'choice of forum' clause.[37] Some commentators have argued that human judges are better equipped than Judge AI to preside over aberrant matters. For example, Wu maintains that the particular legal and contextual nuances of an aberrant matter are likely beyond the capacity of Judge AI systems.[38] Indeed, similar to family law matters, using data from previous cases would likely lead to an erroneous or unjust decision in an aberrant matter for want of useable data.[39] Notably, Wu also points out that hard cases often require the 'balancing of conflicting values' in order to avoid an inappropriate or 'absurd' decision.[40] Sourdin and Cornes concur. They similarly note that judgment on novel cases 'will always require

[33] Sourdin et al, 'COVID-19' (n 29) 240.

[34] Katie Walsh, 'Robots Are Coming to Courts—But They Won't Replace Judges' Australian Financial Rev (2017).

[35] Sourdin et al, 'COVID-19' (n 29) 270.

[36] Marilyn Bromberg, 'Are Court's Backs to the Future Regarding Artificial Intelligence?' (2018) 21(1) Internet Law Bulletin 2.

[37] See William Woodward, 'Legal Uncertainty and Aberrant Contracts: The Choice of Law Clause' (2014) 89(1) Chicago-Kent L Rev 197.

[38] Tim Wu, 'Will Artificial Intelligence Eat the Law? The Rise of Hybrid Social-Ordering Systems' (2019) 119 Columbia L Rev 2001, 2023.

[39] See Surden (n 30) 105-06.

[40] Wu (n 39) 2023.

a fresh evaluation of circumstances beyond the capacity of machine learning.'[41] Thus the authors of this Chapter note that, unless and until Judge AI can make affective and context-specific determinations, it seems likely that aberrant cases will be resistant to automated decision-making although in such cases, supportive technology may be of significant utility.

Another reason why aberrant matters are arguably less receptive to AI relates to coding difficulties. The ease of translating law into code is clearly an important point in the context of AI.[42] Commentators have noted that coding the steps taken to resolve a legal matter is an easier task for more simple cases. As Taruffo explains: 'a simple procedure may be more easily standardized in the form of a computer program for the trivial reason that each step of the procedure has to be translated into part of the program.'[43] In addition to legal procedures, Susskind further notes that although sometimes the legislation can be directly translated into code, case law, in contrast, is harder to turn into computing language due to the difficulty of writing *ratio decidendi* with some simple canonical rule.[44] Consequently it seems unlikely that the coding of factors relevant to an aberrant matter will be a simple task because the operation of the law in such matters is nuanced, contextual, and often discretionary in nature.[45] Thus significant questions arise as to how such nuances will be effectively coded in a way that enables a Judge AI system to make just determinations.[46] For example, in a dispute about a contract Judge AI may be required to consider questions of policy,[47] judicial discretion,[48] and the relative bargaining power of each party[49] when translating the law regarding the enforceability of a choice of forum clause into code.[50] In this regard, there have been queries about the use of AI where the law 'operates within the context

[41] Tania Sourdin and Richard Cornes, 'Do Judges Need to be Human? The Implications of Technology for Responsive Judging' in Tania Sourdin and Archie Zariski (eds), *The Responsive Judge: International Perspectives* (Springer 2018) 100.

[42] Justice Melissa Perry, 'iDecide: Administrative Decision-Making in the Digital World' (2017) 91 Australian LJ 29.

[43] Michele Taruffo, 'Judicial Decisions and Artificial Intelligence' (1998) 6 Artificial Intelligence and Law 311, 318.

[44] Richard Susskind (n 9) 160.

[45] Tania Sourdin, 'Judge v Robot? Artificial Intelligence and Judicial Decision-Making' (2018) 41(4) UNSW LJ 1114, 1127.

[46] However, it can be argued that this consideration is less relevant where the Judge AI system adopts a machine learning approach: Neha Bansal, Arun Sharma, and Rita Singh, 'A Review on the Application of Deep Learning in the Legal Domain' (IFIP International Conference on Artificial Intelligence, Crete, 2019); Fusheng Wei et al, 'Empirical Study of Deep Learning for Text Classification in Legal Document Review' (IEEE International Conference on Big Data, Seattle, 2018).

[47] For example, Greene argues that policy considerations are applicable when considering the enforceability of choice of forum clauses: Janey Greene, 'Party Autonomy in Choice of Law in Contract: Through the Lens of Akai Pty Ltd v The People's Insurance Company' (1997) 25 Australian Business L Rev 330, 330. See also *The Bremen v Zapata Off-Shore Co* 407 US 1, 15 (1972), citing *Boyd v Grand Trunk WR Co*, 338 US 263 (1949).

[48] Andrew Bell, 'Jurisdiction and Arbitration Agreements in Transnational Contracts: Part I' (1996) 10 Journal of Contract Law 53, 58.

[49] ibid 56; Frank Zumbo, 'Franchising: Implied Good Faith and Unconscionability in Franchises: Moving Towards Relational Contract Theory' (2000) 28 Australian Business L Rev 462, 462.

[50] Indeed, Justice Melissa Perry persuasively points out that 'computer programmers are not policy experts and seldom have legal training.' In this sense additional difficulties arise in the coding of aberrant matters for the use of Judge AI: Perry (n 43) 29.

of statutory presumptions and discretionary judgements' as 'ensuring these intricacies are properly coded into an autonomous process is challenging'.[51] Surden has similarly argued that aberrant cases 'may not be well-suited' to AI given the difficulties associated with their digitization.[52] Indeed there is early evidence that translating law into code is 'extremely difficult' in even average cases.[53] Interestingly though, compared to a Judge AI system, concerns may not be as evident where advisory systems are considered given the different roles performed by two types of systems.[54] Nevertheless, some of the same concerns raised above may be present with advisory systems that may result in inaccurate and incorrect outcomes.

Furthermore, not only are some areas of law deemed inappropriate for AI usage, but also some AI tools themselves must be carefully considered and used appropriately in the judicial sphere. One form of AI that must be closely contemplated in this manner are generative AI tools, the most popular of which is ChatGPT.[55] ChatGPT, as a generative form of AI that operates as a large language model (LLM), has the ability to respond and create seemingly organic answers to a range of text-based prompts.[56] It is clear that LLMs, like ChatGPT, could be used to increase efficiency in the legal sector, by being used to analyze and summarize lengthy documents for professionals. A benefit of this is that it can increase the accessibility of legal advice, [57] by being trained to give preliminary responses to legal issues.[58] There are already several examples of judges using ChatGPT in different ways. For example, the Law Society of England and Wales noted that:

> In September 2023, the deputy head of civil justice Lord Justice Birss, while commenting publicly on the potential of tools like ChatGPT at our dispute resolution conference, revealed he used the tool to provide a summary of an area of law, which he subsequently included in his judgment.
>
> This is the first known use of an AI chatbot by a British judge, demonstrating that generative AI tools can and already have been used within our legal system.[59]

[51] Tania Sourdin, 'Judge v Robot?' (n 46) 1127.

[52] Surden (n 30) 105–06.

[53] Taruffo (n 44) 318. However, it is noted that the ability to translate the law into code in more simple matters has become an easier task since 1998 due to recent developments in machine learning. That is, developments in machine learning can mean that coding is now much less relevant in the past as the algorithms or coding that is required is quite different. Newer machine learning processes may not however deal with situations where there is novelty and complexity. For further discussion, see Sourdin, *Judges, Technology and Artificial Intelligence* (n 5).

[54] Tania Sourdin, Jacqueline Meredith, and Bin Li *Digital Technology and Justice* (Routledge 2020) 70.

[55] References to generative AI also include references to other AI forms such as Claude. See also Purvish Parikh, Dinesh Shah, and Kairav Parikh, 'Judge Juan Manuel Padilla Garcia, ChatGPT, and a Controversial Medicolegal Milestone' (2023) 75(1) Indian Journal of Medical Sciences 3.

[56] Analysis and Research Team, 'ChatGPT in the Public Sector—overhyped or overlooked?' (Research Paper, Council of the European Union, 24 April 2023).

[57] See for example use in Singapore reported, Lydia Lam, 'Generative AI tested for use in Singapore Courts, starting with small claims tribunal' (Channel News Asia, 2023) < https://www.channelnewsasia.com/singapore/artificial-intelligence-court-small-claims-singapore-chatgpt-3801756> last accessed 7 June 2025.

[58] Analysis and Research Team, 'ChatGPT in the Public Sector'(n 57).

[59] See Report at The Law Society 'Generative AI—the essentials' (The Law Society, 2024) <https://www.lawsociety.org.uk/topics/ai-and-lawtech/generative-ai-the-essentials> last accessed 7 June 2025.

Judge Juan Manuel Padilla Garcia, a judge in Columbia, has faced serious criticism for consulting ChatGPT in crafting a judgment.[60] However, while defended by Judge Garcia as a tool to help increase efficiently in an overwhelmed legal system, the use of LLMs in judicial decision-making poses significant issues in ethical and appropriate AI usage.[61] Unfortunately, as the accuracy of an LLM's generated responses are wholly based on the quality and diversity of the dataset it draws its answers from, significant biases commonly present in their operation.[62] This is because LLMs are said to 'reflect' the attitudes, standards, and predispositions present within their data sets.[63] This issue is a concern as it has been found that when programmers attempt to remove bias from LLMs' datasets and model outputs, it can lead to greater bias within the system.[64] Further as LLMs are purely reflective models, they cannot critically analyze information, and thus they are unable to deviate from any views present within their data.[65] As previously mentioned this presents a significant issue for hard or 'aberrant' cases in the legal setting as this as this 'reflective' structure significantly limits LLM's ability to respond to issues that may be novel, severely limiting the opportunity for development of precedent and impacting on the ability to provide accurate legal commentary. Such models are also often devised to produce a 'certain' outcome and therefore, there is little likelihood that uncertainty will be reflected in any response.

C. Areas of Application

Despite the potential ethical and practical shortcomings in certain contexts, there are some areas of law where literature has deemed the use of AI to be more appropriate or 'ethical'. One such area is in the context of simple, lower court disputes. It seems clear (at least initially) that Judge AI is more likely to be of use at the lower court level where there are higher caseloads.[66] This is due in part to the fact that, at this level, there is less emphasis on judges to develop or create law.[67] Instead the role of the judge is to focus on the application of law in the finalization of disputes. Thus, coding the steps taken to resolve a dispute at this level is an easier task as the legal 'rules' judges are required to follow are arguably well-established.[68] Indeed Judge AI in small claims disputes are already present to some extent in certain jurisdictions. In Estonia, for example, it has been suggested, but never confirmed, that the Ministry of Justice was working to

[60] Parikh et al (n 56).
[61] ibid.
[62] Analysis and Research Team, 'ChatGPT in the Public Sector' (n 57). Notably some generative AI tools draw upon more specific materials and legal publishers who have 'rolled out' new generative tools (for example 'c counsel' with Westlaw) consider that such tools will revolutionize the legal sector.
[63] ibid.
[64] ibid.
[65] ibid.
[66] Sourdin, *Technology and Artificial Intelligence* (n 5) ch 8.
[67] See Chief Justice Tom Bathurst, 'iAdvocate v Rumpole: Who will Survive? An Analysis of Advocates' Ongoing Relevance in the Age of Technology' (Speech, Australian Bar Association Conference, Boston, 9 July 2015). For an in-depth discussion of the use of AI in the administrative law domain, see Cary Colglianese and David Lehr, 'Regulating by Robot: Administrative Decision Making in the Machine-Learning Era' (2017) 105 Georgetown LJ 1147.
[68] Taruffo (n 44) 318.

develop a 'robot judge' that will adjudicate small claims disputes of less than €7,000 and therefore assist to clear the backlog of small claims disputes in their courts.[69]

Simple, lower court claims may be more amenable to Judge AI on a technical level. As Surden explains, AI systems require a large sample of past cases before 'robust generalizations' can be made. Where there are only a very small number of past cases, Judge AI systems are unlikely to detect patterns that enable just decisions to be made.[70] The higher volumes of caseloads present at lower court levels offer a rich data source for the development of Judge AI. The digitalization of past judicial decisions could enable a Judge AI system to be 'fed with' an appropriate amount of sample data to allow accurate judgments to be made. In this regard, small claims disputes that are: (i) regularly dealt with in the lower courts; and (ii) are subject to clear, well-defined legal principles may be more amenable to the use of Judge AI. Such matters would likely include the payment of fines, debt recovery, consumer issues and simple contract cases.[71] Certainly there may also be more scope for the use of Judge AI in such matters as these disputes are sometimes less likely to involve an emphasis on human behavior and emotion. In this sense additional ethical issues associated with loss of empathy and human involvement are also (arguably) circumvented. On the other hand, unrepresented litigants may be more emotionally involved in their dispute. Therefore, without the proper support and assistance built in together with a lack of human judicial involvement may impact on perceptions of satisfaction and fairness experienced by these self-represented litigants in the judicial process. [72]

Recent developments in the capacity of supportive Judge AI can further be understood in the context of the 'smart court' system in China. The Chinese smart court system was developed to utilize new technology advancements across the entirety of the Chinese courts system.[73] In doing so, the government implemented computer technologies that enable big data use and blockchain formation, to allow advisory and determinative forms of Judge AI to assist in judges' decision-making processes and the daily administration of the court system.[74] The aim of these implementations was to encourage easy access to justice, create faster dispute resolution, reduce costs and strengthen the enforcement of rulings.[75] However this system does not exist without issues, and academics have raised concerns as to the use of such systems of Judge AI. In

[69] This example may be an example of early 'techno hype' and a number of authors have suggested that these arrangements are either not likely to ever be in place or are the result of journalist invention. Thomas Connelly, 'Estonia to Build "Robot Judge" to Clear Case Backlog' (*Legal Cheek*, 26 May 2019) www.legalcheek.com/2019/03/estonia-to-build-robot-judge-to-clear-case-backlog/ last accessed 10 October 2020; Eric Niiler, 'Can AI be a Fair Judge in Court? Estonia Thinks So' (*Wired*, 25 March 2019) <www.wired.com/story/can-ai-be-fair-judge-court-estonia-thinks-so/> last accessed 3 November 2020.

[70] Surden (n 30) 105–06.

[71] Tania Sourdin, *Judges, Technology and Artificial Intelligence* (n 5). See also Peter Suciu, 'AI in the Courts: The Jury is Out' (*Tech News World*, 20 February 2020) <www.technewsworld.com/story/86521.html> last accessed 3 November 2020.

[72] John Zeleznikow, 'Can Artificial Intelligence and Online Dispute Resolution enhance efficiency and effectiveness in Courts' (2017) 8(2) Intl J for Court Administration 30–45.

[73] Changqing Shi, Tania Sourdin, and Bin Li, 'The Smart Court–A New Pathway to Justice in China?' (2021) 21(1) International Journal for Court Administration 4.

[74] ibid.

[75] ibid.

particular, the probable automation of judgment includes risks to the independence of the judiciary, and raises questions about data and privacy protection.[76]

In this sense AI systems may be able to assist human judges towards what Posner terms a 'zone of reasonableness'.[77] This could mean that the closer a judicial decision is to this zone of reasonableness, the more likely ethical issues associated with judicial reasoning (such as bias)[78] can be evaded. However, there is also potential for unjust or inappropriate laws to be applied without judicial commentary or criticism. The imposition of supportive Judge AI without independent judicial review raises particular concern in light of recent discourse highlighting the 'astronomical' conviction rate of Chinese courts.[79] In this sense it is perhaps not surprising that commentators such as Landsman and Zhang have highlighted a decrease in the Chinese public's 'faith in the judiciary' for want of an 'independent adjudicatory system'.[80]

Other courts in China have tackled such issues by developing supportive Judge AI systems that caution judges when they issue an 'abnormal' decision. The system deems a decision abnormal if it 'significantly differs from judgments of similar cases'.[81] The AI system adopts a risk management approach and warns a judge's superior when an abnormal decision is made.[82] The development of such advisory systems have gained some limited support in the literature as they do not pose the risk of usurping the judicial role the same way that fully automated Judge AI does. Rather, as Surden notes, they can 'complement' human work by assisting the judge during their application of precedent.[83] This enables a human judge to turn their mind towards the 'discretionary or social considerations to be made that may be beyond the capacity of the computer program'.[84] However, many might consider that such approaches encroach upon judicial independence and the capacity for judges to exercise discretion (see discussion later in this chapter). However, such developments may also raise issues related to judicial 'anchoring'.[85] This is the phenomenon where judges view AI as infallible and are hence 'anchored' by the decision or prediction propounded by the system. Notably,

[76] ibid.

[77] Richard Posner, 'The Role of the Judge in the Twenty-First Century' (2006) 86 Boston U L Rev 1049, 1053.

[78] Andreas Tsamados et al, 'The Ethics of Algorithms: Key Problems and Solutions' (2021) 36 AI & Society; Eolenka, 'Bias in the AI Court Decision Making—Spot It Before You Fight It' (*Towards Data Science*, 1 July 2019) < https://medium.com/data-science/bias-in-the-ai-court-decision-making-spot-it-before-you-fight-it-52acf8903b11> last accessed 7 June 2025.

[79] Neil Connor, 'Chinese Courts Convict More Than 99.9 Per Cent of Defendants', *The Telegraph UK* (London, 14 March 2016) <www.telegraph.co.uk/news/worldnews/asia/china/12193202/Chinese-courts-convict-more-than-99.9-per-cent-of-defendants.html> last accessed 7 June 2025.

[80] Stephen Landsman and Jing Zhang, 'A Tale of Two Juries: Lay Participation Comes to Japanese and Chinese Courts' (2008) 25(2) Pacific Basin LJ 179, 180.

[81] Meng Yu and Guondong Du (n 17). See also Li Zhonghao and Jiang Hao (n 17).

[82] ibid. Another example of Judge AI that adopts a risk management approach is provided by the Taizhou Intermediate People's Court of Zhejiang Province. That Court has developed a colour-coded AI system that detect judicial risk. Notably, as of April 2019, a total of 248 risks had been detected and alerted by the system: Supreme People's Court of China, 'Chinese Courts and Internet Judiciary' (White Paper, Supreme People's Court of China 4 December 2019) 82.

[83] Surden (n 30) 87, 101.

[84] Tania Sourdin, 'Judge v Robot?' (n 46) 1130–31.

[85] Sourdin, *Judges, Technology and Artificial Intelligence* (n 5).

the discourse by Holler revealed that judges issued a detention sentence that was 32 per cent longer after being presented with a numerical reference point. This numerical reference point was said to have acted as an 'anchor' in the judge's mind upon sentence.[86]

Other commentators have highlighted how Judge AI could be more appropriate for regulatory areas of law.[87] Similar to the arguments raised in relation to lower court disputes, regulatory areas of law are arguably better suited to automation as they may offer fewer opportunities for judicial creativity.[88]

In comparison, Colglianese and Lehr provide an argument in the American context, that administrative law officers are often tasked with making judgments akin to those now made by AI in the private sector.[89] In this regard it is perhaps not surprising that the Social Security Administration (SSA) in the United States has developed a Judge AI tool that 'identifies errors in draft decisions by administrative judges and adjudicates disability benefits cases'.[90] Notably, there exists a dichotomy in the literature about the suitability of such approaches. Several commentators have argued against the use of Judge AI in the administrative context and are concerned that the checks and balances traditionally afforded by an independent judiciary would come under threat. For example, Zalnieriute and Bell argue that the independence of the judiciary may be destabilized where other arms of government are involved in the creation of Judge AI.[91] Moreover, other commentators such as Michaels raise concern about the ability of Judge AI to act as an appropriate 'check' on the executive and legislative arms of government and argues that judges should remain human.[92] Perspectives relating to Judge AI and judicial independence are clearly subject to significant jurisdictional variation. This is especially so as many countries do not operate under a strict separation of powers regime.[93] Such variation further underscores the need to develop an ethical framework for the judicial use of AI that is sensitive to the context in which it is being utilized.

[86] Rod Hollier, 'The Anchoring Bias and Its Effect on Judges' (Report, The Law Project May 2017) <https://www.thelawproject.com.au/insights/anchoring-bias-in-the-courtroom> last accessed 7 June 2025..

[87] Bathurst (n 88).

[88] Sourdin, *Judges, Technology and Artificial Intelligence* (n 5) ch 8.

[89] Colglianese and Lehr (n 68) 1153.

[90] David Engstrom and Daniel Ho, 'Algorithmic Accountability in the Administrative State' (2020) 37(3) Yale Journal on Regulation 1.

[91] Zalnieriute and Bell (n 10). For an in-depth discussion of these issues, see Sourdin, *Judges, Technology and Artificial Intelligence* (n 5) ch 7.

[92] Andrew Michaels, 'Artificial Intelligence, Legal Change, and Separation of Powers' (2020) 88 University of Cincinnati L Rev 1083.

[93] See Juan Ameen, 'European Court Orders Poland to Suspend Judiciary Panel for Lack of Independence', *The Shift* (28 April 2020) <https://theshiftnews.com/2020/04/28/polish-judiciary-disciplinary-panel-suspended-for-lack-of-independence/> last accessed 7 June 2025; Li Ling, 'The Chinese Communist Party and People's Courts: Judicial Dependence in China' (2016) 64(1) American Journal of Comparative Law 66, cited in Björn Ahl, 'Why do Judges Cite the Party? References to Party Ideology in Chinese Court Decisions' (2020) 18(2) *China*: An International Journal 175.

D. AI Regulation

Internationally there has been a significant focus on the general risk of AI, which is well articulated in recent AI literature and regulatory instruments. Of most significant note is the European *Artificial Intelligence Act* ('AI Act').[94] The EU Act aims to regulate 'high risk' AI and legally limit AI that poses too hazardous an outcome[95] while concurrently enabling the investment and innovation in AI and promoting international cooperation.[96] The AI Act has received academic acclaim for this identification of AI systems as 'high risk',[97] including systems used in the legal application and justice administration. Therefore, legal and judicial AI programs must conform to a number of regulations to ensure the quality of the algorithm and administration including the; transparency of information to users, necessity of human oversight, and vigorous cybersecurity.[98] Although, ground breaking in its recognition of the importance of AI regulation, submissions relating to the AI Act suggests that there are potential risk areas, partly due to the Act's focus on the individual rather than mitigating societal harm: 'while many risks from AI technology can be thought of as the potential for harms to an individual's health and safety or of adverse impact on their fundamental rights, AI may also cause significant harm, on a societal level'.[99]

The AI Act outlines in Annexure II that certain judicial activities are automatically described as 'high risk' and will therefore be subject to a different regulatory regime. However, the proposed regulatory approach is somewhat unclear. While it notes that requirements should apply to high-risk AI systems regarding the; quality of data sets used, technical documentation and record-keeping, transparency and the provision of information to users, human oversight, and robustness, accuracy and cybersecurity,[100] - there is too much focus on how AI arrives at a determination rather than the other challenges presented. As a result, the EU approach is limited to addressing the lack of transparency, often termed in the literature as the 'black box' phenomenon.[101] Furthermore, sanctions and penalties for misusing AI by fiduciaries or those in positions of trust are not outlined in the Act. Instead, the act focuses on self-regulation in a narrower context. [102]

[94] See Future of Life Institute, 'The Artificial Intelligence Act: What is the EU AI Act?', *The AI Act*, (Web page) <https://artificialintelligenceact.eu/> last accessed 7 June 2025.

[95] Josh Meltzer & Aaron Tielemans, *The European Union AI Act: Next steps and issues for building international cooperation*, (Policy Brief, May 2022).

[96] ibid.

[97] Sónia Moreira and Patrícia Borges, 'Artificial Intelligence and jurisdictional decisions: is the Robot-Judge imminent?' (Draft Paper, Law and Society Association Conference, 13 –16 July 2022).

[98] ibid.

[99] Sam Clarke et al, 'Submission of Feedback to the European Commission's Proposal for a Regulation laying down harmonised rules on artificial intelligence', *Feedback from: University of Cambridge (Leverhulme Centre for the Future of Intelligence and Centre for the Study of Existential Risk* (Feedback form, August 2021) <https://ec.europa.eu/info/law/better-regulation/have-your-say/initiatives/12527-Artificial-intelligence-ethical-and-legal-requirements/F2665626_en> last accessed 7 June 2025.

[100] Josh Meltzer and Aaron Tielemans, *The European Union AI Act: Next steps and issues for building international cooperation*, (Policy Brief, May 2022).

[101] Colglianese and Lehr (n 68).

[102] Tania Sourdin, Bin Li, and Alexei Brown, 'An Ethical Perspective in the Judicial Use of Artificial Intelligence: Where Will the New EU Artificial Intelligence Act Take Us?'(2023) 97(1) Australian LJ 4.

Black Box code is a term coined to describe the opacity of the programmer's code implemented in an AI's machine learning. This creates difficulties when understanding how the AI is 'weighing' certain values and arriving at a final decision.[103] In the context of the legal domain, there is also evidence that notions of empathy,[104] bias,[105] process rights,[106] and judicial independence[107] are at risk where AI is implemented without regard to ethical considerations such as ensuring the trust in the legal system is maintained.[108] The authors, together with Morley and others, argue that these issues should be targeted proactively.[109] Moreira and Borges raised similar concerns, when discussing the AI Act, [110] where despite praising the identification of 'high risk' systems they identified a seemingly 'loophole'-like annex in the legislation, stating those utilizing AI systems need not use external assessment measures to proceed in the use of the system, provided they conform to internal control assessments.[111] This presents a juxtaposition between transparency and administrative ease, raising significant concerns for their efficacy.[112]

Upon consideration of recent landmark AI regulation in the international context a common thread begins to emerge. While vital in the development of ethical frameworks of AI used all around the globe, there appears a significant dearth between the general principles of what an ethical framework should contain through the risks identified in AI systems, and a concreate outline as to what an ethical AI system in the area of judicial use should and must contain.

In addition, the EU regulatory approach, provides that AI systems "intended to be used by a judicial authority or on their behalf to assist a judicial authority in researching and interpreting facts and the law and in applying the law to a *concrete set of facts*" are classified among the "high-risk" systems. Importantly, the EU provisions appear to draw a distinction where the input if the input refers to a distinct factual situation. This approach means that AI use by the judiciary in searching cases and legislation,

[103] Indeed, there are past examples in the medical context where AI systems have 'weighed' factors incorrectly and ultimately led to a blatantly erroneous and unjust outcome: see Max Brantley, 'How Arkansas Used a Computer Formula to Cut Services to the Disabled' *Arkansas Times* (Arkansas, 22 March 2018) <https://arktimes.com/arkansas-blog/2018/03/22/how-arkansas-used-a-computer-formula-to-cut-services-to-the-disabled> last accessed 7 June 2025.

[104] Jessica Morley et al, 'The Ethics of AI in Health Care: A Mapping Review' (2020) 260 Social Science & Medicine 113, 222.

[105] Tsamados et al (n 79); Eolenka (n 79); Christopher T Bavitz, 'Algorithms and Justice' (Berkman Klein Centre for Internet & Society at Harvard University, 15 October 2019) <https://cyber.harvard.edu/projects/ai-algorithms-and-justice> last accessed 26 April 2024; Jason Tashea, 'Courts are Using AI to Sentence Criminals. That Must Stop Now' (*Sentencing Law and Policy*, 18 April 2017) <https://sentencing.typepad.com/sentencing_law_and_policy/2017/04/courts-are-using-ai-to-sentence-criminals-that-must-stop-now.html> last accessed 7 June 2025.

[106] Monika Zalnieriute, Lyria Moses, and George Williams, 'The Rule of Law and Automation of Government Decision-Making' (2019) 82(3) MLR 425.

[107] Zalnieriute and Bell (n 10); Michaels (n 93). For additional discussion on how judge AI may undermine the rule of law, see Pamela Stewart and Anita Stuhmcke, 'Judicial Analytics and Australian Courts: A Call for National Ethical Guidelines' (2020) 45(2) Alternative LJ 82, 85–86.

[108] Morley et al (n 105) 115–16.

[109] ibid.

[110] Sónia Moreira and Patrícia Borges, 'Artificial Intelligence and jurisdictional decisions: is the Robot-Judge imminent?' (Draft Paper, Law and Society Association Conference, 13–16 July 2022).

[111] ibid.

[112] ibid.

correcting grammar and word use, in organising, paginating, assembling documents is likely to be less problematic provided that sources are referenced and checked. AI use in creating chronologies, summarising, auto inserting precent material and even assisting with complex single issue research is also likely to not raise concerns provided that the AI use does not include research and interpretation of the specific facts and is more generalised and more focussed on administrative and related functions. More questionable judicial usage might involve the use of AI in reframing material, structure creation, more complex research perhaps via specialised generative AI systems or using AI to enhance comprehensibility and translating material. This usage is more questionable in part because of the potential for error. What remains most controversial is AI functions that may impact more significantly on the process of human judgement. Such functions include using AI for evaluation and predictive analytics, using AI 'assistants' to check and comment on drafts or using AI in respect of expert assessment. Drafting judgements in their entirety would of course raise the most significant issues for the reasons noted above and that such concerns can be even more problematic is one considers specific jurisdictions as noted above.

E. Conclusions

The judicial use of AI raises significant ethical and practical concerns. A review of the literature reveals that the nature of such concerns varies depending on the context in which AI is used and the way in which AI is used. For example, matters which involve high levels of emotion (criminal law and family disputes) and those which are aberrant may be less amenable to the use of AI - instead, requiring the empathic and creative abilities of a human judge. In other simpler cases (such as small claims disputes or administrative matters), the use of AI may be more appropriate. Different issues arise where jurisdictional disparities exist in terms of the core ethical principles and underlying values of the justice system. Additionally, there are ongoing questions about whether fully automated Judge AI is ever appropriate. Some commentators have argued that supportive Judge AI will play a more significant role in the future and may not usurp the judicial role in the same way that fully automated Judge AI does. The authors agree with this view in the medium term. However, it is noted that other jurisdictions are in the early stages of implementing more disruptive forms of AI.[113] Given the more extensive and rapid proliferation of AI in recent years, it is not unreasonable to assume that more sophisticated Judge AI systems will eventually penetrate the judicial landscape in the longer term despite the ongoing ethical debate.

As technological use has extended into the judicial realm,[114] there are issues about how justice objectives are being met and the extent to which they are articulated. In particular, AI raises issues not only about how a 'just' justice system can be maintained and developed but also about how human judicial involvement will be retained within the justice system. In this respect there are narrow as well as broader options,

[113] Connelly, 'Estonia to Build "Robot Judge"' (n 70); Niiler, 'Can AI be a Fair Judge in Court?' (n 70).
[114] Milena Heinsch et al, 'Death Sentencing by Zoom: An Actor–Network Theory Analysis' (2020) 46(1) Alternative LJ 13.

even where a limited Judge AI case load is proposed. For example, on a narrow view, the judicial role might be restricted to a reviewing function to enable a litigant to have a review of a decision made by a Judge AI.[115] In such circumstances there should be a clear and accessible judicial review or appeal process. In a broader application, the role would involve supportive Judge AI—that is, decisions which must involve a human 'in the loop' process.[116] In addition, supportive AI tools are likely to become more relevant and arguably do not raise the concerns that arise with any application to a decision that is created to apply to specific case circumstances. As Wang explains, such processes enable the 'efficiency of intelligent automation' to be harnessed 'while remaining amenable to human feedback'.[117] Regardless of the extent of changes, there is a need to develop material specifically tailored to assist judges and policy makers manage the novel ethical issues raised by AI. The development of this framework should be informed by existing guidance on ethics and AI, as well as a detailed consideration of how different levels of society can be protected from developments that could result in unjust outcomes which may change the social fabric of our society.

Bibliography

Ahl B., 'Why do Judges Cite the Party? References to Party Ideology in Chinese Court Decisions' (2020) 18(2) China: An International Journal.

Aletras N, Tsarapatsanis D, Preoţiuc-Pietro D, Lampos V, 'Predicting judicial decisions of the European Court of Human Rights: a Natural Language Processing perspective' (2016) 2(93) Peer J Computer Science.

Ameen J, 'European Court Orders Poland to Suspend Judiciary Panel for Lack of Independence', *The Shift* (28 April 2020) https://theshiftnews.com/2020/04/28/polish-judiciary-disciplinary-panel-suspended-for-lack-of-independence/.

Analysis and Research Team, 'ChatGPT in the Public Sector—overhyped or overlooked?' (Research Paper, Council of the European Union, 24 April 2023).

Australian Research Council, Automated Decision Making in NSW (March 2024) <https://www.ombo.nsw.gov.au/__data/assets/pdf_file/0007/145096/Research-Report-ADMS.pdf>.

Bansal N, Sharma A, and Singh R, 'A Review on the Application of Deep Learning in the Legal Domain' (IFIP International Conference on Artificial Intelligence, Crete, 2019).

Barbas, S, 'Exploring the Experience of Separation in Australia: Perspectives from Formerly Married and Cohabiting Parents' (DPhil thesis, Edith Cowan University 2017).

Bathurst T, 'iAdvocate v Rumpole: Who will Survive? An Analysis of Advocates' Ongoing Relevance in the Age of Technology' (Speech, Australian Bar Association Conference, Boston, 9 July2015).

Bathurst T, 'Who Judges the Judges, and How Should They be Judged?' (Law Society Opening of Law Term Dinner, Sydney, 30 January 2019) 8.

[115] A 'right to review approach' might replicate the approach that is being considered in Europe in respect of ADR so that where an automated decision has been made, there is a right to a natural person review—see Directorate-General for Communication, 'Alternative dispute resolution for consumers' (European Commission) <https://commission.europa.eu/live-work-travel-eu/consumer-rights-and-complaints/resolve-your-consumer-complaint/alternative-dispute-resolution-consumers_en> last accessed on 20 April 2024.

[116] This is distinct from a human 'on the loop' process, where individuals take a more supervisory approach and are less involved in AI decisions. See Sourdin, *Judges, Technology and Artificial Intelligence* (n 5).

[117] Ge Wang, 'Humans in the Loop: The Design of Interactive AI Systems' (*HAI Stanford University,* 20 October 2019) <https://hai.stanford.edu/blog/humans-loop-design-interactive-ai-systems> last accessed on 20 April 2024.

Bavitz CT, 'Algorithms and Justice' (Berkman Klein Centre for Internet & Society at Harvard University, 15 October 2019) <https://cyber.harvard.edu/projects/ai-algorithms-and-justice>.

Bell A, 'Jurisdiction and Arbitration Agreements in Transnational Contracts: Part I' (1996) 10 Journal of Contract Law.

Bell F, 'Family Law, Access to Justice, and Automation' (2019) 19 Macquarie LJ 103.

Brantley M, 'How Arkansas Used a Computer Formula to Cut Services to the Disabled' *Arkansas Times* (Arkansas, 22 March 2018) <https://arktimes.com/arkansas-blog/2018/03/22/how-arkansas-used-a-computer-formula-to-cut-services-to-the-disabled>.

Centre for Innovative Justice, 'Innovative Justice Responses to Sexual Offending—Pathways to Better Outcomes for Victims, Offenders and the Community' (Report , May 2014).

Chin D, 'Sentencing: A Role for Empathy' (2012) 160 University of Pennsylvania L Rev 1561, 1581.

Clarke S et al, 'Submission of Feedback to the European Commission's Proposal for a Regulation laying down harmonised rules on artificial intelligence', *Feedback from: University of Cambridge (Leverhulme Centre for the Future of Intelligence and Centre for the Study of Existential Risk* (Feedback form, August 2021) <https://ec.europa.eu/info/law/better-regulation/have-your-say/initiatives/12527-Artificial-intelligence-ethical-and-legal-requirements/F2665626_en>.

Colglianese C and Lehr D, 'Regulating by Robot: Administrative Decision Making in the Machine-Learning Era' (2017) 105 The Georgetown LJ 1147.

Connelly T, 'Estonia to Build "Robot Judge" to Clear Case Backlog' (*Legal Cheek*, 26 May 2019) <www.legalcheek.com/2019/03/estonia-to-build-robot-judge-to-clear-case-backlog/>.

Connor N, 'Chinese Courts Convict More Than 99.9 Per Cent of Defendants', *The Telegraph UK* (London, 14 March 2016) <www.telegraph.co.uk/news/worldnews/asia/china/12193202/Chinese-courts-convict-more-than-99.9-per-cent-of-defendants.html>.

Corcoran K, 'Psychological and Emotional Aspects of Divorce' (*Mediate.com*, June 1997) <www.mediate.com/articles/psych.cfm>.

Directorate-General for Communication, 'Alternative dispute resolution for consumers' (European Commission) <https://commission.europa.eu/live-work-travel-eu/consumer-rights-and-complaints/resolve-your-consumer-complaint/alternative-dispute-resolution-consumers_en>.

Engstrom D and Ho D;'Algorithmic Accountability in the Administrative State' (2020) 37(3) Yale Journal on Regulation 1.

Eolenka, 'Bias in the AI Court Decision Making—Spot It Before You Fight It' (*Towards Data Science*, 1 July 2019) <https://towardsdatascience.com/bias-in-the-ai-court-decision-making-spot-it-before-you-fight-it-52acf8903b11>.

Family Court of Australia, '2017–18 Family Court of Australia Annual Report' (Report, Family Court of Australia 2018).

Future of Life Institute, 'The Artificial Intelligence Act: What is the EU AI Act?', *The AI Act*, (Web page) <https://artificialintelligenceact.eu/>.

GitHub Let's build from here [online] <https://github.com/>.

Greene J, 'Party Autonomy in Choice of Law in Contract: Through the Lens of Akai Pty Ltd v The People's Insurance Company' (1997) 25 Australian Business L Rev 330.

Heinsch M et al, 'Death Sentencing by Zoom: An Actor-Network Theory Analysis' (2020) 46(1) Alternative LJ 13.

Hollier R, 'The Anchoring Bias and Its Effect on Judges' (Report, The Law Project May 2017) <https://www.thelawproject.com.au/insights/anchoring-bias-in-the-courtroom>.

Justice Martin G, 'How Far Has Technology Invaded the Criminal Justice System?' (Australia and New Zealand Education Law Association, Legal Studies Teachers' Conference, Brisbane, 11 May 2018).

Katz D, Bommarito M, and Blackman J, 'A general approach for predicting the behaviour of the Supreme Court of the United States' (2017) 12(4) PLOS One 1.

Lam L, 'Generative AI tested for use in Singapore Courts, starting with small claims tribunal' (Channel News Asia, 2023) <https://www.channelnewsasia.com/singapore/artificial-intelligence-court-small-claims-singapore-chatgpt-3801756>.

Landsman S and Zhang J, 'A Tale of Two Juries: Lay Participation Comes to Japanese and Chinese Courts' (2008) 25(2) Pacific Basin LJ 179.

Ling L, 'The Chinese Communist Party and People's Courts: Judicial Dependence in China' (2016) 64(1) American Journal of Comparative Law 66.

Macfarlane J, 'The National Self-Represented Litigants Project: Identifying and Meeting the Needs of Self-Represented Litigants' (Report, May 2013).

Maclure J, 'AI, Explainability and Public Reason: The Argument from the Limitations of the Human Mind' (2021) Minds and Machines 13.

McKay C, 'Predicting Risk in Criminal Procedure: Actuarial Tools, Algorithms, AI and Judicial Decision-Making' (2019) University of Sydney Law School Research Paper No 19/67.

Meltzer J and Tielemans A, *The European Union AI Act: Next steps and issues for building international cooperation,* (Policy Brief, May 2022).

Meltzer J, and Tielemans A, *The European Union AI Act: Next steps and issues for building international cooperation,* (Policy Brief, May 2022).

Michaels A, 'Artificial Intelligence, Legal Change, and Separation of Powers' (2020) 88 University of Cincinnati L Rev 1083.

Minku L, 'Will AI Ever Understand Human Emotions?' (Blog Post, The Conversation 10 January 2017)<https://theconversation.com/will-ai-ever-understand-human-emotions-70960>.

Moreira S and Borges P, 'Artificial Intelligence and jurisdictional decisions: is the Robot-Judge imminent?' (Draft Paper, Law and Society Association Conference, 13–16 July 2022).

Morley J et al, 'The Ethics of AI in Health Care: A Mapping Review' (2020) 260 Social Science & Medicine 113, 222.

Niiler E, 'Can AI be a Fair Judge in Court? Estonia Thinks So' (*Wired*, 25 March 2019) www.wired.com/story/can-ai-be-fair-judge-court-estonia-thinks-so/.

Parikh P, Shah D, and Parikh K,'Judge Juan Manuel Padilla Garcia, ChatGPT, and a controversial medicolegal milestone' (2023) 75(1) Indian Journal of Medical Sciences 3.

Perry M, 'iDecide: Administrative Decision-Making in the Digital World' (2017) 91 Australian LJ 29.

Plesničar M, and Stubbs K, 'Subjectivity, Algorithms and the Courtroom' in Završnik A (ed), *Big Data, Crime and Social Control* (Routledge 2018).

Posner R, 'The Role of the Judge in the Twenty-First Century' (2006) 86 Boston U L Rev 1049.

Shi C, Sourdin T, and Li B, 'The Smart Court—A New Pathway to Justice in China?' (2021) 21(1) Intl J for Court Administration 4.

Smyth B and Fehlberg B, 'Australian Post-Separation Parenting on the Smartphone: What's 'App-ening?' (2019) 41(1) J of Social Welfare and Family L 53.

Sourdin T and Zariski A (eds), *The Responsive Judge: International Perspectives* (Springer 2018) 100.

Sourdin T et al, 'COVID-19, Technology and Family Dispute Resolution' (2020) 30(4) Australasian Dispute Resolution J 270 .

Sourdin T, 'Judge v Robot? Artificial Intelligence and Judicial Decision-Making' (2018) 41(4) UNSW LJ 1114.

Sourdin T, Li B, and Brown A, 'An Ethical Perspective in the Judicial Use of Artificial Intelligence: Where Will the New EU Artificial Intelligence Act Take Us?'(2023) 97(1) Australian LJ 4.

Sourdin T, Meredith J, and Li B, *Digital Technology and Justice* (Routledge 2020).

Sourdin T, *Judges, Technology and Artificial Intelligence: The Artificial Judge* (Edward Elgar Publishing 2021).

Stewart P and Stuhmcke A, 'Judicial Analytics and Australian Courts: A Call for National Ethical Guidelines' (2020) 45(2) Alternative LJ 82.

Stobbs N, H unter D, and Bagaric M,'Can Sentencing Be Enhanced by the Use of Artificial Intelligence' (2017) 41 Criminal LJ 261.

Suciu P, 'AI in the Courts: The Jury is Out' (*Tech News World*, 20 February 2020) <www.technewsworld.com/story/86521.html>.

Supreme People's Court of China, 'Chinese Courts and Internet Judiciary' (White Paper, Supreme People's Court of China 4 December 2019).

Surden H, 'Machine Learning and Law' (2014) 89 Washington L Rev 87.

Susskind R, *Online Courts and The Future of Justice* (OUP 2020).

Taruffo M, 'Judicial Decisions and Artificial Intelligence' (1998) 6 Artificial Intelligence and Law 311.

Tashea J, 'Courts are Using AI to Sentence Criminals. That Must Stop Now' (*Sentencing Law and Policy*, 18 April 2017) <https://sentencing.typepad.com/sentencing_law_and_policy/2017/04/courts-are-using-ai-to-sentence-criminals-that-must-stop-now.html>.

The Law Society 'Generative AI – the essentials' (The Law Society, 2023) <https://www.lawsociety.org.uk/topics/ai-and-lawtech/generative-ai-the-essentials> .

Tsamados A et al, 'The Ethics of Algorithms: Key Problems and Solutions' (2021) 36 AI & Society.

Wang G, 'Humans in the Loop: The Design of Interactive AI Systems' (*HAI Stanford University,* 20 October 2019) <https://hai.stanford.edu/blog/humans-loop-design-interactive-ai-systems>.

Wei F et al, 'Empirical Study of Deep Learning for Text Classification in Legal Document Review' (IEEE International Conference on Big Data, Seattle, 2018).

Yu M and Du G, 'Why Are Chinese Courts Turning to AI?' (*The Diplomat,* 19 January 2019) <https://thediplomat.com/2019/01/why-are-chinese-courts-turning-to-ai/>.

Zalnieriute M and Bell F, 'Technology and Judicial Role' in Appleby G and Lynch A (eds), *The Judge, the Judiciary and the Court: Individual, Collegial and Institutional Judicial Dynamics in Australia* (CUP 2021).

Zalnieriute M, Moses L, and Williams G, 'The Rule of Law and Automation of Government Decision-Making' (2019) 82(3) MLR 425.

Zeleznikow J, 'Can Artificial Intelligence and Online Dispute Resolution enhance efficiency and effectiveness in Courts' (2017) 8(2) Intl J for Court Administration 30.

Zhonghao L and Hao J, 'Anhui R & D Case Guide Project and Trial' (*People's Court Daily*, 21 June 2016) <http://rmfyb.chinacourt.org/paper/html/2016-06/21/content_113216.htm>.

Zumbo F, 'Franchising: Implied Good Faith and Unconscionability in Franchises: Moving Towards Relational Contract Theory' (2000) 28 Australian Business L Rev 462.

Conclusions

Fernando Esteban de la Rosa, Pablo Cortés, and Nuria Marchal Escalona

Over the past thirty years, many advanced countries in Europe, America and Asia have made significant progress in the digitalization of their judicial systems, and technological tools are already playing a decisive role in enhancing the efficiency of justice systems. Today, improvements in network capacity and the integration of information and communication technology (ICT) tools with artificial intelligence (AI) tools and blockchain technology present a new opportunity for advancement. The digitalization of justice in many jurisdictions was accelerated during the COVID pandemic. The purpose of this book has been to identify the opportunities and challenges involved in the legal development of technologically advanced judicial systems, as well as to start formulating the key questions and exploring potential answers regarding the integration of AI into justice systems.

Digitalization is transforming courts and their users worldwide and will continue to do so. By digitalizing judicial proceedings, communication across long distances between key stakeholders—judges, lawyers, court administrators, litigants, and the public— is greatly enhanced. It also creates opportunities to simplify procedures and draw valuable insights from past cases. These advancements have already showed their potential to enhance efficiency, accessibility, and fairness within the judicial system. However, digitalization also raises critical concerns, particularly regarding privacy, bias, and the evolving nature of judicial decision-making. The integration of digital processes with emerging AI tools further amplifies the potential benefits, such as improved efficiency, accuracy, and automation. At the same time, it introduces significant risks, including the risk of opaque decision-making, skewed processes, and the embedding of inherent biases. For dispute system designers, the key challenge lies in developing digital processes that maximise these benefits while effectively mitigating and managing the associated risks.

The digitalization of justice initiatives supports the achievement of Goal 16 of the UN 2030 Agenda, which aims to promote peaceful and inclusive societies and improve access to justice. Since the mid-2010s, there has been increasing focus on ensuring that Online Dispute Resolution (ODR) and the use of technology comply with ethical principles, resulting in the creation of various guidelines and standards. However, no universal roadmap for this process exists. As the experiences illustrated in this book have shown, the implementation of ICT innovations in justice systems varies significantly due to the diverse factors that influence digitalization efforts. While the overarching goals of digital transformation are widely shared, the implementation strategies ought to consider each society's unique political, technological, cultural, territorial, and legal contexts. The remainder of this conclusion aims to identify the main findings from each chapter of this collective volume.

The first and second chapters of the book propose conceptual frameworks that support the thoughtful integration of technological tools into dispute resolution, focusing respectively on a people-centred approach and the opportunities created by embracing process pluralism. As highlighted in some chapters, together, these approaches serve as fundamental pillars for navigating the vast potential of technology and identifying secure pathways to advance the digitalization of justice systems. Their aim is to enhance access to justice and promote better procedural justice.

Fernando Esteban de la Rosa observed in chapter 1 that as digitalization advances, addressing the digital divide and prioritizing people-centred justice is increasingly important. Initiatives like the EU's 2022 Declaration on Digital Rights and the OECD's 2023 Recommendation emphasize placing people at the core of justice digitalization, which goes beyond the objective of achieving greater efficiency. To translate this principle into concrete actions that uphold and promote fundamental rights, he argues that the human-centred approach must go beyond merely training justice professionals and users to utilise digital tools effectively. It should also shape the design of dispute resolution processes. Similarly, to ensure digital justice does not become a barrier to access, he advocates for prioritising consent and user choice to foster a fair and accessible digital justice environment. This flexibility is essential to accommodate users' varying levels of digital literacy and to ensure that the transition to a digital justice system does not compromise access to justice. The chapter observes a global trend in legislation emphasizing user consent as a fundamental principle for participating in most online procedures and video hearings, making it mandatory only for certain procedures, courts, specific groups of users or after digital processes have been widely tested and evaluated. Thus, this chapter notes that is a general trend that advocates against imposing digitalization on users, instead supporting a transition that naturally empowers them while avoiding the creation of a digital divide. It also submits that digitalization initiatives, including the creation of online courts to operate entirely online, should incorporate user-focused designs, pilot programs, and data-driven evaluations to ensure their effectiveness.

Orna Rabinovich Einy in chapter 2 unearths another significant conceptual framework, which arises from the growing recognition of procedural pluralism. This approach rejects the rigidity of attempting to fit all cases into a uniform process, acknowledging that a 'one-size-fits-all' model in dispute resolution is often ineffective. Instead, procedural pluralism aims to enhance both procedural justice and access to justice by tailoring processes to the specific needs of individual disputes. The integration of technology into dispute resolution—both within and beyond court systems—has undergone significant advancements, particularly from the emergence of COVID-19 and the recent advancements in AI. This evolution has introduced a new dimension in process pluralism, enabling greater flexibility in the choice of communication methods and facilitating the development of innovative processes and roles that are no longer bound by the constraints of synchronous interaction, human resources, physical spaces, or geographical limitations. This approach allows online processes to be customized to address the distinct requirements of different types of disputes. However, the chapter clarifies that although emerging technologies offer the promise of enhanced efficiency, lower costs, and greater convenience, they also underscore challenges related to individuals' abilities—particularly those from diverse social groups—to access and effectively navigate dispute resolution systems. To maximize technology's potential to empower and create equality, its implementation and design must be tailored to the specific nature of each type of claims and the unique characteristics of its users. In some instances, this may necessitate foregoing technological solutions, while in others, it may require adapting the medium and format of online communication to better accommodate users' needs. For both approaches, the impact of various designs should be systematically analysed over time and across different contexts, fostering research that is essential for generating valuable insights into how design choices influence the principles underlying our procedures and the objectives pursued by our systems. As Rabinovich-Einy observes, AI has the potential to make dispute resolution processes more efficient and accessible, but she also cautions that it is important to ensure that AI is used in a way that is fair and unbiased.

As the digitalization of justice must respect fundamental rights, it is essential to identify specific vulnerabilities associated with judicial digitalization tools, such as remote access to documents and courts, electronic communications, and the use of AI tools. Chapter 3 by Jose Antonio Castillo Parrilla deals with the impact of advances in the digitalization of justice on the right to data protection. The chapter argues that special attention should be given to the following four main aspects: (1) protection of personal data in general; (2) cybersecurity; and (3) automated decision-making and suggestions, and (4) transparency and explainability of AI tools. Based on the analysis conducted, the chapter proposes an impact assessment of AI tools in the administration of justice, intended as a resource for practitioners and public authorities to guide the study and implementation of judicial digitalization, emphasizing the principles to be respected and the recommended measures to achieve these goals. A key distinction is made between fully automated decisions and suggestions, with the freedom of human intervention differentiating the two. Meaningful human involvement ensures that a process is not classified as fully automated and instead falls within the category of assisted tools. The controller, under the principle of accountability, must ensure that human intervention, when required, is meaningful and occurs before producing any effects. Such intervention must go beyond formal or symbolic actions to genuinely influence outcomes. It is also crucial for the legal framework to start distinguishing different types of automated actions, as has already been established in the Spanish Civil Procedural Act.

A common challenge for all technologically advanced judicial systems is the need to develop a secure and reliable digital infrastructure for all stakeholders, including society, legal professionals, and administrative staff. Trustworthiness and security are foundational in designing a virtual space; however, user convenience must also be considered. No single identification method fits all e-justice actions. While traditional digital identity management systems, such as username-password systems and those based on digital certificates, are user-friendly and adaptable to different security needs, they can be unreliable. These systems may be accessed by individuals other than the rightful owner without requiring fraudulent actions to obtain the necessary data. Begoña Fernández Rodríguez in chapter 4 provides a valuable overview of the integration of digital signatures and biometric technologies. Biometric identification systems have transformed security and personal identification via the provision of both, physical and virtual solutions. By linking an individual's identity to unique physical, physiological, or behavioural traits, these systems enhance the reliability of identity verification through intrinsic biometric data. However, biometric identification technology is not without risks, as highlighted by various national and European authorities. The chapter recommends that legislation should mandate the use of electronic identification methods with varying security levels, tailored to the importance and sensitivity of the identification process.

A key aspect of technology's application in the judicial system is its ability to promote settlements both before and during litigation, thereby reducing cost, saving time and enhancing satisfaction in the resolution process. In chapter 5 Pablo Cortés observes that settlement is often the most desirable outcome for parties, as it can save them time, money, and stress. He also notes that promoting settlement can help to reduce the burden on the courts. The chapter explores the experiences in England and Wales, showcasing how ODR processes have been integrated at various stages of a civil dispute's life cycle. It argues that the incorporation of ADR into court proceedings—particularly by making it a mandatory step—is transforming ADR from a supplementary mechanism into an integral component of litigation. The chapter emphasizes that the effectiveness of ADR largely depends on the timing of referrals, as this can significantly influence the parties' willingness to participate in the process. It further highlights that the digitalization of justice systems, especially through the interoperability of pre-action ODR platforms with digital court systems, offers the potential to seamlessly integrate ADR into the civil justice framework. The chapter also recognises the importance of process pluralism, and it argues that parties should have a choice of different dispute resolution processes available to them, so that they can choose the process that is most appropriate for their dispute. He thus observes that technology can play an important role in facilitating process pluralism.

The book advocates for a human-centric approach in the dispute system design, one that is grounded in solid empirical research to inform the development of ODR systems aimed at expanding access to justice. In chapter 6 Schmitz argues that ODR systems should be designed based on solid research to be accessible, fair, and user-friendly. This chapter provides an overview of court related ODR initiatives in the United States and the research that has been conducted on these programs, noting the importance of human-centric design in ODR systems. The creation of online courts represents a key milestone in the advanced digitalization of the justice system. Analysing experiences in the United States since 2014, the chapter finds that not all online court projects have achieved success, with many pilot programs being discontinued. In some cases, courts have begun exploring new providers after earlier collaborations with private ODR platforms failed to meet expectations. The chapter notes that ODR in US courts has entered a new phase, as courts review pilot project outcomes and consider revisions and redesigns to improve performance. It emphasizes the need to return to basics and focus on creating systems that address real problems faced by real people. Thus, it argues for the need to focus on human-centric design based on dispute system design elements and solid empirical research to inform the design of ODR systems aimed to expand access to justice. Designers are encouraged to scrutinize and refine programs over time, leveraging insights from ongoing research to make incremental adjustments and redesigns. At the same time, a research-design feedback loop is highlighted as particularly important for promoting access to justice.

This approach ensures that ODR systems can adapt to the changing needs and challenges of diverse user groups. By prioritizing research-driven redesigns, policymakers are empowered not only to develop systems initially aligned with access to justice principles, but also to continuously optimize and refine these systems as technology evolves. Ultimately, the chapter underscores that system design, informed by ongoing research and a focus on ethics, serves as a powerful driver for the fair and effective evolution of ODR systems.

China provides a compelling example of the successful implementation of online courts, designed to address internet-related disputes and support the rapid growth of its digital economy and e-commerce. In chapter 7 Alex Chung and Ying Yu observe that as traditional courts become increasingly inadequate in the digital age, China has leveraged technologies such as blockchain and AI to launch e-courts and other digital public tools. In China, online litigation is quickly becoming the new norm, marking a significant transition driven by judicial reforms aimed at adapting the legal framework to meet the demands of the digital era. This digital transformation extends beyond online courts to the creation of a comprehensive e-justice ecosystem, requiring continuous collaboration between the judiciary and digital economy sectors. For example, the CMMC applet and the Internet Judicial Blockchain platform exemplify the integration of cutting-edge technologies to enhance judicial processes. The chapter highlights that China's Supreme People's Court has played a central role in modernizing the legal system, issuing directives and developing tools like the CMMC applet, which has registered millions of users and processed vast numbers of cases. The Internet Judicial Blockchain platform, now linked to over 3,500 courts, secures and authenticates digital evidence, while also promoting cross-departmental collaboration. With plans to establish a fully interconnected judicial ecosystem by 2025, China is setting a benchmark for digital transformation. However, cross-border challenges remain, particularly regarding the recognition of blockchain-based evidence, as most legal systems continue to rely on traditional methods for evidence verification. It may take time for such technologies to gain broader acceptance internationally. China's transformation of its judicial landscape through e-courts and digital tools—facilitated by collaboration between the government, judiciary, and industry stakeholders—has improved accessibility, efficiency, and fairness in the digital age. This integrated approach to online litigation and digital solutions offers valuable insights for other countries seeking to modernize their legal systems and address the challenges of the digital economy. China's best practices—such as the use of blockchain technology for securing evidence—can serve as models for many nations. However, implementing such technologies in regions with strict data privacy laws will require careful planning to balance efficiency with privacy protections.

The digitalization of the justice system is a global phenomenon, and as Nauman Reayat observes in chapter 8, Pakistan serves as a relevant case study, especially for low- and middle-income countries facing similar challenges in modernizing judicial systems, including large populations, unstable political, legal, and economic systems, limited access to justice for minorities, massive case backlogs, and decreasing public trust in the justice system. He suggests that Pakistan should learn from the experiences of other countries, such as the United Kingdom and Canada, which have made significant progress in digiting their justice systems. The chapter argues that, to advance its digitalization process, Pakistan's judicial system requires adequate financial resources to cover the high costs of digitalization and the establishment of a suitable legal framework to support implementation. These resources should be directed towards programs designed to enhance access to computers, tablets, and reliable internet for litigants, ensuring the effective use of online judicial services. Additionally, efforts should be made to organise data for efficient processing and machine automation, as well as to develop data-sharing systems across government departments, courts, and the National Database Registration Authority. The establishment of an online portal connecting all levels of courts and government departments is essential, as is the design of software capable of receiving, storing, and processing electronic claims and evidence while facilitating communication with litigants and legal representatives. Furthermore, litigation officers should be appointed in each government department to manage portal access, coordinate responses, and submit documents on behalf of departments. Training programs for judges, lawyers, and staff are necessary to develop digital skills, alongside the recruitment of technical personnel with expertise in data management and technology maintenance to support system operations. Efforts to convert paper-based records into electronic formats, with appropriate categorisation and codification, will ensure compatibility with digital systems. It is also crucial to educate litigants about the potential and usage of digital systems, fostering broader adoption and ease of use. These requirements underscore the technical, structural, and human resource challenges that Pakistan faces in modernising its judicial system. The insights derived from these challenges are also relevant to other jurisdictions, particularly low- and middle-income countries pursuing similar reforms.

Once technology enables remote accessibility and participation, the next natural step is to extend procedures and courts beyond national borders. Chapters 9 and 10 of the book provide an analysis of the new European legal framework designed to facilitate access to justice in cross-border proceedings. This legislation is pioneering in its use of technological and legal solutions to address the challenges involved in achieving this goal. The EU has been advancing a digitalization strategy to balance the efficiency of international judicial cooperation with safeguarding procedural rights and access to justice. In chapter 9 Nuria Marchal Escalona highlights that the current legal framework offers significant potential to adapt judicial cooperation to the digital age, promoting sustainable, people-centred justice that empowers both citizens and businesses while protecting fundamental rights. Key technological pillars of the developed system include the decentred computer system, e-Codex, and electronic points in the states, each playing a crucial role in facilitating connectivity and communication among judicial authorities. However, the chapter argues that to prevent planned digitalization from deepening inequalities, countries should invest in digital infrastructure and provide adequate training for judicial officers and citizens. Additional challenges include ensuring data protection, maintaining the integrity of judicial processes and addressing the digital divide that may prevent certain groups from fully benefiting from these developments. Adequate design will help ensure judicial processes that are faster, more efficient, and transparent. Effective implementation hinges on establishing suitable infrastructure, technical resources, and interoperable communication systems. Achieving these objectives will largely rely on a coordinated, multilevel approach that tackles both technical and organisational challenges.

María José Fernández-Fígares Morales in chapter 10 notes that the European legal framework has also introduced significant innovations in how judicial bodies collect testimony from parties, witnesses, and experts located outside the jurisdiction of the requesting authority but within the territory of most EU Member States. Direct videoconferencing represents a major advancement over previous systems, enabling the sentencing court to establish closer contact with the source of evidence and thereby reinforcing the principle of immediacy. The use of technology in this context is presented to uphold the right to a fair trial, as it allows for greater flexibility and accessibility for all parties involved. However, this progress remains incomplete, as respect for national sovereignty and jurisdictional boundaries means that participation remains voluntary for individuals in other Member States. Moreover, the absence of a uniform European procedural law and a dedicated platform for this purpose across EU countries further complicates efforts to ensure that remote audio-visual evidence collection is accessible to all judicial bodies. To address these limitations, the chapter proposes that legislators consider requiring the presence of a judicial authority from the requested State alongside the requesting authority during evidence collection. Undoubtedly, cooperation between European and national institutions is seen as crucial to ensure that digital technologies are effectively implemented, thereby improving access to justice in an increasingly interconnected legal landscape.

The final section of this book discusses the use of AI in the administration of justice. Chapter 11, authored by Ozana Olariu and John Zeleznikow, underscores the importance of developing a robust regulatory framework for AI that is firmly grounded in international human rights standards. It also emphasises the need for effective enforcement and monitoring mechanisms to ensure that AI systems align with and uphold these principles. It highlights that AI systems should not only avoid infringing upon human rights and freedoms but also actively promote their realization. To achieve this, the chapter proposes that core human rights principles must be translated into actionable legal measures and implementation strategies. It argues that the AI Convention and the AI Act are insufficient, as they either serve only as guidelines for integrating principles into national AI policies or adopt a risk-based approach that grants states flexibility, but lacks detailed guidelines, leaving room for the circumvention of contentious provisions. Therefore, to guarantee the protection of individual rights national legislation should complement these frameworks by enacting targeted laws to address algorithmic bias, data protection, and the use of AI in sensitive areas such as law enforcement, healthcare, and social services. Governments should strive to exceed international minimum standards and lead efforts to advance a human rights-focused AI governance agenda. Key actions should encompass meaningful stakeholder engagement through collaboration with civil society organizations, human rights experts, and affected communities, ensuring the inclusion of diverse perspectives, the identification of risks, and the development of effective mitigation strategies. Furthermore, robust oversight and enforcement mechanisms are necessary to guarantee that AI systems are monitored, audited, and held accountable for violations. Promoting digital literacy is crucial to empowering individuals to engage with AI systems, understand their risks, and challenge biased outcomes. This can be achieved by providing accessible resources, such as plain-language explanations and mechanisms to report algorithmic harm, which encourage public participation in AI governance and accountability processes. Additionally, international cooperation is vital to address global AI challenges and uphold consistent human rights standards across borders. The chapter concludes by underscoring the importance of adopting a comprehensive approach that integrates human rights considerations throughout all stages of AI development and governance. Such an approach would allow society to unlock the transformative benefits of AI while mitigating risks like algorithmic bias. Failing to implement these measures could exacerbate inequalities, erode public trust in democratic institutions, and undermine the protection of human rights.

In chapter 12, Javier Valls Prieto, focused on the European vision of integrating AI into the judicial system. According to the new European legal framework, AI governance systems are based on a hybrid approach that combines self-regulation (ethical principles) and hard law (human rights enshrined in legislation and the new AI regulation). The High-Level Expert Group created by the European Commission launched ethical guidelines for AI, comprising seven principles designed to ensure fairness, accountability, and safety in judicial AI systems. These principles are built on three pillars—lawfulness (respect for human rights), ethics (ethical principles and values), and robustness (technical and social resilience). First, human agency and oversight emphasize that AI must support human decision-making without undermining autonomy or causing harm, ensuring judges and legal professionals maintain control over AI systems and decisions. Second, robustness and safety require AI systems to be secure, resilient to attacks, and error-preventive, particularly in sensitive legal cases, with security measures scaled to match risk levels, from simple tools to predictive parole systems. Third, accuracy ensures AI achieves high-performance standards while protecting privacy and data governance to prevent bias, errors, and breaches of sensitive information. Fourth, transparency mandates that AI decisions must be traceable, explainable, and comprehensible, giving users the right to know when interacting with AI and to demand clear explanations of decisions. Fifth, diversity, non-discrimination, and fairness promote equal access and bias prevention by involving stakeholders throughout AI implementation. Sixth, societal and environmental well-being encourages AI systems to align with the common good, minimize energy consumption, and promote social well-being while avoiding harm to physical and mental health. Finally, accountability requires mechanisms for auditing AI systems, assessing risks, and providing redress for harm, particularly for vulnerable groups, to ensure compliance with human rights standards. These principles aim to enhance efficiency while protecting human rights, democratic values, and public trust in judicial AI systems. Furthermore, the chapter observes that the AI Act imposes human rights impact assessments for the use of high-risk intelligent systems in both the public sector and private companies performing tasks for the public sector. The main risk lies in the use of predictive tools within the criminal justice system; therefore, such applications are classified as high-risk, requiring impact assessments to mitigate or eliminate risks. While Annex III of the AI Act clarifies that criminal justice applications are high-risk, Recital 61 generalizes this classification to civil and administrative justice, reflecting the need for rigorous oversight across all judicial contexts.

Chapter 13, by Roberta Montinaro, criticizes the European AI framework for its insufficient regulation of AI systems and large language models (LLMs) in the legal field, arguing that the AI Act fails to promote the responsible development of AI systems for the legal sector. Under the AI Act, such systems are classified as high-risk only when (1) deployed by the judiciary or ADR bodies in procedures with legal effects for the parties, and (2) used to assist in researching and interpreting facts and applying the law (Art. 6.2 and Annex III (8)). One significant worry is the lack of transparency around AI use in legal settings. If people are not aware that an AI system played a role in their case, it could hinder their ability to seek rightful compensation or challenge the outcome under the AI Act. The rise of LLMs and their growing use by legal professionals has prompted the adoption of *ad hoc* deontological rules at the supranational level, aimed at complementing and clarifying national standards for legal services to ensure that AI systems, especially LLMs, adhere to principles such as care, competence, confidentiality, and transparency. Soft law norms have also been introduced for legal professionals and judges, updating their professional diligence obligations. However, fulfilling these obligations often depends on LLM providers disclosing key information about their systems. For example, deployers need to know the capabilities and limitations of an LLM, including accuracy metrics and training data characteristics, presented in an accessible format. Similarly, evaluating the accuracy and reasoning behind LLM outputs requires providers to adopt a 'by design' approach that ensures transparency. The analysis underscores the lack of accountability among AI developers and providers in the legal sector, raising concerns about whether the current legal framework complies with the Council of Europe's Framework Convention on Artificial Intelligence, which mandates legislative and administrative measures to protect fundamental rights and uphold the rule of law in AI development and deployment.

In the following chapter John Zeleznikow, examines AI's role in the digitalization of justice administration, focusing on its potential to improve access to justice for self-represented litigants (SRLs). Chapter 14 thus observes that these AI tools may eliminate or dramatically reduce the need for lawyer assistance. At the same time, courts have increasingly embraced technology to promote ODR to expand access to justice. The chapter discusses several prototypes that aim to integrate AI into the judicial system, particularly to improve access to justice for SRLs. However, aside from the British Columbia Civil Resolution Tribunal, thus far, very few public AI systems have been adopted, and even those currently employed, like the Solution Explorer used in British Columbia, rely primarily on rule-based AI rather than machine learning. The chapter also examines the Split-Up system, developed in Australia over two decades ago, and its successor, the Amica system, recently implemented by the Australian Government. With the emergence of Generative AI, there is growing enthusiasm and concern about its application in the judicial system. Tools like ChatGPT can assist both lawyers and non-professionals by offering advice on legal processes and outcomes, potentially improving access to justice for SRLs. Yet, the rise of Generative AI also raises ethical challenges, particularly regarding the validity of the advice provided and whether it is being used appropriately, and the potential for AI to perpetuate existing biases.

In chapter 15, David Freeman Engstrom, Ayelet Sela, and Natalie Knowlton analyse the evolving role of AI within US courts, particularly its potential to enhance access to justice. The authors delineate six primary areas of 'courthouse AI' implementation: document management and docketing, procedural screening and compliance, case triage and docket analytics, litigant self-help tools, ODR, and judge work product tools. The authors observe that the reasons why advances in AI are not reaching courts in a smooth and seamless manner can be attributed to the presence of limited technical capacity in courts, legal-cultural barriers, such as the prohibition on unauthorized practice of law and norms of court neutrality, which pose obstacles to AI-powered self-help tools. Although increasingly sophisticated AI tools offer a promising opportunity to reimagine both court operations and service delivery, realizing this potential is far from straightforward. The decentralized structure of American courts, the fragmented state of their technological infrastructure, and concerns about AI's maturity—especially in direct-to-consumer applications—pose significant hurdles. Moreover, courts must address the tension between providing meaningful assistance to litigants and adhering to judicial neutrality and unauthorized practice rules. The future of AI courts may depend on courts' ability to innovate while recognizing the limitations of current technologies. While incremental improvements, such as automating administrative processes and language translation services, can deliver immediate benefits, unlocking AI's full potential may require courts to rethink entrenched norms and structures, taking bolder steps toward procedural innovation, technological integration, and standardization. The chapter concludes by outlining the implications of these challenges. Courts must decide whether to develop their own AI tools or facilitate a third-party legal-tech ecosystem, each with its own set of difficulties. The path forward may involve a mix of approaches, including data standardization, improved technical capacity, and the redesign of legal service delivery and court architecture. However, simply automating court processes does not guarantee improved accessibility; courts must commit to user-centred design of AI tools and carefully oversee their implementation to ensure they meet the needs of all users, including the most vulnerable. Ongoing evaluation and oversight of new AI technologies—whether developed in-house or procured externally—will be crucial to ensuring these tools are both effective and equitable. AI is however not a panacea for the access-to-justice crisis; while it holds significant promise, it cannot address broader systemic issues such as poverty, institutional distrust, and socioeconomic disparities. Therefore, AI tools must be complemented by human support services, particularly for SRLs from disadvantaged backgrounds or with technological constraints. A human-in-the-loop approach can ensure that courthouse AI is accessible, understandable, and genuinely helpful, offering a vital alternative for those who may struggle to effectively utilize AI tools. The choices courts make in the coming years will determine whether AI becomes a transformative force that narrows the justice gap or merely reinforces existing inequalities and inefficiencies.

In the last chapter, authored by Tania Sourdin and Ella Sourdin Brown, it is observed that while supportive AI has potential to improve judicial processes in the medium term, the application of disruptive Judge AI raises significant ethical, practical, and societal concerns that demand careful regulation. Chapter 16 focused on the use of AI by judges. This is already being implemented for various purposes, such as suggesting, guiding, or correcting judicial decisions. Furthermore, several jurisdictions are exploring more disruptive forms of judicial AI designed to replace judges. These AI applications raise ethical concerns, particularly regarding Generative AI, which could potentially undermine public trust in the exercise of judicial authority. Concerns about transparency, bias, and the 'black box' nature of AI decision-making processes further underscore the risks of relying on disruptive AI in sensitive areas like criminal and family law. The judicial use of AI also presents practical and ethical challenges, especially in cases involving high emotional stakes, such as criminal law and family disputes, where the empathy and creativity of human judges remain essential. In contrast, simpler cases, like small claims or administrative matters, may be better suited for AI integration. However, jurisdictional disparities in ethical principles and justice values add complexity, particularly when determining whether fully automated Judge AI is ever appropriate. Some experts advocate for supportive AI systems that assist judges rather than replace them, predicting that such systems will play a more prominent role in the medium term, despite ongoing exploration of disruptive AI in certain jurisdictions. Given the rapid proliferation of AI, it is likely that sophisticated AI systems will become more prevalent in the judicial landscape in the long term, even as ethical debates persist. AI adoption in the judicial system raises fundamental questions about whether justice objectives are being achieved and whether human judicial involvement will be preserved. Narrow applications might limit human judges to a reviewing role, enabling litigants to appeal AI decisions through a clear and accessible review process. In broader applications, supportive AI systems with human oversight—a 'human-in-the-loop' approach—could combine AI efficiency with human feedback, ensuring greater accountability. Regardless of how AI systems are implemented, there is an urgent need to develop ethical frameworks to guide judges and policymakers in addressing the novel challenges posed by AI. These frameworks should draw on existing AI ethics guidelines and safeguard society against unjust outcomes that could reshape social structures.

The integration of digital technologies and AI into judicial systems worldwide marks a transformative era, promising enhanced efficiency, accessibility, and fairness. This collected volume has aimed to explore the ongoing digital journey of justice systems, highlighting both opportunities and challenges. From conceptual frameworks that emphasise people-centred approaches and procedural pluralism to practical considerations of data protection, digital infrastructure, and the ethical use of AI, the chapters collectively underscore the complexity of this evolution.

While advancements in technology offer the potential to streamline processes, reduce backlogs, and improve access to justice, they also raise significant concerns regarding privacy, bias, and the fundamental nature of judicial decision-making. As the digitalization process progresses, an approach that prioritises human rights, ethical considerations, and continuous evaluation will be essential in harnessing the benefits of digitalization while mitigating its risks. This will ensure that technology strengthens, rather than undermines, the foundations of justice.

Index

For the benefit of digital users, indexed terms that span two pages (e.g., 52–53) may, on occasion, appear on only one of those pages.

Tables and figures are indicated by an italic *t* and *f* following the page number.

The manufacturer's authorised representative in the EU for product safety is Oxford University Press España S.A. of el Parque Empresarial San Fernando de Henares, Avenida de Castilla, 2 – 28830 Madrid (www.oup.es/en or product.safety@oup.com). OUP España S.A. also acts as importer into Spain of products made by the manufacturer.

www.ingramcontent.com/pod-product-compliance
Ingram Content Group UK Ltd.
Pitfield, Milton Keynes, MK11 3LW, UK
UKHW020842150926
475595UK00010B/188/J
9780198918721